# Risk Adjustment, Risk Sharing and Premium Regulation in Health Insurance Markets

## Related titles

*Pauly, McGuire & Barros, North Holland* (ISBN 978-0-444-53592-4)

*Culyer & Newhouse, North Holland* (ISBN 978-0-444-50471-5)

*Culyer & Newhouse, North Holland* (ISBN 978-0-444-50470-8)

# Risk Adjustment, Risk Sharing and Premium Regulation in Health Insurance Markets

Theory and Practice

Edited by

**Thomas G. McGuire**

**Richard C. van Kleef**

**ACADEMIC PRESS**
An imprint of Elsevier

Academic Press is an imprint of Elsevier
125 London Wall, London EC2Y 5AS, United Kingdom
525 B Street, Suite 1650, San Diego, CA 92101, United States
50 Hampshire Street, 5th Floor, Cambridge, MA 02139, United States
The Boulevard, Langford Lane, Kidlington, Oxford OX5 1GB, United Kingdom

**Notices**
Knowledge and best practice in this field are constantly changing. As new research and experience broaden
our understanding, changes in research methods, professional practices, or medical treatment may become
necessary.

Practitioners and researchers must always rely on their own experience and knowledge in evaluating and
using any information, methods, compounds, or experiments described herein. In using such information or
methods they should be mindful of their own safety and the safety of others, including parties for whom
they have a professional responsibility.

To the fullest extent of the law, neither the Publisher nor the authors, contributors, or editors, assume any
liability for any injury and/or damage to persons or property as a matter of products liability, negligence or
otherwise, or from any use or operation of any methods, products, instructions, or ideas contained in the
material herein.

**British Library Cataloguing-in-Publication Data**
A catalogue record for this book is available from the British Library

**Library of Congress Cataloging-in-Publication Data**
A catalog record for this book is available from the Library of Congress

ISBN: 978-0-12-811325-7

For Information on all Academic Press publications
visit our website at https://www.elsevier.com/books-and-journals

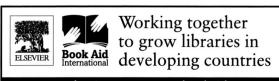

Working together
to grow libraries in
developing countries

www.elsevier.com • www.bookaid.org

*Publisher:* Candice Janco
*Acquisition Editor:* Graham Nisbet
*Editorial Project Manager:* Susan Ikeda
*Production Project Manager:* Debasish Ghosh
*Cover Designer:* Mark Rogers

Typeset by MPS Limited, Chennai, India

# Contents

## 4.  Risk Sharing                                                                  105

*Thomas G. McGuire and Richard C. van Kleef*

**5. Evaluating the Performance of Health Plan
Payment Systems**    133

*Timothy J. Layton, Randall P. Ellis, Thomas G. McGuire
and Richard C. van Kleef*

## 13. Regulated Competition and Health Plan Payment Under the National Health Insurance Law in Israel—The Unfinished Story 365

*Shuli Brammli-Greenberg, Jacob Glazer and Amir Shmueli*

# List of Contributors

**John Armstrong** Erasmus School of Health Policy and Management, Erasmus University Rotterdam, Rotterdam, The Netherlands

**Sebastian Bauhoff** Center for Global Development, Washington, DC, United States

**Konstantin Beck** CSS Institute for Empirical Health Economics, Lucerne, Switzerland; University of Lucerne, Lucerne, Switzerland

**Shuli Brammli-Greenberg** University of Haifa, Haifa, Israel

**Florian Buchner** University Duisburg-Essen, CINCH - Health Economics Research Center, Duisburg, Germany; Carinthia University of Applied Sciences, Villach, Austria

**Frank Eijkenaar** Erasmus School of Health Policy and Management, Erasmus University Rotterdam, Rotterdam, The Netherlands

**Randall P. Ellis** Department of Economics, Boston University, Boston, MA, United States

**Ayman Fouda** University of Bologna, Bologna, Italy; Erasmus University Rotterdam, Rotterdam, The Netherlands

**Inés Galindo-Henriquez** Ministry of Health and Social Protection, Bogota, Colombia

**Jacob Glazer** Tel Aviv University, Tel Aviv, Israel; University of Warwick, Coventry, United Kingdom

**Dirk Göpffarth** State Chancellery of North Rhine-Westphalia, Düsseldorf, Germany

**Ramiro Guerrero** PROESA, Icesi University, Cali, Colombia

**Joeri Guillaume** Socialist Mutualities, Brussels, Belgium

**Josefa Henríquez** Centro de Estudios Públicos, Santiago, Chile

**Lukas Kauer** CSS Institute for Empirical Health Economics, Lucerne, Switzerland; University of Zurich, Zurich, Switzerland

**Timothy J. Layton** Department of Health Care Policy, Harvard Medical School and the NBER, Boston, MA, United States

**Gordon Liu** Peking University, Beijing, China

**Gerald Lux** University Duisburg-Essen, CINCH - Health Economics Research Center, Duisburg, Germany

**Bruno Martins** Department of Economics, Boston University, Boston, MA, United States

**Andrew Matthews** Medibank Private, Melbourne, Australia

**Thomas G. McGuire** Department of Health Care Policy, Harvard Medical School and the NBER, Boston, MA, United States

**Ellen Montz** Department of Health Care Policy, Harvard Medical School, Boston, MA, United States

**Félix Nates** Ministry of Health and Social Protection, Bogota, Colombia

**Alice Ndikumana** Harvard University, Cambridge, MA, United States

**Joseph P. Newhouse** Department of Health Care Policy, Harvard Medical School and the NBER, Boston, MA, United States

**Francesco Paolucci** Murdoch University, Perth, WA, Australia; University of Bologna, Bologna, Italy

**Iván Rodríguez-Bernate** Ministry of Health and Social Protection, Bogota, Colombia

**Sherri Rose** Department of Health Care Policy, Harvard Medical School, Boston, MA, United States

**Sonja Schillo** University Duisburg-Essen, CINCH - Health Economics Research Center, Duisburg, Germany

**Christian P.R. Schmid** CSS Institute for Empirical Health Economics, Lucerne, Switzerland; University of Bern, Bern, Switzerland

**Erik Schokkaert** KULeuven, Leuven, Belgium

**Frederik T. Schut** Erasmus School of Health Policy and Management, Erasmus University Rotterdam, Rotterdam, The Netherlands

**Ana R. Sequeira** Murdoch University, Perth, WA, Australia; ISCTE – University Institute of Lisbon, Lisbon, Portugal

**Igor Sheiman** National Research University High School of Economics, Moscow, Russia

**Mark Shepard** Kennedy School of Government, Harvard University and the NBER, Cambridge, MA, United States

**Julie Shi** Peking University, Beijing, China

**Amir Shmueli** The Hebrew University, Jerusalem, Israel

**Wynand P.M.M. van de Ven** Erasmus School of Health Policy and Management, Erasmus University Rotterdam, Rotterdam, The Netherlands

**Carine van de Voorde** KULeuven, Leuven, Belgium

**Richard C. van Kleef** Erasmus School of Health Policy and Management, Erasmus University Rotterdam, Rotterdam, The Netherlands

**René C.J.A. van Vliet** Erasmus School of Health Policy and Management, Erasmus University Rotterdam, Rotterdam, The Netherlands

**Carolina Velasco** Centro de Estudios Públicos, Santiago, Chile

**Jürgen Wasem** University Duisburg-Essen, CINCH - Health Economics Research Center, Duisburg, Germany

# Regulated Competition in Health Insurance Markets: Foreword by Alain Enthoven

This is an important and very timely book. With Republican attacks on the Affordable Care Act, many people are concluding that competition in the private sector cannot be made to work in health insurance in the U.S. This is ironic because, for many years, competition in the private sector was the Republican answer to proposals for a government monopoly in health care finance, as exemplified by Governor Romney's successful model in Massachusetts. Prominent Democratic leaders and their followers are now advocating for "single payer health insurance" which means a government monopoly on health care finance. They and anyone else interested in health policy should read this book and find that eleven other countries, including Germany, Switzerland and the Netherlands have achieved universal health insurance with regulated competition in the private sector, plus successful efforts in Medicare and Medicaid (covered in this book), and in addition, the Federal Employees Health Benefits Program (FEHBP), the Health Benefits Division of the California Public Employees Retirement System (CalPERS), the Wisconsin State Employees Employee Trust Fund, as well as the Affordable Care Act (ACA). Universal health insurance is not synonymous with "single payer." Readers will also learn that the broad concept of "regulated competition" in the private sector is flexible and can work in a variety of countries with various histories, cultures, and political structures.

It may be helpful to balance the review of current state of affairs with regard to regulated competition contained in this book with some history of the development of the ideas. I have sought to do that in this foreword.

My intellectual journey to regulated health insurance competition in the private sector began with my experience as a member of the Medical Center Committee of the Board of Directors of Georgetown University in the late 1960s, in the era of dominance of open-ended uncoordinated fee-for-service (FFS) for physician services and for cost-reimbursement for hospitals and long before the Medicare Prospective Payment System. I learned that the doctors and hospital managers didn't know and had little reason to care what different types of patients cost to treat, or how those costs might be reduced with no harm to the patient. The incentives providers faced worked against efforts to find and implement less costly ways of caring for patients. The open-ended era fostered cost-unconscious demand. No wonder Medicare expenditures were soaring, exceeding the projections made at the inception of the program. (Those projections ignored the incentives inherent in the payment methods.) And the physicians made cost-unconscious demands for new facilities and equipment.

At about this time, the Health Maintenance Organization (HMO) Act (1973) was being proposed and debated. The original vision of an HMO was a prepaid multi-specialty group practice (PGP) based on the successful experience of Kaiser Permanente. The physicians in the Department of Community Medicine recognized that the FFS model would not be viable over the long run and sought a better more sustainable model to which their students could be exposed. Their search led them to PGP. The economist in me liked the idea because of the alignment of physician incentives with their patients' interests, the teamwork, the opportunity to create systems that could work to improve quality and economy and be held accountable for the results. Department physicians proposed creation of Georgetown University Community Health Plan (GUCHP). I introduced the proposal to the Board of Directors with a positive endorsement. GUCHP came into operation in 1970 and by 1980 had enrolled 50,000 members. In 1980, GUCHP joined Kaiser Permanente, and it now serves over 700,000 enrolled members in the Washington DC area.

After leaving the Department of Defense in January 1969, at the end of the term of President Lyndon Johnson who appointed me, I joined Litton Industries, a diversified conglomerate. After an interlude on the corporate staff, I became President of Litton Medical Products, a collection of 12 acquired companies spread out from Chicago to Germany. I asked what was the "product-market strategy" of the X-ray company. The answer was "a quality cost-effective machine". It turned out that the only hospitals that cared about cost-effectiveness were Group Health Cooperative of Puget Sound (a non-profit PGP) and investor-owned hospitals. More broadly, I observed more of the cost-unconscious demand I had observed at Georgetown. Marketing a product as "cost-effective" was a mistake in a market where customers were unconcerned with cost.

While I was at Litton, a group of physicians from Suburban Maryland came to us and proposed that we join them to form an HMO. I studied it thoroughly and concluded that it would be inappropriate for a short-term profit-oriented company to go into that business. I imagined someone telling the doctors to postpone an operation until the next quarter so that we could meet our quarterly profit target. During that time, at a conference, I met Dr. Sidney Garfield, the founding doctor of Kaiser Permanente. I described the situation and he said "you are talking to the wrong doctors", and he was right. His remarks taught me the fundamental importance of physician culture.

In 1973, I came to Stanford Graduate School of Business to accept a new endowed chair in Public and Private Management. At Stanford, I became close friends with Victor Fuchs and read his landmark book *Who Shall Live?* Victor was and remains a wonderful resource for an economist who wants to learn about health care—full of knowledge in depth. I tested out many ideas on him and got valuable advice.

Around this time, I went to the Headquarters of Kaiser Permanente in nearby Oakland to meet with their CEO and executive vice-president. I told them what I had been doing at Georgetown and earlier in the Department of Defense (including leading the introduction of cost-effectiveness analysis to the Department of Defense), believed in what they were doing, wanted to keep my hand in real-world decision-making, and proposed a consulting relationship that lasted 40 years. I learned a great deal from them about health care finance, and worked on a variety of assignments. I could see the effects of incentives alignment, a service-oriented culture, the potential for improvement in quality and economy. It became clear to me that with an open market and a level playing field, this program and others like it had the potential to replace FFS.

The most important insight I gained came when I asked the Kaiser executives: "Where does your business come from? Who are your customers?" The answer at the time was the Federal Employees Health Benefits Program (FEHBP) and the Health Benefits division of the California Public Employees' Retirement System (CalPERS.) In both programs, Kaiser was the largest supplier of health insurance and care in California. "Something about us that bureaucrats like" someone said. I thought and replied "No, they are the only two large employment groups in the country that offer employees a choice of insurance plan and an opportunity to keep the savings for themselves if they choose wisely." (A few years later, the University of California and Stanford University joined that list.)

EUREKA! We can replace cost-unconscious FFS with competing PGPs and similar systems if we can get other employers, or, indeed, all of America, to adopt a similar model. That was the beginning of regulated competition in my mind. Meanwhile, in 1972, I was elected to the Institute of Medicine of the National Academy of Sciences (now the National Academy of Medicine) signaling that someone thought I had valuable contributions to make to health policy.

In 1976, Presidential Candidate Carter promised Americans universal health insurance, and as President-elect appointed my former colleague at the Defense Department and friend, Joseph Califano, Secretary of Health, Education and Welfare with responsibility for fulfilling the campaign promise to bring us Universal Health Insurance. Secretary Califano invited me to join his administration to develop a plan for universal health insurance. It soon became clear to me that no one in the Carter Administration had any idea what the promise of universal health insurance meant or how to fulfill it. My family and I were happy in California. I didn't want to move back to Washington, so I offered to serve as a consultant, spend full-time on the project, and every other week in Washington. During my time in California I consulted extensively with Victor Fuchs and also Scott Fleming, Senior Vice President of Kaiser Permanente who, in a previous tour in Washington had designed a model he called "structured competition" which was an inspiration for my ideas. I also drew inspiration from Charles Schultze whose Godkin Lecture at Harvard was called "Public Use of Private Interest", that made the case that many public problems such as pollution could best be managed by creating incentives for the private sector to serve the public interest.

I wanted to propose a design that would encourage the forming and growth of high quality cost-effective organized delivery systems that attracted and pleased their enrolled members. Then, the whole health care delivery system could be transformed gradually and voluntarily into systems that improved quality and efficiency and replaced the dominant FFS model.

Naturally, I had PGP and Kaiser Permanente in mind, but I rejected any proposal that specifically favored them or that would admit only PGP into the realm of qualifying health plans eligible to participate in the reformed system. All they and I wanted was to open the market (i.e. everybody could select one if available in their geographic market) and level the playing field (i.e. correct tax laws and other laws favoring more costly health plans.) Of course, the dominant employer-based health insurance system did neither.

Along the way, I was regularly subjected to stern lectures that "everybody knows that competition cannot work in health insurance or healthcare." Why not? One reason skeptics gave was that it was too complicated. People cannot understand and make choices. I agreed. Health insurance could be extremely complicated. Only experts could understand it. And insurance companies found it in their interest to make it so. So step one in regulated competition should be that insurance contracts should be standardized, or if circumstances made variations necessary, then they should be as standard as possible with ease of comparison an important design principle. There are several good reasons why the competitors should be required to offer the same contract:

- Non-standard contracts could be very difficult to understand and compare, making people reluctant to change plans, making demand curves inelastic. If we want lower price and higher quality, the competition should focus on those two issues.
- Non-standard contracts could include tricky exclusions that come back and bite unsuspecting consumers, sometimes seriously. (In fact, later on, when CalPERS and Stanford adopted standard contracts, we found deceptive exclusions embedded in the previous contracts.)

- Non-standard contracts can be designed to repel poor risks and attract good risks. Non-standard contracts could segment markets, reducing the field in which competition takes place.

So to make competition work well, it is best to make all competing coverage contracts as standardized as possible.

Later on, I learned that there were practical reasons why completely standard contracts were not appropriate. As Chairman of the CalPERS Health Benefits Advisory Committee, I recommended and the Executive Director and the Board agreed that we should standardize all the 20-plus HMO plans' contracts. But many people had good reasons for not wanting to choose an HMO including that HMOs did not serve the geographic regions where they lived, or strong attachments to doctors who were not in HMOs. So we had to offer a wide access PPO. But the PPOs, being basically FFS, had to rely on consumer cost-sharing to manage utilization. And as utilization rose, narrower networks had to be offered. But all PPOs offered the same contracts for deductibles and copayments, and the other lists of exclusions were the same as for the HMO contracts.

The next major problem with competition among insurance plans was biased risk selection. For example, at the outset, the FEHBP had a serious design flaw. There were two national contracts: Blue Cross Blue Shield, and Aetna insurance company. In each case, the insurers offered a "high option" and a "low option" with less and more consumer cost sharing. It should not have been surprising that in each case, the high options attracted a much costlier mix of patients than the low options, driving up the premiums so much that they became untenable—a "death spiral" of adverse selection. Both carriers had to withdraw their high options and replace both high and low options with a "standard option."

But there are many reasons other than plan design that one plan or another might attract a disproportionate share of good or bad risks. It is impressive how many ways insurance companies have found to be unattractive to poor risks. One way to avoid poor risks is for a plan or affiliated medical group to cultivate a reputation for not being very good at caring for diabetes or heart disease or cancer. It was clear early on that risk selection was a major issue. Today's risk adjustment technology did not exist 40 years ago, so I proposed a set of "actuarial categories" analogous to the more recent DRGs, using age, sex and diagnoses, grouping patients by predicted relative costs. Plans could then charge more for people in more costly categories, but the government would pay more to people in the more costly categories. This was not very satisfactory, and by 1993, when modern risk adjustment tools had been developed, I favored community rating of premiums, and compensatory payments to health plans so that those attracting more costly patients would not be disadvantaged in the marketplace.

The federal government invested millions of dollars in development of risk adjustment models for HMOs serving Medicare beneficiaries to be sure that HMOs were realizing their savings by more efficient care practices, and not by attracting better risks, as was claimed by their critics. Risk adjustment was not the only way to mitigate concerns with risk selection. Reinsurance or a "stop loss" for plans can compensate them for very high cost patients and achieve some of the same objectives.

Critics of the competition idea argued that there was a complete lack of comparative data on quality of care, which was true, but there were consumer satisfaction surveys that could be of some assistance to patients. I replied that quality of care measures could be and needed to be developed, not just for the sake of competition but also to serve as a basis for quality improvement efforts. And they were. The National Committee for Quality Assurance (NCQA) appeared at the national level, alongside some state-level bodies such as the Integrated Healthcare Association (IHA) in California. The IHA is a non-profit consortium of insurers, medical groups and hospitals, with a Board made up of stakeholders, including a few professors, that formed collaborative working groups to develop valid quality measures. The IHA now publishes annually the comparative quality performance of about 200 participating physician organizations, using about 60 different measures.

The fact that I was working for Secretary Califano on a universal health insurance plan generated publicity and anticipation of what I might find and propose. Dr. Arnold Relman, then Editor of *the New England Journal of Medicine* invited me to prepare a version of my report to Califano for publication. A two-part article appeared in March 1978, and the idea promptly attracted bi-partisan support. That year, two prominent members of Congress, Republican David Stockman, an articulate critic of the regulatory approach in place at the time and subsequently Budget Director for President Reagan, and Richard Gephardt, leader of Congressional Democrats, had my report translated into legislative language in the form of the National HealthCare Reform Act of 1981.

Consumer Choice Health Plan (CCHP), the name I had given my proposal, would provide multiple health plans competing for members in each geographic market area, with the Federal Government deciding on the standard coverage contract, and paying in full for the low-priced qualified plan in each market area. Anyone choosing a different and more costly plan would pay the full difference in premium with net-after-tax dollars. The very costly (in terms of federal tax collections) exclusion of employer contributions to employee health care would be repealed, and the revenues thereby generated would help pay for the government's premium support payments. That alone would not have been enough to pay for the government's costs, but, taking the long view, the inexorable rise of National Health Expenditures as a percent of the GDP would likely have been attenuated or stopped. The inflationary incentives of the existing system would have been reversed. With more cost-effective plans setting lower premiums, consumers would have been attracted to the low-priced plan to save money and health plans and affiliated provider groups would have incentives to innovate and bring down their costs to attract consumers.

I imagined that the most successful competitors would be organized systems like PGPs, in which the organizations' incentives for efficiency would be translated into incentives for medical groups to innovate to find ways to improve outcomes and cut costs.

I argued that the choice of plans must be at the *individual* level, rather than plans competing to serve whole groups. Competition for groups might require a unanimous consent in which all employees must agree to switch from one plan to another, an agreement highly unlikely if switching plans means changing doctors. In competition, plans will select either preferred providers or affiliated medical groups, so choice of plan must mean individual choice. Also, the correct conception of competition should be for informed cost-conscious choice among comprehensive care organizations that offer annual memberships, rather than among individual items of service. The reason for comprehensive care organizations or networks is that it takes systems to improve quality and economy. Quality of care is a system property.

Further debate and discussion brought out the need for a modification to the model for competition to lead to socially desirable results. Enrollment needed to be done through a neutral broker like an exchange or the employee benefits office so that health plans cannot select risks in the enrollment process.

CCHP was not adopted by the Carter Administration. Instead, President Carter, in my view, wasted four years seeking the enactment of price controls on hospitals, an idea that was simplistic and naïve and went nowhere. Thankfully, the idea of Managed Competition did not die. Bills using some of the ideas were introduced by Democratic Ways and Means Committee Chairman Al Ullman, and Senate Finance Committee Member Republican Senator David Durenberger. In 2010, Senator Ron Wyden, ranking Democrat on the Senate Finance Committee teamed up with Republican Senator Bob Bennett and with 16 bi-partisan co-sponsors in the Senate to introduce a plan that was very similar to CCHP. In 1999, the National Bi-Partisan Commission on the Future of Medicare, led by Democratic Senator John Breaux and Republican Congressman Bill Thomas proposed the same idea for Medicare. About 3 years later, the Bipartisan Policy Commission, headed by former Senator and Republican Budget Committee Chairman Pete Domenici and Alice Rivlin, founding Director of the Congressional Budget Office and Director of the Office of Management and Budget for President Clinton, proposed a similar plan for Medicare. CalPERS continues its successful operation, adopting refinements of the Managed Competition idea including standard contracts and risk adjustment of premiums. The FEHBP, the first large-scale competition model continues its successful operation, though without risk adjustment or standard benefits. Interestingly, in nearly 60 years of successful operation, nobody has proposed going back to a fee-for-service or single payer model.

The 2010 Affordable Care Act, struggling to survive in the face of Republican efforts to repeal it, is alive and well, performing particularly well in California. All this suggests that a regulated competition model has a good potential to attract bi-partisan support. It is heartening to me to see how many places around the world, and in important health insurance sectors in my own country, have managed to put these ideas into practice.

**Alain Enthoven**

# Acknowledgments

McGuire acknowledges support from the Linda and John Arnold Foundation. This collaborative project was inspired by the Risk Adjustment Network (RAN) members who contributed as chapter authors and commenters. Sarah Stone devoted part of her Summer 2017 to helping edit the chapters when they were arriving fast and furious. We are grateful to her for skilled help at a critical time. Most gratitude is due to our colleagues from around the world who took the time to assemble such an authoritative set of chapters, and to put up with our repeated calls for revisions. Finally, the editors thank Elsevier's Susan Ikeda for her guidance and assistance throughout the logistically complex writing and production process.

# Part I

# Theory

Chapter 1

# Regulated Competition in Health Insurance Markets: Paradigms and Ongoing Issues

**Thomas G. McGuire[1] and Richard C. van Kleef[2]**

[1]*Department of Health Care Policy, Harvard Medical School and the NBER, Boston, MA, United States,* [2]*Erasmus School of Health Policy and Management, Erasmus University Rotterdam, Rotterdam, The Netherlands*

## 1.1 INTRODUCTION

Around the world we find health insurance systems characterized by "regulated (or managed) competition," systems in which private health insurers compete on price and quality within bounds set by regulation. The institutional antecedents of these systems are diverse; some evolved from market-based insurance systems, such as in the United States, some from private nonmarket institutions such as the sickness funds in Germany and the Netherlands, and some from single-payer public insurance, as in Israel. Despite their different paths of reform, everywhere these systems share, in broad terms, common objectives of access, fairness in financing, and efficiency in both the health insurance products and in healthcare provision. Though the relative importance of these objectives differs across systems, countries and sectors share the challenge of evaluating and mediating the tradeoffs among the objectives.

Again speaking broadly, public systems, even when adequately financed, tend to do well on access and fairness, but do less well on serving diverse preferences (for insurance and health care), promoting innovation, and conveying to providers incentives for quality and cost control. Unfettered private health insurance markets, while generally effective at conferring incentives for innovation, quality, and cost control, also suffer from well-known problems, score poorly on access and fairness, and frustrate social objectives relating to supporting care for sicker, more costly members of society.

The regulated competition approach seeks to draw on the strengths and avoid the shortcomings of pure public or pure market systems. The essence

Risk Adjustment, Risk Sharing and Premium Regulation in Health Insurance Markets.
DOI: https://doi.org/10.1016/B978-0-12-811325-7.00001-4

of this approach is that a "regulator" decides where competition should work to affect health insurance outcomes and where these outcomes should be set by regulation. For example, a "minimum benefit package" might constrain competition on insurance product design, allowing competition for more but not less coverage; premium regulation might permit plans to set the level of premium overall but prohibit setting different premiums for subgroups of the population; and so on. This chapter begins in Section 1.2 with an overview of the intellectual roots of regulated competition, introducing the seminal ideas of Alain Enthoven and Peter Diamond. Section 1.3 illustrates how the forms of regulated competition proposed by these scholars have been put into practice in the United States, Europe, Asia, Australia, and Latin America. Section 1.4 summarizes the menu of regulatory tools used for structuring and monitoring competition in health insurance and places health plan payment—the focus of this volume—in the context of these tools. Section 1.5 sketches the outline of this entire 19-chapter volume and explains how we see the current volume as contributing to policy and research on regulated competition and health plan payment.

## 1.2  INTELLECTUAL ROOTS OF REGULATED COMPETITION

The intellectual roots of regulated competition trace back to Alain Enthoven, an economist and planner who served in the Departments of Defense and the (then-named) Department of Health Education and Welfare in the US federal government. Enthoven sought to "change financial incentives by creating a system of competing health plans in which physicians and consumers can benefit from using resources wisely" (Enthoven, 1978, 1980).[1] Over time, this simple idea was developed by Enthoven himself (e.g., Enthoven, 1989, 1993) and further refined and operationalized in specific contexts by others (e.g., Enthoven and Van de Ven, 1993; Van de Ven et al., 2013; Cutler, 1994). Section 1.2.1 summarizes the main ideas from this stream of literature. A key feature of Enthoven's model is that competition between health plans operates at the *individual (or family) level*. In Section 1.2.2 we call attention to a second major intellectual theme within a broadly defined regulated competition approach which relies on health plan competition at the *group level*. This later idea originates with Peter Diamond (1992), an economist at MIT and an expert in social insurance. Section 1.3 documents how regulated health insurance markets today reflect the ideas of both Enthoven and Diamond.

### 1.2.1  Evolution of the Enthoven Model: Individual-Insurance Markets Managed by a Sponsor-Regulator

The original proposal (Enthoven, 1980) as well as the modified proposals for 1990s (Enthoven and Kronick, 1989) were developed for national policy in the United States. In *Health Plan*, Enthoven (1980) called his approach the Consumer Choice Health Plan (CCHP), and described it succinctly as follows:

> *The most important principles …. are* multiple choice *and* fixed-dollar subsidies. *Once a year, each family (or individual) would have the opportunity to enroll for the coming year in any of the qualified health plans operating in its area. The amount of financial help each family gets toward the purchase of its health plan membership — from Medicare, Medicaid, employer, or tax laws — would be the same whichever plan it chooses. The subsidy might be more for poor than for nonpoor, for old than young, for family than individuals,* but not more for people who choose more costly health plans. *The family that chooses a more costly plan would pay the extra cost itself. Thus it would have an incentive to consider the cost. In addition, physicians would be organized in competing economic units (most would participate in one or another alternative delivery system), so that the premium each group charged would reflect its ability to control costs. (p. xxii, emphases in original)*

Enthoven was adamant about the principle of a subsidy to each individual/family *independent of their plan choice*, as this was critical to create incentives for consumers to choose less expensive plans, and therefore critical for creating incentives to plans to cut costs so as to be able to lower premiums and increase enrollment.

Enthoven's original vision differs from contemporary models of regulated competition based on individual health insurance in two main ways. First, health plans in the original Enthoven model were paid directly by enrollees. A central authority might subsidize purchases, but there was no sponsor collecting funds, risk-adjusting the funds, and then disbursing them to plans. In the late 1970s, when Enthoven first developed his ideas, there was nothing like the risk adjustment formulas available today to use as a basis for health plan payment. Instead of risk rating in plan payments from a central fund, the Enthoven model relied on a simple demand-side risk rating. Specifically, Enthoven proposed allowing insurers to charge more "to people in categories with higher average medical costs":

> *I propose a modified system of community rating called 'community rating by actuarial category.' The idea is to require insurers to charge the same premiums for the same benefits to all persons in the same demographic category, such as 'adults aged forty-five to sixty-five,' but to allow higher premiums to be charged to people in categories with higher average medical costs. Insurance is still made affordable for people in the higher-cost categories by providing them with higher government subsidies. (pp 80–81).*

Second, as evident from the earlier quotation, Enthoven imagined competition to take place among competing delivery systems. Enthoven, influenced by the early health maintenance organization (HMO) movement in the

United States, envisioned closed network provider groups forming the backbone of the competing health plans in the CCHP. Today, plans and providers are distinct economic units in the Netherlands, Germany, Switzerland, and elsewhere, and while closed network plans exist in the United States, they compete with plans with large networks.

The Enthoven model has evolved as its ideas have been applied in particular institutional contexts. Today, sophisticated risk adjustment models give a regulator an effective tool to quantify differences among individuals in their expected healthcare costs. Rather than a system of risk-rated premiums, regulators rely more on risk adjustment to pay plans more for higher-risk enrollees. Also, the countries in which the regulated competition model has become dominant (e.g., Germany, the Netherlands) are characterized by separation of the functions of health insurance and healthcare provision. Regulated competition can and has been implemented without the presence of integrated HMO-type risk-bearing delivery systems. In these countries, and in other settings such as Medicare Advantage in the United States, regulated competition is oriented to the health insurers, not the healthcare delivery system.

Throughout this evolution, the key feature of Enthoven's model remains: an active collective agent on the demand side of health insurance structures and manages the health plan market to overcome market failures. Enthoven calls this agent a "sponsor," a role that can be fulfilled by various organizations. In health insurance markets today, sponsors are mainly governments (as is common in Europe and the United States) and employers (as is common in the United States). In this volume we will generally refer to a "regulator."

## 1.2.2 Diamond Model: "First-Stage" Group-Level Competition

In one of his first acts as chief executive, in 1993, President Bill Clinton initiated a "health care reform." The goal of the ultimately failed attempt in the early 1990s, similar to the later successful reform led by President Barack Obama, was to reform the health insurance (not healthcare) sector, and to do so in a way to promote near universal coverage. The intellectual inspiration of the Clinton health reform came from Diamond who proposed competition at the group level—the second major form of regulated competition. Diamond recommended health insurance for the entire US population be based on the most prevalent and generally successful model of employer-based health insurance in which a sponsor (in this case, the large employer) ran a first-stage competition choosing an insurer to offer a small number of plans to members of the group. Diamond (1992) summarized his plan as follows:

> In a nutshell, the principles for combining regulation and competition that underlie the proposal below are the following. Health insurance should only be provided through large groups. The government forms the groups (on a geographic basis) using its power of compulsion. Market competition is preserved, with

*private insurance companies competing for the large groups. There are multiple large groups in any area to enhance competition and provide yardstick competition. A new semi-autonomous government agency will be created to serve the role for each group now played by employee benefit offices in large firms. Choice from a short menu will be offered individuals in each group, although the organization and pricing of these choices will be different from that currently followed by large firms. Financing is by a combination of taxes and out-of-pocket payments for premiums. Having all individuals in similar large groups will alter the relationship between insurance companies and medical providers, allowing a negotiation approach to cost containment strategies. (1992, pp. 1239–40)*

Diamond proposed organizing the entire US population into groups of 20,000–200,000; initially, these could include large employers. Like large employers, the Diamond approach relied heavily on a first-stage competition to be able to offer plans to members of a group. The Clinton reform, drawing on Diamond's ideas, would have created regional "health alliances" that served the Diamond group function (Cutler, 1994).

The ability to limit choice to a few health plan options gives the sponsor another powerful tool to deal with market failures in health insurance. Rather than relying primarily on regulation of dimensions of a health plan's product, the sponsor can act as an informed buyer and preselect an insurer for its population, based on criteria and priorities established by the sponsor. In Diamond's model, a potential insurer bid applies to the entire menu of offerings (e.g., a more and a less generous plan) so that one insurance entity bears the entire risk for the group. Incentives to engage in risk selection in a second stage would thus be "greatly diminished" (Diamond, 2012, p. 1241). The Diamond groups would not need formal risk adjustment models, for the same reasons such models are not used in employer-based health insurance in the United States (Glazer and McGuire, 2001).

While both the original Enthoven and Diamond approaches rely on competition to establish incentives for efficiency, they did so in different ways. In the Enthoven model insurers compete for individuals, while in the Diamond model they compete for groups. The most obvious difference is that the Diamond model limits consumer choice since the health plan options available for individuals in a group will be much smaller than those available in Enthoven's idea of a marketplace. Table 1.1 summarizes other main features of the original Diamond and Enthoven models of regulated competition.

## 1.3   PREVALENCE OF REGULATED COMPETITION

Part II of this volume covers 14 health insurance systems in which (some of) the ideas by Enthoven and/or Diamond have been implemented. We briefly introduce these systems and give a flavor of the roles of competition and regulation.

**TABLE 1.1** Regulated Competition in Original Enthoven and Diamond Models

|  | Individual-level competition | Group-level competition |
| --- | --- | --- |
| Intellectual origin | Enthoven (1980) | Diamond (1992) |
| Level of competition | Individual or family | Natural groups created by regulation |
| Regulated minimum plan coverage/quality; some coverage/quality competition permitted | Yes | Yes |
| Consumer premium levels | Set by plan in market; subsidized for some or all | Insurer bids to group; subsidized for some or all |
| Open enrollment | Yes, switch frequency regulated | Only within plans offered by group |
| Consumer premium discrimination | Yes, by, e.g., age | Family size |
| Risk adjustment of payments to plans | No | No |
| Primary mechanism to deal with risk selection and adverse incentives | Risk rating of premiums; regulation of plan competition | Informed selection of insurer to offer to members |
| Modern examples | Netherlands National Health Insurance; US Medicare Advantage | Employer-sponsored health insurance in United States; Medicaid, US |

## 1.3.1 Individual and Group-Level Competition in the United States

Fig. 1.1 and Table 1.2 depict the sectors of health insurance in the United States in 2014 that rely on elements of the two forms of regulated competition. Fig. 1.1 displays numbers of people and total spending by a broadly defined procurement method. Beginning at the bottom of the figure, there is no private health plan (and no procurement) involved in some important sectors of the United States, including Traditional Medicare and the Veterans' Administration, as well as some other public programs. Moving up in Fig. 1.1, more than half of the US population has health insurance procured on its behalf by group-level or what we refer to above as "first-stage" competition, whereby a sponsor, in this case a private employer, chooses an insurer to offer limited (oftentimes very limited) choice to its employees. This group-level procurement method is by far the largest health insurance

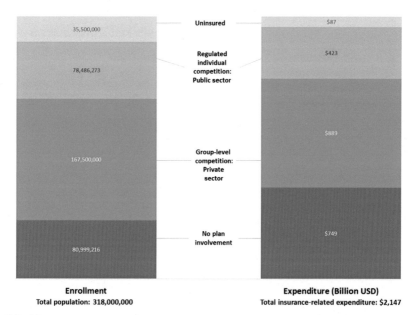

**FIGURE 1.1** 2014 US health insurance enrollment and expenditure by insurance market type. *National Health Expenditure Accounts, CMS, CBO, KFF.*

market type in the United States both in terms of the number of people covered (167.5 million) and in terms of spending ($889 billion).

Regulated competition in individual health insurance markets applies to 78.5 million people in the United States and accounts for $423 billion of healthcare spending. This broad segment is made up of Marketplaces, other individual private health insurance outside of the Marketplaces, Medicaid Managed Care, and Medicare Advantage. Table 1.2 summarizes some of the key features of these regulated competition markets, and breaks out the people and dollars across each. Each sector, the Marketplaces, Medicaid Managed Care, and Medicare Advantage, is the subject of a chapter in this volume—the reader is referred there for more information about these sectors. For purposes of comparison, the largest health insurance market type, that serving large employers, is listed on the right-hand side of the table. Large employers in the United States are squarely within the Diamond model of regulated competition.

## 1.3.2   Individual-Level Competition in Europe

Part II of this volume covers six European health insurance systems with regulated competition. Table 1.3 summarizes some of their general features, in some cases different elements than we used to summarize sectors in the

**TABLE 1.2** Health Insurance Procurement Methods in the United States

|  | Medicare advantage | Marketplaces | Medicaid managed care | Employer-based |
|---|---|---|---|---|
| Role of competition | Individual choice of plans | Individual choice of plans; "Active Marketplaces" use first-stage competition | Individual choice of plans; generally use some first-stage competition | First-stage competition for the contract |
| Price to enrollee | Single price set by plan; mildly income-related; highly subsidized; could be positive or negative | Set by plan; subsidized by income; limited rating categories | No price to enrollees | Subsidized by employer; set by employer |
| Benefits | At least as good as traditional Medicare | Highly regulated; metal tiers defined by actuarial value; maximum out-of-pocket | Very comprehensive though vary by state. Little or no demand-side cost sharing | Limited regulation of coverage. Demand-side cost sharing ranges from very little to very high |
| Choice | Varies. Many choices to highly concentrated; issuer may have many plans in same market | Varies. Many markets to highly concentrated; issuer may have many plans in same market | Usually small number; nonactive choosers may be "auto-assigned" | No choice or choice among 2–3 plans most common |
| Risk adjustment | Yes | Yes | Yes | No |
| Enrollment 2014 | 16.0 m | 5.4 m | 43.4 m | 167.5 m |
| Expenditure 2014 | $156 b | $22 b | $162 b | $889 b |

**TABLE 1.3** Examples of Regulated Health Insurance Markets in Europe

| | Belgium | Germany | Ireland | Israel | Netherlands | Switzerland |
|---|---|---|---|---|---|---|
| Role of competition | Individual choice of plans | Individual choice of plans | Individual choice of plans | Individual choice of plans | Individual choice of plans | Individual choice of plans |
| What is regulated? | Coverage; enrollment; health plan payment | Coverage; enrollment; health plan payment | Coverage; enrollment; health plan payment | Coverage; enrollment; health plan payment | Coverage; enrollment; health plan payment | Coverage; enrollment; health plan payment |
| Dimensions of contract space | Very limited | Very limited | Provider network; benefits on top of minimum coverage; cost-sharing options | Provider network; | Provider network; cost-sharing options; group arrangements | Provider network; cost-sharing options |
| Enrollment | 11.3 m (2015) | 71.5 m (2016) | 2.1 m (2017) | 8.3 m (2016) | 16.9 m (2016) | 8.3 m (2015) |
| Expenditure | €23.8 b (2016) | €218.4 b (2016) | €2.1 b (2016) | €12.8 b (2016) | €42.7 b (2016) | CHF 43.4 b (2015) |

United States. All six rely on Enthoven's approach of establishing incentives for efficiency via individual choice of health plan, and all use some form of risk adjustment to pay plans. Regulation of coverage, enrollment, and health plan payment seeks to avoid market failures and guarantee access and individual affordability. In Part II of the volume, big differences can be observed in the design of these regulatory tools, and health plan payment in particular. There are also differences in the insurers' flexibility in health plan design. Whereas in Belgium and Germany plans are very similar, plans in other countries are allowed to differ in terms of provider network, cost-sharing options, and/or additional benefits on top of the minimum coverage. In terms of spending and enrollment, the German system has the largest market size followed by the Netherlands, Belgium, Switzerland, Israel, and Ireland. Only in Ireland is enrollment voluntary. All five other countries mandate insurance coverage in some way.

### 1.3.3 Regulated Competition in Australia, Asia, and Latin America

Regulated competition in health insurance can be found in country markets around the world. Part II covers five of these countries, i.e., Australia, China, Chile, Colombia, and Russia. Table 1.4 summarizes some general characteristics of these systems. With 736 million enrollees, China has the largest social health insurance system in the world. Some components of this scheme, which are executed by local governments, have elements from the Diamond model. As described in more detail in Chapter 9, Health Insurance and Payment System Reform in China, local governments can—and more and more actually do—purchase insurance via first-stage competition. The other four countries in Table 1.4 rely on individual choices of health plan for establishing competition among insurers, more aligned with the Enthoven model. Though these systems all rely on regulation of coverage, enrollment, and health plan payment to promote access, affordability, and efficiency, they greatly differ in the design of these tools. The same is true for the dimensions of contract space. While the system in Russia provides hardly any flexibility in health plan design, the Chilean, Australian, and Colombian systems allow for variation in provider network, cost-sharing options, and/or additional benefits on top of the minimum coverage.

### 1.4 THE ROLE OF HEALTH PLAN PAYMENT IN REGULATED COMPETITION

The role of health plan payment in regulated health insurance markets depends fundamentally on the form of competition. In Diamond's model of first-stage competition, it is important that total revenues for a group (e.g., employees of a firm) cover total insurance claims for that group. A

**TABLE 1.4** Examples of Regulated Health Insurance Markets in Australia, Asia, and Latin America

| | Australia | China | Chile | Colombia | Russia |
|---|---|---|---|---|---|
| Role of competition | Individual choice of plans | Some regulators (i.e., local governments) purchase insurance via first-stage competition for the contract | Individual choice of plans | Individual choice of plans | Individual choice of plans |
| What is regulated? | Coverage; enrollment; health plan payment | Coverage; enrollment; health plan payment | Coverage; enrollment; health plan payment | Coverage; enrollment; health plan payment | Coverage; enrollment; health plan payment |
| Dimensions of contract space | Provider network; benefits on top of minimum coverage; cost-sharing options; group arrangements | None | Provider network; benefits on top of minimum coverage; cost-sharing options | Provider network; | None |
| Enrollment | 13.3 m (2016) | 736 m (2014) | 17 m (2015) | 46.4 m (2016) | 142 m (2016) |
| Expenditure | AUD $13.9 b (2016) | 289 b yuan (2014) | $12.1 b (2015) | US$ 9.4 b (2015) | 2.7 b roubles (2016) |

(negotiated or market-set) single average premium paid to a plan can achieve that outcome. In the modern version of Enthoven's model of individual choice of health plan, however, the role of plan payment is more complicated: on the one hand the payment system should promote affordability of coverage, while on the other hand it should maintain incentives for insurers and consumers to use resources wisely. Moreover, the role of health plan payment depends on the other regulatory tools in place. For example, greater contract space not only expands the insurers' instruments for efficiency, but also expands the insurers' toolkit for risk selection. Therefore, greater contract space requires better adjustment of health plan payments to variation in individuals' cost risk, e.g., via risk adjustment, risk sharing, and/or risk rating. In this section we first describe the broader menu of regulatory tools (Section 1.4.1) and then elaborate on the role of health plan payment in individual health insurance markets (Section 1.4.2).

## 1.4.1 The Broader Menu of Regulatory Tools

Tools to regulate individual health insurance markets can be clustered into five general categories: (1) regulation of coverage, (2) regulation of enrollment, (3) regulation of market entry, (4) regulation of health plan payment, and (5) market support and surveillance (see Table 1.5). Regulation of coverage refers to the regulator requiring health plans cover a standardized set of benefits with specified demand-side cost sharing or a certain set of cost-sharing options. With this tool the regulator can counteract risk selection on the basis of width and depth of coverage (Enthoven, 1989). Regulators typically specify the terms of coverage but leave some aspects of implementation of this to plans. This could mean, for instance, that health plans are obliged to cover cancer treatment but have some freedom in deciding where and by whom such treatment is to be delivered. Under this form of regulation, health plans can differ in terms of price and quality (e.g., the quality of the contracted network of physicians) but not (or only limited) in terms of coverage. Regulators in many cases limit plans' network and contracting decisions in order to deter some of the same selection-driven incentives associated with coverage.

On the demand side, regulation of enrollment could mean that the regulator requires individuals or families to buy (a certain minimum of) insurance coverage. Such regulation may also specify a standardization of the contract period (typically 1 year) and/or the date and circumstances in which consumers are allowed to switch health plan. For example, plan switching might be possible on January 1 of each year, or upon changes in personal circumstances such as a geographical move or a marriage. Limits on switching prevent consumers from moving in and out of more generous coverage in response to health events, and therefore counteract adverse selection and the threats it poses to efficient plan design (Enthoven, 1989). On the supply side, regulation of enrollment can mean that insurers are

**TABLE 1.5 Regulator's Tools for Structuring and Managing Individual Health Insurance Markets**

| General tools | Examples of specific regulation |
|---|---|
| Regulation of coverage | • Standardization of benefits<br>• Standardization of consumer cost-sharing<br>• Network requirements |
| Regulation of enrollment | • Insurance mandate<br>• Open enrollment<br>• Standardized contract length<br>• Central entry point for enrollment |
| Management of market entry | • Screening of insurers (e.g., in terms of solvency)<br>• Screening of plans (e.g., in terms of transparency)<br>• Screening of provider networks (e.g., in terms of quality) |
| Market support and surveillance | • Promotion of transparency<br>• Quality measurement<br>• Antitrust supervision<br>• Solvency requirements<br>• Monitoring of risk selection |
| Regulation of health plan payment | • Premium regulation<br>• Risk equalization<br>• Risk sharing<br>• Subsidies (e.g., to consumers, health plans, employers and/or providers of care) |

obliged to accept every applicant independent of the applicant's characteristics. This so-called "open enrollment" avoids selective underwriting and guarantees consumers access to health plans.

Regulation of market entry in the context of health plan regulation is a complex issue. On the one hand, competition conveys the usual benefits in terms of pressuring sellers to be efficient, to price near cost, and to design their product and to innovate in response to consumer preferences. On the other hand, in the presence of incentives related to adverse selection, it is well-established that competition in the context of free choice of consumers does not lead to efficiency (Rothschild and Stiglitz, 1976; Glazer and McGuire, 2000). The key point, however, is that with respect to competition and regulation of health insurance, both major forms of regulated competition, Enthoven or Diamond-style, rely on vigorous competition among insurers for good sector performance. Although Diamond-style limits choice at a second stage, when consumers are choosing plans, the initial selection of insurer to offer at the second stage will only serve consumers efficiently if there is vigorous competition at the first stage. Regulation of entry could also concern solvency requirements for insurance companies. Finally, a regulator might exclude plans that offer poor quality, poor service, or biased information (e.g., on coverage and entitlements).

In addition to market regulations, some support and surveillance may be necessary to manage the marketplace. Support could mean that the regulator helps developing product classifications and quality indicators (in order to ease negotiations between insurers and providers). Regulators could promote transparency by developing websites on which consumers can make independent comparisons between health plans. Surveillance may include antitrust regulation and monitoring of market behavior (e.g., naming and shaming of insurers applying risk selection).

The tools described above help to promote access to health insurance coverage, but do not guarantee individual affordability, a central goal of many countries with respect to health insurance markets. Without regulation, competition will push health plans to charge risk-rated premiums. For people with known expensive conditions risk rating can lead to premiums of tens of thousands of euros per year, violating the standard that health insurance should be affordable to all members of society. All systems covered in this volume rely on premium regulation to avoid high premiums for sick people. A well-known drawback of premium regulation, however, is that it exacerbates incentives for risk selection, which can lead to a variety of inefficiencies. Additional tools—such as risk adjustment and risk sharing—are needed to correct for these selection incentives. Moreover, subsidies are generally necessary to make coverage affordable for low-income people. As will be described in more detail in this volume, beginning with Chapter 2, Premium Regulation, Risk Equalization, Risk Sharing, and Subsidies: Effects on Affordability and Efficiency, regulation of health plan payment is a cornerstone in achieving affordability and efficiency. At the same time, health plan payment design is complex and involves a variety of tradeoffs.

## 1.4.2 Regulation of Health Plan Payment

Regulation of health plan payment has become one of the foundations of regulated competition in individual health insurance markets. Both theory and practice have shown that no payment system achieves all goals. Inevitably, payment system design requires tradeoffs between the objectives associated with regulated competition such as access, affordability, and efficiency, with the best choice ultimately depending on how regulators weight these different objectives. Moreover, implementation of payment systems is not only guided by economic criteria for payment design, but also depends on political and cultural aspects of the country or sector. As illustrated in Table 1.6, regulation of health plan payment design substantially varies across systems. We present three here, and highlight some of the differences to introduce the complexity of plan payment design discussed in detail throughout this volume.

**TABLE 1.6** Regulatory Framework in Three Systems of Regulated Competition

| General tools | US Marketplaces | Netherlands | Israel |
|---|---|---|---|
| Premiums | • Limited rating categories on the basis of age, region, and tobacco use<br>• Premiums finance 100% of the insurance claims | • Community-rating per health plan<br>• Premiums finance about 50% of insurance claims | • No premium |
| Risk adjustment | • Risk adjusters based on age, gender, and diagnoses<br>• Zero-sum | • Risk adjusters based on age, gender, region, diagnoses, socioeconomic factors, and prior cost<br>• Risk adjustment payments finance about 50% of insurance claims | • Risk adjusters on age, gender, and region<br>• Health plans' revenues (for the national health insurance) exclusively consist of risk adjustment payments and some additional funds from the government |
| Risk sharing | • Reinsurance and risk corridors from 2014 to 2016 | • None | • None |
| Subsidies | • Income-based subsidies to consumers | • Income-based subsidies to consumers | • None |

In terms of premiums, the US Marketplaces allow for some discrimination on the basis of age, region, and tobacco use, while the Netherlands relies on community-rating per health plan. The choice of rating categories introduces a tradeoff between fairness and efficiency. Risk rating on the basis of age reduces affordability for older people. At the same time it brings the price down for younger people, closer to their costs, and makes insurance more attractive which—in the absence of a strong mandate, as in the Marketplaces—can promote enrollment among this group. Risk rating according to lifestyle factors—like tobacco use—can stimulate healthy behavior and prevention on the side of consumers. Any premium risk rating will have implications for the design of plan payments. The presence of risk rating on age, e.g., means that the risk adjustment system should also not "adjust for age."

Despite the use of some premium rating categories, nonenrollment of the healthy people is indeed a problem in the US Marketplaces (Newhouse, 2017). One obvious solution would be to strengthen the mandate. Alternatively, redesign of the payment system could help as well. As shown in Table 1.6, insurance claims in the US Marketplaces are fully financed via the insurance premium. As a result, premiums might be (far) beyond what healthy people are willing to pay and thereby discourage enrollment. A fixed subsidy can help to bring down premiums. An example comes from the Netherlands where insurers receive a fixed subsidy per enrollee of about 50% of the mean per person insurance claims in the market (see Table 1.6). This subsidy—which is transferred via the risk adjustment system and financed by income-related earmarked taxes—reduces the insurance premium by about 50%, which encourages enrollment among young and healthy people. Marketplace premiums are also subsidized, but based on income (see Chapter 17: Health Plan Payment in US Marketplaces: Regulated Competition With a Weak Mandate).

In the Israeli system there is no premium at all. On the one hand, this maximizes affordability, but on the other hand it can hinder efficiency by limiting the domains of plan competition. In both the US Marketplaces and the Netherlands, competition takes place on the price and quality of health plans. This means that insurers might charge and get higher prices if they provide a more attractive health insurance product. A broader network, perhaps one including more expensive hospitals with a good reputation, e.g., might be a dimension of quality competition that requires higher pricing. Israeli plans can compete on quality but not on price. In Israel it is not possible to pass through savings from more efficient health system management to consumers, nor is it possible to charge higher prices for higher-quality plans.

All three systems rely on risk adjustment to pay insurers more for sick people. While the US Marketplaces and the Netherlands use sophisticated health-based algorithms, Israel uses a much simpler formula based on age, gender, and region only. Empirical research has shown, however, that demographic risk adjustment models correct for only a "small" portion of predictable spending variation (see Chapter 3: Risk Adjustment for Health Plan Payment). Given the absence of premiums and other payment features, this implies that health insurers in Israel are confronted with strong incentives to select healthy enrollees. Limited use of risk adjustors in the Israeli plan payment formula leaves a larger burden for other regulatory tools to limit plans tactics to select healthy enrollees.

In the US Marketplaces and the Netherlands, risk adjustment models also use diagnostic information. Though these models better correct for predictable spending variation, they come with a price since diagnoses-based variables create a link between treatment decisions and future payments to health plans. Such a link reduces incentives to avoid unnecessary treatments or even increases incentives to provide more of such treatments. Similar incentives are associated with the cost-based risk adjusters used in the Netherlands. How these incentives play out depends on the possibilities for health plans to influence treatment or coding decisions by providers.

Recent empirical literature has shown that even the sophisticated risk adjustment models in the US Marketplaces and the Netherlands do not completely correct for variation in predictable spending. As will be discussed in more detail in Chapter 4, risk sharing can be an effective strategy to mitigate the predictable profits and losses remaining after risk adjustment. As indicated in Table 1.6, both the US Marketplaces and the Netherlands have recently moved away from risk-sharing mechanisms. The impact of this decision involves tradeoffs. Risk sharing is effective at reducing incentives for selection but dilutes incentives for cost containment. Research described in Chapter 4, Risk Sharing, and Chapter 5, Evaluating the Performance of Health Plan Payment Systems, helps evaluate the terms of this fundamental tradeoff.

These brief comments on differences in health plan payment systems are meant to introduce some of the choices and tradeoffs faced in the design of policy in regulated competition. The purpose of this volume is to provide a comprehensive conceptual framework for understanding these complexities and a toolkit for designing and evaluating health plan payment systems.

## 1.5 THE OUTLINE OF THIS VOLUME

Section 1.4 has given a flavor of the differences in health plan payment systems and their implications for affordability and efficiency. Chapter 2, Premium Regulation, Risk Equalization, Risk Sharing, and Subsidies: Effects on Affordability and Efficiency, discusses these implications in more detail. Starting from an unregulated market, it describes and illustrates how premium regulation, risk adjustment, risk sharing, and several forms of subsidies affect affordability and efficiency. This conceptual framework helps to identify the specific tradeoffs that come with these different components of payment system design.

Today, plan payment methodologies are a more important feature of regulated competition in individual health insurance markets than in the early Enthoven proposals. One important reason for this is the development of the "technology" of risk adjustment. When Enthoven and Diamond were first developing their ideas, data and risk adjustment methods were primitive in comparison to the methodologies available today. Early risk adjustment models did not include measures of health status, whereas today in many health insurance markets, risk adjustment uses scores of health status variables as a basis of payment. Chapter 3, Risk Adjustment for Health Plan Payment, reviews the huge literature on risk adjustment methods and models. It provides a conceptual framework for risk adjustment design and gives an overview of state-of-the-art methodologies.

Chapter 4, Risk Sharing, dives into the concept and details of risk sharing, another important tool for health plan payment design. Broadly speaking, risk sharing can serve two purposes. First, it can help to mitigate selection incentives remaining after risk adjustment. Second, it can help to reduce financial risks for insurers, e.g., to protect insurers from uncertainties related to outliers in the distribution of healthcare spending or uncertainties produced by the payment system itself. Risk sharing might avoid high loading fees and encourage market entry. After a discussion of these goals, Chapter 4 gives an overview of different risk-sharing modalities and discusses how these modalities help to mitigate selection incentives and protect insurers from extensive financial risk. It also discusses how risk sharing can be integrated with risk adjustment, in terms of estimation of risk adjustment models and in terms of a complementary policy to mitigate incentives for risk selection.

In order to make well-informed choices with respect to health plan payment design, ex-ante information on the performance of different payment modalities is crucial. Chapter 5, Evaluating the Performance of Health Plan Payment Systems, provides a conceptual framework and a series of metrics to perform such evaluations. It starts by discussing some conventional evaluation metrics including the $R$-squared from a risk adjustment regression and under/overcompensations (or predictive ratios) for groups of interest. Though these metrics can be very helpful, in some circumstances, they can be improved. Chapter 5 describes how and in what circumstances modifications are called for. The chapter also develops metrics for measuring the efficiency of consumer sorting among health plan options and incentives for cost control that are new to the literature on health plan payment.

After the conceptual chapters, Part II of this volume turns to the practice of health plan payment and describes the context, design, and challenges of 14 different systems. For each system authors will outline how regulated competition is organized and then focus on the role of health plan payment. After a detailed description of the payment system in place, each chapter reviews the performance of that system and discusses the ongoing issues and reforms.

## ENDNOTE

1. In his early work Enthoven refers to his proposal as "regulated competition" (see, e.g., Enthoven, 1978) while in his later work he uses "managed competition." Since regulation of health insurance markets may stretch further than "managing" competition, we use the original terminology but accept both forms in the material to follow in this volume.

Chapter 2

# Premium Regulation, Risk Equalization, Risk Sharing, and Subsidies: Effects on Affordability and Efficiency

Richard C. van Kleef, Frederik T. Schut
and Wynand P.M.M. van de Ven
*Erasmus School of Health Policy and Management, Erasmus University Rotterdam, Rotterdam, The Netherlands*

## 2.1 INTRODUCTION

A major challenge in regulated health insurance markets is to design a payment system that promotes both affordability and efficiency. By affordability we mean that all consumers are able to buy a certain level of coverage, including people with low income and those in poor health. Efficiency has multiple dimensions of which three are primarily focused on in this chapter: efficiency of production, efficiency of health plan design, and efficiency of consumer sorting (see Box 2.1). The goal of this chapter is to show how different payment system interventions (i.e., premium regulation, risk equalization, risk sharing, and various forms of subsidies) influence these objectives. This exercise helps to understand the tradeoffs involved with these different interventions and provides a conceptual basis for payment system design.

When it comes to promoting affordability, a first question is: "For which coverage?," for instance in terms of the benefits package, provider network, and levels of cost sharing. Obviously, the answer to this question requires a normative decision by the regulator. In what follows we assume the regulator has determined a target level of what we refer to as "basic" coverage. This coverage is not necessarily fully specified. Most regulators define basic coverage in terms of a "contract space" in which insurers have some flexibility with respect to health plan design and consumers have a set of choice options. In the Netherlands, the US Marketplaces, and Switzerland, for instance, consumers

Risk Adjustment, Risk Sharing and Premium Regulation in Health Insurance Markets.
DOI: https://doi.org/10.1016/B978-0-12-811325-7.00002-6

> **BOX 2.1 Dimensions of efficiency focused on in this chapter**
>
> By *efficiency of production* we mean that the cost of health plans (i.e., medical and administrative expenses) are minimized, holding quality constant.
>
> By *efficiency of health plan design* we mean that insurance products are designed in response to consumers' preferences about price and quality (e.g., in terms of coverage and provider network).
>
> Efficiency of consumer sorting has two dimensions: sorting into the market and sorting within the market across plans. By *efficiency of sorting into the market* we mean that consumers who value insurance coverage at more than their expected insurance claims under that coverage plus the loading fee, actually buy insurance. By *efficiency of sorting across plans* we mean that each consumer enrolls in the plan with the highest net value over cost.

can choose among different levels of cost sharing. In many countries, insurers have flexibility regarding network design and provider contracting.

Without regulatory intervention, competitive health insurance markets do not guarantee affordability and efficiency. First, these markets tend towards risk rating, which threatens the affordability of basic coverage for high-risk people, such as those with expensive medical conditions. Moreover, for low-income people, premiums for basic coverage might be unaffordable anyway, even for those who are healthy. Second, to the extent that risk rating is incomplete, these markets tend towards risk selection by consumers and insurers, which threatens both affordability and efficiency. In the remainder of this introductory section, we explain and illustrate these issues with the information in Fig. 2.1. The bars in this figure show the mean per person insurance claims under the Dutch basic health insurance in 2013 for a series of medical conditions derived from the use of prescribed drugs in 2012 (see Box 2.2).

As a starting point of the illustration, we assume that Fig. 2.1 exactly covers the population for which a regulator wants to make basic coverage affordable, and that the bars represent the mean annual per person insurance claims that are expected to occur under that coverage. Moreover, we assume that insurance contracts have a duration of 1 year.

### 2.1.1 Risk Rating: A Threat to the Affordability of Basic Coverage for High-Risk People

By risk rating we mean that the premium for a contract is adjusted to the expected claims under that contract. Assume that both the consumer and the insurer know the medical condition of a consumer as well as the mean expected claims per condition. Now imagine a market with two types of insurers: type A, which charges a community-rated premium equal to the

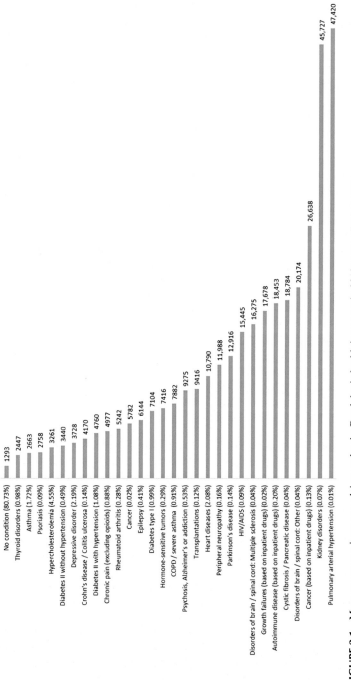

**FIGURE 2.1** Mean per person insurance claims under the Dutch basic health insurance in 2013 per medical condition.
Note: The medical conditions are derived from the use of specific pharmaceuticals in the prior year (see Box 2.2 for further explanation). The overall mean insurance claims are 2160 euros per person per year. The percentages in parentheses represent the frequency of people with a medical condition relative to the total population.

---

**BOX 2.2 A numerical illustration based on the Dutch Pharmacy-based Cost Groups (PCGs)**

The data used for our numerical illustration include individual-level insurance claims and risk characteristics of all individuals with a health plan under the Dutch basic health insurance in 2013 ($N = 16.6$ million). One of the risk characteristics in the dataset is a morbidity-classification based on the use of prescribed drugs in 2012. In practice, this classification is referred to as "Pharmacy-based Cost Groups" (PCGs). More specifically, each PCG represents a medical condition and includes individuals who used a certain quantity (in most cases: >180 defined daily dosages per year) of specific drugs that are known to be used by people suffering from that condition (see also Chapter 14: Health Plan Payment in the Netherlands). Since these PCGs are based on information from 2012, the variation in mean insurance claims across PCGs in 2013 can be considered "predictable." Fig. 2.1 shows that the predictable variation in insurance claims is substantial: for people in none of the 30 PCGs (81% of the population) the mean insurance claims are about 1300 euros per person per year, while for those in a PCG (19%) the mean claims per PCG vary from 2450 to 47,400 euros per person per year. Overall, the mean insurance claims are 2160 euros per person per year. Note that the number of PCGs shown here differs from the number mentioned in Chapter 14. The explanation is that the PCGs shown here correspond to the classification used in the risk equalization model of 2016 while the classification described in Chapter 14 corresponds to the classification used in the risk equalization model of 2017. For the purpose of risk equalization, people can be classified in multiple PCGs. Here we classified people in one PCG only. Those who are eligible for multiple PCGs (due to use of multiple relevant drugs) are classified in the one with the highest mean insurance claims in 2013.

---

*overall* mean claims, and type B, which charges a risk-rated premium equal to the mean expected claims per condition. (For simplicity we ignore loading fees.) In this market, people without a medical condition have a financial incentive to opt for B. For them, the risk-rated premium of 1293 euros offered by B (see the top bar in Fig. 2.1) is much more attractive than the community-rated premium of 2160 euros offered by A. The opposite holds for people *with* a medical condition, for whom the expected insurance claims exceed the community-rated premium. Consequently, A will disproportionally attract high-risk people and must raise the premium to cover insurance claims of those choosing the plan. Under the extreme circumstances that all people with a medical condition opt for A (and all people without a condition opt for B), A has to raise its premium to 5971 euros (i.e., the mean claims of those with a medical condition). After this premium jump, A is no longer the cheapest option for people with expected claims below 5971 euros (e.g., those with thyroid disorders or diabetes type II). These people now have an incentive to switch to B, which implies that A has to raise the premium again. As long as A keeps charging a community-rated premium this process will repeat, resulting in an upward premium spiral driving more and more consumers to B. Thus, in order to survive in this market, A has to charge a risk-rated premium too. This example illustrates how competition, without regulation, drives premiums to expected costs by risk type. Given the huge variation in expected claims, risk rating threatens the affordability of basic coverage for high-risk people. For those with kidney disorders, for instance, a risk-rated premium would exceed 45,000 euros per year (see Fig. 2.1).

## 2.1.2   Risk Selection: A Threat to Both Affordability and Efficiency

In real-world health insurance markets, even without regulation, risk rating is incomplete (Herring and Pauly, 2001). Reasons might be that the required information on individuals' risk is not available (at reasonable costs), or that insurers fear that risk rating may harm their reputation (Schut and Van de Ven, 2011). To the extent that risk rating is incomplete, competitive insurance markets tend towards risk selection by consumers and insurers (Akerlof, 1970; Rothschild and Stiglitz, 1976; Feldman and Dowd, 1982; Newhouse, 1996; Glazer and McGuire, 2000).

In the absence of open enrollment, risk selection on the insurer side can take the form of selective underwriting, which can also be illustrated with the information in Fig. 2.1. Assume that insurers know whether or not consumers have a medical condition but—for whatever reason—cannot (or do not want to) risk rate their premiums on the basis of that information. Instead, insurers charge a community-rated premium equal to the average claims in the population (2160 euros). Under these circumstances, insurers have an incentive to avoid customers with a medical condition since expected claims for these people exceed the premium. This makes coverage less available for high-risk people, which is inefficient. Alternatively, in an attempt to avoid enrollment of unprofitable consumers, insurers can make their plans unattractive for people with specific conditions, which threatens the efficiency of the health plan design (Glazer and McGuire, 2000).

Risk selection on the consumer side can mean that low-risk people buy less than basic coverage (which can be no coverage) when the incremental premium for basic coverage is beyond what they are willing to pay (Einav and Finkelstein, 2011). In terms of our example this can be illustrated as follows. Assume that consumers are risk averse and willing to pay a risk premium of 50% on top of their expected claims. This means that people without a condition (more than 80% of the population) are willing to pay a premium of 1940 euros ($=1.5 \times 1293$ euros). Now assume that the insurers do not anticipate selection by consumers and charge a community-rated premium equal to the mean expected claims in the population (2160 euros).

Under these circumstances, and in the absence of an insurance mandate, those without a condition will not buy basic coverage since the premium is beyond what they are willing to pay. First, this can be considered inefficient, as the people without a condition value basic coverage at more than their expected claims, i.e., 1940 euros (the premium they are willing to pay) versus 1293 euros (their expected claims) plus a loading fee (that we assume to be less than 50% of the expected claims). Second, this "selection by consumers" can also threaten affordability: once insurers learn that those without a medical condition do not enroll in basic coverage, they have to raise the community-rated premium for that coverage to at least 5971 euros (i.e., the mean expected claims for those with a medical condition), which threatens affordability. Moreover, this upward premium spiral might continue, further deteriorating affordability and efficiency (Price and Mays, 1985; Feldman and Dowd, 1991; Cutler and Reber, 1998).

### 2.1.3   The Goal and Outline of This Chapter

To achieve affordability and efficiency, regulators of competitive health insurance markets apply premium regulation, risk equalization, risk sharing, and/or various forms of subsidies to insurers and consumers. The goal of this chapter is to describe how each of these interventions affects the two objectives. The outline is as follows. To simplify our analysis, Section 2.2 introduces some assumptions about other regulations that are in place. After that, in Section 2.3, we will return to our analysis of the effects of risk rating and risk selection. While our illustration above (on the basis of Fig. 2.1) gives a good sense of how risk rating and risk selection affect *affordability*, it does not fully capture the effects on *efficiency*. Section 2.3 extends our analysis of efficiency using elements of a graphical framework developed by Einav and Finkelstein (2011). After that, we will analyze how different payment system interventions affect affordability and efficiency. Section 2.4 describes the benchmark for this analysis and formulates six specific aspects of affordability and efficiency we are interested in. Based on the directions in which interventions work, we categorize them in three groups: premium regulation (Section 2.5), risk equalization, risk sharing and subsidies to insurers (Section 2.6), and subsidies to consumers (Section 2.7). Though regulators often rely on a blend of interventions, we consider each tool in isolation, which helps to identify the specific tradeoffs involved with an intervention.

## 2.2   STARTING POINT OF OUR ANALYSES

The starting point of our analyses is a competitive health insurance market without regulation of *health plan financing*. More specifically, we assume that premiums can vary with health risk and that there are no subsidies to consumers or insurers. Moreover, mechanisms such as risk equalization and risk sharing are absent. Health plan revenues only come from premiums.

To simplify the analyses, we assume that three types of regulation are in place. First, insurers who choose to participate in the health insurance market must offer at least one plan with what we call "basic" coverage. Second, these insurers are bound by an open enrollment requirement for basic-coverage plans. In the absence of other regulation, this means that insurers may offer health plans outside the scope of basic coverage and have full flexibility with respect to premium setting. For example, insurers are free to charge a very high premium for basic coverage, either to all consumers or high risks in particular. In fact, these assumptions transform the problem of *unavailability* of basic coverage into a problem of *unaffordability*. Third, we assume that (by regulation) insurance contracts have a duration of 1 year.

It is worth emphasizing that we do *not* assume an insurance mandate. The reason is that the need for such a mandate depends on the payment system itself. As will be explained in more detail later, affordability requires subsidies to high-risk people (e.g., those with expensive preexisting conditions). An important aspect of payment system design is how these subsidies are financed. In practice, (combinations of) two modalities are applied: "internal" and "external" financing, an issue discussed in Newhouse (2017). In the internal modality, subsidies to high-risk people are financed via the insurance premium. In terms of our numerical example (Fig. 2.1), this could mean that all people pay the same premium of 2160 euros. In such a system, low-risk people (i.e., those without a medical condition) on average pay a contribution of 867 euros (2160 minus 1293) to subsidize the high-risk people (i.e., those with a medical condition). Examples of systems with high levels of internal financing are the Swiss national health insurance (Chapter 16: Health Plan Payment in Switzerland) and the US Marketplaces (Chapter 17: Health Plan Payment in US Marketplaces: Regulated Competition with a Weak Mandate). By external financing we mean that subsidies are financed with external resources, such as tax payment revenues or income-related contributions that people pay to the system independent of having insurance or not. Examples of systems with high levels of external financing are the Belgium national health insurance (Chapter 7: Risk Adjustment in Belgium: Why and How to Introduce Socioeconomic Variables in Health Plan Payment) and US Medicaid (Chapter 18: Health Plan Payment in Medicaid Managed Care: A Hybrid Model of Regulated Competition). Coming back to the need for an insurance mandate, the point is this: with internal financing, contributions by low-risk people (on top of their actuarially fair premium) are directly linked to enrollment. This might discourage low-risk people from enrolling and could call for an insurance mandate. With external financing, contributions are not directly linked to enrollment, making an insurance mandate less necessary. In fact, external financing requires mandatory contributions (e.g., tax payments) rather than mandatory coverage.

## 2.3 HOW RISK RATING AND RISK SELECTION AFFECT EFFICIENCY: A GRAPHICAL FRAMEWORK

This section provides a graphical framework of how risk rating and risk selection affect efficiency. In later sections, this framework will be used to analyze the efficiency effects of payment system interventions. Our considerations will be illustrated with diagrams showing the relationship between expected claims, premiums, and the demand for basic coverage. The spirit of these diagrams finds its origin in the selection framework developed by Einav and Finkelstein (2011) and extensions developed by Geruso and Layton (2017). Readers who are familiar with these studies will notice that we use a slightly different language here, corresponding to the terminology we have used so far. A more important difference with these earlier studies is that we make an explicit distinction between two features that feed into the demand for basic coverage. We refer to these aspects as the consumer's *ability to pay* (i.e., his budget) and his *willingness to pay* (i.e., how he values basic coverage). This approach allows for making a distinction between affordability problems and efficiency problems. When a consumer is *not able to pay* the *actual* premium for basic coverage, we will speak of an *affordability problem*. When this consumer is able but *not willing to pay* the *actual* premium, despite the fact that he values basic coverage at more than his expected claims plus the loading fee, we will speak of an *efficiency problem*. This means that our considerations of efficient sorting into the market are conditional on the population for which basic coverage is affordable under the payment system in place.

We are aware that what we define as an affordability problem can also be considered an efficiency problem. For example, subsidizing a risk-rated premium of 45,000 euros for a person with kidney disorders does not only improve affordability of basic coverage for that person, but can also improve social welfare, i.e., when this person values basic coverage at more than his expected claims plus the loading fee (Nyman, 1999). For simplicity, however, we will not elaborate on this association between affordability and social welfare. Instead, we just assume the regulator wants to make basic coverage affordable, regardless of the underlying motives.

### 2.3.1 Risk Rating: Good for Efficiency

Though risk rating threatens affordability for high-risk people (see Section 2.1) it is good for efficiency. The reason is simple: more-refined rating categories mean less potential for risk selection and thus less potential for selection-related inefficiencies. The working of a competitive health

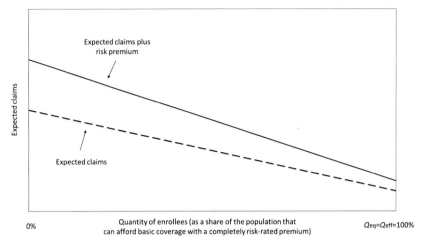

**FIGURE 2.2**    The demand for basic coverage under complete risk rating.
Note: the horizontal axis represents the population that can afford basic coverage with a completely risk-rated premium. Consumers are ordered according to their expected insurance claims for basic coverage. Those with the highest expected claims are on the left and those with the lowest on the right. All consumers are assumed to be risk-averse and thus willing to pay a risk premium on top of their expected claims.

insurance market with *complete* risk rating can be illustrated with Fig. 2.2. Imagine a situation in which consumers have a binary choice between basic coverage and no coverage, and assume that the horizontal axis of Fig. 2.2 represents the population that is able to buy basic coverage in case of complete risk rating. Consumers are ordered according to their expected claims: those with the highest expected claims are on the left and those with the lowest on the right. All consumers are assumed to be risk averse and thus willing to pay a risk premium on top of their expected claims. For simplicity, we assume no loading fee. Complete risk rating means that for each consumer the premium equals his expected claims. Given that all consumers on the horizontal axis value basic coverage at more than their premium, they will all enroll, i.e., $Q_{eq}$ (the equilibrium quantity) = 100%. And because all these people value basic coverage at more than their expected claims, this outcome is efficient, i.e., $Q_{eff}$ (the efficient quantity) = 100%.

Furthermore, in a situation of complete risk rating there is no "unpriced risk heterogeneity," meaning there are no incentives for risk selection by insurers (via health plan design). Moreover, when the expected returns on selection are zero, the only way for insurers to reduce cost is by improving efficiency in production, e.g., via managed care techniques.

As mentioned above, we assume here that consumers have a binary choice between basic coverage and no coverage. In practice, there can be a variety of coverage options in between. For example, there might be health plans with slightly less than basic coverage. Under these circumstances, a complete analysis of consumer sorting into the market takes into account all these options. For simplicity, however, we will not elaborate on this scenario and keep focusing on a binary choice between basic coverage and no coverage. Section 2.3.2 analyzes this choice in a situation of community rating, where risk selection comes into play.

## 2.3.2 Risk Selection by Consumers: Bad for Efficient Sorting

In a situation of incomplete risk rating, the premium will not be based on the per person expected claims but on the *average* expected claims in a premium-risk group, resulting in unpriced risk heterogeneity and selection-related inefficiencies. First, incomplete risk rating can lead to inefficient sorting into the market. This can be illustrated with Fig. 2.3 (drawn from Einav and Finkelstein, 2011), in which we assume a community-rated premium equal to the *average* expected claims of all consumers enrolled in basic coverage. Though we are aware that there is a wide spectrum between complete risk-rating (Fig. 2.2) and complete community-rating (Fig. 2.3), this simplification helps to show the impact of incomplete risk rating. Compared to Fig. 2.2, an additional curve appears in Fig. 2.3, reflecting the average

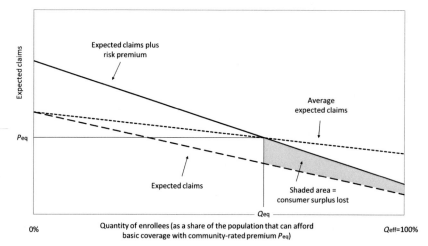

**FIGURE 2.3** The demand for basic coverage under complete community rating.
Note: the horizontal axis represents the population that can afford basic coverage with community-rated premium $P_{eq}$. Consumers are ordered according to their expected insurance claims for basic coverage. Those with the highest expected claims are on the left and those with the lowest on the right. All consumers are assumed to be risk-averse and willing to pay a risk premium on top of their expected insurance claims. Since willingness to pay decreases with expected claims, the "average expected claims" curve is downward-sloping (but above the "expected claims" curve).

expected claims of those enrolled in the market. Since willingness-to-pay (i.e., the expected claims plus risk premium) decreases with expected claims, the "average expected claims" curve is downward-sloping (but always above the "expected claims" curve). In a situation with community-rating the premium will not be based on the expected claims (as was true in Fig. 2.2) but on the *average* expected claims. As Fig. 2.3 shows, this results in inefficient enrollment: low-risk people (those on the right) are not willing to pay a premium equal to the average expected claims. The competitive equilibrium, i.e., the intersection of the "average expected claims" curve and the "expected claims plus risk premium" curve, leads to premium $P_{eq}$ and quantity $Q_{eq}$. This outcome is inefficient since those who do not enroll, i.e., those right of $Q_{eq}$, value basic coverage at more than their expected insurance claims. The lost consumer surplus equals the risk premium these people are willing to pay, indicated by the shaded area.

Note that our comparison of Figs. 2.2 and 2.3 above ignores the effect of different premium structures on affordability. Compared to a situation of complete risk rating (Fig. 2.2), community-rating (Fig. 2.3) makes basic coverage more affordable for high-risk people and less affordable for low-risk people. This means that "the population for which basic coverage is affordable," as depicted on the horizontal axis of our diagrams, can be (very) different in the two situations. And with different populations on the horizontal axis, the slopes of the curves can be different too. For simplicity, however, we will not elaborate on this complication and simply conclude that incomplete risk rating potentially leads to inefficient sorting into the market.

Geruso and Layton (2017) distinguish between selection by consumers *into* the market and selection by consumers *within* the market (i.e., across plans with different coverage). The former refers to the sorting problem analyzed above, i.e., the problem that low-risk consumers choose not to enroll in basic coverage despite the fact that they value this coverage at more than their expected claims. Selection by consumers *within* the market refers to another type of sorting problem, i.e., the sorting of low- and high-risk consumers into different plans (Einav and Finkelstein, 2011; Glazer and McGuire, 2011; Bundorf et al., 2012; Geruso, 2016).

The effect of risk selection on consumer sorting could be illustrated with the type of diagram shown in Fig. 2.3. In contrast to Fig. 2.3, however, that diagram would not show the *total* expected claims (plus risk premium) for basic coverage (compared to no coverage), but the *incremental* expected claims (and incremental risk premium) for one type of basic-coverage plan versus another. For example, this can be a low- versus a high-deductible plan. Rather than introducing another figure, however, we will simply provide some intuition here. Just as with the *total* expected claims (plus *total* risk premium) for basic coverage, the slopes of the *incremental* expected claims (plus *incremental* risk premium) for a low- versus a high-deductible plan are typically downward-sloping. This means that consumers with high expected claims are more likely to enroll in the low-deductible plan than those with low expected claims. In case of a flat premium per health plan, this type of selection increases the incremental premium of the low-deductible plan compared to the high-deductible plan. Consequently, low-risk people who value a low-deductible plan at more than their incremental expected claims might not enroll in that plan because they are not willing to pay the incremental premium. In fact, inefficient sorting across plans can occur in any situation where consumer preferences with respect to "contract space dimensions" are correlated with expected claims. For a graphical illustration of this type of inefficient sorting and more discussion about the welfare effects, see Chapter 5, Evaluating the Performance of Health Plan Payment Systems.

Note that the impact of risk selection by consumers on efficiency critically depends on the position and slopes of the three curves in Fig. 2.3. For example, if the "expected claims plus risk premium" curve is always above the "average expected claims" curve, all consumers will enroll in basic coverage. For a discussion of this and other possible versions of Fig. 2.3, as well as a discussion about the impact of a loading fee, we refer to Einav and Finkelstein (2011).

### 2.3.3 Risk Selection by Insurers: Bad for Efficiency of Plan Design and Efficiency of Production

Incomplete risk rating not only comes with potential for risk selection by consumers, but also with potential for selection by insurers. The explanation is simple: incomplete risk rating results in predictable profits and losses. This can be illustrated with the diagram in Fig. 2.4, which mimics Fig. 2.3. This time, however, we focus on the group that enrolls in basic coverage, i.e., the group to the left of point $Q_{eq}$ (rather than the group to the right that does not enroll). Given the downward slope of the "expected claims" curve, a community-rated premium results in predictable profits (i.e., the scattered triangle to the right) and predictable losses (i.e., the scattered triangle to the left). With a heterogeneous population as depicted in Fig. 2.1 these predictable profits and losses can be substantial. For example, in an extreme situation where all people with a medical condition enroll in basic coverage and those without a condition do not, a community-rated premium equals 5971 euros (i.e., the average expected spending of those with a medical condition). Under these circumstances, the predictable profit on people with thyroid disorders would be 3524 euros per person per year ($= 5971 - 2447$) while the predictable loss on people with pulmonary arterial hypertension would be 41,449 euros per person per year ($= 5971 - 47,420$). Such "unpriced risk heterogeneity" provides insurers with incentives to engage in actions to attract profitable consumers and to deter unprofitable ones.

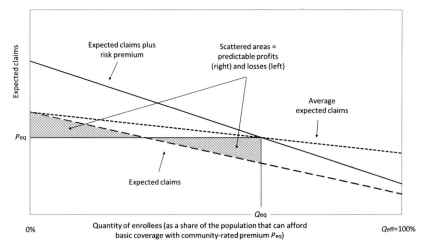

**FIGURE 2.4**  Predictable profits and losses under complete community rating.
Note: the horizontal axis represents the population that can afford basic coverage with community-rated premium $P_{eq}$. Consumers are ordered according to their expected claims for basic coverage. Those with the highest expected claims are on the left and those with the lowest on the right. All consumers are assumed to be risk-averse and willing to pay a risk premium on top of their expected claims. Since willingness to pay decreases with expected claims, the "average expected claims" curve is downward-sloping (but always above the "expected claims" curve). The scattered triangles represent the predictable profits (right) and losses (left) that occur with community-rated premium $P_{eq}$.

Though open enrollment, generally present in regulated health insurance markets and assumed in this chapter for purposes of analysis, precludes selective underwriting, insurers can engage in other forms of risk selection, sometimes referred to as indirect selection (Van de Ven and Ellis, 2000; Breyer et al., 2012). The unprofitable consumers (to the left) are likely to be different than the profitable ones (to the right); e.g., the unprofitable people may suffer more often from specific chronic illnesses. In this case an insurer can structure its marketing and product in a way to appeal differently to these groups. Examples include actions to target profitable consumers via health plan design (e.g., by not covering healthcare services or providers that are particularly attractive to unprofitable people). In principle, any dimension in which basic coverage is allowed to differ (e.g., cost-sharing options, provider network, utilization management, and customer service) is a potential tool for risk selection (Van Kleef et al., 2013a,b).

Risk selection by insurers threatens efficient health plan design. As shown by Glazer and McGuire (2000), competition forces health plans to design their benefits such that the plan is relatively attractive to low-risk people and relatively unattractive to high-risk people. Consequently, plans may cover "too much" of services/providers that are relatively attractive to low risks and "too little" of services/providers that are relatively attractive to high risks. To the extent that health plans do not cover services/providers who are relatively attractive to high risks, healthcare providers have disincentives to offer and invest in these services. This may threaten the availability of high-quality care for high-risk people (Van de Ven et al., 2015).

Risk selection by insurers might also threaten efficiency in production (Van de Ven and Ellis, 2000). The larger the predictable profits resulting from risk selection, the greater the chance that investments in risk selection have higher returns than investments in cost containment. At least in the short run, when an insurer has limited resources available to invest in cost-reducing activities, he might choose to invest in risk selection rather than in improving efficiency of production. If the insurer chooses not to invest in risk selection he might lose market share to insurers who do. Contrary to investments in cost containment, however, investments in risk selection produce no net benefits to society since risk selection is a zero-sum game (Van de Ven and Schut, 2011). So any resources specifically used for risk selection represent a welfare loss.

## 2.4   BENCHMARK FOR ANALYZING THE EFFECTS OF PAYMENT SYSTEM INTERVENTIONS

So far, our analysis has shown that *without* regulation of health plan payment, competitive health insurance markets can lead to risk rating and/or risk selection. In terms of both affordability and efficiency the outcomes of these markets are likely to be unsatisfactory. First, risk rating of premiums threatens affordability of basic coverage for high-risk people. Second, for low-income people basic coverage might be unaffordable anyway, even for those who are healthy (Bundorf and Pauly, 2006). Moreover, adverse selection into the market can drive up premiums, exacerbating problems of affordability. Third, adverse selection into the market also threatens efficiency, namely when low-risk consumers face a price so high they do not buy but still value basic coverage at more than their expected insurance claims (plus loading fee). Fourth, predictable profits and losses in the market confront insurers with incentives for risk selection, which threatens the efficiency of the health plan design. Fifth, risk selection via marketing can be a more attractive strategy to control spending than cost containment (at least in the short term), which threatens efficiency in production. Sixth, selection by consumers across basic coverage plans can lead to price distortions resulting in inefficient sorting of consumers across these plans. The relative importance of these six threats depends on the level of risk rating: with refined risk rating, the main concern might be unaffordability of coverage for high-risk people; with poor risk rating (e.g., community-rating), the main concern might be selection-related inefficiencies. To keep track of the aforementioned threats, we translate them into six objectives associated with payment system

---

**BOX 2.3 Six objectives associated with payment system design**
1. Affordability of basic coverage for high-risk people
2. Affordability of basic coverage for low-income people
3. Efficient health plan design
4. Efficient enrollment in basic coverage
5. Efficient sorting of consumers across basic-coverage plans
6. Incentives for efficiency in production

---

design (see Box 2.3). The next sections describe how premium regulation, risk equalization, risk sharing, and various forms of subsidies affect these objectives. Though we are aware that regulators in practice rely on a blend of tools, we will first analyze each tool in isolation, which helps to identify the specific tradeoffs involved with a tool.

In order to indicate the effects of payment system interventions on the six objectives in Box 2.3, it is helpful to define a benchmark. In what follows, the benchmark will be a competitive health insurance market without payment system regulation, in which both risk rating and risk selection are present. In other words, we assume premiums are risk rated, but not completely (leaving room for risk selection). Under these circumstances, all six objectives in Box 2.3 are potentially threatened. We do not make assumptions, however, about the relative importance of the six objectives. Our primary goal is to indicate the direction in which a payment system intervention affects these six objectives, rather than indicating the size of the effects.

## 2.5 PREMIUM REGULATION

Premium regulation can take several forms, such as community rating per health plan (i.e., one premium for all consumers choosing the same plan), restrictions on rating factors (e.g., no premium differentiation on the basis of medical conditions), rate-banding (i.e., a minimum and maximum premium between rating categories) or guaranteed renewability (see Box 2.4). Around the world, various modalities of premium regulation are applied. In Switzerland, for instance, insurers are not allowed to risk rate premiums for basic coverage according to people's health status, but can risk rate on the basis of certain age groups and regions (Chapter 16: Health Plan Payment in Switzerland). Age can also be used in the US Marketplaces, but with a maximum ratio of 3:1 for the old-to-young premium (Chapter 17: Health Plan Payment in US Marketplaces: Regulated Competition with a Weak Mandate). Other countries, such as Belgium (Chapter 7: Risk Adjustment in Belgium: Why and How to Introduce Socioeconomic Variables in Health Plan Payment), Germany (Chapter 11: Health Plan Payment in Germany),

### BOX 2.4 Guaranteed renewability

Guaranteed renewability generally means that insurers are obliged to renew an insurance contract with their enrollees at the "standard premium and standard conditions" (see, e.g., Pauly et al., 1995; Herring and Pauly, 2006). The rationale for guaranteed renewability is that it protects consumers from rate hikes or being denied coverage if they develop a health condition that would make them high-cost consumers the future. To understand how guaranteed renewability works, let us return to Fig. 2.1 and focus on the group with no medical condition. Assume that, from the insurers' perspective, people in this group have the same risk of developing a serious disease. In the case of guaranteed renewability, insurers' will charge all individuals in this group an additional "guaranteed renewability fee" on top of the standard premium that covers the costs during the contract period. This "guaranteed renewability fee" equals the present discounted value of the cost of protection against the risk that future premiums will be higher than the standard premium because of the onset of a medical condition. The "guaranteed renewability fee" should be sufficient to allow the insurer to ask the same premium for all following contract periods.

Guaranteed renewability can improve affordability for people who develop a (high-cost) disease after enrollment. It does not improve affordability, however, for people with a preexisting condition. These people will still be confronted with a high premium. Moreover, guaranteed renewability does not protect parents for the lifelong healthcare cost of newborn children with serious birth defects. When it comes to market efficiency, guaranteed renewability might mitigate risk selection by consumers as more low-risk people enroll in guaranteed renewability contracts (to protect themselves from rate hikes or being denied coverage in future periods). On the other hand, guaranteed renewability faces practical difficulties due to the fact that it is impossible to define the relevant standard policy conditions for a period of 20–50 years, both in terms of coverage and premium. Due to the development of new diagnostic tests, new treatments, new drugs, and medical technology, in 50 years from now the current benefit package is likely to be largely irrelevant. Consequently, over the course of time, a guaranteed renewability contract might become increasingly incomplete. In addition, consumers have imperfect foresight and might under/overestimate their future needs and enroll in a contract that is either too limited or too generous. In terms of premium, the uncertainty about future developments in medical technologies makes it hard for insurers to make an accurate actuarial calculation of the present discounted value of the future life-long additional expenses of those who in the contract period will become a high risk. For example, in 1967 it was nearly impossible to make a reliable estimate of the level of health expenses in 2017. Consequently, premiums might deviate substantially from the "real" (but unknown) actuarial value. Another reason why guaranteed renewability might distort efficiency is that people who have become a high risk are "married with their insurer." For example, this "lock-in" is a problem when the chronically ill are dissatisfied with the (quality of) coverage offered by their insurer. They cannot switch at an affordable premium to another insurer,

*(Continued)*

**BOX 2.4  (Continued)**

because the other insurers will ask them for a much higher premium. In other words, guaranteed renewability is hard to reconcile with free consumer choice of health insurer for high-risk people. If these people cannot easily change insurer, there might hardly be competition on this group, resulting in a loss of efficiency.

the Netherlands (Chapter 14: Health Plan Payment in the Netherlands), and Russia (Chapter 15: Health Plan Payment in the Russian Federation) rely on community-rating per health plan.

Table 2.1 describes the effects of rate restrictions on affordability and efficiency. As mentioned in Section 2.4, our benchmark is a competitive market in which both risk rating and risk selection are present. In general, rate restrictions reduce or eliminate problems due to risk rating, but exacerbate problems due to risk selection. With respect to affordability, rate restrictions work in two directions. On the one hand, premiums for high-risk people tend to be lower than in a situation with risk rating. On the other hand, the average premium in the market can increase because the lowest risks might choose not to enroll in basic coverage, which threatens affordability for all, starting with the lowest incomes. For an explanation of the effects on efficiency, we simply refer to our analysis of complete community rating in Section 2.3.

Table 2.1 leads to the conclusion that premium regulation as a standalone intervention cannot simultaneously achieve affordability and efficiency. Supplementary tools will be needed to avoid low-risk people not enrolling in basic coverage (e.g., an insurance mandate and/or subsidies). Moreover, additional measures will be needed to avoid risk selection by insurers and inefficient sorting of consumers across plans (e.g., risk equalization and/or risk sharing).

In addition to the efficiency effects listed in Table 2.1, there can be other effects of rate restrictions on efficiency. One additional disadvantage is that rate restrictions reduce the consumer's financial incentive for health-risk-reducing behavior (which would exist in the case of risk-rated premiums). On the other hand, premium rate restrictions might have some advantages as well. A first potential advantage is that rate restrictions might improve transparency of premium schedules, making it easier for consumers to compare health plan prices. This advantage might be particularly relevant if the demand elasticity in health insurance markets is (too) low (Schut and Van de Ven, 2011). A second potential gain of rate restrictions is that it might increase the trust of consumers in health insurers as purchasing agents. Risk

**TABLE 2.1** How Do Rate Restrictions Affect Affordability and Efficiency?

| Objective | | Effect |
|---|---|---|
| Affordability of basic coverage for high-risk people | + | Rate restrictions create implicit cross-subsidies from low-risk to high-risk people, which reduces premiums for high-risk people |
| Affordability of basic coverage for low-income people | − | Rate restrictions increase premiums for low-risk people. As a result, low-risk people might choose not to enroll in basic coverage, which drives up premiums and deteriorates affordability |
| Efficient health plan design | − | Rate restrictions increase unpriced risk heterogeneity which can exacerbate the incentives for risk selection (via plan design) |
| Efficient enrollment into basic coverage | − | Rate restrictions increase premiums for low-risk people. As a result, low-risk people might choose not to enroll in basic coverage. When these people still value basic coverage at more than their expected claims this outcome is inefficient |
| Efficient sorting across basic-coverage plans | − | Rate restrictions increase unpriced risk heterogeneity. To the extent that profitable and unprofitable consumers concentrate in different health plans, incremental premiums will be distorted which can lead to consumers choosing the "wrong" plan |
| Incentives for efficiency in production | − | Rate restrictions increase the expected returns on risk selection. Consequently, insurers may choose to rely on risk selection (e.g., via marketing) rather than cost containment to control costs |

The benchmark for the effects in this table is a competitive market with both risk rating and risk selection (meaning that all six objectives are potentially violated). Symbols indicate whether the intervention promotes the objective (+), (potentially) distorts the objective (−), or has no direct effects (0). The table covers what we think are the *major* effects; there might be additional (indirect) effects not covered here. Symbols indicate the direction of effects rather than their size. We do not make assumptions about the relative importance of the six objectives.

rating may be perceived by consumers as a sign of profit orientation, undermining trust in the agency role of insurers in a system of regulated competition (Schut and Van de Ven, 2011). A third potential gain is that premium regulation protects consumers from "reclassification risk," i.e., the risk of moving to a higher premium category after developing a medical condition (Handel et al., 2015).

## 2.6   RISK EQUALIZATION, RISK SHARING, AND SUBSIDIES TO INSURERS

Regulation of individual health insurance markets can include risk equalization and risk sharing, possibly combined with an external subsidy (e.g., from the regulator) to the risk equalization/sharing fund. This section analyzes the effects of these tools on affordability and efficiency. Again, our benchmark is a competitive market with both risk rating and risk selection. As will be shown, the presence of an external subsidy can crucially affect sorting of consumers into the market. In order to isolate the effects of the different tools, we will first analyze the impact of risk equalization and risk sharing *without* an external subsidy (Sections 2.6.1−2.6.3) and then turn to systems *with* an external subsidy (Sections 2.6.4 and 2.6.5).

### 2.6.1   Risk Equalization Without an External Subsidy

In the absence of an external subsidy, risk equalization basically means that the risk equalization payment (REP) for individual $i$ is based on the difference between some concept of expected claims for individual $i$ ($\hat{y}_i$) and the mean expected claims in the population ($\bar{\hat{y}}$):

$$\text{REP}_i = \hat{y}_i - \bar{\hat{y}} \qquad (2.1)$$

In what follows, we assume that the regulator wants to correct for the variation in expected claims completely (which is not necessarily the case, e.g., when the regulator allows that some of the variation in expected claims is reflected in premiums, such as in the US Marketplaces). In the absence of an external subsidy, REPs to health plans for high-risk people require contributions from plans for low-risk people. This mechanism can be illustrated with Fig. 2.1. Let's assume that the population in Fig. 2.1 represents the pool in which expected claims have to be equalized and that expected claims differ across medical condition groups, but not within these groups. The overall mean claims equal 2160 euros per person per year. Risk equalization according to Eq. (2.1) means that for people with heart disease health plans receive a compensation of 8630 euros per person per year ($= 10{,}790 - 2160$), while for people without a condition plans pay a contribution of 867 euros per person per year ($= 1293 - 2160$).

### 2.6.2   Risk Sharing Without an External Subsidy

Another way to establish cross-subsidies between health plans is risk sharing. For example, insurers can share in a proportion of claims. An essential difference between risk equalization and risk sharing is that risk equalization is based on some concept of *expected* claims, while risk sharing takes place on the basis of *actual* claims. For example, the risk sharing payment (which could be positive or negative) for individual $i$ could be calculated as a share s of the difference between the actual claims for individual $i$ ($y_i$) and the mean actual claims in the population ($\bar{y}$):

$$RSP_i = s(y_i - \bar{y}) \tag{2.2}$$

Next to "proportional risk sharing" (as applied in Belgium, see Chapter 7: Risk Adjustment in Belgium: Why and How to Introduce Socioeconomic Variables in Health Plan Payment), risk sharing can take a variety of other forms. A well-known method is "reinsurance" or "excess loss compensation," meaning that insurers share in a proportion of individual-level claims *in excess of a certain threshold* (as is done in Australia, see Chapter 6: Health Plan Payment in Australia). Another method is that insurers share in a proportion of the average profits and losses per person outside a bandwidth (i.e., "risk corridors"), as formerly applied in the Netherlands (Chapter 14: Health Plan Payment in the Netherlands) and the US Marketplaces (Chapter 17: Health Plan Payment in US Marketplaces: Regulated Competition with a Weak Mandate). Risk sharing can also take the form of a cost-based compensation for specific ex-ante risk types (i.e., "high-risk pooling"). For a discussion of these and other methods, see Chapter 4, Risk Sharing.

### 2.6.3 Effects of Risk Equalization and Risk Sharing Without an External Subsidy

For the first five objectives in Box 2.3, risk equalization and risk sharing (without an external subsidy to the risk equalization/sharing fund) work in the same direction. From the viewpoint of an insurer, both strategies reduce expected costs for high-risk enrollees and increase expected costs for low-risk enrollees. In terms of our graphical illustration this leads to a new curve, i.e., the "expected claims minus RE/RS payment," which results from a rotation of the "expected claims curve." In the extreme case of a *complete* correction for variation in expected claims, the new curve ends up horizontal, as represented by the gray line in Fig. 2.5. From the insurers' perspective, all consumers in the market now represent the same "cost." Note that a *complete* correction for variation in expected insurance claims leads to the same competitive equilibrium as complete community rating. In both situations the market stabilizes at the intersection of the "expected claims plus risk premium" curve and the "average expected claims" curve. In this competitive equilibrium, the sum of (implicit) compensations to high-risk people in the market (in Fig. 2.5: the striped triangle to the left) equals the sum of (implicit) contributions from low-risk people in the market (in Fig. 2.5: the striped triangle to the right).

Table 2.2 summarizes the effects of risk equalization/sharing without an external subsidy on the first five objectives from Box 2.3. Again, the

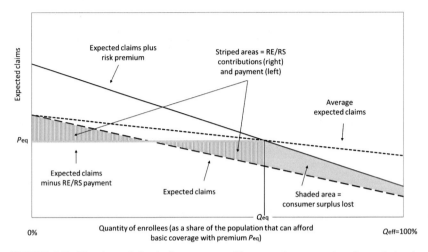

**FIGURE 2.5** The demand for basic coverage with a complete correction for variation in expected claims.

Note: the horizontal axis represents the population that can afford basic coverage with premium $P_{eq}$. Consumers are ordered according to their expected claims for basic coverage. Those with the highest expected claims are on the left and those with the lowest on the right. All consumers are assumed to be risk-averse and willing to pay a risk premium on top of their expected claims. Since willingness-to-pay decreases with expected claims, the "average expected claims" curve is downward-sloping (but always above the "expected claims" curve). With a complete correction for variation in expected claims, the "expected claims minus RE/RS payment" curve ends up horizontal.

benchmark is a competitive market with both risk rating and risk selection. The impact on affordability goes in two directions. On the one hand, these tools can mitigate risk rating and thereby reduce premiums for the relatively high-risk people in the market. On the other hand, they might increase the average premium in the market as low-risk people do not enroll in basic coverage. This would reduce affordability for all, and for low-income people in particular. The effects on efficiency are mixed too. On the one hand, risk equalization and risk sharing reduce unpriced risk heterogeneity and thus mitigate the potential for inefficient sorting across health plans and risk selection by insurers. On the other hand, however, these tools can exacerbate inefficient sorting into the market (Table 2.2).

With respect to the sixth objective in Box 2.3—incentives for efficiency in production—the effects of risk equalization and risk sharing are different (Table 2.3). To the extent that risk sharing mitigates unpriced risk heterogeneity, it reduces the expected returns on risk selection (e.g., via marketing). At the same time, however, it also reduces the returns on cost containment (see Chapter 4: Risk Sharing). The first effect makes cost containment a more attractive strategy to control costs, but the second effect makes it a

**TABLE 2.2** How Do Risk Equalization and Risk Sharing Without an External Subsidy Affect Affordability and Efficiency?

| Objective | Effect | |
|-----------|--------|---|
| Affordability of basic coverage for high-risk people | + | To the extent that risk equalization and risk sharing reduce variation in expected claims that would otherwise be reflected in premiums they reduce premiums for high-risk people |
| Affordability of basic coverage for low-income people | − | To the extent that risk equalization and risk sharing reduce variation in expected claims that would otherwise be reflected in premiums they increase premiums for low-risk people. Consequently, low-risk people might choose not to enroll in basic coverage, which drives up premiums and deteriorates affordability |
| Efficient health plan design | + | To the extent that risk equalization and risk sharing correct for unpriced risk heterogeneity, they mitigate incentives for risk selection (via plan design) |
| Efficient enrollment in basic coverage | − | To the extent that risk equalization and risk sharing reduce variation in expected claims that would otherwise be reflected in premiums they increase premiums for low-risk people. Consequently, low-risk people might choose not to enroll in basic coverage. When these people value basic coverage at more than their expected claims this is inefficient |
| Efficient sorting across basic-coverage plans | + | To the extent that risk equalization and risk sharing reduce unpriced risk heterogeneity within the market they mitigate the potential for price distortions and inefficient sorting |

The benchmark for the effects in this table is a competitive market with both risk rating and risk selection (meaning that all six objectives are potentially violated). Symbols indicate whether the intervention promotes the objective (+), (potentially) distorts the objective (−), or has no direct effects (0). The table covers what we think are the *major* effects; there might be additional (indirect) effects not covered here. Symbols indicate the direction of effects rather than their size. We do not make assumptions about the relative importance of the objectives.

less attractive strategy. This is different with risk equalization based on exogenous risk factors (i.e., factors that cannot be influenced by health insurers such as age and gender). Exogenous risk equalization reduces the expected returns on risk selection *without* reducing the expected returns on cost containment. As will be explained in more detail in Chapter 3, Risk Adjustment for Health Plan Payment, exogenous risk factors insufficiently correct for predictable variation in insurance claims. In practice, many risk

**TABLE 2.3** How Do Risk Equalization and Risk Sharing Affect Incentives for Efficiency in Production?

| Intervention | Effect | |
|---|---|---|
| Risk equalization based on *exogenous* risk factors | + | To the extent that risk equalization mitigates unpriced risk heterogeneity, it reduces the returns on risk selection (e.g., via marketing). When based on exogenous factors, risk equalization does not affect the returns on cost containment. As a result, cost containment becomes a more attractive strategy to control costs |
| Risk equalization based on *endogenous* risk factors | +/− | To the extent that risk equalization mitigates unpriced risk heterogeneity, it reduces the returns on risk selection (e.g., via marketing). When based on endogenous factors, however, risk equalization also reduces the expected returns on cost containment. Moreover, endogenous risk factors can introduce incentives for oversupply when the incremental subsidy associated with a certain treatment exceeds the "cost" associated with that treatment |
| Risk sharing | +/− | To the extent that risk sharing mitigates unpriced risk heterogeneity, it reduces the returns on risk selection (e.g., via marketing). However, it also reduces returns on cost containment |

The benchmark for the effects in this table is a competitive market with both risk rating and risk selection. Symbols indicate whether the intervention promotes incentives for efficiency in production (+), (potentially) distorts incentives for efficiency in production (−), or has no direct effects (0). The table covers what we think are the *major* effects; there might be additional (indirect) effects not covered here. Symbols indicate the direction of effects rather than their size.

equalization models rely on endogenous risk factors (i.e., factors that can be influenced by health insurers) such as morbidity classifications based on (prior) use of health care. Endogenous risk factors create a link between treatment decisions and (future) compensations, which not only reduces the expected returns on cost containment (since cost containment may lower future compensations) but can also introduce incentives for oversupply and upcoding (in case the incremental subsidy associated with a treatment exceeds the "costs" associated with that treatment). The extent to which such incentives are present and may have an effect depends on the specification of these endogenous risk factors, and the possibilities for insurers to influence treatment decisions (Geruso and Layton, 2015). Therefore, it is not clear beforehand whether endogenous risk equalization is better than risk sharing at maintaining incentives for efficient production. Both dilute "power," i.e., the share of costs at the margin borne by the health plan, but the size of this loss depends on a payment system's characteristics and context (Geruso and McGuire, 2016). For more explanation and discussion of this power issue, see Chapter 5, Evaluating the Performance of Health Plan Payment Systems.

### 2.6.4   The Effects of an External Subsidy to Insurers

We will now turn to the effects of an external subsidy (e.g., from the regulator) to insurers. In what follows, we assume that this subsidy is funded with income-based contributions (e.g., income-based tax payments not directly linked to enrollment). In practice, such a subsidy is often, but not necessarily, combined with a risk equalization or risk-sharing scheme. For example, the regulator can make a contribution to the risk equalization/ sharing fund. Before discussing the effects of such a combination (Section 2.6.5), we will first analyze the effects of an external subsidy as a standalone intervention. For this exercise we look at a very simple form, namely a fixed per-person subsidy paid to the insurer, and we ignore the effect of paying the mandatory contribution on affordability. The effects are summarized in Table 2.4.

Though an external fixed subsidy does not fully solve affordability problems due to risk rating, it reduces the premium and thereby improves affordability for low-income people. To the extent that incomplete risk rating results in inefficient sorting into the market, an external fixed subsidy can help. This can be illustrated with Fig. 2.6, in which—for simplicity—we assume complete community-rating. The curves reflecting "expected claims," "expected claims plus risk premium," and "average expected claims" are similar to those in Fig. 2.3. From the insurers' perspective, an external fixed subsidy reduces the average expected claims, which is reflected by the new curve "average expected claims minus subsidy S." If the external fixed subsidy fully compensates for the gap between the "average expected claims" and "expected claims plus risk premium," which is the case in Fig. 2.6, all consumers (who can afford basic coverage in the case of equilibrium premium $P_{eq}$) will enroll in basic coverage, i.e., $Q_{eq} = Q_{eff} = 100\%$.

While an external fixed subsidy leaves the absolute premium differences among plans in place, it increases the relative premium differences. Douven et al. (2017) show that this can affect choice since consumers tend to be sensitive to relative premium differences ("relative thinking"). A fixed subsidy can leverage relative thinking and increase demand elasticity for health plans. Indirectly, this can increase plans' incentives for cost containment (and selection).

**TABLE 2.4** How Does an External Fixed Subsidy Affect Affordability and Efficiency?

| Objective | Effect | |
|---|---|---|
| Affordability of basic coverage for high-risk people | 0/+ | An external fixed subsidy lowers the premium for all, both directly (because of subsidy S) and indirectly (when more of the low-risk people enroll in basic coverage), but does not correct for risk rating. Most likely, premiums will still be unaffordable for high risks (e.g., those with kidney disorders, see Fig. 2.1) |
| Affordability of basic coverage for low-income people | + | An external fixed subsidy lowers the premium for all. Assuming that the subsidies are funded with income-related contributions, affordability for low-income people improves |
| Efficient health plan design | 0 | An external fixed subsidy does not directly affect unpriced risk heterogeneity and has no direct effect on incentives for risk selection (via plan design) |
| Efficient enrollment in basic coverage | + | An external fixed subsidy lowers the premium, which makes it more attractive for low-risk people to enroll in basic coverage. When these people value basic coverage at more than their expected claims this is efficient |
| Efficient consumer sorting across plans | 0 | An external fixed subsidy does not directly affect unpriced risk heterogeneity and has no direct effect on consumer sorting |
| Incentives for efficiency in production | 0 | An external fixed subsidy does not directly affect the returns on cost containment. Neither does it directly affect the expected returns on risk selection |

The benchmark for the effects in this table is a competitive market with both risk rating and risk selection (meaning that all six objectives are potentially violated). Symbols indicate whether the intervention promotes the objective (+), (potentially) distorts the objective (−), or has no direct effects (0). The table covers what we think are the *major* effects; there might be additional (indirect) effects not covered here. Symbols indicate the direction of effects rather than their size. We do not make assumptions about the relative importance of the six objectives.

## 2.6.5   Risk Equalization or Risk Sharing With an External Fixed Subsidy

One disadvantage of risk equalization and risk sharing is, to the extent that they push premiums for all groups towards the mean, that they can discourage low-risk people from enrolling in basic coverage (see Table 2.2). Whether low-risk people in a certain population indeed choose not to enroll

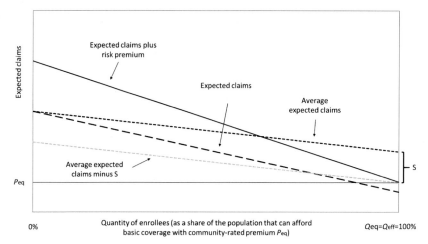

**FIGURE 2.6**    The demand for basic coverage under complete community rating and an external fixed subsidy S.

Note: the horizontal axis represents the population that can afford basic coverage with premium $P_{eq}$. Consumers are ordered according to their expected claims for basic coverage. Those with the highest expected claims are on the left and those with the lowest on the right. All consumers are assumed to be risk-averse and willing to pay a risk premium on top of their expected claims. Since willingness-to-pay decreases with expected claims, the "average expected claims" curve is downward-sloping (but above the "expected claims" curve). From the insurers' perspective, per-person subsidy S reduces the expected cost, which is reflected in the "average expected claims minus S" curve.

depends on the slopes of the "expected claims plus risk premium" curve and the "average expected claims" curve, as well as the presence and strength of an insurance mandate. To the extent that risk selection into the market is actually a problem, supplementing risk equalization or risk sharing with an external subsidy to insurers can help to reduce that problem. In fact, this combines the two effects shown in Figs. 2.5 and 2.6. Risk equalization/risk sharing reduces unpriced risk heterogeneity and thus the potential for inefficient sorting and inefficient health plan design. An external subsidy lowers the equilibrium premium and thus reduces the problem of inefficient sorting into the market. In practice, many risk equalization schemes are combined with an external fixed subsidy to insurers. In these schemes, the REP for individual $i$ can be written as:

$$REP_i = \hat{y}_i - \bar{\hat{y}} + S \qquad (2.3)$$

where, similar to formula (2.1), $\hat{y}_i$ is some concept of expected claims for individual $i$, $\bar{\hat{y}}$ is the mean per-person expected claims in the population, and $S$ is an external fixed per-person subsidy from the regulator. In practice, various combinations of risk equalization (or risk sharing) and a fixed subsidy can be found. In the Netherlands, for instance, the external fixed subsidy equals about 50% of the average expected claims in the population (see Chapter 14: Health Plan Payment in the Netherlands). In Belgium (Chapter 7: Risk Adjustment in Belgium: Why and How to Introduce Socioeconomic Variables in Health Plan Payment), the external fixed subsidy nearly equals the average expected claims in the population. In Israel (Chapter 13: Regulated Competition and Health Plan Payment Under the National Health Insurance Law in Israel—The Unfinished Story), Russia (Chapter 15: Health Plan Payment in the Russian Federation), and US Medicaid (Chapter 18: Health Plan Payment in Medicaid Managed Care: A Hybrid Model of Regulated Competition), the external fixed subsidy fully covers the average expected claims in the population.

## 2.7 SUBSIDIES TO CONSUMERS

In this section, we focus on subsidies to consumers. More specifically, we consider three forms: premium-based subsidies (Section 2.7.1), risk-based subsidies (Section 2.7.2), and income-based subsidies (Section 2.7.3). Again, our benchmark for analyzing the effects of these interventions is a competitive market in which both risk rating and risk selection are present. As with a fixed subsidy to insurers, we assume here that subsidies are funded externally with income-related contributions (e.g., income-based taxes not directly linked to enrollment in basic coverage), and we ignore the effect of paying the mandatory contribution on affordability.

The simplest form of a subsidy to consumers is a fixed subsidy. Since the effects of such a subsidy—in terms of the six objectives in Box 2.3—are similar to those of a fixed subsidy to *insurers* we do not elaborate on this form here, but simply refer to Section 2.6.4.

### 2.7.1   Premium-Based Subsidies to Consumers

In a situation of risk-rated premiums, a simple strategy to promote affordability is to provide consumers with a subsidy depending on the level of their premium (Zweifel and Breuer, 2006). For example, such a subsidy can take the form of a premium-based state allowance or a premium-based employers' contribution. The working of premium-based subsidies can be easily illustrated with Fig. 2.1. Let us assume that the premium is risk-rated according to the mean expected claims per medical condition. Under these circumstances a simple subsidy to promote affordability could take the form of an allowance for individual $i$ equal to the premium for $i$ minus 1293 euros (i.e., the premium for people without a condition). Consequently, the net premium (i.e., the expected claims minus the subsidy) is the same for all, i.e., 1293 euros.

**TABLE 2.5  How Does a Premium-Based Subsidy to Consumers Affect Affordability and Efficiency?**

| Objective | Effect | |
|---|---|---|
| Affordability of basic coverage for high-risk people | + | Though premium-based subsidies do not affect risk rating, they reduce the net premium for high-risk people |
| Affordability of basic coverage for low-income people | + | External premium-based subsidies lower the net premium. Assuming that the subsidies are funded with income-related contributions, affordability for low-income people improves |
| Efficient health plan design | − | A premium-based subsidy reduces the incentive for (high-risk) consumers to shop around for the lowest premium, and thus reduces the insurers' incentive to compete on price |
| Efficient enrollment in basic coverage | 0/+ | To the extent that external premium-based subsidies reduce the net premium for low-risk people, these people will be more likely to enroll in basic coverage. When these people value basic coverage at more than their expected claims this is efficient |
| Efficient consumer sorting across plans | + | A premium-based subsidy reduces the net premium differences among plans, which mitigates the effect of price distortions and promotes efficient sorting of consumers across plans |
| Incentives for efficiency in production | − | A premium-based subsidy reduces the incentive for (high-risk) consumers to shop around for the lowest premium, and thereby reduces the insurers' incentive for cost containment |

The benchmark for the effects in this table is a competitive market with both risk rating and risk selection (meaning that all six objectives are potentially violated). Symbols indicate whether the intervention promotes the objective (+), (potentially) distorts the objective (−), or has no direct effects (0). The table covers what we think are the *major* effects; there might be additional (indirect) effects not covered here. Symbols indicate the direction of effects rather than their size. We do not make assumptions about the relative importance of the six objectives.

Table 2.5 summarizes the effects of a premium-based subsidy. To the extent that premiums are risk rated, a premium-based subsidy clearly improves affordability for high-risk people. To the extent that risk rating is incomplete, the effect of a premium-based subsidy is more complex. To analyze this effect we have to distinguish between two situations: one without and one with premium differences among plans. *Without* premium differences, a premium-based subsidy will be the same for all enrollees and thus works in the same direction as a fixed subsidy (see Section 2.6.4). *With* premium differences among health plans, e.g., due to sorting of different risk types into different health plans, premium-based subsidies mitigate the *net* premium differences. Under these circumstances, premium-based subsidies can mitigate the effects of price distortions due to selection of consumers across plans. A major inefficiency from premium-based subsidies is that they reduce the incentive for consumers to shop around for the lowest premium, and thereby reduce the insurers' incentives for low pricing and cost containment.

It is worth mentioning here that next to the effects in Table 2.5, premium-based subsidies can lead to another efficiency effect: such subsidies reduce the financial incentives for consumers to maintain or improve their health status since premium subsidies (partly) prevent them from paying a higher premium after developing an (expensive) medical condition. However, as long as premium-based subsidies do not fully compensate for premium-rate variation, the reduction in these incentives is not as strong as with community rating.

## 2.7.2    Risk-Based Subsidies to Consumers

Instead of a premium-based subsidy, the regulator can choose to provide consumers with a risk-based subsidy, e.g., in the form of a risk-adjusted voucher, independent of their plan choice. Note that a risk-based subsidy only makes sense when it is based on risk factors that are actually used for premium differentiation. For simplicity, we assume that to be true.

The effects of a risk-based subsidy on affordability are in the same direction as a premium-based subsidy, which can be illustrated as follows. Imagine a situation in which the premium is risk-rated according to the mean expected claims per medical condition. Under these circumstances a risk-based subsidy to promote affordability could take the form of a voucher for individual $i$ equal to the expected claims for $i$ minus 1293 euros (i.e., the expected claims for people without a medical condition). As with the premium-based subsidy, the net premium will be the same for all. A crucial advantage of a risk-based subsidy over a premium-based subsidy, however, is that the subsidy is now independent of the premium. This means that incentives for consumers to shop around for the lowest premium—and thus incentives for insurers to offer low premiums and contain costs—are maintained. When risk rating is incomplete (which we assume to be the benchmark here) risk-based subsidies do not mitigate selection problems.

To the extent that insurers use endogenous factors as rating factors, there is a link between treatment decisions and future premiums. Under these circumstances consumers have an incentive to stay healthy and avoid these treatments. When risk-based subsidies take into account the same endogenous rating factors, they reduce incentives for consumers to avoid these treatments (i.e., an effect comparable to endogenous risk equalization). Though

**TABLE 2.6** How Does a Risk-Based Subsidy to Consumers Affect Affordability and Efficiency?

| Objective | Effect | |
|---|---|---|
| Affordability of basic coverage for high-risk people | + | Assuming that risk-based subsidies are based on the same risk factors as used for premium differentiation, they reduce the net premium for high-risk people |
| Affordability of basic coverage for low-income people | + | External risk-based subsidies lower the average net premium. Assuming that the subsidies are funded with income-related contributions, affordability for low-income people improves |
| Efficient health plan design | 0 | A risk-based subsidy does not directly affect unpriced risk heterogeneity within the market and thus does not directly affect incentives for risk selection (via health plan design) |
| Efficient enrollment in basic coverage | 0 | Given that risk-based subsidies are likely to be based on premium rating factors (instead of the other way around), they will not affect sorting of low-risk consumers to the market |
| Efficient consumer sorting across plans | 0 | A risk-based subsidy does not directly affect unpriced risk heterogeneity within the market and thus has no direct impact on price distortions resulting from selection of profitable and unprofitable consumers into different plans |
| Incentives for efficiency in production | 0 | A risk-based subsidy does not reduce the incentive for (high-risk) consumers to shop around for the lowest premium, and thereby does not reduce the insurers' incentive for cost containment. In addition, a risk-based subsidy does not directly affect unpriced risk heterogeneity within the market, so it does not directly influence the expected returns on risk selection |

The benchmark for the effects in this table is a competitive market with both risk rating and risk selection (meaning that all six objectives are potentially violated). Symbols indicate whether the intervention promotes the objective (+), (potentially) distorts the objective (−), or has no direct effects (0). The table covers what we think are the *major* effects; there might be additional (indirect) effects not covered here. Symbols indicate the direction of effects rather than their size. We do not make assumptions about the relative importance of the six objectives.

this efficiency problem does not directly relate to the six objectives in Table 2.6, it needs to be taken into account when considering subsidies on the basis of endogenous factors. The relevance of this argument depends on the possibilities for consumers to influence treatment decisions.

**TABLE 2.7** How Does an Income-Based Subsidy Affect Affordability and Efficiency?

| Objective | Effect | |
|---|---|---|
| Affordability of basic coverage for high-risk people | 0/+ | An external income-based subsidy improves affordability for high-risk people with low income. Most likely, however, premiums will still be unaffordable for high-risk people (e.g., those with kidney disorders, see Fig. 2.1) |
| Affordability of basic coverage for low-income people | + | An income-based subsidy improves affordability for low incomes |
| Efficient health plan design | 0 | An income-based subsidy does not directly affect unpriced risk heterogeneity within the market and thus does not directly affect incentives for risk selection (via health plan design) |
| Efficient enrollment in basic coverage | 0/+ | To the extent that external income-based subsidies reduce the net premium for low-risk people, enrollment in this group might increase. When these people value basic coverage at more than their expected claims this is efficient |
| Efficient consumer sorting across plans | 0 | Income-based subsidies do not directly affect unpriced risk heterogeneity within the market and thus have no direct impact on price distortions resulting from selection of profitable and unprofitable consumers into different plans |
| Incentives for efficiency in production | 0 | An income-based subsidy does not directly affect unpriced risk heterogeneity within the market. This means it does not directly influence the expected returns on risk selection |

The benchmark for the effects in this table is a competitive market with both risk rating and risk selection (meaning that all six objectives are potentially violated). Symbols indicate whether the intervention promotes the objective (+), (potentially) distorts the objective (−), or has no direct effects (0). The table covers what we think are the *major* effects; there might be additional (indirect) effects not covered here. Symbols indicate the direction of effects rather than their size. We do not make assumptions about the relative importance of the six objectives.

## 2.7.3  Income-Based Subsidies to Consumers

Table 2.7 summarizes the effects of income-based subsidies. Income-based subsidies, which are common in health insurance markets, directly subsidize lower-income groups. Such subsidies can take the form of income-based allowances, tax deductions, tax credits, and income-related employers' contributions. Income-based allowances can be found in the national health insurance schemes in the Netherlands (Chapter 14: Health Plan Payment in the Netherlands) and Switzerland (Chapter 16: Health Plan Payment in Switzerland), among others. Tax credits are applied in the US Marketplaces (Chapter 17: Health Plan Payment in US Marketplaces: Regulated Competition with a Weak Mandate), among others. This strategy does not directly affect affordability problems due to risk rating, but inherently improves affordability for low-income people. To the extent that income-based subsidies reduce the net premium for low-risk people, enrollment in this group might increase, which is efficient when these people value basic coverage at more than their expected claims under that coverage.

## 2.8 SUMMARY AND CONCLUSION

Without regulation of health plan payments, competitive health insurance markets do not guarantee affordability and efficiency. The reason is twofold. First, these markets tend towards risk rating, which threatens affordability of basic coverage for high-risk people. Moreover, for low-income people, premiums for basic coverage might be unaffordable anyway, even for those who are healthy. Second, to the extent that risk rating is incomplete, these markets tend towards risk selection by consumers and insurers, which threatens both affordability and efficiency. On the side of insurers, risk selection can lead to inefficient health plan design. Moreover, in the short term risk selection can be a more attractive strategy to control spending than cost containment, which threatens efficiency in production. On the consumer side, risk selection can mean that low-risk people do not enroll in basic coverage, which drives up premiums and threatens affordability. Moreover, when low-risk people value basic coverage at more than their expected claims (plus loading fee), leaving them uninsured is inefficient. Selection by consumers can also occur *within* the market in a way that profitable and unprofitable consumers sort into different health plans. Consequently, incremental premiums will not only reflect differences in quality and productive efficiency, but also differences in risk composition among plans, which distorts the price/quality tradeoff and ultimately leads to consumers choosing the "wrong" plan.

This chapter has described how typical interventions in health plan payments affect affordability and efficiency. Table 2.8 provides a summary of our conceptual exercise. As above, the benchmark for the effects of the different interventions is a competitive market with both risk rating and risk selection (meaning that all six objectives are potentially violated). An important conclusion that can be drawn from this table is that no single intervention promotes all six objectives simultaneously, which calls for a blend. But what does an appropriate blend look like? Though the answer to this question depends on circumstances of the market in question and how regulators

**TABLE 2.8** Effects of Different Payment System Interventions on Affordability and Efficiency in Competitive Health Insurance Markets

| Intervention | Affordability of basic coverage for high-risk people | Affordability of basic coverage for low-income people | Efficient health plan design | Efficient enrollment in basic coverage | Efficient sorting of consumers across basic-coverage plans | Incentives for efficiency in production |
|---|---|---|---|---|---|---|
| Premium regulation (Section 2.5) | + | – | – | – | – | – |
| *Risk equalization, risk sharing and subsidies to insurers (Section 2.6):* | | | | | | |
| Exogenous risk equalization without an external subsidy | + | – | + | – | + | + |
| Endogenous risk equalization without an external subsidy | + | – | + | – | + | +/– |
| Risk sharing without an external subsidy | + | – | + | – | + | +/– |
| External fixed subsidy | 0/+ | + | 0 | + | 0 | 0 |
| *Subsidies to consumers (Section 2.7):* | | | | | | |
| External premium-based subsidy | + | + | – | 0/+ | + | – |
| External risk-based subsidy | + | + | 0 | 0 | 0 | 0 |
| External income-based subsidy | 0/+ | + | 0 | 0/+ | 0 | 0 |

The benchmark for the effects in this table is a competitive market with both risk rating and risk selection (meaning that all six objectives are potentially violated). Symbols indicate whether the intervention promotes the objective (+), (potentially) distorts the objective (–), or has no direct effects (0). The table covers what we think are the *major* effects; there might be additional (indirect) effects not covered here. Symbols indicate the direction of effects rather than their size. We do not make assumptions about the relative importance of these six objectives.

weight the different objectives, some observations can be made. To start with, risk equalization based on exogenous variables combined with a sufficiently large external subsidy such that all low-risk people choose to enroll in basic coverage, improves outcomes for all of the six objectives, implying that these interventions are part of a smart plan payment policy. Experience has shown, however, that exogenous risk equalization (e.g., demographic models) insufficiently corrects for variation in expected claims, meaning that supplementary tools are needed to achieve the six objectives in Table 2.8. But supplementary tools come with tradeoffs. Premium regulation, for instance, helps to make basic coverage affordable for high-risk people but at the same time distorts all four efficiency goals. Endogenous risk equalization can improve affordability for high-risk people and mitigate selection problems within the market, but comes with a price too: endogenous risk adjusters reduce incentives for cost containment and can even introduce incentives for oversupply. The size of such perverse incentives, however, strongly depends on the specification of these risk adjusters. Chapter 3, Risk Adjustment for Health Plan Payment, provides some guidelines for the selection and design of risk adjusters that help to limit endogeneity problems. As an alternative for endogenous risk equalization, regulators can apply risk sharing. Similar to endogenous risk equalization, risk sharing reduces incentives for cost containment; contrary to endogenous risk equalization, however, risk sharing does not introduce incentives for oversupply. Chapter 4, Risk Sharing, discusses how risk-sharing methods can help to mitigate selection problems without sacrificing too much on incentives for cost containment. In sum, we conclude that choosing the "right" blend involves complex tradeoffs. Chapter 5, Evaluating the Performance of Health Plan Payment Systems, provides a toolkit for quantifying some of these tradeoffs in order to compare alternative payment systems.

## ACKNOWLEDGMENTS

The authors thank Thomas McGuire, Konstantin Beck, and Frank Eijkenaar for their valuable comments on previous versions of this chapter. Remaining errors are the authors' responsibility.

# Chapter 3

# Risk Adjustment for Health Plan Payment

**Randall P. Ellis[1], Bruno Martins[1] and Sherri Rose[2]**
[1]*Department of Economics, Boston University, Boston, MA, United States,* [2]*Department of Health Care Policy, Harvard Medical School, Boston, MA, United States*

## 3.1 INTRODUCTION

This chapter reviews how risk adjustment can be developed and used for health plan payment, with an emphasis on practical aspects of risk adjustment model design, estimation, and implementation in healthcare insurance markets, using information at the individual level to allocate funds to competing health plans. Since our interest is in health plan payment rather than provider reimbursement, we concentrate on predictions of plan obligations for a 1-year period rather than on predicting other measures, such as the cost of hospitalizations, episodes, or spells of treatment, which are more commonly used for provider or provider network payment. We provide a brief review of the theoretical literature on risk adjustment before turning to the practical issues of specification, estimation, estimator selection, and payment implementation of risk adjustment models. We touch upon issues related to premiums, risk sharing, and market regulations in this chapter only to the extent that these issues create special considerations in the design and estimation of risk adjustment; the main discussion of these issues is elsewhere in this volume.

Risk-adjusted plan payment is only possible if there is an agent, here called the regulator,[1] which could be a government, independent agency. or employer, willing to reallocate payments to plans based on the predicted costs for each enrollee. Three other ways for a regulator to pay a health plan for their enrollees are to pay actual cost incurred by the plan (plus an administrative fee), to pay a fixed lump sum (equal say to the average cost), or to pay a competitively determined premium for each enrollee. Paying actual costs provides no incentive for plans to control costs, but does eliminate the incentive for plans to avoid unprofitable enrollees. Paying a fixed lump sum amount equal to the average cost does the opposite: maximizing cost-saving incentives, but creating strong selection incentives to avoid high-cost

*Risk Adjustment, Risk Sharing and Premium Regulation in Health Insurance Markets.*
DOI: https://doi.org/10.1016/B978-0-12-811325-7.00003-8
**55**

enrollees. Premiums can be determined through competitive bidding, or by allowing health plans to charge a premium directly to enrollees based on enrollee characteristics. The disadvantages of premiums are that plans may not be perfectly competitive, and unacceptably large differences in the break-even premiums can arise. Moreover, premiums might become unaffordable for high-risk people. More than 10-fold differences in premiums can emerge based on age and gender alone, with much larger differences possible if health status or other information is used for premium setting. Elsewhere in this volume, we explore risk sharing, in which plan payments reflect combinations of actual costs, lump sum payments, and premiums. The motivation for risk adjustment is that it can correct for (some of the) predictable spending variation, while maintaining cost containment incentives.

There are many issues to consider when designing, estimating, and implementing a risk adjustment model for health plan payment. Box 3.1 organizes these issues into nine dimensions, which can be broken down into estimation and implementation issues. We organize the presentation in this chapter around these nine issues after first discussing the criteria guiding the design of risk adjustment models in the next section.[2]

---

**BOX 3.1 Nine dimensions of risk adjustment**

*Risk adjustment model estimation*

1. The sample on which the risk adjustment model is to be calibrated (e.g., the entire population, or specific subsets of the population).
2. The types of services for which spending is to be predicted (e.g., for the total benefit package, specific services, or specific cost elements of certain services).
3. The types of information to be used for predicting annual spending (sociodemographic, diagnostic, pharmacy, or other information).
4. The timing of the information to be used for predicting annual spending (e.g., lagged or concurrent information, or both).
5. The objective function, functional form, and statistical methodology used for selection and estimation.

*Risk adjustment model implementation*

6. The group of members for which risk is to be equalized (e.g., entire population, each state, or certain plan types).
7. The adjustments made for the time lag between estimation and implementation of the formula.
8. The sources of funds paid into the equalization fund to which the risk adjustment formula is applied (premiums or taxes paid by consumers, funds from the regulator, or revenues from health plans).
9. The integration of the risk adjustment with risk sharing and premiums for plan payments.

In order to illustrate key features of empirical risk adjustment models, we intermingle our discussion of concepts with empirical examples, using results from existing studies as well as new results from commercial claims data. For our new empirical results, we use a sample of US privately insured enrollees from the widely used IBM Watson/Truven MarketScan Commercial Claims and Encounter data (the "MarketScan data"). MarketScan data were used to develop and evaluate the risk adjustment formula used in the Health Insurance Marketplace for populations aged 0−64, created as part of the Affordable Care Act (ACA) of 2010 (Kautter et al., 2014). For illustrating issues related to the practical application of risk adjustment models we use an enhanced version of the hierarchical condition category (HCC) model first described in Ash et al. (2000), commonly called the DxCG-HCC model.[3]

## 3.2    CRITERIA GUIDING THE DESIGN OF RISK ADJUSTMENT MODELS

We discuss here criteria guiding the design of risk adjustment models, as developed and reviewed in Van de Ven and Ellis (2000), Ash et al. (2000), Kautter et al. (2014), and Van Veen et al. (2015b). We group our discussion into three categories: incentives for efficiency, fairness, and feasibility. We also discuss and expand upon the principles for model development first presented in Pope et al. (2000) and used in the United States and elsewhere.

### 3.2.1    Efficiency

When developing risk adjustment models, a central objective is maintaining appropriate incentives for efficient provision of care. Efficiency raises concerns about the quality of information used to set payments, and concerns about creating incentives to provide the wrong quantities or qualities of healthcare services.

#### 3.2.1.1    Avoiding Endogenous Signals

A central concern when selecting risk adjusters is that they should not be gameable, which is to say that plans or providers cannot readily manipulate them to increase plan payments. Ideal risk adjusters are exogenous to health plan influence and readily verifiable. Age and sex are ideal risk adjusters, although unfortunately by themselves they are not highly predictive of plan obligations. Variables such as counts of visits or dollars of healthcare spending for an enrollee are much more predictive, but also more endogenous variables. Diagnoses and pharmaceutical use are also endogenous, although researchers are still documenting the extent. Endogenous variables such as prescriptions, visits, and spending can directly cause welfare losses due to treatment or quality changes; the social and other costs of changes in diagnoses made to increase payments are less clear.

Papers that document or quantify the degree of endogeneity in the United States include MEDPAC (1998), Newhouse et al. (1999), Wennberg et al. (2013), and Geruso and Layton (2015). While there is no disagreement that manipulation of risk adjustment signals does occur, there are differences of opinions about the magnitude and seriousness of the problem. Bauhoff et al. (2017) estimate that in Germany the share of diagnoses recognized for payment grew by 3%−4% over a 5-year period, which is a rate of about 0.7% per year, an amount that could be removed through the payment formula, or accommodated as an estimate of technological change. Chapter 11, Health Plan Payment in Germany and Chapter 14, Health Plan Payment in the Netherlands, discuss the presence of endogenous signals in Germany and the Netherlands, where it appears to be a growing concern.

### 3.2.1.2 Avoiding Noisy Signals

In addition to endogeneity, efficiency (and fairness) concerns arise if risk adjusters are noisy. Variables such as homelessness, income, race/ethnicity, and indicators of need for long-term care services are examples of risk adjusters that can be predictive, but difficult to verify. Unfortunately, few variables that predict healthcare costs are fully exogenous and readily verifiable. Diagnoses from health claims are both noisy and potentially influenced by plan effort to change coding or utilization. Fig. 3.1 documents that among the commercially insured in the United States; there is a remarkable amount of year-to-year variation in the prevalence of specific chronic conditions. Evidence on the lack of persistence of diagnoses is also evident in Abbas et al. (2012) for Germany, which now requires outpatient diagnoses to appear

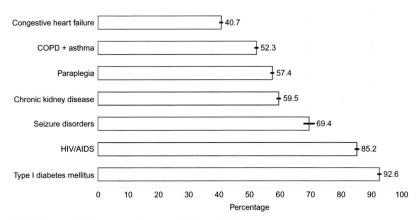

**FIGURE 3.1** HCC Persistence between 2013 and 2014.
Note: Each bar shows, for individuals that had a given HCC in 2013, the percentage that had the same serious related condition in 2014. Sample corresponds to MarketScan individuals who were enrolled for 12 months in both 2013 and 2014, $N = 15,711,896$. Dark bars around the values correspond to 95% confidence intervals.

in two different quarters to affect plan payments. This evidence suggests both noisy coding and the potential for upcoding through greater plan effort.

### 3.2.1.3 Avoiding Incentives Not to Prevent or Cure

A related but slightly different issue for designing risk adjustment models is to avoid incentives for health plans to underspend on prevention or cure treatable conditions because this reduces future plan revenue (Pope et al., 2004). Eggleston et al. (2012) develop a two-period theoretical model of this problem, and show that achieving the first best requires a pay-for-performance type of incentive payment for prevention, and that this is difficult to implement when people can switch plans. The empirical magnitude of this problem has not been established.

### 3.2.1.4 Maintaining Incentives for Cost Control ("Power")

The efficiency issue that has received the greatest attention by developers of risk adjusters is to maintain incentives to control costs, which Laffont and Tirole (1993) define as the "power" of the contract to control costs. Newhouse (1996) characterizes health plan power conceptually, while more recently Geruso and McGuire (2016) develop empirical measures of power of risk-adjusted payments. Geruso and McGuire observe that because indicators for clinical conditions come from instances of healthcare utilization, a risk-adjusted payment system links costs to revenues, diluting plans' incentives to control costs. In their framework, full cost-based payments will have a power of zero, since any reductions in costs reduces revenues equally (and therefore there are no incentives to control costs). With exogenous risk adjusters like age and sex, the power of the payment system is one, which is to say that plans will face the full marginal cost of paying for each service provided. Geruso and McGuire calculate that concurrent risk adjustment has a power of 0.62 for inpatient events and 0.77 for outpatient events, versus 0.91 and 0.85, respectively, for a prospective model using the same risk adjustors. Power is one element of evaluation of health plan payment systems discussed in Chapter 5, Evaluating the Performance of Health Plan Payment Systems.

### 3.2.1.5 Avoiding Overpayment

Although the power of a payment system is a useful measure in terms of the *marginal* revenue generated by an incremental dollar of spending, the overall *average* revenue can also have direct effects on cost containment incentives. Even with fully capitated payments, under competition, overly generous payments can motivate providers to overprovide services, even when the calculated power is one (Ellis et al., 2016). This can be the result of either the overall payment rate being too generous or the capitated payment for a population subgroup being too high. Since consideration of payment generosity affects cost-saving incentives in every health plan payment system, generosity is not solely a risk adjustment issue; therefore we circumvent the effects of overpayment here, and focus on risk adjustment payment schemes in which total plan payments exactly match total plan costs.

### 3.2.1.6  Avoiding Service-Level Selection Incentives

The central issue for risk adjustment is to avoid service-level selection incentives. Glazer and McGuire (2000) were the first to formally model how risk adjustment formulas should be modified to reduce service-level selection. Layton et al. (2017), along with many chapters in this volume, discuss how undesirable selection incentives can be reduced or quantified in the design and implementation of risk adjustment models, as well as through regulation, premium design, and risk sharing. Mitigating service-level selection incentives is perhaps the most important efficiency rationale for risk adjustment, but it is not the only efficiency concern.

## 3.2.2  Fairness

Although economists often focus solely on efficiency issues, a majority of health planners and consumers also care about fairness. For example, regulators might want to achieve a certain concept of equity in individuals' contributions to the health insurance system. Such objectives have implications for the design of risk adjustment. As discussed below, fairness can matter across multiple dimensions, and fairness across age and health status can conflict with fairness of payments across income, geography, or other socioeconomic variables like education and race. In the United States, fairness considerations commonly guide the choice of risk adjusters to use in payment formulas. For example, Ash et al. (2000) and Pope et al. (2004) discuss why certain variables like race and income are not appropriate risk adjusters, even if predictive, and why payments should not be lower for certain conditions such as dementia and severe developmental disability, which can lead to undertreatment. Ash et al. (2017) describe how the Massachusetts Medicaid program started using homelessness and neighborhood variables for risk adjustment in 2016 to improve the fairness of the state's Medicaid risk adjustment formula. In Europe, fairness is commonly spoken of in terms of "solidarity" across income or health when discussing risk adjustment (Chinitz et al., 1998a,b; van de Ven and Ellis, 2000; Van Kleef et al., 2009). Solidarity and fairness issues are discussed below when discussing sociodemographic variables, and in Chapter 7, Risk Adjustment in Belgium: Why and How to Introduce Socioeconomic Variables in Health Plan Payment (Belgium) and Chapter 14, Health Plan Payment in the Netherlands.

### 3.2.3  Feasibility

Some risk adjusters may be desirable but infeasible to implement. For example, using diagnoses from all sources may be infeasible in a health plan setting if such diagnoses are not already collected and available for use in calibrating a risk adjustment model. Data availability can be changed by regulations, and provision of data does respond to financial incentives. In the early 2000s, Germany's office-based physicians greatly improved their coding of diagnoses on office-based claims once the government announced that office-based diagnoses would be used along with inpatient diagnoses for risk adjustment. In a similar way, the prospect of using office-based diagnoses for risk adjustment in the United States for Medicare Advantage risk adjustment led to a remarkable improvement in diagnostic coding practice in the early 2000s when the change was phased in. Regulators and risk adjustment model developers should not think of imperfect data as an irremediable flaw.

Feasibility issues can also arise for other reasons. In every country, it is infeasible to obtain prior year data for new immigrants. Frequent health plan changes and the absence of unique identifiers that permit linking individuals across health plans make it infeasible in most of the United States to calibrate risk adjustment models in the private sector that span different insurers. Switching from private to Medicaid or Medicare health insurance creates similar data issues. Feasible risk adjustment in the United States must always accommodate new, partial-year enrollees for other reasons than birth and migration, at rates that vastly exceed rates of partial-year enrollment in most other countries.

Policymakers often feel that a simpler system is more feasible to implement. This view is reflected in the early efforts in the US Medicare and German systems to develop and implement risk adjustment models with only a modest number of disease categories, and simple data burdens. Early risk adjustment models have often used a "rate cell" approach (preferred by many US actuaries and currently used as a large part of the payment system in Switzerland (Chapter 16: Health Plan Payment in Switzerland) and elsewhere) in which each person is assigned to one unique rate cell, and the mean cost of people in that cell serves as a basis for the payment for that category. Such models are easy to explain, and have some implementation advantages. For example, in a rate cell system, there are no interactions between cells, and predictions for one cell can be adjusted without affecting the predictions for other cells. Rate cell payments can also be generated using aggregated rather than individual-level data, which can be a big plus. The disadvantages of rate cells are that sample size limits the number of cells for which means can be reliably estimated, and they generally have less predictive power than additive models with more variables.

More recently, and perhaps in response to growing challenges of upcoding, and worsening service-level selection, risk adjustment models in the

Netherlands, Germany, and the United States have become more complex, with separate models for different population groups and/or medical services, and increased numbers and variety of risk adjusters. In an interesting twist on the argument for simplicity, Rose (2016) has argued that complex empirical methods for estimation, such as machine learning algorithms (discussed below) confer an advantage rather than a disadvantage. If providers and plans cannot reverse engineer the payment model, they may not be in a good position to manipulate it by upcoding or other tactics.

### 3.2.4 Ten Principles in Pope et al. (2004)

Box 3.2 summarizes the 10 principles that guided the creation of the diagnostic classification system of the first HCC system for Medicare Advantage, and that have remained influential in the development of the Medicare Part D prescription drug (Kautter et al., 2012) and Marketplace. (Kautter et al., 2014) risk adjustment formulas. Similar principles also guided the initial development of the German diagnosis-based classification system. The advantage of specifying principles is that, once agreed upon, they can be

---

**BOX 3.2 Principles guiding HCC model development**

1. Diagnostic categories should be clinically meaningful.
2. Diagnostic categories should be predictive.
3. Diagnostic categories that will affect payments should have adequate sample sizes to permit accurate and stable estimates of expenditures.
4. Hierarchies should be used to characterize the person's illness level within each disease process, while the effects of unrelated disease processes accumulate.
5. The diagnostic classification should encourage specific coding.
6. The diagnostic classification should not reward coding proliferation.
7. Providers should not be penalized for recording additional diagnoses (monotonicity).
8. The classification system should be internally consistent (transitive) with regard to costs.
9. The diagnostic classification should assign all ICD-9-CM codes (i.e., be exhaustive).
10. Discretionary diagnostic categories should be excluded from payment models.
11. *Designers should anticipate induced changes in coding and treatment.*
12. *Designers should optimize given likely selection effects induced by payment system.*
   Note: The first 10 principles are from Pope et al. (2004).

applied by researchers repeatedly without having to return to clinicians, statisticians, and policymakers as frequently for guidance.[4]

Principle 1 seems obvious but may be violated by machine learning or other algorithms that group diseases with similar costs but diverse clinical meaning. Principle 2 warns against creating categories that are clinically meaningful but not predictive. Principle 3 guides how finely to create clusters of conditions as a priori protection against overfitting ($N \geq 500$ is a common minimum cell size). Principles 4, 5, and 6 speak to designing risk adjusters to reduce sensitivity to gaming. Principles 7 and 8 reflect desirable properties for fairness and consistency. Principle 9 is primarily for bookkeeping, making it easier to identify new or unclassified diagnoses. Principle 10 recognizes that payment models can differ from predictive models (also a prominent theme with machine learning models) and can justify substantial reductions in predictive power in order to improve incentives. The final two principles, shown in italics, were not in the original Pope et al. (2004) list. We added them to reflect recent insights into risk adjustment discussed below: designers should anticipate the effects of the payment system on the risk adjusters, and try to optimize the formula against anticipated selection effects.

We now turn to a discussion of the nine dimensions of risk adjustment described in Box 3.1.

## 3.3 CHOICE OF ESTIMATION SAMPLE

The first decision to make in risk adjustment model development is what sample to use for model calibration. Although it would seem obvious to use a large sample from the same population as the one on which the risk adjustment model will be applied, this is often not done. One reason is feasibility, related to data availability. The US Medicare Advantage program (Chapter 19: Medicare Advantage: Regulated Competition in the Shadow of a Public Option) continues to use the traditional Medicare enrollee sample, not its own enrollee data, for calibrating its risk adjustment formula more than 30 years after first adopting risk adjustment, since the Medicare Advantage data needed for this purpose are not collected. The US Marketplace (Chapter 17: Health Plan Payment in US Marketplaces: Regulated Competition With a Weak Mandate) uses privately insured claims data from large employers for its formula for the new individual insurance market. Germany used data from only a subset of all plans to initially develop its first risk adjustment formula, although Germany now uses a national sample.

Beyond feasibility explanations, Newhouse (2017) argues that if the population on which the risk adjustment formula is to be applied for payment reflects service-level distortions, then using a sample unbiased by selection effects may be desirable. This rationale underlies the calibration of formulas on traditional Medicare used for the Medicare Advantage enrollees. This argument is further extended in Bergquist et al. (2018), who point out that it may be not only service-level distortions, but also under- or overconsumption by various population subgroups in the estimation sample that may cause problems during estimation.

A number of empirical studies have shown that for predicting total spending, risk adjustment formulas developed on one sample are often relatively robust for prediction on different samples. Ash et al. (2000) examined correlations of risk scores generated between privately insured, Medicare, and Medicaid enrollees, while Ash and Ellis (2012) demonstrate the stability of a US formula over 6 years and seven plan types. Ellis et al. (2013a,b) found that an HCC formula calibrated using US data had predictive power nearly as strong as using 117 related condition categories, which are aggregates of HCCs, calibrated using Australian data. Rose et al. (2015) show that fit results for the US Marketplaces are similar when using the privately insured claims data versus a sample of that data selected to more accurately reflect Marketplace enrollees.

### 3.3.1 Sample Exclusions

It is common for risk adjustment models to be estimated on data after elimination of troublesome records. This often includes purging partial year (less than 12 month) eligibles, or, in prospective models, dropping people when the full 12 months of prior-year claims are not available. Also common is to drop extreme outliers, or alternatively to "top-code" outliers, i.e., to replace spending on individuals above a threshold (such as $250,000) with that threshold.[5] For evaluating different risk adjustment models, it is also common to focus on relatively homogeneous subgroups, such as adults, by excluding infants and children. Table 3.1 uses 2014 MarketScan data to illustrate how these exclusions affect sample means, and three measures of variability, all of which are unit-free measures and hence comparable across samples.[6] These variability measures are the coefficient of variation (CV, which is the standard deviation divided by the mean), skewness (which captures how asymmetric spending is around the mean), and kurtosis (which captures how thick the tails are). Excluding partial-year eligibles has a particularly large effect on these latter two measures, and will particularly bias risk adjustment formulas since it drops most deaths and newborns from the sample, both of which have unique characteristics and may have (very) high spending.[7] For diseases like chronic heart failure and pancreatic cancer, only including people who survive for an additional 12 calendar months in the estimation sample generates a very biased subset of these populations. Methods for incorporating and adjusting for partial-year eligibles are discussed in Section 3.3.6.

**TABLE 3.1** Alternative Estimation Sample Summary Statistics on 2014 Plan Payments per Enrollee

|  | Number of observations | Mean spending | CV | Skewness | Kurtosis |
|---|---|---|---|---|---|
| Full sample | 21,832,612 | 4429 | 1660 | 184.9 | 219,009 |
| Removed if less than 12 months eligible in 2014 | 18,041,199 | 4322 | 1521 | 36.4 | 5061 |
| As above, plus removed if less than 12 months eligible in 2013 | 15,710,699 | 4416 | 1507 | 35.8 | 5135 |
| As above, plus removed if aged 0–21 | 10,894,520 | 5473 | 1322 | 29.1 | 4071 |
| As above, plus removed if spending more than 1000 times mean | 10,894,517 | 5471 | 1305 | 21.3 | 1177 |

Sample is the IBM Watson/Truven MarketScan Commercial Claims and Encounter. Variable used is plan obligations per enrollee divided by the fraction of the year eligible. All statistics generated use sample weights equal to the fraction of months enrollee was eligible in 2014. Observation counts are unweighted counts of enrollees.

## 3.3.2    Separate Formulas for Population Subgroups

It is relatively common to estimate separate regression models for distinct subpopulations in recognition of different patterns of disease and cost. The 2017 CMS Medicare Advantage model uses nine different formulas for different subpopulations (Chapter 19: Medicare Advantage: Regulated Competition in the Shadow of a Public Option). These formulas differ according to whether the enrollee is aged (age 65 and over) or disabled (age $< 65$), ineligible, fully, or partially eligible for Medicaid. In addition, three more formulas are used for institutionalized enrollees (i.e., those in a nursing home), for new enrollees with less than 9 months of prior year eligibility, and for a subset of new enrollees in chronic condition special needs plans. The US Medicare Part D risk adjustment formula uses the first eight but not the final model. The Swiss (Chapter 16: Health Plan Payment in Switzerland) have separate risk adjustment formulas within each canton (similar to a county in the United States), using age, gender, and whether people are hospitalized or not. Since they use primarily a rate cell approach rather than a regression-based approach for risk adjustment, it is equivalent to having separate models for each geographic area canton.

Estimating separate models for population subgroups is generally a good idea if sample sizes are adequate, and there is evidence that cost patterns differ among the groups. Germany, despite having an enormous sample size, uses a single risk equalization formula for the full population, although the formula does include age-specific HCC terms that allow it to better predict certain age-related spending patterns (Chapter 11: Health Plan Payment in Germany). Estimating a single formula, but including dummy variables for population subgroups—alone or interacted with other risk adjusters—is more appropriate where sample sizes are a concern. From a modeling perspective, there is a tradeoff between obtaining greater fit by having separate models with fewer risk adjusters versus gaining from information learned across subgroups by having more complex single equation models with interactions. The Netherlands (Chapter 14: Health Plan Payment in the Netherlands) uses the latter approach extensively. Machine learning approaches, discussed below, provide an empirical basis for choosing model structure based on statistical grounds.

### 3.3.3 Separate Formulas for Different Health Plan Benefits

In some countries there is not one formula used for risk adjustment for a given person, but rather a family of formulas that depend on the plan the person chooses. The US Marketplace risk adjustment formula has five variants that vary according to whether the enrollee is in a platinum, gold, silver, bronze, or catastrophic plan. The Marketplace formulas were developed on the basis of one sample of enrollees, on which the effects of different degrees of benefit coverage were simulated. More concretely, Kautter et al. (2014) started with total covered spending in an estimation sample, without correcting for the existing level of plan coverage. They simulated the effects of the platinum, gold, silver, bronze, and catastrophic plan benefit levels on out-of-pocket costs, subtracted these costs from covered spending and used the resulting simulated plan obligations to estimate separate risk adjustment formulas. Empirically the risk scores from formulas estimated by Kautter et al. for different benefit plans are highly correlated, but are scaled to reflect the differences in coverage.

Adjusting payments for differences in benefit design clearly helps with predicting means correctly, but it introduces issues of fairness: how large should the subsidies be (through risk equalization) for consumers choosing more generous benefit when this generosity induces greater healthcare utilization? A significant concern, about which there is relatively little research, is how to incorporate consumer and provider behavioral response to benefit design differences across plans into the risk adjustment formula.

### 3.3.4    Separate Formulas for Different Types of Services

The correct dependent variable in risk adjustment modeling is plan-obligated spending, which implies calculating both the services covered and plan obligations after deducting enrollee cost-sharing payments and any payments a plan would receive from risk sharing (such as reinsurance). In the United States, Medicare Advantage plans are only required to cover specified inpatient and outpatient spending, notably not including prescription drugs (although many plans nonetheless choose to include pharmacy coverage) hence the Medicare Advantage formulas predict plan obligations only for inpatient and outpatient services covered by traditional Medicare. The Medicare program uses a separate risk adjustment formula for its prescription drug plans that cover only prescription drugs (Chapter 19: Medicare Advantage: Regulated Competition in the Shadow of a Public Option). The Netherlands has separate formulas for subsets of spending rather than subsets of the population. Their main model covers somatic health care (medical plus pharmaceutical spending, excluding certain specified categories) that encompasses about 80% of total healthcare spending under the benefits package. Separate models predict and equalize payments for short-term mental health care, long-term mental health care, and further calculations correct payments for differences in out-of-pocket payments for deductibles (Chapter 14: Health Plan Payment in the Netherlands).

Estimating separate formulas for distinct services does not create implementation problems if the formulas are combined when making plan payments, as they are in the Netherlands. But separate formulas for different services can create problems when there is a separate contract or risk adjustment equalization for these different services (which are called "carve outs" in the United States). Separate contracts may encourage inappropriate substitution between different services. For example, in the US Medicare program, risk equalization and payments for outpatient prescription drugs in the Part D program are done separately from the Medicare Advantage risk adjustment, in which some of the plans also include prescription drugs. When payments for different services come out of different bundled payments, providers may have an incentive to change care patterns and take advantage of these different payment flows. Carve outs also add budgetary complexity and encourage lobbying for favorable funding.

### 3.3.5    Predicting Only Covered Services

Countries vary in how fully they specify the services that must be covered by the health plans. In some systems coverage of all qualified providers and drugs is determined nationally, whereas in others considerable discretion is exercised at the plan level. An example from the United States is pharmaceutical spending where formularies, subject to some regulation, may include or exclude a wide number of drugs. In principle, developers of risk adjustment models would also know what costs are to be included when estimating formulas. Coverage is standardized for traditional Medicare in the United States, while there is meaningful heterogeneity in what services are covered or not covered in Medicare Advantage, prescription drug plans, and the Marketplace.

Payment formulas can be adjusted when new technologies or costs are anticipated. For example, in 2016, a new hepatitis C drug in the US marketed by Gilead Sciences had a list price of $75,000 for a 12-week drug treatment, and was recommended for virtually everyone infected with hepatitis C. This had a noticeable one-time cost increase for this illness. The Medicare Part D prescription drug program (CMS, 2016a) as well as the Massachusetts Medicaid risk adjustment program (Clements et al., 2016) built these additional drug costs into their risk adjustment payment formulas in a relatively ad hoc manner without relying on regression recalibration.

In some contexts, data show that total paid and covered amounts are extremely highly correlated ($\rho = 0.998$ in our US MarketScan data, whether top-coded at $250,000 or not). In these cases, the differences in risk scores at the aggregate for a given sample are relatively small according to whether paid or total spending are used for estimating risk adjustment models. Using payments rather than total spending will matter for certain diseases or types of spending where drugs or outpatient services have higher or lower rates of coverage, and this coverage varies across health plans. In settings in which demand-side cost sharing is modest and there is little risk sharing by the regulator, the differences in relative risk scores (RRS) using total and plan-paid amounts is likely to be modest at the plan level, but differences of even a few percent may be troubling. We have not seen this issue explored empirically in settings other than the United States.

### 3.3.6 Accommodating Partial-Year Eligibles

For research studies, researchers often choose to focus on the cleanest sample, which usually means samples in which everyone is enrolled for all 12 months in a calendar year. For payment purposes, one still needs to make predictions for people with less than 12 months of eligibility. Using estimates based on only full-year eligibles is undesirable because partial-year enrollments are nonrandom, and have different patterns of costs, as we already illustrated in Table 3.1. Births, deaths, retirements, and changing jobs or health plans are all correlated with specific diseases and levels of health spending, and hence if partial-year enrollees are dropped, or this issue is ignored, then serious biases can result.

Ellis and Ash (1995) advocated, and many regulators adopted, a method for estimating linear risk adjustment models with annualized spending and then weighting the sample by the fraction of the year a person is eligible.

This is equivalent to using the average monthly spending on health care and then weighting by the number of months eligible. It is straightforward to show that this results in unbiased predictions of monthly spending which exactly match actual spending in every mutually exclusive cell created by the dichotomous risk adjusters (like HCCs), i.e., the formula correctly predicts actual spending for people in each HCC.

The importance of annualizing is easily seen by considering newborns. Newborns are relatively expensive on average compared to 1−10-year-olds. Suppose that on average in their first year, newborns cost $6000. Unlike most 1−10-year olds, babies are on average only eligible for coverage for about half of the year. Therefore their average monthly cost should be $1000 per month eligible. Without annualizing and weighting, a risk adjustment model will predict that babies cost only $500 per month, half of the actual value. This problem is fixed by annualizing and weighting the spending. Annualizing and weighting is particularly important in the United States where people change health plans frequently, and hence partial-year coverage is relatively common. It is also particularly important when enormous resources are spent on people in the year in which they die, which is true in the United States as well as other countries.

Using unweighted spending can be preferred when health plan eligibility data are missing or of poor quality or when supplementary plan coverage is only used rarely even when continuously available. One example is US Department of Veterans Affairs health claims data, since US veterans remain eligible for veterans' benefits continuously once eligible. Even if a veteran does not use any VA services, they are still eligible. This is true in other settings, such as with private insurance in Australia, where a supplementary benefit means that enrollees often obtain insurance from other sources.[8] With very intermittent use of the benefit, perhaps only every few years, assigning individuals to a geographic region or provider group can be problematic.

Partial-year eligibles create two problems for risk adjustment. One problem is that annual spending in the prediction year for which payments are made will be biased downward, which is addressed by predicting annualized spending, as described. A different problem arises because the base period during which diagnoses (or other risk adjusters) are observed is shortened. Chen et al. (2015) examine the bias and weaker fit from ignoring the duration of the base period and propose formulas that incorporate duration information in the prospective Medicare Advantage formula. Ericson et al. (2017) document the undercount of diagnoses in concurrent models such as the Marketplace formula and propose adjustments to improve fit and lessen bias for partial-year eligibles.

Adjustment for partial year enrollment is done differently in various countries. The United States and Switzerland use monthly eligibility to annualize spending and perform risk equalization. Germany and the Netherlands use the number of days in the year covered for both annualizing and weighting. The choice between using monthly or daily information for annualizing and weighting could be influenced by at least two issues. In smaller sample sizes, weighting by days can introduce some very large outliers for people only eligible for a few days, and hence is less desirable than a monthly annualization.[9] The second issue is how premiums and plan revenue payments are paid. In the United States, most employers and the government pay health plans a monthly premium for each enrollee, even when an enrollee is only eligible for a fraction of the month, while Germany and the Netherlands adjust payments to health plans based on the number of days each individual is enrolled.

### 3.3.7 Normalizations to Create Relative Risk Scores

In the United States, risk adjustment model results are generally presented in terms of RRS rather than monetary predictions. RRS express predicted spending as a multiple of mean spending. Fig. 3.2 presents normalized spending rather than dollar amounts, which are akin to RRS. RRS are presented in most tables and figures in various government publications and software (e.g., Kautter et al., 2012, 2014). RRS always reflect a

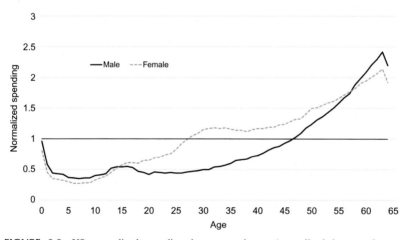

**FIGURE 3.2** US normalized spending by age and sex (normalized by sample mean; $N = 21,832,612$).

Note: This figure shows normalized spending by 1-year age increments, for males and females, aged 0–64, in the 2014 US MarketScan Commercial Claims and Encounter Data using only people with no capitation payments. Normalized spending was calculated by first annualizing spending by dividing actual spending by the fraction of the year enrolled, and then calculated the weighted mean using eligibility fractions. Annualized spending was then divided by the weighted annualized average to create a normalized spending measure.

normalization to some period of time and sample, which should be specified for results to be interpreted easily.

Normalizations are particularly important to use when pooling data for estimation across different years, or multiple population subsets, where medical inflation and/or treatment intensity tends to change costs over time. To increase sample size, multiple years of claims data are often combined using medical cost deflators, such as in the United States the personal consumption expenditure medical cost index. For large samples, an alternative strategy is to normalize spending in each year by the average spending in that year before pooling.

## 3.4    INFORMATION USED FOR PREDICTING SPENDING (RISK ADJUSTERS)

This section discusses the types of information potentially used for risk adjustment, commonly called risk adjusters.

### 3.4.1    Age and Gender

The classic risk adjusters are age and gender. Fig. 3.2 illustrates the 1-year average spending per enrollee on all types of health care—inpatient, outpatient, and pharmaceutical—for a sample of 21.8 million individuals from age 0 to age 64 among the commercially insured population in the United States in 2014 by 1-year age intervals for males and females, where spending is normalized by the overall mean. Males and females show similar patterns until age 15, at which point spending starts to diverge and women have higher mean spending until around the age of 58.[10]

Fig. 3.2 reveals that the relationship between age and spending is nonlinear, and the difference between males and females is particularly noticeable during childbearing years. A similar although dampened pattern typically holds even when other risk adjusters are included. Thus, there is a strong argument for not using a simple additive sex term, but at least to use age−sex interaction terms. The HCC-CMS and HCC-HHS systems use 32 age−sex categories, with 5- or 0-year increments, approximating the curve for each sex with a step function. Even this step function approach introduces imperfect fits just before and after the break points that could be avoided by using finer age categories, including 1-year increments. As long as the overall sample size is large, then the age gender patterns can be reliably estimated with little risk of overfitting.

### 3.4.2    Diagnoses on Submitted Claims or Encounter Records

Both in the United States and elsewhere, diagnoses on claims or encounter records.[11] submitted by providers are the preferred set of information for risk

**TABLE 3.2 Risk-Adjustment Model Results—$R^2$ (in Percentages) With 95% Confidence Intervals**

| Model | Untop-coded spending | Spending top-coded at $250,000 | Log(1 + spending) |
|---|---|---|---|
| *Concurrent* | | | |
| Age—sex (Marketplace age groups) | 1.4 (1.2, 1.6) | 2.9 (2.9, 3.0) | 10.68 (10.6, 10.7) |
| Age—sex (1-year increment) | 1.5 (1.2, 1.7) | 3 (3.0, 3.0) | 11 (11.0, 11.1) |
| DxCG-HCC with age—sex (Marketplace age groups) | 41.5 (35.2, 46.5) | 57.9 (57.8, 58.0) | 59.1 (59.1, 59.2) |
| *Prospective* | | | |
| DxCG-HCC with age—sex (Marketplace age groups) | 15.3 (12.9, 17.3) | 23.2 (23.1, 23.3) | 29.7 (29.7, 29.7) |

Each cell provides the within-sample $R^2$ (in percentage) for an OLS regression model that predicts total (outpatient, inpatient, and pharmacy) spending normalized by sample mean. $N =$ 21,832,612. Age—sex variables are interactions of sex and age dummies variables using either the Marketplace age groups or 1-year age increments. DxCG-HCC refers to DxCG 394 Hierarchical Conditional Categories. 95% confidence intervals (in parentheses) are based on 500 bootstraps.

adjustment, currently in use in the United States, Germany, the Netherlands, Belgium, and Israel. Diagnoses have the advantage of being potentially veri-fiable in most cases by reviewing the patient's medical records. Furthermore, diagnoses are much more predictive than simply age and sex. As shown in Table 3.2, the R-squared for diagnoses-based prospective and concurrent models are 15.3% and 41.5%, versus only 1.5% for age—sex alone in US commercial data. Improvements in the root mean squared error (RMSE) and mean absolute error (MAE), two other commonly used metrics of fit (Table 3.3), are also impressive. This improvement in predictive power is even greater once the data are top-coded at $250,000, where we also see that the confidence bands are reduced to close to a zero range.

The quality of diagnoses recorded varies across providers and settings, with inpatient diagnoses generally viewed as more accurate than office-based diagnoses. Sometimes nonclinicians (e.g., home health workers or massage therapists) may report diagnoses on claims or encounters, which in the United States and in most countries are not recognized in risk adjustment models (Kautter et al., 2014; Department of Health and Human Services, 2016). We will have more to say later about how the very large number of the International Classification of Diseases (ICD) diagnoses (approximately

**TABLE 3.3** Two Alternative Risk-Adjustment Model Measures of Fit

| Model | Root mean squared error | | Mean absolute errors | |
|---|---|---|---|---|
| | Untop-coded spending | Spending top-coded at $250,000 | Untop-coded spending | Spending top-coded at $250,000 |
| *No risk adjustment (constant only)* | 14.8 (14.0, 16.1) | 9.9 (9.9, 10.0) | 1.26 (1.25, 1.26) | 1.19 (1.18, 1.9) |
| *Concurrent* | | | | |
| Age−sex (Marketplace age groups) | 14.7 (13.8, 16.1) | 9.8 (9.8, 9.8) | 1.2 (1.19, 1.20) | 1.13 (1.13, 1.13) |
| Age−sex (1-year increment) | 14.7 (13.8, 16.1) | 9.8 (9.8, 9.8) | 1.2 (1.19, 1.20) | 1.13 (1.13, 1.13) |
| DxCG-HCC with age−sex (Marketplace age groups) | 11.3 (10.2, 13.0) | 6.5 (6.4, 6.5) | 0.71 (0.71, 0.72) | 0.65 (0.65, 0.65) |
| *Prospective* | | | | |
| DxCG-HCC with age−sex (Marketplace age groups) | 13.6 (12.7, 15.1) | 8.7 (8.7, 8.7) | 1 (0.99, 1.00) | 0.93 (0.93, 0.94) |

Each cell provides the root mean squared error or mean absolute error for an OLS regression model that predicts total (outpatient, inpatient, and pharmacy) spending normalized by sample mean. $N = 21,832,612$. Age−sex variables are interactions of sex and age dummies variables using either the Marketplace age groups or 1-year age increment dummies. DxCG-HCC refers to DxCG 394 Hierarchical Conditional Categories. 95% confidence intervals (reported in parentheses) are based on 500 bootstraps.

68,000 legal codes in the ICD-10-CM versus 14,000 ICD-9-CM codes) are collapsed into a limited number of categories below.

It is worth mentioning that, in most years, the World Health Organization (WHO) makes changes to the ICD diagnoses. Most of these ICD changes are limited to descriptions and criteria for existing diagnosis codes, but occasionally new diagnoses are added. Less frequently, approximately once every 20 years, the WHO changes the version of its classification system more fundamentally, such as when it went from ICD-9 (1975) to ICD-10 (1994) to ICD-11 (scheduled for 2018). Many countries do not adopt the WHO ICD codes immediately or without modification. The United States (through the US National Center for Health Care Statistics together with CMS) modifies these codes to create its own ICD-9-CM (clinical modification), which are updated annually on October 1. ICD-10-CM was only adopted in the United States in 2014, two decades after the WHO version change. These differences matter to risk adjusters since they create a necessity for each country to create and maintain risk adjustment classification systems consistent with their own coding system.[12]

### 3.4.3 Pharmacy Information

Pharmacy information is increasingly being used for risk adjustment, despite there being differing opinions about the desirability of doing so. On the positive side, drug use can often signal chronic conditions that are being controlled by medications, and which will be missed if only diagnoses are used for prediction. For some conditions, the pharmacy cost is an important component of plan obligations, and using pharmacy information can help predict this. Advocates of using pharmaceutical information argue that a drug prescription represents a validation of a doctor's opinion, whereas a diagnosis from a visit might only reflect a suspicion. On the negative side, using prescription drug information for risk adjustment may lead to too many prescriptions. Many drugs are given for prevention or maintenance, and basing payments on this information creates strong incentives for overuse.[13]

The Netherlands was the first to use pharmacy information for risk adjustment; it started in 2002 even before the use of diagnostic information in 2004. In 2017, the Dutch risk adjustment system used 33 pharmacy-based cost groups for risk adjustment in addition to diagnostic cost groups and diverse other measures (Chapter 14: Health Plan Payment in the Netherlands). Germany (Chapter 11: Health Plan Payment in Germany) also uses pharmacy information, although largely to validate or fill in for missing diagnoses. The United States is not currently using pharmaceutical information in its risk adjustment systems, although there was a proposal to do so for the Marketplaces (CMS, 2016c).

There are several challenges with using pharmaceutical information for prediction in risk adjustment. One challenge is the large number of different drugs prescribed. Individual drugs are identified by rich classification systems: National Drug Codes (NDC) in the United States and Anatomical Therapeutic Chemicals (ATC) in Europe. These highly detailed codes are mapped into categories of drugs, and selections of these categories are then incorporated in risk adjustment models. The US Food and Drug Administration (FDA) maintains a directory of allowed drugs that is updated daily, so keeping the list of allowed prescriptions up to date requires more effort than keeping up with the much more modest, and less frequent, diagnostic coding changes.[14] The World Health Organization updates the EU's ATC system only twice per year.

Even more challenging is that prescription practices and the plan predicted cost implications of individual drug categories can change rapidly and dramatically. The extremely popular allergy drug loratadine (better known by its brand name Claritin) went off patent in the United States in 2002, and then almost simultaneously switched from being a prescription drug to being sold over the counter (i.e., without a prescription). As a result, prescriptions for this drug, and indeed many other allergy medicines, plummeted. Visits to allergists and recordings of the diagnosis for allergies also declined. Diagnosis-based formulas predicting covered pharmacy spending overpredicted plan costs in this category until it was recalibrated, while pharmacy-based models tended to underpredict because of the disappearance of a large block of prescriptions.

The use of prescription pharmaceuticals for prediction is also complicated by the phenomenon of free samples dispensed by hospitals and clinics, unobserved pharmaceutical use in inpatient settings, and the fact that many drugs have more than one use. On this last point, some antihypertensive drugs have proven effective for preventing hair loss, while specific heart drugs have benefits in terms of sleep, acne, and weight loss. Changes in off-label uses of pharmaceuticals can change the prevalence and cost predictions of many drugs, requiring further attention. Having highlighted the challenges, one strength of pharmaceuticals is that the prescription information is generally available quickly. Moreover, some drugs are highly predictive of specific illnesses: insulin use is a very strong predictor that a person has type II diabetes. Both Germany and the Netherlands require more than one prescription of drugs in their payment formulas in order for that drug variable to be included. In the Netherlands most pharmacy-based cost groups require use of at least 181 defined daily dosages.

### 3.4.4   Prior-Year Spending Information

A frequently considered but rarely used risk adjuster is lagged spending. In our US MarketScan data on the commercially insured, spending in 2013 predicts spending in 2014 with a validated R-squared of 9.08%. This predictive power can be improved to 14.40% by top-coding spending used on the right-hand side at $250,000 and further improved to 21.41% by top-coding both the dependent and right-hand side variables at this level. The coefficient on the lagged spending variable in this last model is 0.49, implying that each extra dollar spent in year 1 predicts 49 cents in year 2. In terms of the Geruso and McGuire (2016) definition of power, these results imply that predictive models using lagged spending (in the form of a continuous variable) have a minimum power of 0.50 (i.e., half of spending this year is returned in payments next year. The reward to a plan is lost if a person changes plans.). While not a power of 1.0 this is still far from cost-based fee-for-service incentives where there is little incentive to reduce costs (power = 0).

Ellis and McGuire (2007) and Ellis et al. (2013a) demonstrate that one can improve prediction of year 2 spending using spending by type of service rather than total spending. Their work, using very large samples, finds that spending by type of service is even more predictive than diagnostic information (their R-squared increased from 10% to 15%). Such models would probably not be attractive to use as a payment model, in that there exist some types of spending for which a dollar spent on that service predicts more than a dollar of costs (and hence risk-adjusted payment) for the following year. Still, it is useful as a reminder that other information not desirable to use in risk adjustment will always be available for health plans to use for risk selection.

Although lagged spending is not used directly as a risk adjuster, the Dutch risk adjustment model (Chapter 14: Health Plan Payment in the Netherlands) includes dummy variables based on risk classes for people with high spending in multiple prior years, on the rationale that these people suffer from a chronic condition that may not be fully recognized by the existing diagnostic risk adjustors. Van Kleef and Van Vliet (2012) show that inclusion of these risk classes leads to substantial improvements in predictive value, even in a risk adjustment model including diagnoses- and pharmacy-based risk adjusters. Moreover, the Dutch risk adjustment model currently includes risk classes based on prior-year spending for two specific services, i.e., home care and geriatric rehabilitation care.

### 3.4.5 Healthcare Utilization Measures

In addition to diagnoses, pharmaceutical information, and spending, certain measures of prior-year utilization are also sometimes used as risk adjusters. The Netherlands uses flags for durable medical equipment, while Switzerland uses a dummy variable for whether or not a person has been hospitalized in the prior year. Moreover, diagnosis-based models include a reward for at least one claim associated with service with a diagnosis. It is difficult to assess the incentive effects of prior utilization on cost containment incentives, but certainly, including this as a risk adjustor reduces the power of the payment system, while improving the fit. Whether they are better or worse than much simpler cost-sharing or reinsurance programs remains to be investigated.

### 3.4.6 Medical Record Information

Ever since medical records became computerized there has been a desire to utilize this information for improved risk adjustment (Parkes, 2015). While the focus of this chapter is prediction of healthcare spending, the use of record information for predicting other outcomes is even more compelling. The attraction of medical record information is primarily that it is more detailed, containing not only the diagnoses reported on claims, but also more secondary diagnoses and suspected conditions, lab test results and their interpretation, timing information, and information about who made the diagnosis. Despite the great promise of using medical record information, it has yet to be used in any risk-adjusted payment system. Medical record information is being used extensively for severity adjustment of outcomes other than spending,[15] and for reconciling and buttressing claims submissions that affect plan payments. There is an active industry in the US advising providers and plans on how to capture more diagnoses so as to increase plan revenue, but similar efforts to use this information to refine risk adjustment predictive models have not to our knowledge been developed. There are several obstacles to overcome before this can happen. First, medical records in the United States are not sufficiently standardized so that they can be easily used across different information systems or merged into a common format. Second, both privacy limitations and market competitiveness mean that many providers do not necessarily share their information with other providers, or even pharmacies and hospitals, so the medical records are often highly incomplete, both from using out-of-network providers and from whenever a patient changes their provider. Third, medical record information is inherently intermittent and, similar to diagnoses, only collected in the course of active medical treatment. Records tend to be collected when a patient is diseased, injured, in stress, being tested, or seeking preventive care. None of these is a random event, and the information collected is often very specific to that setting. None of the reviews and comparisons of risk adjusters by the Society of Actuaries in the United States or government health systems in Europe and Australia have used medical record information.[16]

### 3.4.7    Self-Reported Measures

Self-reported measures, which typically are collected via surveys, have long been considered good candidates for risk adjustment models. The central challenges are feasibility and bias. Feasibility relates to the high cost of surveys relative to using diagnoses from submitted claims, while bias relates to the challenges of getting adequate and representative response rates. A common type of self-reported information is perceived health status, either in its simplest form, which asks whether the respondent's health is excellent/very good/good/fair/poor, or in more elaborate forms such as the Short Form 36, which measures perceived health status along eight dimensions (Ware and Sherbourne, 1992). A different class of information measures functional health status, for which two common instruments ask about activities of daily living (ADLs) and instrumental activities of daily living (IADLs). A third class of self-reported measures relates to chronic conditions (e.g., diabetes, high blood pressure, asthma, etc.). Other self-reported measures include information about lifestyle (smoking, drinking, and food), marital status, employment education, and whether a person can drive.

The usefulness of many of these self-reported measures for prediction has been evaluated numerous times. Much of the analysis of the Rand Health Experiment in the mid-1970s was conducted using survey information, although the modest sample size of about 10,000 person years of spending information substantially limited the statistical power for population-based prediction. Van de Ven and Ellis (2000) report fit measures ($R$-squared) for six early studies, all of which suffer from overfitting because they use very small sample sizes, with fewer than 30,000 respondents, but together question the value of using self-reported information.

Ellis, Fiebig et al. (2013b) report results using data from New South Wales, Australia, on 267,188 individuals over a 4-year panel data set, yielding a panel size of 787,000 person-years. Interestingly, the self-reported measures perform well in predicting use even 2 years before or after the survey was taken. Yet adding survey information in the form of 76 responses capturing each of the dimensions discussed above achieved an R-squared of only 10.2%, which was lower than those achieved by coarse diagnostic, pharmacy, or lagged utilization models. Survey results only added 0.8% points onto the 23.8% achieved using diagnosis, pharmacy, and lagged utilization measures. Gravelle et al. (2011) also explored the incremental information that can be acquired using surveys in addition to diagnostic information using UK data and found modest gains. Rose et al. (2016) examined the inclusion of self-reported health measures in risk adjustment formulas for accountable care organization (ACO) benchmarking and found that they decreased variation in differences between ACOs and local average FFS spending.[17] Similarly to socioeconomic variables, to which we now turn, the main value of including survey-based information is not its contribution to the overall fit of the risk adjustment model, but rather its value in improving predictions for identifiable individuals of concern.

### 3.4.8 Socioeconomic Variables

Demand-related variables such as race/ethnicity, income, poverty, housing, homelessness, unemployment, and language, and supply-related variables such as numbers of doctors and hospitals, provider distance and waiting time, and other measures of access are sometimes used to allocate funds geographically or to provider groups, but such information may not be available at the individual level. The UK payment system has gradually evolved from using aggregated information to using individual-level information to allocate budgets regionally and to providers such as hospitals and primary care providers. Gravelle et al. (2011) demonstrated that diagnosis-based risk adjusters largely eliminated the statistical contribution of most of the demand- and supply-side variables for hospital budgets, while Dixon et al. (2011) found similar results for primary care trusts.

A major effort to improve risk adjustment and other payment formulas in the United States to better recognize "social risk factors" is currently mandated by Congress (US Department of HHS, 2016). Efforts are being made to incorporate these social determinants of health not only in risk adjustment, but also in hospital and other bundled payments.

A key challenge in using certain socioeconomic variables like race, language, income, or education, is that they may not be politically or socially feasible to include in a payment model: simply put, policymakers may not want to pay plans based on race, income, or language. Furthermore, if discrimination or access barriers are a problem, a subgroup (say a minority or nonnative language group) may currently receive too little health care. A regression-based model without any further adjustment will tend to perpetuate this inequity, paying less for this subgroup because it better predicts current spending. The classic risk adjustment solution is to simply omit this information from the predictive model, which makes this underpayment less visible, but does not address the inequity.

A related problem can arise when there are predictive variables that the regulator wants to exclude from a payment model for fairness reasons. For example, suppose spending is high in some region because of higher provider prices or higher intensity of treatment, and that these costs are correlated with other variables that the regulator does want to include. Simply dropping these variables can lead to an omitted-variable bias in the final payment formula. A correction for this problem is discussed in Box 3.3.

Ash et al. (2017) explore alternative ways of incorporating socioeconomic information while estimating individual-level risk adjustment models for Medicaid enrollees in Massachusetts. Using a relatively large sample ($N > 800,000$ when pooled) they explore adding both individual-level administrative information, such as income-related Medicaid eligibility, as well as population-based measures merged on using the enrollees zip code and census block. Merging on census data at the census block level is interesting since potentially this can be done much more easily and cheaply than using survey information. Ash et al. (2017) collapse seven variables primarily related to income from the enrollee's neighborhood into a single neighborhood stress variable, and collapse two variables related to homelessness and frequent changes in mailing address into an insecure housing variable for inclusion in a regression model. Inclusion of these two new variables in the Fiscal Year 2017 payment formula for the state meaningfully improved predictive ratios for key vulnerable groups in this population although the contribution to model fit was trivial. This study is one of several in support of

**BOX 3.3 Omitted-variable bias**

An interesting consideration related to fairness is the distinction between risk factors for which cross-subsidization is desired (the so-called S-type factors) and risk factors for which cross-subsidization is not desired (the N-type factors; Van de Ven and Ellis, 2000). In most countries age, gender, and health status will probably be considered S-type factors, at least to a certain extent. But the regulator may decide that spending variation related to other factors, such as regional differences in supply and prices, should not be reflected in the subsidies. This has implications for risk adjustment.

When N-factors are independent of S-factors, compensation for N-factors can be avoided by simply omitting these factors from the regression model used to estimate risk-adjusted payments. Things are more complicated in the case that these two types of risk factors are correlated (Schokkaert et al., 2017). An example of such a correlation can be that sick people (S-factor) are concentrated in geographical areas with relatively high levels of supplier-induced demand (N-factor). If weights for S-factors are simply determined by a regression of observed spending on the S-factors, these weights will suffer from an omitted-variable bias. Consequently, the subsidies will (partly) reflect the spending variation due to the N-factors. Empirical illustrations by Schokkaert et al. (2004), Van Kleef et al. (2008), and Stam et al. (2010) have shown that this bias can be substantial. Different solutions have been proposed to overcome this omitted-variable bias, including Schokkaert and Van de Voorde (2004) Van Kleef et al. (2008), and Stam et al. (2010). Further discussion is provided in Chapter 7, Risk Adjustment in Belgium: Why and How to Introduce Socioeconomic Variables in Health Plan Payment, and Chapter 14, Health Plan Payment in the Netherlands.

new US initiatives to reflect social risk factors in healthcare payments by the National Quality Forum (NQF, 2014) and the National Academy of Science, Engineering and Medicine (NAS, 2016).

In Europe, sociodemographic variables are commonly used in risk adjustment models. The Dutch risk adjustment model includes risk adjusters based on household income, household size, and employment status (see Chapter 14: Health Plan Payment in the Netherlands for more details). Similar types of information are used in Belgium (see Chapter 7: Risk Adjustment in Belgium: Why and How to Introduce Socioeconomic Variables in Health Plan Payment). Though these risk adjusters do not generally lead to substantial increases in $R$-squared, including them in the predictive model can redistribute large amounts of money (e.g., from plans with relatively many self-employed to plans with many unemployed. See Chapter 7: Risk Adjustment in Belgium: Why and How to Introduce Socioeconomic Variables in Health Plan Payment for an extensive discussion of this point.

## 3.5    CHOICE OF TIMEFRAME FOR DATA USED FOR PREDICTION

The time interval over which risk adjusters are observed is called the "base period" by risk adjustment modelers, while the period for which spending is predicted is called the "prediction period" (Ash et al., 1989, 2000; Kautter, 2014). Several alternatives for choosing the base and prediction periods are possible.

### 3.5.1    Prospective Versus Concurrent Risk Adjusters

Two broad empirical frameworks are commonly used to characterize the information used for risk adjustment. Prospective risk adjusters come from a base period that precedes and does not overlap with the prediction period. Concurrent risk adjusters use information from a base period that coincides with the prediction period. For example, diagnoses and/or pharmaceuticals from year 1 are used to "predict" spending in year 1 in a concurrent model. Concurrent models require that the regulator must wait until the end of the year to observe all of the information used for prediction.[18]

It used to be easy to classify risk adjustment formulas as either prospective or concurrent. However, many formulas today use both types of information. Prospective models have more power (Geruso and McGuire, 2016) than concurrent models, and are less prone to endogenous signals, since diagnoses for acute conditions that are treated and resolved within 1 year matter little for prospective models. On the other hand, prospective models require more data and require a separate formula to use with newly arriving enrollees, for whom prior year information is never available. Another disadvantage of prospective models is that they have lower predictive power, leaving more risk and uncertainty for health plans. Concurrent plans suffer from greater endogeneity of diagnoses, and the data arrive for payment 1 year later, which creates its own uncertainty, administrative burdens, and planning challenges. Typically, concurrent models use provisional payments, but some plans and providers strongly resist the revenue uncertainty of retroactive payment adjustments, even though the same plans readily accept cost uncertainty.

Prospective diagnosis-based information is used for the US Medicare Advantage and Part D payment systems, and in Germany, Switzerland, the Netherlands, and Belgium. However, each system also uses concurrent information for age and sex, as well as for diverse other variables such as institutionalization and Medicaid eligibility (United States), and income (Belgium). Concurrent risk adjustment is used in some US Medicaid systems, and for Marketplace enrollees, where it is particularly attractive since turnover tends to be high in such programs, so prior year information is commonly missing for many enrollees.

### 3.5.2 Hybrid Risk Adjusters

In addition to prospective and concurrent risk adjustment, another possibility receiving attention is hybrid risk adjustment, which uses both concurrent and prior year information for prediction. This hybrid could be in diagnostic information, procedures, or specific types of services that are calculated separately. Dudley et al. (2003) were perhaps the first to examine such a framework, and introduce the terminology of "hybrid risk adjustment".[19] In their framework, anyone with a specified high-cost event, including pregnancies, heart attacks, and other high cost events, mostly inpatient driven, would be paid on a concurrent basis. Specifically, they identified 100 verifiable, expensive, predictive conditions that occurred among 9.3% of the population, and used a concurrent framework to pay for this subsample of the population while paying for the remaining 90.7% of the population using a prospective HCC framework. Their pioneering early work achieved an $R$-squared of 26% versus a prospective R-squared of only 8%. Further research in this direction was conducted by García-Goñi et al. (2009) to predict drug expenditures using Spanish data with similar gains in predictive power. Belgium and the Netherlands use a hybrid approach in which concurrent socioeconomic information and age and sex are combined with prospective diagnoses and utilization measures.

Any payment system that uses ex post information, such as reinsurance or outlier payments, is also a form of hybrid risk adjustment. In particular, the recent proposal by Layton and McGuire (2017) to use dollars of spending above a threshold as a risk adjuster and fixing the coefficient at the desired share (making it equivalent to reinsurance) is inherently a hybrid framework. Chapter 4, Risk Sharing, contains a more detailed discussion on this point.

### 3.6  CHOICE OF THE OBJECTIVE FUNCTION FOR ESTIMATING RISK ADJUSTMENT

Perhaps the most important topic for risk adjustment is the choice of the objective function to be maximized and the algorithm for maximizing it. This section reviews the key concepts relevant to objective functions, and how they are incorporated in risk adjustment model design and selection. We start by distinguishing two broad approaches to risk adjustment: traditional risk adjustment and optimal risk adjustment. While there is considerable overlap between the two approaches, one interesting theme is that traditional risk adjustment has often focused on the selection of risk adjusters for a given objective function, while optimal risk adjustment takes the risk adjusters as given and focuses on the selection of coefficients to maximize the objective function. New approaches, including machine learning techniques discussed below, try to do both simultaneously.

## 3.6.1   Traditional Risk Adjustment

The traditional approach to risk adjustment, as embodied in Ash et al. (2000), Pope et al. (2004), Kautter et al. (2014) and the payment systems of the Netherlands and Germany, has emphasized accuracy in matching plan obligations to predictable spending at the individual level while incorporating concerns about selection, gaming, coding accuracy, and fairness, as presented in the first 10 principles of Box 3.1.[20]A commonly stated objective is to "level the playing field" so that health plans do not gain from attracting profitable enrollees, nor lose from attracting unprofitable ones (Ash et al., 1989). Traditional risk adjustment changes health plan profit incentives by paying more for enrollees predicted to cost more and less for enrollees predicted to cost less. It has generally focused on the careful choice of risk adjusters, as well as the constraints and functional form issues. At its heart, traditional risk adjustment attempts to pay each health plan the predicted cost of each enrollee conditional on the choices of risk adjuster variables and model structure, while minimizing the unexplained variation in spending or equivalently, maximizing the model fit. Although diverse objective functions are often considered, the overwhelming favorite objective function of traditional risk adjustment is to minimize the variance of the unexplained part of spending, i.e., the sum of squared residuals between actual and predicted costs, which when normalized by the sum of squared deviations of the dependent variable to its mean is called the R-squared.

Because of its central role as a metric of risk adjustment performance, it is worth reviewing the formula and properties of the R-squared (Van Veen et al, 2015a). This metric has several attractive features. One is that because it is a unit free number, it can be compared across specifications, dependent variables, time, and samples. It also has an easy conceptual interpretation as the fraction of the total variance in the dependent variable explained by the model. We follow Ash et al. (1989, 2000) and report the $R$-squared as a percentage rather than a ratio. The $R$-squared can be calculated as

$$R^2 = 1 - \frac{\sum_i (y_i - f_i)^2}{\sum_i (y_i - \bar{y})^2} \qquad (3.1)$$

where $f_i$ is the prediction for observation $i$ and $y_i$ is the actual value, and $\bar{y}$ is the sample mean of $y_i$. Note that the $R$-squared can be calculated using this formula for any predictive model, even when $f_i$ is not the result of a least squares regression. Table 3.2 presents within-sample $R$-squared measures using our test sample for three alternative dependent variables and four alternative sets of right-hand side variables, which we discuss further below.

### 3.6.2 Optimal Risk Adjustment

Economic models of risk selection (Glazer and McGuire, 2000; Layton et al., 2017) imply that traditional risk adjustment, by focusing on explaining as much of the variance as possible, will in general not fully solve efficiency problems related to selection except under strong and implausible assumptions.[21] Glazer and McGuire (2000) show that simply maximizing the fit of a model can still lead to inefficiencies when health plans can distort premiums, plan characteristics, or the availability of specific services to attract profitable enrollees. These new models have led to an expanded set of objective functions, or welfare metrics for measuring the performance of health plan or provider payment formulas. The term "optimal" is used to characterize the maximization of a specific economic objective, rather than to signify that there is no possibility that even better risk adjustment models are not possible.

Optimal risk adjustment models start with a theory-based objective function and conceptualize risk adjustment as a tool for selecting risk adjustment weights to maximize that objective. A variety of different objective functions has been used. Glazer and McGuire (2000) use efficiency of service provision as the objective and assume health plans maximize profits through their choice of shadow prices that ration consumer access to various services. Since risk adjustment signals are imperfect, they propose overpaying (underpaying) for weak signals to correct capitation incentives to undersupply (oversupply) certain services. Building on this insight Ellis and McGuire (2007), and more recently McGuire et al. (2014) and Ellis et al. (2017b) calculate how various risk adjustment models moderate plan incentives to distort benefits and services. Minimizing incentives to distort is a conceptually attractive concept, although not a complete objective function to assume for a health plan payment system, since it reflects the health plan's private objective, not society's social objective. Einav and Finkelstein (2011), McGuire et al. (2014), and Layton et al. (2017) show how premium subsidies, risk sharing, and fairness objectives can also be incorporated into the risk adjustment calculations by specifying a social objective function to use when calculating the payment system. Insights from these papers are discussed in Chapter 4, Risk sharing and Chapter 5, Evaluating the Performance of Health Plan Payment Systems.

### 3.7 FUNCTIONAL FORM AND MODEL SPECIFICATION

We now turn to discussing how risk adjusters are incorporated in the prediction formulas, which includes consideration of the structure of how predictors are used, the functional form of the dependent variable, and the use of constraints and manipulations on the risk adjusters.

### 3.7.1   Categorical Versus Additive Models

Since the origins of risk adjustment in the 1980s, two different frameworks have been advocated: Categorical models that place each individual uniquely in a single cell, and additive models that do not classify each individual into one category but instead classify consumers along multiple dimensions. Categorical models, which reduce the estimation problem to calculating the mean for each rate cell, are used in Switzerland and Colombia, as well as in 3M's Clinically Related Groups (CRG) system in the United States.[22] An additive regression approach is more flexible than a categorical model in that a larger number of interaction terms can be incorporated in the formula without loss of power.[23] The essential difference in the modeling approach is whether predictions are additive in the explanatory factors or fundamentally mutually exclusive, as with a branching structure.

In head-to-head comparisons of models by research on large samples (i.e., with over one million observations), such as that conducted by the US Society of Actuaries (SOA) (Dunn et al., 1996; Winkelman and Mehmud, 2007; Hileman and Steele, 2016), additive models have consistently performed as well or better than other models (including categorical ones) on standard statistical measures of performance ($R$-squared, RMSE, and predictive ratios for policy-relevant subgroups). Cid et al. (2016) provides a summary of eight different international studies comparing various risk adjustment models, including both categorical and additive models, supporting the superior predictive power of additive models. The last two SOA studies also include machine learning models among the set of models analyzed, but in each case the attention given to machine learning was fairly cursory. We discuss further machine learning techniques below, some of which also use a categorical rather than an additive framework.

### 3.7.2   Transformations of the Dependent Variable

All risk adjustment performance measures are affected by transformations of the dependent variable, as discussed in Van de Ven and Ellis (2000). Such transformations are commonly done to reduce model sensitivity to skewness and kurtosis. One common transformation is to top-code the dependent variable at some level such as $250,000.[24] Hence, if Y is total spending, the transformed dependent variable $Y^{TC}$ is the minimum of actual spending and $250,000. This has the effect of minimizing the impact of extreme outliers. It, of course, means that predicted spending does not hit the mean spending conditional on the regressors, although depending on the distributions, the resulting bias may not be large, and it may be outweighed by better precision in the estimated coefficients.

Top-coding, which retains individuals with very high levels of payments, is preferred to dropping high cost observations altogether, because extremely high costs are often predictably associated with specific conditions. In samples of ten million or more individuals, top-coding may not be needed, since even random high-cost enrollees will be averaged out, however, for smaller samples these extreme outliers can have a dramatic effect on individual coefficients. Alternative values for top-coding ranging from $50,000 to $1 million have sometimes been used.[25] Resetting negative spending amounts to zero is also commonly done.[26]

A second, more dramatic transformation is to use natural logarithms of spending as the dependent variable. Since annual health spending is often zero, it is common to add one to spending before taking logs. If negative values of spending, $Y$, occur, these must also be eliminated by resetting them to one. Hence the natural log of $Y$, $LnY$, is calculated as

$$LnY = Ln(max(1, Y + 1)) \tag{3.2}$$

Tables 3.2 and 3.3 present $R$-squared, RMSE, and MAE, respectively, for a variety of model specifications, where explanatory variables vary across rows, while dependent variables vary across columns. Across the three columns, three different dependent variables are used: untop-coded spending, $250,000 top-coded spending, and natural log of spending.[27] The R-squared shown here was calculated in the log form. For comparison across specifications, predictions from the log linear model need to be transformed back into their raw dollar level, such models invariably do worse than linear models once this is done.

Results from four model specifications are shown across rows, with three concurrent specifications, and one prospective. The first two rows use only age−sex categorical variables to predict concurrent spending, while the third row adds 394 DxCG-HCCs variables to the concurrent model. The final row in each table shows prospective model results, using the same specification as for the concurrent model. Among the two age−sex models, the first uses 28 age−sex groups, as used by the ACA Marketplace risk adjustment model,[28] while the second row uses 130 age−sex dummies, with sex interacted with 1-year age dummies. The take away from the comparison of the two age−sex-only models is that saturating the model with annual dummies, while capturing the full nonlinearity shown in Fig. 3.2, does not meaningfully improve model performance by any of the three metrics.

The first column of Table 3.2 shows the results of the model for predicting spending (with no top-coding). Using only age and sex information predicts 1.5% of the total variation but the fit can be improved simply by redefining the outcome variable. Indeed, top-coding spending at $250,000 improves the fit to almost 3% of spending variation. This improvement is explained by the large variation in spending among the top spenders of the distribution, for which their spending levels are better related to their unobserved individual characteristics rather than their age or sex. As discussed in Chapter 4, Risk Sharing, outlier policies such as reinsurance deal with the same concerns about outliers as top-codings. Another way of removing the effect of the outliers is the logarithmic transformation (column 3), which smooths the variation in spending, specifically for larger values. Furthermore, because of skewness, this transformation also helps at the bottom tail of the distribution. Numerous studies have shown that the residuals after a log transformation do a better job of predicting the logged value (e.g., Jones, 2011). Simply using the logarithmic transformation improves the $R$-squared to over 10% in a model with age and gender only, but the gain is illusory: payments have to be made in monetary levels, not log of spending. Every loglinear model estimated to date is inferior in terms of R-squared in large samples to linear regression models when used to predict levels of spending while accommodating partial-year eligibles, i.e., for the primary purpose of risk adjustment models (Winkelman and Mehmud, 2007; Jones, 2011; Ellis et al., 2013a,b).

Transforming the dependent variable also has implications for the precision of the goodness-of-fit measures. In fact, the confidence intervals around the $R$-squared when the data are not top-coded are close to 30% of the point estimate, even with 21 million observations. These large confidence intervals arise due to the influence of outliers affecting the unexplained spending variation in the data. Top-coding these outliers—or removing them completely from the risk adjustment model—not only increases the $R$-squared of the model but also decreases the confidence interval to negligible amounts. The log transformation has the same impact on the confidence interval since it also removes the effect of outliers.

Model comparisons based on spending with no top-coding might lead to misleading results, as the estimated R-squared is sensitive to the particular draw of observations. In this sense, top-coding the dependent variable before the analysis is a more robust approach to compare different models.

### 3.7.3   Diagnostic Hierarchies

Even after grouping diagnoses into a manageable number of discrete categories, there are a number of strategies for introducing them into a predictive model. The simplest way is to just include them all, and decide ex ante which, if any interaction, terms enter in. The problem with this approach is that for a reasonably well-specified system with over 200 categories, there are potentially 20,000 two-way interactions terms that could be considered, with a vastly larger number of three- and higher-level interactions. Machine learning algorithms can be considered to choose among this large number of potential interactions; however, they may sacrifice accuracy for simplicity when too many variables are introduced for consideration.

The overfitting problem is particularly problematic when diagnosis categories are strongly related, which is to say that they are highly collinear: either condition A or B is needed in the model but perhaps not both. To address this, as well as to reduce sensitivity to endogenous diagnostic coding, Ash et al. (1989) developed the concept of diagnostic hierarchies, captured in the Diagnostic Cost Group (DCG) classification system. The DCG single-hierarchy approach was further elaborated in what came to be known as the HCC approach that underlies the risk adjustment models used in the United States for Medicare Advantage, Medicare Part D, and the Marketplace, as well as in Germany. In the original DCG system 78 disease categories (or cost groups) were entered into an algorithm in which only the highest cost or most severe group overall in the sample was used for predicting individual payments. A version of the DCG approach is still used in the Netherlands. The HCC system expanded the DCG framework by considering multiple rather than only one hierarchy. The current CMS HCC system defines 30 broad body systems when imposing hierarchies, so that conditions affecting one body system do not affect risk adjusters arising from other body systems. Rather than the DCG predictions using only the single most serious condition a patient has in the year, the HCC framework uses one or more of the most serious conditions within each of 30 body systems for prediction.

Consider the following extended example to see how the hierarchical grouping works. Assume there are two diseases of interest, called A and B. For prediction, one could consider using dummy variables $D_A$, $D_B$, and $D_{A+B} = D_A \cdot D_B$. Several specifications are possible. One possibility is that A and B are simply additive, so that the first two direct effects are statistically significant, while the interaction term is not. The insignificance of the interaction term occurs frequently because spending on most diseases affecting different body systems is additive: the incremental cost of a broken arm or an allergy diagnosis is hardly affected by coexisting conditions.

Another second possibility is that conditions A and B complicate one another. Diabetes, cancer, immune disorders, heart conditions, pregnancy, and liver disorders, for instance, tend to complicate the treatment and hence the cost of other conditions. For these conditions, not only will $D_A$ and $D_B$ be significant but also their interaction $D_{A+B}$ will be positive, and including this interaction term may be desirable. Indeed, the risk adjustment models used in the United States for Medicare Advantage, prescription drug spending, and the Marketplace, and the German risk adjustment formula contain a small number of interaction terms across body systems for some such situations.

A third and very common possibility is that conditions A and B are related conditions such that A represents a more serious manifestation of a given disease than B. For example, condition A might differ from condition B due to the presence of a complicating condition. Here, $D_A$ will have a higher coefficient than $D_B$, but for a person with both A and B coded, then only having the more serious diagnosis A may matter. If true, then when all three terms, $D_A$, $D_B$, and $D_{A+B}$ are included in a regression, then the $D_{A+B}$

dummy coefficient will be equal to the negative of the coefficient on $D_B$, signifying no incremental cost of B conditional on A.

Imprecise diagnostic coding in practice increases the frequency of this third possibility. Physicians choose how much effort to put into coding: even when a more serious diagnosis is present (diabetes with renal manifestations) they may only code a less specific condition (diabetes, unspecified) since that is all that matters for their reimbursement for the current visit. In such cases, the less specific condition can be uninformative in combination with the more serious code. If the two codes only appear for the same patient jointly due to imprecise coding of this form, then a regression model will estimate the coefficient on $D_{A+B}$ to be the negative of the coefficient on $D_B$, just as with the complicating condition example above. For this third possibility, whereby coding is imprecise or only the more serious manifestation matters, imposing hierarchies makes use of this knowledge to specify a more parsimonious model and reduce the problem of overfitting. Instead of including three terms in the regression, $D_A$, $D_B$, and $D_{A+B}$, the modeler imposes the constraint that the coefficients on $D_B$, and $D_{A+B}$ are equal but of opposite signs. Imposing this constraint is numerically equivalent to including only two terms $D_A$, and $D_{B \sim A}$, where $D_{B \sim A}$ is an indicator variable for the presence of disease B without A being present, which is what imposing a hierarchy does: only recognizes B when not accompanied by A. In effect, hierarchies embody a clinical rationale for excluding the vast majority of potential two-way interactions in the risk adjustment model. The 2017 CMS-HCC classification system includes 79 HCCs but imposes 57 hierarchical restrictions that reduce the number of regressors. Pope et al. (2004) document that adding additional interactions or omitting hierarchies has very little impact on model fit.

The ability to use a priori clinical criteria to constrain interaction terms and exclude variables from a risk adjustment formula is a major argument in favor of hierarchical classification systems. This statistical argument is true whether the system uses a single hierarchy, such as the DCG system used in the Netherlands, or multiple hierarchy systems, such as the various HCC models used in the United States and Germany. A second and equally important rationale is that hierarchies also reduce the sensitivity of formulas to gaming. One of the simplest ways of upcoding is to add all of the less serious conditions (cough, chest pain) to patients with more serious conditions (lung cancer). Additive models, without hierarchies, will tend to keep increasing predictions as more (less serious) conditions are reported.[29]

Similar issues over hierarchies arise with the combinations of diagnostic and pharmaceutical information. For example, type I diabetes can either be detected through a diagnosis code, or through prescriptions for insulin. What is to be done when both signals are encountered? Following Germany, the 2016 proposal for the ACA Marketplace is only to recognize the insulin prescription when the diagnosis has not been recorded, which is a form of hierarchy imposed across sources of information. Other possibilities for informed variable selection also exist when adding demographic information, or considering models for specialized populations, to which we now turn.

### 3.7.4 Excluding Risk Adjusters

We have just argued that imposing hierarchies is equivalent to including interaction terms but constraining the coefficient on the interaction to be the negative of the coefficient of the lower-cost HCC. A related approach for traditional risk adjustment is to exclude risk adjusters when estimating the formula due to clinical or policy-motivated criteria when selecting the preferred risk adjustment model. Traditional risk adjustment often excludes eligibility or socioeconomic adjusters even when they are highly significant, in order to avoid undesirable incentives or to reduce unfairness. (See Box 3.3 for an example involving fairness.) The 2017 HHS-HCC model increased the number of HCCs from 201 in the CMS-HCC Medicare Advantage program to 264 HHS-HCCs for the Marketplace, of which 137 HCCs were excluded, leaving 127 HCCs for potential inclusion in the model. Constraints were then imposed across 26 of these remaining HCCs, thereby reducing the total number of HHS-HCCs in the model to 101 (CMS, 2016c). Although Kautter et al. (2014) provides a valuable overview of the final HHS-HCC model chosen, details of the process used for the selection of HCCs are not available. The 10 principles shown in Box 3.2 above likely played a central role. Based on the earlier work for CMS documented in Pope et al. (2004), principle 2—excluding conditions that are not predictive, principle 5—encouraging specific coding, and principle 10—excluding discretionary categories, are the three most important reasons for omitting HCCs. Principle 6—not to include coding proliferation, is another important reason why some HCCs are omitted.

### 3.7.5 Constrained Regression Models

An important new direction for risk adjustment estimation is reflected in a series of recent papers by Van Kleef et al. (2016), Layton et al. (2016), and Bergquist et al. (2018) who demonstrate the value of constrained regression models to simultaneously balance model fit with achievement of other goals. Van Kleef et al. (2016) extend the conceptual work of Glazer and McGuire (2002) and argue that selection incentives for specific types of services can be addressed by using constrained least squares regression techniques. If the traditional risk adjustment formula allocates too little money for people receiving home care services, e.g., then imposing constraints on the estimated coefficients can ensure more funding goes to this group, mitigating selection-related incentives. This method can reallocate funds without increasing the total budget. Van Kleef et al. (2016) use a large sample of

Dutch enrollees to show proof of concept in which underpayment for both physiotherapy and home healthcare services can be completely eliminated in constrained regressions in which the sum of squared residuals is minimized while at the same time forcing predicted payments for the group of people using these two types of services exactly match total spending on this group. Constraints will change the payments for other groups as well. Notably, as Van Kleef et al. (2016) show, a number of other previously underpaid groups have payments increased with the introduction of the constraint on home care underspending. Funding for some other groups must go down, of course, to compensate for the increase for the previously underfunded groups.

Constrained regressions can be used to address other objectives of plan payment as well. Layton et al. (2016) introduce a selection incentive metric to be minimized while estimating a regression model. In their framework, rather than estimating a model and then evaluating how well it does at reducing selection incentives, they choose a social objective function that includes both selection incentives and profit variation as objectives, and estimate models that weight both objectives. They illustrate their model using Dutch data to demonstrate how it can reduce selection incentives for 10 healthcare services. Constrained regression risk adjustment is attractive conceptually, and deserving of further research. For practical implementation, it remains to be seen whether the methodology embodied in the constraint is acceptable to policymakers, whether the models are sufficiently understandable, and whether the effects on other groups in aggregate are acceptable.

### 3.7.6 Quantile Regression Models

An alternative method for incorporating an "optimal risk adjustment" perspective concerns into the risk adjustment estimation is exemplified in the work of Normann Lorenz (2015, 2017). This new approach conceptualizes insurers' activities for risk selection as a contest in which insurers compete to attract enrollees. For the contest success function used in most of the contest literature, optimal transfers for a risk adjustment scheme should be determined by maximizing the Cummings Prediction Measure (CPM) via a quantile regression for the median. Depending on whether it is easier to attract healthy or repel sicker subsets of the population, other percentiles than the median should be estimated. However, quantile regressions for the median (and other percentiles) result in very biased estimates of the mean (because the median is smaller than the mean). Therefore, a constraint to ensure that mean spending is also the mean of predictions can be incorporated. With this constraint, estimates do not depend on the percentile used, so the optimal payments do not depend on whether insurers compete in attracting or repelling individuals. Empirical results show that constrained quantile regressions increase the CPM somewhat, but computation times for estimation are still an issue for complex models and very large data sets

(Lorenz et al., 2017). Whether this approach will prove attractive for policy adoption remains to be seen.

### 3.7.7 Machine Learning Methods

Machine learning algorithms provide automated tools to learn adaptively, based on the data, about the relationships between variables. This can be attractive since the underlying functional form of the data is generally unknown, and the algorithms can also select variables from among a large set of predictors. Incorporation of both investigator knowledge and automation may help yield improved yet interpretable prediction functions. Given the complexity involved in designing risk adjustment formulas, there is growing interest in exploring the potential of machine learning techniques, particularly as computational demands have become less onerous over time. In this section, we provide an overview of the use of machine learning for risk adjustment model selection, focusing attention on the class of nonparametric statistical models of the set of possible probability distributions of our data.

#### 3.7.7.1 From Objective Functions to Loss Functions

Machine learning algorithms for general prediction problems have been developed across the computer science, statistics, and data science literature. The starting point is typically to define the goals for performance of an algorithm, often specified as a loss function to be minimized. One candidate loss function is to simply use the sum of squared errors commonly used for traditional risk adjustment, called the general $L_2$ loss function:

$$\min_{\hat{E}(Y|X)} \left\{ \sum_{i=1}^{N} \frac{1}{N} (y_i - \hat{y}_i)^2 \right\} \tag{3.3}$$

This $L_2$ loss function, which can be used with regression methods or a machine learning approach, is minimized by the conditional mean of our outcome, thus we minimize over candidate estimators $\hat{E}(Y|X)$ of the conditional mean $E(Y|X)$. For each algorithm (i.e., estimator that takes our covariate predictors and maps them to the real line as predicted outcome values) we can evaluate performance based on the chosen loss function and, preferably, out-of-sample validation criteria. A well-known limitation of the $L_2$ loss function is that it can lead to poor performance when the data deviate dramatically from the normal distribution, particularly when sample sizes are less than a million observations.

Other loss functions can be considered including a quasi-log-likelihood loss for bounded continuous outcomes, which would be an interesting approach given the bounded nature of spending. This quasi-log-likelihood loss allows for a transformed continuous outcome variable bounded within

[0,1] combined with the negative log likelihood loss function often used with binary outcomes. This approach can also be used to reduce the impact of outliers on the payment formula without either top-coding or excluding outliers. The quasi-log-likelihood loss has been used for continuous outcomes in earlier statistics literature (Wedderburn, 1974; McCullagh, 1983), and recently for effect estimation (Gruber and van der Laan, 2010), but has not been used to date for plan payment risk adjustment or machine-learning-based prediction. Transformed outcomes on the log scale can also guide the choice of loss function.

### 3.7.7.2  Algorithms

There are many broad classes of machine learning methods we might consider for the development of risk adjustment formulas. One of the most straightforward approaches that can be understood in the context of the regression-based OLS techniques is penalized regression, which allows for greater bias in exchange for smaller variance.[30] For linear regressions, the function to minimize can be characterized in its simplest form by:

$$\min_{\beta} \left\{ \sum_{i=1}^{N} \frac{1}{N} (y_i - X\beta)^2 + \lambda R[\beta] \right\} \tag{3.4}$$

where the first term is the familiar mean squared error and the second term, $R[\beta]$, is the regularizer or penalty function, intended to capture the nature and extent of the bias accepted, or alternatively to punish the predictive model for using too many regressors or allowing coefficients to deviate too widely, which may be a priori implausible. There are many possibilities to use for regularizer function, including the sum of the absolute value of the coefficients (referred to as the lasso—least absolute shrinkage and selection operator—estimator) or the squared sum of the coefficients (a ridge estimator). Since lasso estimators put a penalty on the number of coefficients, they generate more parsimonious estimators with fewer coefficients (the functional form specification). Ridge regression will produce an estimator with coefficients shrunk toward zero, but none will be exactly zero. General elastic nets that consider combinations of the ridge and lasso penalties can also be implemented. Lasso, ridge, and general elastic net estimators have been used within ensembles for risk adjustment, discussed below.

Decision trees are another popular technique and can be described as dividing the covariate space based on homogeneity for the outcome. Trees have become widely used due to their ability to "let the data speak" and discover potentially important interactions among covariates data-adaptively. Given the sheer volume of possible interaction terms that could enter a risk adjustment formula, automating this choice with a tool such as decision trees may be desirable. To demonstrate briefly the potential advantages of tree-based methods for capturing unique interactions, consider the following simple example. Suppose a substantial increase in spending was associated with having disease condition A, but only when age is higher than 35. A regression tree could find such an interaction that was not known a priori nor simple to include in a parametric regression without some type of data-adaptive technique to discover it.

Several papers have studied single regression trees as a primary alternative method for predicting healthcare spending. Relles et al. (2002) examined the use of a simple single regression tree for payment in inpatient rehabilitation and found that its predictive performance was very similar to other techniques. Other work, by Drozd et al. (2006), explored psychiatric payments using simple single regression trees, and their results showed an improved performance of about 20% compared to a proposed traditional nontree-based estimator. Buchner et al. (2017) implemented a regression tree approach to assess interaction terms for improving model fit. Using a sample size of 2.9 million individuals from a major German health plan, they obtain an improvement in the adjusted R-squared of from 25.43% to 25.81%, which they describe as a marginal improvement. In a similar exercise based on the Dutch risk adjustment formula of 2014, Van Veen et al. (2017) find an improvement in the adjusted R-squared of from 25.56% to 27.34%. In general, using only a single regression tree will generate a formula with high variance: averaging over many trees can improve performance. Another popular method is to create "random forests" that average over many trees (e.g., 500 or 1000) using bootstrapped samples and random subsets of covariates, to reduce variability. However, even when incorporating cross-validation, random forests may still overfit, so it is important to consider imposing constraints on the algorithm, such as on the number of terminal nodes, observations per terminal node, number of trees, or covariates allowed for each tree.

Random forests are therefore a specific type of "ensemble" algorithm, which we will define broadly as an algorithm that incorporates multiple algorithms, selecting either a single algorithm from among the collection or an average of the collection of algorithms. Random forests average over only a collection of trees, whereas a generalization of stacking algorithms (Wolpert, 1992; Breiman, 1996) called "super learning" (van der Laan et al., 2007) averages over a collection of (potentially) disparate algorithm types that may search the model space in different ways. This is accomplished by running each algorithm with K-fold cross-validation and then regressing the spending outcome on the cross-validated predicted values for each algorithm to estimate the weight vector. A key advantage of a general ensembling approach, such as a super learner, is that investigators do not need to decide beforehand which single algorithm to select; there is no penalty for implementing many in this a priori specified framework. The researcher protects against a potentially poor choice of an estimator by running multiple algorithms.

Rose (2016) developed a super learner for total annual spending in a sample of MarketScan data comparing the performance of 14 algorithm implementations to the super learner based on a validation R-squared, considering a full set of variables, including demographic information and 74 HHS-HCCs, as well as a data-adaptively selected set of 10 variables identified by random forests for each algorithm. The collection of algorithms included OLS, penalized regressions, single regression trees, and random forests, among others. Super learner yielded a minor improvement in $R^2$ and the results also showed that the reduced set of 10 variables retained much of the predictive performance of the full set in most of the algorithms (e.g., OLS regression had a validation $R$-squared of 25% for the full set vs 23% for the reduced set). Further work is needed to adequately understand the policy implications of removing such a large number of variables, especially on the basis of R-squared, without considering predictive ratios and other metrics. Replication studies in other populations, including Medicare, are ongoing. Shrestha et al. (2017) present a super learner prediction function for mental health spending in MarketScan using mental health diagnosis information and comparing three sets of mental health diagnosis variables joined with demographic information: HHS-HCCs, AHRQ's clinical classification software (CCS) categories, and HHS-HCC plus CCS categories. Here, OLS regression was nontrivially outperformed by both super learning (14% better) and random forests (10% better) with respect to validation $R$-squared. This paper also finds CCS categories to be more predictive of mental health spending than HHS-HCCs. The flexibility of the super learning framework allowed these comparisons to be a priori specified and run in one global algorithm: considering many different algorithms with alternative tuning parameters and comparing different sets of variables within each algorithm. There are many other machine learning techniques; for a thorough discussion see Friedman et al. (2001).

Although the machine learning results are encouraging, machine learning techniques are not ready to replace more traditional risk adjustment models for plan payment purposes. Machine learning techniques can identify subsets of variables or interactions to include in more traditional methods, but have not yet shown their superiority in validated predictive power on large samples with millions of enrollees. We suspect that this is so for two reasons. One reason is that the greater computational burdens of machine learning techniques have until recently meant that the methods were only commonly used on samples of less than one million observations, which precludes being able to estimate additive or categorical models that allow as many risk adjusters to be used as in traditional risk adjustment. A second reason is that machine learning methods generally result in prediction functions that clinicians and policymakers find unintuitive or hard to explain. As noted above, this lack of transparency could, however, be advantageous to prevent strategic responses to the risk adjustment formula, such as by "upcoding" diagnoses or undersupplying services to unprofitable enrollees. More work is needed to understand the policy implications of deploying these techniques.

## 3.8 RISK ADJUSTMENT MODEL IMPLEMENTATION ISSUES

We now turn to the implementation of risk adjustment formulas, which is sometimes called risk equalization. Risk equalization involves choosing the plan enrollees among whom payments are to be reallocated, and defining precisely how available funds are used to make payments at the plan level. Since these allocations depend upon many detailed implementation decisions that tend to be country-specific, the interested reader should consult the individual country/sector chapters in Part II of this volume. Here we try to touch on some common challenges and selected solutions.

### 3.8.1 The Population Groups for Which Risk Is to Be Equalized

In Box 3.1 we note that in addition to choosing the sample on which to estimate the formulas, one must also define the population to whom the formula is applied. The two need not be the same. In the United States, it is often a completely separate population from the one on which the risk adjustment formula is estimated. Moreover, many systems decide to equalize payments only within certain subsets of the full population. In the US Medicaid, and US Marketplace, for instance, risk adjustment is only used to reallocate funds within each state, although for the Marketplace, risk sharing is done at a national level. In Switzerland, risk adjustment and risk sharing are done at a canton level.

The choice of region, demographic subsets, or an all-encompassing group for risk equalization is often driven by political considerations. From a risk perspective, using a national population rather than regional or demographic subsets would appear to be superior. Adjusting for cost of living differences may be necessary when doing national equalization, and hence may be a consideration in using smaller regions.

### 3.8.2 "Zero-Sum" Versus "Guaranteed" Risk Adjustment

A key implementation issue is how payment flows among plans are calculated. One approach is "guaranteed payment" risk adjustment, in which payments to one plan are not affected by the health status of enrollees in other health plans (Dorn et al., 2017). In this system, typically the regulator specifies the overall mean payment per standardized risk enrollee, and a health plans' revenue for an enrollee is the product of this mean payment and the person's average risk score. Adjustments are also made for the number of months eligible or geographic cost factors. This guaranteed payment approach is used in US Medicare for its Medicare Advantage program and for its part D prescription drug formulas. Box 3.4 illustrates with hypothetical numbers how a fixed budget of $100 million might be divided up among four health plans using normalized risk scores and monthly eligibility counts.

**BOX 3.4 Hypothetical risk equalization with guaranteed (average) payment**

| Health plan | Number of eligible months | Average relative risk score (RRS) | Renormalized RRS | Risk-adjusted total revenue ($) |
|---|---|---|---|---|
| | *A* | *B* | *C = B*/Mean of *B* | *D = A\*C\** (Mean payment) |
| P1 | 50,000 | 0.900 | 0.874 | 17,475,728 |
| P2 | 50,000 | 1.100 | 1.068 | 21,359,223 |
| P3 | 30,000 | 1.450 | 1.408 | 16,893,204 |
| P4 | 120,000 | 0.950 | 0.922 | 44,271,845 |
| Totals | 250,000 | | | $ 100,000,000 |
| Means (per month) | | 1.030 | 1.000 | $ 400 |

A second approach, as used in the Netherlands, Germany, and the US Marketplaces, is called "zero-sum" risk adjustment in that risk equalization payments sum up to zero for a specified budget across plans.[31] Conceptually, in a zero-sum system funds are reallocated from funds with low average risks or high average revenues and given to health plans with high average risk. Zero-sum payments can be made to adjust health plan payments, as is done in the Netherlands, or designed to adjust health plan revenues, as is done in the US Marketplace. The key feature of a zero-sum payment system is that if one plan has sicker enrollees and gets more equalization funds, then payments to other plans must be decreased. The hypothetical example provided in Box 3.5 illustrating how premium revenue to four health plans from the previous example (Box 3.4) might be reallocated in a zero-sum manner if premium revenue determines the size of the total payments and payments to health plans are calculated as the net differences between their risk adjusted revenue and their premium revenue. The first five columns in the two textboxes are the same. A similar approach can be used if total plan obligations rather than premium revenue determines total payments to be allocated among the four plans.

One advantage of zero-sum payment systems is that there is no need to forecast levels of revenue or total budgets before risk equalization. Zero-sum payments also insulate the regulator from financial risk. As discussed in van de Ven and Ellis (2000) and in various country and sector chapters in this book, diverse institutional arrangements do this equalization in practice using various sources of funding.

**BOX 3.5 Hypothetical risk equalization with "zero-sum" payment**

| Health plan | Number of eligible months | Average relative risk score (RRS) | Renormalized RRS | Risk-adjusted total revenue ($) | Average premium per month ($) | Total premium revenue ($) | Net transfers into plan ($) |
|---|---|---|---|---|---|---|---|
| | A | B | C = B/Mean of B | D = A*C* (mean of E) | E | F = A*E | G = D – F |
| P1 | 50,000 | 0.900 | 0.874 | 17,475,728 | 400 | 20,000,000 | –2,524,272 |
| P2 | 50,000 | 1.100 | 1.068 | 21,359,223 | 400 | 20,000,000 | 1,359,223 |
| P3 | 30,000 | 1.450 | 1.408 | 16,893,204 | 500 | 15,000,000 | 1,893,204 |
| P4 | 120,000 | 0.950 | 0.922 | 44,271,845 | 375 | 45,000,000 | –728,155 |
| Totals | 250,000 | | | $100,000,000 | | $100,000,000 | 0 |
| Means (per month) | | 1.030 | 1.000 | | $400 | | |

### 3.8.3    Accommodating Lags Between Model Estimation and Implementation

In risk adjustment payment systems implemented to date, the payment formula has been estimated using historic data and then implemented on current experience.[32] This introduces a need to consider how adjustments can be made either to the formula or to overall payments to deal with this time lag.

In the United States, there is typically a 3—5-year lag between the data used to calibrate the risk adjustment formula and the year in which payments are calculated. In the intervening years, new diagnoses or new drugs and technologies may have occurred. New diagnostic variables are added to the CMS-HCC model approximately every 2—3 years when the payment formulas are updated. The HHS-HCC risk adjustment model, originally calibrated using 2010 data when introduced in 2014, was updated for 2016 and 2017 to use a simple average of models from 2012 to 2014 data, which enabled changes in coding and cost patterns to be incorporated (CMS, 2016c).

Further challenges arise when the risk adjustment method payment uses guaranteed payment risk equalization, which is used in the US Medicare and Part D prescription drug risk adjustment programs. In this case, healthcare cost inflation needs to be estimated and used to update mean payments, and changes in the demographic or mean risk scores of enrollees is needed. Whereas a zero-sum equalization system automatically balances spending and risk score changes over time, guaranteed payment systems must forecast levels of both the mean payment per normalized enrollee as well as changes in risk scores into the future when planning payments.

Both zero-sum and guaranteed payment risk equalization require that enrollments and potentially other demographic information at the end of the payment year are available. Hence, payments to health plans are always made or at minimum adjusted after the end of the year. This is a serious challenge when using concurrent risk adjustment formulas, since it can take a number of months for claims to arrive and be fully adjudicated. To deal with this some systems make interim payments to plans, and in other cases some portion of payments is held back (in the US funds are "sequestered" pending final reconciliation). In the US Marketplaces, the 2017 sequestration rate was 7.1% of payments for risk adjustment and 6.9% of payments for the reinsurance program (US Department of Health and Human Services, 2016). Together this means that 14% of plan revenue was withheld pending final reconciliation of risk-adjusted payments and reinsurance. In the Netherlands, risk equalization is done by continuing to make zero sum adjustments to revenues for up to 3 years after the payment period (Chapter 14: Health Plan Payment in the Netherlands).

### 3.8.4 The Sources of Funds Used for Equalization

In many countries diverse sources of funds finance payments to health plans. Revenues can include general taxes; designated taxes; enrollee premiums (whether calculated as fixed dollar amounts, a percent of income, from an age−sex schedule, bids from health plans); cost sharing at the time that services are received from consumers, or designated ("earmarked") budgets funded through other sources such as cigarette or alcohol taxes. A key feature for risk equalization is that funds from any of these sources can be pooled and used to reallocate funds to health plans. Funds can be captured and used either to compensate for a guaranteed payment scheme, or used for zero sum reallocation.

Along with the diversity of sources of funds used for risk equalization, a variety of institutional arrangements can be used for risk equalization. Sometimes a national government agency does redistribution (e.g., the Centers for Medicare and Medicaid Services in the United States), while other times it is an autonomous agency (Germany). Van de Ven and Ellis (2000) characterize two different organizational structures for the entity that does the equalization, but there are other possibilities, including devolving responsibilities to individual states (US Medicaid), or an association of private health plans (Chile).

Newhouse (2017) raises an important issue often overlooked, bearing on whether guaranteed payment rather than zero-sum risk equalization is appropriate. In many countries, there are options outside of the risk-adjusted pool that can be chosen by consumers. In the United States this includes traditional Medicare (with a 70% market share—see Chapter 19: Medicare Advantage: Regulated Competition in the Shadow of a Public Option), and the private insurance outside of the Marketplace (Chapter 17: Health Plan Payment in US Marketplaces: Regulated Competition With a Weak Mandate), or in Germany (Chapter 11: Health Plan Payment in Germany), the private, nonstatutory insurance plans retain 10% of the market and do not participate in the insurance risk equalization. Newhouse's analysis implies that if the payment system includes corrections for adverse selection, then either a guaranteed payment structure is needed or a zero-sum payment program will need budget adjustments for plans to break even.

### 3.8.5 Integrating Risk Adjustment With Risk Sharing

A key theme of this volume is that risk sharing can complement risk adjustment for reducing risk selection incentives, and reducing plan level risk. Some forms of risk sharing discussed in Chapter 4, Risk Sharing, can be implemented by modification of the risk adjustment formula. The observation to make here is that the distinction between risk adjustment and risk sharing is blurry. Furthermore, implementation of a risk adjustment formula should at least take into account the presence of any risk-sharing program so that risk adjustment adjusts for the risks that plans are actually responsible for.

## 3.9 CONCLUDING THOUGHTS

This chapter has attempted to provide an overview of the huge empirical literature on the estimation, selection, use, and interpretation of risk adjustment models for health plan payment. We have tried to provide abundant references for those interested in estimating risk-adjustment models. We end by speculating on a few likely directions for future research and implementation. First, better use of timing information can be made. There are a number of new estimation approaches that use hybrid risk adjustment models, in which both concurrent (year $t$) as well as prospective (year $t-1$) information is used to predict and determine year $t$ payments. More broadly, using longer prior time periods for risk adjusters, and potentially using more information about the timing during the year of new information appears promising. Second, constrained regression techniques are another promising direction. The statistical and incentive properties of these new approaches are just beginning to be understood. Third, there is enormous diversity across countries in the risk adjusters and methods used. Opportunities exist for cross-fertilization and a convergence in their approaches. Fourth, new machine learning algorithms show promise for better specifying and designing risk adjustment models. Whether these approaches can satisfy the feasibility criteria that policy decision-makers seem to desire remains an open question. Fifth, to our knowledge, none of the existing risk adjustment models has fully taken advantage of the rich new diagnostic detail included in the new ICD-10 diagnosis system (only implemented in the United States in 2014) or of the rich new information contained in electronic medical records or consumer self-reported information. Sixth, and finally, researchers need to consider how to incorporate diverse social risk factors—education, income, language barriers, homelessness, and more—into risk adjustment formulas so as to improve fairness and efficiency. Better data, methods, objectives, and payment formulas lie ahead and suggest a busy future for developers of risk adjustment models.

## ACKNOWLEDGMENTS

We thank Arlene Ash and Wenjia Zhu for useful input to this chapter on early drafts, and above all Tom McGuire and Richard van Kleef for their detailed and useful comments.

## ENDNOTES

1. Van de Ven and Ellis (2000) call this agent the "sponsor," emphasizing that this agent is willing to take losses on some enrollees by cross-subsidizing from the gains on others.
2. These nine dimensions parallel the dimensions of risk sharing defined in Van Barneveld et al. (2001) which are discussed in Chapter 4: Risk Sharing of this volume.
3. The DxCG-HCC predictive model, (licensed by Verscend Technologies as Version 4.2), with 394 HCCs is currently used for payment by the Massachusetts Medicaid program (which covers low-income and high-health-cost individuals) for plan payment (Ash et al., 2017), and has also been used for risk-adjusted quality and performance measures (Iezzoni, 2013; Song et al., 2011; Ash and Ellis, 2012) where more disease-specific HCCs and greater predictive power are desirable.
4. For a discussion of the rationale for each principle see Kautter et al. (2014). Principles for including or imposing hierarchies on pharmacy clusters are presented in CMS (2016b).
5. see Ash et al., 2000; Pope et al., 2004.
6. As discussed in Section 3.3.6, spending for partial-year eligibles has been annualized by dividing by the fraction of the year for which their utilization is observed.
7. In our 2014 MarketScan sample, we discovered 26 people with annualized plan obligations that exceeded 1000 times the sample mean, and hence covered costs that exceeded $369,000 per month. This including one person who was in the sample costing over $26 million in less than 12 months. Only four of these individuals were eligible for all 12 months of the year. Hence dropping partial-year eligibles eliminated 85% of these extreme outliers from the estimation sample. The last line of Table 3.1 eliminated the remaining three, with a further dramatic reduction in skewness and kurtosis, but a modest effect on the mean and CV.
8. The challenge of veterans or other secondary insurance enrollees is that they may move around without being detected, and hence it is difficult to know months of eligibility in a specific region. The modeling choices are either to assume full-year eligibility in the region in which a claim is made or to assume eligibility starts only when the first claim is made in that region. The former may be preferred. Primary insurance plans generally do a better job at tracking geographic mobility, although seasonal movements still present similar problems.
9. Consider an individual that incurs $50,000 of plan obligation in the first 5 days of the year and then dies. In terms of a daily weighting, this will be a person costing an annualized $3.65 million dollars per year with a weight of 1.36%. With monthly weighting, this will be a person costing an annualized $600,000 per year with a sample weight of 8.33%. The latter observation is much less skewed and will lead to more stable estimation results.
10. Fig. 3.2 reveals a dip in spending between 63 and 64 years old for both groups, possibly reflecting an anticipatory effect of postponing treatment until covered by Medicare, or that sicker workers are more likely to retire early, improving the pool of remaining enrollees, or the effect of deductibles which make the partial year enrollees have a lower average plan payments in the final year before exiting to Medicare (Ellis et al., 2017a).
11. The distinction between claims and encounter records is that the former is used by health plans to pay providers and charge consumers, whereas encounter records may be recorded in settings that do not use fee for service reimbursement, and hence may be devoid of the financial incentives to report the same degree and quality of information. In the United States and abroad some capitated plans do not require claims, and hence only encounter records are available.
12. Revisions to ICD-9-CM introduced by the ICD-10-CM include:
    - Relevant information for ambulatory and managed care encounters, such as whether it is an initial or follow-up encounter.
    - Expanded injury codes.
    - New combination codes for diagnosis/symptoms to reduce the number of codes needed to describe a problem fully.

- Addition of sixth and seventh digit classification.
- Classification specific to laterality (right versus left side).
- Classification refinement for increased data granularity.

  Existing risk adjusters, and notably the US HCC system, although allowing mappings with the new ICD-10-CM codes, have not fully taken advantage of their greater specificity and refinements in the design of their classification and prediction systems. This is impossible to do here until data on both diagnoses and spending under the new system are available.).

13. It is not hard to find a preventative drug for a high-cost health condition that is itself inexpensive, but which is predictive of higher annual spending. Paying a plan a lot for the prescription of this drug creates incentives to overprescribe it.
14. US Food and Drug Administration, National Drug Code Directory, https://www.accessdata.fda.gov/scripts/cder/ndc/.
15. see especially Iezzoni, 2013.
16. The first author of this chapter participated in unpublished exploratory work that attempted to use simple lab test results on a moderately large sample and did not find meaningful increases in predictive measures from doing so once diagnoses were used.
17. In unpublished related work removed from the manuscript for space, the authors found that inclusion of self-reported health measures and other survey information improved validation R-squared values by 1%−3% points depending on model specification.
18. The concept of retrospective risk adjustment should be reserved for models that use a base period that follows the prediction period. For example, researchers may want to study the costs of a year that includes a heart attack, a hospitalization, or a delivery, using information from a subsequent period, such as the characteristics of the cancer, infection, or newborn that ultimately resulted. Such a retrospective analysis could also be used to reward (or punish the lack of) preventive effort.
19. (Hybrid risk adjustment is also used sometimes to refer to including diverse risk adjusters that may differ in source and not just timing.
20. Glazer and McGuire (2000) coined the term "conventional risk adjustment," which they characterize as having the goal of paying providers as close as possible to the amount the enrollee is expected to cost. Conventional risk adjustment is a statistical and data-oriented approach that is often characterized as trying to maximize the fit of the predictive model. In this chapter we use traditional risk adjustment to reflect the attention to selection incentives and coding accuracy, which lead to the imposition of constraints that intentionally sacrifice predictive power to improve incentives and fairness.
21. Sufficient assumptions so that maximizing the R-squared achieves the social optimum are that plans can discriminate at the individual level, and that there are no other plan payment features such as premiums and risk-sharing that can affect revenue (Layton et al., 2017).
22. Fuller et al. (2016) advocates for mutually exclusive categories.
23. To illustrate with one concrete example, a categorical rate cell approach, if it includes a rare condition such as HIV/AIDS, it will generally not be able to distinguish the additional costs of adding further conditions to individuals in the HIV/AIDS rate cell, while an additive approach is able to make predictions that take into account not only other common conditions, but even other rare ones among the HIV/AIDS patients.
24. Top-coding has been evaluated in research but is rarely adopted for payment models. See the two SOA reports (Winkelman and Mehmud, 2007; Hileman and Steele, 2016) for extensive analysis for the commercial setting.
25. It might seem that a correction for the bias from top-coding might be desired, such as to multiply all spending by a constant so as to maintain the same sample mean. Once it is remembered that the purpose of estimating any risk adjustment model is to come up with RRS, then this bias is immediately rectified once its predicted value, whether Y or YTC, is divided by its mean.

26. Negative values for spending can occur in the United States when a health plan reconciliation reduces the payment to a provider in the year following the original claim. Or it can occur when a claim reconciliation is incorrectly attributed to the wrong patient, or coverage for a service in the previous year is denied and the consumer pays the plan for a service previously paid for by the plan. There is no easy way to correct these negative payments just using claims data. As described in Pope et al. (2004), the US Medicare Advantage risk adjustment program leaves observed negative values unchanged in case they are correlated with specific health conditions, so that resetting spending to zero could introduce a biased payment for these conditions.

27. We also tested a model that predicts untop-coded spending, but uses the results from estimating the top-coded model. However, this model did not improve our results in any statistical measure.

28. Age groups for the DxCG model are defined as [0, 1], [2, 4], [5, 9], [10, 14], [15, 20], [21, 24], [25, 29], [30, 34], [35, 39], [40, 44], [45, 49], [50, 54], [55, 59], [60, 64].

29. Consider the following example from the Clinical Classification Software (CCS) system created by the Agency for HealthCare Quality and Research (AIIRQ, 2017), which has the great advantage of being open source software. As of 2017, the CCS classification system allows different degrees of fineness, including 285 mutually exclusive diagnostic categories. But the CCS system does not propose any suggested hierarchies among CCS categories. Consider for example two single-level diagnostic categories: CCS 98 (Essential hypertension) and CCS 99 (Hypertension with complications and secondary hypertension). Here 99 is clearly a more serious manifestation of 98, but 98 will commonly be coded along with 99 on different claims. Although a modeler can include flags for both 98 and 99 and their interaction (i.e., three terms) in a model to be considered, it may be preferable to include instead only two flags: one for CCS 99 and a flag for (CCS 98 but not 99). This saves a degree of freedom, improves clinical coherence, reduces overfitting, and reduces the incentive for upcoding.

30. For a brief economist-accessible description of penalized regressions for prediction, see Kleinberg et al., 2015.

31. The budget to which the risk equalization is applied needs not be the total budget of the health plans. In the Netherlands, for instance, health plans can charge an additional premium to enrollees. These funds are not included in the zero-sum budget that is then allocated across plans. The payments are still zero-sum in the sense that if one plan has a higher risk score from coding more disease, its revenue increases by decreasing the payments to other plans.

32. In theory, the principles for estimating the payment model could be specified and the concurrent risk adjustment formula could be estimated even after the utilization and claims were observed. This has been done in some pay-for-performance systems, such as is described in Vats et al. (2013) for one health plan in Albany New York. High-quality data and speedy action would be needed, along with tolerance for delayed payments.

# Chapter 4

# Risk Sharing

**Thomas G. McGuire[1] and Richard C. van Kleef[2]**

[1]*Department of Health Care Policy, Harvard Medical School and the NBER, Boston, MA, United States,* [2]*Erasmus School of Health Policy and Management, Erasmus University Rotterdam, Rotterdam, The Netherlands*

> *The extreme skewness of medical spending — in any one year, the top five percent of the spenders account for half of spending — emphasizes the money at stake for plans that insure bad risks at average rates.*
>
> (Newhouse, 1996, p. 1245)

## 4.1 INTRODUCTION

The three primary tools of a health plan payment system are pricing of health plan premiums, risk adjustment, and risk sharing. This chapter is concerned with the third of these tools. Risk sharing can be combined with premium regulation and risk adjustment to improve the performance of the health plan payment model. More specifically, risk sharing can be very effective in protecting health plans against financial risk (e.g., due to skewness of spending or any risk associated with system reform) and in mitigating problems related to risk selection (such as inefficient sorting of consumers into health plans and actions by insurers to attract profitable consumers and to deter the unprofitable ones).

In health insurance parlance, "risk" sometimes means simply "cost," with the implication that the realization of healthcare cost for an individual is uncertain.[1] "Risk sharing" in this context is thus synonymous with "supply-side cost sharing," moving financial responsibility for some of the (uncertain) costs of health care in a population away from the plan to the regulator (or other reinsurer).[2] The cost sharing is supply-side in contrast to the demand-side cost sharing that takes place in the form of deductibles, coinsurance, and coverage limits. From the standpoint of a health plan, demand-side cost sharing transfers financial responsibility for some of the healthcare costs to consumers, whereas supply-side cost sharing transfers some financial responsibility to what we will refer to here as a regulator, usually a public agency. Demand-side cost sharing generally appears on the

Risk Adjustment, Risk Sharing and Premium Regulation in Health Insurance Markets.
DOI: https://doi.org/10.1016/B978-0-12-811325-7.00004-X
**105**

---

**BOX 4.1  Health plan risk (cost) sharing with a consumer and the regulator: an example**

Demand-Side Cost Sharing: the consumer has a $500 deductible after which 20% coinsurance applies up to a maximum on total out-of-pocket spending of $2500. The consumer would be fully covered after spending $10,500.

   Supply-Side Cost Sharing: the regulator covers 20% of costs after $60,000 total spending per consumer.

   Plan Obligations: What is not paid by the consumer or the regulator. For example, if a person spends $75,000 on health care, $2500 would be paid by the consumer and 0.2(75,000 − 60,000) = $3000 would be paid by the regulator as reinsurance, leaving the plan obligation at $69,500. In addition, the health plan may have to pay a reinsurance premium to the regulator.

---

front-end of coverage (e.g., deductibles) and often does not apply to ranges of high costs (i.e., most schemes include limits on total out-of-pocket spending rather than limits on total coverage). Supply-side cost sharing most frequently applies to costs on the back end. Box 4.1 gives a particular example of a health plan design (in dollars) with both demand- and supply-side cost sharing, and illustrates how both of these features work to determine plan obligations.

Fig. 4.1 shows the same plan graphically, depicting the distribution of financial responsibility for healthcare costs among the consumer, the health plan, and the regulator. The range of the plan's responsibilities falls in the middle section (shaded in the figure). Just as the plan sits on top of the consumer and takes responsibility for most of the costs above a deductible, protecting the consumer against financial risk, the regulator or reinsurer sits on top of the plan and takes responsibility for a share of the costs above a reinsurance threshold.

## 4.2   MOTIVATIONS FOR RISK SHARING

Risk sharing can supplement risk adjustment and premium regulation. Some of cost risk is predictable and may be accounted for by the risk adjustment formula.[3] To the extent that predictable cost variation is not accounted for by risk adjustment, risk sharing can be an effective way to contend with selection problems. Another component of costs/risks is the "unpredictable" component not captured by the risk adjustment formula, and this component can be quite large for a high-cost person. Risk adjustment models are inevitably subject to underprediction for very high-cost cases since they are based on predicted means conditional on the risk adjustor variables. As we show empirically later in this section, profits and losses for a plan, even after taking account of risk adjustment, strongly depend on the proportion of

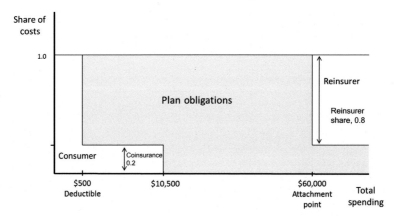

**FIGURE 4.1**  Plan obligations with some demand-side cost sharing and some supply-side risk sharing.

high-cost cases. High-cost cases thus threaten plan viability, especially for smaller plans, and may discourage plan entry and efficient pricing. Risk sharing is an effective way to contend with these types of problems. In sum, the two principal motives for risk sharing are mitigating problems related to risk selection not dealt with by risk adjustment and plan risk protection (including any risk associated with system reform).

## 4.2.1  Protecting Plans Against Financial Risk

The distribution of healthcare costs in a year is highly skewed, with a small share of the high-cost cases accounting for a large share of the costs, an empirical regularity documented in many European and US contexts.[4] Cattel et al. (2017) trace spending patterns under the Dutch national health insurance in 2013, with some results shown in Fig. 4.2. The nine bars on the left (10−90) show the mean per-person spending for the bottom nine deciles and the 10 bars on the right (91−100) show the same information for the top decile split into percentiles. The distribution is highly skewed: the top percentile (100) accounts for 24% of total spending. The top decile (91−100) accounts for 62% of total spending.

In an updated version of the data used to calibrate plan payment models in the US Marketplaces, Layton and McGuire (2017) find a similar pattern: a few very high-cost patients account for a large share of annual costs. In the 2 million people, the 99th percentile of spending (identifying the top 1% of the insured population) was $67,393 and above. This 1% of the population accounted for 28% of total costs. The top 10% of the population, those spending more than $10,537 in a year, accounted for 70% of all spending.

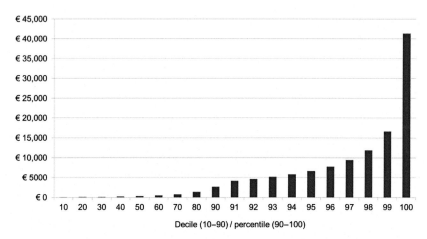

**FIGURE 4.2** Mean annual medical spending per decile/percentile based on administrative information of the entire Dutch population in 2013 ($N$ = 16.75 million).
Notes: Spending includes hospital care, pharmaceuticals, ambulatory care, and primary care, among others, but excludes mental care, long-term care in nursing homes, and home care. *Source: Cattel, D., F. Eijkenaar, R.C. van Kleef, R.C.J.A. van Vliet en A.A. Withagen-Koster, 2017. Evaluatie normbedragen van somatische risicovereveningsmodellen 2010-2013 (English translation: "Evaluation of the payment weights of the risk equalization models for somatic care in 2010-2013"), Research report, Erasmus University Rotterdam.*

The average spending in the top decile was $35,175, more than 35 times the median spending.

Risk adjustment, paying more for enrollees predicted to be high-cost, helps in plan financial protection, but tends to systematically underpredict for persons with high realized costs, a result found, e.g., in the US Medicare program (Table 3 in Brown et al., 2014). After estimation of the risk score for each individual based on the HHS-HCC model used in the US Marketplaces, Layton and McGuire (2017) computed the difference between actual spending and the spending predicted by risk adjustment. Such an approach isolates the portion of high costs not captured by the risk adjustment model. The few high-cost cases impose plan losses, even with risk adjustment. Fig. 4.3 presents average profits after risk adjustment by selected percentiles of spending. Plans lose, on average, $69,787 for persons in the top 1% of spenders. Enrollees are profitable over a large range of cost. Risk adjustment leads to a nearly flat distribution of profits of around $2000 per person from the 1st to the 60th percentile of the spending distribution. Plans make money on average on all enrollees up through the 80th percentile of spending. Even after application of sophisticated risk adjustment models, high-cost cases remain a financial threat to plans.

Note that although Fig. 4.2 for the Netherlands and Fig. 4.3 for the US Marketplaces have the same horizontal axis, however the vertical axis tracks different things. Fig. 4.2 graphs total cost by place in the cost distribution,

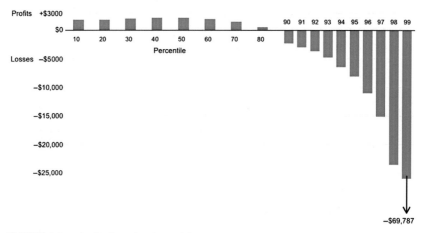

**FIGURE 4.3**  Distribution of gains and losses post risk adjustment for deciles/percentiles of costs in the US Marketplace population.
Notes: This figure presents average profits for each decile/percentile of spending. Profits are equal to simulated revenues minus costs. Simulated revenues are based on the Marketplace transfer formula and incorporate risk adjustment but not reinsurance. *Layton, T.J., McGuire, T.G., 2017. Marketplace plan payment options for dealing with high-cost enrollees. Am. J. Health Econ. 3(2): 165–191.*

whereas Fig. 4.3 graphs gain/loss post risk adjustment by place in the cost distribution.

Variance in healthcare costs is even more concentrated in the high-cost cases than cost itself. Because of the squaring property of a measure of variance,[5] the contributions to the variance in spending are more highly skewed than the contributions to the mean spending. Among the 2 million enrollees (a different 2 million than in the study by Layton and McGuire mentioned above), the top 1% of the spending distribution accounts for 27.7% of the spending (this is the statistic usually reported) but 85.4% of the variance (Geruso and McGuire, 2016). Fig. 4.4 depicts the skewness of costs and of variance of costs based on these results.

In finance, a high variance of return on a portfolio of investments is a measure of risk. Exposing insurers to large cost risk can adversely affect the health insurance market by discouraging plan entry by small innovative plans, and causing plans to raise prices to compensate for bearing risk. In the US Marketplaces, reinsurance provided some protection to plans against this high-cost risk and encouraged entry and lowered initial prices in the Marketplaces. In interviews with the GAO (2015, p. 33), insurers participating in the Marketplaces cited reinsurance as positively influencing their entry decision, with some reporting that reinsurance was the most important of the premium stabilization programs. Industry analysts cite loss of reinsurance protection as a contributor to high anticipated premium increases for 2017.[6]

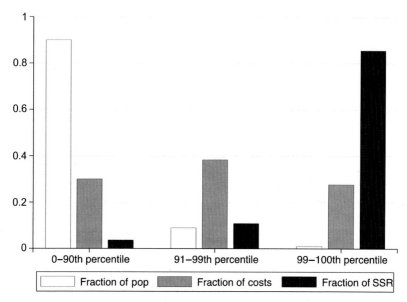

**FIGURE 4.4**    Skewness in spending and variation in spending.
Notes: Figure taken from Geruso and McGuire (2016). The bars show the fraction of population, total costs, and sum of squared residuals (a measure of variation) for various population groups.

(Recent regulations for payments in the Marketplaces reinstate a form of reinsurance, though with a much higher attachment point. See Chapter 17: Health Plan Payment in US Marketplaces: Regulated Competition With a Weak Mandate for some discussion.)

The best way to reduce the variance in returns in a plan's portfolio of health-cost risks is to target the losses on the very high-cost cases, a task well-suited to risk sharing.

## 4.2.2    Contending With Selection Problems

More important than protecting plans against risk is the objective of mitigating problems related to risk selection, such as inefficient sorting of consumers into health plans and actions by insurers to discourage enrollment by the loss-imposing high-cost cases. This fundamental argument for risk sharing was made by Newhouse (1996) who cast the choice about risk sharing as a tradeoff between selection and cost containment.

A central theme of this volume is that unpriced risk heterogeneity might lead to selection problems. By compensating for predictable cost variation risk adjustment mitigates unpriced risk heterogeneity. Even highly developed risk adjustment models, however, such as the Dutch risk equalization model, systematically over/undercompensate health plans for certain groups. For example, Van Kleef et al. (2016) show that the Dutch model of 2016 under-compensates for groups of consumers with high expected spending such as those who report ex ante that they suffer from one or more chronic conditions.

The HHS-HCC model used in the US Marketplaces systematically under-pays for persons with some common chronic illnesses. Using an updated version of the data used for calibration of risk adjustment models in the Marketplaces, Layton et al. (2017) find that underpayments expressed as a percent of average costs for the groups are cancer (8.0%), diabetes (4.4%), heart disease (17.5%), and mental illness (19.3%).

Risk sharing, like risk adjustment, can mitigate unpriced risk heterogeneity and thus can be used as a strategy to contend with selection problems.

## 4.3  FORMS OF RISK SHARING

Van Barneveld (2001) identifies four dimensions of risk sharing (see Box 4.2). Since multiple options are available for each aspect, risk sharing can take numerous forms. In this chapter we will focus on four of the most common forms, i.e., proportional risk sharing (Section 4.3.1), reinsurance (Section 4.3.2), high-risk pooling (Section 4.3.3), and risk corridors (Section 4.3.4). In terms of Van Barneveld's taxonomy these forms mainly differ in terms of the group of enrollees for whom (some of) the risk is shared and the extent of the risk that is shared.

Risk-sharing modalities can be combined with risk adjustment or even with each other (e.g., reinsurance and risk corridors as in the US Marketplaces through 2017). In this section, however, we present each of the major forms of risk sharing in isolation.

---

**BOX 4.2 Four dimensions of risk sharing**

1. The group of members for whom (some of) the risk is shared (e.g., the entire population, people with spending above a certain threshold, or a specific group of high-risk people)
2. The types of care for which the risk is shared (e.g., for the total benefit package, specific services, or specific cost elements of services)
3. The extent of the risk that is shared (e.g., a proportion of total spending, spending above a threshold, or a proportion of spending above a threshold)
4. The price that insurers have to pay to share some risk (e.g., a flat-rate premium, a risk-rated premium, or no premium in case the pool is financed by the regulator)

Source: Van Barneveld et al. (2001).

## 4.3.1 Proportional Risk Sharing

The simplest form of risk sharing is proportional risk sharing, where a plan is paid a fixed combination of a prospective component and a cost-based payment. Suppose the population average spending is $\bar{x}$ and the spending during a year for person $i$ is $x_i$. In a proportional risk sharing arrangement, the plan is paid $\lambda\bar{x} + (1-\lambda)x_i$ for person $i$ where $(1-\lambda)$ is the portion of the risk (cost) retained by the regulator. As $\lambda$ approaches 1 the payment system becomes fully prospective, and as $\lambda$ approaches 0 it becomes fully cost-based. The incentive properties of what has been referred to as a "mixed system" were first studied in the context of provider payment (Ellis and McGuire, 1986),[7] and were generalized and applied to plan payment by Newhouse (1996). The prospective component, $\bar{x}$ from above, can be risk-adjusted. Box 4.3 describes a modality of proportional risk sharing currently applied in Belgium.

Some analytic properties of a mixed system can be described easily, useful for introducing the power of risk-sharing methods for improving the performance of a health plan payment system. The key observation is this: a little bit of proportional risk sharing can substantially improve the fit between payment and cost. To make this concrete, consider the risk-adjustment model used for prospective payments to Medicare Advantage plans in the United States (described in Chapter 19: Medicare Advantage: Regulated Competition in the Shadow of a Public Option) containing about

---

**BOX 4.3 Proportional risk sharing in Belgium**

In Belgium the total budget for healthcare expenditures (called $\omega$ here) is distributed over the insurers according to a weighted formula:

$$F_v = \left(\frac{\text{RAS}_v}{\omega}\right)r\omega + \frac{E_v}{\sum_k E_k}(1-r)\omega,$$

where $\text{RAS}_v$ stands for the risk-adjusted subsidies of insurer $v$ and $E_v$ is its actual cost. The interpretation of this expression is obvious: only a fraction $r$ of the budget $\omega$ is distributed on an ex ante (risk-adjusted) basis, the remainder is distributed on the basis of actual cost. In terms of Van Barneveld's taxonomy, this modality can be described as follows:

1. The group of members for whom some risk is shared: the entire population
2. The types of care for which the risk is shared: all services covered
3. The extent of the risk that is shared: $1-r$
4. The price that insurers have to pay to share some risk: $\left(\frac{\text{RAS}_v}{\omega}\right)(1-r)\omega$

   See Chapter 7, Risk Adjustment in Belgium: Why and How to Introduce Socioeconomic Variables in Health Plan Payment, for more details about health plan payment in Belgium.

---

**BOX 4.4 The R-squared equivalent of a mixed system**

R-squared measures the portion of variation in costs "explained" by the risk-adjustment model predictions. In a mixed system, the "prediction" is a weighted average of the population mean and of actual costs. Writing the mixed system in general form with a weight of $\lambda$ on the population mean cost and $(1-\lambda)$ on the individual's realized cost, the predicted value for person $i$ is: $\hat{x}_i = \lambda\bar{x} - (1 - \lambda)x_i$. The R-squared equivalent of explained variance can be expressed as usual as 1 minus the "unexplained variance" as a function of $\lambda$:

$$R\text{-squared of mixed system with } (\lambda) = 1 - \frac{\sum_i (x_i - \lambda\bar{x} - (1-\lambda)x_i)^2}{\sum_i (x_i - \bar{x})^2} = 1 - \lambda^2.$$

In the text we mention the example of $\lambda = 0.9$ (90% of the weight on the mean) and the formula shows R-squared equivalence is $1-(0.9)^2$ or 0.19.

---

100 variables and decades in development. The R-squared statistic describing the fit of predicted to actual spending at the person level is about 0.11. Proportional risk sharing of only 6% in combination with a simple *flat* prospective payment set equal to the population average, with no risk adjustment at all, can attain the same fit at the person level. Specifically, a mixed system in which a health plan is paid 94% of the overall population average and then 6% of the actual costs of an enrollee produces a fit of payments to costs with an R-squared equivalent of 0.11.[8] This level of fit can be calculated and holds true for any underlying data. In other words, the R-squared equivalent of a proportional risk-sharing plan can be calculated without any data analysis (see Box 4.4).

A mix with more proportional cost sharing can easily outperform the current Medicare Advantage model in terms of person-level fit. A mixed system 90/10 with 90% of the weight on the population average and 10% on costs produces an R-squared equivalent of 0.19, almost twice the fit of the current model. To give just one more example, a 50/50 mix produces an R-squared equivalent of 0.75, vastly exceeding the fit of any risk adjustment formula. Box 4.4 shows the general formula relating the degree of mix to the R-squared equivalent.

While R-squared is an appropriate measure for indicating the extent to which a certain payment system mitigates a plan's financial risk, it may not be the best metric for measuring the extent to which a payment system mitigates selection problems. As will be discussed in Chapter 5, Evaluating the Performance of Health Plan Payment Systems, the appropriate selection metric depends on the particular selection problem to be analyzed and the underlying market mechanisms. For example, when it comes to measurement of incentives for health plans to select in favor or against particular groups, predictive ratios and measures of under/overcompensation are more meaningful than the *R*-squared, improvements in these measures can also be readily described when risk-sharing takes the form of a simple mix.[9] Our purpose beginning with proportional risk sharing is to preview the power of risk sharing generally, and to set the stage for the value of risk sharing targeted at the high-cost range of the cost distribution.

### 4.3.2 Reinsurance

Reinsurance generally takes the form of the reinsurer (perhaps the regulator) paying a share of costs of an individual (sometimes referred to as the "coinsurance"[10]) above a threshold (sometimes referred to as the "attachment point"). For example, reinsurance might be defined by a threshold of $60,000 and a reinsurer coinsurance share of 80% as in Box 4.5. Then, if a person has realized costs during a year of $160,000, the reinsurance portion is 0.80*($160,000–$60,000) = $80,000. Reinsurance would return nothing to the plan if costs were below $60,000 for an enrollee during a year. Reinsurance payments need to be financed in some way, such as from the public sector, or from a small premium the regulator might assess on every enrollee.

The favorable properties of reinsurance in individual health insurance markets have been appreciated for some time (Schwartz, 2006; Van Barneveld, 2001). In many empirical contexts, research shows that reinsurance is very effective at fitting individual-level plan payments to plan liabilities for high-cost cases using numerous data sets from the United States,[11] as well as in data from the Netherlands (Van Barneveld et al., 1998, 2001).

---

**BOX 4.5 Reinsurance in the US Marketplaces**

Section 1341 of the ACA created a reinsurance program for the first 3 years of the Marketplaces, from 2014 to 2016. In terms of Van Barneveld's taxonomy, reinsurance in 2014 took the following form:

1. The group of members for whom some risk is shared: all enrollees.
2. The types of care for which the risk is shared: all services covered.
3. The extent of the risk that is shared: 80% of a health plan's annual costs for an enrollee above an "attachment point" of $60,000 and up to a $250,000 cap (HHS, 2012). The attachment point was raised (and thus the reinsurer share was decreased) in 2015 and 2016. Plans were expected to buy commercial reinsurance covering costs above $250,000.
4. The price that insurers have to pay to share some risk: a flat-rate premium determined by the Treasury and set annually, i.e., assessed for all covered lives in nongrandfathered health plans in the United States, including some self-funded plans (see Chapter 17: Health Plan Payment in US Marketplaces: Regulated Competition With a Weak Mandate).

Schmid and Beck (2016) use data from one large private insurer to simulate the properties of reinsurance in Switzerland. As explained in Chapter 16, Health Plan Payment in Switzerland risk adjustment model from 2012 to 2016 was based on age, gender, and prior hospitalizations, so we can expect reinsurance to make big improvements in the fit of payments to costs. (In 2017, pharmacy groups were added as a risk adjustor.) The $R$-squared of the current risk adjustment formula is about 0.15, and this goes up to about 0.41 with a reinsurance threshold of 60,000 CHF and a reinsurance coinsurance rate of 80% (see their Table 1).

Schillo et al. (2016) study a plan to finance high-cost cases in Germany in which a plan receives extra reimbursement for enrollees with large "funding gaps," defined as the difference between actual expenses in a year and the capitation amount associated with the risk adjustment model.[12] At thresholds beginning at 15,000 euros, the fit of payment to costs jumps from 27.6% with risk adjustment only to 78.1% (Table 2 in Schillo et al., 2016).

Layton and McGuire (2017) study how reinsurance protects health plans from the unpredictable appearance of high-cost cases within their covered population. They evaluate some properties of continuing a reinsurance feature for the US Marketplaces for 2017 and beyond, using an updated version of the data used for calibrating Marketplace risk adjustment models. All of their analyses study the contribution of reinsurance to plan risk reduction over and above the risk adjustment model used in the Marketplaces. The reinsurance options vary in attachment points from a high of $1 million to a low of $100,000, all with a reinsurer coinsurance share of 80%.[13]

Some results from Layton and McGuire (2017) are summarized in Table 4.1. For reference, the first column shows results for a risk-adjustment model only (i.e., with no reinsurance). The payment system fit (the same as $R$-squared with risk adjustment only) is 0.438 with the concurrent HHS-HCC model. Simulations taking random draws from the population find that a health plan with 10,000 enrollees would lose more than 5% of revenues in a year about 5.4% of the time. This is referred to as the "risk of ruin" in the table.

The first two rows of Table 4.1 characterize the "touch" of reinsurance in terms of people and dollars. At a high attachment point of $1 million, only 0.002% of the population, only 2 in 100,000 people, are affected by reinsurance. The percent of costs affected is of course higher since costs are concentrated in this group, but still, well less than 1% of costs are impacted by reinsurance. The payment system fit, however, is incremented notably to 0.499. Reducing the attachment point to $500,000 still touches only 1% of costs, but adds 0.13 to the payment system fit. Risk of ruin also falls steadily as the attachment point is lowered, and it is basically eliminated at an attachment point of $100,000. This analysis shows that fit at the individual level and plan risk of large losses are reduced effectively with reinsurance at attachment points affecting a very small share of the population.[14]

**TABLE 4.1** Properties of Reinsurance at Various Attachment Points

| Attachment point | N/A | | $1,000,000 | $500,000 | $100,000 |
|---|---|---|---|---|---|
| | Risk adjustment only | | | | |
| Percent of people above attachment point | N/A | | 0.002% | 0.020% | 0.530% |
| Share of dollars above attachment point | N/A | | 0.22% | 1.01% | 9.95% |
| Payment system fit | 0.438 | | 0.499 | 0.572 | 0.784 |
| "Risk of ruin" for a health plan with 10,000 members | 5.4% | | 4.3% | 3.1% | 0.3% |

Data are 2M sample from MarketScan described in Layton and McGuire (2016), and updated version of the data used to calibrate plan payment models in the US Marketplaces. All reinsurance programs feature 80% reinsurer coinsurance. The table presents statistics describing high-cost cases in our sample. Each column shows the number of people above a cutoff, the percent of people above a cutoff, and the share of dollars covered by reinsurance for a given cutoff. The "attachment point" is the cutoff. Risk adjustment model is the concurrent version of the HHS-HCC model. Risk of ruin is defined as the probability of costs exceeding revenues by at least 5% for a health plan of size 10,000 members.

A number of research papers assess the extent to which reinsurance mitigates health plans' incentives to attract or deter particular risk groups. They do so by calculating conventional metrics of over/underpayment for certain groups or the more sophisticated metrics discussed in Chapter 5, Evaluating the Performance of Health Plan Payment Systems. Unsurprisingly, since reinsurance adds revenue for enrollees that would otherwise be financial losers, it mitigates selection problems. Zhu et al. (2013) use survey data from the United States to study selection incentives for four major disease groups (heart disease, cancer, mental health, and diabetes) in payment system alternatives for the US Marketplaces. The metric is a predictive ratio, where the numerator is the total payments a plan receives for a group and the denominator is the total cost for the group. Adding reinsurance to a prospective risk-adjustment payment formula pushes the predictive ratios towards 1.0 for all groups as the reinsurance attachment point is lowered. Using the same large health insurance claims database used to calibrate risk adjustment models for the Marketplaces in the United States, Layton et al. (2017) calculate predictive ratios for these same four disease groups adding reinsurance of 80% with a $60,000 attachment point to a prospective risk adjustment model. The predictive ratio for the cancer group moves from 0.64 to 0.80, and the predictive ratios for other groups improve as well. The authors apply a version of the more economic-based selection incentives discussed below and in Chapter 5, Evaluating the Performance of Health Plan Payment Systems, and show that a prospective risk adjustment model with reinsurance matches the performance of a concurrent risk adjustment model in Marketplaces in terms of incentives for selection.

### 4.3.3  High-Risk Pools

High-risk pooling (HRP) can be useful to protect health plans against high spending of an identified group of high-risk enrollees. Usually, enrollees are assigned to the HRP pool ex ante on the basis of information known before the start of the contract period (in contrast to reinsurance which relies on ex post or realized costs). The workings of an HRP can vary according to (1) the regulator or other agent doing the assignment and (2) the rules used for assignment. Regarding the first aspect, the regulator decides on a rule and administers it, possibly with the assistance of the health plans themselves. With respect to the second aspect, prior high cost, prior diagnosis, or prior rejection by private health insurers could all serve to identify high-risk enrollees.

Based on data from the Netherlands, Van Barneveld et al. (1998, 2001) examined the extent to which HRP would mitigate health plans' incentives for risk selection and compared the outcomes with those of reinsurance and proportional risk sharing. By keeping the amount of money involved in risk sharing fixed (and thereby keeping cost containment incentives roughly constant), the authors find that HRP leads to greater reductions in selection incentives (in terms of under/overcompensations) than the other forms. The intuitive explanation for this finding is that HRP does a better job in moving additional funds to specific ex ante risk groups. So, HRP targeted at groups for which selection concerns are greatest, can outperform reinsurance and proportional risk sharing. Van Barneveld et al. (1998, 2001) do not explicitly examine other types of selection problems such as inefficient sorting of consumers into health plans. It can be expected, however, that in any case where selection problems are related to identifiable groups, HRP can be an effective measure to mitigate these problems.

To the best of our knowledge, no country has implemented HRP so far as part of a national health insurance policy. In the Netherlands, however, the regulator was very close to implementing the form of HRP described in Box 4.6. In the almost-implemented Dutch system described in Box 4.6, the identified high-risk individuals would have been kept in the main health insurance pool, but special risk-sharing provisions were proposed for their costs.

Van Kleef and Van Vliet (2012) studied the properties of the HRP considered in the Netherlands and described in Box 4.6, illustrating design choices for an HRP and the tradeoffs involved. They examined the effects of

---

**BOX 4.6 High-risk pooling considered for implementation in the Netherlands**

In the Netherlands, the following modality of high-risk pooling was considered for implementation in 2012:

1. The group of members for whom some risk is shared: those belonging to the top 15% of spending in each of three previous years (to be determined by the regulator)
2. The types of care for which the risk is shared: all services covered by the benefit package
3. The extent of the risk that is shared: a proportion $p$ of realized costs with $p$ such that the average undercompensation of those in the high-risk pool equals zero
4. The price that insurers have to pay to share some risk: a proportion of the prospective payment for enrollees not assigned to the high-risk pool

(Instead of implementing HRP, the Dutch government finally decided to include multiple-year high costs as a risk adjustor in the risk equalization model.)

---

**TABLE 4.2 Mean Costs and 85th Percentile of Costs Covered by the Dutch Basic Health Insurance in 2004, 2005, and 2006**

| Year | Mean costs in euros (std dev) | 85th percentile of costs in euros |
|------|-------------------------------|-----------------------------------|
| 2004 | 1369 (5081) | 1668 |
| 2005 | 1571 (5297) | 2054 |
| 2006 | 1568 (5209) | 2087 |

*Source:* Van Kleef, R.C., Van Vliet, R.C.J.A., 2012. Improving risk equalization using multiple-year high cost as a health indicator. Med. Care 50(2), 140–144.

---

HRP as a supplement to a sophisticated risk equalization model (based on the Dutch approach) including demographic risk adjustor variables, socioeconomic variables, pharmacy-based cost groups, and diagnoses-based cost groups. As a first step in their empirical analysis, they estimated this risk equalization model using 2007 information on costs and risk characteristics of about 14.9 million enrollees ($R$-squared = 0.2465). In a second step, they identified enrollees whose costs were in the top 15% in each of the years 2004–2006. Table 4.2 presents the cost thresholds that had to be exceeded in these years to become eligible for the high-risk pool. The choice of a look-back period of 3 years was based on the judgment that a period of just 1 or 2 years would include too many people with a temporary condition while a period of 4 or more years would exclude too many people who just incurred a long-term condition. Enrollees exceeding the 85th percentile in each of the years 2004–2006 represented 4.6% of the population in 2007. The mean realized spending for this group in 2007 was 9140 euros, while the mean predicted spending was 6567 euros, implying an undercompensation of on average 2573 euros per person per year (= 6567 − 9140).

In a third step, the prospective risk equalization payment was supplemented with the HRP option described in Box 4.6. The value of risk sharing $p$ necessary to eliminate the initial undercompensation of the high-risk group turned out to be 0.28. In order to finance the retrospective compensation, health plans would have to pay a proportion of 0.10 of predicted spending for enrollees not assigned to the high-risk pool. In terms of our classification of risk-sharing options, this HRP could also be described as proportional risk sharing, with proportion $p$, for a subset of the population in the pool.

The HRP described here eliminates the initial undercompensation of the high-risk group as well as the initial overcompensation of the complementary group. Table 4.3 shows the effect of HRP for another split of the population, i.e., those with undercompensation in each of the years 2004, 2005, and 2006 (4% of the population) and the complementary group (96%). Though HRP does not fully eliminate the under/overcompensation for these groups, incentives for risk selection are substantially mitigated compared to risk

**TABLE 4.3** Predictive Ratios (PR) in 2007 for Subgroups Based on Undercompensation in 2004–2006, After Applying the Risk-Equalization Model of 2010 (Estimated on Administrative Data From 2007; $N$ = 14.9 million) Supplemented With High-Risk Pooling

| Subgroup | Population frequency in 2007 | Mean actual costs in 2007 | PR in 2007 after applying the risk-equalization model 2010 | PR in 2007 after applying the risk-equalization model 2010 plus high-risk pooling |
|---|---|---|---|---|
| Not 3 × undercompensated in 2004–2006 | 4% | 6107 | 1.07 | 1.04 |
| 3 × undercompensated in 2004–2006 | 96% | 1563 | 0.52 | 0.72 |

Predictive ratio equals the total compensation divided by realized costs. The modality of high-risk pooling applied here is that health plans receive a proportion $p$ of realized costs for enrollees whose costs were in the top 15% in each of the years 2004–2006. Proportion $p$ equals 0.28 and was chosen such that the expected undercompensation in 2007 for the group with spending in the top 15% in each of the years 2004–2006 was eliminated.
*Source:* Van Kleef, R.C., Van Vliet, R.C.J.A., 2012. Improving risk equalization using multiple-year high cost as a health indicator. Med. Care 50(2), 140–144.

equalization alone. At the same time, however, the retrospective compensation reduces incentives for efficiency, since the health plans' compensation for year t becomes dependent on realized costs in year t in this form of HRP. More specifically, health plans will be liable for on average "only" 72 cents of each euro spent on the high-risk group.

HRPs can be structured in other ways, and need not involve supply-side cost sharing. Prior to the ACA in the United States, 35 states operated high-risk pools, with eligibility mostly determined by having a "preexisting condition," which interfered with enrollment in individual health insurance markets when insurers had the ability to exclude enrollees based on prior conditions (Pollitz, 2016). States regulated premiums, but these were generally higher than those available in the regular market, and deductibles were high. States subsidized the pools to keep HRP plans reasonably affordable. At their peak, HRPs enrolled about 2% of the population in the individual health insurance market. Returning to subsidized HRPs is part of some proposals in the United States to replace the ACA Marketplaces (Pollitz, 2016).

### 4.3.4   Risk Corridors

Risk corridors define ranges of plan-level profits or losses over which the regulator shares cost risk. A simple form of a one-sided risk corridor allows a plan to keep any profits but limits losses to, e.g., 5% of revenues. Under such a plan, the regulator is in effect responsible for 100% of plan-level costs above 105% of revenues. This form of risk corridor is referred to as "one-sided" because it applies only to losses and not profits.

Risk corridors have been applied in several health insurance markets; they may be particularly useful during transition periods in which the financial consequences of reforms are uncertain. From 2006 to 2016 temporary risk corridors were used in the Netherlands in connection to several reforms in that period. Box 4.7 describes what the risk corridor looked like in 2006. Fig. 4.5 shows the relationship of profits and average plan spending in the presence of the temporary risk corridor policy in the Netherlands.

Temporary risk corridors were also part of the initial setup of the Marketplaces in the United States (see Chapter 17: Health Plan Payment in US Marketplaces: Regulated Competition With a Weak Mandate). Section 1342 of the ACA established a symmetric risk corridor program for the Marketplaces which operated from 2014 to 2016. Under this program a "target amount" of medical expenditures was calculated for each health insurer's covered risk pool, equivalent to their total premiums collected minus an allowed amount for administrative costs and profits. If a plan's actual expenditures for medical care for its enrollees exceeded the target by at least 3%, the plan would receive a payment from the risk-corridor program. This program was intended to be "symmetric" because if a plan's actual medical expenditures are lower than the target by 3% or greater the

### BOX 4.7  Risk corridors in the Netherlands

Right after the introduction of the Health Insurance Act (2006) Dutch health plans faced financial uncertainty due to the implementation of a new product classification among others. Because of this uncertainty a risk corridor was applied. In terms of Van Barneveld's taxonomy, this risk-sharing modality took the following form (in 2006):

1. The group of members for whom some risk is shared: the entire population.
2. The types of care for which the risk is shared: all services covered in the benefit package.
3. The extent of the risk that is shared: 90% of a health plan's mean financial result outside a bandwidth of −35 euros and +35 euros. The mean financial result for a plan is calculated as the difference between realized spending and predicted spending (by the risk equalization model) divided by the number of premium payers (i.e., those 18 years and older).
4. The price that insurers have to pay to share some risk: health plans with a positive (negative) mean financial result of >35 euros per premium payer pay into (receive from) the fund. The balance is financed by the regulator.
   Source: Zorginstituut (2005).

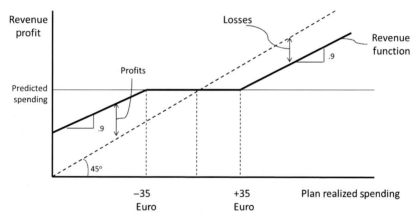

**FIGURE 4.5**  Relationship of profits and average plan spending in the presence of the temporary risk corridor policy in the Dutch national health insurance in 2006.

plan must make a payment to the risk-corridor program. It turned out that plan losses were more frequent and larger than plan profits and the self-financed risk-corridor program was only able to return a fraction of the intended funding to plans with losses (Layton et al., 2016).[15]

In principle, a symmetric risk corridor program could be self-financed so long as the regulator's share of profits is sufficient to meet the regulator's responsibilities to share losses. Risk corridor payments to Medicare Part D plans for greater than expected costs are financed by recouping funds from plans with greater than expected profits, and the expected net cost of the program to Medicare is zero (MedPAC, 2012). Balanced budget financing of risk corridor payments is obviously not feasible with a one-sided risk corridor limiting plan losses, and generally, risk corridor programs tend to be more oriented to loss-sharing than profit-sharing and thus require infusions from the regulator to operate the program.

We now consider how a risk corridor addresses plan financial risk and selection incentives. With respect to plan financial risk we can say definitively that—for any fixed amount of money involved in risk sharing—risk corridors dominate reinsurance. In contrast to reinsurance, defined at the person level, a risk corridor is defined at the plan level, making risk corridors a more efficient use of funds from the standpoint of plan risk protection (Ellis and McGuire, 1988; Keeler et al., 1988; Layton et al., 2016). This is because risk corridor payments apply only when a plan's total costs fall in the extreme tails of the insurer's cost distribution, whereas reinsurance results in payments to plans when individuals are costly, even if the plan is making profits on average on their other enrollees. From the standpoint of plan protection against losses on their enrollees, it is the experience of all enrollees in aggregate that matters.

In terms of contending with selection problems, the comparison of risk corridor and reinsurance is less clear cut. Both types of policies tend to reduce unpriced risk heterogeneity, and in that respect diminish selection problems; comparisons, however, would have to be empirical, depend on the setting, and would not be straightforward. The research and policy literature tends not to analyze risk corridors with respect to their effects on selection problems. The reason is likely that this would require simulations of health plan experience, not just analysis of individual-level gains and losses relative to risk adjustment.

When it comes to health plans' incentives to attract or deter particular risk types, reinsurance and risk corridors would affect these incentives differently. Reinsurance is more oriented to high-cost individuals, and if individual-level selection were the main worry (e.g., surreptitious denial of enrollment to likely high-cost individuals), reinsurance would be a better option. If health plans' selection actions are oriented to groups of users (e.g., persons likely to use home care), evaluation of the two approaches would need to rely on simulations of plan experience under alternative payment options.

Generalization is also difficult when it comes to selection problems related to market segmentation (such as inefficient sorting of consumers into health plans). Both reinsurance and risk corridors tend to move funds to plans attracting high-cost individuals, mitigating segmentation. We speculate that since this is a plan-level not an individual-level problem, for a given level of costs shared, risk corridors are a better choice.

When applied at the insurer level (rather than the health plan level) risk corridors have the disadvantage of being vulnerable to manipulation if a health plan can book profits and losses across organizational boundaries. Suppose Plan A is part of Parent Company. If Plan A will get risk corridor payments for some losses, Parent Company might overcharge Plan A for management services, creating profits at Parent Company and booking losses at Plan A. The same vulnerability to transfer pricing manipulation exists if Plan A is integrated with a hospital system. Plan A might overpay Hospital System, transferring profits there and booking losses, subject to risk corridor payments, at the plan level.

## 4.4    RISK SHARING AND INCENTIVES FOR COST CONTAINMENT

One fundamental element of regulated competition is setting capitation payments to plans, making them risk bearing. This encourages plans to use the tools available to them to restrain spending in order to keep costs (and premiums) low. Plan payment policies that reduce insurer risk bearing, including reinsurance and risk corridors, diminish a plan's incentives to control costs, presenting the regulator with a tradeoff between mitigating selection problems/reducing insurer risk and providing insurers with the incentive to control costs—precisely the tradeoff identified and discussed by Newhouse (1996).

### 4.4.1    The Share of Dollars/Euros Touched by Risk-Sharing Measures Incentives Affected

What is the magnitude of the effect of risk sharing on incentives to a health plan? In the case of a mixed system covered in Section 4.3.1 this is simple to describe. If the mix is such that 50% of the weight is put on a prospective payment and 50% on costs, one could say that the payment system is "50% cost-based."

The idea of the share of costs covered as a measure of incentives can be generalized. Payment systems can be thought of as not prospective or retrospective but as a mix, and the degree of "cost-basedness" of a payment system can be characterized by asking, "What share of the plan costs is the responsibility of the regulator?" In the Dutch HRP proposal described above, for qualified individuals, a fixed share of 28% of the costs associated with those designated to the pool would be the responsibility of the regulator. In this system, the overall share of costs that is the responsibility of the regulator is equal to the share of spending attributable to people in the HRP times 28%.[16] Thus, if 25% of spending were associated with those in the pool, the regulator would be responsible for 7% of the costs (Van Kleef and Van Vliet, 2012). This serves as a measure of how much a particular cost-sharing plan affects incentives, which can be compared among payment system options. For example, if the Dutch HRP included more people in the pool (amounting to say 10% of the spending) but paid a lower share (say 20% of costs), the regulator's share could be determined and compared to the alternative policy (in this case 2.0%, a greater effect on incentives).

Table 4.1 showed some similar calculations in the case of some reinsurance options in US Marketplaces. With an attachment point of $500,000, only 1% of the costs would be the responsibility of the regulator via reinsurance; with the lower attachment point of $100,000, this share was 10%. On the basis of this, one would conclude that the incentive effect of reinsurance at an attachment point of $500,000 had a negligible effect on incentives for cost containment.

The idea of this simple measure is that a plan would have incentives to reduce costs to the degree that it was responsible for those costs. Just as we can compare demand-side cost sharing in terms of its incentives to consumers as measured by the share of costs they pay, we can do the same with plans and grade the incentive effects of risk-sharing alternatives in terms of the share of costs passed off to the regulator.

## 4.4.2 Risk Sharing and the Tradeoff Between Incentives for Cost Reduction and Financial Uncertainty

The terms of the tradeoff introduced by risk sharing between incentives for cost containment and reducing plan financial uncertainty depend on the form of risk sharing. Targeting the high-cost cases or losses at the plan level is generally a better way to use risk sharing in terms of reducing plan financial uncertainty.

Table 4.1 can be consulted to see this point, illustrated with a reinsurance example. At a "cost" in incentives for efficiency of only 1%, the payment system fit is augmented by 0.13 (0.572−0.438) and the risk of ruin falls by 40% (5.4%−3.1%) with the reinsurance attachment point of $500,000. This is a very favorable tradeoff and a very general result. Certainly in this Marketplace example, concerns about incentives are negligible until the attachment point is $500,000 or less. Given the higher distribution of healthcare costs characterizing the United States in comparison to other countries, attachment points considerably lower would exhibit this very favorable tradeoff outside the United States.

## 4.4.3 Risk Sharing and the Tradeoff Between Incentives for Cost Reduction and Selection

As discussed in Section 4.3, risk sharing can reduce unpriced risk heterogeneity, thereby mitigating selection problems. With respect to the quantification of the tradeoff between selection and incentives for cost containment, two important observations can be made. First, to evaluate the tradeoff, a clear identification and way of measuring the selection problem is needed. As we will show in Chapter 5, Evaluating the Performance of Health Plan Payment Systems, different forms of selection problems call for different metrics. So far, the limited empirical literature on the effects of risk sharing on selection has focused on health plans' incentives to selectively attract or deter particular risk types. In these analyses, specifying the risk types is necessary, and even this offers choices to the investigator. It will generally not be fully known on which dimensions plans might implement tactics to effect selection. Furthermore, the effect of risk sharing on other types of selection problems, such as the inefficient sorting of consumers, is an unexplored area for research. A second observation is that the evaluation of risk-sharing options should take into account other elements of a health plan payment system in place that affect "unpriced heterogeneity" (i.e., risk adjustment and premium differentiation). For example, risk sharing is likely to add less in terms of selection-related incentives reduction to a plan payment system with a sophisticated risk adjustment system compared to a plan payment system with very limited risk adjustment. Chapter 5, Evaluating the Performance of Health Plan Payment Systems, addresses some of these issues where measures of selection-related problems are presented and discussed.

## 4.5   ESTIMATION OF RISK ADJUSTMENT MODELS IN THE PRESENCE OF RISK SHARING

This section considers a practical aspect of integrating some risk sharing as a complement to a health status-based risk adjustment model. For example, suppose the Dutch HRP proposal were implemented. What would this mean for how estimation of the risk adjustment model should be modified? Obviously something should change, since the health plans paid by risk adjustment are responsible for a different set of costs. This section explains how estimation of risk adjustment models should be modified in the presence of some supply-side cost sharing. We base our comments on an analogy to demand-side cost sharing. Simply stated, if a plan is not responsible for certain costs, they should not be part of the dependent variable in a risk adjustment model. We explain the specifics of how to conduct such an empirical analysis in one step with a typical claims data set.

Risk adjustment models are designed to predict the costs that a health plan is responsible for, a principle recognized and put into practice by regulators in many contexts. For example, demand-side cost sharing moves some costs to consumers, and regulators recognize that these costs should not be part of the dependent variable in risk-adjustment models. In the Netherlands, risk adjustment models are estimated on total spending including the out-of-pocket expenses under the deductible. In order to compensate insurers for (differences in) out-of-pocket expenses (between high-risk and low-risk individuals) there is a separate prediction model for out-of-pocket spending. The payment to a health plan is based on the prediction of total spending minus the prediction on out-of-pocket spending. An analogous approach has been used in the US Marketplaces where separate risk adjustment models are estimated according to the average amount of demand-side cost sharing in a plan, as indicated by the metal level. If a type of healthcare service where, e.g., long-term mental health care, is not a plan responsibility, costs for this type of care are not included in the model.

The same logic applies to supply-side cost or risk sharing. If the health plan is not responsible for the costs, they should not be part of the dependent variable. Risk adjustment weights should predict the costs a plan is responsible for. There are two ways to do this, both straightforward, and both leading to exactly the same result. Analogous to the way demand-side cost sharing is handled in empirical models of risk adjustment, one way would be to literally pull out costs covered by risk sharing prior to estimation. For example, if the attachment point were $500,000 and the coinsurance were 80%, pull out 80% of costs over $500,000, and then estimate. The risk adjustment weights would be optimized for the costs the plan is responsible for. This approach was applied in the Netherlands in the period 2006–2014, when reinsurance was part of the plan payment. In 2006, e.g., a reinsurance attachment point of 12,500 euros was applied after which 90% of costs were shared with the regulator. Risk adjustment weights for 2006 were estimated by a regression model in which the dependent variable equaled the sum of cost below the 12,500 euros attachment point and 10% of the cost above this point. This approach requires two empirical steps: pulling out the costs not the responsibility of the plan, and then estimating the model.

A second analytically equivalent way to achieve the same objective is to include a variable in the risk adjustment model equal to (in the reinsurance example) "costs above the attachment point" and constrain the coefficient on this variable to be the reinsurer's coinsurance share, say 0.8. In the case of a $500,000 attachment point, if a person spends less than $500,000, the value of this variable is zero.[17] If a person spends above, e.g., $532,000, the value would be $32,000. With this method, the "usual" risk adjustment model coefficients will be optimized to fit the part of costs not picked up by the reinsurance variable. The resulting coefficients will be exactly the same as if the first method of pulling out costs were applied. This second approach is a one-step empirical procedure.

In this second approach it is necessary to restrict the coefficient to be equal to the reinsurance share. To not do so and let this coefficient simply be estimated along with the others would be undesirable for two reasons: first, an estimated coefficient different than this share would defeat the purpose of substituting precisely for a particular form of reinsurance, and second, the estimated coefficient on costs above the attachment point is likely to be greater than 1.0, introducing unacceptable incentive properties in the payment system.[18] Restricting the coefficient to 0.8 or some other value in an OLS regression is simple to implement, a one-line modification of SAS code.

A related approach to including current costs in a risk adjustment formula was proposed by Schillo et al. (2016) who consider inclusion of up to three (0,1) indicators of "high-cost groups," where high cost was post risk adjustment defined in terms of a "funding gap," equal to the difference between the observed cost and the revenue from the risk adjustment formula. Funding gap is defined based on costs in the current period. A single dummy variable for a "funding gap above 30,000 euros" increases the $R$-squared of the risk adjustment model from 27.6% to 51.0%.[19] The Schillo et al. approach is related to reinsurance, with the threshold defined in terms of a funding gap rather than a cost threshold.

Note that the approaches just described are distinct from using past indicators of high-cost use into a prospective risk adjustment model. A similar empirical approach using an indicator for *past* high costs was studied earlier in the Netherlands; specifically, an indicator for exceeding a cost threshold in multiple past years (Van Kleef and Van Vliet, 2012), which was subsequently included in the Dutch risk adjustment methodology.

Risk sharing refers to current costs playing a role in plan payment. The methods described here for incorporating risk sharing based on *current* costs within a risk adjustment estimation methodology can be grafted on risk adjustment systems that include indictors for *past* high cost (which only imperfectly predicts current high cost).

## 4.6   CONCLUSION: RISK SHARING AS A COMPONENT OF A HEALTH PLAN PAYMENT SYSTEM

This chapter has described how risk sharing can be used as a supplement to risk adjustment and premium regulation. Two main objectives of risk sharing have been identified. First, risk sharing can reduce financial uncertainty for health plans. Regulators might consider excessive financial uncertainty undesirable since it can adversely affect the health insurance market by discouraging plan entry, especially by small innovative plans, and causing plans to raise prices to compensate for bearing risk. Moreover, regulators may want to protect plans against (temporary) uncertainty about the financial consequences of specific system reforms. The second main objective of risk sharing is to mitigate problems related to risk selection such as inefficient sorting of consumers and health plan actions to selectively attract or deter certain risk types. Even sophisticated risk adjustment formulas do not completely account for predictable cost variation.[20] Risk sharing can reduce unpriced risk heterogeneity.

When it comes to the design of risk sharing, four main dimensions can be distinguished: (1) the group of members for whom (some of) the risk is shared (e.g., the entire population, people with spending above a certain threshold, or a specific group of high-risk people); (2) the types of care for which the risk is shared (e.g., for the total benefit package, specific services, or specific cost elements of services); (3) the extent of the risk that is shared (e.g., a proportion of total spending, spending above a threshold, or a proportion of spending above a threshold); and (4) the price that insurers have to pay to share some risk (e.g., a flat-rate premium, a risk-rated premium, or no premium in case the pool is financed by the regulator). Since multiple options are available for each aspect, risk sharing can take numerous forms. In this chapter we have focused on four of the most common forms, i.e., proportional risk sharing, reinsurance, high-risk pooling, and risk corridors. The best use of risk sharing within a health plan payment system depends on the objectives of the regulator as well as the other tools the regulator has available, such as risk adjustment. Recognizing that much will depend on the particular circumstances, some general observations can be made.

The main drawback of risk sharing is that it reduces health plans' incentives for cost containment. Research can contribute to evaluating the tradeoff between the benefits of risk sharing and the loss of cost-containment incentives. The preferred risk sharing design is the one that provides the greatest benefits (in terms of the regulator's objectives) for a given level of incentives for cost containment. Some forms of risk sharing are likely to be more effective than others in these terms.

When it comes to protecting health plans against excessive financial uncertainty due to the variation in individual-level medical spending, reinsurance is particularly attractive for the simple reason that healthcare spending is very skewed, and a small fraction of the population is responsible for a major fraction of (the variance in) spending. By targeting risk-sharing payments to this high-spending group, reinsurance reduces plan risk while affecting cost incentives for only a very small fraction of costs.

A different objective of the regulator might lead to other choices for risk sharing. If a regulator is introducing health system reforms (e.g., expansions of the benefit package or the introduction of a new product classification), plan uncertainty will not be due to the risk of drawing a few high-cost cases, but from the uncertain redistributions associated with the reforms themselves. In this case, risk sharing directed at the plans might be a better choice, e.g., risk corridors might do a better job since they limit plan- or insurer-level profits and losses more directly.

When it comes to mitigating selection problems, identification of the selection problem to be tackled is crucial for deciding on the best form of risk sharing. For example, when the objective of the regulator is to mitigate incentives for health plans to deter particular risk types, if those individuals can be identified with data available, high-risk pooling of the type proposed for the Netherlands can be an effective strategy since it targets extra payments to the groups of interest. Actual cost during a year is data normally available for plan payments. A general strategy, such as reinsurance, uses cost realization to target funds to individuals with high costs, a strategy likely to be helpful if there are many potential forms of selection concerns, or if targeted groups cannot be easily identified with available data. Risk corridors, working at the plan level, may be particularly useful when the concern is with the adverse effects of market segmentation, such as inefficient sorting of consumers.

In sum, the optimal risk-sharing design depends on the regulator's goals regarding payment fit, avoidance of selection problems and incentives for cost control, and the other characteristics of the plan payment system. Some form of risk sharing to deal with high-cost cases is generally a component of good policy for plan payment.

## ACKNOWLEDGMENTS

We thank Konstantin Beck, Sonja Schillo, Wynand van de Ven, and René van Vliet for their valuable comments on early drafts of this chapter.

## ENDNOTES

1. The word "risk" is used in two senses in this chapter: risk in the sense of cost in the term "risk sharing" and risk in the sense of uncertainty as in the phrase, "reducing the variation in the distribution of net profit outcomes for a plan reduces risk to the plan." The meaning should be clear in this context.
2. Given the focus of this volume we will say throughout this chapter that the risk is shared with the "regulator." This should be interpreted broadly. For example, the regulator could contract a reinsurer to carry the risk or setup a special fund that organizes risk-sharing payments/contributions to/from health plans.
3. "Predictable" depends on the perspective. Cost risk accounted for in the risk adjustment formula is predictable by definition. What consumers and plans can predict is another matter.
4. Cutler and Zeckhauser (2000, pp. 571−572) review some of this literature. The skewness in the distribution is lessened somewhat but remains substantial when the time period of observation extends beyond a year.
5. Variance is the sum of the squares of the deviation of each observation and the mean for the distribution.
6. http://www.msn.com/en-us/money/healthcare/obamacare-sticker-shock-price-hikes-are-on-the-way/ar-BBtnQ8N?li=BBnb7Kz&ocid=iehp. Accessed May 24, 2016.
7. Medicare hospital payment for hospitals and units exempt from the DRG-based prospective payment system were paid on the basis of a mixed system. Payment to primary care practitioners or groups in a number of contexts reviewed in McGuire et al. (2011) feature a fixed payment component associated with the patient enrolling with the provider or group, and then some payment associated with services provided. One example is the payment model that evolved in California in the 1990s where health plans contracted with physician groups to bear some but not all of the financial risk of health care, paying the groups by a form of mixed system (Robinson, 2001).

8. This *R*-squared equivalent is the payment system fit metric which generalizes the *R*-squared, explained in Chapter 5: Evaluating the Performance of Health Plan Payment Systems.

9. For example if undercompensation for a group is $100 using a certain risk-adjusted prospective payment system, if the mix of 80% risk-adjusted average and 20% costs were substituted instead, the undercompensation would fall to $80. Under/overcompensation changes proportional to the mix, whereas the *R*-squared equivalence changes in proportion to the square, since *R*-squared is based on squared deviations.

10. The term "coinsurance" is also used to describe consumer demand-side cost sharing. From the standpoint of the plan, consumers and a sponsor are "coinsuring" the cost risks so the usage makes sense from that standpoint. Here we will use the term "reinsurer coinsurance" to avoid any confusion with demand-side cost sharing.

11. The following papers all use payment systems modeled on the Marketplaces. Geruso and McGuire (2016) use MarketScan data from 2008 to 2009, and Zhu et al. (2013) and Layton et al. (2016) use data from the Medical Expenditure Panel Survey (MEPS) with characteristics matching likely Marketplace participants. Using an updated version of the data used for calibration of the ACA risk adjustment models, the same data as are used in this paper, Layton et al. (2017) show that reinsurance paired with prospective risk adjustment produces a fit of payments to costs much higher than concurrent risk adjustment with no reinsurance. Simulations assume that a prior year's data are unavailable for 50% of Marketplace participants and risk adjustment (as is done in Medicare for new enrollees) must be based only on age and gender. The reinsurance policy was 80% above $60,000. Dow et al. (2010) used data from a Medicare population.

12. Schillo et al. refer to this as a high-cost pool, but we discuss it here in the reinsurance section since the assignment of people to the pool is based on ex post spending, a particular feature of reinsurance.

13. Layton et al. (2016) address similar empirical issues with a smaller sample in survey data from the United States, the Medical Expenditure Panel Survey, and find similar results. The simulation methods used in Layton and McGuire (2017) are described in more detail in the earlier paper.

14. In the simulations in Table 4.1, risk adjustment is optimized for the presence of reinsurance in a way described in Section 4.5. Results in fit improvements with reinsurance are also found in Zhu et al. (2013). For example, using survey data from the United States, Zhu et al. find that adding reinsurance of 80% with an attachment point of about $105,000 improves the payment system fit using a prospective risk adjustment system for the Marketplaces from 0.14 to 0.31. See their Figure 1.

15. Risk corridors are also used in provider payment settings. An example is the payment scheme for Accountable Care Organizations (ACOs), a risk-bearing entity in the US Medicare program. Risk corridors are also a permanent feature of health plan payments in the case of drug insurance in Medicare (Part D), and of the ACO program established by the Affordable Care Act. The Medicare Shared Savings and Pioneer ACO Programs allow ACOs to choose between a one-sided and two-sided arrangement. Under the one-sided arrangement, ACOs share up to 50% of savings in excess of a minimum loss ratio. Under the two-sided model, ACOs share in 60% of savings, but they will also be liable for up to 60% of costs above the target amount. The one-sided model was much more frequently chosen by ACOs (Centers for Medicare and Medicaid Services, 2013.

16. The "responsibility of the regulator" should be interpreted as applying at the time the costs are incurred. Obviously the regulator must obtain the funds from somewhere, either from taxes directly or indirectly from mandatory contributions from health plans as in the case of the proposed Dutch HRP.

17. See Layton and McGuire (2017) where this method is applied to data used to calibrate risk adjustment weights for the US Marketplaces.

18. The incentive problems stem from the fact that a coefficient above 1.0 implies that, above the threshold, for each additional dollar that an insurer spends, it receives back more than one dollar via risk adjustment. The reason for the estimated coefficient greater than 1.0 is that even after reinsurance payments, high-cost cases still have costs higher than predicted with the conventional risk adjustor variables. The unrestricted estimated coefficient on costs above the threshold reflects the correlation of these costs with the "losses" on cases for which reinsurance does not activate, moving the estimated coefficient above 1.0.

19. Schillo et al. (2016) first compute the conventional risk-adjusted payment, and compare this to cost to determine the "funding gap".

20. Risk sharing can also repair mispricing in a risk adjustment formula as pointed out by Newhouse (1996), which can arise from a number of sources. A main source is the lack of sufficient risk adjustor variables. Another source can be shortcomings in the underlying data used for estimating risk adjustment weights. For example, risk adjustment models are always estimated with some lag in the data used, and changes in medical technology can alter cost patterns in treatment after risk adjustment models have been estimated. Suppose, for example, that a new highly effective but expensive device is available to treat heart disease. A risk-adjustment model estimated on 5-year-old data would underpay for heart disease in relation to this new state-of-the-art treatment. If, however, there were some risk sharing built into the payment system that applied over the range of costs involved, health plans would be partly protected against "cost shocks" to technology not built into the risk adjustment model.

# Chapter 5

# Evaluating the Performance of Health Plan Payment Systems

**Timothy J. Layton[1], Randall P. Ellis[2], Thomas G. McGuire[1] and Richard C. van Kleef[3]**

[1]*Department of Health Care Policy, Harvard Medical School and the NBER, Boston, MA, United States,* [2]*Department of Economics, Boston University, Boston, MA, United States,* [3]*Erasmus School of Health Policy and Management, Erasmus University Rotterdam, Rotterdam, The Netherlands*

## 5.1 INTRODUCTION

Social objectives for health plan payment systems include efficiency and fairness, each with multiple dimensions. Efficiency is concerned with matching the form of insurance to consumer preferences, and encouraging provision of efficient health care. Fairness has to do with individual affordability of health insurance and health care, access to high-quality providers, and with the distribution of the burden of financing health insurance.[1] This chapter deals primarily with efficiency, although fairness implications are noted as they arise. We explain the nature of efficiency goals and then review methods for evaluating a plan payment system against these goals. We look for evaluation metrics that satisfy two criteria. First, measures should be *valid*, i.e., be linked to an objective of the health plan payment system. Second, measures should be *practical*, i.e., feasible to construct with the data typically available to researchers charged with design of payment system methods.[2]

Other objectives for health plan payment systems are covered elsewhere in this volume. Fairness and access concerns are discussed extensively in Chapter 2, Premium Regulation, Risk Equalization, Risk Sharing, and Subsidies: Effects on Affordability and Efficiency. Risk adjustment is often a crucial part of health plan payment. Some criteria for evaluation specific to the risk adjustment component of plan payment, such as that the risk adjustment scheme should not be "gameable," are covered in Chapter 3, Risk Adjustment for Health Plan Payments.

*Risk Adjustment, Risk Sharing and Premium Regulation in Health Insurance Markets.*
DOI: https://doi.org/10.1016/B978-0-12-811325-7.00005-1
**133**

As in the rest of this volume, the institutional setting for our discussion of methods for evaluation is regulated competition. Individuals choose their health insurance plan from among a set of competing insurers offering products subject to premium and benefit regulation. Regulation notwithstanding, plans may have the ability to discourage/encourage membership by, among other things, distorting some elements of their coverage and services. We assume throughout that regulation includes open enrollment provisions, which, though perhaps working imperfectly, require that health plans accept all applicants.

Our primary perspective is at the market design phase: with data on patterns of utilization representative of the population to be covered, researchers and regulators need to assess how well a payment system—meaning the set of policies regulating both the premium structure and the plan payment scheme—will achieve social objectives of efficiency and fairness. The market-design phase is when most evaluations of plan payment methods take place. Statistical analysis and simulations prior to putting a payment system in place are the primary way regulators evaluate and decide on payment systems for the US state-based Marketplaces, Medicare's payment system for private health plans, and plan payment systems in the Netherlands, Switzerland, Israel, Germany, and elsewhere.[3]

The (ex ante) market-design phase contrasts with the postmarket-performance phase commonly studied in the empirical literature in economics, where econometric methods are used ex post to study the impact of payment system changes. While this form of research obviously feeds into the choice of plan payment system, evaluations of changes in complex healthcare systems (such as, e.g., US Medicaid or Marketplace expansions) usually cannot identify the causal effects of distinct design components of a health plan payment system, necessarily relying on ad hoc model calibrations, and therefore fall short of answering questions critical to regulators.[4] We include some discussion of these ex post evaluation studies as we go, using them to substantiate that the selection-related distortions payment systems are designed to combat actually play out in insurance markets.

### 5.1.1 Efficiency Problems in Individual Health Insurance Markets

Individual health insurance markets are vulnerable to economic inefficiencies caused by adverse selection, the tendency of sicker, higher-cost consumers to choose more generous coverage. This natural pattern of demand causes two central problems: (1) equilibrium premiums reflect selection as well as coverage differences, leading to pricing distortions that cause consumers to choose the "wrong" plans (Einav and Finkelstein, 2011), and

(2) insurers distort the coverage of their health plans, or take other discriminatory actions, to make them less attractive to unprofitable (typically sicker) enrollees (Glazer and McGuire, 2000). The relative importance of these two forms of inefficiency varies across regulated competition markets. In the US Medicare program, sorting of beneficiaries between the private managed care plans (Medicare Advantage (MA) plans) and traditional Medicare has received the most attention (see Chapter 19: Medicare Advantage: Regulated Competitionin the Shadow of a Public Option), whereas in the national health insurance system in the Netherlands with common regulation and coverage for the entire population, underprovision of some services (e.g., exclusion of high-quality doctors or healthcare facilities from provider networks) is the larger concern (see Chapter 14: Health Plan Payment in the Netherlands). Other markets, such as the Marketplaces established in the US as part of the Affordable Care Act (ACA) (Chapter 17: Health Plan Payment in US Marketplaces: Regulated Competition With a Weak Mandate) feature both concerns: inducing participation among those eligible to purchase coverage on the Marketplace (Newhouse, 2017) and ensuring that plans provide adequate coverage for all conditions (Shepard, 2016; Geruso et al., 2017).

For many years, motivated by concerns with adverse selection, studies of and reports on health plan payment methods have focused on the $R$-squared from a risk adjustment regression as the main metric of health plan payment system performance. Some papers and official reports also include ratio or difference measures of over/undercompensation for specific groups. In the United States, researchers tend to use the ratio of predicted costs to actual costs for selected groups in the population ("predictive ratios"), such as those with a chronic illness, whereas in Europe researchers tend to use the difference between projected revenues and costs ("over- and undercompensation"). Typically, in calibration of risk-adjusted payments, $R$-squared is given primacy. The statistical regression procedure maximizes $R$-squared, and then under/overcompensation for various groups is checked to see if it is satisfactory. One goal of this chapter is to explain when and what modifications of these measures are called for to assess the efficiency consequences of health plan payment systems.

The health plan payment system in all countries and sectors is also expected to help with the moral hazard—or cost control—problem in health care: the tendency of providers and patients to decide on "too much" health care when the patient is close to fully insured and does not bear the full cost of the care she receives. The health plan payment system should pay health plans so as to give them incentives to discourage overutilization of health care, where overutilization is defined as care for which the cost exceeds the value consumers place on it. In discussions of regulated competition, beginning with Enthoven, this objective motivated the idea of paying plans "prospectively," i.e., independent of the quantity of health care an individual uses during the current year. If, at the plan level, revenues are set in advance, any costs incurred by an individual reduce net revenue of the plan. In this way, while the consumer may not care about cost control, the plan will, and the plan will take actions to restrain spending, such as setting copays and deductibles, managing care, negotiating efficient prices from providers, or creating networks of selected providers.

It turns out, however, that in the complex payment systems in use in many countries, the "prospectiveness" of a payment system is not a yes/no characteristic, but a matter of the degree to which revenues depend on costs incurred. It has been infrequently recognized that most health plan payment systems are not fully prospective. Less common still is the application of measures of prospectiveness to health plan payment systems. While some payment system features such as reinsurance obviously incorporate some amount of cost-reimbursement, other features like risk adjustment also incentivize use though in less transparent ways, making accurate measurement of this aspect of payment critical. An objective of this chapter is to explain how researchers and policymakers can measure the degree of prospectiveness of a health plan payment system, and bring forward for discussion this policy-relevant aspect of health plan payment.

**TABLE 5.1** Metrics for Evaluating Efficient Performance of Health Plan Payment Systems

| Section of chapter: Dimension of efficiency | Traditional metric | Modified/New metric |
|---|---|---|
| 5.2: Selection: Fit at the Individual Level | R-squared or other fit statistics from a risk-adjustment regression | Payment system fit using predicted payments (not regression predictions) |
| 5.3: Selection: Fit at the Group or Action Level | Predictive ratios (United States); under- and overcompensation (Europe) | Group payment system fit; measure for potential plan actions |
| 5.4: Selection: Individuals Choose the Right Plan | No incentive metric in common use | Summary measure of the gap between efficient incremental premium and the actual premium; payment system fit |
| 5.5: Incentives for Cost Control | No incentive metric in common use | Power of the payment system |

## 5.1.2    Plan of the Chapter

Table 5.1 previews treatment of four efficiency issues associated with plan payment methods covered in the next four sections. The purpose of each section is to propose valid, practical metrics for each dimension of efficiency.

## 5.2    MEASURES OF FIT AND INCENTIVES AT THE INDIVIDUAL LEVEL

This section explains the rationale for a measure of fit at the individual level as a metric of the efficiency properties of a health plan payment system. After review of the rationale for the $R$-squared from a risk-adjustment regression, we present a generalization of the $R$-squared measure that is easy to compute and takes into account other aspects of the health plan payment system, not just the predicted values from a risk-adjustment model. This generalization is desirable when health plan payment systems contain other features in addition to a capitation rate based on a risk adjustment regression, such as premium categories and risk sharing. Assuming that fit at the individual level is a valid and relevant metric for the efficiency of health plan payment, the generalized fit measure we propose integrates other health plan payment features.

## 5.2.1    Rationale for $R$-Squared From a Risk Adjustment Regression

By far the most commonly reported measure of the performance of a health plan payment system is the $R$-squared from a regression of spending at the individual level on the variables used as risk adjustors. Letting $Y_i$ be the actual spending of individual $i$ in the data used for calibrating the risk adjustment model, $\overline{Y}$ be the average spending in the population, and $\hat{Y}_i$ be the predicted spending from the regression of $Y_i$ on the risk adjustors, the $R$-squared of the risk adjustment model is:

$$R^2_{\text{reg}} = 1 - \frac{\sum_i (Y_i - \hat{Y}_i)^2}{\sum_i (Y_i - \overline{Y})^2} \tag{5.1}$$

We label this $R$-squared with a subscript "reg" to indicate that it comes from the risk adjustment regression (most commonly in practice a variant of ordinary least squares).[5] The denominator in Eq. (5.1), $\sum_i (Y_i - \overline{Y})^2$, is the total sum of squares of individual spending, with higher values indicating that spending is more dispersed around the mean $\overline{Y}$. The numerator, $\sum_i (Y_i - \hat{Y}_i)^2$, is the "residual" sum of squares measuring the dispersion of spending in relation to the value predicted in the risk-adjustment regression. The better the risk adjustment model does fitting predicted to actual spending, the smaller is the residual sum of squares. If predicted values exactly fit actual values, the numerator is zero and $R^2_{reg} = 1$. If the regression equation explains none of the variation in individual costs, the predicted value is just the mean, implying the numerator equals the denominator and $R^2_{reg} = 0$. Real-world risk adjustment models typically fall somewhere in between with $0 \leq R^2_{reg} \leq 1$. It is common to report the $R$-squared as a percentage of the total variance explained by the model, so that they range between 0% and 100%.[6]

The $R$-squared from risk-adjustment regressions can strike those new to the field as being surprisingly low. Although age and gender are important predictors of healthcare costs, a regression with age and gender cells often explains only 1%−4% of the variation in healthcare costs. This is due to the enormous variation in spending even within an age−gender cell. The risk adjustment formula used in the US Medicare program based on a previous year's diagnoses raises the $R$-squared from a least squares regression to around 12%. The Dutch risk adjustment model for somatic care, which is the most sophisticated prospective risk adjustment system in the world, using 186 variables from a number of domains, including prospectively defined clinical variables, has an $R$-squared of about 31% (see Chapter 14: Health Plan Payment in the Netherlands). Chapter 3, Risk Adjustment for Health Plan Payment, contains an extensive discussion of the methods behind and the results of various risk adjustment models.

A higher $R$-squared is generally regarded as an improvement in the performance of a risk adjustment model. Buchner et al. (2013) for Germany, Beck et al. (2010) for Switzerland, and Van Veen et al. (2014) for the Netherlands use $R$-squared to compare individual-level fit across different risk adjustment models. Examples from the United States include the risk adjustment work by Kautter et al. (2012, 2014) and the assessment of alternative risk adjustment specifications in the Society of Actuaries evaluation by Hileman and Steele (2016). While $R$-squared is by far the most common, it is not the only statistic used to evaluate risk adjustment models: each of these studies also includes others. The mean absolute prediction error (MAPE) uses the absolute value of the difference between actual and predicted spending, rather than squaring that difference as is done with an $R$-squared measure.[7] Arguments for the less-common alternatives to $R$-squared are generally made on statistical rather than economic grounds.[8]

The $R^2_{reg}$ is the right metric to use to evaluate the efficiency of a payment system under four assumptions: (1) health plans can take actions to encourage or discourage enrollees at the individual level (this is why fit would be figured person-by-person), (2) any inefficiency associated with those actions is proportional to the square of the gains and losses associated with the revenue and cost for the person (this is why we square the prediction-cost deviation),[9] (3) observed spending levels ($Y_i$) are the socially efficient spending levels, and (4) the predicted values from the regression are the exclusive basis for health plan payment (otherwise the predictions don't fully represent the actual payment model).[10] We discuss each assumption in turn before presenting our generalized measure.

Assumption (1), health plans can discriminate at the individual level for all potential enrollees, is unlikely to hold. Economic analysis of the dangers associated with adverse selection regard the health plan as discriminating in favor or against groups of enrollees, not individual enrollees; e.g., persons with a certain diagnosis who are underpaid in the risk adjustment formula, or persons using a certain service (such as home care). If the plan acts at a group rather than an individual level, a group level measure of fit is the appropriate one. For example, a plan might be underpaid by 20% for users of home care, and have incentives to underprovide this care. It is not important to plan incentives that some people within the group of home-care users are underpaid more or less leading to the 20% underpayment.[11] Risk adjustment researchers are aware of this issue and often present group-level measures of fit (such as group over/undercompensation) and group $R$-squared to supplement reports of model fit at the person level.

Assumption (2) has a sound basis in welfare economics, where it is normally assumed that the efficiency cost of a distortionary incentive is proportional to the square of the distortionary incentive. A distortion may move a decision maker (consumer, producer, plan) away from the optimal decision in some linear fashion, but a small movement near the optimum may have little efficiency effect, whereas the same size movement far away from the optimum will have a large efficiency effect. Fig. 5.1 illustrates the rationale for squaring the price distortion as a measure of inefficiency in the familiar context of a tax. If a tax t is imposed, price rises t above marginal cost (MC).

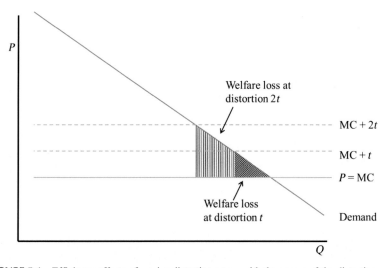

**FIGURE 5.1**  Efficiency effects of a price distortion go up with the square of the distortion.

The welfare loss associated with price MC + t is shown in the figure. Also shown is how the welfare loss quadruples (squaring) with a doubling of the tax to 2t.

Assumption (3) is unlikely to be true. Observed spending levels are likely to be different from efficient levels unless the optimal payment system is in place and competition is perfect, among other things. However, because efficient spending levels are typically unknown, and the efficient levels are the correct benchmark for welfare analysis (see Fig. 5.1) the researcher must specify some spending to be efficient. Observed spending, especially observed spending from a well-functioning setting (such as employer-provided insurance in the United States), has sometimes been assumed to be efficient by researchers.[12]

Assumption (4) will be true in some institutional circumstances and not in others. It is reasonable to assume that the degree of fit of revenues to costs is captured by the $R$-squared from a regression in Germany, Israel, and the US MA program where a plan's revenue is tied closely to the empirical risk adjustment model. In other contexts where premium categories influence payment (US Marketplaces, Ireland, Switzerland) or where there is risk sharing (US Marketplaces, Ireland, Switzerland, Australia), or where the risk equalization payment is made up of more than one predictive model (the Netherlands) the payments a plan receives for a person depend on more than the statistical fit of the risk adjustment formula. In Switzerland, a plan receives a risk equalization payment and a payment for each day an enrollee is hospitalized. Any incentives for or against individuals or groups are generated by the full set of payments a plan gets, not just from one feature of the payment system.

Judging how well the full payment system fits costs ideally includes taking all features into account. Even if the purpose of an analysis is to assess only the risk adjustment methodology, taking account of the other features of payment is necessary to more accurately gauge the incremental contribution of risk adjustment.

## 5.2.2   Generalizing the *R*-Squared: Payment System Fit

Providing a rationale for a fit measure at the person level requires acceptance of the first three assumptions: (1) plans can discriminate at the person level, (2) efficiency loss goes up with the square of the distortionary incentive, and (3) observed spending levels are equal to optimal levels. Our generalization has to do with assumption (4); more specifically, our modified metric generalizes the $R$-squared to account for other payment system features. In healthcare systems where predicted values from the risk adjustment model nearly fully capture payments, our generalized metric reduces to the $R$-squared from the risk adjustment model. When other payment features (e.g., risk sharing) are present, the metric takes them into account in a way consistent with assumptions (1)−(3).

The generalization is based on the simple idea that incentives are created by the relationship of plan revenues to costs. Revenues to a plan for a person are what matters for how much the plan chooses to allocate to that person, and the revenue function can have more components than the predicted values from the risk adjustment regression model. Payment system fit (PSF) is constructed by substituting the revenue a plan would receive for a person for the predicted value from the regression. Then, an $R$-squared-type measure describes the population-level individual fit of payments to costs. PSF measures the "explained variance" in costs accounted for by the full set of payment system features, not just the variance explained by the risk adjustment model (Box 5.1).

Geruso and McGuire (2016, p. 9) compare conventional $R$-squared fit with PSF in the US Marketplaces (using data from Marketscan, which are those used to calibrate Marketplace risk adjustment). Concurrent risk adjustment alone has an $R$-squared of 0.37. During 2014−16, plan payments in Marketplaces also included reinsurance. Adding the 2014 version of reinsurance (100% coverage after $45,000 in annual expenses), increases the PSF to 0.61. A conventional $R$-squared measure has no way to consider the fit of both elements when used in tandem.

### 5.2.3    Comments on Individual-Level Fit Measures

In spite of its tenuous basis as an economic efficiency metric, the $R$-squared from a risk adjustment regression remains a natural and easy-to-compute metric for the performance of a risk adjustment model. It is intuitive that

---

**BOX 5.1 Payment system fit**

PSF substitutes the simulated payment that a plan would receive for enrolling an individual for the predicted value from the risk adjustment regression model. In relation to the formula for the regression $R$-squared presented above ($R^2_{\mathrm{reg}}$), PSF replaces the predicted value $\hat{Y}_i$ with the revenue $R_i$ a plan receives for each person. Thus,

$$PSF = 1 - \frac{\sum_i (Y_i - R_i)^2}{\sum_i (Y_i - \overline{Y})^2} \tag{5.2}$$

This is analogous to an $R$-squared and is in fact equal to the $R$-squared if risk adjustment is the only factor determining plan payment. It differs from $R$-squared from a regression if plan revenues depend on other payment system features, such as through premium categories or risk sharing.

better fit at the person level should improve the performance of a payment system with respect to selection problems. In settings in which only relative risk scores from a regression model determine payments, and discrimination at the individual level is an issue, the $R$-squared has a sound basis in economics. It is a short hop from there to account for other payment system features, should they exist, within a concern for individual-level discrimination. Our proposed PSF makes that hop.

Replacing predicted values from the risk adjustment regression model by revenues a plan receives for an individual is called for even if the deviations are not squared and summed as in the $R$-squared. Other metrics of individual fit, such as the MAPE, also benefit by the generalization to PSF. Replacing simple predicted values with revenues that reflect predictions minus imputed premiums and risk sharing at the person level is also part of what we recommend for measures of fit at the group level, a topic we turn to next.[13]

## 5.3 MEASURES OF FIT AND INCENTIVES AT THE GROUP (OR ACTION) LEVEL

Restrictions on risk rating of premiums and open enrollment provisions in individual health insurance markets are intended to prevent health plans from discriminating on the basis of price or access to health insurance at the individual level. Health plans can, however, still take actions to discourage or encourage enrollment by targeted groups of consumers, referred to in the research literature as "indirect selection," "service-level selection," "supply-side selection," or "cream skimming."[14] The potential for this type of insurer behavior raises two key questions: "What groups?" and "What actions?" The answers to these questions will depend on the market being studied. For example, in the Netherlands, individuals reporting low health status or multiple chronic illnesses have been identified as potential targets for plan underservice (Van Kleef et al., 2013a,b; Eijkenaar et al., 2018). In the United States, researchers have studied users of particular classes of drugs (Carey, 2017a,b; Han and Lavetti, 2017; Geruso et al., 2017), users of certain hospitals (Shepard, 2016), users of certain types of services (Ellis and McGuire, 2007; McGuire et al., 2014), and population subgroups such as nursing home residents and amputees (Pope et al., 2011).

At the close of this section we will recommend that for this purpose groups be defined on the basis of discriminatory actions available to plans in the market under study. We will also explain that for a tactic to be effective as a selection device, it must be recognized by consumers (otherwise they do not respond). We begin with a discussion of some of the general issues regarding measurement of incentives to discriminate against (or in favor of) a group of potential enrollees.

The risk of under- and overservice for certain groups of enrollees is well-recognized by architects of health plan payment systems. In Europe, incentives to serve certain groups (e.g., those with multiple chronic illnesses) is typically assessed by measuring over- and undercompensation for a group. Researchers in the US concerned with the same issue form a ratio rather than a difference between predicted values and costs.

This section first presents the rationale for group-fit measures such as over/undercompensation and predictive ratios. We note some shortcomings of these measures and suggest three lines of improvement: (1) recognizing other elements of the payment system (as in Section 5.2 and fit at the person level), (2) developing a comprehensive plan-wide measure of group fit covering the service of interest as well as all others, and (3) improving the measure of plan incentives by recognizing that incentives created by a given amount of over- and undercompensation will differ for different people.

### 5.3.1 Rationale for Over-/Undercompensation and Predictive Ratio Measures

Presently used metrics to assess incentives at the group level compare predicted values from a risk-adjustment regression to actual costs for a defined group of consumers. We will thus refer to these as measures of group (as opposed to individual) level fit. An example would be a group of consumers who used home care in a previous period. The question these measures address is, "Does the payment system adequately pay plans for enrollees who used home care in a previous period?" The concern is that if the system does not pay adequately, a plan might take actions to discourage membership from among this group, by, e.g., unduly restricting access to home-care services.

As in the previous section, let $\hat{Y}_i$ be the predicted value from the risk adjustment regression for individual $i$, and $Y_i$ be $i$'s actual cost. Let $i \in g$ indicate the individuals in the group, $g$, of concern, and $n_g$ be the number of consumers in group $g$. A commonly used measure of possible over- or undercompensation for group g is:[15]

$$\text{Over/Undercompensation} = \frac{\sum_{i \in g}\left(\hat{Y}_i - Y_i\right)}{n_g} \qquad (5.3)$$

The over/undercompensation measure is the average for group g and is measured in monetary terms (e.g., euros or dollars). When Eq. (5.3) is positive it indicates overcompensation and when it is negative, undercompensation.

A predictive ratio uses the same elements:

$$\text{Predictive ratio} = \frac{\sum_{i \in g}\hat{Y}_i}{\sum_{i \in g}Y_i} \qquad (5.4)$$

The predictive ratio is a unit-free number. When Eq. (5.4) is greater than 1.0 it indicates overcompensation, and when less than 1.0, undercompensation.

Over/undercompensation and predictive ratios are both useful measures of group-level incentives. We will, however, argue in favor of modifying them to better reflect the full set of payment system features. The usual interpretation of these metrics is that if over/undercompensation is near zero, or the predictive ratio is near one, a plan has little incentive to discriminate in favor or against members of group g. As overcompensation grows more positive (negative) or the predictive ratio goes above (below) one, a plan has an incentive to attract (deter) members of the group. Expression (5.3) makes clear that over/undercompensation is a group-level measure, which is appropriate if insurer actions operate at the group level.

Over/undercompensation, either in the form of a difference or a ratio, is routinely assessed for selected groups in many risk adjustment contexts. For example, Van Kleef et al. (2013a,b) merged survey information with health claims for a subset of people in the Netherlands to calculate "undercompensation" (defined as the difference in costs and predicted revenue rather than their ratio) for various groups of people, including those with low physical and mental health scores and those with chronic conditions. They compare seven different risk adjustment models with different sets of explanatory variables. For the risk-adjustment model used in US Marketplaces, Kautter et al. (2014, E22) computed predictive ratios for various subgroups defined by predicted costs. In their evaluation of the CMS-HCC model, Pope et al. (2011) report predictive ratios for a large number of subgroups, including groups defined by disease, numbers of prior hospitalizations, demographic characteristics, and others.

Other papers assess the evidence for service-level distortions without measuring the incentives to engage in service-level selection. Cao and McGuire (2003) in Medicare and Eggleston and Bir (2009) in employer-based insurance find patterns of spending on various services consistent with service-level selection among competing at-risk plans.

Some papers do both, assessing incentives and checking for evidence of under/oversupply. Ellis et al. (2013a) rank services according to incentives to undersupply them. Consistent with service-level selection, they show that HMO-type plans tend to underspend on predictable and predictive services (in relation to the average) just as the selection index predicts. This pattern of spending is not observed among enrollees in non-HMOs.

A number of recent papers focus on groups defined by use of a certain class of drugs. The "action" here is a plan's decision to cover a group of drugs generously or not by tier placement on the drug formulary. This active area of recent research confirms that with respect to this readily measured "action," payment models create incentives and plans respond. In particular, plans distort coverage to attract the healthy and avoid the sick. Carey (2017a,b), and Han and Lavetti (2017) study incentives for selection in Medicare Part D and document evidence that Part D insurers respond to those incentives when designing their drug formularies. Other recent work has focused on identifying evidence of service-level selection among Marketplace plan formulary contracts. Geruso et al. (2016) use data on Marketplace plan and self-insured employer plan formularies to determine whether differences between Marketplace formularies (where selection incentives are strong) and employer formularies (where there are no selection incentives) correspond to the strength and the direction of the selection incentive associated with a particular drug class. They find that selection incentives are minimal in this setting due to a well-functioning payment system, but for the drugs where payment "errors" exist, they find robust evidence that Marketplace plans severely limit coverage and access for drug classes that are used by the most unprofitable enrollees.

Finally, another recent paper analyzes groups defined by their use of a particular "star" hospital system in Boston. Shepard (2016) shows that people who switch plans in response to one plan's decision to drop the hospital system from its network have costs that greatly exceed the revenue they bring to the plan. Using counterfactual simulations, he finds that in equilibrium, this underpayment would lead to this star hospital system being dropped from all health plan provider networks, a finding that has effectively played out in this market in recent years.[16]

## 5.3.2 Identifying Potential Actions and Groups of Interest

In thinking about group-level measures, what groups are relevant? How should a population be grouped with respect to incentives for plans to act at the group level? Some years ago, Newhouse (1993) defined risk selection as "actions by consumers and health plans to exploit unpriced risk heterogeneity..." A key word in this definition is "actions." Plan actions to exploit unpriced risk heterogeneity consist of tactics to discourage enrollment of the unprofitable and encourage enrollment of the profitable. Groups should therefore be defined as those that may be affected by a plan action. For example, if plans can *only* take actions that discriminate between people under the age of 65 and those above the age of 65, these become the groups of concern when it comes to (measuring) risk selection (incentives). If plans can only discriminate on the basis of "yes/no chronic condition" then these are the two relevant groups. If health plans can discriminate on combinations of "yes/no >65" and "yes/no chronic condition," there will be four groups of concern, and so on.

Some research defines groups according to geography under the thinking that a health plan might favor or disfavor certain regions because of systematic regional differences in medical spending, as was done in a study of risk selection in Germany by Bauhoff (2012). Other research defines groups according to the services used, the idea being that a health plan could favor or disfavor primary versus some kinds of specialty care, e.g., to encourage/discourage potential enrollees anticipating making use of those services.[17] Studies of selection and drug formulary design discussed in the previous section typically assume that insurer actions take place at the level of the drug class (Carey, 2017a,b; Geruso et al., 2017; Han and Lavetti, 2017). Studies of selection and network design assume insurer actions take place at the level of the hospital or physician group (Shepard, 2016).

Since the instruments for health plans to engage in risk selection differ across healthcare schemes, there is no universal set of relevant groups. Thus, an important step for evaluating incentives for risk selection in a particular setting is to identify the possible selection actions in that setting and to derive the relevant groups. For example, in the Netherlands health plans are unable to discriminate at the individual level due to open enrollment requirements. On the other hand, plans can discriminate across groups on the basis of network design. For example, contracting with first-best physicians for treatment of disease X will attract patients with disease X; conversely, a poor network in terms of quality or convenience will deter patients in that disease group. When a plan can make a network decision hospital-by-hospital, study of groups defined by those using individual hospitals may be called for.

Van de Ven et al. (2015) identify a number of specific selection actions in the Netherlands that can occur as a consequence of over/undercompensation, including selective advertising, offering choice of deductible, making supplementary insurance (un)attractive for certain groups, offering group contracts, and quality skimping on certain services. To measure the incentives involved requires a designation of the group affected. Advertising may be targeted to certain populations, e.g., young families, or group contracts may be offered to only selected groups among the population.

An important corollary of this discussion is that if there is no action a plan can take with respect to a group, there is no point, and indeed, it may be misleading, to construct incentive measures for that group.

### 5.3.3 Generalizing Over-/Undercompensation and Predictive Ratios to Include Other Elements of Plan Payment

Once the simulated payment amount for each person is available, ratio and difference measures of over- and undercompensation can be easily modified to incorporate other plan payment features, such as risk sharing, a modification that improves the validity of the measures of incentives at the group level. Incentives to a plan to attract/deter members of a group are governed by net revenues. Inclusion of all elements of net revenues yields the valid measure of these incentives.

McGuire et al. (2014) modify predictive ratios incorporating premium differences and risk sharing in the US Marketplaces. The numerator of the "payment system predictive ratio" for a subgroup is the sum of the payments for the group (which can depend on all payment system features) rather than the regression predicted values. The denominator in these predictive ratio measures remains the actual costs for the groups. Geruso et al. (2016) modify predictive ratios and under/overcompensation measures in the same way.

### 5.3.4 Generalizing Group Fit to the Entire Population

Studies of fit at the group level typically report under/overcompensation or predictive ratios for a subset of the population (e.g., those with a chronic illness). When predictive ratios are computed for the entire population (e.g., those with a chronic illness and those without a chronic illness), the statistics are not summed or aggregated in any way to provide an *overall measure* of fit at the group level. By contrast, the PSF measure noted above for assessing fit at the person level summarizes fit for the entire population (in the form of the reduction in sum of squares of the payment-cost residuals).

A summary measure may be useful for group fit as well. While we can agree that reducing undercompensation for a group of interest is an improvement for that particular group, what if a payment system alternative decreases undercompensation for one group but increases it for another? Which alternative is preferred? If payment alternatives are all subject to the same overall budget constraint, moving payments more towards one group inevitably lowers payments for another group. This could be a good thing if the group experiencing lower payments was initially overpaid; it would be a bad thing if the group were initially underpaid and the policy change exacerbated an underpayment problem.

A group-level measure analogous to the individual-level measure discussed above is a natural way to summarize group fit at the population level (Van Kleef et al., 2017). Suppose potential actions by a plan allow health plans to discriminate among G mutually exclusive groups indexed by g with $g = 1, \ldots, G$. We can then use data to determine:

$s_g$   the share of the population in group g, with $\sum_g s_g = 1$,
$\overline{R}_g$   the average plan revenue for a person in group $g$,
$\overline{Y}_g$   the average plan cost for a person in group $g$,
$\overline{R}_g - \overline{Y}_g$   the average under/overcompensation for a person in group $g$.

Given these parameters, under- and overcompensations can be summarized in several different ways. One possibility is $\sum_g s_g |\overline{R}_g - \overline{Y}_g|$, i.e., the sum of absolute under- and overcompensations weighted by the size of the groups as a share of the population. As this metric falls, fit improves.

Most closely analogous to the PSF measure above, however, is a group fit measure that weights the squared group-level payment-cost residuals and is scaled to fall between zero and one (like an *R*-squared or a PSF). Our measure is analogous to the one presented by Ash et al. (1989), who measured regression fit at the group level by a grouped *R*-squared. We generalize this measure and call it the group payment system fit (GPSF) because it incorporates other payment features.

$$GPSF = 1 - \frac{\sum_g s_g \left(\overline{Y}_g - \overline{R}_g\right)^2}{\sum_g s_g \left(\overline{Y}_g - \overline{Y}\right)^2} \tag{5.5}$$

The denominator of Eq. (5.5) is the total sum of squared residuals at the group level. The numerator is the sum of squared group-level residuals after the payment system is in place. Analogous to an $R$-squared or PSF measure at the individual level, $0 \leq GPSF \leq 1$, with higher values indicating the payment system is doing a better job at matching revenues to costs at the group level.

Squaring the group-level payment-cost residuals has a grounding in welfare economics, where the efficiency loss associated with a price distortion (such as a tax) is proportional to the square of the distortion at the group level. A related argument supporting raising the group-level residual to a power greater than 1.0 comes from Van Barneveld et al. (2000), who contend that small predictable profits and losses are likely to be irrelevant for a health plan. Selection can be costly and the net benefits are uncertain, and small incentives may simply not induce a health plan to act.

Depending on the institutional circumstances, other functions of the group-level payment-cost residuals may be justified. Van de Ven et al. (2015) point out that overcompensation may lead to an improvement in quality, whereas undercompensation leads to a deterioration of quality. It may be that undercompensation is worse than overcompensation. A metric to represent this would be the group population-weighted sum of only the negative deviations (squared or not), similar to that used in Shen and Ellis (2002).[18]

In the end, while we believe squaring and summing group-level errors with population weights is a natural way to measure incentives around group fit, depending on the circumstances, researchers may justify and choose other functions of the weighted residuals.

### 5.3.5   Taking Account of Consumer Response

Measures based on predictive ratios or under/overcompensation are missing a key element of selection incentives: how consumers (in a group) will respond to the action in question. If consumers cannot or simply do not respond to the action in question, the plan has no incentive to take it, even if the group in question is under- or overcompensated. Here is a simple example. Suppose the targeted group is young families for whom a plan is overcompensated. The action is advertising in newspapers and television. If young people do not respond (perhaps because they get their news elsewhere) to newspaper advertising, in spite of the overpayment, plans have no incentive to take the action of newspaper advertising.

The same point applies to healthcare services. Unless consumers respond to skimping or overprovision of services, the plan has no incentive to take the action. Another example is the following: suppose plans are undercompensated for members who use ambulance services during a year. But suppose also that use of an ambulance cannot be anticipated by consumers. Specifically, consumers do not know whether they are at high or low risk for using an ambulance. In that case, skimping on ambulance services will not disproportionately discourage enrollment by the group for which the plan was undercompensated. Indeed, the more consumers can correctly anticipate that they will or will not be users of a certain service, the more effective an action on that service will be with respect to separating risks. Well-baby care will be very appealing to young families anticipating have a child, but irrelevant to young couples who have decided not to have children. Young families might well know into what group they fall. More generally, it is the profitability of the consumers whose choice to enroll in a plan is marginal to the plan's decision of how much of a particular service to provide who matter for plan incentives (Veiga and Weyl, 2016). Consumers whose plan choice does not depend on the plan's actions with respect to the service do not matter, even if they are heavy utilizers of the service in question.

With that qualification in mind, it remains true that services affecting those with a chronic illness are likely to be effective selection tools. The idea of a chronic illness is that it is persistent, and therefore likely to be anticipated. Those with diabetes this year are very likely to have diabetes next year, and these people are likely to be well-aware of their health situation. In this case, plan choice of those with diabetes are very likely affected by the level of diabetes-related services offered by the plan. Restricting access to care important to consumers with diabetes is thus likely to be an effective strategy, should plans be undercompensated for this group.

A key factor in determining whether a consumer is likely to respond to changes in the level of a service offered by a plan is likely to be the "predictability" of the service. Research papers in health economics have studied the role of predictability of healthcare use by consumers and its role in incentives to plans to under/over provide services (Ellis and McGuire, 2007). Because predictability is measureable, at least in part, the concept has played a prominent role in measuring which services are more likely to affect consumer plan choices. In the research literature, the total selection incentive is measured by combining a measure of over/undercompensation with a measure of how well consumers can anticipate their use of a service. Research papers show that the incentive to select against a service is a function of its predictability, how well it predicts profitability (termed its "predictiveness"), the variation of profits, and the demand elasticity.[19]

### 5.3.6 Summary Comments About Action/Group-Level Measures of Incentives

In summary, one of the key distortions that plan payment systems are designed to combat is distortions to health insurance contracts to attract profitable enrollees and deter enrollment by unprofitable ones. An insurer's incentive to distort its plans in such a way is related to the extent to which a group is over/undercompensated. The extent to which over/undercompensation matters for a given group depends on (1) whether an insurer can target the group in some way, (2) whether members of the group would respond to distortions targeted at them, and (3) the size of the over/undercompensation. We developed measures of incentives for insurers to engage in these distortions where the researcher determines (1) and (2), while (3) is estimated from data.

## 5.4 MEASURES OF INCENTIVES FOR CONSUMERS TO CHOOSE THE RIGHT PLAN

Many individual health insurance markets allow for a variety of plan types (e.g., more/less coverage, variation in network design, or other differences) for the purpose of serving consumer preferences and rewarding plans for successful innovation. In the Netherlands, consumers can choose among plans with a range of deductibles, with lower premiums associated with higher-deductible plans. Dutch plans also contract with different networks of providers. In the US Marketplaces, consumers choose among metal levels with a gold plan covering a larger share of costs than a silver plan, which in turn covers more than a bronze. Marketplace plans also construct different provider networks. An element of the efficiency of the market for health insurance is to encourage consumers to enroll in the "right" plan for them, defined as the plan that offers them the most net benefits over cost. This is not only a static issue; it is also important in a dynamic framework with innovation. As consumers move to plans with better value, incentives are conveyed to the plans to innovate in ways to improve value to consumers.

Using consumer choice to reward high-value plans and punish low-value plans is the essence of the "competition" element of Enthoven's vision of "managed competition." If plans innovate by improving value, it might be more expensive and they would have to charge more, but if the innovation is worth more than the cost consumers will reward the plan with enrollment. If plans innovate by reducing costs, competition will press them to pass on the savings to consumers in the form of lower premiums. In this setting, with consumers facing different prices approximating the costs of the alternative insurance products, Enthoven argued that the market would lead to an efficient allocation of consumers across plans. There are two factors that interfere with a market producing the premiums that lead to efficient choice of plans. We explain these, and how to measure the problems they cause, after first describing what efficient pricing looks like.

## 5.4.1 Efficient Premium Pricing

We now turn to the role that premium pricing plays in influencing efficient enrollee plan choices. It is worth recognizing up front that no health insurance market could realistically achieve the set of premium prices necessary to fully meet the ideal of efficient sorting of consumers across plans. To see this, consider a simple setting with just two plans, Plan A and Plan B, with somewhat different characteristics. For concreteness, suppose Plan A offers full coverage and Plan B has a large deductible. Consumers are heterogeneous in their costs (at each plan) and in their tastes with respect to the presence of a deductible (because of risk aversion or other reasons).

Consumer 1 "should be" in Plan A if that consumer's extra or incremental valuation of Plan A with the full coverage is greater than the incremental plan cost Consumer 1 would incur in a plan without a deductible compared to one with a deductible. This rule for efficiency leads consumers to the plan in which their benefits most exceeds the costs.[20] The same statement of efficient sorting could be made for consumers, 2, 3, ... N. It is immediately clear that in the case where each consumer faced a price difference (referred to in the literature as an incremental price) between the two plans equal to *that particular consumer's cost difference in plan cost* between the plans, consumers will sort efficiently.[21] If consumer 7 certainly will go over the deductible, the incremental price to 7 is approximately the deductible,[22] and, at that price, 7 would choose whether Plan A is preferred at that price, and this choice would be efficient. If consumer 11 faces a low probability of having any medical spending, the price to 11 should be much lower. 11 might prefer choice and be willing to choose A at the premium right for her. If consumers 7 and 11 face the same incremental price for Plan A, the resulting choices may not be efficient. This is the "single-premium problem" in the research literature (Bundorf et al., 2012; Geruso, 2017). Generally, no single premium can sort consumers efficiently between two plans.[23]

## 5.4.2 First Source of Deviation From Efficient Pricing: Limited Premium Categories

It is obviously not realistic to expect a market, regulated or not, to generate incremental premiums to be person-specific, even in this simple setting of just two plans. Asymmetric information can be one barrier. Consumers may know if they are likely to be high cost but some of this information may be unavailable to plans. More important, however, is that regulation constrains plan risk rating. As shown in Part II of this volume, in most markets with

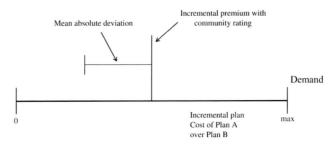

**FIGURE 5.2** A community-rated premium leads to a large average gap between the incremental premium and incremental costs.

regulated competition, risk-rating of premiums is proscribed for purposes of fairness and access. It is understood that such regulation comes at some cost in terms of efficiency,[24] but this cost is generally regarded as tolerable in exchange for the gain in fairness achieved by having the healthy subsidize the sick in health insurance purchase.[25] Even so, there are alternatives for regulating premiums in pursuit of fairness, e.g., subsidizing the sick by a special risk pool, allowing age bands or not, restricting differences between the old and the young, etc.; but there are always unavoidable tradeoffs between fairness and efficiency. It is therefore worthwhile to be able to measure the comparative efficiency in terms of sorting of the various approaches to fairness.

The discussion here is in terms of *incremental* plan costs, *incremental* benefits, and *incremental* premiums. Incremental plan costs of a person refer to the *difference* in plan costs (not the total or out-of-pocket cost) for that person between plans; incremental benefits refer to the person's individual subjective *difference* in the valuation of alternative plans. Incremental premiums are differences in premiums in a market and will be group- rather than person-specific. For example, if the community-rated premium for Plan A is 800 euros per month and the community-rated premium for Plan B is 600 euros, the incremental premium—the amount a consumer can save by choosing the lower-priced plan—is 200 euros.[26]

The intuition behind the measure we propose for the inefficiency associated with limited premium categories can be illustrated in Fig. 5.2, which shows, in the case of two plans (again, Plan A and Plan B), the distribution of the incremental cost of consumers in Plan A compared to Plan B along the horizontal axis. We assume these differences are all positive (Plan A costs more for everyone), and that the incremental costs are distributed uniformly on the line. (Neither of these simplifications is important for the argument.) As was said in the previous section, if each consumer faced an incremental premium between the plans equal to her specific difference in cost, all consumers would sort themselves efficiently between Plans A and B.

Suppose premiums are community-rated so that premiums are different for Plan A and Plan B, but everyone pays the same premium for each plan. If Plan A drew a representative set of consumers from the population, the difference in average cost between Plan A and Plan B would be the average of the incremental costs. With competition, the premium difference for Plan A compared to Plan B would then also be the average of the incremental cost differences, shown in Fig. 5.2 as a vertical line at the midpoint (the average) of the incremental costs. Except in special cases, this incremental premium will not lead to efficient sorting: the premium difference is too high for the consumers to the left of the vertical line and too low for the consumers to the right. Too few of the low-cost consumers are likely to choose Plan A and too many of the high-cost consumers will choose Plan A (we come back to the implications of this for premiums shortly).

Measures of the misaligned incentive from community rating are based on the gap between the efficient incremental premium (the person's incremental plan cost) and the incremental premium they face because of community rating, a measure analogous to the "price distortion" measure common in welfare economics. This gap can be summed (or averaged) in a linear accounting of the distortion, or greater deviations can be given more weight by squaring the gaps before summing. The mean absolute deviation of the distribution of incremental cost, the expected value of this divergence, is the linear measure of the gap. The mean absolute deviation is shown in Fig. 5.2. The quadratic measure would square the differences before summing to yield the variance of the incremental cost distribution.

We now illustrate how this premium efficiency measure can be used to compare policy alternatives. Suppose instead of community rating, regulators set two premium categories, one for the young and one for the old. Assume there are equal numbers of young and old in the population. Since the old tend to be more costly, raising the incremental price for the old and lowering it for the young will tend to improve the match between the incremental premium consumers face and their incremental cost. More young, facing a lower incremental premium, will be induced to correctly choose Plan A and

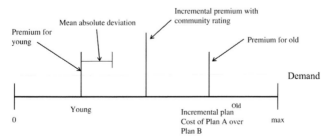

**FIGURE 5.3** Risk rating by age reduces the average gap between incremental premiums and incremental costs.

fewer old, facing a higher incremental premium, will be correctly discouraged from choosing the more generous plan.

The change in the average gap between prices and incremental costs measures the improvement in sorting incentives achieved by risk rating by old and young. Fig. 5.3 shows consumers divided into the young and old, and to keep the illustration simple, the young are assumed to be to the left with lower incremental costs and the old are to the right with higher incremental costs. If we allow risk rating by these two age categories, the incremental premium for the young will fall at the midpoint of the young distribution of incremental costs and the incremental premium for the old will fall in the middle of the old distribution, as shown in the figure. The figure also shows that the new mean absolute deviation (which is the same for the young and the old), is smaller than the standard deviation with community rating. In this example, the mean absolute deviation falls to exactly half of the previous value. We could also use a squared measure of the deviations in terms of the variance of the gap between incremental costs and premiums, and that would also fall. In this example, the variance would fall to one-quarter of the previous level.

This example makes clear that a measure of the fit of incremental premiums to incremental costs is the natural way to measure how well a set of premium categories conveys efficient incentives to consumers regarding choice of plan.[27] Following the approaches proposed earlier in this chapter, we measure fit of (incremental) premiums to (incremental) costs with a linear and a quadratic metric.

The linear measure is the MAPE associated with a set of premium categories, normalized by the MAPE with a single community-rated premium (equal to the difference in average cost). Taking one minus this measure transforms it into a measure with range 0 to 1 with higher values better (like other measures of fit):

$$\text{Premium MAPE} = 1 - \frac{\sum_i |\Delta Y_i - \Delta P_i|}{\sum_i |\Delta Y_i - \overline{\Delta Y_i}|} \qquad (5.6)$$

The premium MAPE in Eq. (5.6) linearly accumulates the individual-level price distortions associated with a given payment system. In making such a summation, it may be easier to think of $i$ as representing types of individuals, who have an average or expected incremental cost, than $i$ representing each person.

A case can be made that the metric should be quadratic rather than linear. In that case the measure is simply the $R$-squared from a regression of incremental costs on incremental premiums. Obviously, one incremental premium (the average) explains none of the variance. As the premium categories bring incremental premiums closer to incremental costs, the fit improves. We call the quadratic measure premium $R$-squared, also normalized and subtracted from one (like a conventional $R$-squared):

$$\text{Premium } R^2 = 1 - \frac{\sum_i (\Delta Y_i - \Delta P_i)^2}{\sum_i (\Delta Y_i - \overline{\Delta Y_i})^2} \tag{5.7}$$

Although simple and intuitive, there are three notable limitations to both the linear and quadratic measures presented in Eqs. (5.6) and (5.7), respectively, which limit the applicability of our metric in many settings. First, as is the case with all the ex ante measures presented in this chapter, Eqs. (5.6) and (5.7) stop short of measuring welfare loss due to adverse selection. Instead, they measure price distortions. A measure of welfare requires information (or assumptions) about demand/willingness to pay, and demand response. In particular, these price distortions do not *necessarily* lead to inefficient sorting: While a price equal to the individual's incremental cost ensures efficient sorting, there is an infinite number of other prices that will result in the individual making the same choice. However, while other prices induce efficient sorting only under a specific level of demand/willingness-to-pay, the incremental cost induces efficient sorting under *any* level of demand, making it the natural benchmark with which to evaluate price distortions.

Second, measures (5.6) and (5.7) require information not readily available in claims data, including information about incremental costs and equilibrium premiums under different regulatory regimes. Estimating incremental costs between plans would likely need to be done by making assumptions about the demand response of different individuals to alternative plan designs.[28] Evaluation of payment systems at the market design stage, prior to observing market equilibrium, or evaluating alternative payment systems different from the system currently in use also requires an estimate of the equilibrium incremental premiums, as these premiums are not observed. The analyst needs to make an assumption about what they would look like under the modified payment system rules.

Finally, individual health insurance markets are likely to have a number of types of plans. The expressions (5.6) and (5.7) can be generalized to multiple plan types, by, e.g., measuring incremental costs for all plans relative to a base plan, but this might get complicated fast as the number of plan types proliferates. We recommend the analyst choose two plans, those representing the most important choice facing the largest body of consumers. In some markets, this will be natural—MA versus traditional Medicare, a Silver plan versus a Gold plan in the Marketplaces, a high versus a low deductible plan in the Netherlands—but in other settings, some consideration will be necessary to make the choice. Once the two plans are chosen, *incremental premiums* can be observed for each person. For two plans in the community-rated Netherlands, e.g., this is simply the difference in the plans' premiums.

### 5.4.3 Second Source of Deviation From Efficient Pricing: Adverse Selection

The second source of deviation from efficient pricing is due to adverse selection. As we noted above in our discussion of Fig. 5.2, with community rating (or, even with other limited premium categories), too few of the low-cost and too many of the high-cost members of an insurance pool will tend to

---

**BOX 5.2 Theoretical and empirical literature on adverse selection and the inefficiency of plan pricing**

Building on work by Cutler and Reber (1998), Einav and Finkelstein (EF) and their colleagues have proposed an elegant and influential model of sorting between two plan types (Einav and Finkelstein, 2011; Einav et al., 2010a). The population is ordered by their willingness to pay for the more generous plan. Adverse (or favorable) selection is related to the slope of the average cost curve (the average of the incremental costs as a function of incremental price of the more generous plan). With competition and average cost pricing, the more generous plan sets too high a price and too few consumers join the plan. This form of pricing with a feedback loop between selection and pricing can lead to the dreaded "death spiral" for the generous option in health insurance markets (Cutler and Reber, 1998).

With empirical estimates of the shapes of the demand and cost curves, the EF model can be used to estimate a welfare triangle related to the inefficiency of pricing due to adverse selection. The EF framework has been frequently applied to study premiums and efficient sorting of consumers among plans. For example, Hackmann et al. (2015) use the EF model to evaluate the welfare consequences of the Massachusetts health care reform of 2006, the precursor to the national reform. Kowalski (2014) applies the HKK version of the EFC model to estimate the welfare consequences of the implementation of the ACA.

EF-type models have also recently been applied to MA. Cabral et al. (2014) use a modified version of the EF framework to estimate the extent of selection into MA, finding little evidence of selection on the margin. Curto et al. (2014) also estimate important structural elements of demand and cost using changes in MA premiums over time, again finding little evidence of selection into MA at the margin (as premiums move up and down) but, on average, costs were lower in MA, even after risk adjustment, by 2%–3%. More recently, Glazer and McGuire (2017) use the EF conceptual framework to derive the implications for setting the level of subsidy to MA plans.

Note that the EF model is concerned with the second form of pricing problem, that due to selection, and not the first, due to limited premium categories. Welfare losses estimated with the EF framework thus are only a partial measure of the welfare loss from inefficient premium pricing. Bundorf et al. (2012) and Geruso (2017) use a more general framework to study the interaction between premium regulation and selection, highlighting the issues we discuss here.

choose Plan A, the more generous plan in our example. With the more generous plan drawing an adverse selection of the risks, it must price higher not just for its more generous coverage, but for the higher costs of the risks the plan attracts. Efficient sorting is promoted when Plan A prices higher for its more generous benefits—this is the incremental plan cost standard. Efficient sorting is undermined when Plan A prices higher because it draws more expensive risks (Einav et al., 2010a). Some of the highly developed theoretical and empirical literature on this subject is summarized in Box 5.2.

We do not anticipate that policy researchers will have, ex ante, a measure of the degree of adverse selection in the relevant individual health insurance market. Rather than basing a measure on the extent of the problem (which will typically not be known), we base our measure on the degree to which the payment system, including risk adjustment and any risk sharing, addresses the problem. Risk adjustment, and other plan payment features such as reinsurance, transfer funds from plans attracting healthier enrollees to plans attracting sicker, more expensive enrollees. This transfer requires the plans with the healthier pool (likely the plan with lower premiums/less generous coverage) to raise its premium and enables the plans with the sicker pool (those with more generous coverage) to lower their premiums. Risk adjustment transfers thus counteract the adverse selection effect, raising the incremental premium in the less generous plan and reducing the degree to which the incremental premium difference is affected by selection.

The previously discussed PSF from Eq. (5.2) is a suitable measure of how much the payment system contributes to blunting the problems adverse selection causes for premium setting. Our approach here is to note that there is a second reason to be interested in PSF: it is also a good measure of how the payment system contends with adverse selection and premium pricing.

### 5.4.4 Summary Comments on Measures of Incentives for Efficient Sorting

The issue of the efficiency of plan sorting has different importance in different institutional settings. The underlying problem of efficient sorting is less salient in health insurance markets where the differences among the plans are small, as, e.g., in Germany where plans have the same regulated benefit package and can do little in terms of selective contracting or managed care. In such a setting, the fairness associated with community rating comes at a small cost in inefficient sorting. In other settings, however, available plans differ considerably, and there the efficiency cost of the fairness of community rating is higher. In some cases some fairness can be maintained even with efficient incremental pricing. Box 5.3 explains this with an example showing the fairness improvement with some risk adjustment and risk rating only the incremental premium.

> **BOX 5.3 Risk rating of incremental premiums can combine with fairness-related subsidy of higher-cost groups**
>
> Suppose the population is half young and half old, with cost structure in Plans A and B as follows:
>
> | | Costs | |
> |---|---|---|
> | | Young | Old |
> | Plan A | 100 | 200 |
> | Plan B | 150 | 300 |
>
> Risk rating of Plan A and B premiums would lead the old to have to pay more than the young for both Plan A (200 vs 100) and for Plan B (300 vs 150). This would lead to efficient sorting of both groups between the plans because the incremental premium for the young to join Plan B (50 = 150–100) and for the old (100 = 300 − 200) is equal to the incremental cost for each group. It may be regarded to be unfair that the old pay more than the young.
>
> An alternative is to make Plan A free to both groups (preserving fairness). The regulator then pays Plan B 100 for every young that joins and 200 for every old (these are the group costs in Plan A). If we then allow Plan B to risk rate, the young will be charged 50 for Plan B and the old will be charged 100, ensuring efficient sorting.

## 5.5   MEASURES OF INCENTIVES FOR COST CONTROL

An important objective of managed competition is conveying incentives to health plans to control costs. Making a fixed payment to a plan per person per month is intended to do just that. It is clear, as we discussed in Chapter 4, Risk Sharing, that risk sharing in plan payment with, e.g., reinsurance, reduces a plan's incentives to control costs. Traditionally, diagnosis-based risk adjustment has not been seen as also sacrificing incentives for cost-control incentives, under the premise that risk adjustment compensates for patient characteristics rather than services provided (Pope et al., 2011). This position, however, is not correct. In risk adjustment formulas with diagnosis-based risk adjustment, plan revenues are *not* independent of cost. After a very brief reminder about risk sharing and incentives for cost control, this section explains why diagnosis-based risk adjustment also dilutes incentives, and then proposes a metric, incorporating the effects of both risk sharing and risk adjustment, for measuring the degree to which a payment system deviates from full incentives to control costs.

### 5.5.1   Risk Sharing Affects Incentives for Cost Control

Section 4.4.1 was titled, "The Share of Dollars/Euros Touched by Risk-Sharing Measures Incentives Affected," telling the story of how the effect of risk sharing on incentives can be measured. For example, a common form of risk sharing is reinsurance. If the reinsurance attachment point implies 5% of the costs are above the attachment point, and if the reinsurance share is 80%, the share of dollars/euros touched by risk sharing is 80% of 5%, or 4%. As we say in Section 4.4.1, the idea of this simple measure is that a plan would have incentives to reduce costs to the degree that it was responsible for those costs, and it is responsible in this example for 96% of the costs, so would retain, with this reinsurance example, very strong incentives to contain costs.

### 5.5.2   Diagnosis-Based Risk Adjustment Affects Incentives for Cost Control

It is important to dispel the belief that paying plans by health status risk-adjusted capitation leaves cost-control incentives unaffected. The belief would hold true if the capitation payment were based on age and gender (or other characteristics independent of utilization), but predominantly, risk classification systems are based on diagnoses that emerge with healthcare treatments. In practice, the conditions used to determine risk adjustment are established during provider—patient interactions in which a claim is generated. For example, in the CMS-HCC system paying MA plans in the US Medicare system, a single physician office visit at which a patient receives a new diagnosis of "diabetes without complications" changes a patient's risk score and results in an additional payment of approximately $1500 annually. The visit generating the diagnosis, and the follow-up events the visit triggers, such as further diagnostic testing, are components of cost to the plan, creating a link between payments a plan receives from risk adjustment and the plan's realized costs. Thus, utilization affects both costs and risk-adjusted payments, implying that insurers are compensated at least in part for their patients' utilization. The diabetes case is of course not an isolated example; diagnoses emerge only in the course of diagnostic visits or treatment so that plans are paid more when new diagnosis-generating health care takes place. This is true in concurrent risk adjustment systems, such as in the US Marketplaces, and in prospective systems used in most other settings in which diagnoses are from a previous period, so long as the enrollee has some likelihood of remaining enrolled in the plan.

The connection between a prospective capitation payment and plan spending is obvious in systems that use some explicit indicator of costs as a risk adjustor. As noted in Chapter 4, Risk Sharing, Van Kleef and Van Vliet (2012) compared a form of high-risk pooling with the option of including "membership in the high-risk group" as a risk adjustor in the Dutch equalization model. Presently, the Dutch system includes risk adjuster variables that provide insurers with additional compensation for consumers who were in the top 15% of the spending distribution in each of the three preceding years. As long as there is some continuity in plan enrollment, it may be financially attractive for plans to provide extra care to individuals in order to induce them to exceed the cost threshold and assure assignment to the high-risk group.

The degree to which cost-containment incentives are affected by health-status-based risk adjustment can be measured (and ultimately compared to the incentive of other plan payment options such as risk sharing). Building on analysis of the incentive effects of hospital "prospective payment" by McClellan (1997), who measured the de facto risk sharing in the DRG payment system to hospitals, Geruso and McGuire (2016) in the US Marketplaces and Schmid and Beck (2016) in Switzerland measure the de facto cost sharing in risk adjustment payment systems by simulation methods. These papers ask: suppose some component of health care were not provided to a patient during a year. How much would this affect the payment the plan receives for the person? Averaged over the experience of a group of enrollees, the payment reduction associated with the cost reduction describes the portion of the costs shared by the regulator (or by the market depending on the risk-sharing modality). In a fully cost-based system, payments to the plan would go down one-for-one with any reduction in services. In a pure prospective system (where, for instance, capitation was based only on age and gender as in Israel), payments would not fall at all and there would be no risk sharing. But in capitation payment systems using health status indicators, for some patients randomly removing certain office visits (e.g.) along with their costs and any diagnoses generated in that visit does lead to a payment reduction, indicating and measuring the degree of de facto risk sharing built into the capitation payment system.

Schmid and Beck (2016), for Switzerland, find that the de facto risk sharing in the Swiss risk adjustment model is 0.09, meaning that on average 9% of plan spending is returned in the form of higher payments given the risk adjustment model.[29] Reinsurance with a cutoff of 60,000 CHF and a reinsurance rate of 80% increases the return to about 17% on average. This 8% additional reduction in cost control incentives, however, boosts the fit of the payment model at the individual level from 0.15 to 0.41 (Table 1 in Schmid and Beck, 2016), serving as a reminder of the essential tradeoff between reducing incentives for risk selection against the loss of incentives for cost control in having costs drive revenues.

"Upcoding" of diagnoses, another persistent problem with risk-adjusted payment systems, is another indicator of the incentive effects of diagnosis-based risk adjustment. Upcoding takes place not only when plans change codes in isolation, but decide to "do stuff" in order to generate codes, such as engaging in home-based diagnostic visits. Under the prospective health-status-based risk adjustment model in MA, an individual generates a risk score in a MA plan that is about 6%−7% larger than the risk score the same person would generate in Traditional Medicare by some combination of more services and simple upcoding (Geruso and Layton, 2017).

### 5.5.3   Defining Incentives for Cost Control: The Power of a Plan Payment System

We base our measure on the concept of *power* as the term is used in contract theory, the share of costs at the margin borne by the health plan.[30] Power in health insurance contracts is tightly linked to the goal of cost control, as it describes the payment system's impact on the insurer's marginal incentive to limit healthcare spending. Power characterizes how a plan's expenditures impact a plan's net payment from the regulator. This connection is obvious with risk-sharing features of plan payment and present but not-so-obvious when it comes to risk adjustment. Our definition and method of operationalizing power is intended to expose the full incentives in a payment scheme.

If an insurer's payment $R_i$ is invariant to changes in realized costs $Y_i$, as it would be in a plan paid by an age−gender-only risk adjustment system, the power of the payment system would be at the maximum of 1.0. That is, the share of costs borne by the plan at the margin is 1.0. Conversely, in a cost-based system where payment tracked costs exactly, the power would be 0. Away from these polar cases of payment systems, the change in payment for a person with respect to a change in cost for a person could vary over people, vary over ranges of cost, and vary over types of services. For example, the first healthcare event in a diagnostic area will trigger higher payment, but subsequent ones may not.

Imagine a thought experiment in which 10% of each person's healthcare costs were reduced by randomly eliminating part of the use of that person during a year. Individuals' risk scores would fall and the revenue of the plan would go down by $X$ percent. The share of the cost reduction kept by the plan, the power of the payment system, is $1 - \frac{X}{10}$. More formally, we define power as:

$$\text{Power} \equiv 1 - \frac{1}{N}\sum_i \frac{dR_i}{dY_i} \tag{5.8}$$

where $N$ is the number of enrollees in a plan, and $\frac{dR_i}{dY_i}$ is the derivative of payment for person $i$ with respect to a marginal change in their utilization (Geruso and McGuire, 2016).

## 5.5.4 Measuring Power in Plan Payment Systems

Power, as defined in Eq. (5.8), has been measured in research studies in Switzerland and in the US Marketplaces, but at present, the technology of power measurement is not easily applied by policy researchers. It is likely that the simulation methods proposed by Geruso and McGuire (2016) will be refined (or replaced) as research continues. In the meantime, policy researchers can put to use the basic findings from the research literature.

The power of a prospective system is greater than a concurrent system because diagnoses given last year are less predictive of costs this year than diagnoses received this year. Roughly speaking, Geruso and McGuire (2016) find that the power of the HCC-based concurrent risk adjustment system is about 70%, and the power of the same diagnostic system when applied prospectively is about 80%.[31] High year-to-year turnover does not affect power in a concurrent system (because the past doesn't matter), yet strengthens the power of a prospective system (because a diagnosis made for a person last year returns nothing to a plan if the person leaves the plan). The 70% power for a concurrent system and 80% power for a prospective system (before figuring in turnover) are the best power numbers for the two types of HCC-based systems, in our view, based on current research. We look for both more conceptual and empirical research to refine these estimates and to extend them to other institutional settings and risk adjustment models.

A complete power analysis takes account of any risk-sharing features of the plan payment model. For example, suppose the policymaker was considering a prospective system with a reinsurance component that affected 5% of total costs. We have argued above that the power loss from such a risk-sharing policy is 5%. Prospective risk adjustment plus the reinsurance policy would have a power of 75% (80%−5%). This metric can be useful in the following way: based on the (limited) research literature, the prospective system plus reinsurance has greater power than a concurrent system (with no reinsurance). Policy researchers can readily compare the fit at the individual and group level of the two alternatives. If the fit is at least as good in the prospective plus reinsurance system, the policymaker can obtain better fit with more power in the prospective plus reinsurance system than in a concurrent risk adjustment system.[32]

## 5.5.5 Final Comments on Measuring Incentives for Cost Control

The main message of this section is that diagnosis-based risk adjustment systems, prospective as well as concurrent, weaken incentives for cost control. A patient must have a medical encounter in which a diagnosis is made in order to turn on the diagnosis flag in a risk adjustment model. The higher revenue associated with the appearance of the diagnosis rewards the encounter where the diagnosis takes place, weakening incentives to control costs. This is true both for a concurrent risk adjustment system where the plan is paid more this year if the flag goes on, and for a prospective risk adjustment system, where the plan is paid more next year if the patient stays in the plan.

Once this point is accepted, it becomes a matter of degree to which a particular plan payment system maintains the power of cost containment incentives. We have proposed a way for analysts to conduct such an assessment without need to undertake extensive new research. We recognize the "evidence base" for the power of alternative systems is thin. The simulation methods used to assess power in the few papers doing so also need reconsideration and refinement. Much more work is needed on alternative systems in different settings in order to gain an appreciation of how payment models affect incentives, and ultimately to quantify the fundamental tradeoff between incentives for cost control and incentives related to selection that have been recognized to be the fundamental issues in plan payment design (Newhouse, 1996).

**TABLE 5.2** Circumstances in Which Proposed Metrics Do Better at Measuring Incentives for Efficiency

| Section of chapter: Issue | Proposed/Traditional metrics | Circumstances where new metrics are called for |
|---|---|---|
| 5.2: Selection: Fit at the Individual Level | Payment system fit preferred to $R$-squared from a risk-adjustment regression | Payment system includes other elements than predictions from a single risk adjustment model |
| 5.3: Selection: Fit at the Group or Action Level | Group payment system fit preferred to predictive ratios or under- and overcompensation | Payment system includes other elements than predictions from a single risk adjustment model |
| 5.4: Selection: Individuals Choose the Right Plan | New metric: gap between incremental premiums and incremental costs; payment system fit | Major differences in characteristics and premiums of plans available to consumers, and changes in premium regulation are under consideration; a second reason to recognize payment system fit |
| 5.5: Incentives for Cost Control | New metric: power of a payment system (in retaining incentives for cost control) | When diagnosis-based risk adjustment, risk sharing, or possible major change in encounter-based variables in model are under consideration |

## 5.6   SUMMARY AND DISCUSSION

In a nutshell, this chapter intends to equip researchers and regulators with a toolkit for practical ex ante evaluation of health plan payment systems. We hope to advance the field by proposing simple modifications of currently used approaches that, in many circumstances, do a better job than conventional metrics of measuring incentives for efficiency.

### 5.6.1   When Does It Matter to Make Use of the Proposed Metrics?

Table 5.2 briefly summarizes our views about when our proposed metrics will be more informative than existing metrics. With respect to both individual and group-fit measures, using predictions from a risk adjustment regression to compute $R$-squared and conventional measures of over/undercompensation is fine if the payment system is fully described by those predictions. We regard this to be essentially true in Germany and MA in the United States, but not elsewhere. In Switzerland, risk sharing figures into plan payment; in the Netherlands there are four predicted values that need to be aggregated to describe plan payment; in Marketplaces, premium categories and reinsurance features play a role. PSF is what is called for generally, and in special circumstances this will be approximated by regression predicted values.

We proposed two metrics related to consumer sorting. Our first, based on the gap between incremental premiums and incremental costs, is problematic from a practical standpoint in many settings, and may not be of interest in a context where policymakers are committed to community rating. Our second measure, capturing the inefficiency in pricing and sorting caused by adverse selection, is simply the individual-level fit measure, PSF. A necessary condition for either of our sorting metrics to be worthwhile is that there are some meaningful differences in plans that affect their cost. This latter condition is true in most settings but not all (again, Germany is in the minority).

Measuring power is important when alternatives being considered might differ in the degree to which they affect cost-control incentives. For example, adding diagnoses from outpatient claims in a prospective risk adjustment model will affect power. Adding a risk-sharing feature will affect power.

### 5.6.2   Mathematical Properties of the Measures

We close this chapter with a couple of brief reminders about the mathematical properties of the measures proposed.

First, we present linear and quadratic forms of measures of fit of plan payments to plan costs at the individual and group levels, and linear and quadratic forms of the fit of incremental premiums to incremental costs. Our power measure is simply linear. Though we lean towards the quadratic forms on the basis of the general property of the increasing economic harm from price distortions, the analyst needs to make a choice about whether they would regard the linear or the quadratic (or some other power) most helpful.

Second, in the quadratic form, all of our measures are between 0 and 1. They are unit-free numbers that cannot be added. The measures are useful for identifying potentially dominant policies. In the example discussed above, if prospective risk adjustment plus a small amount of reinsurance yields better PSF and higher power, it can be regarded as superior to the alternative of concurrent risk adjustment. The measures could be useful for designing a policy that is equivalent to another policy in one dimension so as to focus policy choice on the other. Sticking with the same example, our method for assessing power would allow the analyst to identify the degree of reinsurance that, when paired with prospective risk adjustment, yields the same power as concurrent risk adjustment. With this in place, the analyst can compare various fit properties of the models.

The metrics cannot be added (this would be a meaningless number) nor, in the presence of tradeoffs—i.e., one payment system is better on one metric but worse on another—can the metrics value the tradeoff involved. A 0.01 change in power cannot be compared with a 0.01 change in PSF. This comparison must be based on the values of the decision maker.

## ENDNOTES

1. Some aspects of "fairness" are related to efficiency. Specifically, redistribution from healthy to sick consumers provides implicit insurance against the financial consequences of shifting from a healthy to a sick state, which can be welfare-enhancing (Handel et al., 2015).
2. For a technical presentation of some of the ideas in this chapter, see Layton et al. (2017).
3. See, as examples, Kautter et al. (2014) on US Marketplaces; Pope et al. (2011) on US Medicare; Shmueli et al. (2010) on Israel; Beck et al. (2010) on Switzerland; Breyer et al. (2003) on Germany; Van Kleef et al. (2013) on the Netherlands.
4. Exceptions occur when there is variation in program implementation geographically, over time, or across eligible populations that may enable the impact of specific reform features to be identified.
5. Most real-world risk adjustment models use weighted least squares (WLS) to accommodate partial-year enrollees or population sampling weights. WLS weights then enter into the $R$-squared formula in the usual way. For simplicity, we ignore those issues here and refer simply to "ordinary" least squares.
6. Although the within-sample $R^2_{reg}$ is always guaranteed to be nonnegative, outside of sample (validation) measures, or measures generated using simulation models that change the model specification can have negative values.
7. See, e.g., Van Barneveld et al. (2001) and Ettner et al. (2001). Van Veen et al. (2015) summarize fit measures used in this literature.
8. Some papers propose an empirical measure of "how much of healthcare costs are predictable" by using extensive sets of information that consumers might have available for prediction, such as 5 years of past healthcare spending in Van Barneveld et al. (2001) or something similar in Newhouse et al. (1989), who estimate individual fixed effects based on several years of data. These predictions may of course under- or overstate how much consumers can actually predict. Researchers then compare the $R$-squared from a particular risk adjustment formula to this "maximum explainable $R$-squared."

9. For example, suppose a health plan can direct treatment resources at the individual level and respond to the incentive to spend too much or too little based on whether the individual is a winner or a loser. In that case, a consumer's declining marginal benefit curve implies squaring the measure of incentive at the individual level is correct. See Layton et al. (2017) for a formal development including other assumptions necessary for the $R$-squared to be the exact metric to compare payment models in terms of incentives for economic efficiency.

10. And the assumption that plan actions to discriminate in favor/against some enrollees is the main efficiency issue. The $R$-squared measure is not well-suited to measuring efficiency incentives with respect to enrollee choice of plan or incentives for cost containment.

11. An assumption here is that within-group variation of profits and losses is not correlated with differences in consumer response to selection actions. We come back on this assumption in Section 5.3.5.

12. This is a rationale for why data from traditional Medicare are used to calibrate payment models for MA plans. See Bergquist et al. (2018) for discussion of this issue.

13. Chapter 4: Risk Sharing discusses empirical methods for incorporating the presence of premium categories and risk sharing into the estimation of the risk adjustment model. The PSF measure remains the relevant one because it incorporates the "explanatory power" of all payment system features.

14. The literature on service-level or "supply-side" selection began with studies of the incentives of insurers to distort service-level offerings to attract good risks based on models of health plan profit maximization. Geruso and Layton (2017) provide a recent review of this literature.

15. This over/undercompensation measure is the negative of the more familiar mean prediction error which is widely used in statistics. Using the negative makes positive values correspond to positive profits when the predictions are thought of as a measure of revenue.

16. See also Kuziemko et al. (2014) for a study of Medicaid managed care plans attempting to attract lower-cost births based on the race/ethnicity of the mother.

17. See Ellis and McGuire (2007) for implementation of this approach in Medicare and McGuire et al. (2014) for its application in Marketplaces.

18. A related argument is made by Lorenz (2014) who also identifies empirical methods that weight over- and undercompensation asymmetrically.

19. The theory of plan incentives to use services to affect selection is presented in Frank et al. (2000) and Ellis and McGuire (2007). The ideas are developed and applied empirically in McGuire et al. (2014) and Ellis et al. (2017).

20. Note that the efficiency rule has to do with plan costs, not total costs. If a deductible only shifts costs from the plan to the consumer, only the portion of spending covered by the plan should be part of the efficient incremental premium. All plan costs, including administrative costs, should be considered when evaluating efficiency. We proceed by effectively assuming that administrative costs for a given consumer are constant across plans.

21. This argument is made in Keeler et al. (1998), among other places. The argument is the same as that for prices generally: when consumers face prices equal to costs, utility-maximizing consumers make socially efficient choices. For now, we ignore the distinction between expected and realized cost. We will recognize the importance of expected costs in developing our proposed measure below. We also ignore deviations between willingness-to-pay (demand) and underlying valuation that may be caused by behavioral frictions (Spinnewijin, 2017).

22. This is the incremental plan cost for the plan without a deductible. All other costs are covered similarly in the two plans.

23. A single premium can sort efficiently in some special cases. For example, if all heterogeneity in preferences is perfectly collinear with expected costs, a single premium can achieve efficient sorting. This is the special case in Cutler and Reber (1998).
24. For an early treatment, see Pauly (2008).
25. Gains in fairness may also represent efficiency gains. The transfers from healthy to sick consumers induced by limited premium categories also effectively provide insurance against the financial consequences of transitioning from a healthy to a sick state. Indeed, Handel et al. (2015) show that in a setting similar to the ACA Marketplaces, efficiency gains from limiting "reclassification risk" exceed efficiency losses due to adverse selection when comparing risk-rated premiums to a single premium policy.
26. The analysis here assumes that consumers choose on the basis of premium differences across plans, i.e., would make the same choices if plan premiums were 100 euros and 300 euros as when the premiums were 600 euros and 800 euros. If consumers react to relative prices rather than differences in absolute prices, this assumption is questionable. Douven et al. (2018) question whether consumers decide on the basis of price differences independent of the level of prices.
27. Incremental costs can be thought of in terms of expectation if the metric developed here is applied ex ante. The expectation is an objective expectation (not necessarily what the consumer might be able to forecast). In implementing this idea we use data on actual costs averaged over the types of interest to estimate expected costs.
28. Assumptions about demand response to metal tier plans in the US Marketplaces are made prior to estimating the separate models for each metal tier.
29. Schmid and Beck (2016) report the "power" of the payment models which is 1 minus the de facto cost sharing.
30. Power is maximized with a fixed-price contract and decreases as the price is tied to realized costs. See Laffont and Tirole (1993, p. 11).
31. Geruso and McGuire (2016) in their Table 2 report power for specific disease areas, and then a range for inpatient and outpatient overall. Our 80% and 70% are summary numbers not found in the Geruso and McGuire table.
32. This is the comparison made by Geruso and McGuire (2016) in the context of US Marketplaces. There a prospective HCC-based system with Marketplace reinsurance policy fits better than concurrent risk adjustment (as measured by PSF) and preserves higher power.

# References for Part I

Abbas, S., Ihle, P., Köster, I., Schubert, I., 2012. Estimation of disease incidence in claims data dependent on the length of follow-up: a methodological approach. Health Services Res. 47 (2), 746−755.

Agency for HealthCare Policy and Research (AHRQ), 2017. Clinical Classifications Software (CCS) for ICD-9-CM Fact Sheet. <https://www.hcup-us.ahrq.gov/toolssoftware/ccs/ccsfactsheet.jsp>.

Akerlof, G.A., 1970. The market for 'Lemons': quality uncertainty and the market mechanism. Quart. J. Econ. 84 (3), 488−500.

Ash, A.S., Ellis, R.P., 2012. Risk-adjusted payment and performance assessment for primary care. Med. Care 50 (8), 643−653.

Ash, A.S., Porell, F., Gruenberg, L., Sawitz, E., Beiser, A., 1989. Adjusting medicare capitation payments using prior hospitalization data. Health Care Financing Rev. 10 (4), 17−29.

Ash, A.S., Ellis, R.P., Pope, G., Ayanian, J., Bates, D., Burstin, H., et al., 2000. Using diagnoses to describe populations and predicts costs. Health Care Financial Rev. 21 (3), 7−28.

Ash, A.S., Mick, E., Ellis, R.P., Kiefe, C., Clark, M., 2017. Adding Social Determinants of Health Factors to Medically-Based Risk Adjustment Improves Risk Equalization Payment in a US Low-Income Population. Working paper, University of Massachusetts Medical School, Worcester, MA.

Bauhoff, S., 2012. Do health plans risk select? An audit study on the Germany's social health insurance. J. Public Econ. 96, 750−759.

Bauhoff, S., Fischer, L., Göpffarth, D., Wuppermann, A.C., 2017. Plan responses to diagnosis-based payment: evidence from Germany's morbidity-based risk adjustment. J. Health Econ. 56, 397−413.

Beck, K., Trottmann, M., Zweifel, P., 2010. 'Risk adjustment in health insurance and its long-term effectiveness'. J. Health Econ. 29 (4), 489−498.

Bergquist, S.L., Layton, T.J., McGuire T.G., Rose S., 2018. Intervening on the Data to Improve the Performance of Health Plan Payment Methods. Working paper, Department of Health Care Policy, Harvard Medical School.

Breiman, L., 1996. Stacked regressions. Mach. Learn. 24 (1), 49−64.

Breyer, F., Heineck, M., Lorenz, N., 2003. Determinants of health care utilization by German sickness fund members − with application to risk adjustment. Health Econ. 12 (5), 367−376.

Breyer, F., Bundorf, K., Pauly, M.V., 2012. Health care spending risk, health insurance, and payment to health plans. In: Pauly, M., McGuire, T., Barros, P. (Eds.), The Handbook of Health Economics, vol. 2. Elsevier, Amsterdam.

Brown, J., Duggan, M., Kuziemko, I., Woolston, W., 2014. How does risk selection respond to risk adjustment? Evidence from the Medicare Advantage program. Am. Econ. Rev. 104 (10), 3335−3364.

Buchner, F., Göpffarth, D., Wasem, J., 2013. The new risk adjustment formula in Germany: implementation and first experiences. Health Policy 109, 253–262.

Buchner, F., Wasem, J., Schillo, S., 2017. Regression trees identify relevant interactions: can this improve the predictive performance of risk adjustment? Health Econ. 26 (1), 74–85.

Bundorf, M.K., Pauly, M.V., 2006. Is health insurance affordable for the uninsured? J. Health Econ. 25 (4), 650–673.

Bundorf, M.K., Levin, J.D., Mahoney, N., 2012. Pricing and welfare in health plan choice. Am. Econ. Rev. 102 (7), 3214–3248.

Cabral, M., Geruso, M., Mahoney, N., 2014. Does Privatized Health Insurance Benefit Patients or Producers? Evidence from Medicare Advantage. NBER Working Paper 20470.

Cao, Z., McGuire, T., 2003. Service-level selection by HMOs in medicare. J. Health Econ. 22 (6), 915–931.

Carey, C., 2017a. Technological change and risk adjustment: benefit design incentives in medicare Part D. Am. Econ. J.: Econ. Policy 9 (1), 38–73.

Carey, C., 2017b. Time to Harvest: Evidence on Consumer Choice Frictions from a Payment Revision in Medicare Part D. Working Paper. Retrieved from: <https://drive.google.com/file/d/0B2TeS7lispKBQ21RLV9PckE2eWs/view>.

Cattel, D., Eijkenaar, F., van Kleef, R.C., van Vlieten, R.C.J.A., Withagen-Koster, A.A., 2017. Evaluatie normbedragen van somatische risicovereveningsmodellen 2010-2013 (English translation: "Evaluation of the Payment Weights of the Risk Equalization Models for Somatic Care in 2010-2013". Research report, Erasmus University Rotterdam.

Centers for Medicare &Medicaid Services, 2016a. Advance notice 2017. <https://www.cms.gov/Medicare/Health-Plans/MedicareAdvtgSpecRateStats/Downloads/Advance2017.pdf>.

Centers for Medicare & Medicaid Services, 2016b. Patient Protection and Affordable Care Act: Benefit and Payment Parameters for 2018. 45 CFR Parts 144, 146, 147, 148, et al. September 6, 2016. <https://www.gpo.gov/fdsys/pkg/FR-2016-09-06/pdf/2016-20896.pdf>.

Centers for Medicare & Medicaid Services, 2016c. HHS-Operated Risk Adjustment Methodology Meeting Discussion Paper. <https://www.cms.gov/CCIIO/Resources/Forms-Reports-and-Other-Resources/Downloads/RA-March-31-White-Paper-032416.pdf>.

Chen, J., Ellis, R.P., Toro, K.H., Ash, A.S., 2015. Mispricing in the Medicare advantage risk adjustment model. INQUIRY: J. Health Care Organization Provision Financing 52, 1–7.

Chinitz, D., Preker, A., Wasem, J., 1998a. Balancing competition and solidarity in health care financing. In: Saltman, R.B., Figueras, J., Sakellarides, C. (Eds.), Critical Challenges for Health Care Reform in Europe. Open University Press, Buckingham, pp. 55–77.

Chinitz, D., Shalev, C., Galai, N., Israeli, A., 1998b. Israel's Basic Basket of Health Services: the importance of being explicitly implicit. Br. Med. J. 317, 1005–1007.

Cid, C., Ellis, R.P., Vargas, V., Wasem, J., Prieto, L., 2016. Global risk-adjusted payment models. In: Scheffler, R. (Ed.), Handbook of Global Health Economics and Public Policy, vol. 11 (1), pp. 311–362.

Clements, K.M., Clark, R.E., Lavitas, P., Kunte, P., Graham, C.S., O'Connell, E., et al., 2016. Access to new medications for hepatitis C for Medicaid members: a retrospective cohort study. J. Manag. Care Specialty Pharm. 22 (6), 714–722b.

Curto, V., Einav, L., Levin, J., Bhattacharya, J., 2014. Can Health Insurance Competition Work? Evidence from Medicare Advantage. National Bureau of Economic Research Working Paper 20818, December.

Cutler, D., 1994. A guide to health care reform. J. Econ. Perspect. 8 (3), 13–29.

Cutler, D., Zeckhauser, R., 2000. The anatomy of health insurance. In: Newhouse, J., Culyer, T. (Eds.), Handbook of Health Economics, vol. I. Elsevier, Amsterdam.

Cutler, D.M., Reber, S.J., 1998. Paying for health insurance: the tradeoff between competition and adverse selection. Quart. J. Econ. 113 (2), 433−466.

Diamond, P., 1992. Organizing the health insurance market. Econometrica 60 (6), 1233−1254.

Dixon, J., Smith, P., Gravelle, H.S.E., Martin, S., Bardsley, M., Rice, N., et al., 2011. A person based formula for allocating commissioning funds to general practices in England: development of a statistical model. BMJ 343 (nov 22 1), d6608-d6608.

Dorn, S., Garrett, B., Marks, J., Holtz-Eakin, D., Holt, C., Book, R., et al., 2017. Stabilizing the Individual Market: Risk Adjustment and Risk Mitigation. June 28, Downloaded 9/25/2017 from: <https://www.americanactionforum.org/research/stabilizing-individual-market-risk-adjustment-risk-mitigation/>.

Douven, R. Ron van der Heijden, R., McGuire, T., Schut, E., 2017. Premium Levels and Demand Response in Health Insurance. National Bureau of Economics Research Working Paper 23846.

Dow, W.H., Fulton, B.D., Baicker, K., 2010. Reinsurance for high health costs: benefits, limitations, and alternatives. Forum Health Econ. Policy 13 (2), 1−21. Art 7.

Drozd, E., Cromwell, J., Gage, B., Maier, J., Greenwald, L., Goldman, H., 2006. Patient casemix classification for medicare psychiatric prospective payment. Am. J. Psychiatry 163 (4), 724−732.

Dudley, R.A., Medlin, C.A., Hammann, L.B., Cisternas, M.G., Brand, R., Rennie, D.J., et al., 2003. The best of both worlds? The potential of hybrid prospective/concurrent risk adjustment. Med. Care 41 (1), 56−69.

Dunn, D.L., Rosenblatt, A., Tiaira, D.A., Latimer, E., Bertko, J., Stoiber, T., et al., 1996. A Comparative Analysis of Methods of Health Risk Assessment. Final Report to the Society of Actuaries. SOA Monograph M-HB96-1.

Eggleston, K., Bir, A., 2009. Measuring selection incentives in managed care: evidence from the Massachusetts State Employees Insurance Program. J. Risk Insurance 76, 159−175.

Eggleston, K., Ellis, R.P., Lu, M., 2012. Risk adjustment and prevention. Can. J. Econ./Revue canadienne d'économique 45 (4), 1586−1607.

Eijkenaar, F., van Vliet, R.C.J.A., van Kleef, R.C., 2018. Diagnosis-based cost groups in the Dutch risk-equalization model − effects of clustering diagnoses and of allowing patients to be classified into multiple risk-classes. Med. Care 56, 91−96.

Einav, L., Finkelstein, A., 2011. Selection in insurance markets: theory and empirics in pictures. J. Econ. Perspect. 25 (1), 115−138.

Einav, L., Finkelstein, A., Cullen, M.R., 2010. Estimating welfare in insurance markets using variation in prices. Quart. J. Econ. 125 (3), 877−921.

Ellis, R.P., Ash, A.S., 1995. Refinements to the Diagnostic Cost Group (DCG) model. Inquiry 32 (4), 418−429.

Ellis, R.P., McGuire, T.G., 1986. Provider behavior under prospective payment: cost sharing and supply. J. Health Econ. 5 (2), 129−151.

Ellis, R.P., McGuire, T.G., 1988. Insurance principles and the design of prospective payment systems. J. Health Econ. 7 (3), 215−237.

Ellis, R.P., McGuire, T.G., 2007. Predictability and predictiveness in health care spending. J. Health Econ. 26 (1), 25−48.

Ellis, R.P., Jiang, S., Kuo, T.-C., 2013a. Does service-level spending show evidence of selection across health plan types? Appl. Econ. 45 (13), 1701−1712.

Ellis, R.P., Fiebig, D.G., Johar, M., Jones, G., Savage, E., 2013b. Explaining health care expenditure variation: large sample evidence using linked survey and health administrative data. Health Econ. 22 (9), 1093–1110.

Ellis, R.P., Martins, B., Miller, M.M., 2016. Provider payment methods and incentives. In: Heggenhougen, H.K., Quah, S. (Eds.), International Encyclopedia of Public Health, second ed., Elsevier, Amsterdam.

Ellis, R.P., Martins, B., Zhu, W., 2017a. Health care demand elasticities by type of service. J. Health Econ. 55, 232–243.

Ellis, R.P., Martins, B., Zhu, W., 2017b. Demand elasticities and service selection incentives among competing private health plans. J. Health Econ. 56, 352–367.

Enthoven, A.C., 1978. Rx for health care economics: competition, not rigid NHI. Hosp. Prog. 59 (10), 44–51.

Enthoven, A.C., 1980. Health Plan. Addison-Wesley Publishing, Reading, MA.

Enthoven, A.C., 1993. The history and principles of managed competition. Health Aff. 12, 24–48.

Enthoven, A.C., Kronick, R., 1989. A consumer-choice health plan for the 1990s. Universal health insurance in a system designed to promote quality and economy (2). N. Engl. J. Med. 320 (2), 94–101.

Ericson, K.M., Geissler, K., Lubin, B., 2017. The Impact of Partial-Year Enrollment on the Accuracy of Risk Adjustment Systems: A Framework and Evidence. NBER Working Paper 23765.

Ettner, S., Frank, R., McGuire, T., Hermann, R., 2001. Risk adjustment alternatives in paying for behavioral health care under medicaid. Health Services Res. 36 (4), 793–811.

Feldman, R.G., Dowd, B.E., 1982. Simulation of a health insurance market with adverse selection. Oper. Res. 30 (6), 1027–1042.

Feldman, R.G., Dowd, B.E., 1991. Must adverse selection cause premium spirals? J. Health Econ. 10, 349–357.

Frank, R.G., Glazer, J., McGuire, T.G., 2000. Measuring adverse selection in managed health care. J. Health Econ. 19 (6), 829–854.

Friedman, J., Hastie, T., Tibshirani, R., 2001. The Elements of Statistical Learning. Springer, New York, NY.

Fuller, R.L., Averill, R.F., Muldoon, J.H., Hughes, J.S., 2016. Comparison of the properties of regression and categorical risk-adjustment models. J. Ambulatory Care Manage. 39 (2), 157–165.

GAO (Government Accounting Office), 2015. Patient Protection and Affordable Care Act: Despite Some Delays, CMS has made Progress Implementing Programs to Limit Health Insurer Risk. GAO-14-447. Washington, DC, April.

García-Goñi, M., Ibern, P., Inoriza, J.M., 2009. Hybrid risk adjustment for pharmaceutical benefits. Eur. J. Health Econ. 10 (3), 299–308.

Geruso, M., 2017. Demand heterogeneity in insurance markets: implications for equity and efficiency. Quant. Econ, 8 (3), 929–975.

Geruso, M., Layton, T., 2015. Upcoding: Evidence from Medicare on Squishy Risk Adjustment. NBER Working Paper 21222.

Geruso, M., Layton, T., 2017. Selection in insurance markets and its policy remedies. J. Econ. Perspect. 31 (4), 23–50.

Geruso, M., McGuire, T.G., 2016. Tradeoffs in the design of health plan payment systems: fit, power and balance. J. Health Econ. 47, 1–19.

Geruso M., Layton, T., Prinz D., 2016. Screening in Contract Design: Evidence from the ACA Health Insurance Exchanges. NBER Working Paper 22832.

Glazer, J., McGuire, T.G., 2000. Optimal risk adjustment in markets with adverse selection: an application to managed care. Am. Econ. Rev. 90 (4), 1055–1071.

Glazer, J., McGuire, T.G., 2002. Setting health plan premiums to ensure efficient quality in health care: minimum variance optimal risk adjustment. J. Public Econ. 84 (2), 153–173.

Glazer, J., McGuire, T.G., 2001. Private employers don't need formal risk adjustment. Inquiry 38 (3), 260–269.

Glazer, J., McGuire, T.G., 2011. Gold and Silver health plans: accommodating demand heterogeneity in managed competition. J. Health Econ. 30 (5), 1011–1019.

Glazer, J., McGuire, T.G., 2017. Paying medicare advantage plans: to level or tilt the playing field. J. Health Econ. 56, 281–291.

Gravelle, H., Dusheiko, M., Martin, S., Smith, P., Rice, N., Dixon, J., 2011. Modeling Individual Patient Hospital Expenditures for General Practice Budgets. CHE Research Paper 73.

Gruber, S., van der Laan, M., 2010. A targeted maximum likelihood estimator of a causal effect on a bounded continuous outcome. Int. J. Biostat. 6 (1), A26.

Hackmann, M.B., Kolstad, J.T., Kowalski, A.E., 2015. Adverse selection and an individual mandate: when theory meets practice. Am. Econ. Rev. 105 (3), 1030–1066.

Han, T., Lavetti, K., 2017. Does Part D abet advantageous selection in medicare advantage? J. Health Econ. 56, 368–382.

Handel, B., Hendel, I., Whinston, M.D., 2015. Equilibria in health exchanges: adverse selection vs. reclassification risk. Econometrica 83 (4), 1261–1313.

Herring, B., Pauly, M.V., 2001. Premium variation in the individual health insurance market. Int. J. Health Care Finance Econ. 1, 43–58.

Herring, B., Pauly, M.V., 2006. Incentive-compatible guaranteed renewability health insurance premium. J. Health Econ. 25, 395–417.

Hileman, G., Steele, S., 2016. Accuracy of Claims-Based Risk Scoring Models. Society of Actuaries.

Iezzoni, L.I. (Ed.), 2013. Risk Adjustment for Measuring Healthcare Outcomes. fourth ed. Health Administration Press, Ann Arbor, MI.

Jones, A.M., 2011. Models for health care. In: Clements, M.P., Hendry, D.F. (Eds.), Oxford *Handbook of Economic Forecasting*. Oxford University Press, New York, NY.

Kautter, J., Ingber, M., Pope, G.C., Freeman, S., 2012. Improvements in medicare Part D Risk adjustment: beneficiary access and payment accuracy. Med. Care 50 (12), 1102–1108.

Kautter, J., Pope, G.C., Ingber, M., Freeman, S., Patterson, L., Cohen, M., et al., 2014. The HHS-HCC risk adjustment model for individual and small group markets under the Affordable Care Act. Medicare Medicaid Res. Rev. 4 (3), E1–E11.

Keeler, E., Carter, G., Newhouse, J., 1998. A model of the impact of reimbursement schemes on health plan choice. J. Health Econ. 17 (3), 297–320.

Keeler, E.B., Carter, G.M., Trude, S., 1988. Insurance aspects of DRG outlier payments. J. Health Econ. 7 (3), 193–214.

Kleinberg, J., Ludwig, J., Mullainathan, S., Obermeyer, Z., 2015. Prediction policy problems. Am. Econ. Rev.: Papers Proc. 105 (5), 491–495.

Kowalski, A., 2014. The early impact of the affordable care act, state by state. Brookings Papers on Economic Activity, Economic Studies Program, The Brookings Institution 49 (2 (Fall)), 277–355.

Kuziemko, I., Meckel, K., Rossin-Slater, M., 2014. Do Insurers Risk-Select Against Each Other? Evidence from Medicaid and Implications for Health Reform. NBER Working Paper No. 19198.

Laffont, J.-J., Tirole, J., 1993. A Theory of Incentives in Procurement and Regulation. The MIT Press, Cambridge, MA.

Layton, T., McGuire, T.G., Sinaiko, A.S., 2016. Risk corridors and reinsurance in health insurance marketplaces: insurance for insurers. Am. J. Health Econ. 2 (1), 66−95.

Layton, T.J., McGuire, T.G., 2017. Marketplace plan payment options for dealing with high-cost enrollees. Am. J. Health Econ. 3 (2), 165−191.

Layton, T.J., McGuire, T.G., Van Kleef, R.C., 2016. Deriving Risk Adjustment Payment Weights to Maximize Efficiency of Health Insurance Markets. NBER Working Paper 22642.

Layton, T.J., Ellis, R.P., McGuire, T.G., Van Kleef, R.C., 2017. Measuring efficiency of health plan payment systems in managed competition health insurance markets. J. Health Econ. 56, 237−255.

Lorenz, N., 2015. The interaction of direct and indirect risk selection. J. Health Econ. 42, 81−89.

Lorenz, N., 2017. Using quantile and asymmetric least squares regression for optimal risk adjustment. Health Econ. 26 (6), 724−742.

Lorenz, N., Schillo, S., Wasem, J., 2017. Quantile regression in risk adjustment: an application to the German risk adjustment system. IBES Diskussionbeitrag.

McClellan, M., 1997. Hospital reimbursement incentives: an empirical analysis. J. Econ. Manage. Strategy 6 (1), 91−128.

McCullagh, P., 1983. Quasi-likelihood functions. Ann. Stat. 11, 59−67.

McGuire, T.G., 2011. Physician agency and payment for primary medical care. In: Glied, S., Smith, P. (Eds.), The Oxford Handbook of Health Economics. Oxford University Press, Oxford.

McGuire, T.G., Newhouse, J.P., Normand, S.L., Shi, J., Zuvekas, S., 2014. Assessing incentives for service-level selection in private health insurance exchanges. J. Health Econ. 35, 47−63.

Medicare Payment Advisory Commission (MEDPAC), 1998. Report to the Congress: Medicare Payment Policy, vol. 2.

Medicare Payment Advisory Commission (MEDPAC), 2012. Report to the Congress: Medicare Payment Policy.

National Academies of Sciences, Engineering, and Medicine, 2016. Accounting for Social Risk Factors in Medicare Payment. National Academies Press, Washington, DC.

National Quality Forum, August 15, 2014. Risk Adjustment for Socioeconomic Status or Other Sociodemographic Factors, Technical Report. <http://www.qualityforum.org/WorkArea/linkit.aspx?LinkIdentifier = id&ItemID = 75398> (accessed 05.01.17).

Newhouse, J.P., 1996. Reimbursing health plans and health providers: efficiency in production versus selection. J. Econ. Lit. 34 (3), 1236−1263.

Newhouse, J.P., 2017. Risk adjustment with an outside option. J. Health Econ. 56, 256−258.

Newhouse, J.P., Manning, W.G., Keeler, E.B., Sloss, E.M., 1989. Adjusting capitation rates using objective health measures and prior utilization. Health Care Financing Rev. 15 (1), 39−54.

Newhouse, J.P., Buntin, M.B., Chapman, J.D., 1999. Risk Adjustment and Medicare. The Commonwealth Fund.

Nyman, J.A., 1999. The value of health insurance: the access motive. J. Health Econ. 18, 141−152.

Parkes, S., 2015. Producing actionable insights from predictive models built upon condensed electronic medical records. Health Watch.

Pauly, M., 2008. Adverse selection and moral hazard: implications for health insurance markets. In: Sloan, F., Kasper, H. (Eds.), Incentives and Choice in Health Care. MIT Press, Cambridge, MA, 2008.

Pauly, M.V., Kunreuther, H., Hirth, R., 1995. Guaranteed renewability in insurance. J. Risk Insurance 10, 143−156.

Pollitz, K., 2016. High Risk Pools for Uninsurable Individuals. Kaiser Family Foundation, Issue Brief, July.

Pope, G.C., Ellis, R.P., Ash, A.S., Ayanian, J.Z., Bates, D.W., Burstin, H., et al., 2000. Diagnostic Cost Group Hierarchical Condition Category Models for Medicare Risk Adjustment, Final Report. Health Care Financing Administration, Contract No. 500-95-048.

Pope, G.C., Kautter, J., Ellis, R.P., Ash, A.S., Ayanian, J.Z., Ingber, M.J., et al., 2004. Risk adjustment of medicare capitation payments using the CMS-HCC model. Health Care Financing Rev. 25 (4), 119−141.

Pope, G.C., Kautter, J., Ingber, J.J., Freeman, S., Sekar, R., Newhart, C., 2011. Evaluation of the CMS-HCC Risk Adjustment Model. In Final Report, RTI Project Number 0209853.006, RTI International, March.

Price, J.R., Mays, J.W., 1985. Biased selection in the federal employees health benefits program. Inquiry 22, 67−77.

Relles, D., Ridgeway, G., Carter, G., 2002. Data mining and the implementation of a prospective payment system for inpatient rehabilitation. Health Services Outcomes Res. Method. 3 (3), 247−266.

Robinson, J., 2001. Theory and practice in the design of physician payment incentives. Milbank Quart. 79 (2), 149−177.

Rose, S., 2016. A machine learning framework for plan payment risk adjustment. Health Services Res. 51 (6), 2358−2374.

Rose, S., Shi, J., McGuire, T., Normand, S.L., 2015. Matching and imputation methods for risk adjustment in the health insurance marketplaces. Stat. Biosci. Available from: https://doi.org/10.1007/s12561-015-9135-7. Advance online publication.

Rose, S., Zaslavsky, A.M., McWilliams, J.M., 2016. Variation in accountable care organization spending and sensitivity to risk adjustment: implications for benchmarking. Health Aff. 35 (3), 440−448.

Rothschild, M., Stiglitz, J., 1976. Equilibrium in competitive insurance markets: an essay on the economics of imperfect information. Quart. J. Econ. 90 (4), 629−649.

Schillo, S., Lux, G., Wasem, J., Buchner, F., 2016. High-cost pool or high-cost groups? How to handle the high(est) cost cases in a risk adjustment mechanism. Health Policy 120, 141−147.

Schmid, C., Beck, K., 2016. Reinsurance in the Swiss Health Insurance Market: fit, power and balance. Health Policy 120 (7), 848−855.

Schokkaert, E., Van de Voorde, C., 2004. Risk selection and the specification of the conventional risk adjustment formula. J. Health Econ. 23, 1237−1259.

Schwartz, K., 2006. Reinsuring Health. Russell Sage Foundation.

Shen, Y., Ellis, R.P., 2002. Cost minimizing risk adjustment. J. Health Econ. 21 (3), 515−530.

Shepard, M., 2016. Hospital Network Competition and Adverse Selection: Evidence from the Massachusetts Health Insurance Exchange. Harvard University, unpublished.

Shmueli, A., Messika, D., Zmora, I., Oberman, B., 2010. Health care costs during the last 12 months of life in Israel: estimation and implications for risk adjustment. Int. J. Health Care Finance Econ. 10 (3), 257−273.

Shrestha, A., Bergquist, S., Montz, E., Rose, S., 2017. Mental Health Spending Risk Adjustment Using Clinical Categories and Machine Learning. Working Paper.

Song, Z.S., Safran, D.G., Landon, B.E., He, Y., Ellis, R.P., Mechanic, R.E., et al., 2011. Health care spending and quality in year 1 of the alternative quality contract. N. Engl. J. Med. Available from: https://doi.org/10.1056/NEJMsa1101416.

Stam, P.J., van Vliet, R.C., van de Ven, W.P., 2010. Diagnostic, pharmacy-based, and self-reported health measures in risk equalization models. Med. Care 448−457.

U.S. Department of Health and Human Services, 2016. Patient Protection and Affordable Care Act; HHS notice of benefit and payment parameters for 2018. Fed. Regist. 81 (17), 61456−61535.

U.S. Department of Health & Human Services, Office of the Assistant Secretary for Planning and Evaluation, 2016. Report to Congress: Social Risk Factors and Performance Under Medicare's Value-Based Purchasing Programs. Washington, DC. <https://aspe.hhs.gov/pdf-report/report-congress-social-risk-factors-and-performance-under-medicares-value-based-pur-chasing-programs> (accessed 03.05.17).

Van Barneveld, E.M., Lamers, L.M., van Vliet, R.C.J.A., van de Ven, W.P.M.M., 1998. Mandatory pooling as a supplement to risk-adjusted capitation payments in a competitive health insurance market. Social Sci. Med. 47 (2), 223−232.

Van Barneveld, E.M., Lamers, L.M., van Vliet, R.C.J.A., van de Ven, W.P.M.M., 2000. Ignoring small predictable profits and losses: a new approach for measuring the incentives for cream skimming. Health Care Manage. Sci. 3, 131−140.

Van Barneveld, E.M., Lamers, L.M., van Vliet, R.C.J.A., van de Ven, W.P.M.M., 2001. Risk sharing as a supplement to imperfect capitation: a tradeoff between selection and efficiency. J. Health Econ. 20 (2), 147−168.

Van de Ven, W.P.M.M., Ellis, R.P., 2000. Risk adjustment in competitive health plan markets. In: Culyer, A., Newhouse, J. (Eds.), Handbook of Health Economics. North Holland, Amsterdam, pp. 755−845.

Van de Ven, W.P.M.M., Schut, F.T., 2011. Guaranteed access to affordable coverage in individual health insurance markets. In: Glied, S., Smith, P.C. (Eds.), The Oxford Handbook of Health Economics. Oxford University Press, Oxford, pp. 380−404.

Van de Ven, W.P.M.M., Beck, K., Buchner, F., Schokkaert, E., Schut, F.T., Shmueli, A., et al., 2013. Preconditions for efficiency and affordability in competitive healthcare markets: are they fulfilled in Belgium, Germany, Israel, the Netherlands and Switzerland. Health Policy 109, 226−245.

Van de Ven, W.P.M.M., van Kleef, R.C., van Vliet, R.C.J.A., 2015. Risk selection threatens quality of care for certain patients; lessons from Europe's Health Insurance Exchanges. Health Aff. 34, 1713−1720.

Van der Laan, M.J., Polley, E., Hubbard, A., 2007. Super learner. Stat. Appl. Genet. Mol. Biol. 6 (1), A25.

Van Kleef, R.C., Beck, K., Van de Ven, W.P.M.M., Van Vliet, R.C.J.A., 2008. Risk equalization and voluntary deductibles: a complex interaction. J. Health Econ. 27 (2), 427−443.

Van Kleef, R.C., Van de Ven, W.P.M.M., Van Vliet, R.C.J.A., 2009. Shifted deductibles for high risks: more effective in reducing moral hazard than traditional deductibles. J. Health Econ. 28, 198−209.

Van Kleef, R.C., Van Vliet, R.C.J.A., 2012. Improving risk equalization using multiple-year high cost as a health indicator. Med. Care 50 (2), 140−144.

Van Kleef, R.C., Van Vliet, R.C.J.A., Van de Ven, W.P.M.M., 2013a. Risk equalization in the Netherlands: an empirical evaluation. Expert Rev. Pharmacoecon. Outcomes Res. 13 (6), 829−839.

Van Kleef, R.C., van de Ven, W.P.M.M., van Vliet, R.C.J.A., 2013b. Risk selection in a regulated health insurance market: a review of the concept, possibilities and effects. Expert Rev. Pharmacoecon. Outcomes Res. 13 (6), 743−752.

Van Kleef, R.C., McGuire, T.G., Van Vliet, R.C.J.A., Van De Ven, W.P.M.M., 2017. Improving risk equalization with constrained regression. Eur. J. Health Econ. 18 (9), 1137−1156.

Van Veen, S.H.C.M., Van Kleef, R.C., Van De Ven, W.P.M.M., Van Vliet, R.C.J.A., 2015a. Improving the prediction model used in risk equalization: cost and diagnostic information from multiple prior years. Eur. J. Health Econ. 16 (2), 201−218.

Van Veen, S.H.C.M., Van Kleef, R.C., Van De Ven, W.P.M.M., Van Vliet, R.C.J.A., 2015b. Is there one measure of fit that fits all? A taxonomy and review of measures-of-fit for risk-equalization models. Med. Care Res. Rev. 72 (2), 220−243.

Van Veen, S.H.C.M., Van Kleef, R.C., Van De Ven, W.P.M.M., Van Vliet, R.C.J.A., 2017. Exploring the predictive power of interaction terms in a sophisticated risk equalization model using regression trees. Health Econ. Available from: https://doi.org/10.1002/hec.3523.

Vats, S., Ash, A.S., Ellis, R.P., 2013. Bending the cost curve? Results from a comprehensive primary care payment pilot. Med. Care 51 (11), 964−969.

Veiga, A., Weyl, E.G., 2016. Product design in selection markets. Quart. J. Econ. 131 (2), 1007−1056.

Ware, J.E., Sherbourne, C.D., 1992. The MOS 36 item short form health survey (SF-36). Med. Care 30 (6), 473−483A.

Wedderburn, R., 1974. Quasi-likelihood functions, generalized linear models, and the Gauss-Newton Method. Biometrika 61, 439−447.

Wennberg, J.E., Staiger, D.O., Sharp, S.M., Gottlieb, D.J., Bevan, G., Mcpherson, K., et al., 2013. Observational intensity bias associated with illness adjustment: cross sectional analysis of insurance claims. BMJ 346, F549.

Winkelman, R., Mehmud, S., 2007. A Comparative Analysis of Claims-Based Tools for Health Risk Assessment. Society of Actuaries.

Wolpert, D.H., 1992. Stacked generalization. Neural Networks 5 (2), 241−259.

Zhu, J.M., Layton, T.J., Sinaiko, A.D., McGuire, T.G., 2013. The power of reinsurance in health insurance exchanges to improve the fit of the payment system and reduce incentives for adverse selection. Inquiry 50 (4), 255−275.

Zorginstituut Nederland, 2005. Regeling beleidsregels vereveningsbijdrage zorgverzekering 2006.

Zweifel, P., Breuer, M., 2006. The case for risk-based premiums in public health insurance. Health Econ. Policy Law 1, 171−188.

# Part II

# Practice

# Chapter 6

# Health Plan Payment in Australia

Francesco Paolucci[1,2], Ana R. Sequeira[1,3], Ayman Fouda[2,4] and Andrew Matthews[5]
*[1]Murdoch University, Perth, WA, Australia, [2]University of Bologna, Bologna, Italy, [3]ISCTE − University Institute of Lisbon, Lisbon, Portugal, [4]Erasmus University Rotterdam, Rotterdam, The Netherlands, [5]Medibank Private, Melbourne, Australia*

## 6.1 INTRODUCTION

The Australian healthcare system is characterized by a mix of public and private financing and provision of healthcare services. The main component of the public scheme is "Medicare," which is, in essence, a national health insurance that (partly) covers a broad set of healthcare services to all lawful residents. Medicare was introduced in 1984, and is funded through general taxation and earmarked income taxes. Medicare partly covers three main health services: first, the private outpatient care[1]; second, inpatient services listed in the Medicare Benefit Schedule (MBS); and third, prescription drugs listed in the Pharmaceutical Benefits Schedule (PBS). In addition to Medicare there is a market for voluntary private health insurance (PHI), which provides supplementary coverage for healthcare services excluded from the MBS and PBS (e.g., dental care, optometry, and private hospital care delivered in a private hospital) and duplicative coverage for services already covered by Medicare such as treatment in a public hospital as a "private" patient (Paolucci et al., 2011).

Until the introduction of Medicare, voluntary PHI was the sole form of coverage. Box 6.1 provides an historical overview of the main regulations, conditions, and financing principles of the PHI market since then. From the start, open enrollment and community rating have been the backbone of health plan regulation (Parliament of Australia, 1953; Colombo and Tapay, 2003; Hurley et al., 2002). The policy objectives backing the introduction of these two regulatory instruments were to broaden health insurance coverage and to improve affordability of health plans, particularly for high-risk individuals. In 1984, with the introduction of Medicare, the PHI market predictably suffered from what many economists refer to as an adverse selection spiral. PHI take up dropped from 50% to 30% in less than a decade, which

Risk Adjustment, Risk Sharing and Premium Regulation in Health Insurance Markets.
DOI: https://doi.org/10.1016/B978-0-12-811325-7.00006-3

**181**

**BOX 6.1  A timeline of health plan regulation and financing (based on Connelly et al., 2010)**

| | | Conditions | Financing |
|---|---|---|---|
| Before 1953 | Private health insurance market was largely unregulated | | |
| 1953 | Parliament of Australia (1953) | • Annual caps on benefits payments for chronic diseases and preexisting conditions<br>• Open enrollment | • Community rating regulations<br>• Federal government subsidies for hospital and medical services that are given to private patients |
| 1958–76 | Amendment establishing the Special Accounts (SA)[a] | • SAs were introduced for members with preexisting ailments and chronic conditions<br>• The Special Accounts comprised hospital and medical benefits | • Comprised members' premiums and Commonwealth subsidies<br>• Any deficits in the Special Accounts would be funded by the Commonwealth<br>• No risk redistribution between insurers |
| 1976–2007 | Reinsurance Scheme<br>Lifetime Health Cover<br>Medicare Levy Surcharge (MLS)<br>Premium Rebates (PRs)[b] | • The replacement of the Medibank scheme (national health insurance scheme with no voluntary opt out) by Medibank Mark II (national health insurance scheme with the option to opt out if insured by PHI) | • Deficit in the Special Accounts to be financed by the fixed Commonwealth contribution through MLS & PRs and risk redistribution between insurers |
| 2007–Present | Private Health Insurance Act (2007)<br>"Risk Equalization Trust Fund" | • Insured patients can receive care in state-owned hospital and private hospitals | • Lifetime Community rating<br>• Open enrollment<br>• Premium Rebate & Medicare Levy Surcharge (means-testing) |

[a]*Caps restriction on benefit payments for chronic diseases and preexisting conditions which was introduced in 1953 did not ease from 1953 to 1958 as was expected with the anticipated growth of PHI.*
[b]*Reinsurance replaced SAs to contain the anticipated SA deficit resulting from the introduction of the opt-out option in the Medibank Mark II scheme.*

led to government intervention in the mid-1990s in the form of implicit and explicit subsidies. The goal of this intervention was to alleviate the financial and fiscal pressure from the public system (Paolucci et al., 2011). As a result of these regulatory interventions, PHI uptake increased to the pre-Medicare level (nearly 50%).

In 2007, the PHI Act established the "Risk Equalization Trust Fund" (RETF). The objective was to mitigate problems caused by community rating. As explained by Connelly et al. (2010), the RETF would promote equity among insurers and "increase industry stability in the context of community rating" (Connelly et al., 2010, p. 5). A particular feature of the RETF is that health plan payments to/from insurers are based on a combination of risk equalization and risk sharing. In this chapter we will refer to this hybrid system as "claims equalization." Note, however, that in some papers, the terms "ex-post claims equalization scheme," "ex-post risk equalization," and "Risk Equalization Trust Fund" are used. When citing specific legislation in this chapter, we will employ the original terminology.

This chapter is organized as follows. The next sections will describe the organization of the current health insurance system (Section 6.2) and the design of the health plan payment system (Section 6.3). Section 6.4 addresses the evaluation of the payment system and Section 6.5 discusses the ongoing issues and reforms.

## 6.2 ORGANIZATION OF THE HEALTH INSURANCE SYSTEM

This section describes the main features of the PHI regulations, governance, consumer choice options, and mechanisms used by insurers to promote efficiency in the delivery of care. We will also pay attention to PHI's link with Medicare.

### 6.2.1 Health Plans and Regulatory Bodies

The Australian PHI market includes 33 competing insurers of which 25 are open to the general public. The other eight are "closed" insurers, which are not-for-profit insurers who typically provide health plans to specific professions, unions, or syndicates (APRA, 2016b; Commonwealth Ombudsman, 2015). Closed insurers currently cover only 5.3% of PHI enrollees (APRA, 2016a). At the national level, the five largest health insurers account for around 80% of the market (APRA, 2015a). The eight next-largest have a joint market share of 11% (APRA, 2015a). In June 2016, Australia's PHI market accounted for a total premium revenue of A$22bn and total assets[2] comprising A$12bn (APRA, 2016b). Based on the latest reports of the Australian Prudential Regulation Authority, private health insurers paid A$18.3bn of total benefits, which resulted in an average net margin of 2.3% (APRA, 2016b).[3]

The PHI market is regulated by the Australian Prudential Regulation Authority (APRA) and the Private Health Ombudsman (s96-20, Parliament of Australia, 2007). APRA is the national prudential regulator of financial institutions and is responsible for the registration and supervision of health plans. This includes establishing prudential standards and directions, regulating the Health Benefits Funds, and publicly disclosing quarterly key statistics about the insurers' membership, finances, benefits paid, and the policy coverage for each Territory and State where the insurers operate (Stavrunova and Yerokhin, 2014). APRA comes under the Treasury of the Australian government and is responsible for prudential supervision. The policy responsibility for PHI is with the Department of Health. The Private Health Ombudsman is an independent government body representing the interests of the general public by assisting PHI members in resolving discordance through a fair complaints handling service, and by providing advice to the industry and the government about insurers' performance and consumers' rights (Commonwealth Ombudsman, 2015).

In June 2016, the APRA reported that about 46.9% (11.3 million) of the Australian population held PHI with hospital coverage, including accommodation and medical services in public and private hospitals. As of June 30, 2016, 55.6% (13.4 million) of the Australian population had general treatment coverage (ancillary table cover) covering items such as dental care, optometry, and remedial massage. Despite the high percentage of PHI policyholders, PHI accounts for only 8% of total health expenditure. The majority of costs are funded through public sources (41% from the Federal Government and 27% from State and Territory budgets) and 18% from out-of-pocket (OOP) spending[4] (APRA, 2016a; AIHW, 2015, 2016).

In September 2016, the Minister for Health and Aged Care announced the establishment of the Private Health Ministerial Advisory Committee. The committee's charge is to examine the industry and to provide the government with advice on reforms including the following topics: the development of easy-to-understand categories of health insurance plans, standardization of definitions for medical procedures across insurers, simplification of the billing system, and assurance that private health plans meet the specific needs of Australians living in remote and rural Australia (Department of Health, 2016b).

## 6.2.2 Health Plan Market Regulation

Following the regulatory interventions introduced by the government since 1995, the Private Health Insurance Act (2007) was enacted with the aim of strengthening incentives to stimulate consumer choice, while maintaining high levels of PHI take-up and retention. Another goal of the Act was to mitigate the pressure on the public scheme (s3-1, Parliament of Australia, 2007). The PHI Act consolidated the main principles and regulations set by previous legislation, which are summarized in Box 6.2.

> **BOX 6.2  Fundamental principles and regulations of Australian PHI markets**
> - Community-rating and open enrollment
> - Maximum waiting periods for hospital and medical treatments
> - Portability requirements
> - Minimum benefits to be covered
> - Claims equalization

The community-rating and open enrollment principles (firstly articulated in the National Health Act, Parliament of Australia, 1953) remain the central regulatory instruments of PHI markets in Australia. Under these arrangements, insurers are obliged to charge the same premium to consumers with the same health plan and to accept any applicant. Secondly, insurers have to respect maximum waiting periods for hospital and medical treatment: 12 months for preexisting ailments and obstetrics; and 2 months in other cases (s75-1, Parliament of Australia, 2007). If PHI holders decide to switch to a health plan with similar or lower benefit levels, the new plan must provide continuity with respect to waiting periods (Division s78-1, Parliament of Australia, 2007). This means that if a (part of the) waiting period has already been served with another insurer, (that part of) the waiting period must be waived by the new health plan. This specific regulation is referred to as "portability requirements".[5] If the new health plan includes new or more benefits than the consumer's previous plan, the waiting periods for these benefits are as stipulated in the new policy, meaning that "if a person is switching to a new policy with a higher level of cover, he/she will have to serve the entire relevant waiting period for that higher level of coverage" (PHIAC, 2015c).

In addition to the aforementioned regulations, the Private Health Insurance Act 2007 reinforces the prescription that minimum benefits are to be covered (s72-1, Parliament of Australia, 2007), to which four types of regulatory instruments (continue to) apply in order to maintain incentives for PHI to be attractive and affordable. This includes the introduction of the claims equalization scheme, which will be described in Section 6.3.

The first incentive is the so-called Premium Rebate (PR) which prescribes that PHI-holders with at least hospital cover[6] are eligible for a means tested ad valorem premium-based subsidy. This subsidy is a percentage of the premium, decreasing with income and increasing with age (see Table 6.1 for details). The second incentive is the Medicare Levy Surcharge (MLS), which is calculated as a percentage (i.e., 1.0%−1.5%) of taxable income above an annual threshold (i.e., A\$90,000 for singles and A\$180,000 for families). Australian taxpayers are exempt from paying MLS when their income is below the annual threshold of A\$90,000 or when their individual

**TABLE 6.1** The Australian Government Private Health Insurance Rebate and Medicare Levy Surcharge Tiers

| Singles | ≤ A$90,000 | A$90,001–105,000 | A$105,001–140,000 | ≥ A$140,001 |
|---|---|---|---|---|
| Families | ≤ A$180,000 | A$180,001–210,000 | A$210,001–280,000 | ≥ A$280,001 |
| | | Rebate | | |
| | Base tier (%) | Tier 1 (%) | Tier 2 (%) | Tier 3 (%) |
| < Age 65 | 25.934 | 17.289 | 8.644 | 0 |
| Age 65–69 | 30.256 | 21.612 | 12.966 | 0 |
| Age 70+ | 34.579 | 25.934 | 17.289 | 0 |
| | | Medicare levy surcharge | | |
| All ages | 0.0 | 1.0 | 1.25 | 1.5 |

Source: Australian Government Private Health Insurance Rebate. (n.d.). Australian government private health insurance rebate. [Web page] Retrieved from http://www.privatehealth.gov.au/healthinsurance/incentivessurcharges/insurancerebate.htm

income is below A\$21,335, even if their family income exceeds the threshold of A\$180,000. The PR and the MLS thresholds and percentages are shown in Table 6.1.[7]

The third incentive is the introduction of Lifetime Health Cover, which has been created with the purpose of encouraging younger people to take up PHI by the age of 31 and to maintain it thereafter. This surcharge only applies to hospital cover (i.e., services that require hospital admission) and works as follows: for every year beyond the age of 30 that the purchase of PHI is foregone, individuals pay a 2% loading fee on top of the community-rated premium. In 2016, 7.1 million Australian adults under the age of 31 held hospital cover (APRA, 2016a).

## 6.2.3    Health Plan Choice Options for Consumers

The affordability of PHI and the sustainability of the industry are two of the founding principles motivating the salient features of the PHI regulatory framework, which ultimately aims at encouraging consumers to purchase PHI. The underlying rationale to support PHI and private healthcare provision is to remove pressure from the public system by enabling mixed public and private services to meet healthcare needs. From a consumer's perspective, the main benefits of being treated as a private patient include free choice of doctors (ABS, 2009; Ward et al., 2015), shorter waiting times (ABS, 2009; Johar & Savage, 2010), and avoidance of tax penalties such as the Medicare Levy Surcharge (ABS, 2009). Once consumers are enrolled in PHI they have several options (see Box 6.3) which are described in more detail below.

Health insurance products differ in terms of type and level of benefits, with distinct levels of coverage among states. Summed over all states, there are currently more than 50,000 PHI products in the market (Department of Health, 2016b). Information on how products differ is largely unavailable and, to date, no systematic review of the degree of product differentiation has been undertaken. APRA discloses aggregate lists of products, grouping them under three main categories: hospital, general, and hospital and general combined. However, a number of factors that might contribute to the

---

**BOX 6.3 Consumer choice options regarding PHI**
- Voluntary enrollment (though some consumers are subject to substantial tax penalties for not purchasing PHI)
- Choice of health plan and coverage (benefits)
- Choice of deductible and copayment options
- Choice of contract period

proliferation of products have been identified and typically reflect individuals' or groups' features and needs, such as (PHIAC, 2013, pp. 45−48):

1. Temporary residents—all residents (students and workers) under a temporary visa must have a PHI plan.
2. Urban versus rural/remote—The available segments and services vary according to location and access to private hospital services. The availability of these services also varies immensely from state to state, and even among towns.
3. Online-only products—These products are more attractive to young profile consumers and highly mobile workers.

### 6.2.4    Link Between Private Health Insurance and Medicare

The existing public/private mix in health insurance and financing is characterized by a partial duplication in hospital coverage for PHI holders. More specifically, this means that PHI holders, unlike individuals without PHI, can choose between being treated as a public or a private patient in public hospitals. If treated as private patients in public hospitals, they would still retain entitlements under the public scheme (e.g., Medicare) and would also have:

- Choice of physician, rather than a doctor assigned by the treating hospital (ABS, 2009; Ward et al., 2015);
- Prioritized admission and shorter waiting times (ABS, 2009; Johar and Savage, 2010);
- Reduced (albeit uncertain) out-of-pocket spending. The Medicare Schedule fee covers 75% of services and procedures. In many instances, private insurers contract with medical specialists to cover (at least part of) the remaining 25% of costs (Shmueli and Savage, 2014).[8]

PHI also covers services that aren't covered (fully) under Medicare, e.g., private ambulance services, dental care, physiotherapy, and occupational therapy expenses.[9]

### 6.2.5    Instruments for Health Plans to Promote Efficiency in the Delivery of Care

The most commonly used instrument to promote efficiency in the delivery of care is "selective contracting." This happens within a relatively flexible negotiation framework between insurers and providers. As far as hospital care is concerned, some insurers enter agreements with private hospitals. These agreements are called Hospital Purchaser Provider Agreements (HPPAs) and specify the prices insurers pay for treatments provided to health plans' members (APRA, 2015b). To improve efficiency and share the risk between insurers and hospitals, the agreed price is based on the type of activity (i.e., episode of care) instead of the length of stay. Selective contracting instances and associated negotiations have been reported to the Australian Competition and Consumer Commission (ACCC). Examples include a large private health insurer contracting with one hospital while excluding others, and a large hospital group adopting a "one-in, all in" position (one provider for all services), resulting in a debilitated bargaining position for insurers (ACCC, 2011). Furthermore, HPPAs allow hospitals to demonstrate compliance with a set of quality and service criteria, and be assessed by the Second Tier Advisory Committee. This assessment authorizes hospitals to rate on 85% of the average rate for a particular service as reflected in each insurer's contract (Australia Private Hospitals Association, 2015), which is especially relevant for areas that are underserved.

Insurers also negotiate with other providers via the so-called Medical Purchaser Provider Agreements (MPPAs). These negotiations differ significantly from the negotiations with hospitals. Contrary to the HPPAs, MPPAs include a fixed excess fee over the Medicare Benefits Schedule (MBS) fees for the practitioners' services. From the consumers' perspective, these agreements limit or possibly eliminate any payable out-of-pocket costs or copayments.

Insurers vertically integrate to achieve more control over providers, such as in dental and optical care. Other insurers turned to network design, which is relatively new to the Australian PHI market and focuses mainly on non-hospital services. Thus, at this point it is relatively small and is mainly available in urban areas (Private Health Insurance Administration Council, 2013).

## 6.3 HEALTH PLAN PAYMENT DESIGN

The payment flows between the consumer, the insurer, and the Special Account are summarized in Fig. 6.1. Consumers pay a community-rated premium to their insurer, denoted by P. The flows between the insurer and the Special Account, denoted by S, are a combination of risk equalization and

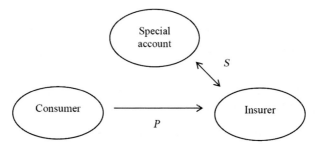

**FIGURE 6.1** Payment flows in Australia's claims equalization scheme.
S = Claims equalization payment; P = Premium. *Paolucci, F. den Exter, A. van de Ven, W., 2006. Solidarity in competitive health insurance markets: analysing the relevant EC legal framework. Health Econ. Policy Law 1(2), 107−126 (Paolucci et al., 2006).*

risk sharing: at the end of every quarter insurers with an over-representation of elderly and high-cost insured receive a payment from the Special Account, and insurers with an under-representation of elderly and high-cost insured contribute a payment to the Special Account. The age-based portion of the payment is a combination of risk equalization and risk sharing, and the high-cost portion of the payment is a form of risk sharing. In this chapter, we will refer to this hybrid health plan payment system as "claims equalization."

Consumers pay solely to their insurer; they do not contribute to the Special Account directly. Moreover, no payments and contributions are made by a government agency (Connelly et al., 2010). All transfers from and to the Special Account occur at the state level.

### 6.3.1 Premium Regulation and Contributions

Under the Private Health Insurance Act, premium changes for existing health insurance products must be approved by the Minister of Health. New products do not require premium approval. The approval of premium changes needs to be in accordance with the public interest (APRA, 2015b). Stated objectives of premium regulation include (APRA, 2015b, p. 27):

- Ensuring an attractive PHI product for consumers;
- Keeping downward pressure on PHI premiums;
- Protecting the government's interest in PHI;
- Transparency in the approval of PHI premiums;
- Timeliness in the approval of PHI premiums; and
- Consistency in the approval of PHI premiums.

The process of premium approval involves the submission of specific information, such as an application form, the appointed actuary report, the APRA operations reports, the APRA quarterly data on health insurance business, and the Standard Information Statements (APRA, 2016b). By convention, this process is done annually, although insurers can apply anytime. In the last 6 years, the average premium increase was 5.7% per year, which is higher than the 2.2% per year increase in the consumer price index (Department of Health, 2016a).

### 6.3.2 Claims Equalization: A Combination of Risk Equalization and Risk Sharing

#### 6.3.2.1 General Principles

In a nutshell, claims equalization in Australia works as follows. First, the regulator (i.e., APRA) determines the individual-level insurance claims that are eligible for claims equalization (Section 6.3.2.2). Second, the regulator calculates the average eligible claims per insurer per state. Insurers with above-average eligible claims in a state receive from the Special Account while those with below-average eligible claims pay to the Special Account (Section 6.3.2.3).

### 6.3.2.2 Claims Costs Eligible for Claims Equalization

Claims equalization applies to claims costs for three types of services (Connelly et al., 2010): hospital services (i.e., services that require hospitalization as a private patient), hospital substitute services provided by ancillary providers (e.g., dental treatment, home nursing, physiotherapy, and chiropractic treatment) and chronic disease management programs (i.e., treatments aimed at reducing complications and enhancing the prognosis of patients with diagnosed chronic diseases).

The individual-level claims allocated to the claims equalization pool consist of two components. The first component is referred to as the Age-Based Pool (ABP) and is calculated as the product of claims costs (for the above-mentioned services) and an age-specific weight. The second component is referred to as the High-Cost Claimants Pool (HCCP) and based on the claims costs (for the above-mentioned services) that remain after subtracting the allocation to the ABP. The sum of ABP and HCCP allocations is the "claims costs eligible for claims equalization" and forms the basis for transfers between insurers and the Special Account (see Section 6.3.2.3).

### Age-Based Pool (ABP)

Allocations to the ABP in quarter $q$ are calculated by multiplying specific age weights with the claims in quarter $q$. As shown in Table 6.2, the weights increase with age. The ABP constitutes a combination of risk sharing and risk equalization based on age only. This part of the system compensates insurers for the above-average claims costs of elderly people. More specifically, insurers with relatively many elderly enrollees will receive from the Special Account while those with relatively few elderly people will contribute to the Special Account. This mitigates incentives for risk selection and levels the playing field for insurers.

Table 6.2 provides an illustration of the allocation to the ABP. Column B shows the weight per age group. Columns C and E demonstrate the claims costs (for hospital services, hospital substitute services, and chronic disease management programs) for two hypothetical insurers in a given quarter. The total ABP allocation for an insurer is obtained by multiplying the claims per age group with the relevant age-based weight in column B. The resulting ABPs for insurers 1 and 2 are contained in columns D and F, respectively. The bottom row shows the column totals which reveal that the ABP allocation is larger for insurer 1 than for insurer 2.

**TABLE 6.2 The allocation to the Age-Based Pool (ABP): Two Hypothetical Insurers**

| A | B | C | D = BC | E | F = BE |
|---|---|---|---|---|---|
| Age group | ABP weight | Claims costs Insurer 1 | ABP allocation Insurer 1 | Claims costs Insurer 2 | ABP allocation Insurer 2 |
| 0–54 | 0.000 | A$13,818,135 | A$0 | A$10,242,164 | A$0 |
| 55–59 | 0.150 | A$1,765,650 | A$264,848 | A$1,308,721 | A$196,308 |
| 60–64 | 0.425 | A$2,516,052 | A$1,069,322 | A$1,864,927 | A$792,594 |
| 65–69 | 0.600 | A$4,025,683 | A$2,415,410 | A$2,983,884 | A$1,790,330 |
| 70–74 | 0.700 | A$6,843,661 | A$4,790,563 | A$5,072,603 | A$3,550,822 |
| 75–79 | 0.760 | A$12,044,844 | A$9,154,081 | A$8,927,781 | A$6,785,114 |
| 80–84 | 0.780 | A$21,439,823 | A$16,723,062 | A$15,891,449 | A$12,395,330 |
| 85 + | 0.820 | A$39,020,477 | A$31,996,791 | A$28,922,438 | A$23,716,399 |
| Totals | | A$101,474,325 | A$66,414,077 | A$75,213,967 | A$49,226,898 |

Source: APRA Australian Prudential Regulation Authority (APRA), 2015a. Operations of the Private Health Insurers Annual Report 2014–20015. Australian Prudential Regulation Authority, Canberra; Connelly, L. Paolucci, F. Butler, J. Collins, P., 2010. Risk equalization and voluntary health insurance markets: the case of Australia, Health Policy 98, pp. 3-14, p. 7.

### High-Costs Claimants Pool (HCCP)

Once individual-level allocations to the ABP have been determined, the regulator subtracts the ABP allocation for individual $i$ from the claims (for the three relevant types of services) of individual $i$ in quarter $q$. The remaining claims for individual i in quarter q are referred to as the "residual" ($r_{i,q}$). This residual forms the basis for the allocation to the HCCP (Parliament of Australia, 2007). Contrary to the ABP, allocations to the HCCP in quarter $q$ are not only based on claims in quarter $q$, but also on those in $q$-1, $q$-2, and $q$-3 (Connelly et al., 2010, p. 8). Before explaining the reason for taking into account the three previous quarters we first provide a technical description of how allocations to the HCCP are calculated. First, the regulator determines the so-called "cumulative residual" $cr$ for individual $i$ in quarter $q$ as:

$$cr_{iq} = r_{i,q} + r_{i,q-1} + r_{i,q-2} + r_{i,q-3} \qquad (6.1)$$

Second, the regulator determines the allocation to the HCCP for individual $i$ in quarter $q$ as:

$$\text{HCCP}_{iq} = \max\left(0.82\left(cr_{iq} - T\right) - \text{HCCP}_{i,q-1} - \text{HCCP}_{i,q-2} - \text{HCCP}_{i,q-3}, 0\right) \qquad (6.2)$$

in which $T$ is the cost threshold after which risk sharing applies, 0.82 is the rate of risk sharing above the threshold, and $\text{HCCP}_{i,q-1}$, $\text{HCCP}_{i,q-2}$, and $\text{HCCP}_{i,q-3}$ are the allocations to the HCCP for individual $i$ in quarters $q$-1, $q$-2, and $q$-3, respectively. The rationale for taking into account these previous quarters is that the threshold applies to spending over the past year (rather than the past quarter). Since medical costs can be billed in multiple quarters, the regulator takes into account four quarters ($q$, $q$-1, $q$-2, and $q$-3) to determine whether an individual's cumulative residual exceeded the threshold in the past year. The idea behind the HCCP is that insurers are compensated for their high-cost cases, a form of risk sharing. Ceteris paribus, insurers with relatively many high-cost cases will receive from the Special Account while those with relatively few high-cost cases will contribute to the Special Account. This mechanism mitigates incentives for risk selection and levels the playing field for insurers.

To illustrate the calculation of allocations to the HCCP, Table 6.3 provides a hypothetical example for a 63-year-old enrollee. From Table 6.2 we know that the age-weight for this individual equals 0.425 (see column B of Table 6.2). Assume that the amounts in column B of Table 6.3 represent the individual's claims costs (for the three relevant services) per quarter. In $q$-3 and $q$-2, no claims are allocated to the HCCP: in $q$-3 there were no claims at all, and in $q$-2 the cumulative residual did not exceed the threshold. In $q$-1 and $q$, the situation is different as the cumulative residual exceeds the threshold, resulting in an allocation to the HCCP. In $q$-1 the allocation to the HCCP equals A\$34,588, i.e., 0.82 times the difference between the

**TABLE 6.3** Hypothetical Example of the Working of the High-Cost Claimant Pool (HCCP)

| A | B | C = 0.425(B) | D = B − C | E | F | H |
|---|---|---|---|---|---|---|
| Quarter | Claims | Age-Based Pool (ABP) allocation | Residual | Cumulative Residual (cr), See Formula (6.1) | Threshold (T) | Allocation to HCCP, See Formula (6.2) |
| q-3 | Nil | Nil | Nil | Nil | Nil | Nil |
| q-2 | A$75,292 | A$31,999 | A$43,293 | A$43,293 | A$50,000 | Nil |
| q-1 | A$85,021 | A$36,134 | A$48,887 | A$92,180 | A$50,000 | A$34,588 |
| q | A$60,000 | A$25,500 | A$34,500 | A$126,680 | A$50,000 | A$28,290 |

Note: In this example we assume that in q-3, q-2, and q-1 the sum of allocations to the HCCP over the three preceding quarters is zero. In quarter q the sum of allocations to the HCCP over the three preceding quarters equals A$34,588.
Source: Connelly, L. Paolucci, F. Butler, J. Collins, P., 2010. Risk equalization and voluntary health insurance markets: the case of Australia, Health Policy 98, pp. 3-14, p. 8.

cumulative residual in $q$-1 (A\$92,180) and the cost threshold of A\$50,000. In quarter $q$ the allocation to the HCCP equals A\$29,290, i.e., 0.82 times the difference between the cumulative residual in $q$ (A\$126,680) and the cost threshold of A\$50,000, minus the allocation to the HCCP in $q$-1 (A\$34,588).

### 6.3.2.3   Calculation of Transfers

The claims equalization scheme is depicted in Fig. 6.2. In sum, the Special Account pools the eligible claims costs (i.e., the ABP and HCCP allocations) of all insurers in a state. Transfers between the insurers and the Special Account are made every quarter and based on the difference between the average eligible claims costs for an insurer and the average eligible claims costs in the state. The result is that insurers with relatively high per-person eligible claims will be net receivers while those with relatively low per-person eligible claims will be net payers. This mechanism reduces incentives for risk selection and levels the playing field for insurers.

Table 6.4 illustrates the calculation of transfers, which is based on two types of information: (1) the allocations to the ABP (column B) and HCCP (column C), and (2) the so-called Average Single Equivalent Unit (SEU), which is shown in column D. The SEU indicates the number of enrollees (APRA, 2016b): one SEU for a policy that covers only one adult (possibly with children), or two or more children; two SEUs for a policy that covers two or more adults.

The calculation of transfers proceeds as follows. First, the state-level pooled claims per SEU (column F) are calculated by dividing the total

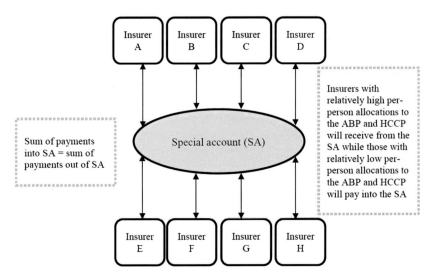

**FIGURE 6.2** The claims equalization scheme. *Source: Connelly, L. Paolucci, F. Butler, J. Collins, P., 2010. Risk equalization and voluntary health insurance markets: the case of Australia, Health Policy 98, 3–14.*

**TABLE 6.4** Hypothetical Example of a Payment Transfer Calculation: One State With Two Insurers

| A | B | C | D | E = B + C | F = E/D | G | H = E − G |
|---|---|---|---|---|---|---|---|
| | Allocation to ABP | Allocation to HCCP | SEUs | Actual pooled claims = | State total pooled claims per SEU | Normative pooled claims = D * State pooled claims per SEU | Transfer |
| Insurer 1 | A$66,414,077 | Nil | 463,024 | A$66,414,077 | — | A$66,431,819 | − A$17,742 |
| Insurer 2 | A$49,226,897 | A$30,000 | 343,193 | A$49,256,897 | — | A$49,239,155 | A$17,742 |
| State Total | A$115,640,974 | A$30,000 | 806,217 | A$115,670,974 | A$143.47 | A$115,670,974 | A$ 0 |

SEU, Single Equivalent Unit; ABP, Aged-Based Pool; HCCP, High-Cost Claimant Pool.
Source: APRA Australian Prudential Regulation Authority (APRA), 2015a. Operations of the Private Health Insurers Annual Report 2014–20015. Australian Prudential Regulation Authority, Canberra.

pooled claims (bottom row of column E) by the total number of SEUs (bottom row of column D). Second, the normative pooled claims for an insurer (column G) are calculated by multiplying the insurer's SEUs (column D) by the state-level pooled claims per SEU (bottom row of column F). In a final step, the transfer to/from an insurer (column H) is calculated as the difference between the insurer's actual pooled claims (column E) and normative pooled claims (column G). For details, see Connelly et al. (2010).

### 6.3.3    Implementation and Maintenance

The maintenance of the claims equalization scheme in Australia is carried out by both the Department of Health and APRA. Although the Health Minister is required to consult APRA prior to any changes in the claims equalization policy, failing to consult APRA does not nullify the changes. APRA is an independent regulator that is largely funded by the industries it regulates. It is responsible for the supervision and administration of the Special Account as well as the supervision of insurers' compliance with the PHI Act (2007) and subsequent rules (2015). Through consultation with stakeholders, APRA sets the prudential policy for PHI. APRA takes part in the process of maintaining the claims equalization scheme and calculating health plan payments. For example, it analyzes all the reports received from the insurers which are used as a basis for the health plan payments. These reports include financial and capital data, and detailed information about the health insurance business (APRA, 2016c), such as the number of insured people and type of policies. The APRA website provides templates for these reports, which insurers need to submit every quarter. According to the PHI (Council Administration Levy) Rules 2007, the census day refers to the last day of March, June, September, and December (APRA, 2015c), and the insurers have the following 28 days to submit the reports (APRA, 2016d). After compiling all the insurers' data, APRA publishes quarterly statistics and an annual report on the functioning of the claims equalization scheme on its website.

### 6.4    EVALUATION OF HEALTH PLAN PAYMENT

To the best of our knowledge, no formal public evaluation of the health plan payment scheme has been conducted. This section summarizes some research papers that have focused on the impact of the regulatory framework and the claims equalization scheme.

### 6.4.1    Sustainability of the Private/Public-Mix Services Provision

King (2013) studied the trend in the number of private patients in public hospitals. He found that the percentage of private patients in public hospitals increased from 7.8% in 2005−2006 to 10.5% in 2010−11. The author concludes that the increase in the number of private patients is a direct result of the capped Commonwealth and State funding arrangements. These arrangements limit the expenditure budget for public hospitals, thereby stimulating hospitals to attract private patients in order to get additional revenue (King, 2013).

In 2009, a survey concluded that 24% of Australians with PHI did not disclose their health plan in the admission and received services as public patients (ABS, 2009). This is considered as undesirable since it leads to a shift of costs from the private to the public domain.

## 6.4.2 Price and Premium Regulation

As described in Section 6.3.1, premium levels are subject to control and approval by the Ministry of Health (PHIAC, 2015b). Over time, consumer organizations have been complaining about premium increases, which negatively affect the affordability of PHI. Some have argued that premium increases should be linked to the national consumer price index (CPI) to increase PHI uptake. Currently, the weighted average premium increase doubles the CPI (ABS, 2017) (see Table 6.5).

Some have complained about "overregulation" of premiums by the Ministry of Health and several proposals have been made to address this

**TABLE 6.5** Average Premium Increases in Comparison With the National Consumer Price Index, by Year

| Year | Industry-weighted average premium increase (Department of Health, 2016) (%) | National Consumer Price Index (ABS 2016b) (%) |
| --- | --- | --- |
| 2017 | 4.80 | 1.50 |
| 2016 | 5.59 | 1.30 |
| 2015 | 6.18 | 1.30 |
| 2014 | 6.20 | 2.90 |
| 2013 | 5.60 | 2.50 |
| 2012 | 5.06 | 1.60 |
| 2011 | 5.56 | 3.30 |
| 2010 | 5.78 | 2.90 |
| Total average | 5.59 | 2.16 |

Note: The national consumer price index corresponds to the value recorded in March for each year.

issue (Deloitte, 2012; PHIAC, 2013). These proposals recommend the development of better data collection and analytics and the creation of a consumer charter: "Such a charter would stipulate commitment to standards of service and actions that the industry can take if these standards are not met. The charter would define the timelines for the regulatory process," as well as "release guidelines outlining definition of assessment criteria and process" (Deloitte, 2012). Another recommendation is to shorten the process of premium approval and to align this process with the financial year (Deloitte, 2012).

### 6.4.3 Instruments for Health Plans to Promote Efficiency in the Delivery of Care

In Australia, some medical associations have expressed their opposition to contractual arrangements with insurers as these can lead to interference from insurers with clinical independence (ACCC, 2011).[10] On the other hand, the Australia Competition and Consumer Commission has warned that the absence of agreements with medical specialists can increase prices due to the scarcity and uniqueness of their expertise (APRA, 2015b).

Regarding the newly developed vertical integration of ancillary services by insurers, the extent of this integration and its repercussions on the PHI market competitiveness require further studying and investigation. Nevertheless, there has been a specific concern that, when both insurers and service providers often have different financial incentives, "there is a risk that vertical integration will require compromise on one or other side of the equation" (Private Health Insurance Administration Council, 2013). However, this premise of vertical integration of ancillary services is still developing and will continue to be of interest to regulators.

### 6.4.4 Claims Equalization Scheme, Risk Selection, and Adverse Selection

Prior to the introduction of the Private Health Insurance Act in 2007, the Productivity Commission (1999) reported that the then low percentage of PHI membership in Australia was driven by the requirement for insurers to keep the premium flat regardless of the contract length. Such regulation, at that time, exacerbated adverse selection as high-risk consumers showed a tendency to enroll in PHI, while low-risk consumers showed a tendency to opt out.

Connelly et al. (2010) empirically investigated the effect of the then new claims equalization scheme in Australia on risk selection—precisely 1 year after its commencement. It was found that the net transfers between insurers, which were relatively small at the industrial level and relatively large for small insurers, did not provide a clear indication regarding the extent of risk selection under the claims equalization scheme using only 1 year's data. Connelly et al. (2010) concluded that more time is needed—to collect data (time-series) and to be able to measure the effect on the risk arrangements on risk selection in Australia.

Based on the requirement of community rating and given the information asymmetry, Buchmueller et al. (2013) tested the theory that consumer knowledge of their health risk would predict "a positive correlation between insurance coverage and expected claims." Buchmueller et al. (2013) found no positive correlation in the Australian PHI market and also found that PHI holders' inpatient and outpatient utilization are less than non-PHI holders. These findings suggest the presence of advantageous selection rather than adverse selection and also suggest the presence of other factors that drive the demand for PHI. It was found that an important factor for the PHI demand is the opportunity cost of time as PHI allows consumers to skip long waiting times (PHI insures consumers against the opportunity cost of time).

### 6.4.5 Health Plan Choice Options for Consumers

To some extent product proliferation is also regulation-induced. As pointed out by Paolucci et al. (2011), product proliferation is a way to get around the requirement of community-rating. Armstrong et al. (2010) have reported plan proliferation in Ireland and South Africa. Product proliferation is also induced by regulations prohibiting insurers from discontinue existing policies while allowing them to discontinue their availability to new members. Additionally, the absence of regulations restricting the creation of new products, including new ways of bundling benefits without prior authorization, has contributed greatly to product proliferation. Increasingly, insurers have been bundling traditional products with preventative programs to promote healthy living and reduce members' health risks. The great variety of options within the preventative programs space seems to have contributed to product proliferation as well.

An important tool for product differentiation is cost sharing flexibility. For a policy covering only one person, the maximum deductible is A$250 per year; for all other policies, it is about A$1000 (PHIAC, 2015a). Similarly, copayments are unregulated and do not impact consumers' eligibility for Premium Rebate and/or Medicare Levy Surcharge (PHIAC, 2015d).

### 6.5 ONGOING ISSUES AND REFORMS

The current public/private mix in healthcare financing and provision in Australia, with fragmented governance and a multitude of healthcare purchasers (e.g., the Commonwealth, State governments, consumers, and private insurers), suffers from fundamental design inconsistencies that have led to inefficiencies and affordability issues. This section summarizes the main shortcomings of the PHI regulations and the claims equalization scheme, and proposes some reforms.

## 6.5.1  Duplication Between Public and Private Coverage

The overlap between public and private coverage is one of the main sources of inefficiency in the funding of the Australian healthcare system. Duplication arises from the fact that individuals voluntarily purchasing PHI gain faster access and greater choice of care delivered in public hospitals, while remaining entitled to public services (no opt out). It is interesting to observe that, despite the high PHI take up ($\sim 47\%$), PHI spending represents only 8.3% of total expenditure (AIHW, 2016). If any inference can be deduced from these numbers, it is that the service utilization by private patients is not proportional to the PHI overall coverage or that there is no clear distinction or disclosure of the health plan in public hospitals by PHI holders due to the duplication between both the public and private schemes. Nevertheless, private patients using public hospitals constitute a significant financial resource to the state hospital expenditure budget (King, 2013). To tackle these inefficiencies, Paolucci et al. (2008, 2011) recommend allowing individuals to opt out of Medicare voluntarily. In this same discussion, Seah et al. (2013) suggest three other directions. The first alternative is to expand what already is being done by private patient liaison officers in hospitals: informing patients about their PHI benefits. The second alternative is to "create a mandated PHI policyholder registry to allow public hospitals to identify patients with PHI." And lastly, the third option is a "primary payer model" for insurers in the hospital. In this model, which is also used in the United States, "When there is more than one payer an established procedure for 'coordination of benefits' exists. In the US, the PHI company is always the 'primary payer' and Medicare is the secondary payer" (Seah et al., 2013). In the Australian context, mirroring the US model would mean that insurers would have the primacy in hospital bills over Medicare, so that for PHI patients admitted in a public hospital, the PHI would be the primary payer and Medicare would solely cover costs not covered by PHI (Seah et al., 2013).

Between 2008 and 2009, the National Health and Hospital Commission set up by the government also indicated competitive integrated national health insurance with risk-adjusted subsidies (the so-called "Medicare Select" proposal) as the preferred long-term strategy for a sustainable, efficient, equitable, and modern healthcare system insurance and financing design (National Health and Hospital Reform Commission, 2009). These proposals have been put forward in a context of a shifting burden of diseases towards chronic conditions, which requires adequate and integrated responses. The legal inability for private health insurers to cover GP care, and the increasing out-of-pocket expenditures (as a share of total healthcare expenditures) resulting from this, have been impeding integration and coordination of care to address the needs of chronic patients (Paolucci and Goni, 2015).

## 6.5.2 Issues Related to Health Plan Payment

Paolucci et al. (2011) have argued that, to improve efficiency while reducing selection, it is necessary to add ex ante risk-adjusted subsidies to those based only on share of elderly.

### 6.5.2.1 Risk Adjusters

When it comes to the development of ex ante risk equalization, age/gender-based risk adjusters can be readily introduced. In addition, the Australian diagnosis-related groups (DRGs) could be used as a basis for risk adjustor variables, as DRGs allow for identification of individuals' health status and the associated claims (Fouda et al., 2017). Paolucci and Shmueli (2011) argued that the current scheme can be improved through tweaks in the demographic risk adjusters (i.e., adding gender). They point out, however, that demographic factors alone cannot deter risk selection. Adding health-based indicators or retaining some risk sharing will be crucial. This approach requires the linking of the state hospital and expenditure data with the federal medical and pharmaceutical expenditure data at the individual level (Paolucci and Shmueli, 2011).

### 6.5.2.2 Claims Equalization Transfers and Pool Size

The size of the claims equalization pool has increased from A$1.3bn in 1999−2000 (Ahluwalia et al., 2011) to A$5.7bn in 2014−15, with consequences for the competitiveness of small insurers. The Australian PHI market has a small number of large insurers and a large number of small insurers (Private Health Insurance Administration Council, 2013). A closer look at the absolute value of claims equalization transfers shows that smaller insurers, with a market share under 2%, receive a significantly low absolute value/amount of risk-pooled transfers, threatening their viability, compared to bigger insurers which are net receivers of transfers. This trend, which favors the big insurers, poses a threat to the sustainability of the market and to the competitiveness of the small insurers. As reported by PHIAC (2013), in 2011−12 BUPA (one of the largest insurers) received risk-pooled transfers equal to 4.5% of total claims paid in that period. On the other side, 15 small insurers who account for around 1% of the market each transferred 10% in excess of their actual claims in 2011−12. The justification for these transfers should be investigated. If smaller insurers have a systematically healthier (lower-cost) population, the transfers are justified. Furthermore, big insurers have a larger-volume internal claims transaction which tends more to the national average, leading to a lower level of net transfers (less than 5%) as a proportion of their actual claims paid (PHIAC, 2013).

### 6.5.2.3   Costs of Chronic Disease Management Programs

After passing the Private Health Insurance Act in 2007, Broader Health Cover (BHC) benefits were introduced to offer preventive or substitute services for hospitalization, disease management, and wellness programs, especially for chronic diseases. BHC was offered in the form of Chronic Disease Management Programs (CDMP) (Biggs, 2013). Biggs (2013) argues that the introduction of CDMPs led to more service utilization and improved health outcomes for some members, but further studies will be needed to determine the cost-effectiveness of the programs and also further discussions will be needed with the industry stakeholders over the adequacy of BHC and CDMPs arrangements. Connelly et al. (2010) say that one of the problems in the CDMPs arrangement is that only some CDMP benefits are eligible for inclusion in the claims equalization scheme as mentioned in Subsection 6.3.2.2. The unclear definitions of these benefits regarding the inclusion of which CDMP benefits are eligible for claims equalization and which are not eligible pose a challenge for insurers to develop CDMPs (Biggs, 2013; Hamar et al., 2015). Moreover, this unclear definition/inclusion of CDMPs complicates the claims equalization scheme.

## 6.6   FINAL COMMENTS

In Australia a number of proposals have been made that support structural reforms with a clear focus on promoting consumers' choice of insurers, the integration of the dual system (i.e., removal of the duplication), and universal guarantee for a uniform broad package of services (Paolucci and Goni, 2015; Stoelwinder, 2008, 2013; Paolucci et al., 2011; Stoelwinder and Paolucci, 2009). Major reforms are needed to integrate the management of chronic and complex diseases at the primary care level, and to keep health expenditure "under control." The roles and funding schemes that will be assigned to the Commonwealth funding, State funding, PHI, and out-of-pocket financing are still undefined. Improving sustainability and efficiency of the Australian healthcare system requires industry and government commitment.

## ACKNOWLEDGMENTS

We would like to express our gratitude to Richard van Kleef and Tom McGuire, whose support and work on the chapter has been exceptionally valuable.

## ENDNOTES

1. General Practice (GP) expenses are solely subsidized by the Medicare Schedule fee, which is usually transferred directly to the private GP practices, or paid by the patient - usually when a price higher than the Schedule Fee is paid and then reimbursed by Medicare. Most PHI policies do not cover GP consultations (PHIO 2015).
2. These assets include equities, interest-bearing assets, properties, subsidiaries and associated entities, loans, receivables, intangibles, deferred acquisition costs, and prepaid expenses, among others.
3. Shamsullah (2011, p. 24) characterizes health insurance organizations as "licensed agents of the Commonwealth," the objective of which is to strengthen the accumulation of reserves instead of the return to shareholders. As many private health insurers are now for-profit entities, to the extent this may be true, those firms presumably treat this as an objective constraint.
4. The remaining 6.1% of total health expenditure came from accident compensation schemes (AIHW, 2016).
5. To further empower consumers' choice, the Standard Information Statements (SISs) is a complementary tool to ensure that consumers receive timely and standardized information to make informed choices about insurance products (s93-1, Parliament of Australia 2007).
6. See Australian Taxation Office (https://www.ato.gov.au/individuals/medicare-levy/private-health-insurance-rebate/private-health-insurance-rebate-eligibility/). (accessed March 14, 2017).
7. The rebate is calculated based on the income tiers, the family composition, and recently age, where the income is divided based on tiers (four in total: one basic and three other tiers) and the family composition is basically divided based on the distinction of singles and families (single parents and couples are included as families). The tiers of the PHI rebate are also the same tiers used for the Medicare Levy Surcharge (MLS). The rebate is claimed through a reduced premium or through tax returns.
8. Under these arrangements, the insurers pay practitioners an amount above the Medicare Schedule Fee and their enrollees are entirely or partially indemnified against the out-of-pocket costs (i.e., the remaining 25% of the costs) of the included medical services.
9. Other services include speech therapy, eye therapy, chiropractic services, podiatry or psychology services, most surgical and other therapeutic procedures performed by doctors, glasses and contact lenses, hearing aids and other appliances, and home nursing (Department of Human Services, s/db).
10. The United States is a well-known case where medical practitioners need to confirm certain procedures with insurers before advising patients.

## REFERENCES

ABS Australian Bureau of Statistics (ABS), 2009. National Health Survey: Summary of Results, 2007–2008 (Reissue), (cat. no. 4364.0), ABS, Canberra.

ABS Australian Bureau of Statistics (ABS), 2016b. Consumer Price Index. [Web page]. Available from: http://www.abs.gov.au/AUSSTATS/abs@.nsf/Lookup/6401.0Explanatory%20Notes1Sep%202016?OpenDocument. [23 December 2016].

ABS Australian Bureau of Statistics (ABS), 2017. Consumer Price Index. [Web page]. Available from: http://www.ausstats.abs.gov.au/ausstats/meisubs.nsf/0/374225B092E1E9B9CA25810C001B87A7/$File/64010_mar%202017.pdf [23 May 2017].

Ahluwalia, A. Reid, J. Tripolano, S. 2011. Risk equalizsation 2020. Is the current system sustainable? Presented to the Institute of the Actuaries of Australia, Biennal Convention, Finity Consulting Pty Limited, Sydney.

AIHW Australian Institute of Health and Welfare, 2015. Health expenditure Australia 2014−15. AIHW, Health and welfare expenditure (series no. 57. Cat. no. HWE 67), Canberra.

AIHW Australian Institute of Health and Welfare, 2016. Australia's Health 2016. Australia's health series no. 15. Cat. no. AUS 199, AIHW, Canberra.

APRA Australian Prudential Regulation Authority (APRA), 2015a. Operations of the Private Health Insurers Annual Report 2014−20015. Australian Prudential Regulation Authority, Canberra.

APRA Australian Prudential Regulation Authority (APRA), 2015b. Competition in the Australian Private Health Insurance Market: Research Paper 1. Australian Prudential Regulation Authority, Sydney.

APRA Australian Prudential Regulation Authority (APRA), 2015c. Private Health Insurance (Council Administration Levy) Rules 2007. Australian Prudential Regulation Authority, Canberra.

APRA Australian Prudential Regulation Authority (APRA), 2016a. Private Health Insurance Membership and Coverage. Australian Prudential Regulation Authority, Canberra.

APRA Australian Prudential Regulation Authority (APRA), 2016b. Private Health Insurance Operations Report data 2015-16. Australian Prudential Regulation Authority, Sydney.

APRA Australian Prudential Regulation Authority (APRA), 2016c. Financial Sector (Collection of Data) (reporting standard) determination, No. 22 of 2016. Australian Prudential Regulation Authority, Canberra.

APRA Australian Prudential Regulation Authority Authority(APRA), 2016d. Information to assist Private Health Insurers to complete reporting forms. [Web page]. Available from: http://www.apra.gov.au/PHI/Reporting-Framework/Pages/Information-to-assist-PHI-reporting.aspx. [29 December 2016].

Armstrong, J., Paolucci, F., McLeodc, H., van de Ven, W., 2010. Risk equalisation in voluntary health insurance markets: A three country comparison. Health Policy 98, 39−49.

Australia Private Hospitals Association, 2015. Second Tier Default Benefit Eligibility. [Web page]. Available from: http://www.apha.org.au/resource/2nd-tier-default-benefit-eligibility/ [12 June 2017].

Australian Competition and Consumer Commission, 2011. Report to the Australian Senate on Anti-competitive and Other Practices by Health Funds and Providers in Relation to Private Health Insurance. Australian Competition and Consumer Commission, Canberra.

Biggs, 2013. Chronic disease management: the role of private health insurance. Parliam. Australia 2013, 9.

Buchmueller, T., Fiebig, D., Jones, G., Savage, E., 2013. Preference heterogeneity and selection in private health insurance: The case of Australia. J. Health Econ. 32 (5), 757−767.

Colombo, F., and Tapay, N. (2003). Private health insurance in Australia: a case study. OECD Health Working Paper No. 8. Paris: OECD.

Commonwealth Ombudsman, 2015. Private Health Insurance Ombudsman. State of the Health Funds Report 2015 (Financial Year 2014-15). Commonwealth Ombudsman, Canberra.

Connelly, L., Paolucci, F., Butler, J., Collins, P., 2010. Risk equalization and voluntary health insurance markets: The case of Australia. Health Policy 98, 3−14.

Deloitte, 2012. The Future of Private Health Insurance Premium-Setting: Seeking Integrative Solutions. Deloitte, Sydney.

Department of Health, 2016a. Premium Round Individual private health insurer average premium increases, [Web page]. Available from: http://health.gov.au/internet/main/publishing.nsf/content/0B815BFEB8EDECA7CA257BF000195929/$File/Table-of-premium-increases-2016.pdf. [13 November 2016].

Department of Health, 2016b. New Committee to provide recommendations on private health insurance reform, Available from: http://www.health.gov.au/internet/ministers/publishing. nsf/Content/health-mediarel-yr2016-ley056.htm. [10 December 2016].

Department of Human Services, s/db. Medicare Services: Cleft lip and cleft palate scheme, [Web page]. Available from: https://www.humanservices.gov.au/customer/services/medicare/cleft-lip-and-cleft-palate-scheme. [23 December 2016].

Fouda, A., Fiorentini, G., Paolucci, F., 2017. Competitive health markets and risk equalisation in australia: Lessons learnt from other countries. Appl. Health Econ. Health Policy. Available from: https://doi.org/10.1007/s40258-017-0330-1.

Hamar, G.B., Rula, E.Y., Coberley, C., Pope, J.E., Larkin, S., 2015. Long-term impact of a chronic disease management program on hospital utilization and cost in an Australian population with heart disease or diabetes. BMC Health Serv. Res. 15 (1), 174.

Hurley, J., Vaithianathan, R., Crossley, T.F., and Cobb-Clark, D.A. (2002). Parallel private health insurance in Australia: a cautionary tale and lessons for Canada. IZA Discussion Papers 515, Institute for the Study of Labor (IZA).

Johar, M., Savage, E., 2010. Do private patients have shorter waiting times for elective surgery? Evidence from New South Wales Public Hospitals. Economic Papers 29 (2), 128–142.

King, D., 2013. Private Patients in Public Hospitals, Sponsored by Australian Health Service Alliance & Australian Centre for Health Research. Australian Centre for Health Research.

National Health and Hospital Reform Commission, 2009. A Healthier Future for All Australians: Final Report. Commonwealth of Australia, Canberra.

Paolucci, F., Goni, M.G., 2015. The Case for Change Towards Universal and Sustainable National Health Insurance & Financing for Australia: Enabling the Transition to a Chronic Condition Focussed Health Care System. Technical paper No. 2015-07, November 2015. Australian Health Policy Collaboration.

Paolucci, F. Shmueli, A., 2011. Demographic scales for ex-ante risk equalizsation in the Australian Private Health Insurance Market, ACERH Working Paper Number 9, The University of Queensland and The Australian National University.

Paolucci, F., Shmueli, A., 2011. The introduction of ex-ante risk equalizsation in the australian private health insurance market: a first step. Agenda: J. Policy Anal. Reform 18 (2).

Paolucci, F., den Exter, A., van de Ven, W., 2006. Solidarity in competitive health insurance markets: analysing the relevant EC legal framework. Health Econ. Policy Law 1 (2), 107–126.

Paolucci, F., Butler, J., van de Ven, W., 2008. Subsidizing private health insurance in Australia: why, how, and how to proceed? Working paper series 2, Australian Centre for Economic Research on Health, The Australian National University, Canberra.

Paolucci, F., Butler, J.R., van de Ven, W.P., 2011. Removing duplication in public/private health insurance in Australia: Opting out with risk-adjusted subsidies? Agenda: J. Policy Anal Reform 18, 49–70.

Parliament of Australia, 1953. National Health Act 1953. No. 95 of 1953. Canberra.

Parliament of Australia, 2007. Private Health Insurance Act 2007, as amended. No. 31 of 2007. Canberra.

PHIAC Private Health Insurance Administration Council (PHIAC), 2013. Competition in the Australian Private Health Insurance Market: Research Paper 1. PHIAC, Canberra.

PHIAC Private Health Insurance Administration Council (PHIAC), 2015a. Risk sharing in the Australian private health insurance market: Research Paper 4. PHIAC, Canberra.

PHIAC Private Health Insurance Administration Council (PHIAC), 2015b. Barriers to entry in the Australian private health insurance market: Research Paper 3. PHIAC, Canberra.

PHIAC Private Health Insurance Administration Council (PHIAC), 2015c. Portability, switching and competition in the Australian private health insurance market: Research Paper 2. PHIAC, Canberra.

PHIAC Private Health Insurance Administration Council, 2015d. Competition in the Australian private health insurance market. PHIAC, Australia.

PHIO Private Health Insurance Ombudsman, 2015. What is covered? Private health insurance ombudsman [Web page]. Retrieved from www.privatehealth.gov.auAvailable from: http://www.privatehealth.gov.au/healthinsurance/whatiscovered/ [14 January 2017].

Productivity Commission, 1999. Annual Report 1998-99. AusInfo, Canberra.

Seah, D., Cheong, T., Anstey, M., 2013. The hidden cost of private health insurance in Australia. Australian Health Review 37, 1−3.

Shamsullah, A., 2011. Australia's private health insurance industry: structure, competition, regulation and role in a less than 'ideal world'. Aust. Health Rev. 35 (1), 23−31.

Shmueli, A., Savage, E., 2014. Private and public patients in public hospitals in Australia. Health Policy 115, 189−195.

Stavrunova, O., Yerokhin, O., 2014. Tax incentives and the demand for private health insurance. J. Health Econ. 34, 121−130.

Stoelwinder, J., 2008. Medicare Choice? Insights from Netherlands health insurance reforms. http://www.achr.com.au/pdfs/MedicareChoice.pdf.

Stoelwinder, J., 2013. Sustaining universal health care in Australia: Introducing dynamic efficiency. Healthcare: Reform or Ration. CEDA. Available from: http://www.ceda.com.au/media/302619/healthcarefinal1.pdf.

Stoelwinder, J., Paolucci, F., 2009. Sustaining Medicare through consumer choice of health funds: lessons from the Netherlands. MJA 191, 30−32.

Ward, P., Rokkas, P., Cenko, P., Pulvirenti, M., Dean, N., Carney, S., et al., 2015. A qualitative study of patient (dis)trust in public and private hospitals: the importance of choice and pragmatic acceptance for trust considerations in South Australia. BMC Health Serv. Res. 15, 297.

## FURTHER READING

ABS Australian Bureau of Statistics (ABS), 2016a. Patient Experiences in Australia: Summary of Findings, 2015-16, (cat. no. 4839.0), ABS, Canberra.

APRA Australian Prudential Regulation Authority (APRA), 2017. Private Health Insurance Membership Trends. Australian Prudential Regulation Authority, Canberra.

Australian Competition and Consumer Commission, 2015. Information and informed decision-making in private health insurance: A report to the Australian Senate on anti-competitive and other practices by health insurers and providers in relation to private health insurance (For the period of 1 July 2013 to 30 June 2014). Australian Competition and Consumer Commission, Canberra.

Australian Taxation Office, 2017. Private health insurance rebate eligibility. [Web Page] Available from: https://www.ato.gov.au/individuals/medicare-levy/private-health-insurance-rebate/private-health-insurance-rebate-eligibility/ (14 March 2017).

Department of Health, 2013. Allied health workforce, [Web page]. Available at: http://www.health.gov.au/internet/publications/publishing.nsf/Content/work-review-australian-government-health-workforce-programs-toc ∼ chapter-8-developing-dental-allied-health-workforce ∼ chapter-8-allied-health-workforce [15 September 15, 2017].

Department of Human Services, s/da. Medicare Service: Chronic Disease Management Plan. [Web page]. Available from: https://www.humanservices.gov.au/customer/services/medicare/chronic-disease-management-plan. [23 December 2016].

Ministry for Health, 2015a. Private Health Insurance (Risk Equalization Policy) Rules 2015: Explanatory Statement. [Web page]. Available from: Access date: 15 November 2016 https://www.legislation.gov.au/Details/F2015L01051/Explanatory%20Statement/Text Access date: 15 November 2016.

Ministry for Health, 2015b. Private Health Insurance (Health Insurance Business) Rules 2016. [Web Page] Available from: https://www.legislation.gov.au/Details/F2016L00503/ Explanatory%20Statement/Text Access date: 15 November 2016.

Parliament of Australia, 2015. Private Health Insurance (Prudential Supervision) Act 2015. No. 85 of 2015, Canberra.

# Chapter 7

# Risk Adjustment in Belgium: Why and How to Introduce Socioeconomic Variables in Health Plan Payment

Erik Schokkaert[1], Joeri Guillaume[2] and Carine van de Voorde[1]

[1]KULeuven, Leuven, Belgium, [2]Socialist Mutualities, Brussels, Belgium

## 7.1 INTRODUCTION

Belgium introduced a (new) system of financial accountability of its health insurers in 1995. The health insurers active in the Belgian mandatory health insurance system are nonprofit organizations with strong ideological roots, commonly called "sickness funds" or "mutualities." These sickness funds are locally organized, but they are grouped in national associations. The latter are the risk-bearing entities at the national level. We will use the term "sickness funds" for the local organizations and the term "health insurers" for the national associations. In addition, private for-profit health insurers are active on the supplementary insurance market. They are not part of the risk-adjustment system. If we refer to them we will always add the term "for-profit" to avoid confusion with the national associations of sickness funds. At first sight, the system introduced in 1995 looks like regulated competition, in which consumers can freely choose among insurers and the latter are financed partly on the basis of risk-adjusted capitation amounts. However, the financial risk of the Belgian health insurers is limited and they did not receive the instruments to control healthcare expenditures. Moreover, socioeconomic variables are important in the risk-adjustment formula. In the policy debate, an explicit distinction is made between statistically significant and normatively relevant variables. These specific features of the system can only be understood in the light of the history of health plan payment in Belgium. More details about the historical background can be found in Companje et al. (2009) and, more specifically on risk adjustment, in Schokkaert and Van de Voorde (2000).

Risk Adjustment, Risk Sharing and Premium Regulation in Health Insurance Markets.
DOI: https://doi.org/10.1016/B978-0-12-811325-7.00007-5

## 7.1.1 The Health Insurance Law of 1963

As in many European countries, the basic structure of the Belgian system of social insurance was laid out after the Second World War. Belgium opted for a Bismarckian system, in which a crucial role is played by the social organizations of employers and workers. Health insurance was part of that broader structure. Whereas it was voluntary before 1945, it became mandatory afterwards, first for workers and their families and later for the self-employed. The financing of the system was largely public, but it was implemented by private nonprofit sickness funds and provider associations. These sickness funds had strong ideological roots.

The Health Insurance Law of 1963 elaborated further the basic structure of the Belgian health insurance system by introducing a system of collective price setting through negotiations, including rules for reimbursement by the sickness funds and out-of-pocket payments for the patients. It created the National Institute for Health and Disability Insurance (RIZIV/INAMI), a government agency responsible for health and disability insurance, supervising the sickness funds, and coordinating health policy in general. The Law had as one of its main principles the condition of a yearly fixed budget for healthcare expenditures. This budget was financed by social security contributions proportional to income and by state subsidies from taxation. The health insurers received the social contributions paid by their own members. For the government subsidy, the 1963 Law proposed a risk-adjustment mechanism, taking into account the number of members in "expensive" categories such as pensioners, widows/widowers, and the disabled. The health insurers financed the health expenditures of their members. If these expenditures were larger than the revenues, the Law imposed on the health insurers the obligation to cover their deficits with (community-rated) additional premiums. In broad terms, this financial structure contained features of regulated competition with risk adjustment.

However, although officially a form of financial accountability was introduced by the 1963 Law, it has never been applied, as later governments could not agree on the application of the Law. Instead, medical expenditures were "provisionally" reimbursed with advances, distributed among the health insurers according to their expenditures in the previous year. The main reason why the legal mechanism was not implemented was the weakness of the formula for distributing the revenue to the health insurers, which did not compensate sufficiently for the differences in the risks of their members. High-income members provided higher revenues from social contributions while their medical expenditures were lower. The primitive correction through the government subsidy was insufficient to make up for this contribution effect. If the Law had been strictly applied, the health insurers would have had to bear a substantial financial risk and they would have had strong incentives for risk selection, both on the basis of income and on the basis of morbidity characteristics that were not taken up in the simple risk-adjustment formula.

There was thus a large discrepancy between the law on one hand and on the other hand the actual practice of full reimbursement of all medical expenditures with implicit subsidies from "surplus" insurers to "deficit" insurers, where the latter were mainly characterized by the lower socioeconomic status of their members. This situation was unsustainable in the long run. With all expenditures effectively reimbursed, the health insurers had no incentive to control healthcare costs and to administer benefits efficiently. On the contrary, unpopular cost-reduction efforts could lead to a loss of members with no offsetting benefit to insurers. Moreover, from a political and legal point of view, the large accounting deficits and surpluses of some health insurers could not fail to create tensions. As an illustration: in 1994 the largest sickness fund had a cumulated (theoretical) surplus of €775 million in the system of employed workers, the second largest had a cumulated (theoretical) deficit of €1.9 billion (see Schokkaert and Van de Voorde, 2000). These considerations led to a change in the legal framework in 1993.

## 7.1.2   The Introduction of Financial Accountability in 1995

The 1993 Law kept to the same principles as the Health Insurance Law of 1963, but aimed at organizing the system in a more rational and transparent way. The idea of financial accountability of the health insurers was revived, but now with the explicit intention to tackle the Achilles' heel of the weak risk-adjustment system. The concrete details of the system were contained in a Royal Decree (1994), the specific features of which strongly influenced the later developments of risk adjustment in Belgium.

This historical background helps to explain why, despite the fact that Belgium has the formal structure of regulated competition (including a model of risk adjustment), regulated competition is absent from the political debate. The idea of the regulator in 1993 was to give some financial accountability to all the actors (including the health insurers), within a Bismarckian negotiation structure. In fact, in the Belgian political culture there is strong opposition to the explicit introduction of competition both for health insurance and for healthcare provider markets. The emphasis is on equal access and on cross-subsidies from the rich to the poor and the general opinion among policymakers is that these values would be threatened by introducing too much competition. As we will see in Section 7.2, the perception and the political discourse are not fully in line with the Belgian reality, in which there is in fact a lot of competition on provider markets.

We will describe the payment flows to the insurers and the risk-adjustment system in more detail in Sections 7.3 and 7.4, where it will become clear that the financial risks of the health insurers remain limited, certainly compared to many other countries relying on regulated competition.

The possible future development of the system is discussed in Section 7.5. The current discussion on the organization of the Belgian health insurance system is dominated (or overshadowed) by the problem of the structure of the Belgian state: will health insurance/health care be defederalized? Regulated competition is still not on the agenda in Belgium. Yet, the issue of the future role of the insurers (in whatever political setting will come out of the debate) is unsettled.

Throughout the chapter we will focus on three features of the Belgian risk-adjustment system that may be relevant to other countries. First, the Belgian risk-adjustment system includes more socioeconomic variables than the risk-adjustment systems used in other countries (as far as we know). Second, Belgium applies a method that "neutralizes" the effects of variables that are significant determinants of healthcare expenditures but are regarded as inappropriate for compensation in the risk-adjusted subsidies. Third, the payment formula integrates both prospective and retrospective elements. To some extent, all these features originated from the specific formulation of the 1994 Royal Decree.

## 7.2 ORGANIZATION OF THE HEALTH INSURANCE SYSTEM

We first sketch the broad financing structure and then describe in more detail the choice options for consumers and the policy instruments for health insurers.

### 7.2.1 Broad Financing Structure

The Belgian health insurance system is of the Bismarck-type with a highly regulated insurance market (but free choice of sickness fund) and liberal provider markets. The mandatory health insurance system covers in principle the whole population of about 11.2 million people. It also covers a broad service package, including, e.g., long-term (medical) care, home health care, and large fractions of dental and mental care. This package is identical for all insured persons. The estimated total claims for 2016 were 23.8 billion euros (Source: RIZIV/INAMI, Note CGV 2016/288, 20 September 2016). In addition to these expenditures at the federal level, local governments also have some responsibilities (such as prevention and, recently, nursing homes). Expenditures at the local level are not included in the risk-adjustment mechanism.

The general financing structure is illustrated in Fig. 7.1. The 1993 Law kept the principle of a fixed budget for healthcare expenditures. This total budget is administered by the central fund (in Belgium: RIZIV/INAMI). The large bulk (85%) of the financial resources of RIZIV/INAMI comes from the National Social Security Office. The remaining 15% of RIZIV/INAMI revenues comes from earmarked financing sources (such as tobacco taxes). Since

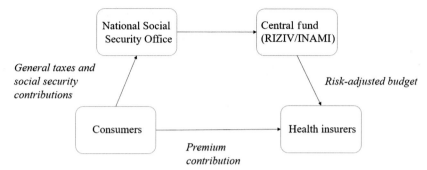

**FIGURE 7.1**    Payment flows in the Belgian health insurance system.

**TABLE 7.1  Public Financing Sources of Social Insurance**

| Financing source | 2000 (%) | 2012 (%) | 2015 (%)[a] |
|---|---|---|---|
| Social security contributions | 73.50 | 62.94 | 72.46 |
| Government subsidies | 13.39 | 14.37 | 10.49 |
| Alternative financing | 8.20 | 18.31 | 9.16 |
| Other | 4.91 | 4.38 | 7.89 |

[a]*After the state reform transferring competencies from the federal to the federated authorities.*
Source: Federal Planning Bureau and http://www.rszjaarverslag.be/2015/nl/kerntaken/financieren/inkomsten.html.

1995, the different social insurance sectors in Belgium (these also include, in addition to health insurance, pensions and unemployment benefits) are financed together, with financing surpluses in some sectors used to finance the deficits in other sectors. It is therefore not possible to separate the financing of medical expenditures from that of the other sectors. Table 7.1 shows the development of the revenue sources of the National Social Security Office. Income-related social security contributions (a mixture of employee and employer contributions) cover the largest part of total social insurance expenditures. These contributions are not collected by the insurers but are directly deducted at the source. In addition, there is also a transfer from general taxes. Part of this is alternative financing (mainly value-added taxes), which is earmarked for the financing of social insurance.

Fig. 7.2 offers another perspective on health spending in Belgium. First, it goes beyond the federal level (RIZIV/INAMI) and also includes the other sources of public financing (e.g., prevention policies financed by local governments). Public sources cover 78% of total medical expenditures. Second, Fig. 7.2 also includes spending on the market of supplementary insurance

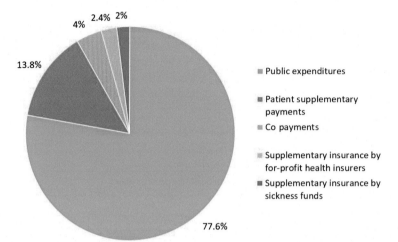

FIGURE 7.2 Public and private health spending in 2014, in percentage of total health spending. "Public expenditures" refers to healthcare spending by all the public authorities, including also the local governments that are responsible, e.g., for prevention. This notion is therefore broader than that used in the main text, which only focuses on the expenditures within the federal system (RIZIV/INAMI). "Copayments" refers to the difference between the official price of the healthcare services and the reimbursements by the health insurers. "Patient supplementary payments" refer to the supplements (extra- billing) above the official prices. *Source: Assuralia, 2017. De nationale uitgaven in de gezondheidszorg, Brussels, Assuralia (Assurinfo No. 13) (Assuralia, 2017).*

(offered both by for-profit private health insurers and by nonprofit sickness funds) which covers about 4.4% of total expenditures. Thirdly, it also shows the out-of-pocket payments by patients, which are quite substantial. The working of provider markets is covered in Section 7.2.3.

In the remainder of this chapter "healthcare budget" refers to the global budget at the federal level that is managed by RIZIV/INAMI. This budget is the main revenue source for insurers and is allocated to them on the basis of a risk-adjustment formula (see Section 7.3). The individual premium contributions are negligible (<€20 per year).

## 7.2.2 Choice Options for Consumers in the Insurance Market

Consumers can freely choose their sickness fund. They can change sickness fund at the beginning of each trimester, with a minimum enrollment period of 1 year. Less than 1% of the population switches sickness fund in any year (source: RIZIV/INAMI). In 2016, there were 53 local sickness funds, grouped in five national associations. For the mandatory insurance these national associations are the relevant risk-bearing entities. There is also a government fund acting as an insurer of last resort. As stated before, the health insurers are private nonprofit organizations with strong ideological roots. The market—and therefore also the negotiations between insurers, providers, and government—are dominated by three health insurers (Christian, Socialist, and "Independent") that are nonuniformly distributed over the regions. The Christian Mutuality dominates the northern Dutch-speaking Flanders, the Socialists and the Independents are relatively stronger in French-speaking Wallonia and in Brussels. The latter are the most market-oriented. The mandatory insurance market is closed to new insurer entrants. As the Belgian health insurance system is seen as part of "social insurance," the European antitrust regulations on service markets do not apply.

Within the mandatory insurance, the package of covered services is identical for all insurers (also with respect to prices as explained below). The local sickness funds offer in addition a differentiated "mandatory supplementary insurance," covering mostly dental care, speech therapy, home care, and psychotherapy (to the extent these are not covered in the mandatory benefits package), alternative medicine such as homeopathy, and (to an increasing extent) the copayments to be paid in the universal mandatory system. More often than not, this "mandatory supplementary package" also offers different types of fringe benefits like gifts at the birth of a child or cheap holiday arrangements. Members of a sickness fund (for the mandatory system) are obliged to take the supplementary package of that fund, giving funds a tool for competition and differentiation from their competitors.

On top of all this there is a market for voluntary supplementary (mainly hospital) insurance. The main items covered by hospital insurance are the extra-billing by providers (the "supplements") and the copayments associated with hospital stay. We will explain that system in the next section. Private for-profit insurers are active in this market. If a person opts for the hospital insurance of a sickness fund, (s)he necessarily has to enroll in the same sickness fund for the mandatory (and the "mandatory supplementary") package. Since 2012, sickness funds have had to make a strict legal and accounting distinction between their activities in the mandatory and the voluntary supplementary insurance markets. In the former they have to satisfy additional social conditions, such as community rating and pay-as-you-go financing. The law stipulates the kind of services that can be offered on both markets.

Price competition in the mandatory health insurance system is very limited, given the very small personal premium contributions. Competition between the sickness funds is mainly on service quality and on the composition of the "mandatory supplementary insurance." Before giving an overview of the possibilities they have to control healthcare expenditures, we first briefly describe the organization of healthcare provider markets.

## 7.2.3    Healthcare Provider Markets

In provider markets patients have a great deal of freedom of choice. Moreover, travel times are generally limited and waiting times are short (except for specialized nonurgent surgery). Provider payments are largely fee-for-service. Hospitals are not-for-profit. "Official prices" and reimbursement rules are set through negotiations between the providers and the ("cartel of") insurers, supervised by the government. However, there is also a possibility of extra-billing. In fact, all this means that there is a lot of competition between providers to attract patients. There is a sharp contrast between the reality of liberal provider markets and the proclaimed antimarket ideology of most players in the system.

Although the precise estimates differ somewhat depending on the definition of nonreimbursed healthcare expenditures, out-of-pocket payments are usually regarded to amount to nearly 20% of total spending (see also Fig. 7.2). Official copayments and extra-billing constitute an important share of these out-of-pocket payments. For medicines and hospital expenditures there are third-party payer arrangements. In the ambulatory sector, patients (except those with low incomes and, in some cases, the chronically ill) first pay the full price and receive reimbursement afterwards. This probably increases their price awareness. There are some social protection mechanisms such as copayment reductions for low-income patients. Moreover, there are income-dependent ceilings (a "maximum billing system") at the level of the household: as soon as the total amount of copayments paid reaches the ceiling, the patient is notified and does not have to pay anymore. Extra-billing in hospitals is excluded from the maximum billing system and regulated separately (basically it is only paid by patients in one-person rooms).

The Belgian structure of differentiated copayments has some features of "value-based insurance design" (Chernew et al., 2007; Cleemput et al., 2012). For example, copayments vary across categories of medicines and prices of brand drugs are higher if there is a generic drug available. Moreover, patients pay lower copayments if they opt for a regular family doctor. This differentiated "price structure" is common for all insurers and subject to the negotiations between insurers, providers, and government.

While patients have greater freedom of choice on provider markets, most of them are poorly informed about the prices (including the extra-billing component) and about the quality of care. It is therefore likely that the competition between providers is mainly based on the quality of the personal service provided.

## 7.2.4    Instruments for Insurers

As mentioned above, the "official fees" (and the copayments) for medical services are set through negotiations between insurers and providers within the context of RIZIV/INAMI. In these negotiations the insurers act as a cartel. While the 1993 Law refined the system of financial accountability of the insurers, it did not give them the necessary instruments at the individual level to control expenditures: as an example, in the mandatory system they are prohibited from engaging in selective contracting. In principle, the insurers would be in a good position to spread information about the quality of individual providers and hospitals among their members. For three reasons, however, they remain reluctant to do so. First, good-quality information is not always available (despite the recent improvement in the development of quality indicators for hospitals). Second, insurers are afraid to thwart the collective negotiations with the providers. Third, privacy legislation prohibits distribution of information on individual providers (when these are natural persons).

In sum, individual health insurers have little scope to increase the efficiency of the healthcare system. One can then wonder whether it made sense to introduce financial accountability with the ensuing incentives for risk selection. The "downside" of risk selection has been introduced without the "upside" of plans responding to financial accountability. However, an interesting open question is whether the introduction of financial accountability changed the incentives of (the cartel of) insurers in the negotiations with the providers about the official fees and the size of the healthcare budget. We will return to these issues in the final section.

In recent years, there has been a movement in the direction of "managed care," reflected in an increasing share of prospective provider payments and in the setting up of care programs with integrated provider networks. However, these developments are not initiated by the health insurers but by the government. The role of the insurers in this respect will also be discussed in the final section.

## 7.3 HEALTH PLAN PAYMENT DESIGN

### 7.3.1 Contributions and Premium Regulation

Each year the government (together with the social partners) fixes ex ante the healthcare budget on the basis of a so-called "growth norm," which is heavily debated during the negotiations about the government budget. If that ex ante healthcare budget turns out to be unrealistic in the course of the year, it can be adjusted (again after negotiations between the government, the provider's associations, and the health insurers) or ad hoc policy measures are implemented to curtail the expenditures. All these measures are taken at the central level.

As mentioned before, the bulk of the financing is through income-related social security contributions and government subsidies from general taxation. The individual yearly premium for the mandatory system is very small. On top of that comes the contribution for the "mandatory supplementary" package that differentiates the different health plans offered by the local sickness funds. Yet, even including this additional cost, the total yearly premium paid directly to the sickness fund remains less than €100 per person. These individual contributions are community-rated (at the level of the individual local sickness funds).

The total budget for healthcare expenditures is allocated to the insurers according to a formula that mixes prospective ("risk-adjusted") and retrospective payments. We first describe the risk-adjustment system and then explain the risk-sharing mechanism (i.e., the retrospective payments).

## 7.3.2 Risk Adjustment

### 7.3.2.1 Historical and Institutional Background

As described before, the financial accountability of the health insurers was introduced in a very cautious way. Moreover, it was based on a political compromise rather than a coherent blueprint for a new system. This institutional background has had a strong and lasting impact on the design of the risk-adjustment scheme. Indeed, the Royal Decree of 1994 included the following sentence: *For 1995 and 1996, variables that can be included (if relevant and available) are professional and social status (e.g., pensioners, social minimum recipients), age, gender, mortality, population density, unemployment rate, household composition, income.*

The first and most striking feature of this formulation is that it specifies a limited list of variables that could be taken into account for the calculation of the risk-adjusted subsidies in the first 2 years of the system. Other variables could only be included from 1997 onwards ("if relevant and available"). From the very start, this confronted the designers of the formula with the question of how to handle variables with a statistically significant effect on expenditures that were not on the list of the Royal Decree.

Second, the 1994 list did not include many indicators of morbidity (except for mortality). The focus was on socioeconomic variables. This was mainly driven by considerations of data availability: in the mid-1990s there was no adequate morbidity information available. However, an additional factor was the observation that the insurers with the largest expenditures per capita were those with relatively more enrollees with lower socioeconomic status. Therefore, socioeconomic differences were seen as the main explanation for the differences in expenditures. The rationale for including socioeconomic variables in the formula as a proxy indicator of need was to achieve a level playing field for insurers, compensating them for the expected cost of their enrollees. In that initial stage the danger of risk selection did not play any role in the policy discussions.

Note that the list of variables in the Royal Decree did not include a regional indicator, despite the fact that there were significant regional differences in expenditures, mainly along the north–south divide (and therefore the linguistic divide between Dutch- and French-speaking regions). Healthcare expenditures per capita are lower in the north, if one does not correct for differences in needs. Introducing "region" explicitly as a variable would have been extremely sensitive from a political point of view. Therefore, the approach taken was to explain regional differences as far as possible by other indicators such as population density or the regional unemployment rate. While driven by political considerations, this approach is defensible from a scientific and a normative point of view.

### 7.3.2.2   From Predicted Spending to Health Plan Payment: Neutralizing the Effect of the N-Variables

As noted above, the Royal Decree of 1994 specified a restricted set of variables that could enter the risk-adjustment formula. In the first stage of the design of the risk-adjustment formula, only aggregate data (at the level of the local sickness funds) were available. With these data an indicator of (regional) medical supply (the first principal component of indicators such as the number of hospital beds per capita and the number of physicians per capita) was highly significant. Of course, the interpretation of this result raises a well-known identification problem: does the significant coefficient of medical supply capture a phenomenon of supply-induced demand (SID), or is medical supply larger where needs are larger? With the available data, it was impossible to settle this question on statistical grounds. Moreover, the highly sensitive political discussion on the regional differences in expenditures centered exactly on the possibility of SID and the resulting political compromise had been not to include medical supply in the limited list of "acceptable" risk adjusters of the Royal Decree. Yet omitting it from the regression had a substantial impact on the other coefficients. The estimated effect of medical supply, an indicator deliberately excluded from the list of risk adjusters, would have been partially taken up by estimated coefficients of variables correlated with medical supply.

While the discussion about medical supply was triggered by the fact that the Royal Decree had imposed a restricted set of variables, it raises a general methodological issue. In general, there is no reason to think that the observed medical expenditures are the "optimal" ones (in the sense of reflecting only legitimate variation caused by differences in needs), certainly not if the data are generated in a system where overconsumption might be expected a priori. The Belgian setting before 1995 with its large degree of freedom of choice and fee-for-service remuneration for the providers, and no incentives for the insurers to control expenditures, was a case in point. The variation in observed expenditure also reflects differences in efficiency between the different insurers. While some of the significant variables point to differences in needs (call these *S*-variables, for which cross-subsidies are seen as legitimate), other variables capture these efficiency differences (call these *N*-variables, for which compensation is not desirable). *Explaining* expenditures is not the same as *specifying normative expenditures*, or "acceptable" risk-adjusted subsidies. How to handle the distinction between *S*- and *N*-variables (Van de Ven and Ellis, 2000) is an issue in many contexts. Omitting from the regression *N*-type variables that are correlated with the included *S*-type variables will lead to biased estimates of the effects of the latter. Including these *N*-type variables raises the question of how to treat them when calculating the risk-adjusted subsidies.

Belgian policymakers confronted this from the beginning. Their preferred solution was to include medical supply in the estimated regression, but to neutralize its effect in the risk-adjustment formula using methods developed in Schokkaert et al. (1998), and further developed in Schokkaert and Van de Voorde (2004, 2006, 2009). The availability of a methodology to neutralize *N*-type variables (while having them included in the statistical model) made it possible to formulate the political issues explicitly. Estimating the best possible model is a scientific question. Defining what the *S*- and *N*-variables are is a political choice. We will see in the next sections that the distinction did indeed come to the table at various occasions. Let us first describe the method in general terms.

Suppose one estimates the linear model

$$E_i = \alpha + \theta X_i + u_i \tag{7.1}$$

where $E_i$ is the expenditures of individual $i$, $X_i$ is a vector of explanatory variables, $\alpha$ and $\theta$ are coefficients to be estimated, and $u_i$ is a disturbance term. At the estimation stage the aim is to find the best explanatory model without making a distinction between *S*- and *N*-type variables. This distinction only becomes relevant when one goes from the estimated equation to the risk-adjusted subsidies.

The split between *S*- and *N*-variables involves value judgments concerning the desirable extent of cross-subsidies (or, on the other side of the coin, of individual and collective responsibility). These decisions have to be taken through the democratic process. Ultimately politicians will decide about how to partition $X_i = (S_i, N_i)$ and (correspondingly) $\theta = (\beta, \gamma)$. When the decision about the partitioning has been made, Eq. (7.1) can be rewritten as

$$E_i = \alpha + \beta S_i + \gamma N_i + u_i. \tag{7.2}$$

One can then calculate "normative expenditures" by using the estimated values of the coefficients (indicated by hats) and putting the *N*-type "responsibility variables" at a fixed value. Any fixed reference value would do, but taking the average is intuitively appealing and makes it possible to implement the budget constraint in a transparent way. This yields:

$$NO_i = \hat{\alpha} + \hat{\beta}S_i + \hat{\gamma}\overline{N}. \tag{7.3}$$

By construction, differences in these normative expenditures are only influenced by differences in the $S$-variables, for which cross-subsidies are desirable:

$$NO_i - NO_j = \hat{\beta}(S_i - S_j)$$

Insurers remain responsible for differences in expenditures, due to differences in the $N$-variables. Indeed, given that premium contributions are community-rated, these cannot be used to shift the burden towards the individual patients.

Eq. (7.3) implicitly assumes that the unexplained residual can be interpreted as an $N$-variable, i.e., that it does not capture $S$-type variation. This assumes that all the relevant $S$-variables are included in the regression model, which is highly unlikely. Of course, this problem is common to all regression-based risk-adjustment systems. The decomposition in Eq. (7.2) just makes it more explicit. Note that it is impossible to remove all incentives for risk selection without lowering the incentives for efficiency, if the model is not separable between S- and N-variables (see, e.g., Schokkaert and Van de Voorde, 2004, 2009).

In a country (like Belgium) with a fixed global budget $\omega$, it is natural to require that the total amount of normative expenditures equals $\omega$. One therefore defines "corrected normative expenditures" as

$$CNO_i = NO_i + \frac{1}{n}\left(\omega - \sum_i NO_i\right)$$

where $n$ is the total number of insured individuals. Using the definition in Eq. (7.3) of $NO_i$ and aggregating to the level of the insurer one obtains the following expression for the risk-adjusted subsidies $RAS_v$ that can easily be applied:

$$RAS_v = n_v\left[\frac{\omega}{n} + \hat{\beta}(\overline{S}^v - \overline{S})\right] \tag{7.4}$$

with $n_v$ being the number of members of insurer $v$. The term between brackets in Eq. (7.4) is a capitation amount per member of insurer $v$. The reference point is an equal distribution of the budget $(\omega/n)$. This reference value is corrected by a term capturing the estimated effect of the $S$-variable on expenditures $(\hat{\beta})$ and the difference between the average value of that $S$-variable for insurer $v$ and the country average. These "correction terms" $\hat{\beta}(\overline{S}^v - \overline{S})$ can be interpreted in a straightforward way.

## 7.3.2.3 Risk Adjusters: Socioeconomic Variables and Morbidity Indicators

As mentioned above, for the design of the initial risk-adjustment scheme only aggregated data at the level of the local sickness funds were available. The sample was small and there was not even enough variation in age to estimate the age effect in a reliable way. The first formula was dominated by the insurance status of the members (i.e., different models were estimated for the groups with preferential treatment regarding copayments) and by socioeconomic indicators: the unemployment rate, the number of public sector workers, the degree of urbanization (population density). As described, medical supply was treated as an $N$-type variable.

From 1998 onwards, the limitation of the Royal Decree was no longer present. Moreover, gradually more and better data at the individual level were collected. In fact, the collection by the health insurers of rich data at the individual level was motivated by the need for a better risk adjustment model and would probably not (or much later) have taken place if the system had not been introduced in 1995. With hindsight, this has been one of the most positive effects of the whole process, since these individual-level data are now used for the empirical evaluation of different aspects of healthcare policy on a sound scientific basis. With individual-level data, it became possible to estimate in a robust way the effects of age and gender. Until 2008, however, the morbidity information remained rather limited. At that time the formula was essentially based on demographic and socioeconomic information such as income support, allowances for handicapped and chronically ill, social isolation, population density, preferential treatment regarding copayments. Remarkably, with the individual-level data, being unemployed no longer had a significant effect. This suggests that the significance of the regional unemployment rate in the aggregate data captured some other environmental effects.

Initially, some insurers objected to the use of individual-level data with the argument that the explanatory power (in terms of $R^2$) of the aggregate model was larger. This is not merely an anecdote reflecting a misinterpretation of $R^2$: it perfectly illustrates the state of mind of many players in the Belgian setting. They were primarily interested in creating a level playing field for insurers, in the sense that insurers had to be compensated for predicted cost differences among their *actual* enrollees. There was hardly any concern about incentives for risk selection. The discussion about the advantages of using individual-level data brought the latter issue into the Belgian debate for the first time.

Some of the variables included in the model (e.g., the indicator of whether the individual received a special allowance for the chronically ill) could in principle be manipulated by the insurers, since the latter play a key role in determining whether their members are entitled to such an allowance.

However, in the light of the almost complete lack of good morbidity indicators, there were never real doubts about keeping these variables in the risk-adjustment system. Still, the lack of discussion about this issue illustrates again, how different the mindset is in Belgium, compared to that in other countries with regulated competition.

From 1998 onwards, medical supply could in principle have been taken up in the risk-adjustment formula. Yet, the method for neutralizing the effect of the $N$-variables was by then well understood and accepted, which meant that the question of how to treat medical supply was seen as a matter for political discussion. That discussion focused on the degree of responsibility of the insurers. The question was raised whether the effect of medical supply reflected differences in needs or rather inefficient practice variation. In the case of the latter, the next question was whether the insurers had the instruments to control (the effect of) medical supply. Although the answer is likely to be negative, the discussion resulted in the compromise that medical supply remained in the regression model, but was neutralized in the risk-adjusted payment formula.

The possibility of "neutralizing" the effects of variables was also discussed in other settings. One interesting example concerns the treatment of income support recipients in the subsidy scheme for the voluntary insurance of the self-employed (see Box 7.1). This example raises the (interesting and underexplored) issue of how to handle underconsumption in risk adjustment.

---

**BOX 7.1  A negative coefficient for social minimum recipients in the subsidy scheme for the self-employed**

Until 2008, mandatory health insurance covered only a part of the medical expenditures of the self-employed (i.e., only the "large risks"—mainly hospital costs). They could take a voluntary insurance for their "small risks" (mainly ambulatory expenditures) on the market for supplementary insurance (with the local sickness funds and private for-profit health insurers as suppliers). While this was essentially a private market, the premiums of the sickness funds were partly subsidized. After the introduction of the financial accountability of the sickness funds in 1995, this subsidy became risk-adjusted.

In 2006, the estimated model had a statistically significant negative coefficient for (self-employed) social minimum recipients. This unexpected finding called for an interpretation: did the negative coefficient reflect a real difference in "needs" or did it rather point to a problem of underconsumption? If the negative effect were treated as an $S$-variable, the sickness funds would get *less* for social minimum recipients; if it was neutralized, it would become profitable for them to attract these people and this would create some room to enact policies to fight underconsumption. Finally, the decision taken was indeed to neutralize the negative effect.

## 7.3.2.4 The Present Formula

In December 2008 a new model was introduced which remains in place today. This model includes extensive morbidity information on a concurrent basis (i.e., the morbidity indicators take values in year $t$ and are used to explain year $t$ expenditures). A full list of the included variables can be found in Box 7.2. First, the model includes 13 illness groups, identified for

---

**BOX 7.2 Variables included in the current Belgian risk-adjustment model (2017)**

- 41 *gender—age* combinations (with age defined in 5-year brackets). For males the age group >95 was merged with the age group 90—95 because of the small number of observations. For females these two age groups were kept separate.
- *Sociodemographic and socioeconomic information*: widow/widower/orphan, living alone, preferential reimbursement, incapacity to work (<1 year), entitled to allowance for handicapped, subsistence income beneficiary, self-employed.
- *Environmental variables*: living in urbanized area.
- *Mortality* (died in the relevant year).
- *Illness groups of disabled* (>1 year incapacity to work) *(13)*: infectious and parasitic diseases, tumors, endocrine and metabolic diseases, blood diseases, psychological disorders, diseases of nervous system, respiratory diseases, diseases of the digestive system, urogenital diseases, congenital malformations, accident injuries, ill-defined conditions.
- *Chronic conditions based on prescribed drugs (16)*: cardiovascular disease (general), cardiovascular disease (cardiac therapy), COPD (> 50 years), asthma (≤ 50 years), cystic fibrosis, diabetes + cardiovascular disease, diabetes with insulin, arthritis and Crohn, psychosis (≤ 70 years), psychosis (>70 yrs), Parkinson's disease, epilepsy, HIV, chronic hepatitis, multiple sclerosis, organ transplant.
- *Chronic conditions based on hospital diagnoses (66)*: metastatic cancer, mouth/pharynx cancer, liver/pancreas cancer, colon cancer, rectal cancer, lung cancer, breast cancer, blood and lymphatic cancer, cancer male genital organs, cancer urinary organs, carcinoma in situ, diabetes without complications, diabetes with chronic complications, other endocrine and metabolic disorders, pancreatic disorders, diseases of esophagus, peptic ulcer, inflammatory bowel disease, diverticula of intestine, gallbladder disorders, anal and other intestinal disorders, rheumatoid arthritis, bone/joint infections, osteoarthritis, iron-deficiency anemia, blood/immune disorders, dementia, major depression, nonpsychotic depression, drug dependence, headache, mononeuropathy, valvular heart disease, hypertension, coronary atherosclerosis, postmyocardial infarction, unstable angina, angina pectoris, heart rhythm disorder, atrial arrhythmia, cardiorespiratory failure, congestive heart failure, cerebral hemorrhage, precerebral arterial occlusion, stroke, transient

*(Continued)*

**BOX 7.2 (Continued)**

cerebral ischemia, atherosclerosis major vessel, arterial aneurysm, thrombo-embolic vascular disease, peripheral vascular disease, COPD, other lung disorders, renal failure, kidney infection, other renal and urethral disorders, hyperplasia of prostate, genital prolapse, decubitus, hip fracture, complications of medical procedures, major congenital disorders, other infectious diseases, aggregate of small groups ($\leq 200$ cases).

- *Medical supply* (neutralized).

individuals who are recognized as disabled (which means that they have been unable to work for health reasons for more than 1 year and have obtained the right to receive a disability allowance). More importantly, it also includes 16 chronic conditions identified based on (outpatient) pharmaceutical consumption (the threshold consumption to allocate a patient to a specific group was 90 defined daily doses) and 66 DxGroups defined on the basis of diagnostic information derived from hospital stays. The pharmaceutical and diagnostic information was selected by two independent commissions of medical experts who also took into account the degree of manipulability of the resulting indicators.

As noted, before 2008 the Belgian risk-adjustment model included a long list of socioeconomic variables. These were mainly seen as indirect indicators of needs. It could have been expected that many of them would no longer have a significant effect after the introduction of the detailed morbidity information. However, this turned out not to be the case. For most of the socioeconomic variables the effect remained highly significant and the exclusion of these variables from the model led to a sharp decrease in the explanatory power of the regression. This is in line with earlier research on Belgian hospital financing which also suggested that length of stay within the traditional diagnostic groups varies with socioeconomic status (Perelman and Closon, 2011). There are different explanations for this result. Socioeconomic variables can be indirect indicators of severity of illness that add to the usual diagnostic information, e.g., because they act as a proxy for comorbidity or because they are related to lifestyle differences. Indeed some of these variables (e.g., recipients of a lump sum for the chronically ill) identify relatively small groups of patients with large expenditures. Socioeconomic variables can also capture differences in behavior towards the healthcare system, e.g., different attitudes towards the use of emergency rooms (perhaps also as a consequence of postponing GP visits for economic reasons). Other variables (such as population density) can capture contextual effects, e.g., differences in social capital. In principle, there would have been room for a discussion about the classification of some of these socioeconomic variables as $N$-variables, but in practice dropping the significant socioeconomic variables from the risk-adjustment scheme was never seriously considered. Given the substantial differences in the socioeconomic composition of the membership of the different insurers, there was a general feeling that including socioeconomic variables was necessary to level their playing field. Moreover, more than at the time financial accountability was introduced, there was a (slightly) growing awareness of the danger of risk selection. It was felt that socioeconomic variables would be a prime candidate for risk selection if they were omitted from the risk-adjustment scheme.

The effect of medical supply remained significant, and it continued to be neutralized in the risk-adjustment system. A new $S-N$ question arose regarding the treatment of the dummy "self-employed," which was significantly negative. Again, there are different possible explanations for this result, the relevance of which could not be identified with the available data. Due to a selection effect, the self-employed may be healthier than the general population: this would be an argument in favor of treating it as an $S$-variable. On the other hand, the time costs of consulting a medical care provider are larger for the self-employed: this may lead to underconsumption or to a decrease in moral hazard. In the moral hazard interpretation, it would be inefficient to give insurers any incentives to change this behavior. As in other situations, the possibility of allowing for premium differentiation was never seriously considered. Neutralizing the "self-employment" effect would then make the self-employed preferred risks. After some discussion, it was decided to work in a first transition period of 2 years with separate budgets for the self-employed and the rest of the population, with the overall budget split on the basis of the actual expenditures of both groups (and therefore lower per capita for the self-employed). This basically boils down to treating "self-employment" as an $S$-variable. After the transition period, this implicit choice was made explicit through the application of the full model to all expenditures without neutralization of the self-employment variable.

### 7.3.3 Risk Sharing

As mentioned before, the financial accountability of the health insurers was introduced in a cautious and gradual way, with the explicit intention of shielding them from large financial risks. The 1993 Law therefore included a mechanism of risk sharing, in which the total budget for healthcare expenditures $\omega$ is distributed over the insurers according to the formula:

$$F_v = \left(\frac{RAS_v}{\omega}\right) r\omega + \frac{E_v}{\sum_k E_k}(1 - r)\omega, \tag{7.5}$$

where $RAS_v$ stands for the risk-adjusted subsidies to insurer $v$ (as defined in Eq. (7.4)), and $E_v$ is its actual expenditures in the current year. As Eq. (7.5) makes clear, only a fraction $r$ of the budget $\omega$ is distributed on an ex ante (risk-adjusted) basis. The remaining fraction $(1 - r)$ is divided proportionally to the actual expenditures of the insurers. Remember that the sum of the risk-adjusted subsidies $(\sum_v RAS_v)$ is equal to the fixed budget $\omega$ by construction.

The Law introduced what is known in the research literature as a "mixed system," where the mix refers to a combination of prospective and retrospective elements. (See Chapter 4, Risk Sharing or Geruso and McGuire (2016) for a discussion.) In addition, in another form of risk sharing, individual health insurers are only responsible for a fraction $\delta$ of the difference between their actual expenditures $E_v$ and $F_v$.

The logic behind the proposed system was to start initially from low values for both parameters controlling risk sharing in 1995 ($r = 0.10$ and $\delta = 0.15$), but let them grow steadily over time in line with the improvement of the risk-adjustment formula. The gradual accumulation of experience with the system would give the health insurers (and the regulator) the experience to adapt to the new system. In 2016 the parameters have reached the values of $r = 0.30$ and $\delta = 0.25$. A rough calculation then shows that insurers are financially accountable for about 7.5% of total expenditures. Indeed, the deficit to be covered by an insurer $v$ is given by $DEF_v = \delta(E_v - F_v)$. Using Eq. (7.5) (and assuming that $\omega \approx \sum_k E_k$), we can see that $\frac{dDEF_v}{dE_v} \approx \delta r$. For $\delta$, the value of 0.25 is the maximum that was allowed by the 1993 Law. In principle the government has the legal possibility to increase $r$ further to a maximum of 0.40. There are currently no signs that this step will be taken.

There is still an additional safety margin limiting the degree of financial accountability of the insurers. If the total expenditures of the system exceed the ex ante budget $\omega$ by more than 2%, the deficit of the individual insurers is limited to 2% of their real expenditures. The logic of this measure is easily understood: the ex ante budget is set in the first place by the government, and insurers should not have to bear the consequences of huge (strategic?) miscalculations. This upper limit of 2% has seldom been reached in the period 1995−2015.

### 7.3.4 Implementation Issues

The implementation of the risk-adjustment system follows the mechanisms described in Eqs. (7.4) and (7.5). Using Eq. (7.4), the information stream from the insurer to the central fund is simple: the insurers have to communicate only the number of their members and the average values of the $S$-variables for their membership. Of course, given that the risk-adjustment model is based on concurrent variables and that the risk-sharing system in Eq. (7.1) makes use of the actual expenditures, the closing of the accounts can only take place with a delay of a couple of years.

The 2008 model is comparable to good international examples. However, it was estimated with data for 2002 and it has not been reestimated since 2008. The only "update" has been the proportional adjustment of the payment weights in line with the increase in the total budget. This is especially bad for the pharmaceutical groups, for which there certainly have been important changes in spending patterns in the last decade. In fact, this situation illustrates how unimportant the risk-adjustment model is for the main decision-makers.

Recently (in 2016) RIZIV/INAMI initiated a fundamental update and reestimation of the model, including a redefinition of the morbidity indicators. It is symptomatic that the main motivation was the fact that the previous government had taken the decision to transfer some health competencies (e.g., nursing home care) from the federal to the regional level. This transfer of competencies involved some changes in the financial flows. However, it is unlikely that the basic structure of the 2008 model will be changed in the near future.

## 7.4  EVALUATION OF HEALTH PLAN PAYMENTS

As emphasized before, from the beginning the main objective of the system was to guarantee a level playing field to all health insurers. Therefore, the main criterion regarding the design of the risk-adjustment model was its statistical performance. Moreover, for the risk-adjustment model to be accepted by the main players in the system, it had to be transparent and easily applicable.

As for the statistical performance, the focus was on $R^2$ and on the statistical significance and theoretical interpretability of the estimated coefficients. The present estimated model had an $R^2$ of 0.4029. This rather large value is due to the inclusion of the mortality variable and to the fact that the morbidity information is used on a concurrent basis, a choice that was made because of data availability. Moreover, the overall fit of the payment model taking into account the risk-sharing mechanism (Eq. (7.5)) is much larger: following Geruso and McGuire (2016) it can be calculated as $1 - r^2\left(1 - R^2\right) = 0.95$, under the simplifying assumption that actual expenditures are equal to the ex ante budget, i.e., $\sum_k E_k = \omega$.

Transparency and simplicity were essential in the choice of the final version of the 2008 model. It was explicitly decided to stay as closely as possible to medically homogeneous indicators, i.e., to the groups as defined by the medical experts (see Box 7.2). No hierarchical structure was imposed. The only aggregation was to bring together the diagnostic groups with a too limited ($\leq 200$) number of cases.

Efficiency considerations were at the heart of the discussion about the treatment of the medical supply variable. The danger of risk selection was mentioned in passing when considering different models, at least in recent years. However, neither the incentives for efficiency nor those for risk selection were ever calculated in a quantitative way. As mentioned already, a possible concern for risk selection did not play any role when the system was introduced in the first place. At that time there was no evidence of risk selection. In fact, with full reimbursement of all expenditures by the central fund, there were no incentives for it either. In recent years the concern about possible risk selection has increased. However, this is not really taken up in the political debate and there certainly has not been any attempt to monitor the problem on a regular basis. Moreover, until now there has been no relevant scientific research on the topic. As for efficiency, all initiatives in this regard have been taken by the regulator and it has never been considered to give the insurers a more important role.

## 7.5   ONGOING ISSUES AND REFORMS

Belgium has introduced a system of risk adjustment in a Bismarckian system of negotiations between insurers, providers, and the government. Still, at least three features of the Belgian risk-adjustment system may also be relevant for other countries with a more outspoken market perspective. We summarize these in Section 7.5.1. The performance of the system is briefly discussed in Section 7.5.2. This will help us to explain the present discussions about the future role of the health insurers and, hence, the future of the health plan payment system (Section 7.5.3).

### 7.5.1   Important Features of the Belgian Risk-Adjustment System

First, even after introducing morbidity indicators, socioeconomic variables made a significant contribution to the explanation of differences in healthcare expenditures. This may be a relevant finding for other countries, where social risk factors now also get more attention attention in other countries also—see, e.g., Kwan, Stratton and Steinwachs (2017) for an analysis applied to Medicare payments. Indeed, if socioeconomic variables turn out to be highly significant, what would be a good reason not to include them in the risk-adjustment formula? In many settings (including the Belgian one) socioeconomic groups can be the prime target for risk-selection initiatives. If insurers have limited possibilities for selective contracting, their main instrument for risk selection is differentiation of marketing efforts: and it is much easier for them to differentiate based on socioeconomic status than on morbidity differences. Including relevant socioeconomic variables in the risk-adjustment formula then attacks directly the incentives to do so.

Second, as soon as one starts introducing variables that are not directly related to morbidity (such as socioeconomic variables), the discussion about "neutralizing" some of them becomes highly relevant. Regional variables are a prime candidate in this debate. The distinction between "predictions" and "defining normative expenditures" has worked very well in the Belgian context. This could be an inspiring example for other countries, where the problem is more acute because they have gone much further in the direction of regulated competition, so that it is more important to avoid that variation in efficiency is compensated by the risk-adjustment model.

Third, the mixed payment system with an a priori set path for the development of the weight given to risk-adjusted and actual expenditures, respectively, has been a rather effective way to introducing prospective elements in the social insurance system and letting the players adjust to the new rules.

### 7.5.2 Risk Selection and the Growth of Total Healthcare Expenditures

Although Belgium has introduced a risk-adjusted financing system for its health insurers, there has never been an open discussion on the pros and cons of regulated competition. Apparently, risk-adjusted prospective financing (rather than just reimbursing expenditures) was seen as a mechanism to create incentives for the insurers in a setting with negotiations. Viewed from a theoretical perspective on regulated competition, the architecture of the Belgian system is questionable. Financing the health insurers partly with a prospective risk-adjusted capitation scheme has given them incentives for risk selection, which may be significant for some specific patient groups, even with the extensive risk sharing discussed in Section 7.3.3. At the same time, the individual insurers did not get any instruments to control healthcare expenditures and to increase the efficiency of the system. The introduction of financial accountability has even given them strong incentives to lobby as a cartel (and together with the providers) for increasing the total ex ante budget. While regulated competition tries to reconcile efficiency (through the market) with equity (through risk adjustment), Belgium could have ended in the worst possible scenario: risk selection with at the same time increasing and sometimes wasteful expenditures. This has not happened.

First, the evidence for risk selection remains rare. This is striking, because the Belgian health insurers do have the instruments for risk selection. They can target their advertising campaigns on profitable consumer groups. Importantly, they also have the freedom to differentiate the content of their "mandatory supplementary" package to attract specific groups of patients (Paolucci et al., 2007). The main explanation for the limited occurrence of risk selection seems to be the absence of strong competition on the insurance market. The fact that the market is closed for new entrants has made it impossible for aggressive for-profit insurers to undermine the ideological foundations of the traditional dominating health insurers. In recent years there seems to be a limited shift of mainly young insured from the two large "ideological" health insurers to the other ones, but it is not clear that this is the result of intended selection actions by insurers.

Second, the growth of total medical expenditures is comparable to that in other countries, including countries with regulated competition. This may be because the total budget is in the first place set by the government with only indirect influence of the health insurers through the political process. If the government is able to fix a tight budget, the insurers have incentives to control expenditures, at least as long as the expected deficit is not larger than 2%. However, it is striking that even in the period 2010−11, when there was no federal government, the negotiations between health insurers, providers, and social partners within RIZIV/INAMI kept the budget reasonably well under control. This raises interesting questions for further research. How do financial incentives work in a noncompetitive setting? More specifically, how does the introduction of financial accountability change the incentives for the insurers in the process of collective negotiations? And what is the relevance of the fact that these insurers are social organizations with a strong ideological background?

### 7.5.3    The Future Role of Belgian Health Insurers

Although the strange architecture of the Belgian system has not had very negative effects until now, a coherent reform of the Belgian healthcare system cannot avoid the question of the future role of the insurers. Belgium is at a crossroads: either it takes the direction of regulated competition between insurers, or it goes into the direction of a largely government regulated, regionally decentralized structure, with a strong focus on provider competition. The latter option is by far the more realistic. It is highly unlikely that choice on provider markets will be severely restricted in the near future, given the strong opposition by the lobbies of providers, the general acceptance of cost sharing by patients, and, most importantly, the large degree of subjective satisfaction of Belgian citizens. According to the Eurobarometer (2014) survey not less than 97% of Belgians evaluate their health system positively—and 67% consider it to be better than that of other EU countries. With these results, Belgium is at the top of the subjective satisfaction ranking. There is some evidence that this high level of subjective satisfaction is due to the large degree of freedom of choice on provider markets (Costa-Font and Zigante, 2016). Finally, there are not even small steps in the direction of selective contracting by insurers. If regulated competition means giving more and better instruments to the individual insurers, this is certainly not going to happen in the near future.

In that situation, it is important to improve the process of choice on provider markets. "Empowering" the patients (starting by giving better-quality information) is a key requirement in this respect. Insurers can play an important role here. Recent agreements between the insurers and the government seem to point in this direction.

Virtually no one in the Belgian system advocates a move towards more competition in the insurance market. On the contrary, recent government proposals go in the direction of stimulating collaboration rather than competition between the insurers. It is even considered (but not yet decided) to increase again the collective component in the payment of the insurers and to move even further away from increased accountability of the individual insurers. At the same time, it is also unlikely that the system of risk adjustment will be abolished. Some financial accountability for the insurers will remain. As mentioned above, a significant update and actualization of the system is on course. In fact, the need for risk-adjusted financing schemes has become clear also in other healthcare domains. For lack of better alternatives, the formula that is used for the financing of the health insurers is also used in these other settings, although this formula has not been conceived for these other applications. Two examples are especially significant.

First, while the large majority of general practitioners are financed on a fee-for-service basis, some so-called "medical houses" have opted for capitation financing. They can provide GP consultations, physiotherapy, and nursing care. For each of these three categories a formula similar to Eq. (7.4) is applied directly (without the risk-sharing features embodied in Eq. (7.5), but with a protection clause: the capitation amount for a given medical house cannot decrease by more than 1% each year. The constant reference amount ($\omega/n$ in Eq. (7.4)) is in this system not linked to a given budget, but to the average expenditures of the stable population of the mature medical houses in the three categories. The "stable population" is defined as patients who have been registered for more than 1 year in a medical house, "mature" medical houses have a stable membership of at least 500 patients and have been active for at least 2 years. The risk adjustor variables included in the model are the same as in the model for the health insurers with the coefficients adapted to changes in the average level of expenditures. This is highly illogical, since that model has never been estimated separately for the three specific categories of expenditures involved.

Second, the government has recently initiated a call for the introduction of new experimental programs aiming at integrated care for specific groups of chronic patients. These experimental pilot projects bring together different categories of providers and are financed through a system of bundled payment. Health insurers are involved in some of them. The projects can keep the profits made, calculated as the difference between the risk-adjusted capitation amount and the costs of the treatment in the actual system. The capitation amounts would again be risk-adjusted with the same formula as used for the health insurers. While the objectives of the introduction of these projects are clear and commendable, there are obvious dangers. The projects have a large degree of freedom in choosing which services are included in the bundled payment and which are not: this offers much room for gaming given that it is well-known that some medical services actually are overfinanced, while others are underfinanced. Moreover, the setup of the experimental projects also creates the possibility of risk selection through service selection.

If this trend toward application of the risk-adjustment formula in other domains continues, there will be growing pressure to adapt the formula to the specific settings in which it is applied. It is possible that there will also be more interest in regular updates. At the moment, it is impossible to predict what the consequences will be for the risk-adjusted financing of health insurers.

## REFERENCES

Assuralia, 2017. De nationale uitgaven in de gezondheidszorg. Assuralia, Brussels (Assurinfo No. 13).

Chernew, M., Rosen, A., Fendrick, M., 2007. Value-based insurance design. Health Aff. w195−w203.

Cleemput, I., Devos, C., Devriese, S., Farfan-Portet, M.-I., Van de Voorde, C., 2012. Principles and Criteria for the Level of Patient Cost-sharing: Reflections on Value-based Insurance. Belgian Health Care Knowledge Centre (KCE): KCE Report 186B, Brussels.

Companje, K., Hendriks, R., Veraghtert, K., Widdershoven, B., 2009. Two Centuries of Solidarity. German, Belgian and Dutch Social Health Insurance 1770-2008. Aksant, Amsterdam.

Costa-Font, J., Zigante, V., 2016. The choice agenda in European health systems: the role of middle-class demands. Public Money Manage. 36, 409−416.

Eurobarometer, Patient safety and quality of care, 2014, Special Eurobarometer 411/ Wave EB80.2.

Geruso, M., McGuire, T., 2016. Tradeoffs in the design of health plan payment systems: fit, power and balance. J. Health Econ. 47, 1−19.

Kwan, L., Stratton, K., Steinwachs, D.M. (Eds.), 2017. Accounting for Social Risk Factors in Medicare Payment. National Academies Press, Washington, DC.

Paolucci, F., Schut, E., Beck, K., Van de Voorde, C., Gress, S., Zmora, I., 2007. Supplementary health insurance as a tool for risk-selection in mandatory basic health insurance markets: a five countries' comparison. Health Econ. Policy Law 2, 173−192.

Perelman, J., Closon, M.-C., 2011. Impact of socioeconomic factors on in-patient length of stay and their consequences in per case hospital payment systems. J. Health Serv. Res. Policy 16, 197−202.

Schokkaert, E., Van de Voorde, C., 2000. Risk adjustment and the fear of markets: the case of Belgium. Health Care Manage. Sci. 3, 121−130.

Schokkaert, E., Van de Voorde, C., 2004. Risk selection and the specification of the conventional risk adjustment formula. J. Health Econ. 23, 1237−1259.

Schokkaert, E., Van de Voorde, C., 2006. Incentives for risk selection and omitted variables in the risk adjustment formula. Ann. d'Economie et de Statistique 83-84, 327−351.

Schokkaert, E., Van de Voorde, C., 2009. Direct versus indirect standardization in risk adjustment. J. Health Econ. 28, 361−374.

Schokkaert, E., Dhaene, G., Van de Voorde, C., 1998. Risk adjustment and the trade-off between efficiency and risk selection: an application of the theory of fair compensation. Health Econ. 7, 465–480.

van de Ven, W., Ellis, R., 2000. Risk adjustment in competitive health plan markets. In: Culyer, A., Newhouse, J. (Eds.), Handbook of Health Economics 1. North-Holland, Amsterdam, pp. 755–845.

Chapter 8

# Health Plan Payment in Chile

**Carolina Velasco[1], Josefa Henríquez[1] and Francesco Paolucci[2,3]**
[1]*Centro de Estudios Públicos, Santiago, Chile,* [2]*University of Bologna, Bologna, Italy,*
[3]*Murdoch University, Perth, WA, Australia*

## 8.1 INTRODUCTION

### 8.1.1 Historical Background

The origins of the current healthcare system in Chile date to the beginning of the 20th century, when the Ministry of Hygiene, Assistance and Social Security[1] was founded and mandatory insurance for blue-collar workers (*obreros*) was introduced.[2] Another important landmark was the National Employees Medical Service (NEMS), established in 1942, which provided insurance coverage to public and private employees.[3] At its origins, NEMS was a semipublic entity, funded by contributions from employers and employees, who could choose their healthcare providers with copayments at the point of delivery (Giaconi & Concha, 2005). Ten years later, the National Health Service (NHS) was established[4] to administer and operate the public provision of healthcare services. It served the workers and indigents of Chile's 13 regions by providing coverage through its public providers' network. The NHS was funded by state subsidies (originating from general taxation revenues) that complemented the mixed contributions from employers and employees (Aedo, 2001; Quesney, 1995). In 1968, the so-called "Social insurance against occupational accidents and diseases"[5] was introduced to protect employees against the financial consequences of such events. Each employer is obligated to obtain this insurance.

At the end of the 1970s and beginning of the 1980s, the following reforms took place:

1. In 1979, the responsibilities of the Ministry of Health were expanded in terms of the design, evaluation, supervision, and coordination of the healthcare system;
2. Also in 1979, public primary healthcare provision was devolved to municipalities and to the 27 new health services (i.e., decentralized

*Risk Adjustment, Risk Sharing and Premium Regulation in Health Insurance Markets.*
DOI: https://doi.org/10.1016/B978-0-12-811325-7.00008-7

public entities that coordinate, manage, and develop the local public needs and provision of services);

3. Two parallel health insurance components were created: In 1979, the *Fondo Nacional de Salud* (i.e., Fonasa) resulted from a merger between the NEMS and the NHS; and, in 1981, the private health insurance market known as *Instituciones de Salud Previsional* (i.e., Isapres) was created;

4. At the end of the 1980s, the Superintendent of Isapres was created.[6] Its objective was to supervise the functioning of Isapres, a task that was previously the responsibility of Fonasa (Aedo, 2001).

Between 2003 and 2005, further reforms sought to increase access to care and coverage for vulnerable groups (i.e., people with low income and/or high risk), while improving the efficiency of healthcare delivery. The Superintendent of Isapres was replaced by the Superintendent of Health. The latter was made responsible for monitoring the healthcare system as a whole.[7] In relation to Isapres, two laws were passed,[8] which aimed to protect Isapres' beneficiaries from Isapres' financial problems and regulated health plan benefits, entitlements, and premiums. The most relevant change was the extension of the minimum coverage requirements for some services (diagnosis and treatment) associated with certain health conditions (of which there are currently 80). These so-called GES (*Garantías Explícitas en Salud*[9]) services are guaranteed in four aspects: access, timely attention (i.e., maximum waiting times), financial protection, and quality. The reform also included the introduction of a risk equalization scheme regarding GES services, but only for Isapres.

Most recently, in 2015 a new law was passed[10] which introduced a special fund to cover the diagnostics and treatments of high-cost diseases.[11]

## 8.1.2 Organization of the Current Health Insurance System

Box 8.1 summarizes the main components of the current health insurance system in Chile. Mandatory health insurance can be obtained from Fonasa or from one of the Isapres.[12] It mainly covers hospital and ambulatory services, in-patient drugs, and sick leave.[13] In both Fonasa and Isapres, employees pay a mandatory income-related contribution (i.e., 7% of their gross salary).

In 2015, 92% of the population was covered either by Fonasa or Isapres (77.3% and 15.1%, respectively), and 2.4% by the army scheme. Only 3.1% of the population reported not having any health plan and 0.6% had insurance coverage through a different mechanism.[14]

Voluntary health insurance in Chile covers (part of) the copayments under the mandatory insurance, as well as some services excluded from mandatory insurance (including health care in medical centers, catastrophic expenses after a predetermined ceiling, and specific benefits such as dental care), and can be offered by any insurance company other than Isapres.[15]

**BOX 8.1  Tiers of the Chilean health insurance system**

*Layer 1*    *Mandatory insurance*
- Executed by Fonasa (public insurer) and Isapres (private insurers).
- Coverage: hospital and outpatient care, some pharmaceuticals.
- Employees' contribution (7% of gross salary).
- Regulated by the government.
- Supervised by the Superintendent of Health.
- Number of enrollees: 13,226,811 in Fonasa and 3,363,022 in Isapres (2015).

*Layer 2*    *Voluntary insurances (insurance companies)*
- Executed by private insurance companies.
- Private insurance covering copayments of mandatory insurance, catastrophic expenses (after a predetermined ceiling), assistance in medical centers, other benefits.
- Regulated as any other insurance company.
- Supervised by the Superintendent of Securities and Financial Services.
- One-year contracts.
- Policies issued: 400,297 in 2015.
- Policies in force: 933,712 in 2015.

*Source: The authors' summary based on data from Fonasa, Superintendent of Health, and CASEN, 2015.*

Premiums, coverage, and provider contracting under voluntary health insurance are not subject to Isapres regulation but only to general insurance regulation (e.g., solvency requirements),[16] and fall under the oversight of the Superintendent of Securities and Financial Services. In 15% of nuclear families, at least one member has voluntary private insurance. Of the nuclear families in Fonasa, 8.2% have at least one member covered by voluntary private insurance; in Isapres, this percentage equals 45% (CASEN, 2015).

Despite the variety of schemes and coverage options, mandatory and voluntary health insurance plans (as well as other governmental programs) cover 67% of total health expenditures (2013). The remaining 32% is paid out-of-pocket (OECD, 2017).[17]

In what follows, we will concentrate on the mandatory health insurance, specifically on Isapres (i.e., private insurers), as regulated competition mainly applies to this sector. In the next section, we will describe the major features of the mandatory health insurance system (Section 8.2). After that, we will describe the health plan payment system (Section 8.3) and a series of evaluation studies (Section 8.4). In Section 8.5 we will discuss some ongoing issues and reforms.

## 8.2 ORGANIZATION OF THE MANDATORY HEALTH INSURANCE SYSTEM

This section describes the regulatory aspects of Isapres, as well as the tools insurers have to promote efficiency in the delivery of care. After that, we will describe Fonasa and discuss its interaction with Isapres.

### 8.2.1 Regulation of and Access to Health Plans

There are currently 13 regulated, privately owned insurers, called *Instituciones de Salud Previsional* or Isapres, which cover 15.1% of the population. Seven of these are "open" Isapres (covering 97.2% of Isapres population).[18] The other six are "closed" Isapres (i.e., employment-specific, allowing access to employees only, and their families, covering 2.8% of Isapres population). There is no open enrollment, meaning that Isapres can reject applicants.[19]

Isapres can offer as many plans as they wish. In 2016, there were around 7600 health plans available in the market (Superintendent of Health, 2016b).[20] These plans can differ in terms of benefits included (i.e., on top of the minimum benefits), financial coverage, and type/quality of the contracted network of healthcare providers. However, the plans' premiums and some aspects of design are regulated. During the 2000s reforms, regulation focused mainly on product design. For example, it was decided that health plans must cover the following services: (1) a preventive medicine exam with no copayments, (2) curative medical assistance for a list of diseases or conditions established by the Ministry of Health, (3) dental care for specific groups, (4) sick leave, (5) maternity leave and other benefits of the Labor Code for female workers (paid by the state), and (6) a list of health services associated with a set of health conditions (i.e., the GES services, currently 80, see Appendix). GES services are guaranteed with respect to: (1) access, i.e., assurance that all beneficiaries can access the guaranteed benefits; (2) timeliness, i.e., maximum waiting times; (3) financial protection, i.e., copayments are fixed and capped; and (4) quality, i.e., each healthcare provider that delivers any guaranteed service must be certified by the Superintendent of Health. The set of GES services is subject to review and updated every 3 years by the Ministry of Health, based on epidemiological criteria, burden of disease, cost-effectiveness, and financial viability. The proportion of the population that uses GES services is small, however, and concentrated in Fonasa.[21] The 2000s reforms also imposed (for GES services) community-rating per insurer per product, and introduced a risk equalization scheme for the Isapres market with the objective of mitigating incentives for risk selection (see Section 8.3). Complementary plans, which include all services other than GES services, can be purchased voluntarily. Insurers are required to offer at least the same benefits and financial coverage that Fonasa offers to its enrollees in the Free Choice modality (see Section 8.2.3). On top of that, Isapres can offer any other benefit such as out-of-network services. The premiums for complementary plans are allowed to vary with age and gender within a certain band.

In principle, individuals in an Isapre can switch.[22] In 2015, the percentage of Isapres' beneficiaries that switched Isapre was 5.5%, while 11.6% of the Isapres' pool newly enrolled and 7.1% left for Fonasa.

As in most healthcare and health insurance markets, general solvency and financial viability norms apply for both health insurers and providers.[23]

## 8.2.2   Instruments for Health Plans to Promote Efficiency in the Delivery of Care

Isapres plans have some tools to promote efficiency in the delivery of care, such as selective contracting with private providers, payment methods, and specific coverage requirements. Nevertheless, there is no evidence that these tools are used for efficiency purposes.

Regarding selective contracting, the usual practice is that GES and catastrophic services are delivered by a restricted network of providers. For other services, insurers can offer three types of plans (defined by law): (1) free choice plan, covering all providers; (2) preferred provider plan, providing better coverage for preferred providers than for other providers; and (3) closed network plan, providing no coverage for out-of-network spending. Currently, 46.5% of health plans are free choice plans, 52.8% are preferred provider plans and only 0.7% are closed plans. The proportions of individuals enrolled in each plan type are 41%, 55.3%, and 3.7%, respectively.

Isapres plans also have substantial contracting freedom with respect to private provider payments (i.e., prices and payment methods). This freedom does not extend to public providers.[24] Though some innovations in provider payments have been discussed, piloted, and even implemented (e.g., Diagnosis-Related Groups (Riesco, 2015)), fee-for-service is still the standard practice.

In 2005, Law 2015 established that the only objective of Isapres is to fund health services and benefits (article 22), de facto prohibiting vertical integration between insurers and providers. However, integration occasionally and partly occurs indirectly since some organizations participate as shareholders in both businesses (insurance and healthcare provision).

Finally, copayments are applied. These can vary across plans, except for GES services, for which copayments are fixed. Deductibles are not employed (Box 8.2).

**BOX 8.2 Instruments for insurers to promote efficiency**
- GES and catastrophic services are delivered by a restricted network of providers.
- Isapres have substantial contracting freedom. Nevertheless, FFS is the standard and setting conditions (i.e., gatekeeping) is not a common practice.
- Copayments are applied.
- Isapres plans cannot contract with public providers.
- Vertical integration is forbidden.

## 8.2.3 Fonasa: The Outside Option

Fonasa, the public insurer, covers 77.3% of the population (CASEN, 2015). It offers a standardized benefit package (e.g., including GES services). Levels of coverage, however, vary across different types of beneficiaries according to socioeconomic status (see Table 8.1). One of the reasons is that, except for individuals classified in group A (no income), beneficiaries can choose whether to receive health care through the institutional modality, i.e., public providers, or through the free-choice modality, i.e., private providers. Copayments are generally lower in the institutional modality. In the free-choice modality, copayments differ principally in relation to the type of care (i.e., ambulatory or inpatient care). However, GES services and catastrophic coverage are delivered in a closed network of mainly public providers. In these cases, as in the institutional modality, gatekeeping is applied through primary care providers.

There are no premiums for Fonasa coverage. Funding comes from the 7% gross salary contribution of its affiliates and a state subsidy (which, in 2017, accounted for 66% of Fonasa's total budget). Affiliates' dependents are also covered, as well as people without income and their dependents.

Fonasa cannot reject applicants; therefore it acts as an insurer of last resort, enrolling those who cannot enroll in an Isapre. This, combined with the fact that Fonasa is more restricted in terms of tools available to promote efficiency in the delivery of care, implies that Fonasa operates under different conditions than Isapres. In fact, Fonasa must deliver care mainly through public providers, it cannot spend more than 10% of the institutional modality budget on services from private providers, and provider payment methods are defined by law.

Table 8.2 summarizes the main features of Fonasa and Isapres.

**TABLE 8.1** Classification and Coverage for Fonasa's Beneficiaries

| Beneficiary group | Beneficiaries' description | Financial coverage | | |
|---|---|---|---|---|
| | | Institutional modality | Free choice modality | Guaranteed services (GES) |
| A | Indigent or destitute persons, receiving governmental pensions and subsidies | AC: 100% IC: 100% | – | 100% |
| B | Workers (from 18 to 65 years old) receiving a monthly income until minimum wage | AC: 100% IC: 100% | | 100% |
| C | Workers (from 18 to 65 years old) receiving a monthly income above the minimum wage but below 146% of the minimum wage. Those with three or more dependents classified into group B | AC: 100% (GP)/90% (specialists) IC: 90% | AC: Max. 60%<br><br><br>IC: Max. 50% 75% in DAP | Copayments are capped |
| D | Workers (from 18 to 65 years old) receiving a monthly income over 146% of the minimum wage. Those with three or more dependents classified into group C | AC: 100% (GP)/80% (specialists) IC: 80% | | |

AC, ambulatory care; IC, inpatient care; GP, general practitioner. Only dental services have a different (less) coverage in ambulatory and inpatient care.
Source: Authors' own.

## 8.3 HEALTH PLAN PAYMENT DESIGN

The payment flows of the private health insurance market are described in Fig. 8.1. Each beneficiary pays a premium for the health plan of his choice (i.e., health plan premium). A risk equalization scheme is in place, in which a virtual Solidarity Compensation Fund collects a flat contribution charged to open Isapres and then allocates risk-adjusted payments to insurers. As the Fund is virtual, the actual transfers occur between Isapres under the supervision of the Superintendent of Health.

**TABLE 8.2 General Features of the Chilean Health Insurance System**

|  | Public component | Private component |
|---|---|---|
| Insurers | One entity (Fonasa): 77.3% of population | 13 entities (Isapres), seven compete ("open") and six belong to some enterprise ("closed") 15.1% of population |
| Funding | Salary contribution (7%), state subsidy | Salary contribution (7%), voluntary contributions (3% of salary, on average) |
| Health plans | • Standardized coverage in terms of benefits, but differences in financial coverage (i.e., copayments are related to income and type of provider) <br> • Two main modalities (i.e., institutional and free choice) <br> • Low coverage of outpatient pharmaceuticals <br> • Should cover minimum services (GES) + other mandatory services | • Great variety regarding benefits covered, financial coverage, and providers <br> • Low coverage of outpatient pharmaceuticals <br> • Should cover minimum services (GES) + other mandatory services + same financial coverage as Fonasa's free choice modality |
| Premium / contribution | No premium. Only 7% gross salary contribution. Thus, payments depend on income level | Two components: <br> • Guaranteed services premium: community-rated in each Isapre <br> • Complementary plan premium: regulated sex and age risk factors. |
| Providers | Publicly and privately owned | Privately owned (publicly owned in special cases) |
| Risk equalization | No | Yes. For GES services |
| Enrollment | Open | Not open |

Source: Authors' own.

## 8.3.1 Contributions and Premium Regulation

As mentioned above, workers and pensioners contribute 7% of their gross salary or pension to their insurer. When this contribution is less than the private insurance premium, individuals must pay the difference. On average, they pay an extra 3% of their gross salary.

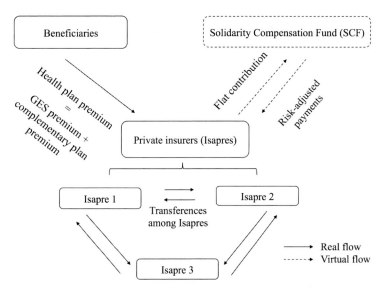

**FIGURE 8.1**    Financing scheme of Isapres. *Authors' own.*

As also mentioned above, health plan design and premiums are regulated. Each plan's premium has two components: a community-rated part for GES services (GES premium) and a regulated risk-rated (i.e., gender and age) part for additional services covered by the plan. The community-rated part is a relatively small component, approximately 13% of the plan's total premium (data from Superintendent of Health for 2016).[25]

The base premium of each plan can be modified yearly (within a defined range). However, courts have been ruling in favor of any member suing Isapres for their allegedly excessive premium increases. Premium regulation requires for each Isapre that increases should not be greater than 1.3 times and less than 0.7 times the average increase of all base premiums of the Isapre. The Superintendent monitors the applicability of the changes and once a year reports on premium adjustments (Superintendent of Health, 2016c).

## 8.3.2  Risk Equalization

The Chilean risk equalization system was first introduced in 2005[26] with the aim of achieving risk-solidarity through cross-subsidies from low-risk to high-risk people and reducing the incentives for risk selection in the presence of community-rating without open enrollment regulations (Superintendent of Health, 2005). Risk equalization applies only to GES services and to open Isapres (seven in 2016), covering about 6.7% of Isapres' total expenditures in health services (data from Superintendent of Health, 2013).

The Superintendent of Health governs the risk equalization scheme, performing computations as well as monitoring the transfers among Isapres. The risk equalization process involves three main steps: (1) calculation of the flat contributions that go into the virtual Solidarity Fund; (2) calculation of the expected costs per cell; and (3) calculation of the transfers among Isapres.

### 8.3.2.1 Calculation of the Flat Contribution (Step 1)

The flat contribution ($FC$) is calculated by the Superintendent of Health and equals the total expected expenditure on GES services, divided by the total number of beneficiaries enrolled in the seven Isapres ($B$) participating in the risk equalization scheme:

$$FC = \frac{\sum_s (Rt_s \times Q_s)}{B} \tag{8.1}$$

In Eq. (8.1) $Q_s$ refers to the quantity of services that is multiplied by the tariff rate for that service $Rt_s$. The numerator takes the sum of this product over the relevant services (which are called the Group of Services, i.e., GS). An example of the quantity and tariff levels used for the Group of Services (i.e., treatments and diagnoses) associated with acute myocardial infarction (one of the 80 health conditions guaranteed through GES services) is presented in Table 8.3.

$Q_s$ is obtained from two sources: (1) for new and modified GES services the cost verification study[27] is used and (2) for the unchanged and existing GES services administrative claims data from the prior year are used.

According to the Ministry of Health (2009), the tariff ($Rt_s$) for each Group of Services is calculated for an average beneficiary considering providers' prices of both Fonasa and Isapres. Tariffs are reviewed every 3 years. The same holds for the set of GES services.[28]

In 2016, the $FC$ charged by the virtual fund (Solidarity Compensation Fund) to each Isapre equaled US \$52.20,[29] obtained by the division of US \$173,401,759 (total expected spending on GES services) and 3,321,748 (beneficiaries of open Isapres).

### 8.3.2.2 Calculation of the Expected Costs per Rate Cell[30] (Step 2)

Risk adjustment is based on an actuarial cell method, which classifies beneficiaries into 36 cells according to age and gender (18 classes for men and 18 classes for women). The age classes are: 0–1 years, 2–4 years, 5–9 years, 10–14 years, 15–19 years, 20–24 years, 5-year cohorts up to the age of 80, and finally a class for people of 80 years or older. The expected costs for an individual in cell $j$ are calculated as follows:

$$\overline{EC}_j = \frac{\sum_s (Rt_s \times q_{sj})}{b_j} \tag{8.2}$$

**TABLE 8.3** Example of the quantity and tariff levels used for the Group of Services associated with Acute Myocardial Infarction.

| Health problem | | Service or Groups of Services (GS) | Tariff without copayment (US $) | Annual GS cases |
|---|---|---|---|---|
| Acute myocardial infarction | Diagnosis | Suspected acute myocardial infarction | 11.4 | 116 |
| | Treatment | Confirmation and treatment of acute myocardial infarction (emergency without thrombolysis) | 44.7 | 590 |
| | Treatment | Confirmation and treatment of acute myocardial infarction (emergency with thrombolysis) | 488.2 | 105 |
| | Treatment | Medical treatment of acute myocardial infarction | 476.4 | 19 |
| | Follow-up | Secondary prevention of acute myocardial infarction | 11.6 | 25,092 |
| | | Average expenditure (US $) | 379,075.2 | |

Source: Circular N°20 of 2016. Info8rma los montos de las compensaciones originadas en el sexto semestre de vigencia del D.S N°4, de 2013, Superintendencia de Salud, from http://www.supersalud.gob.cl/normativa/668/w3-article-14412.html.

where:

- $\overline{EC}_j$ is the average expected costs of an individual in cell $j$;
- $q_{sj}$ is the expected number of people using service $s$ in cell $j$;
- $b_j$ is the total number of beneficiaries in cell $j$;

For example, the expected costs for a male aged over 80 are obtained by dividing the total expected expenditure of his risk cell (in practice US $2,892,288 in 2016) by the number of males aged 80 + years (9986), which equals US $289.60. In contrast, the expected costs for a male in the age group 15–19 are only US $19.20.

### 8.3.2.3 Calculation of Transfers between Isapres (Step 3)

The transfer $(T_i)$ from/to Isapre $i$ is calculated as the difference between $TC_i$, the total "contribution" of that Isapre to the virtual SCF (the virtual amount the insurer pays to the fund), and $EC_i$, the total expected costs of GES services, based on the rate cells, of that Isapre (the virtual amount the insurer receives from the fund).

$$T_i = TC_i - EC_i \qquad (8.3)$$

where

$$TC_i = FC \times b_i,$$

$$EC_i = \sum_j b_{ji} \times \overline{EC}_j$$

and

- $b_{ji}$ = Beneficiaries in cell $j$ of Isapre $i$.

If the expected costs of an Isapre exceed (fall below) his "contribution," that Isapre will receive (or pay) a transfer from (to) another Isapre, subject to the Superintendent of Health instructions and supervision (Box 8.3).

## 8.3.3 Risk Sharing

For GES services, there is currently no risk sharing. However, some proposals have been made to include risk sharing (particularly in the form of ex-post compensation schemes for high-risk individuals), to counteract selection activities against individuals with preexisting conditions, which have been deemed responsible for limiting mobility among Isapres (Superintendent of Health, 2009).

---

**BOX 8.3 Characteristics of the risk equalization scheme**

- Risk equalization scheme only applies to GES services and to open Isapres.
- Risk adjustment is based on an actuarial cell method.
- Cells are based on age and gender (18 classes for men and 18 classes for women).
- Expected expenditure for GES services in a cell is based on the expected cases in that cell and the services' tariffs.
- The transfer from/to an Isapre is based on the difference between the total virtual contribution of that Isapre and its total expected costs for GES services.

## 8.4 EVALUATION OF HEALTH PLAN PAYMENT

In the following subsections, we discuss some studies that evaluated the health plan payment system.

### 8.4.1 Risk Selection Incentives and the Risk Equalization Scheme

The Superintendent of Health is the main governmental institution in charge of monitoring and evaluating the functioning of the Isapres market and the Isapres' behavior and compliance with law (Decree with Force of Law 1 of 2005). Among its key functions, the Superintendent of Health operates and supervises any activity related to the risk equalization scheme (including gathering information about claims, prices, etc., in particular of GES services). The Superintendent of Health has not evaluated empirically the impact of the risk equalization scheme regarding risk selection incentives. It has published only one report that focused on the risk equalization scheme (Superintendent of Health, 2007c). Nevertheless, studies have been commissioned by the Superintendent and also been performed by independent researchers. The Superintendent of Health (2007c) concluded that the current risk equalization scheme does little to reduce selection incentives. The limited impact of risk equalization, however, is due to the insensitivity of transfers to risk differentials rather than the (small) size of the transfers. On average, the per capita compensations represented 2.3% of GES services premium and 0.07% of income in open Isapres (Superintendent of Health, 2007c). Fig. 8.2 shows the updated evolution of the compensations with respect to profits and income in Isapres. The Superintendent of Health (2007c) also suggests that the predictive accuracy of the risk adjustment model could be improved by moving from a cell-based approach to a regression-based approach, by adding socioeconomic and morbidity variables to the formulae, and by using real costs.[31]

The Superintendent of Health itself uses no statistic (e.g., $R$-squared, mean absolute prediction error, root mean square error, etc.) to monitor the functioning of the risk equalization scheme. Henríquez et al. (2016) performed an independent empirical evaluation of the current cell-based risk adjustment model and found that the overall payment fit and predictive performance are rather poor (an $R$-squared of 0.72%). The authors also simulated the impact of "enhanced" risk-adjustment models,[32] by adding new sociodemographic and diagnosis-related adjusters[33] showing that they performed strongly as expected, with an increase in $R$-squared up to 18.1% (Box 8.4).

As extensively described in the economic literature, premium-rate restrictions exacerbate incentives for risk selection (Paolucci et al., 2006;

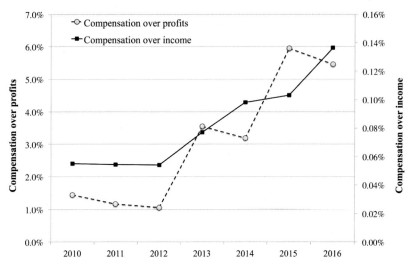

**FIGURE 8.2**    Ratio of compensation to profits and income of Isapres (updated statistics as in Superintendent of Health, 2007c).

Values correspond to the ratio of total compensations for each year (addition of compensations for each semester) and total profits/income for open Isapres in the period. Source: own elaboration based on Superintendent of Health, 2007c; Circular N°9 of 2016; Circular N°20 of 2016, and data published by Superintendent of Health's webpage (available at: http://www.supersalud. gob.cl/documentacion/666/w3-propertyvalue-3741.html).

---

**BOX 8.4  Evaluation of the risk equalization scheme**

- The Superintendent of Health operates and supervises any activity related to the risk equalization scheme.
- The Superintendent of Health has not evaluated empirically the impact of the risk equalization scheme in risk selection incentives. Nevertheless, the scheme has been evaluated by independent researchers.
- Evaluations have focused on: (1) the scope of the fund and (2) how well the cell model explains GES services expenditure.
- Evaluation studies have found a modest impact of the risk equalization scheme on risk selection incentives.

---

Cutler et al., 2010; Connelly et al., 2010; Einav & Finkelstein, 2011; Paolucci & Zweifel, 2011; McGuire et al., 2014; Handel et al., 2015; van de Ven et al., 2017). In Chilean healthcare policy, however, this topic has been largely neglected (Paolucci, 2016; Paolucci & Velasco, 2017).

As already mentioned, courts are ruling in favor of beneficiaries who sue their Isapres when they increase premiums. De facto the so-called "judicialization" creates a further restriction to premium setting and price competition, which provides additional incentives to risk select, and/or to differentiate premiums via product design (Paolucci et al., 2007; Paolucci, 2011−16).

## 8.4.2 Risk Selection Actions

Insurers in Chile have many potential tools for risk selection, such as rejection of applicants (no open enrollment) based on their health status (a form of direct selection, which is prohibited in countries including the Netherlands, Germany, Switzerland, and major US private insurance sectors), and product differentiation (e.g., in terms of services covered and copayment schedules). As in other countries, a number of subtle forms of risk selection can also take place, including selection via complementary insurance, provider network design, and selective advertising (Paolucci, 2016). Nonetheless, the Superintendent, except for product differentiation, does not systematically monitor risk selection actions.

Cid (2011) and Pardo & Schott (2014) have examined how risk selection influenced the distribution of risk types across Isapres and Fonasa. The evaluations show that the population in Isapres is wealthier and healthier than that in Fonasa (Henríquez & Velasco, 2015). Selection activities against individuals with preexisting conditions have been found to limit mobility among Isapres (Superintendent of Health, 2008; Pardo & Schott, 2014). Product differentiation is the main tool for risk selection in the Isapres market. GES services are tied-in with complementary benefits, which can lead to extensive product differentiation in the market (and thereby premium differentiation and consequent market segmentation).

The main evaluations of the Superintendent of Health (2007a,b, 2008) found that Isapres' risk profiles homogenized and displayed a consistently diminished risk variation from 2000 to 2006. An increase in the membership of the elderly population was observed, whilst the number of dependents and low-income individuals decreased. The Superintendent of Health is continuously monitoring the number of health plans and the associated premium and composition of the plans (both in terms of copayments and services covered). However, in January 2016, 64,012 health plans were reported in the system with 7610 of these plans actually being traded in the market (Superintendent of Health, 2016b).[34] The attractiveness of risk selection via supplementary insurance (that in the case of Chile, is easy since GES services must be bought together with the complementary plan) has been documented in the literature (Paolucci et al., 2007; Paolucci, 2011) (Box 8.5).

---

**BOX 8.5 Risk selection actions**

- Direct risk selection is allowed (i.e., there is no open enrollment).
- The only risk selection action systematically monitored is product differentiation.
- Evaluations have shown that risk selection led to selection of unfavorable risk types into Fonasa (and favorable risk types into Isapres).
- Selection activities have limited mobility among Isapres.
- No studies conducted to provide evidence of indirect selection actions.

---

## 8.5 ONGOING ISSUES AND REFORMS

### 8.5.1 Unresolved Issues

Chile represents an interesting and unique case of public/private mix in the financing and provision of health care. The private health insurance market (i.e., Isapres) combines premium regulation (i.e., community-rating) with no restrictions on plan design and no open enrollment. These structural features have led to a proliferation of plans (more than 7000 products), making the market quite opaque, with robust risk selection and de facto hindering of consumer choice, which have effectively made access to private insurance coverage for good-quality care difficult for low-income and high-risk individuals.

The risk equalization scheme has proven to have very limited, if any, impact. The reasons are that it only applies to Isapres for a minimalistic package of GES services, and that it is based solely on age and gender. Also, regulations (e.g., community-rating and no open enrollment) have offset the benefits of competition, creating incentives for insurers to compete by risk selection instead of improving efficiency and quality of care for high-risk individuals. In this context, the risk equalization scheme could play an important role. As argued in Section 8.4, however, substantial improvements to the current risk equalization scheme are necessary to effectively discourage risk selection (Henríquez et al., 2016).

Growing evidence suggests that the current public/private mix has shown signs of a two-tier system (Henríquez & Velasco, 2015; Paolucci, 2016). In particular, low-income/high-risk people have been increasingly experiencing exclusion or reduced coverage from Isapres compared to high-income/low-risk people, leaving Fonasa with the elderly, the sick, and the poor. The difference in the beneficiaries' risk profiles between Isapres and Fonasa has not been reduced to the expected level (Cid, 2011). Fonasa and Isapres face different regulatory frameworks and thus cannot compete on equal terms. Contrary to Isapres, Fonasa cannot act as a strategic buyer for its beneficiaries, since it faces many restrictions related to contracting (including a

**BOX 8.6 Unresolved issues**

- Proliferation of plans and untransparent private health insurance market.
- Low levels of choice and affordability for low-income and high-risk individuals.
- High levels of risk selection due to the absence of open enrollment and the poor risk equalization scheme.
- Signs of emergence of a two-tier system where the elderly, sick, and poor cannot stay in Isapres.
- Fonasa and Isapres face different regulations and thus cannot compete on equal terms.
- Quality of care gap between Fonasa and Isapres (i.e., longer waiting times in Fonasa).
- High premiums in Isapres lead to an increase in people suing their Isapres.

public service obligation). Moreover, the presence of voluntary insurances to cover for the increasing copayments offsets incentives to reduce moral hazard (Box 8.6).

## 8.5.2    Proposals for Reform

The following directions for reform have been considered: a single-insurer system, a social health insurance system including all insurers and a social health insurance system only for Isapres (Butelmann et al., 2014; Comisión Asesora Presidencial para el Estudio y Propuestas de un Nuevo Régimen Jurídico para el Sistema de Salud Privado, 2014; Velasco, 2016; Paolucci, 2016; Paolucci &Velasco, 2017).

In 2011, a draft bill sent to the Congress by President Sebastián Piñera[35] focused on the private health insurance market, proposing the creation of a standardized plan (Plan Garantizado en Salud [PGS]) that must be offered by Isapres, with community-rated premiums, open enrollment, and risk equalization.[36] In addition, a report of the committee of 2014 (i.e., Comisión Asesora Presidencial) presented two options for the long run. The first, supported by the majority of its members, was to establish a single-payer, tax-based mandatory insurance and to regulate voluntary complementary private insurance. The second proposes the creation of a social health insurance system for Fonasa and Isapres, supported by a risk compensation scheme. For the short run, both groups proposed a model similar to that designed in the draft bill of 2011 for Isapres.

Velasco (2016) and Paolucci (2016) proposed a comprehensive modification of the structure of the current mandatory health insurance schemes with two main stages: (1) transformation of the Isapres into social health insurers and (2) integration of the public insurer into the social health insurance system. These measures would require a reduction of the quantity of health plans offered (e.g., standardized basic package), a redefinition of the minimum coverage of the health plans, an improvement of the risk equalization scheme, the introduction of open enrollment, and subsidies for low-income people. The proposal developed by Butelmann et al. (2014) includes the creation of a standardized plan as the draft bill does. Similar to Paolucci and Velasco (2017), it adds the possibility of buying the plan from both Isapres and Fonasa, and it also supports risk equalization for the whole system.

Although there are many common elements in the various proposals, there has not been a new draft bill or improvement of previous ones for a number of reasons, including:

- The proposed reforms clash with other current legislation imposing extensive broad-spectrum legislative changes;
- The technical aspects of the proposals have proven to be politically challenging, as well as the economic impact of the reforms that might affect public finances unpredictably.

The current design has the potential foundations on which to build a modern regulated competition model employed by countries such as Belgium, Germany, Israel, the Netherlands, Switzerland, and important sectors in the United States (Velasco, 2016; Paolucci, 2016; Paolucci & Velasco, 2017).

Chile can capitalize first on its quasicompetitive private insurance market, Isapres, while taking a long-term approach by designing a system that could eventually be implemented nationally to include Fonasa and the other public entities, notably the army.

Basic reform elements that can help Chile in a transition towards a system that effectively combines competition with solidarity concern the structure and composition of the basic benefit package, the sources of funding, system organization and management, risk-adjusted payments, and prudent purchasing and contracting with providers.

The key challenge remains to coherently and efficiently overcome the duality of the mandatory insurance system while promoting managed or regulated competition. This would require insurers to take a leading role in managing Chileans' health risks, and the demand for health services through prudent purchasing and selective contracting. The challenge is thus to promote competition in the Isapres system by turning each of them into competing, risk-bearing insurers open to all Chileans. This can be achieved by regulating open admission and eliminating underwriting by Isapres for the basic and complementary packages. Fonasa should also be incorporated into this market, but it would need some adjustments beforehand.

To increase efficiency and transparency in the market and reduce premium differentiation via product differentiation, Chile might consider introducing some elements of previous proposals (Paolucci, 2016; Velasco, 2016; Paolucci & Velasco, 2017):

1. A basic common benefits package shared by all (GES is too small) insurers public and private with risk-adjusted subsidies (Henríquez et al., 2016);
2. Income-related deductibles to mitigate moral hazard (hence not covering for copayments or deductibles).
3. A flexible supplementary package for benefits excluded from the basic coverage with clear regulatory separation between basic and supplementary health insurers.

In terms of improving access to coverage and reducing risk selection, several promising directions for improvement of the risk equalization scheme have been made: expansion of the set of services covered by risk equalization, use of regression methods, inclusion of more risk adjustors (especially those related to health status) and use of real prices as also suggested (Henríquez et al., 2016; Ellis et al., 2008).

Overall, the Chilean insurance markets and their regulation provide an informative reference case for other middle-income countries and markets in transition to a more competitive structure. The past risk equalization reforms in the Chilean competitive market offer a promising system foundation but also leave many critical issues to be addressed in order to make the system more fair and more competitive.

## ACKNOWLEDGMENTS

We would like to especially thank Dov Chernichovsky, for his valuable comments on the analysis of the future steps of health plan payment policies in Chile, and Fabián Duarte, for his insights into the challenges that the Chilean healthcare system faces, which are an essential part of the ongoing issues section, and his remarks on previous versions of this chapter. Finally, we would not have been able to write this chapter without the support and work of the editors of this book: Richard van Kleef and Tom McGuire.

## ENDNOTES

1. Law Decree 44 of 1924.
2. Law 4054 of 1924.
3. Decree with force of law 32 of 1942.
4. Law 10383 of 1952.
5. Law 16744 of 1968.
6. Law 18933 of 1990.
7. Law 19937 of 2004.
8. Law 19895 of 2003; Law 20015 of 2005.
9. Law 19966 of 2004.

10. Law 20850 of 2015.
11. A new publicly subsidized fund was created, which initially covered about 45 million dollars in annual spending on diagnostics and treatments of high-cost diseases. This fund is expected to grow (Law 20850 of 2015).
12. There are two other mandatory schemes: the occupational accidents and diseases insurance scheme for workers (which covers all costs related to prevention and treatment of occupational accidents and diseases and also considers some subsidies, indemnities, and pensions associated with these events) and the army's plan for health and pensions (i.e., mandatory for army officers).
13. In 2014, sick leave was accountable for 23% of total spending in Fonasa and for 17.6% of total spending in Isapres. Data from Superintendent of Health and Fonasa (financial statistics of Isapres available at: http://www.supersalud.gob.cl/documentacion/666/w3-propertyvalue-3741.html; financial statistics of Fonasa available at: https://www.fonasa.cl/sites/fonasa/institucional/archivos.
14. The remaining group consists of individuals reporting "not knowing" to which insurance they are affiliated are not counted (CASEN, 2015).
15. Along with these insurances, there are other institutions, such as provident funds, that also offer some health benefits, such as dental coverage in agreed providers.
16. Decree with Force of Law 251 of 1931.
17. Bruzzo et al. (2018) used data from 2011 to 2012 to analyze out-of-pocket spending. The major share (38%) was spent on pharmaceuticals, followed by doctor visits (19.8%), lab and imaging services (11.8%), and dental services (9.3%).
18. Superintendent of Health for 2015 (available at http://www.supersalud.gob.cl/documentacion/666/w3-propertyvalue-3757.html
19. As a result, Fonasa de facto acts as the insurer of last resort.
20. Premium rate restrictions (e.g., community-rating age−gender rating) have been identified as the main cause of product proliferation (premium differentiation via product differentiation) (Paolucci, 2016; Henriquez et al., 2016.
21. In 2015, 12.6% of people in Isapres reported having at least one illness covered by GES services. Only 48% of these people actually used GES services to treat that illness. In Fonasa these percentages were 20.1% and 82.6% (data from CASEN, 2015).
22. During the first contract year they can switch with a special agreement. After the first year, they can change Isapre at any given time, subject to contractual terms and conditions.
23. Health insurers must comply with financial norms (i.e., minimum reserves) and healthcare providers must be certified by the Superintendent of Health to provide GES services. It is important to mention that there is no specific antitrust regulation for the health sector.
24. With the exception of emergency services, and a nationally predetermined number of beds for intensive care beds in public hospitals that can be used by Isapres' beneficiaries. As a reference, in 2015, there were 37,570 hospital beds available in Chile, where 6773 correspond to private providers.
25. (As there are also compulsory services included in the complementary plan, people must purchase GES services and the complementary plan together (tie-in sale). The premium of any complementary plan, for additional services on top of GES services, results from the multiplication of the health plan's base premium and the risk factor (i.e., weight of each risk class in each Isapre) of the beneficiary. For example, for a plan with a base premium equal to US $40 and a family of three where, the risk factor of the affiliate is 1, that of the spouse 2, and that of the son 0.5, the complementary plan premium will reach up to US $140 (1 US $40 + 2 US $40 + 0.5 US $40 − Nancuante & Romero 2008).
26. Decree with force of law 1 of 2005.
27. Contracted by the Ministry of Health every 3 years through an open call for international and national external consultants.

28. Most recent tariffs for GES services are stipulated under Law Decree N̲o3 of 2016 (Ministry of Health, 2016).
29. These amounts reflect the limited use of GES services.
30. Hereafter, cell is used to describe the combination of age and gender classes
31. In relation to risk adjustment, the Superintendent engaged an external group of consultants to review the risk equalization model (e.g., methods, risk adjusters, transfers modality, etc.) (Ellis et al., 2008). This review concluded that morbidity and comorbidity, as wells as new sociodemographic variables, should be considered as additional risk adjusters to improve the current risk equalization formula's ability to reduce incentives for risk selection. Improvements in the formula in terms of adding new risk adjusters (especially, diagnosis), has also been pointed out in the international literature (Van Kleef et al., 2013; Buchner et al., 2013). Ellis et al. (2008) also proposed to replace the actual estimated costs with real cost data of the services, and to move from a cell-based to a regression-based model.
32. Also using GES services expenditure as a dependent variable. The model that uses total expenditure (in all services) as dependent variable, sociodemographic and diagnosis- related adjusters shows an R2 of 27.8%.
33. The diagnosis-related adjusters were developed based on the International Classification of Diseases in its tenth version (ICD-10). Sixty-eight groups of chronic conditions were created using the existing Classification—CCS 2003 (Agency for Healthcare Research and Quality [AHRQ]) and in collaboration with physicians.
34. Half of the plans being sold in 2015 (15,050) were discontinued.
35. Boletin N° 8105-11 of 2011.
36. The PGS would include GES services; catastrophic coverage; vital emergency events; preventive care; and other services and financial coverage defined by the Ministry of Health. Sick leaves would be taken out of the health plan and funded separately. Isapres could also offer complementary benefits, but they must be sold separately from the PGS. Finally, it created an index to validate increases in the premium of the PGS in each Isapre

## REFERENCES

Aedo, C., 2001. Las reformas en la salud en Chile. In: Larraín, F., Vergara, R. (Eds.), La transformación económica de Chile. Centro de Estudios Públicos, Santiago, pp. 605–640.

Boletín N° 8105-11 of 2011. Modifica el Sistema Privado de Salud, incorporando un plan garantizado, from https://www.camara.cl/pley/pley_detalle.aspx?prmID = 8504.

Bruzzo, S., Henríquez, J., Velasco, C., 2018. Radiografía del gasto de bolsillo en salud en Chile: una mirada desagregada, Puntos de Referencia, 478. Centro de Estudios Públicos.

Buchner, F., Geopffarth, D., Wasem, J., 2013. The new risk adjustment formula in Germany: implementation and first experiences. Health Policy 109, 253–262.

Butelmann A., Duarte, F., Nehme, N., Paraje, G. and Vergara, M., 2014. Tratamiento para un enfermo crítico. Propuestas para el sistema de salud chileno. Informe de Políticas Públicas 04, Espacio Público.

CASEN, Encuesta de Caracterización Socioeconómica, 2015, Ministerio de Desarrollo Social. http://observatorio.ministeriodesarrollosocial.gob.cl/casen-multidimensional/casen/casen_2015.php.

Cid, C., 2011. Problemas y desafíos del seguro de salud y su financiamiento en Chile: el cuestionamiento a las ISAPRE y la solución funcional, Temas de la agenda pública, 49. Centro de Políticas Públicas UC.

Circular N°9 of 2016. Informa los montos de las compensaciones originadas en el quinto semestre de vigencia del D.S N°4, de 2013. Superintendencia de Salud, from http://www.supersalud.gob.cl/normativa/668/w3-article-13632.html.

Circular N°19 of 2016. Informa primas y modelo de compensación de riesgos que corresponden a la vigencia del D.S N°3 y N°21 rectificatorio, de 2016. Superintendencia de Salud, from http://www.supersalud.gob.cl/normativa/668/w3-article-14411.html.

Circular N°20 of 2016. Informa los montos de las compensaciones originadas en el sexto semester de vigencia del D.S N°4, de 2013. Superintendencia de Salud, from http://www.supersalud.gob.cl/normativa/668/w3-article-14412.html.

Comisión Asesora Presidencial para el Estudio y Propuestas de un Nuevo Régimen Jurídico para el Sistema de Salud Privado, 2014. Informe Final. Gobierno de Chile.

Connelly, L.B., Paolucci, F., Butler, J.R.G., Collins, P., 2010. Risk equalisation and voluntary health insurance markets: the case of Australia. Health Policy 98 (1), 3−14.

Cutler, D., Lincoln, G., Zeckhauser, R., 2010. 'Selection stories: understanding movement across health plans'. J. Health Econ. 29 (6), 821−838.

Decree with Force of Law 1 of, 2005. Fija texto refundido, coordinado y sistematizado del decreto ley N° 2.763, de 1979 y de las leyes N° 18.933 y N° 18.469. Ministerio de Salud, República de Chile.

Decree with Force of Law 32 of, 1942. Refunde en el "servicio médico nacional de empleados', los servicios médicos de las instituciones de previsión social que se mencionan. Ministerio de Salubridad, Previsión y Asistencia Social, República de Chile.

Decree with Force of Law 251 of, 1931. Compañías de seguros, sociedades anónimas y bolsas de comercio. Ministerio de Hacienda, República de Chile.

Einav, L., Finkelstein, A., 2011. Selection in insurance markets: theory and empirics in pictures. J. Econ. Perspect. 25 (1), 115−138.

Ellis, R., Ibern, P., Wasem, J., Vargas, V., 2008. Panel de expertos para la evaluación del fondo de compensación solidario entre Isapres. Ministerio de Salud.

Giaconi, J., Concha, M., 2005. El sistema de salud chileno reformado. Ediciones Universidad Mayor, Santiago.

Handel, B., Handel, I., Whinston, M., 2015. Equilibria in health exchanges: adverse selection versus reclassification risk. Econometrica 83 (4), 1261−1313.

Henríquez, J., Velasco, C., 2015. Las desigualdades en la atención médica en los últimos 20 años, Debates de Política Pública, 13. Centro de Estudios Públicos.

Henríquez, J., Velasco, C., Mentzakis, E., Paolucci, F., 2016. Más equidad y eficiencia en Isapres: Evaluación y propuestas al mecanismo de compensación de riesgos, Debates de Política Pública, 18. Centro de Estudios Públicos.

Law 4054 of, 4054. Seguros de enfermedad, invalidez y accidentes del trabajo. Ministerio del Interior, República de Chile.

Law 10383 of, 1038. Modifica la ley 4054 relacionada con el seguro obligatorio. Ministerio de Salubridad, Previsión y Asistencia Social, República de Chile.

Law 16744 of, 1674. Establece normas sobre accidentes del trabajo y enfermedades profesionales. Ministerio del Trabajo y Previsión Social, República de Chile.

Law 18933 of, 1893. Crea la superintendencia de instituciones de salud previsional, dicta normas para el otorgamiento de prestaciones por isapre y deroga el decreto con fuerza de ley n°3, de salud, de 1981. Ministerio de Salud, República de Chile.

Law 19895 of, 1989. Establece diversas normas de solvencia y protección de personas incorporadas a instituciones de salud previsional, administradoras de fondos de pensiones y compañías de seguros. Ministerio de Salud, República de Chile.

Law 19937 of, 1993. Modifica el D.L. N̲o̲ 2.763, de 1979, con la finalidad de establecer una nueva concepción de la autoridad sanitaria, distintas modalidades de gestión y fortalecer la participación ciudadana. Ministerio de Salud, República de Chile.

Law 19966 of, 1996. Establece un régimen de garantías en salud. Ministerio de Salud, República de Chile.

Law 20015 of, 2001. Modifica Ley N° 18.933, sobre instituciones de salud previsional. Ministerio de Salud, República de Chile.

Law 20850 of, 2085. Crea un sistema de protección financiera para diagnósticos y tratamientos de alto costo y rinde homenaje póstumo a don Luis Ricarte Soto Gallegos. Ministerio de Salud, República de Chile.

Law Decree 3 of, 2016. Aprueba garantías explícitas en salud del régimen general de garantías en salud. Ministerio de Salud, República de Chile.

Law Decree 44 of 1924. Ministerio del Interior, República de Chile.

McGuire, T., Newhouse, J., Normand, S.-L., Shi, J., Zuvekas, S., 2014. Assessing incentives for service-level selection in private health insurance exchanges. J. Health Econ. 47−63.

Ministry of Health, 2009. Estudio de Verificación del Costo Esperado Individual Promedio por Beneficiario del Conjunto Priorizado de Problemas de Salud con Garantías Explícitas, Santiago.

Ministry of Health, 2016. *Glosa 06. Lista de espera no GES. Garantías de Oportunidad GES retrasadas.* Octubre, http://web.minsal.cl/wp-content/uploads/2016/12/Glosa_06_octubre-VF.pdf [26 December 2016].

Nancuante, U., Romero, A., 2008. La reforma de la Salud. Editorial Biblioteca Americana, Universidad Andrés Bello, Santiago.

OECD, 2017. Health at a Glance 2017: OECD Indicators. OECD Publishing, Paris.

Paolucci, F., 2011. Health care financing and insurance. Options for design. In: Frech III, H.E., Zweifel, Peter (Eds.), Developments in health economics and public policy, vol. 10. Springer-Verlag, Berlin Heidelberg.

Paolucci, F., 2016. Designing Efficient & Affordable National Health Insurance for Chile' [presentation], Seguros sociales en salud: una propuesta para Chile, Centro de Estudios Públicos, 15 June 2016.

Paolucci, F., Velasco, C., 2017. Reformando el sistema de seguros de salud chileno: Elección, competencia regulada y subsidios por riesgo, Debates de Política Pública, 25. Centro de Estudios Públicos.

Paolucci, F., Den Exter, A., Van de Ven, W.P., 2006. Solidarity in competitive health insurance markets: analysing the relevant EC legal framework. Health Econ. Policy Law 2006 (Pt 2), 107−126. Available from: https://doi.org/10.1017/S1744133105000137.

Paolucci, F., Schut, E., Beck, K., Greß, S., Van de Voorde, C., Zmora, I., 2007. Supplementary health insurance as a tool for risk-selection in mandatory basic health insurance markets. Health Econ. Policy Law 2, 173−192.

Pardo, C., Schott, W., 2014. Health insurance selection in Chile: a cross-sectional and panel analysis. Health Policy Plann 29, 302−312.

Quesney, F., 1995. El sector privado en salud. In: Giaconi, J. (Ed.), La salud en el siglo XXI, Cambios necesarios. Centro de Estudios Públicos, Santiago, pp. 149−176.

Riesco, X., 2015. Mejorando la salud hospitalaria: Alternativas para el financiamiento y la gestión (II), Puntos de Referencia, 417. Centro de Estudios Públicos.

Superintendent of Health, 2005. Los beneficios de un modelo de ajuste de riesgo en el sistema Isapre, Departamento de Estudios y Desarrollo, from http://www.supersalud.gob.cl/documentacion/666/articles-1065_recurso_1.pdf [20 June 2017].

Superintendent of Health, 2007a. Avances en el monitoreo de la reforma y su impacto en los beneficiarios del sistema Isapres, Departamento de Estudios y Desarrollo, from http://www.supersalud.gob.cl/documentacion/666/articles-3901_recurso_1.pdf [27 December 2016].

Superintendent of Health, 2007b. Avance en el monitoreo de la reforma y su impacto en los beneficiarios del sistema ISAPRE. Parte II. Departamento de Estudios y Desarrollo, from http://www.supersalud.gob.cl/documentacion/666/articles-3900_recurso_1.pdf [29 December 2016].

Superintendent of Health, 2007c. Fondo de ajuste de riesgo en el sistema Isapre. Superintendencia de Salud de Chile, from http://www.supersalud.gob.cl/documentacion/666/articles-3902_recurso_1.pdf.

Superintendent of Health, 2008. Evaluación de la reforma de salud en el sistema Isapres y su impacto en los beneficiarios: informe final 2008. Departamento de Estudios y Desarrollo, from http://www.supersalud.gob.cl/documentacion/666/articles-5408_recurso_1.pdf [27 December 2016].

Superintendent of Health, 2009. Magnitud y Características de la Cautividad en el Sistema Isapre, from http://www.supersalud.gob.cl/documentacion/569/articles-5543_recurso_1.pdf [26 December 2016].

Superintendent of Health, 2013. Prestadores de salud, isapres y holdings: ¿Relación estrecha? from http://www.supersalud.gob.cl/documentacion/666/articles-8826_recurso_1.pdf [26 December 2016].

Superintendent of Health, 2016b. Análisis de los planes de salud del sistema Isapre. Documento de trabajo, Departamento de Estudios y Desarrollo, http://www.supersalud.gob.cl/documentacion/666/articles-13913_recurso_1.pdf [27 December 2016].

Superintendent of Health, 2016c. Análisis de la banda de precios en el sistema Isapre. Documento de Trabajo, Departamento de Estudios y Desarrollo, http://www.supersalud.gob.cl/documentacion/666/articles-13719_recurso_1.pdf [29 December 2016].

van Kleef, R., van de Ven, W., van Vliet, R., 2013. Risk selection in a regulated insurance market: a review of concept, possibilities and effects. Expert Rev. Pharmacoecon. Outcomes Res. 13 (6), 743−752.

van de Ven, W., van Vliet, R., van Kleef, R., 2017. How can the regulator show evidence of (no) risk selection in health insurance markets? Conceptual framework and empirical evidence. Eur. J. Health Econ. 18 (2), 167−180.

Velasco, C., 2016. ¿Hacia dónde vamos en salud? Cómo avanzar hacia un sistema de seguros sociales, Puntos de Referencia, 436. Centro de Estudios Públicos.

## FURTHER READING

Bossert, T., Leisewitz, T., 2016. Innovation and change in the chilean health system. New England J. Med. 374, 1−5.

Clínicas de Chile, 2014. Dimensionamiento del sector de salud privado en Chile. Actualización a cifras año 2014'.

Galetovic, A. & Sanhueza, R., 2013. Un análisis de la integración vertical entre isapres y prestadores. Requested by Inversiones La Construcción, from http://www.consalud.cl/estudioscostosdesalud/Estudios/Un%20analisis%20economico%20de%20la%20integracion%20vertical.pdf [30 December 2016].

Ibáñez, C., 2016. Demanda por seguros complementarios de salud e hipótesis de selección adversa y riesgo moral en base a CASEN 2015. Superintendencia de Salud.

Isapre Banmédica, Estudio Prima GES 2016. http://www.banmedica.cl/Portals/0/Documentos%20GES%202016/GES%202016%20-%20Banmédica_vFINAL.PDF [23 December 2016].

Law 20531 of, 2011. Exime, total o parciamente, de la obligación de cotizar para salud a los pensionados que indica. Ministerio de Hacienda, República de Chile.

Law Decree 21 of, 2016. Rectifica el Decreto N°3 de 27 de enero de 2016, que aprobó garantías explícitas en salud del régimen general de garantías en Salud. Ministerio de Salud, República de Chile.

Pontificia Universidad Católica de Valparaíso, 2012. Mercado de la salud privada en Chile. Estudio solicitado por la Fiscalía Nacional Económica.

Sapelli, C., 2004. Risk Segmentation and Equity in the Chilean Mandatory Health Insurance System. Social Science & Medicine 58, 259−265.

Superintendent of Health, 2016a. Diferencias y heterogeneidad en los precios de un conjunto de prestaciones en prestadores privados de la Región Metropolitana, from http://www.supersalud.gob.cl/documentacion/666/articles-14341_recurso_1.pdf [26 December 2016].

Superintendent of Health, 2016d. Análisis Estadístico del sistema Isapre con enfoque de género. Documento de Trabajo, Departamento de Estudios y Desarrollo, http://www.supersalud.gob.cl/documentacion/666/articles-14689_recurso_1.pdf [27 December 2016].

van de Ven, W., Beck, K., Buchner, F., Schokkaert, E., Schut, E., Shmueli, E., et al., 2013. Preconditions for efficiency and affordability in competitive healthcare markets: Are they fulfilled in Belgium, Germany, Israel, the Netherlands and Switzerland? Health Policy 109, 226−245.

# APPENDIX

List of health problems and year of inclusion to the guaranteed basic plan

| 2005 | | 2007 | |
|------|--|------|--|
| | Chronic renal disease stage 4 and 5 | | Medical treatment knee/hip osteoarthritis |
| | Congenital heart diseases (eligible for surgery) in children under 15 years | | Bleeding from brain aneurysms |
| | Cervical/uterine cancer | | Primary CNS tumors |
| | Pain relief and palliative care for advanced cancer | | Lumbar pulp nucleus hernia |
| | Acute myocardial infarction | | Leukemia adults 15 years and over |
| | Diabetes mellitus type 1 | | Ambulatory odontological emergencies |
| | Diabetes mellitus type 2 | | Oral health (adults 60 years old) |
| | Breast cancer | | Severe polytraumatized |
| | Spinal disorders | | Moderate or severe cranioencephalic trauma |
| | Surgical treatment of scoliosis in people under 25 years | | Serious eye trauma |
| | Surgical treatment of cataracts | | Cystic fibrosis |

|  | | | |
|---|---|---|---|
|  | Osteoarthritis of the hip |  | Rheumatoid arthritis |
|  | Cleft lip and palate |  | Alcohol and drug dependence |
|  | Cancer in children under 15 |  | Analgesia of childbirth |
|  | Schizophrenia |  | Burns |
|  | Testicular cancer (adults) |  | Bilateral hearing loss |
|  | Lymphoma in adults | 2010 |  |
|  | HIV (tritherapy treatment) |  | Retinopathy of prematurity |
|  | Acute respiratory infection |  | Bronchopulmonary dysplasia of prematurity |
|  | Pneumonia |  | Bilateral neurosensory hypoacusia of prematurity |
|  | Essential hypertension |  | Nonrefractory epilepsy in persons 15 years and older |
|  | Nonrefractory epilepsy |  | Bronchial asthma in persons 15 years and older |
|  | Oral health (pregnant) |  | Parkinson's disease |
|  | Prematureness |  | Juvenile idiopathic arthritis |
|  | Pacemaker |  | Secondary prevention for terminal chronic renal failure |
| 2006 |  |  | Hip dysplasia |
|  | Preventive cholecystectomy |  | Oral health during pregnancy |
|  | Gastric cancer |  | Multiple sclerosis (recurrent) |
|  | Prostate cancer |  | Hepatitis B |
|  | Disorders of visual acuity |  | Hepatitis C |
|  | Squint | 2013 |  |
|  | Diabetic retinopathy |  | Bipolar disorder |
|  | Retinal detachment |  | Colorectal cancer |
|  | Hemophilia |  | Ovarian cancer |
|  | Depression |  | Bladder cancer |
|  | Prostate hyperplasia |  | Osteosarcoma |
|  | Orthosis |  | Hypothyroidism |
|  | Cerebrovascular accident |  | Treatment of moderate hearing loss in children under 2 years |

| | Chronic obstructive pulmonary disease | | Lupus erythematous |
|---|---|---|---|
| | Bronchial asthma | | Surgical treatment of aortic valve injuries |
| | Respiratory distress syndrome | | Surgical treatment of mitral and tricuspid valve injuries |
| | | | Treatment of *Helicobacter pylori* |
| Source: Authors' own. | | | |

# Chapter 9

# Health Insurance and Payment System Reform in China

Julie Shi and Gordon Liu
*Peking University, Beijing, China*

## 9.1  INTRODUCTION

The Chinese healthcare system has experienced three different consecutive periods of reform since the establishment of communist China in 1949: the central planning era (1949−78), the market-based era (1978−2002), and the healthcare reform era (2003 to the present). The structures of health insurance and healthcare delivery systems varied in different periods. Wagstaff et al. (2009a,b) and Ma et al. (2008) have provided detailed reviews of system changes during these periods.

Between 1949 and 1978, the Chinese economy was governed by a command and control model. Both health insurance and healthcare delivery systems were under direct control of the government. Health insurance was determined based on people's working status and residence. In urban areas, the Government Insurance Scheme (GIS) covered government officials and staff, and the Labor Insurance Scheme (LIS) covered employees at state-owned enterprises (SOEs). In rural areas, the Cooperative Medical Scheme (CMS) covered much of the population. All programs were government-based. No private insurance was available in that period. As for the delivery system, all healthcare facilities, including village clinics, township health centers, and county and city hospitals, were owned and operated by the government, at different levels. Providers were subsidized by the government. Prices of healthcare services were kept low by regulation, with the aim— "equal access to the healthcare system for all."

In 1978, China implemented economic reforms, and the healthcare system quickly transformed to a market-based system. Due to the breakup of communes there has been a lack of funding, which resulted in an almost total collapse of CMS in rural areas. As many SOEs faced financial difficulties, a large number of SOE employees in urban areas lost insurance coverage. In 2003, 78% of the population was uninsured (Ministry of Health, 2008).

Risk Adjustment, Risk Sharing and Premium Regulation in Health Insurance Markets.
DOI: https://doi.org/10.1016/B978-0-12-811325-7.00009-9

Private health insurance was introduced in the early 1980s, but its development was limited. As for the delivery system, subsidies received by healthcare institutions decreased dramatically. Since hospitals had become financially autonomous, they had incentives to oversupply healthcare services in order to increase revenues. Although private hospitals and clinics were permitted to enter markets, the percentage of private providers was relatively low. In 2003, there were only 2037 private hospitals, compared to 15,727 public hospitals (National Health and Family Planning Commission, 2015). The percentage of number of visits in private institutions was even smaller.

In 2003, because of increasing social discontent about the accessibility and affordability of medical care, and triggered by the severe acute respiratory syndrome (SARS) outbreak, the Chinese government implemented a series of healthcare reforms. From 2003 to 2008, reforms focused on building an insurance system with universal coverage. In the process, public medical expenditure kept increasing, and several insurance programs were launched. In 2008, the uninsured rate dropped dramatically to 12.9% (Ministry of Health, 2013), which was regarded as an outstanding achievement for the government. Since 2009, the government launched a new round of reforms focusing on institutional features, such as reforms of the public hospital management and payment systems.

The rest of this chapter is organized as follows. Section 9.2 introduces the current health insurance system in China, which serves as a basis for reforms going forward. Section 9.3 describes the payment system and how it is changing, focusing on the role and potential of capitation payment. Sections 9.4 and 9.5 evaluate and discuss ongoing issues and policies related to payment system reform.

## 9.2 HEALTH INSURANCE SYSTEM

As mentioned above, following economic reforms, much of China's population had lost insurance coverage in the 1990s. During that time, most people were paying their medical bills out-of-pocket. Catastrophic medical spending became one of the leading reasons behind the impoverishment of low- and middle-income households. In 2003, among households living below the poverty line, 30% claimed medical spending to be the reason behind their impoverishment (Ministry of Health, 2004). The population was generally dissatisfied with the health system; "Kanbingnan, kanbinggui" (expensive and poor access to medical care) had become a serious public concern.

With a view to addressing this problem, the Chinese government started to rebuild its insurance system gradually. In 1998, Urban Employee Basic Medical Insurance (UEBMI) was introduced to cover urban employees. In the period 2003−2008, the New Rural Cooperative Medical Scheme (NRCMS) was piloted in certain local areas and then expanded nationwide to cover rural residents. In 2009, Urban Resident Basic Medical Insurance

(URBMI) was formally introduced nationwide to cover urban residents who were not eligible for UEBMI. The above programs, which covered over 95% of the population, remained the three basic insurance programs in China. In 2012, Catastrophic Health Insurance (CHI) was also introduced to provide coverage for enrollees in URBMI and NRCMS who had catastrophic medical spending. In recent years, private insurance was also allowed and encouraged to act as a supplement to public insurance. Fig. 9.1 illustrates the structures of the five types of insurance programs.

Since CHI is most relevant to the theme of this volume, the following description largely focuses on the implementation of CHI. The government had gathered much experience by implementing previous programs, but faced problems in the process. It was risky and expensive to reform the existing system. CHI is the latest program, and has provided the government with an opportunity to design alternative policies. The scheme has a smaller budget than the other programs. As the financial risk is smaller, the government has been willing to pilot new policies. A significant difference between CHI and other programs is that the private insurance firms involved participated more actively in the system. This was due to the fact that there were mechanisms designed to incentivize private firms. We also briefly discuss the other four types of insurances.

Information about the three basic insurance programs is summarized in Table 9.1. UEBMI provides coverage to urban residents who are either working in the formal sector or are retired. The scheme covers employees but not their spouses or dependents. In 2014, the program covered 283 million enrollees, or 20.7% of the population. The total claims amounted to 670 billion RMB. The program provides the most generous coverage to its enrollees,

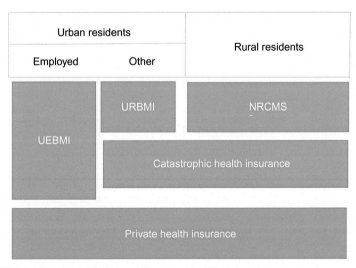

**FIGURE 9.1** Structure of five types of insurance in China.

with the mean per-person claims at 2367 RMB (or about $385) in 2014, which was four to five times the claims made in the other two programs. The premiums are contributed jointly by employees and employers. The employers' contribution is about three-fourths of the total premiums.

URBMI provides coverage to urban residents who are not eligible for UEBMI, including children, students, the elderly without previous employment, and the unemployed. In 2014, the program covered 315 million

**TABLE 9.1** Summary of Three Social Health Insurance Programs

| | UEBMI | URBMI | NRCMS |
|---|---|---|---|
| Who is eligible? | Formal sector employees and the retired | Urban residents who are not eligible for UEBMI (children, students, the elderly without previous employment, and the unemployed) | Rural residents |
| Is enrollment mandatory? | Yes | No | No |
| Individual or family contract? | Individual | Individual | Family |
| Minimum contract period | No | 1 year | 1 year |
| Maximum contract period | No | 1 year | 1 year |
| Number of people covered | 283 million (2014) | 315 million (2014) | 736 million (2014) |
| Total claims | 670 billion RMB (2014) | 144 billion RMB (2014) | 289 billion RMB (2014) |
| Total claims relative to GDP | 1.05% (2014) | 0.23% (2014) | 0.45% (2014) |
| Mean per person claims | 2367 RMB (2014) | 457 RMB (2014) | 393 RMB (2014) |

Source: Statistical report on health and family planning development in 2014; Health and family planning statistical yearbook, 2014; Annual report on social insurance development, 2014.

enrollees, or 23.0% of the population. The total claims were 144 billion RMB. The mean value of per-person claims in 2014 was 457 RMB (or about $74), a little higher than the claims in NRCMS, but much lower than that in UEBMI. The government heavily subsidizes the program, and individuals only pay a proportion of the total premiums.

NRCMS provides coverage to rural residents. In 2014, the program covered 736 million enrollees, or 53.8% of the population. It is the largest insurance program not only in China, but around the world. The total claims were 289 billion RMB. The government heavily subsidizes the program. Again, individuals only pay a proportion of the total premiums. Though both government subsidies and individual premiums kept increasing, financing of the program has continued to be limited. The mean per-person claims were 393 RMB (or about $64) in 2014, which is the lowest among the three programs.

As the coverages of URBMI and NRCMS are limited, enrollees in the two programs have continued to face a risk of high out-of-pocket medical spending. Since 2012, the government started to implement the CHI, with the aim of providing additional financial protection for individuals facing catastrophic spending. The program was initially piloted in some regions, and was then rapidly extended to the entire nation. Enrollees of URBMI and NRCMS automatically enroll in the CHI, without paying additional premiums. CHI plays the role of a supplemental insurance coverage. It reimburses enrollees when their medical spending reaches the ceiling stipulated for the two basic programs.

Indeed, the introduction of the CHI is equivalent to extending the coverages of URBMI and NRCMS in terms of reimbursements to enrollees. However, it is difficult for the government to predict the magnitudes of the enrollees' responses to changes in reimbursement policies. The government is concerned that the program funding could become insufficient for compensation, if the coverage becomes too generous. This was the reason for initiating a separate program, CHI, with a limited budget. Even if the reimbursement rate was inappropriately designed, the program would have only borne limited financial risk. In addition, the government has been encouraging private firms to manage CHI and to share in the risks associated. This is another benefit of the separate implementation of the CHI.

The risk pools of all three basic insurance programs and CHI are at the county or city levels, so the programs are all administered by the local government. Most of the basic programs are directly undertaken by the government, which collects premiums and makes payments to hospitals. There are only a few exceptions where private insurance firms participate in managing the public programs. However, experience has indicated that the government is inefficient in managing the insurance in terms of controlling medical cost and improving quality of care. In many places the objective of the local governments seems to be balancing the budget and to achieve a small surplus. The authorities have little incentive to spend funds efficiently. Many government employees in charge of the programs have lacked the professional skills needed to engage in insurance administration. Hence, in CHI, instead of direct management, a large portion of local governments have been choosing to contract out their reimbursement processes to private insurance firms, or they have been purchasing catastrophic insurance from private firms and providing it to the population.

Each local government selects one insurance firm among competing candidate insurers, and contracts with the firm on insurance services for a given period. The government determines the level of funding, designs the reimbursement policy, and supervises the work of the private insurer. The firm is given the responsibility of implementing the insurance program, and it mainly undertakes four types of tasks. First, it provides consulting services for enrollees and explains the insurance policy to them. Second, it constructs an electronic system to collect and manage the medical claims information of the enrollees. Third, it reviews medical bills, controls unnecessary care, and tries to detect fraudulent behaviors on the parts of the enrollees or providers. Fourth, it implements the reimbursement procedures and makes payments to providers. In some areas, the insurance firms in question do not take the risk of loss from excess payment. In some regions, the private firms share financial risk with the government. The model depends on communication and negotiation between the government and insurance firms in local areas.

Even though the private firms do not determine the premium levels or design the insurance policy, they still actively participate in the CHI program. In places where the private insurers share risk with the government, the insurers could earn profits if the funding is managed efficiently. In addition, the private firms have other considerations. In the course of administering the insurance, firms could collect abundant medical information concerning the enrollees. This information could be used to support the design and management of supplemental private insurance. Furthermore, recognition by the enrollees and the government is important for the reputation of private insurers. Enrollees are more likely to purchase private insurance plans provided by the same insurer, if they are satisfied with their CHI services. The same insurer is more likely to be selected to undertake the three basic medical insurance programs, in the case that the service-purchase model continues to be applied by the government in the future. The markets for the basic programs are much larger than the CHI, and are more attractive to the private firms.

There are no statistics on the number or fraction of CHI programs administered by private firms nationwide, but financial reports of private firms are available. Between January and September, 2014, the total premium revenue of private insurance firms from public programs was 22.48 billion RMB, of which 64% was from CHI and the rest was from URBMI (27%), UEBMI (3%), NRCMS (4%), and medical aid (1%) (Yan, 2015).

A good example of how a private firm can become involved successfully in the public insurance sector is from the city of Zhanjiang in Guangdong province. In 2008, the government combined URBMI and NRCMS into a single insurance program, namely, the Urban and Rural Resident Basic Medical Insurance (URRBMI). In 2009, the government made a contract with a private insurance firm to manage URRBMI, including making payments, reviewing medical bills, and managing financial risk. The firm—the PICC Health Insurance Company—was the first health insurance company in China. It was founded jointly by the People's Insurance Company of China (PICC) and the DKV in 2005. The former has continued to be one of the top comprehensive insurance companies in China, and the latter is the largest commercial insurance company in Europe. The firm was given permission to sell supplemental private insurance plans in the market. In 2012, the city implemented the CHI, and the firm continued to manage the associated CHI services. In that year, over 86% of the population in Zhanjiang was being served by the private firm.

In 2014, the individual premium for CHI was 15.8 RMB. Individuals were reimbursed by URRBMI, if the spending was below 20,000 RMB. Spending above the threshold was compensated by CHI. In Zhanjiang, the insurer shared financial risk with the government under a symmetric risk corridor policy and a ceiling design. The range of profit/loss rate was 3%. Within this range, the insurer took full responsibility for the profit or the loss. In the case that the profit or loss exceeded 3%, the insurer only took half of the profit/loss, and the other half was shared by the government. At the same time, CHI had a ceiling on coverage. The programs were only responsible for compensating for medical spending under 500,000 RMB. Spending above that amount should be paid out-of-pocket or by supplemental private health insurance, if applicable.

Though there has been little academic research on the impact of private participation in the public insurance system, there is some evidence in public reports that private insurers have been performing well (Chen, 2013). Insurers have comparative advantages while providing professional services. For example, in Zhanjiang, about 700 employees would be hired to implement the CHI if the program was directly provided by the government. Instead, by purchasing services from private firms, no additional positions were added to the government.[1] In addition, the electronic system and office equipment are provided by the private firms, which has also saved the government from providing funding.[2] For instance, in Zhanjiang, this privatization was estimated to have saved the government about 8 million RMB in relevant investment. While collaborating with the government, the insurer has to make an effort to provide high-quality services while controlling the medical costs, such as helping the enrollees to understand the insurance policy, reviewing the medical bills to reduce fraud, and improving the information system to speed up the reimbursement process. Per capita inpatient medical spending decreased from 8851 RMB in 2007 to 3869 RMB in 2011 in Zhangjiang (Chen, 2013). As a result, the work conducted by the private insurer has been applauded by the government, and the Zhanjiang model is being considered for expansion to other areas.

Besides public insurance, consumers could also purchase private health insurance in commercial markets, though the markets are less developed. Not only is there little information on private health insurance in public reports, but there is almost no academic research on private insurance markets, probably because almost no data are available. In 2011, only 0.3% of the population, or about 4.0 million people, were covered by private insurance (Ministry of Health, 2013). The majority were urban residents with relatively higher incomes. In 2013, the total claims of private insurance only accounted for 1.3% of total healthcare expenditure (Yan, 2015). In general, private insurance is much more expensive than public insurance and the coverage is usually more generous. Both adverse selection and moral hazard appear to be at work in the market for private insurances. The average medical spending for the population with private insurance is therefore much higher than that for the population without it.

In China, private insurance is largely provided by comprehensive insurance firms. Such firms provide not only health insurance, but also other types of insurance, such as life insurance, property insurance, and auto insurance. Premium revenues on health insurance account only for a small fraction of the total premium revenue. For example, the fraction was 1.74% in 2012 in the PICC (China Insurance Regulatory Commission, 2013). Further, commercial insurance markets are highly fragmented. For example, there were 62 nationwide insurance firms providing health insurance plans in 2012, and different firms focus on services in different regions.

As the coverage of basic insurance is limited, there is an increasing demand for supplemental insurance coverage for the population. Fig. 9.2 shows the premium revenue and growth rate of private health insurance for the period 2006–15.[3] Though the magnitudes are limited, it is clear that private insurance has been growing rapidly in recent years; growth rates have been above 20% since 2012. In 2014, the government issued an administrative document to encourage private insurance in the healthcare sector, which largely stimulated the private insurance markets (State Council, 2014). The growth rates in premiums in 2014 and 2015 were around 40% and 50%, respectively. It is anticipated that the private insurance markets will continue to grow.

## 9.3 PROVIDER PAYMENT DESIGN

In China, payment largely takes the form of public funding transferred from the government to providers. As the participation of private insurance firms in the insurance system in China is quite limited at present, a major concern

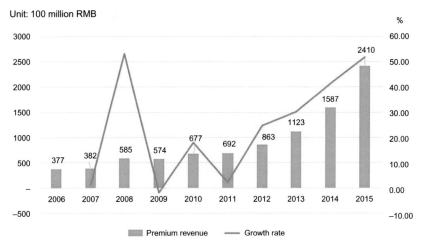

**FIGURE 9.2**  Premium revenue and growth rate of private health insurance between 2006 and 2015. Note: Data are taken from page 76 of China Insurance Market Report 2016, written by Sun and Zheng (2016).

of the government is how to make payments to providers, most importantly, to hospitals. In the US Medicare system and in some European models, payment methods are tools for the government to regulate private insurers. In China too, the government, represented by public insurance authorities, uses payment tools to influence providers' behavior with the same targets of cost control and efficiency improvement.

It is worth noting that the issue of payment methods arises only after the government has rebuilt its public insurance system. Prior to 1998, as there was almost no public insurance, there were no payments transferred from public insurance to providers. A large proportion of hospital revenues come from patients at the time of service use, and only a small fraction comes from government subsidies. The amount of subsidy was not large enough to influence providers' behavior. Along with the expansion of the insurance system, hospital revenues have relied more and more heavily on payments from public insurance, so payment methods have become an important tool to regulate provider's behavior. Also, as government's funding of the healthcare sector keeps increasing, the government has incentives to use payment methods to control the growth of medical costs.

In China's healthcare system, fee-for-service has remained the major payment method, as it is simple and easy to be implemented in practice. Take UEBMI as an example. In 2011, 77.1% of regions made payments based on a fee-for-service method.[4] Recognizing that fee-for-service was inefficient, many regions have reformed their payment system to alternative methods, including global budget, capitation, bundled payment, and payment by inpatient days. For example, the UEBMI in Beijing started to pay some hospitals under the Diagnosis Related Groups (DRG) in 2011, which is one of the earliest DRG pilots in China (Jian et al., 2015). Since the intention here is to discuss health plan payments which are usually based on capitation, the following description focuses on that method.

There are three types of capitation model applied in China. All vary according to their degree of risk-sharing and the use of risk adjustment in determining payments. The first is a simple capitation system with no risk sharing or risk adjustment. The capitation rate is calculated as the total premium divided by the number of enrollees. The second model is capitated global budget (CGB) combined with the notion of a risk corridor. The global budget is determined by a simple capitation rate. At the end of the compensation period, government and providers share the surplus or the loss of the fund. This method reduces the financial risk borne by providers. The third model is similar, but determines the capitation rate with a more sophisticated method. Similar to risk adjustment models in other countries using regulated competition in the health insurance sector, age and diagnoses are considered while determining the capitation rate for each enrollee.[5] Different models are applied in different regions to suit the skills and policy choices of the local government. Eggleston et al. (2008) reviewed how local systems moved away from fee-for-service and the consequences. We mainly summarize findings of the reforms after 2007.

## 9.4   EVALUATION OF CAPITATION-BASED FINANCING PAYMENT REFORM

The capitation payments in China are made from the government to providers, or specifically, from the public insurance authority to hospitals. This section will review some of the policy initiatives and studies regarding capitation-based payment reforms.

Payment reform was part of a more comprehensive reform on the local health systems, and is of great policy relevance. Accompanied by insurance expansion, medical costs were escalating in China. Studies have shown that enrollees' out-of-pocket spending had not reduced (Wagstaff et al., 2009a,b; Lei and Lin, 2009). At the same time, there is no evidence showing that the quality of care has been improved. A key concern was overprescription of drugs, especially of antibiotics. The issue was particularly severe among primary healthcare providers, as they have limited training and capacity to perform examinations and tests and have a high incentive to overprescribe drugs. In view of this problem, Yip et al. (2014) conducted a payment reform in Ningxia province between 2009 and 2012. Yip et al. (2014) collaborated with the government and implemented the reform at township health centers and village clinics. After piloting the reform in two counties, the government of Ningxia province later expanded it to cover the entire province.

In the Ningxia case, the payment methods changed from fee-for-service to a capitated budget with pay-for-performance in the NRCMS. The capitated rate was set to cover the estimated cost of outpatient services for enrollees, and the capitated budget was estimated based on the rate and number of enrollees in each township health center and village clinics. Performance measures included antibiotic prescription rates and patient satisfaction. It is found that the policy change led to a reduction of 15% in antibiotic prescription and 6% in total spending per visit to village clinics. Yip et al. (2014) did not find a significant impact on total spending per visit to township health centers, or drug expenditure per visit to both types of institutions.

In Changde City, the URBMI scheme paid hospitals based on a capitation model for inpatient care since its implementation. Prior to 2007, there were only two public programs in the city, UEBMI and NRCMS. In 2007, the local government decided to implement URBMI to expand insurance coverage to urban residents who were not eligible for UEBMI. The new program faced great pressure to control medical costs, largely because the size of the funding was limited and the program was facing the risk of not being able to pay providers under fee-for-service.

Therefore the insurance authority of Changde City changed the traditional payment method and paid hospitals monthly on a per capita base rate. The rate was determined by city bureau each year, and payments to hospitals differed by the number of contracted enrollees. Two supplemental policies were implemented at the same time to support the capitation model. The first was an equalization fund, which constituted an additional fund used to compensate for the loss of small hospitals ex post. The second was open enrollment. Enrollees could freely choose any in-network provider as a gatekeeper when seeking care and were allowed to change the gatekeeper each year. Thus hospitals were incentivized to compete with each other to attract patients. Enrollees were able to get reimbursed only when they received services from or were referred by the gatekeepers. The gatekeeper was responsible for all costs related to the enrollees, including the referrals. Gao et al. (2014) found that the capitation payment had reduced out-of-pocket inpatient costs by 19.7% and length of stay by 17.7%. However, they found little impact on the overall inpatient expenditure.

In two counties of Shandong province, a payment reform was conducted between 2011 and 2012 for township health centers. Prior to this reform, all centers were being paid through the fee-for-service method. In the reform, some of the hospitals were paid by CGB, and the rest by a combination of CGB and pay-for-performance. There was a third group which would keep the original fee-for-service model and act as a control group. However, owing to pressure from the central government, the local government was not willing to retain the old model, and shifted away. The experiment was only able to compare the impacts of CGB with CGB combined with pay-for-performance. Sun et al. (2016) found that, compared to the CGB model, the combined payment model significantly reduced inappropriate prescribing, but had no impact on out-of-pocket spending.

In Fengsan township of Guizhou province, a 5-year community-based rural health insurance program was conducted between 2003 and 2007. In the program, village doctors were paid a salary plus a bonus based on performance. The performance measures included service quality (such as appropriate drug use or intravenous injections), cost containment, and patient satisfaction. Wang et al. (2011) found that unnecessary care and prescription drugs were reduced. Medical spending was reduced at the village level, but patients were more likely to be referred to township or hospital facilities, where the costs were higher. Hence, total healthcare spending was not significantly reduced.

In summary, all studies found no significant impact of capitation payment on total medical expenditure. There are several possible reasons to explain why no significant impacts are found. First, providers may not change their behavior immediately. As stated in Yip et al. (2014), it takes almost a year for providers to understand the incentives embedded in the reform. It is possible that impacts might appear if studied over a longer time period, though current studies contain no evidence about this. Second, the reforms were implemented for some but not all insurance programs that made payments to providers, thus potentially diluting their effects. For example, the Ningxia reform only implemented NRCMS, and the Changde reform only implemented URBMI. It is possible that the share of revenue from the reformed programs, or the reformed services, was insufficient to change the behavior of providers. Third, some reforms imposed limits on policy designs. For example, in the Shandong reform, the comparison is between CGB and CGB combined with pay-for-performance, so the conclusion is that pay-for-performance had not significantly affected medical spending under the capitation payment system. The reason could be that the performance measures were not appropriately selected, at least, measures on total spending, or the incentives were not strong enough to influence physician behaviors.

In regions where pay-for-performance was implemented, unnecessary care, such as inappropriate prescription, was reduced. There were other regions that had implemented capitated payment reform in recent years, such as for outpatient care in Hangzhou, Zhejiang province, and in Dongguan, Guangdong province. Largely because of lack of data, there have been no rigorous research studies available evaluating the reform impacts.

Two lessons can be learnt from the reform experiences narrated above. First, reform can be successfully implemented only when the government, as the major payer, has an incentive to do so. In the sample described above, the reforms were either initiated by the government or were using policies designed by researchers, but with strong government support.

Payment system reform was first recognized as a direction for reform by the government in 2009, and its importance kept increasing since then (State Council, 2009). In 2011, the Ministry of Human Resources and Social Security issued a special document promoting payment system reform, stating that local governments were to be encouraged to explore alternative payment methods, including global budget, capitation on outpatient care, and bundled payment on inpatient care (Ministry of Human Resources and Social Security, 2011). In the government document issued in November 2016, payment system reform was one of the major tasks listed by the government, along with public hospital reform and referral system implementation. It is expected that there will be more reforms in the future, and the implementation would progressively become easier. Second, pay-for-performance works well, at least with respect to the designated performance measures. In most reforms where pay-for-performance was introduced, inappropriate prescribing was reduced. The change of incentives in this realm indeed changed the behaviors of providers. However, combined with the observation that total spending had not changed, it is difficult to draw a general conclusion that the quality of care had been improved or costs reduced. It is possible that the unnecessary prescribing had been replaced by unnecessary examinations and tests. Changes of provider behavior need to be assessed more comprehensively in future research.

## 9.5 ONGOING ISSUES AND REFORMS

Though the government has encouraged participation of private capital in recent years, there is an ongoing debate on whether this is the correct reform direction. The debate has concentrated not only on promotion of private investment in hospitals, but it has also influenced the insurance sector. On the one hand, compared to government bureaucracies, insurance firms are professional institutions with more up-to-date methods and skilled personnel. They have come up with incentives to perform well and reduce unnecessary care. On the other hand, as the goal of a firm is to earn profits, the quality of services may be affected if public supervision is insufficient. How the private insurance firms are managed and supervised remains an empirical question. Though many CHI programs are being operated by private insurers, there has been sparse analysis comparing privately operated and publicly operated models.

If it is found that private firms are more efficient in operating public insurance, a further question is how the government should structure competition in the market. At present, each region has chosen a single insurer to manage the insurance. The model is simple, and payment can be easily transferred. However, the disadvantage is that the government may have less negotiation power while purchasing services from a single firm. It may also be hard to switch to another insurer, as those compensating services require a large amount of investment on fixed cost in early stages, such as equipment and staff training. If competition were introduced, perhaps in a way similar to the Medicare Advantage system of the United States, insurers would face competitive pressure and may have greater incentives in controlling costs.

When capitation is implemented in China, it would raise concerns about narrow provider selection. In the capitation model, patients are usually restricted to seeking medical care in contracted hospitals. In some models, referrals are allowed, but primary facilities have little incentive to do so as they have to bear the cost of transferred patients. This is the reason why a lot of capitation reforms were firstly piloted on outpatient services. Inpatient services involve more serious illnesses, and it may be inefficient to restrict patients to specific hospitals that may be able to treat them. However, even with regard to outpatient care, it remains a question whether it is appropriate to keep all or the majority of the care in one facility. Medical resources are unequally distributed, and there is a large portion of the population living away from their place of registration. An example is rural-to-urban migrants, usually registered in rural towns but working in cities. As they enroll in NRCMS, the capitation payments are more likely to be paid to the township hospitals. In such a scheme, they may have no access to hospitals where they live and work. Therefore, accessibility and quality of care are likely to be affected. Unfortunately, largely because of lack of data, little evidence is available on this issue.

Since 2009, the focus of Chinese healthcare reform has been shifting from universal insurance coverage to policy changes in delivery and financing. Payment system reform plays a crucial role in this transition. The reform is still at an early stage. Both payment policies and the Chinese healthcare system are large, complicated, and differ in different regions. The Chinese government is seeking to explore payment methods that better fit the Chinese environment.

It is commonly agreed that fee-for-service is not an efficient payment method. Different payment reforms have been piloted in different regions. Theoretically, payment methods, such as capitation and bundled payment, are likely to perform better than fee-for-service in cost control. However, according to the Chinese experience so far, none of the capitation reforms has reduced total medical expenditures. Careful research is needed to explain the gap between theoretical predictions and actual outcomes.

## ACKNOWLEDGMENTS

The authors are grateful to the two editors, Thomas McGuire and Richard van Kleef, for helpful comments, and to Liang Zhang for research assistance. This research is supported by the National Natural Science Foundation of China youth program (71503014).

## ENDNOTES

1. In China, the number of government positions is highly regulated. Usually it is difficult to fire a government employee. So, for a position providing the same services, the cost is higher if it is provided by the government than by a private firm.
2. The fixed cost for the equipment is high for the private firms. However, as mentioned above, private firms have other considerations. So, in practice they are willing to make the investment.
3. Statistics are cited from Sun et al. (2016).
4. Each region represents a risk pool, which could be a county, a city, or a province.
5. No detailed information is available on the diagnoses used or the weights given to diagnoses for purposes of payment.

## REFERENCES

Chen, W., 2013. An Analysis on Development Model of Catastrophic Health Insurance for Chinese Urban and Rural Residents. China Economy Press [Chinese].

China Insurance Regulatory Commission, 2013. Monthly Report of Statistics on Insurance in 2012. Internal Materials [Chinese].

Eggleston K., Ling L., Qingyue M., Lindelow M., Wagstaff A., 2008. Health Service Delivery in China: A Literature Review. 17(2), 149−165.

Gao, C., Xu, F., Liu, G., 2014. Payment reform and changes in health care in China. Soc. Sci. Med. 111, 10−16.

Jian, W., Lu, M., Chan, K., Poon, A., Han, W., Hu, M., et al., 2015. Payment reform pilot in Beijing hospitals reduced expenditures and out-of-pocket payments per admission. Health Aff. 34 (10), 1745−1752.

Lei, X., Lin, W., 2009. The new cooperative medical scheme in rural China: does more coverage mean more service and better health? Health Econ. 18 (S2), S25−S46.

Ma, J., Lu, M., Quan, H., 2008. From a national, centrally planned health system to a system based on the market: lessons from China. Health Aff. 27 (4), 937−948.

Ministry of Health, 2004. An Analysis Report of the 3rd National Health Services Survey in China, 2003. http://www.moh.gov.cn/mohwsbwstjxxzx/s8211/201009/49162.shtml [accessed on January 8th, 2017] [Chinese].

Ministry of Health, 2008. Summary Statistics on Health in 2008. http://www.moh.gov.cn/mohwsbwstjxxzx/s7967/201307/86e8372308a94261af1cf4829816d388.shtml [accessed on January 8th, 2017] [Chinese].

Ministry of Health, 2013. Summary Statistics on Health in 2013. http://www.nhfpc.gov.cn/mohwsbwstjxxzx/s7967/201404/f3306223b40e4f18a43cb68797942d2d.shtml [accessed on January 8th, 2017] [Chinese].

Ministry of Human Resources and Social Security, 2011. Opinions on further reinforcing reforms on health insurance payment schemes. http://www.mohrss.gov.cn/yiliaobxs/YILIAOBX Szhengcewenjian/201105/t20110531_83732.htm [accessed on January 8th, 2017] [Chinese].

National Health and Family Planning Commission, 2015. Statistical Yearbook on Health and Family Planning in 2014 [Chinese].

State Council, 2009. Opinions on Deepening the Reforms on Health Care and Drug System. URL: http://www.gov.cn/test/2009-04/08/content_1280069.htm [accessed on January 8th, 2017] [Chinese].

State Council, 2014. Opinions on Speed Up Development of Commercial Health Insurance. http://www.gov.cn/zhengce/content/2014-11/17/content_9210.htm [accessed on January 8th, 2017] [Chinese].

Sun, Q., Zheng, W., 2016. China Insurance Market Report 2016. Peking University Press [Chinese].

Sun, X., Liu, X., Sun, Q., Yip, W., Wagstaff, A., Meng, Q., 2016. The impact of a pay-for-performance scheme on prescription quality in Rural China. Health Econ. 25, 706–722.

Wagstaff, A., Lindelow, M., Jun, G., Ling, X., Juncheng, Q., 2009a. Extending health insurance to the rural population: an impact evaluation of China's new cooperative medical scheme. J. Health Econ. 28 (1), 1–19.

Wagstaff, A., Yip, W., Lindelow, M., Hsiao, W.C., 2009b. China's health system and its reform: a review of recent studies. Health Econ. 18, S7–S23.

Wang, H., Zhang, L., Yip, W., Hsiao, W., 2011. An experiment in payment reform for doctors in rural china reduced some unnecessary care but did not lower total costs. Health Aff. 30 (12), 2427–2436.

Yan, J. (Ed.), 2015. Development Report of China Health Insurance in 2015. China Finance Press [Chinese].

Yip, W., Powell-Jackson, T., Chen, W., Hu, M., Fe, E., Hu, M., et al., 2014. Capitation combined with pay-for-performance improves antibiotic prescribing practices in rural China. Health Affairs 33 (3), 502–510.

## FURTHER READING

State Council, 2016. Opinions on Further Expanding and Deepening the Experience of Reforms on Health Care and Drug System. http://news.xinhuanet.com/health/2016-11/08/c_111 9874837.htm?from = groupmessage [accessed on January 8th, 2017] [Chinese].

# Chapter 10

# Health Plan Payment in Colombia*

Sebastian Bauhoff[1], Iván Rodríguez-Bernate[2], Dirk Göpffarth[3],
Ramiro Guerrero[4], Inés Galindo-Henriquez[2] and Félix Nates[2]

[1]*Center for Global Development, Washington, DC, United States,* [2]*Ministry of Health and Social Protection, Bogota, Colombia,* [3]*State Chancellery of North Rhine-Westphalia, Düsseldorf, Germany,* [4]*PROESA, Icesi University, Cali, Colombia*

## 10.1 INTRODUCTION

In 1993, the Colombian Congress approved a reform that completely reorganized the healthcare sector and created a universal social health insurance system based on regulated competition. This was part of a wave of reforms that swept the country following the adoption of a new Constitution in 1991, at a time when the "Washington Consensus" discourse had an important influence in Latin America and inspired policy change to incorporate market forces into public services. The Colombian healthcare reform was both socially progressive and market-friendly, following the three guiding principles that the new Constitution had stipulated for social insurance: universality, solidarity, and efficiency.[1] The reform established a universal entitlement to a comprehensive package of healthcare services, subsidies for those within the population that could not afford the contributions, and choice among competing options of care for citizens. It was passed alongside a pension reform that generated substantial debate and effectively provided a window of opportunity to also enact healthcare reforms.

Prior to the 1993 reform there had been a social insurance institute, set up as a public monopoly, that provided health and pension benefits for workers in the formal sector. Workers of contributing employers were eligible for health services that were mostly funded and provided by the institute in its own facilities. Only 23% of the population was enrolled (MSPS, 2015a). Another 10% of the population purchased private health insurance, and the rest sought care in state-owned and -funded hospitals.

---

* The interpretations and conclusions expressed in this chapter are those of the authors. They do not necessarily represent the views of the Ministry of Health and Social Protection.

**Risk Adjustment, Risk Sharing and Premium Regulation in Health Insurance Markets.**
DOI: https://doi.org/10.1016/B978-0-12-811325-7.00010-5

The 1993 reform created two insurance schemes aimed at different populations. Individuals with formal jobs, or with the capacity to contribute, are obligated to enroll in the Contributory Regime (CR) as before. The reform extended this coverage to first-degree family members. In contrast, the Subsidized Regime (SR) is designed for populations unable to contribute, usually those not working or employed in the informal sector (businesses that are not registered, monitored, or taxed by the government, including self-employment).

Since the introduction of universal health insurance in 1993, enrollment has increased to 96% of the population, as of 2014 (MSPS, 2015a). In May 2016, around 21.3 million individuals were covered by the CR and 22.9 million were covered by SR. A total of 2.1 million individuals were covered by special coverage programs, e.g., for members of the military and teachers (MSPS, 2016a). In the latest data available, from 2007, about 90% of hospitalizations and outpatient consultations were financed through the CR and SR (Giedion et al., 2014).

In both the CR and SR there are multiple competing insurers, called *Entidades Promotoras de Salud* (EPS; Spanish for "health-promoting entities"). As we describe below, each insurer bears risk and offers only a single standardized product (i.e., health plan), at a common premium, so that the terms insurer/issuer and health plan are synonymous; in the following we use the term "insurer." These institutions can be public or private (for-profit or not-for-profit). Enrollees are free to choose their insurer and can switch to another at any time after 1 year, unless there are compelling circumstances that warrant an earlier change. Except for emergency services, enrollees can only access the network of providers that has been contracted by the insurers, with no coverage of out-of-network spending.

Insurers may selectively contract with public or private health service providers and rearrange their networks according to the conditions they negotiate in the market. There is, thus, competition in both the insurance and service provision markets. All insurers provide the same basic benefits package, the content of which is regulated by the government. The contributions enrollees make are set by regulation and are the same across all insurers. Some insurers in the CR offer supplemental coverage, which is voluntary, at an additional cost to the insured. The extra benefit does not cover more or different medical services, but provides more direct access to specialists and better rooms in case of hospitalization.

Not being able to compete on price or content of benefits, insurers can attract enrollees through the quality of their customer service and provider network. The prices of health services that insurers purchase are largely determined by the market, although the government regulates some of them. In particular, between 2013 and 2014 the prices of 79 pharmaceutical products, corresponding mainly to expensive biological drugs, were capped by the government.

When this healthcare system was setup in the early 1990s, it set an ambitious goal of achieving universal coverage, with equal benefits for the whole population by 2001. During this decade-long transition, the SR had a less comprehensive benefits package.

Public spending in health care went up from 1.4% of GDP in 1993 to 3.1% in 2003, whereas total health spending went from 6.2% to 7.8% of GDP in the same period (Barón-Leguizamón, 2007). Despite this increase, by the mid-2000s, universal coverage was far from being achieved, and the original goals were found in hindsight to have been overly ambitious (Guerrero, 2008). In 2008, the Constitutional Court reiterated the government's mandate to equalize benefits between the CR and SR systems, a goal that was finally achieved in 2012.

## 10.2 ORGANIZATION OF THE HEALTH INSURANCE SYSTEM

Prior to 2012, the SR benefits excluded secondary services, like access to certain specialties and diagnostic technologies. Benefits, as well as payments to insurers, were formerly set by a National Social Health Insurance Council, with representatives from government, insurers, providers, employers, and unions. This function was passed to a regulatory commission in 2009 and to the health ministry in 2012.

Since equalizing the benefits for CR and SR in 2012, both systems cover primary, secondary, and tertiary care, diagnostic and therapeutic services (both inpatient and outpatient), prescription drugs, and mental health.[2] Other types of care, such as dental (with restrictions), palliative and home health care, and some indigenous traditional medicine are also covered with a list of exclusions.

In 2015, a legal change facilitated shifting from an explicitly defined benefits package to an implicitly defined package with a negative list. In the new regime, individuals are entitled to most health services by default, with limits for only a few areas, such as medically ineffective and esthetic services and treatments that are experimental, unapproved, or unavailable in Colombia (Giedion et al., 2014; Government of Colombia, 2015).

Although the benefits for CR and SR have been equalized, several important differences in regulation remain between the two regimes. First, since the late 1990s, the law mandates that insurers in the SR have to contract at least 60% of services with public providers. Prior to the reform, public providers had guaranteed budgets. In the new system they compete with private providers for revenue from payers. Political pressure led to this exogenously set market share. Second, CR and SR insurers originally had the flexibility to insource or outsource the services delivered to enrollees with service providers. In 2007, they were limited by law to insource at most 30% of the value of services. Limits on vertical integration have been a highly contentious policy issue.

Consumers can switch between SR and CR, although switching rates are very low, at less than 1% in 2014. In the CR and in the context of standardized premiums and benefits, a 2013 survey found that the main reasons for switching relate to customer service (e.g., delays in receiving services) and the quality of services available (Prada, 2016).

In 2015, there were 50 insurers in the overall market. Insurers can choose their operating area (state). As a result, states had between 7 and 24 insurers in 2015 (MSPS, 2015b). Insurers have always had the opportunity to choose whether to operate in either or both regimes, although historically they tended to specialize in one. Prior to 2013, when an enrollee in the SR found a job in the formal sector, he or she typically had to switch to an insurer in the CR. Since 2013, enrollees have been allowed to switch back and forth between CR and SR according to employment status without having to change insurers. CR and SR populations within insurers have begun to mix. Two of the 50 insurers have only CR enrollees, 11 have only SR enrollees, and 37 have enrollees from both regimes. Allowing insurers to operate in both regimes was a deliberate policy decision and allows consumers to stay with a specific insurer even if they alternate between eligibility for SR or CR, e.g., due to casual or seasonal labor.

The 1993 law enabled health insurers to promote efficiency in the delivery of healthcare services in several ways. Insurers can create provider networks and separately contract with individual providers. Except for emergency services, they are not obliged to cover out-of-network spending. Insurers are also allowed to configure the geography of their network. Although they must comply with waiting times targets, these requirements do not imply having to contract any specific provider. In addition, insurers have discretion in the payment mechanism they use. A total of 46% of CR payments in 2011 were based on fee-for-service, while capitated contracts accounted for 35% (Carranza et al., 2015); the former are mostly used for specialty care and the latter for primary care. However, package and diagnosis-based (using Diagnosis-Related Groups, DRG) payments are also used in both regimes and constitute two percent of payments in the CR.

There are restrictions on the insurers' contractual arrangements. As noted above, they can contract with their own providers for up to 30% of expenditures and SR insurers are mandated to use public providers for at least 60% of their expenditures. In addition, insurers' negotiating power is constrained by the availability of specialized services, as tertiary providers tend to have high occupancy rates. Insurers tend to contract with most of these providers but vary the volume of patients they send to each based on the conditions they negotiate.

## 10.3 HEALTH PLAN PAYMENT DESIGN

### 10.3.1 Payment Flows

Fig. 10.1 shows the financing flows for the CR and SR. Most payments for both regimes flow through a central health fund (*Fondo de Solidaridad y*

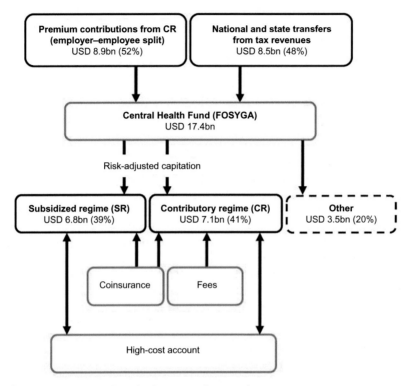

**FIGURE 10.1**  Payment flows for the two enrollment regimes.
Based on MSPS (2013). Exchange rate COP 1950/USD 1. The 2014 tax reform, partly earmarked to replace the employer contribution to health insurance, introduced a new source of
funding and reduced the relative importance of contributions. CR plans provide additional benefits, including payments for sick and maternity leave.

*Garantía*, FOSYGA), which pools revenues and distributes these to
insurers. In 2013, the central fund managed about USD 17.4bn (MSPS,
2013). Revenues consist of the contributions of CR members (52% in
2013), government transfers (48%) and, since 2014, an earmarked tax on
employers. Expenditures consist primarily of risk-adjusted payments to CR
and SR insurers (80% of expenditures), with additional outflows for programs outside the health insurance market, such as disaster relicf and
replacement income for short-term disability and maternity/paternity
leaves. While all contributions are equalized through the central fund, revenues from coinsurance and flat "moderating fees" (described in
Section 10.3.2) are not pooled and directly accrue to the insurer. As
described in Section 10.3.2, the structure of these payments is administratively set and uniform across insurers.

## 10.3.2 Contributions

In Colombia, enrollee contributions to the insurance scheme are paid to the central fund rather than to the insurer, and do not vary across insurers so that there is no competition on price.[3] Enrollees in the CR contribute 12.5% of their monthly income to the central fund. For the employed, 8.5% is nominally paid by the employer and 4% is deducted from the employee's salary. The self-employed pay 12.5% on 40% of their estimated gross income, but at least 12.5% on the full-time monthly minimum wage (about USD 230 in 2016). In 2012 a tax reform exempted private companies from paying the 8.5% health contribution on behalf of their employees, in exchange for a corporate tax surcharge earmarked for health. For public and not-for-profit employers, there was no change. The reform was meant to lower labor costs to encourage formal employment. Fernández and Villar (2016) estimate that this policy caused a reduction of between 1.2% and 2.2% in the national share of informal employment, while Morales and Medina (2016) estimate that 213,000 new formal jobs were created in preexisting firms due to this tax reform.

Both the CR and SR employ cost-sharing features that are uniform and administratively set. Insurers in both regimes collect coinsurance that varies by income (relative to the monthly base income). All enrollees are exempt from coinsurance for some services, such as labor and delivery, certain high-cost services and preventive services. In 2016 the coinsurance rate was 10% for SR and between 11.5% and 23% for CR, depending on the income bracket (MSPS, 2016b). Coinsurance is capped by staggered out-of-pocket maxima per visit and per year. The out-of-pocket maxima are low: for instance, the annual cap for a CR member earning less than twice the monthly base income was about USD 130 in 2016, or about 2.4% of annual income. CR enrollees are also subject to fixed "moderating fees" that ranged from USD 1−10 in 2016, also depending on the income bracket.

The CR pools these contributions and pays each insurer a monthly capitation payment for each enrollee. This payment is risk-adjusted, and is unrelated to the enrollee's income. Age, sex, and geographic area are the three categories of risk adjusters that have been used since the system started, as explained in more detail below.

Eligibility for SR is based on a proxy means test, the *Sistema de Identificación y Clasificación de Potenciales Beneficiarios para Programas Sociales* (SISBEN). SISBEN accounts for several dimensions of poverty measured in household surveys which include labor market participation, education, assets, family structure, housing, and access to water and sanitation. Individuals with low SISBEN scores are eligible for SR, as long as they are not already enrolled in CR. Prior to 2012, when universal enrollment was achieved, this means test was critical for gaining access to scarce slots in the SR. Since 2012, eligibility for the SR has become, de facto, open to those not covered in the CR, and the importance of SISBEN in health insurance access has faded.[4]

In terms of funding, the SR was originally structured around the transfers that the central government makes to local governments, which come from general national tax revenues. Mayors were given the role of applying the SISBEN means test for defining eligibility to the SR, organizing enrollment, and of making the capitation payments to the insurer mainly with fiscal transfers from the national government and cross-subsidies from the CR. (The 12.5% contribution consists of transfers to the CR [11%] and a solidarity contribution to the SR [1.5%].) Operationally the SR and CR were very different. Since universal enrollment with equal benefits was achieved in 2012, the regulation and operation of both schemes have begun to converge. Municipal governments are no longer managing capitation payment monies; their main remaining responsibility is managing collective public health programs designed by the national government. In 2017, the central health fund was replaced by a new entity that will pool all contributions and earmarked taxes for both regimes and distribute capitated payments to all insurers.

An important feature of the Colombian system is the active role played by the judiciary branch, led by the Constitutional Court. When patients or doctors demand a service not included in the benefits package, they can bring their claim to the courts based on a constitutional right to health, through an expedited legal action called *Tutela* (Spanish for "safeguard" or "protection"), which has to be ruled on within a few days. Judges generally have granted coverage for whatever service the physician deems necessary. When exceptional benefits are granted, the insurer has to file a claim for reimbursement with the central fund (in the case of the CR) or the provincial government (in the case of the SR). The value of these exceptional claims has risen to be the equivalent to approximately 20% of the revenue flow of the capitation payments, and has altered incentives for both payers and providers in a fundamental way. These payments are outside the risk adjustment system. Reducing these exceptional claims through an alternative payment mechanism was one motivating factor for switching to the implicit benefits package.

### 10.3.3    Prospective and Concurrent Risk Adjustment

There are two types of risk-based payments to the health insurers. First, the central health fund issues risk-adjusted capitation payments and, if applicable, an add-on payment for insurers with a disproportionate share of elderly insured. Second, insurers may receive payments from a high-cost account for three conditions: stage 5 kidney disease, HIV/AIDS, and hemophilia A.

### 10.3.3.1 Risk-Adjusted Capitation Payments From the Central Health Fund

The main transfer from the central health fund is the risk-adjusted Capitation Payment Unit (*Unidad de Pago por Capitación*, UPC), which represents the per capita value that the system pays to health insurers for each enrollee. The two enrollment regimes (CR and SR) share the same set of UPCs, although their specific values are estimated separately. The risk adjustment considers three factors, age, sex, and geographical zone. For both the CR and SR, there are 14 age−sex groups and four geographical zones, with higher payments for remote areas (to reduce barriers to access) and urban areas (because of expected higher demand). Together, there are 56 cells for each regime, for a total 112 different UPCs (Box 10.1).

The UPCs are the estimated annualized spending per enrollee in each of the 56 cells. They are calculated in two steps, as described in Box 10.2. First, the Ministry of Health forecasts a variety of factors that affect spending and, on that basis, calculates the expected change in spending for each actuarial cell. Second, each cell's current-year UPC is calculated by applying the expected change to the prior UPC values. In practice, these calculations are implemented using actuarial methods that do not rely on statistical estimations (for further details, see MSPS, 2016c).[5]

In the past, the UPC for the CR has exceeded the UPC for the SR, because of differences in the benefits package, utilization, as well as differences in risk groups. However, the UPCs for CR and SR have been converging in recent years because the benefits packages have been equalized. Small differences persist due to differences in utilization and risk composition between CR and SR.

### 10.3.3.2 Additional Payment for a Disproportionate Share of Elderly

The central health fund also issues payments to insurers in the CR that have a high concentration of enrollees older than 50 years. Whereas the risk-adjusted UPC payment for the elderly is available to all insurers, this add-on

---

**BOX 10.1 Risk adjustors used in the risk adjustment as of 2016**

*Age interacted with gender:* 12 age−sex groups, of which two are further separated by gender: 0 year, 1−4 years, 5−14 years, 15−18 years, 19−44 years, 45−49 years, 50−54 years, 55−59 years, 60−64 years, 65−69 years, 70−74 years, and 75 years and older. The classes for 15−18 and 19−44 years are further separated by gender.

*Geography:* four groups based on geographic zones: "regular" areas, dispersed areas, cities, and remote areas.

BOX 10.2 **Estimation procedure for the 2017 Capitation Payment Unit (UPC)**

1. Data. The basis for UPCs of year $t$ are spending and claims data from year $t-2$, i.e., data from the year 2015 are used to calculate the 2017 UPCs.
2. Forecasts. Several adjustments are made to the data from $t-2$ to make them representative for year $t$, for each actuarial cell:
   a. Expected inflation (inflation trending) for year $t$,
   b. Expected claims volume (frequency) for year $t$, calculated with a time series model,
   c. Expected covered or enrolled population for year $t$ in each actuarial cell,
   d. Expected expenditure due to changes in the benefit package according to budget impact analyses,
   e. Adjustment for IBNR and IBNER reserves enough reported.[6]
3. Estimation of the UPC. For each insurance regime and each cell, the new UPCs are derived by adjusting the prior $(t-2)$ UPCs according to the forecasts and allowing for administrative costs and profits. The latter two factors are administratively set to a combined value of 10% for the CR and 8% for the SR.

payment is only available to CR insurers that meet one or both of two conditions: the insurer's share of elderly is relatively high in a given year, or its share has grown relatively rapidly (MSPS, 2011).[7] If the insurer meets at least one of these criteria, it receives an additional payment for each enrollee that is an administratively determined fraction (6% in 2016) of the average UPC (MSPS, 2015c).

### 10.3.3.3  Payments From the High-Cost Account

The third source of revenue for insurers is the high-cost account (*cuenta de alto costo*). This account is an ex-post mechanism that amounts to a form of concurrent risk adjustment with respect to three conditions: Stage 5 of chronic kidney disease (5CKD), HIV/AIDS, and hemophilia A severe (HAs). This mechanism is funded by the insurers and is fiscally neutral: the account's revenues equal its disbursements. In 2016, the account represented less than 0.2% of total payments.

- *Stage 5 of chronic kidney disease (5CKD).* This mechanism disburses based on two criteria. One is the distribution of enrollees with 5CKD. Specifically, the high-cost account issues or deducts funds if the share of an insurer's enrollees with 5CKD in each age group (UPC cell) is above or below the average share of 5CKD patients (MSPS, 2014). In that case, the payment (or deduction) is calculated as the product of the average cost for enrollees with 5CKD and the difference between the expected and actual number of such patients with the respective insurer. The second criterion, introduced in 2014, is a set of four performance metrics related to the prevention of end-stage renal disease.

- *HIV/AIDS.* The high-cost account for HIV/AIDS is funded through contributions by the insurers (in proportion to their size) and redistributes funds in accordance with the achievement on four process indicators and outcome indicators (MSPS, 2015d):
  - Percentage of pregnant women screened for HIV/AIDS,
  - Percentage of enrollees with HIV receiving antiretroviral therapy and having adequate viral load,
  - Percentage of enrollees with early detection of HIV/AIDS,
  - Prevalence of HIV/AIDS among the enrollees.

  The first three indicators each account for 30% of the payment and the fourth for 10%. The funds are distributed according to the insurer's performance on each indicator relative to the performance of all insurers.
- *Hemophilia A severe (HAs).* As for the HIV/AIDS high-cost account, the mechanism for HAs (also called factor VIII deficiency) is funded through a contribution based on the insurers' relative size (MSPS, 2016d). Currently, the funds are redistributed according to the prevalence of HAs, but from 2018 on, the mechanism will account for performance on processes and outcome indicators.

### 10.3.4 Practical Aspects

#### 10.3.4.1 Issues Related to the Approach for Prospective/Ex-Post Adjustment

The Ministry of Health maintains the risk adjustment and ex-post mechanisms, and has implemented several changes over recent years. For instance, prior to 2005, the risk adjustment formula included only seven age—gender groups and two geographic zones. The high-cost account was introduced in 2006, initially only for chronic kidney disease. HIV/AIDS was added to the high-cost account in May 2015 and hemophilia A severe (HAs) was added in March 2016.

#### 10.3.4.2 Issues Related to Data

Currently, the UPCs for both regimes are estimated based only on data from the CR and extrapolated to the SR because data for the SR are more frequently missing or of low quality. The quality of the CR data itself remains problematic despite recent improvements (Giedion et al., 2014).

The main data elements submitted by insurers and used for computing the UPC include beneficiary information, principal and additional diagnosis codes, service provider identifiers, and details of procedures and treatments, such as date of service, length of stay, procedure and/or medication codes, and patient cost-sharing for procedures and/or medications (MSPS, 2016c).

The data used in the risk adjustment are subject to several verification steps, including checks for completeness; uniqueness; internal consistency (e.g., between diagnoses and age and sex, and whether reported lengths of stay are consistent with procedures); high-use and high-cost (unusually high costs or number of encounters); and identity and status of the provider.

## 10.4  EVALUATION OF HEALTH PLAN PAYMENT

Colombia's approach to health plan payments has been evaluated with regards to the fit of the risk adjustment, overall incentives for risk selection, and regulation to contain such behavior.

The risk adjustment scheme has been evaluated at the individual level (by researchers) using measures of statistical fit and the level of actuarial cells (by the Ministry) using predictive ratios as criteria (MSPS, 2016c). At the individual level, the current model's explanatory power as measured by $R^2$ is low, at less than 2% (in-sample and out-of-sample), and the model underpredicts for high-cost individuals while overpredicting for low-cost individuals (Riascos et al., 2014). This is consistent with the explanatory power of age−sex models in other countries (Van de Ven and Ellis, 2000). Research using 2009 data from Colombia suggests that incorporating diagnosis information can increase the fit at the individual level to an $R^2$ of 10% or more (Riascos et al., 2014).

At the level of the actuarial cells, an evaluation of the CR compared actual spending in the second half of 2014 with predicted spending for the same period (applying the method outlined in Box 10.2 on reconciled 2013 data). This assessment found that the current model has a good predictive ratio for dimensions included in the risk adjustment as would be expected (MSPS, 2015e). The CR's "cities" zone is the largest area by population and therefore closely tracks the performance of the overall system (predictive ratio of 1.01). The predictive ratio for the "dispersed" zone is substantially higher at 1.56, reflecting the higher payments to incentivize insurers' operation in these areas.[8] Performance is more variable at the level of the age−gender groups, where children aged 1−4 years and women aged 19−44 are overcompensated, while infants, children aged 5−14 years, and males aged 15−18 years are undercompensated. The oldest age group is also somewhat undercompensated. There is currently no assessment of predictive ratios for dimensions that are not included in the risk adjustment formula.

A review of the Colombian context in 2012 suggested that, in principle, there are several mechanisms for risk selection that are available to Colombian insurers, including selective advertising by insurers to attract lower-risk enrollees and deter those of higher risk; using shortages of specialists in the insurers' network to be less appealing to enrollees that may potentially need such care; supplemental insurance; and choosing low-cost geographic zones as operating areas (Ellis and Fernandez, 2013).

The Ministry of Health regularly reviews selection incentives and indirect measures of selection. The former are assessed through group-level over- and undercompensation. The latter are assessed through information provided by the insurers, including on their financial position.

Although the regulators' data show differences in risk pools, there is no conclusive evidence that insurers engage in risk selection. Similarly, there is no recent evidence on how well the risk adjustment reduces the incentives for and actually prevents risk selection, i.e., how well it mitigates the existence and exploitation of unpriced risk heterogeneity (Newhouse, 1996). A study on 1997 data reported no evidence of risk selection by insurers (Alvarez, 2000).

## 10.5    ONGOING ISSUES AND REFORMS

Current debates regarding payments to health insurers center around two issues: how to respond to the substantial changes introduced by the 2015 reform, and how to continue technical development of risk adjustment so as to encourage efficiency and innovation while maintaining solvency and minimizing the risk of manipulation by providers and insurers.

The 2015 reform has far-reaching implications for payments to and operations of health insurers. The law has been interpreted as requiring coverage for all services that are not explicitly mentioned on a negative list. It also restricts insurers' ability to require prior authorization and strengthens provided autonomy to decide on medications and treatments, although insurers can continue to define provider networks. One implication of the law change is that fewer patients may need to go through the judicial system to claim services that were excluded in the previous explicit benefits package (see Section 10.3.2). As a result, there may be fewer "exceptional claims" that insurers will file with the central health fund or the provincial governments.

Related to the 2015 legal change, the government has reformed the way that exceptional benefits outside the package will be paid. Until 2016 these services had to be approved by medical exception committees (called *Comités Técnico Científicos*, CTC). In 2016, these committees were abolished and replaced by an online prescription/medical order system through which doctors order and justify the exceptional service. The government has declared that this is consistent with mandates for greater autonomy of the medical profession, and that it is counting on peer accountability to curb potential abuse and moral hazard.

Another development in 2017 was the replacement of the FOSYGA central health fund with a new and differently structured entity called ADRES (*Entidad Administradora de los Recursos del Sistema General de Seguridad*

*Social en Salud*) that is expected to simplify the collection processes, improve the flow of monetary resources, and directly control and reduce the operating costs of the financing system.

The future role of the high-cost account is another important policy issue. The account was created partly in response to potential risk selection in dialysis patients: the distribution of these patients was highly skewed against one public EPS, even after accounting for its market share. Once in operation, the emphasis of its regulation and payment mechanisms shifted from correcting risk selection to placing stronger incentives for prevention and paying for performance. The question of whether the account will remain a complement to ex-ante risk adjustment for preventing risk selection, or a vehicle for stimulating prevention and rewarding performance, remains open.

With regards to incentives for risk selection, an important policy issue looking forward is whether the country will continue to use disease-specific mechanisms (adding more pathologies) or shift towards more general risk-sharing mechanisms that are not disease-based. Risk-sharing arrangements that are not disease-specific have been examined in terms of how they would change incentives for insurers if implemented. Duarte and Guerrero (2014) and Camelo and Riascos (2017) have evaluated alternative designs proposed in the international literature by Van Barneveld et al. (2001) with Colombian claims data. These include risk sharing for high risks (RSHR), risk sharing for high costs (RSHC), outlier risk sharing (ORS), and proportional risk sharing (PRS). All of these policies imply a reduction in the selection incentives at the cost of reduced incentives for efficiency, so they are evaluated in terms of this selection-efficiency trade-off. Each of these mechanisms is compared, in turn, with the current ex-ante payment formula (demographic risk adjustment), under the assumption that all insurers are required to participate. The analysis assumes that the regulator uses a demographic model to adjust payments and the insurers have a model that incorporates morbidity variables and yields more accurate predictions of future individual costs. Selection incentives are measured as the gain an individual insurer would expect of attracting good risks and avoiding bad ones, given its model, under each risk-sharing scheme compared to the demographic capitation formula.[9] Incentives for efficiency are measured as the fraction of any costs savings that the insurer is allowed to keep under the respective risk-sharing arrangement. Using these metrics, both studies conclude that risk sharing for high costs would have the greatest reduction in incentives to select with the least detriment on incentives for efficiency.

Another crucial policy issue that relates to the development of risk adjustment is the solvency regulation for health insurers. In 2014, the government updated the requirements insurers must meet in terms of reserves and minimum capital levels, with the intent of controlling the risk of bankruptcy. In the medium term, insurers must have an amount of capital equivalent to at least 10% of the annual revenue they receive from capitation payments.

However, the financial risk insurers face depends not only on their risk pool, but also on how well the payment formula captures ex ante that risk. Riascos et al. (2017) have estimated the amount of capital that would be required to keep bankruptcy risk within a certain threshold, under alternative payment scenarios. If the capitation that insurers receive were adjusted ex-ante for morbidity, their revenue streams would be better aligned with the risk they assume, and they would have to set aside less capital in comparison to what they have to set aside under the current demographic adjustment that the government uses. Not using up-to-date methods for the risk adjustment formula carries an inefficiency in the form of additional capital on the balance sheets of insurers.

Other reforms may indirectly affect the payment system. For instance, the government is considering the development of a standardized payment system for providers, such as Diagnosis Related Groups for hospitals. In the medium term, this could make available diagnosis data that, in turn, could be used in the risk adjustment formula. Larger issues include the shift to the new benefits plan and lack of cost-effectiveness criteria, which raises questions about financial sustainability. However, the inclusion of new technologies is expected to be gradual, and approval is to involve analyses of their budgetary impact.

## ENDNOTES

1. The Constitution does not explicitly define these three principles, except for a reference to the irrevocable right to social security.
2. The equalization is regulated in Agreement 04 of 2009 (for children from 0 to 12 years old); Agreement 011 of 2010 (for children and adolescents under 18); Agreement 027 of 2011 (for adults aged 60 and over); and Agreement 032 of 2012 (for adults between 18 and 59 years.
3. For logistical reasons, the contributions are collected by the insurers on behalf of the central fund.
4. This means test, however, continues to be used for targeting social programs and subsidies in other sectors.
5. The specific actuarial method used is the loss-ratio method.
6. IBNR: incurred but not reported; value for the services and procedures that occurred during the period but that have not been reported. IBNER: incurred but not enough reported; value of the services and procedures for claims, filed but not well reserved.
7. The additional payment is available if one or both of two conditions are met. The first condition requires that an insurers' share of elderly in its enrolled population is high relative to the average share (across all insurers) in a given year. Specifically, the insurers' share must exceed the average share by 1.5 standard deviations of the distribution of shares among all insurers. The second condition focuses on the growth of the share and consists of two subcomponents that must both be met: the insurers' share of elderly must be high relative to the prior year average share and the growth in enrollment of elderly in the insurer must exceed a certain threshold.
8. In 2015, the geographic adjustment for "dispersed" areas was 1.379, compared to 1 for the "regular" areas (MSPS, 2015c).
9. The implementations by Camelo and Riascos (2017) and Duarte and Guerrero (2014) implicitly make the unrealistic assumption that insurers can perfectly predict future individual costs. The original framework by Van Barneveld assumes that insurers have a feasible model that has better predictive performance than the demographic model used by the regulator.

# REFERENCES

Alvarez, H.M., 2000. Riesgo del aseguramiento en el sistema de salud en Colombia en 1997. CEPAL Naciones Unidas, Santiago de Chile. Available from: http://econpapers.repec.org/paper/col000140/003474.htm.

van Barneveld, E.M., Lamers, L.M., van Vliet, R.C.J.A., van de Ven, W.P.M.M., 2001. Risk sharing as a supplement to imperfect capitation: a tradeoff between selection and efficiency. J. Health Econ. 20, 147–168.

Barón-Leguizamón, G., 2007. Gasto nacional en salud de Colombia 1993–2003: composición y tendencias. Rev. Salud Pública 9, 167–179.

Camelo, S.A., Riascos, A., 2017. A Note on Risk-Sharing Mechanisms for the Colombian Health Insurance System. Universidad de los Andes, Facultad de Economía, Bogota, Colombia. Available from: https://ideas.repec.org/p/col/000089/015604.html.

Carranza, J.E., Riascos, Á.J., Serna, N., 2015. Poder de mercado, contratos y resultados de salud en el sistema de salud colombiano entre 2009 y 2011. Banco de la Republica de Colombia, Bogota, Colombia.

Duarte, J., Guerrero, R., 2014. Propuesta de mecanismos de pagos ex post para reducir la selección de riesgos en el Sistema de Salud colombiano. Coyuntura Económica: Investigación Económica Y Social 44, 211–238.

Ellis, R.P., Fernandez, J.G., 2013. Risk selection, risk adjustment and choice: concepts and lessons from the Americas. Int. J. Environ. Res. Public Health 10, 5299–5332.

Fernández, C., Villar, L., 2016. The Impact of Lowering the Payroll Tax on Informality in Colombia (Fedesarrollo). Available from: http://www.banrep.gov.co/sites/default/files/eventos/archivos/sem_452.pdf.

Giedion, U., Bitran, R.A., Tristao, I., Inter-American Development Bank, and Social Protection and Health Division, 2014. Health Benefit Plans in Latin America: A Regional Comparison. Inter-American Development Bank, Washington, DC.

Government of Colombia, 2015. Ley 1753 De 2015. Available from: http://www.secretariasenado.gov.co/senado/basedoc/ley_1753_2015.html.

Guerrero, R., 2008. Financing universal enrollment to social health insurance: lessons learned from Colombia. Well-Being Soc. Policy 75–98.

Morales, L.F., Medina, C., et al., 2016. Assessing the Effect of Payroll Taxes on Formal Employment: The Case of the 2012 Tax Reform in Colombia (Banco de la Republica de Colombia). Available from: http://www.banrep.gov.co/sites/default/files/publicaciones/archivos/be_971.pdf.

MSPS, 2011. Comisión de Regulación en Salud. Acuerdo 26 de 2011. Ministerio de Salud y de Protección Social. Available from: http://www.achc.org.co/documentos/afiliados/Acuerdos/Acuerdo26CRES2011.PDF.

MSPS, 2013. Cifras financieras del sector salud: fuentes y usos de los recursos del SGSSS. Ministerio de Salud y de Protección Social. Available from: https://www.minsalud.gov.co/sites/rid/Lists/BibliotecaDigital/RIDE/VP/FS/Boletin%20Cifras%20finacieras%20del%20Sector.pdf.

MSPS, 2014. Resolucion Numero 0248 De Feb 2014. Ministerio de Salud y de Protección Social. Available from: http://icbf.gov.co/cargues/avance/docs/resolucion_minhacienda_0248_2014.htm.

MSPS, 2015a. MSPS Calculations Based on the Quality of Life National Survey. Ministerio de Salud y de Protección Social, Unpublished.

MSPS, 2015b. Base de Datos Única de Afiliados, March 2015 (Ministerio de Salud y de Protección Social). Available from: http://www.fosyga.gov.co/BDUA/Consulta-Afiliados-BDUA (accessed September 21, 2015).

MSPS, 2015c. Resolucion Numero 5593 De 24 Dic 2015. Ministerio de Salud y de Protección Social. Available from: https://www.minsalud.gov.co/Normatividad_Nuevo/Resoluci%C3%B3n%205593%20de%202015.pdf.

MSPS, 2015d. Resolucion Numero 1912 De 29 May 2015. Ministerio de Salud y de Protección Social. Available from: https://www.minsalud.gov.co/sites/rid/Lists/BibliotecaDigital/RIDE/DE/DIJ/resolucion-1912-de-2015.pdf.

MSPS, 2015e. Measuring the Goodness of Fit of the UPC Model in Colombia. Ministerio de Salud y de Protección Social, Unpublished working paper.

MSPS, 2016a. Sistema Integral de Información de la Protección Social (SISPRO). Ministerio de Salud y de Protección Social. Available from: http://www.sispro.gov.co/Pages/Contruya%20Su%20Consulta/Aseguramiento.aspx (accessed September 29, 2016).

MSPS, 2016b. Ajuste De Cuotas Moderadoras Y Copagos Para 2016. Ministerio de Salud y de Protección Social. Available from: https://www.minsalud.gov.co/Paginas/Ajuste-de-cuotas-moderadoras-y-copagos-para-2016.aspx.

MSPS, 2016c. Estudio De Suficiencia Y De Los Mecanismos De Ajuste De Riesgo Para El Cálculo De La Unidad De Pago De Capitación Para Garantizar El Plan De Beneficios En Salud Para El Año 2016. Ministerio de Salud y de Protección Social. Available from: https://www.minsalud.gov.co/sites/rid/Lists/BibliotecaDigital/RIDE/VP/RBC/estudio-suficiencia-upc-2016.pdf.

MSPS, 2016d. Resolucion Numero 975 De 18 Mar 2016. Ministerio de Salud y de Protección Social. Available from: https://www.minsalud.gov.co/sites/rid/Lists/BibliotecaDigital/RIDE/DE/DIJ/resolucion-0975-2016.pdf.

Newhouse, J.P., 1996. Reimbursing health plans and health providers: efficiency in production versus selection. J. Econ. Literat. 34, 1236−1263.

Prada, S.I., 2016. Traslados entre eps en Colombia: ¿Qué dicen las historias laborales de cotizantes en cinco ciudades del país? Gerencia y Políticas de Salud 15, 176−192.

Riascos, A., Sierra, A., Andres, E., Romero, M., 2014. The Performance of Risk Adjustment Models in Colombian Competitive Health Insurance Market. Universidad de los Andes, Facultad de Economía, Bogota, Colombia. Available from: http://papers.ssrn.com/abstract = 2489183.

Riascos, Á., Serna, N., Guerrero, R., 2017. Capital Requirements of Health Insurers Under Different Risk-Adjusted Capitation Payments. Universidad de los Andes, Facultad de Economía, Bogota, Colombia. Available from: https://ideas.repec.org/p/col/000089/015292.html.

Van de Ven, W.P.M.M., Ellis, R.P., 2000. Risk Adjustment in Competitive Health Plan Markets. Elsevier, Amsterdam, pp. 755−845.

# Chapter 11

# Health Plan Payment in Germany

Jürgen Wasem[1], Florian Buchner[1,2], Gerald Lux[1] and Sonja Schillo[1]
[1]*University Duisburg-Essen, CINCH - Health Economics Research Center, Duisburg, Germany,*
[2]*Carinthia University of Applied Sciences, Villach, Austria*

## 11.1 INTRODUCTION

Unlike most European countries, Germany does not have one universal health insurance system. Instead, it has a two-tiered system, with 90% of the population being insured in one of (at present) about 110 social health insurance institutions (GKV-Spitzenverband, 2016), so called "sickness funds"[1] and the remaining 10% of the population having their coverage primarily with one of about 45 private health insurance companies (Verband der privaten Krankenversicherung, 2016). These private health insurance companies also offer complementary health plans for the insured of the sickness funds. Since 2009, each citizen is obligated to have health insurance in one of these two systems. Moreover, citizens are obliged to enroll in long-term care insurance. In this introduction, we will briefly elaborate on the evolution of these health insurance systems.

### 11.1.1 Evolution of Social Health Insurance for Curative Care

The social health insurance system in Germany dates to the end of the 19th century, with the implementation of mandatory insurance for blue collar workers by Bismarck in 1883. To a certain extent, social health insurance was competitive from the beginning. This was due to the fact that it was a complex system with many types of sickness funds (e.g., local funds, company-based funds, funds for certain branches of the economy) which had evolved during the 19th century by initiative of local governments, employers, trade unions, etc. (Tennstedt, 1983). Bismarck included most types of these sickness funds in the new system. Each of the—initially, several thousand—sickness funds in the Bismarckian system was a legally independent

Risk Adjustment, Risk Sharing and Premium Regulation in Health Insurance Markets.
DOI: https://doi.org/10.1016/B978-0-12-811325-7.00011-7

body, having full financial responsibility when calculating its income-related contribution rate to cover its expenditures for health benefits and administrative costs.

With the extension of mandatory insurance to other groups of the population in the 20th century (white collar workers, later also nonworkers like students or certain categories of the self-employed, for example farmers) the competitive structure was maintained (Zöllner, 1981). Local sickness funds were the backbone and insurers of last resort of the system, but consumers had ample opportunity to switch to other funds. On the one hand, there was a kind of *collective choice*—for instance, companies and their workforce could decide to found a company-based sickness fund with the consequence that the insured had to switch from the local fund in which they usually were enrolled into the newly founded company-based fund. This collective choice was increasingly used in the 1970s and 1980s as consultancy firms advised employers to establish a company-based fund to profit from lower contribution rates in comparison to their employees being insured with the local sickness fund. On the other hand, from the beginning, employees with certain occupations had *individual choice* among various types of sickness funds. Most white collar workers, whose numbers grew sharply in the second half of the 20th century, had an individual choice between a local fund and special professional sickness funds. So, by the 1980s it was estimated that more than 50% of the members of the social health insurance system had an individual choice between two or more sickness funds (Smigielski, 1982).

With more collective and individual choice options for selected groups being exercised, financial performance diverged, especially between local funds and the other types of health insurers, and became an issue for debate. On average, local funds insured a population with below-average income and above-average age. Consequently, these funds had to charge relatively high income-related contribution rates. Blue collar workers and their trade unions challenged the existing situation as a violation of the constitutional provision requiring equal treatment for all, and it was seen as possible that the German Federal Constitutional Court would follow that claim (Gitter, 1991). In 1977, the parliament introduced a pooling mechanism by which health insurance expenditures for pensioners were financed by payments from all sickness funds. As contribution payments by insured are income-related according to the principle of solidarity, the mandatory payments into that pool were income-related as well. The federal Ministry of Health commissioned several studies to analyze potential mechanisms for further financial equalization (Huppertz et al., 1981).

At the same time, health economics started to become an academic discipline in Germany, introducing international perspectives on managed or regulated competition (Enthoven, 1980) as a tool to increase efficiency in healthcare provision (Cassel, 1984; Gitter and Oberender, 1987). Early on, health economists identified risk adjustment among sickness funds as an important element of plan payment within regulated competition (Hofmann and Hühne, 1988; Leber and Wasem, 1989).

By the end of the 1980s, the agenda was thus set for a debate about a major "organizational reform" of the social health insurance system (Wasem, 1989). Two major options were discussed: (1) Abolishing the existing limited choice of sickness funds and the resulting competition completely, following the example of social old-age insurance in Germany, where every insured is allocated to one of the regional or occupational funds, or (2) moving towards free choice of sickness funds for all members of social health insurance. In a major healthcare reform in 1992 (Reiners, 1993), the parliament decided to implement free choice of sickness funds for almost all insured enrolled in social health insurance, starting in 1996, and—with a lead time of 2 years—to introduce risk adjustment among sickness funds from 1994 onwards (Wasem, 1993a).

Whereas for some politicians, the major reason for this step was to establish equity in terms of affordability for all insured, for others the driving force was to establish competition among sickness funds. Therefore, there was no common understanding of the consequences of that decision for the regulatory framework of the healthcare system. Many politicians in particular rejected the idea (and some still do today) that sickness funds should compete via selection of healthcare providers. In contrast, the idea that control of social health insurance expenditures would be easier in a system of monopsony had prevailed since the 1970s (Griesewell, 1985), and still is popular today. Consequently, a system of collective negotiations and contracts of regional associations of all sickness funds with regional associations of all providers still plays an important role in the provision and reimbursement of many services within Germany's social health insurance system (van de Ven et al., 2013).

## 11.1.2   Social Health Insurance for Long-Term Care

In the 1990s, after 20 years of intense discussion, social *long-term care insurance* was established as another branch of the German welfare state (Igl, 2007). There was a debate about whether long-term care insurance should be based on a competitive model, but the political decision was not to go that way. Instead, a long-term care fund is attached to each sickness fund, albeit the two funds are legally and financially independent of each other. Switching to a new sickness fund automatically includes switching the long-term care fund as well. It was also decided that no discretion would be given to individual long-term care insurance funds with regard to reimbursement of providers and with regard to the level of contributions to be paid by insured to the funds. The individual long-term care funds bear no financial risk. Consequently, there is no need for a risk adjustment mechanism with standardized cost weights; instead all expenditures are financed out of a common pool of all long-term care insurers (Hustadt and Wasem, 1993).

### 11.1.3 Private Health Insurance

The market of private health insurance is highly regulated, but the system is completely different from the regulated competition among sickness funds. Insurers do not contract with providers, and on the provider market reimbursement is primarily determined by law and public regulation. In principle, premiums are risk-rated, which means that insurers apply medical underwriting. There are three important regulatory mechanisms, however, designed to enhance accessibility to health insurance. First, insurers have to apply a capital-funded approach, so young insured accumulate capital within their insurance contract to subsidize the, on average, higher premium when growing older. Second, insurers are required to offer a basic health plan for insureds who do not get regular coverage from private insurers; for this basic health plan, insurers are not allowed to risk rate premiums. Consequently, as a third regulation, some type of financial equalization among the funds is established for the basic health plan which resembles risk adjustment (Weber, 2010). The same is true for private long-term care insurance, which is mandatory for the privately insured and for which risk-rated premiums are also ruled out by the regulator.

## 11.2 ORGANIZATION OF THE HEALTH INSURANCE SYSTEM

In what follows, we will only address the scheme in which regulated competition is most prominent, i.e., the social health insurance for curative care, also known as the "sickness fund insurance." In 2015, this scheme covered 90% of the population and about 200 billion euros of medical expenditures, which were about 58% of total health expenditures and 6.6% of GDP in Germany. Moreover, social health insurance also covers about 11 billion euros for sick leave payments. In this section, we describe the legal framework of social health insurance, the choice options for the insured, the benefit package, entry and exit of sickness funds, and instruments that sickness funds can use in their contractual relations to providers.

### 11.2.1 Legal Framework

The legal foundation for social health insurance in Germany is a federal law: The Sozialgesetzbuch (Social Code Book). Especially code book No. 5 ("Health Insurance") regulates who is insured, what is included in the benefit package, and how sickness funds are established, internally organized, and financed. Moreover, the book stipulates who can become a healthcare provider within the social health insurance and how contractual relations between sickness funds and providers work.

Within the federal government the Ministry of Health carries the main responsibility for social health insurance. However, other ministries are also involved, e.g., the Ministry for Commerce (regarding drug prices) and the Ministry for Agriculture (regarding health insurance for farmers). The health insurance law delegates many decisions to a self-governing body: the Joint Federal Committee (JFC, Gemeinsamer Bundesausschuss). The committee includes delegates from the Federal Association of Sickness Funds (GKV-Spitzenverband), the Federal Association of Office-Based Physicians (Kassenärztliche Bundesvereinigung), the Federal Association of Office-Based Dentists (Kassenzahnärztliche Bundesvereinigung), and the German Hospital Association (Deutsche Krankenhausgesellschaft). Patient representatives may take part and speak in the meetings of JFC but do not have a vote. The JFC specifies the benefit package, gives directives for quality management, and sets norms for capacity planning for providers. Decisions by the JFC are binding for sickness funds, providers, and the insured (Busse and Blümel, 2014).

Responsibilities of agencies at the federal level are, in some areas, shared with the states—for instance, the 16 states have a strong influence in capacity planning and the financing of investments for hospitals. The states are also granted authority by the German Constitution to supervise regional sickness funds, whereas sickness funds with a nationwide scope of activity are supervised by the federal government. This division of supervision is increasingly under debate because it may undermine the level playing field for competition among plans. Sickness funds are nonprofit, self-governing entities to which public law applies. Insureds as well as healthcare providers can challenge administrative acts by sickness funds at special courts for social law.

The relationship between sickness funds and healthcare providers is strictly regulated. A total of 95% of sickness funds' expenditures are determined by regional collective contracts between all sickness funds and all healthcare providers and cannot be influenced by any individual sickness fund. Only the remaining 5% are managed in a competitive setting. As collective contracts are mandatory by law, EU and federal antitrust law is applicable only to a limited extent (van de Ven et al., 2013).

## 11.2.2 The Insured and Their Choice Options

Social health insurance is primarily based on an obligation to insure employees and certain other groups in the population (e.g., students) within the system. The obligation to employees applies up to a certain threshold of annual income (in 2017, 57,600 euros) and does not apply to self-employed and certain types of civil servants. Those insured whose obligation to enroll in social health insurance ends can choose to stay within the social health insurance system. Alternatively, they can switch to private health insurance. In general, those in private health insurance can only switch to social health insurance when they are obligated to do so (e.g., because their income falls below the threshold), not on a voluntary basis (Lisac et al., 2010).

Since 2009, each citizen is required to have health insurance in one of the two systems, social or private health insurance. When uninsured people join the insurance system now, they must pay all contributions dating from the time that they should have had insurance, plus a late payment fine. People who do not pay their contributions are entitled only to services in case of "acute need" (which has not been defined by law). It is estimated that less than 0.5% of the German population does not have coverage.

The German law distinguishes between the "member" of social health insurance, who is obliged to enroll (e.g., the employee), and his or her family dependents (children below a certain age, nonworking spouses), whose entitlement to benefits is linked to the insurance of "their" member. Both members and family dependents are called "insured." For members, there is a complicated system of options among sickness funds. Most sickness funds have free enrollment for all members of social health insurance, with about half of them only serving one or a few of the 16 German states, the others nationwide. Some company-based sickness funds are open only to employees of the company they work with. Farmers (less than 1% of the insured of social health insurance) have a separate sickness fund and cannot switch to other sickness funds, nor can the farmers' sickness fund be chosen by nonfarmers; farmers also have a special system of contributions and their sickness fund does not take part in risk adjustment.

Sickness funds are not allowed to reject anyone eligible for insurance or exclude benefits, e.g., due to poor health status, and they cannot terminate coverage. They can, however, use more subtle instruments for risk selection, like informing "bad-risk" citizens about better options for insurance with other sickness funds or being less friendly in their communication to "bad risks" than to "good risks" (Höppner et al., 2006). They can choose the regions in which they are active in marketing, and it has been shown that sickness funds react to applicants for insurance differently depending on the region they live in (Bauhoff, 2012). However, most sickness funds object vigorously to the contention that they engage in risk selection.

Members can transfer after staying a minimum period of 18 months with their sickness fund. However, if the sickness fund raises its additional contribution rate (see Section 11.3), members can switch with a notice period of 2 months even if the minimum period is not fulfilled. A member's sickness fund choice is binding for his or her family dependents. Switching from one sickness fund to another is relatively easy: the change takes effect when the switcher proves that he or she has chosen a new sickness fund.

Several studies have examined individual choice of sickness funds (Andersen and Grabka, 2006; Andersen et al., 2002). Around 5% of the insured switch sickness funds from one year to the next. Price variation (in terms of the contribution rate; see Section 11.3) among sickness funds is the most important motive for switching. Those who switch are, on average, relatively healthy (Drösler et al., 2011).

Other studies have examined the effects of price variation on market shares, finding that sickness funds with above average contribution rates have shrinking market shares (Schmitz and Ziebarth, 2016; Schut et al., 2003; Tamm et al., 2007).

### 11.2.3   Benefit Package

Sickness funds are obligated to cover all medical services included in the benefit package as specified by the JFC. In addition, they can offer supplementary benefits, such as more generous services with regard to home nursing or nonprescription drugs. These additional benefits add up to less than 1% of total spending under sickness fund insurance, but they may influence the choice of sickness fund for some members. In addition, for some options (e.g., deductibles, sick leave payments for self-employed, reimbursement instead of benefits in kind), sickness funds can request a minimum insurance duration of up to 3 years, limiting the right of members to switch funds; the insured can freely decide to contract for these options.

Benefits are delivered primarily in kind, with members showing their health insurance card to the healthcare provider. Members have, by and large, free choice among all providers that are part of the collective contract system. Ambulatory specialists in most cases can be seen without a referral by a general practitioner; for inpatient care (with the exception of emergency care) a referral is needed. Sickness funds must make sure that their members have access to sufficient health care with their health insurance card; with regard to hospital care, this responsibility is with the states; in outpatient physician care, it is with state-level physicians' organizations.

Insureds can use services without their health insurance card, in which case the healthcare provider bills them for the service and the insured receive a (partial) cash reimbursement from their sickness fund. If members do so, their physicians are not restricted to the fee schedule of social health insurance, and some members expect that the physician will give them better service if they pay higher fees. Sickness funds may also offer special tariffs with a premium rebate for insureds opting for partial cash reimbursement. They may also offer financial incentives for using services within networks of preferred providers and for choosing deductibles. Only a small number of insureds choose such options.

Sickness funds are not permitted to offer complimentary health insurance themselves. However, a sickness fund can partner with a private health insurer who may develop a special policy (with a discount) for the insured of that sickness fund which is unavailable for the insureds of other sickness funds. This tie-in may hinder switching between sickness funds.

### 11.2.4   Entry and Exit of Sickness Funds

In general, entry to the market for sickness funds is closed. Only company-based sickness funds may enter; with the approval of a majority of their employees, employers can found a new sickness fund. However, since the introduction of risk-based and income-based transfers among sickness funds (see Section 11.3), this has rarely happened in recent years. Voluntary market exit is also only possible for company-based sickness funds. All other sickness funds (more than 80% of market share in terms of membership) can only be closed by their supervisory agency if they are threatened by insolvency. Another option for economically weak sickness funds is to merge with a financially more powerful sickness fund. Via mergers, the number of sickness funds has decreased from more than 1,000 in 1992 to about 110 in 2017.

### 11.2.5   Instruments for Insurers in Relation to Providers

Individual sickness funds have only limited instruments to behave as "prudent buyers" (van de Ven and Schut, 1994) of health care in their relation to healthcare providers. They are not allowed to own healthcare facilities or to integrate vertically with providers.

In hospital care, the DRG tariff and cost weights are negotiated on the federal level between GKV-Spitzenverband and Deutsche Krankenhausgesellschaft; the base rate of a DRG is collectively negotiated between the associations of sickness funds at the state level and their counterparts on the hospital side. All sickness funds that have a relevant share in the services delivered by a specific hospital collectively negotiate with the hospital future volumes of services, thus generating the hospital's budget. The capacity of hospitals is determined by state governments. Hospitals that the states find to be necessary have to be contracted by all sickness funds, which applies to about 97% of hospital capacities. The remaining hospitals that are not under the states' protection cannot contract with individual sickness funds. They can only contract collectively with all sickness funds operating in their region and all sickness funds must agree jointly to contract with the hospital.

With regard to outpatient care, which is primarily delivered by office-based general practitioners and specialists, the situation is similar: The fee schedule tariff and other important regulations are negotiated by GKV-Spitzenverband and Kassenärztliche Bundesvereinigung. On the state level, the monetary value of the fee schedule positions is negotiated between state-level organizations of sickness funds and physicians. There is also collective planning on the state level to determine the number of physicians in counties and cities. Although sickness funds can selectively contract outpatient care on top of the collectively organized care, physicians decide ultimately whether to accept the contract. In addition, the insured decide whether they want to join these contracts that limit their choice of physicians.

Sickness funds are allowed to contract selectively for generic drugs by organizing tenders. In these cases, the insured are limited to the generic that won the tender. The funds can also organize tenders for medical aids. They can choose the rehabilitation clinics to which they send their insured. Contracts for integrated care are voluntary for all sides. Finally, while performing selective contracts, sickness funds have an obligation to guarantee that their insured get the services to which they are entitled, and members can bring a case to court if they think that they have been unfairly denied access to services.

## 11.3   HEALTH PLAN PAYMENT DESIGN FOR THE SOCIAL HEALTH INSURANCE SYSTEM

Solidarity is a core concept of the German social health insurance system. van de Ven and Ellis (2000) distinguish between risk solidarity and income solidarity, with the former referring to the cross-subsidies between the healthy and the (chronically) ill and the latter referring to the cross-subsidies from high-income earners to low-income earners. Both concepts of solidarity are realized in the German system with income-related contributions independent of any preexisting medical condition and with medical benefits according to need and independent of level of contributions paid. This section describes in more detail how the health plan payment system is organized.

### 11.3.1   Financial Flows in the Social Health Insurance System

Until 2008, sickness funds received contributions paid directly by employers and sickness fund members and had to participate in a risk adjustment mechanism, in which they paid solidarity contributions according to their members' income and received subsidies according to the risk structure of their insured (Buchner and Wasem, 2003).[2] In 2009, the system was changed along the following lines: A "Central Health Fund" (CHF) was established, and since then the payment flow goes from sickness fund members and their employers to the CHF, and sickness funds get their resources from the CHF according to the risk structure of their insured.

The financial architecture of the current system is summarized in Fig. 11.1, with the arrows representing the major money flows. The central payment flow to the CHF is determined by the uniform contribution rate (14.6% in 2017). For employees, this contribution is partly paid by the employer (7.3%) and partly by the employee (7.3%). Some sickness fund members (e.g., the self-employed) pay the full contribution themselves. Sickness funds may raise an additional sickness fund-specific contribution rate (ACR) which is paid completely by their members. There is also a payment from the federal government to the CHF financed by general tax revenues, which amounted to some 14.5 billion euros in 2017. The distribution of resources from the CHF to the sickness funds via the risk adjustment system

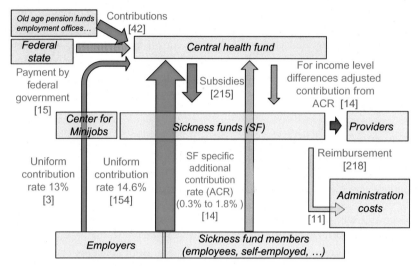

**FIGURE 11.1** Financial flows in social health insurance in Germany: the current system. Note: the numbers in square brackets refer to the amounts in 2017 in billions of euros; official prognosis for all sickness funds participating in Central Health Fund.

(called "Subsidies" in the figure) is explained in the next paragraph (for more detailed information, see Buchner et al., 2013). From their revenue from subsidies and additional contributions, sickness funds have to reimburse health care providers and they must cover their own administrative costs.

The sum of subsidies flowing from the CHF to the sickness funds for year $t$ is determined at the end of year $t−1$. The amount of subsidies for all sickness funds together, once set, remains unchanged, regardless of how the revenues of the CHF develop—therefore, the CHF bears the risk of revenues from income-related contributions falling short of expectations. On the other hand, the sum of subsidies does not change either, regardless of how expenditures of sickness funds materialize—therefore, the risk of expenditure growing faster than expected is with the sickness funds, which have to adjust their additional contribution rates accordingly (see Section 11.3.2).

## 11.3.2 Regulation of Premiums and Contributions

From the insureds' perspective, the contribution rate to their sickness fund consists of the fixed uniform contribution rate (14.6% in 2017) and the sickness fund's specific ACR. The uniform contribution rate is set by federal law, and thus every change needs an amendment of law by parliament. The ACR is determined by each sickness fund and is the same for all members of a fund, but differs among funds. Sickness funds are required by law to have a balanced budget.

With the uniform contribution rate fixed at 14.6%, payments from CHF to the sickness funds only suffice on average for 94% of sickness funds' expenditure. Therefore, all sickness funds need to raise an ACR. Each sickness fund's board must decide on an amendment of the fund's statutes, specifying the ACR and each change of it. The amendment also has to be approved by the supervisory authority of the sickness fund. In general, the decision on a change of ACR is made by the end of a year and valid for the next year. In February 2017, the ACR varied between 0.3% and 1.8%, with an average value of about 1.1%.

As the contributions from the uniform contribution rate flow directly to the CHF, members' income has no impact on the payments a sickness fund gets from these resources. However, with respect to the fund-specific ACR rate, the sickness fund may profit (or suffer) from the high (low) average income of its members. To correct for this, the CHF transforms the contributions from the income-related ACR into payments that correspond to the overall average income level in social health insurance.

Given that the whole contribution payment to sickness funds is income-related, there is no need for a premium subsidy for low-income people in Germany.[3]

## 11.3.3    Risk Adjustment

Risk adjustment was implemented in the German social health insurance system in 1994, with major changes in 2002 and 2009. In contrast to other countries, the German system started without any retrospective risk-sharing elements. A high expenditure pool was temporarily in place from 2002 until the end of 2008 (see Section 11.3.4).

Below, we describe the main characteristics of the German risk adjustment system, called "Risikostrukturausgleich" (RSA). We will successively discuss the risk adjuster variables included in the German model, the selection of diseases included in the RSA, the special treatment of sick leave payments, and persons insured in Germany but residing abroad,[4] and we show the calculation of subsidies in detail.[5] The selection of diseases is a special attribute of the German system due to the fact that the number of diseases the RSA should adjust for is limited by law to 50−80, the result of a political compromise in 2007.

### 11.3.3.1    Risk Adjuster Variables

Each sickness fund receives resources from the CHF according to its risk structure. Since the implementation of the risk adjustment scheme in 1994, age, gender, and a variable for reduced earning capacity interacted with age and gender have been used as risk adjusters in the formula.

During a transition period (from 2002 until 2008), enrollment into certified Disease Management Programs (DMP) for up to seven chronic conditions was used as an additional risk adjuster. When morbidity was directly included in the German risk adjustment formula in 2009, the enrollment into a DMP was abolished as a risk factor, but a fixed payment for each insured enrolled in a DMP is still made.

Morbidity is integrated in the model in a prospective regression approach, which means that diagnoses of year $t-1$ and expenditures of year $t$ are used. Age and gender are used as concurrent variables (of year $t$) to include newborns.

The morbidity classification model is based on the HCC (hierarchical condition categories) developed by Ash et al. (2000). The model was adapted to the German system, by splitting morbidity groups according to age, gender, or prescription of drugs (for more detail see below, e.g., Table 11.1), resulting in the so-called Hierarchical Morbidity Groups (Hierarchisierte Morbiditätsgruppen, HMGs).

HMGs are assigned to the insured according to diagnoses from inpatient stays and outpatient visits. Diagnoses are coded using ICD-10-GM (German Modification); the GM is updated every year by the "Deutsches Institut für Medizinische Dokumentation und Information"[6](DIMDI), a federal agency. In general, for a major *inpatient* diagnosis no further condition has to be satisfied. For a quality assurance of diagnoses in case of *outpatient* visits the so-called M2Q-criterion (minimum two quarters) has to be met: at least two diagnoses belonging to the same disease have to be documented in two different quarters of year $t-1$ for an insured to be allocated to the respective HMG. Since 2012, minor inpatient diagnoses are treated in the same way as outpatient diagnoses and have to fulfill the M2Q-criterion. For some diseases, instead of the M2Q-criterion, the requested validation of the diagnoses is based on prescribed drugs in the form of defined ATC codes for a minimum of 10 days (in case of acute-recurrent diseases), respectively, 183 days (in case of chronic diseases) of treatment derived on the basis of DDDs (Defined Daily Doses, which are also defined and regularly updated by the DIMDI).

As described in Section 11.2, insureds have the right to choose cost reimbursement instead of the standard option of benefits in kind. For each of the two options, age-group stratified variables are included in the model. Box 11.1 briefly describes the risk adjusters in 2017.

### 11.3.3.2 Selection of Diseases Included in the RSA

The number of diseases to be included in the German risk adjustment system is limited to 50−80 by a political decision. The term "disease" was defined by the regulator on the basis of 781 DxGroups of the HCC classification model (Ash et al., 2000) resulting in, at present, 360 diseases. Only diseases

**TABLE 11.1** Top 10 and Bottom 5 HMG Subsidies in 2017[a]

| Risk group | Description | Annual incremental subsidy | Number of insured |
|---|---|---|---|
| HMG285 | Mucopolysaccharidosis type II or VI with ERT[b] | 569,261 € | 81 |
| HMG284 | Pompe's disease with ERT | 385,236 € | 194 |
| HMG281 | Gaucher's disease with ERT or SRT[c], Niemann–Pick disease with SRT, mucopolysaccharidosis type I with ERT | 310,301 € | 235 |
| HMG035 | Hemophilia or von Willebrand disease (long-term medication) | 265,139 € | 2,523 |
| HMG282 | Fabry's disease with ERT | 232,674 € | 493 |
| HMG036 | Hempophilia in men (prn[d] medication) | 95,203 € | 591 |
| HMG259 | Complete traumatic lesion of cervical spinal cord | 92,548 € | 142 |
| HMG250 | Disorders of the urea cycle with sodium phenylbutyrate therapy, PKU/HPE with BH4-responsiveness, disorder of tyrosine metabolism with NTBC-medication | 56,232 € | 364 |
| HMG038 | Willebrand disease (prn medication) | 47,128 € | 110 |
| HMG130 | Dialysis | 45,852 € | 70,245 |
| ... | ... | ... | |
| HMG114 | Other diseases of the pleura | 236 € | 17,670 |
| HMG228 | Other systemic rheumatic diseases | 234 € | 1,303,024 |
| HMG024 | Metabolic disorders after medical treatment, congentinal anomalies of endocrine glands | 106 € | 613,511 |
| HMG099 | Other diseases of the vascular system and the arteries | 68 € | 91,962 |
| HMG289 | Chronic hepatitis (not caused by virus), other secondary liver disorders | 66 € | 54,261 |

[a]For a complete list of all risk adjusters and the respective surcharges for 2017, see http://www.bundesversicherungsamt.de/risikostrukturausgleich/bekanntmachungen/bekanntmachung/article/bekanntmachung-zum-gesundheitsfonds-nr-12017.html
[b]ERT: enzyme replacement therapy.
[c]SRT: substrate reduction therapy.
[d]PRN: pro re nata, as needed.

> **BOX 11.1   Risk adjusters used in the German risk adjustment model (in 2017)**
>
> *Age interacted with gender (AGGs):* 20 classes for men and 20 classes for women. The age classes are: 0 years, 1−5 years, 6−12 years, 13−17 years, 18−24 years, 5-year cohorts up to the age of 94, and finally a class for people of 95 years or older.
>
> *Reduced earning capacity interacted with age and gender (EMGs):* three classes for men and three classes for women who are entitled to a reduced earning pension. The age classes are: below 45 years, 46−55 years, 56−65 years.
>
> *Hierarchical morbidity groups (HMGs):* 80 selected diseases covered by 199 clusters (originally 106) which are organized in 26 hierarchies (originally 25) based on inpatient and outpatient diagnoses from the previous year, drug prescriptions, and (in some cases) age are used for fine-tuning or confirmation of some diagnoses.
>
> Enrollees with multiple diagnoses may be allocated to multiple HMGs. Within one hierarchy insured are allocated only to the most expensive HMG with respect to their diagnoses or drug prescriptions.
>
> Enrollees allocated to a cost reimbursement group cannot be allocated to any HMG.
>
> *Cost reimbursement groups interacted with age (KEG):* five age classes for insured with cost reimbursement instead of benefits in kind for at least 183 days in year $t-1$ (option 1): 0−29 years, 30−59 years, 60−69 years, 70−79 years, 80 years and older (age in year $t$).
>
> Two age classes for insured with cost reimbursement instead of benefits in kind for at least 183 days in year $t-1$ (option 2): 0−65 years, 66 years and older (age in year $t$).
>
> The allocation to one of these cost-reimbursement groups excludes the allocation to any HMG.

that meet the following criteria are considered for inclusion in the risk adjustment formula:

- "costly": the average per capita expenditure for those diseases has to exceed 1.5 times the average per capita expenditure of all insured in the German social health insurance system[7]

and, in addition, diseases have to be,

- either "severe": at least 10% of all cases with this disease have to be hospitalized within the year of observation
- and/or "chronic": in at least 50% of cases, the disease has to be diagnosed in at least two quarters of the year of observation.

Among the diseases fulfilling these criteria, the 80 most expensive diseases are selected. Selection of diseases for year *t* is done based on data

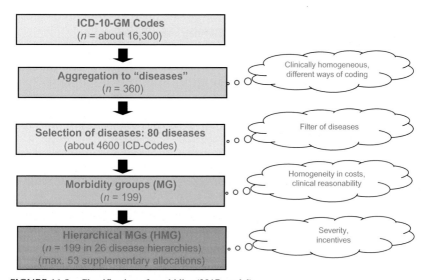

**FIGURE 11.2**   Classification of morbidity (2017 model).
In the text we describe two special topics in the German risk adjustment system that are not covered by the approach described above: sick leave payments and expenditure for insured residing abroad (IRA).

from earlier years. Specifically, to incorporate the impact of disease prevalence into the ranking and selection process, the average annual expenditure per capita of a disease in year $t-3$ (derived from a prospective regression model) is multiplied by the square root of the number of cases of this disease in year $t-4$. The top 80 diseases of this ranking are included in the risk adjustment formula for year $t$. Weighting by the square root of the number of cases is a compromise between a choice based on cost per insured with the disease and a choice based on total cost (average cost weighted by population).

The list of diseases included in the risk adjustment of year $t$ has to be determined and published by the regulator by September 30 of year $t-1$; this is usually done in the first half of year $t-1$. The updating of the list of 80 diseases according to new data generally affects 3−4 diseases per year.

The current system of classification of morbidity is shown in Fig. 11.2.

### 11.3.3.3   Risk Adjustment for Sick Leave Payments

When an employee falls ill, he or she is entitled by law to 6 weeks of wage continuation by his or her employer. If the employee cannot take up work after these 6 weeks, the sickness fund has to pay the so-called sick leave payment for up to 78 weeks. Since the entitlement to sick leave payment is linked to employment, only around 45% of the insured in social health insurance (approximately 31.5 million people) are entitled to sick leave payments

> **BOX 11.2 Risk adjusters used in the German risk adjustment for sick leave payment**
>
> *Age interacted with gender (KAGGs)*: 91 classes for men and 91 classes for women in 1-year age groups up to the last age group for 90 years and older.
>
> *Reduced earning capacity status interacted with age and gender (KEMGs)*: 30 1-year-age-groups for men and 30 1-year age groups for women for age from 36 to 65 years and one age group, respectively, for 35 years and younger.

and only these persons are taken into account in the risk adjustment scheme for this type of benefit. Sickness funds spent about 11 bio. euro on sick leave payment, which is approximately 5% of their total expenditures.

Sick leave payment is unique because it is payed for every day of sick leave and the payable amount is dependent on the income of the insured. It has thus a price component determined by the income of the insured and a quantity-component corresponding to the number of days of sick leave payment.

In contrast to the regression approach for medical expenditures described in the last section, the expenditure for sick leave payment is adjusted using a concurrent cell approach with cells based on 1-year age groups, gender, and reduced earning capacity status. Box 11.2 briefly describes the design of the risk adjusters for sick leave payments.

Although the sick leave payment is dependent on the income level and the number of days out of work, neither component is reflected in the risk adjustment formula. Sickness funds with members of above average income and/or members with above average sick leave days may be disadvantaged by the current regulation. Although these components work in opposite directions and might cancel each other out to a certain degree, significant over- and undercompensations do appear, especially for smaller sickness funds.

To take these over- and undercompensations at least partly into account, a transitional arrangement was implemented in 2014 and came into effect retroactively for 2013. Since then, 50% of subsidies are based on actual expenditure for sick leave payments of the individual sickness fund, thus introducing a retrospective element in the system, and the other 50% of subsidies are distributed as before, according to the cell approach.

### 11.3.3.4 Risk Adjustment for Insureds Residing Abroad

In many cases, morbidity information for insureds residing abroad (IRAs) is lacking or incomplete. Additionally, according to agreements between Germany and other states, which are binding for all sickness funds who insure IRAs residing in specific countries, the German sickness funds have

---

**BOX 11.3  Risk adjusters used in the German risk adjustment for IRA**

*Age interacted with gender (AusAGGs)*: 20 classes for men and 20 classes for women. The age classes are: 0 years, 1−5 years, 6−12 years, 13−17 years, 18−24 years, 5-year cohorts up to the age of 94, and finally a class for people of 95 years or older.

---

to pay a lump-sum per insured (e.g., in Macedonia), or even for all family members covered by family insurance (e.g., in Turkey). These IRAs are not grouped according to the same classification system as the insured living in Germany. Instead, they are grouped into special risk groups called Auslands-Alters-und Geschlechtsgruppen (AusAGGs = Foreign-Age-and-Gender-Groups). Every insured who resides abroad more than 183 days in year $t-1$ is classified in one of 40 age-gender-abroad cells. These AusAGGs are built analogously to the AGGs of the main system, the subsidies for AusAGG cells are calculated by a cell approach and equal the average subsidies of all domestic insured of the same age and gender group. The subsidies for IRA in a given AusAGG are the same, independent of their country of residence and regardless of the compensation agreements with the individual country. Box 11.3 briefly describes the design of the risk adjusters for IRA.

Because of a systematic overcompensation for IRAs as a whole using this method, the subsidies are reduced retroactively to the sum of expenditures documented in the relevant accounts for expenditures abroad of all sickness funds. This arrangement was implemented in 2014 and came into effect retroactively for 2013. It is relevant for about 300,000 insured, and the sickness funds pay approximately 650 mio. euro for IRA expenditures, which is just 0.3 % of their total expenditures.

### 11.3.3.5   Procedure for Deriving Risk Adjuster Coefficients

In the German model, risk adjusters enter as (0,1) dummy variables. The final risk adjuster coefficients for year $t$ are derived in year $t + 1$: an individual-level regression of sickness funds' healthcare expenditure in year $t$ on the dummy variables from year $t-1$ (morbidity and reduced earning capacity), respectively, year $t$ (age, interacting with gender). Data of all insured with at least 1 day of insurance in year $t$ in the social health insurance system are used (details of implementation and of the reconciliation process are given in Section 11.3.5). Details are given in Box 11.4.

### 11.3.3.6   How to Go From Predicted Spending to Risk-Adjusted Payment

Fig. 11.3 shows in a systematic flow how risk adjustment payments for the standardized benefit package are calculated.

**BOX 11.4 Key features of the procedure for deriving risk adjuster coefficients for year *t*, final regression**

- Spending data: from year *t*
- Risk adjuster variables: from year *t*−1, only age and gender from year *t*
- Estimation procedure: individual-level regression of sickness funds' health-care expenditure per day of coverage on dummy variables
- Estimation method: weighted linear least-squares
- Weighting: individuals are weighted with the fraction of the year the individual is enrolled
- Frequency of reestimation of risk adjuster coefficients: every year
- Updating list of diseases for morbidity risk adjusters every year in *t*−1 with data from *t*−4 and *t*−3

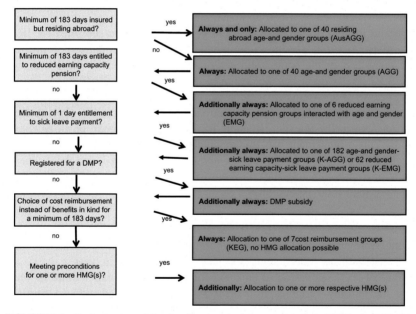

**FIGURE 11.3**  Basic structure of the algorithm to calculate payments from CHF for individual *i*.

As noted above, if an insured resides abroad for at least 183 days with German health insurance coverage in year *t*−1, he or she is classified into one of the 40 abroad-age-gender cells for year *t*. The insured who live in Germany for more than 183 days in year *t*−1 are grouped into one of the 40 age−gender groups. Insureds entitled to a reduced earning capacity (REC) pension for at least 183 days in year *t*−1 are additionally allocated to exactly one of the six REC age−gender groups. Insured with entitlement to sick leave payment of at least 1 day in year $t-1$ are additionally allocated to exactly one of the 182 age−gender sick-leave-payment groups or to one of the 62 REC age−gender sick-leave-payment groups. The clustering for the subsidies of sick leave payment works slightly differently from that of medical expenditure: in the latter case, insured with reduced earning capacity are allocated to both the general age−gender groups and the REC age−gender groups, whereas in the sick leave payment clustering they are allocated only to an REC age−gender group. If an insured is registered for a DMP, the DMP administration surcharge is included in the payment calculation. If an insured opts for cost reimbursement instead of benefit in kind (for at least 183 days in year $t-1$), the insured is assigned to exactly one of seven age-cost reimbursement groups, and the allocation to one of these cost reimbursement groups excludes the allocation to any of the hierarchical morbidity groups. Those insured not grouped to a cost reimbursement group are assigned to one or more HMGs in the case that they meet the respective preconditions of the HMG.

The calculation of the subsidies for an insured individual starts with a so-called basic allocation (Grundpauschale), which is the average predicted per capita expenditure for the standard benefit package minus the average DMP administration expenditure per insured (in 2017 the basic allocation amounted to 2,989 euros). Most of the age−gender groups therefore have a negative coefficient, because "healthy" insureds (meaning those without any HMG) are below average in terms of cost. The values in Table 11.1 represent the top 10 and bottom five preliminary coefficients for HMGs in 2017, to be added to the basic allocation. It also shows the numbers of insured with these HMGs.

To sum up, the basic allocation and the surcharges of the subgroups an insured belongs to result in the payment a sickness fund gets for an insured to cover the expenditure for the standardized benefit package.

There is room for some additional voluntary health service or products beyond the standardized benefit package. To finance this expenditure, each sickness fund gets a standardized amount for each insured (for 2017, the surcharge amounted to 14 euros). To cover administration cost, insurers receive a standardized amount of 78 euros (in 2017) for each insured, plus 2.6% of the risk-adjusted subsidy.

## 11.3.4 Risk Sharing

When the risk adjustment scheme was introduced in 1994, direct morbidity measures were not available and morbidity adjustments could only be implemented in an indirect way using age, gender, and reduced earning capacity. Intensive discussions at the end of the 1990s regarding the introduction of direct measures for morbidity (Buchner and Wasem, 2003) led to a legislative initiative in 2001 to implement them starting in 2007. Until then—to address inequities due to the uneven distribution of the morbidity burden across sickness funds—risk sharing was introduced with a stop-loss high expenditure pool coming into effect in 2002.

Through this high expenditure pool, sickness funds were reimbursed for healthcare expenditures above a certain threshold (20,450 euros per annum in 2002, which increased to 21,352 euros in 2008). In contrast to commercial reinsurance policies, this was financed by all sickness funds collectively and independently of the respective risk profile of a sickness fund. To maintain efficiency incentives only 60% of the expenditures above the threshold were reimbursed, with 40% remaining the responsibility of the sickness funds.

When the morbidity-based risk adjustment was belatedly implemented in 2009 the high expenditure pool was abolished. The expectation was that the morbidity-based risk adjustment would be sufficient to compensate sickness funds adequately for high-expenditure cases.

In the current system, the only retrospective risk-sharing element is the transitional arrangement for sick leave payment, as described in the previous section.

### 11.3.5   Implementation and Maintenance

Responsibility for the development, maintenance, implementation, and evaluation of the risk adjustment scheme lies with the German Federal Social Insurance Authority (BVA). A scientific advisory board supports the process. Specific issues may be addressed by contracting studies with external experts.

The selection of the 50−80 included diseases as a rule is revised every year to keep up with changes in healthcare provision, coding, and shifts in expenditures.

Data needed for the risk adjustment are structured in five areas and provided for every insured person:

- Basic information on the insured person;
- Information on prescribed drugs;
- Diagnoses from inpatient treatment;
- Diagnoses from outpatient treatment;
- Expenditure.

Basic information encompasses, e.g., birth year, gender, number of days the person has been insured with the sickness fund, number of days with reduced earning capacity, number of days the insured has been treated within a disease management program, number of days the insured has been residing abroad, etc. This information is readily available with the sickness funds.

Data on medication are transmitted from the pharmacies to the sickness funds within the accounting procedure. Prescribed drugs are taken into account only when the prescription is filled. Relevant for the classification of the insured to the HMGs are the date the prescription was issued, the count of DDD, and the pharmaceutical identification code.[8]

Diagnoses are documented throughout the treatment and transferred from medical practices and hospitals to the sickness funds for auditing of accounts.

Data are collected, audited, and deidentified by the sickness funds. The personal identification number in the German health insurance and an algorithm that creates a pseudonym ensure that an individual gets the same pseudonym regardless of the sickness fund he is enrolled in. Through this technique, the data of individuals switching from one sickness fund to another can be merged by the BVA and the information for the whole insurance period is available. Only two consecutive years' worth of data are necessary for the calculations, and thus, for data privacy reasons, the pseudonym code changes regularly to ensure that an individual can be followed for only 2 years.

Sickness funds must submit these data to GKV-Spitzenverband by July 31 of the next year. This organization checks the data again for plausibility and completeness and sends it to the BVA no later than August 15.

The BVA itself also checks the data for errors. Some data errors lead to deletion of data sets, others to adjustments of the data. There is an extensive and concerted procedure for addressing irregularities. The health insurance law provides a three-step process: In the first step, diagnostic information from sickness funds is statistically checked for irregularities by the BVA. If the information from a specific sickness fund is puzzling or if the BVA knows of manipulation by a sickness fund, the BVA will do a specific check in the second step that includes on-site verification of a random sample of data from that sickness fund. If the BVA finds irregularities in a third step, it does an extrapolation on the amount of subsidies the sickness fund has received because of these irregularities. The sickness fund then has to pay this amount plus a penalty into the CHF.

### 11.3.5.1    A Chronological Description of the Technical Steps Before, During, and After the Year for Which Risks Are Equalized

In the following, we describe the technical course of action chronologically: At the end of year $t-1$, a council of evaluators (the so-called "Schätzerkreis") predicts the total expenditure of all insured of all sickness funds participating in the risk adjustment system for the following year $t$. The volume of subsidies distributed by the CHF in year $t$ is finally defined as the lower of (1) the volume of expected contributions and the defined payment of the federal government in the CHF in $t$ and (2) the prediction of total expenditure in $t$.

For every year $t$, two regressions are calculated: before and after the year. In both regressions, the expenditure per day for each insured is calculated and used. Therefore, the calculated coefficients are daily values. The first regression in November of year $t-1$ is based on morbidity data of year $t-3$

and expenditure data of year $t-2$. The calculated coefficients are used for the monthly preliminary subsidies in year $t$. The second regression in November of year $t + 1$ uses morbidity data of year $t-1$ and expenditure data of year $t$ for the final pay subsidies.[9] Until the final settlement, the monthly subsidies are adjusted regularly as more data become available.

Beginning in January of year $t$, the sickness funds get monthly preliminary subsidies based on a per capita risk-adjusted allocation multiplied with the current number of insured. This per capita risk-adjusted allocation of each sickness fund is calculated using the coefficients of the first regression in $t-1$ and the morbidity classifications of their current insured claims data. The insured claims data are updated every half year (in the middle and at the end of the calendar year). The sickness funds get monthly reports of their subsidies; every 6 months, the subsidies of the last months are adjusted based on new morbidity data and updated insured basis claims data that affect the per capita risk-adjusted allocation of the sickness fund. These adjustments and the resulting financial demand or supplementary compensations are shown in an additional financial report called "Grundlagenbescheid" and "Korrekturbescheid." Sickness funds get five of these financial reports (in November of year $t-1$, in March and September of year $t$, and in March and September of year $t + 1$) until the final settlement of year $t$ in November of year $t + 1$. In the fifth and last "Grundlagenbescheid" in September of year $t + 1$, the monthly subsidies of year $t$ are no longer calculated on the basis of the number of insured but on the number of insured days of year $t$. Two months later, in November of year $t + 1$, the final settlement, based on the newly calculated regression, is published. As in other countries, the final regression is based on spending per day of insurance coverage: The expenditures for each insured are divided and weighted by the number of days he or she was enrolled in $t$. This is similar to an approach in which expenditures for insured who had coverage in social health insurance for an incomplete year are annualized and weighted by their number of days of insurance (van den Ven and Ellis, 2000). Before 2013, expenditures of insured with incomplete coverage were annualized, however, those of insured who died were not annualized (see, for the effects, Drösler et al., 2011).

In sum, the final payments to sickness funds for year $t$ are determined in November of year $t + 1$. The coefficients used to calculate these payments are estimated by a regression of risk factors from year $t$ and $t-1$ on the actual spending in year $t$. The total sum of payments to all sickness funds remains the same as set at the end of year $t-1$ by the council of evaluators. Compared to the preliminary payments, the final payments do not change the total amount of money to be distributed to all sickness funds but may change the payment to individual sickness funds as the relative weights of the risk factors may change. In order to meet the sum of subsidies set at the end of year $t-1$, a risk-neutral correction term is subtracted or added in November of year $t + 1$.

## 11.4   EVALUATION OF HEALTH PLAN PAYMENT

In 2010, the scientific advisory board on risk adjustment was commissioned by the government to evaluate the 2009 risk adjustment system. In its evaluation report, the advisory board develops its evaluation methods and presents the results (Drösler et al., 2011). Since then, it applies these methods annually when proposing changes in the classification system to the BVA (e.g., Bundesversicherungsamt, 2016), which is a regular task of the advisory board. The BVA usually also publishes these data once the whole process of risk adjustment has been finalized for a given year.

The BVA and the advisory board have a full data set of all 71 million insured available, covering their annual spending and the values of the risk adjuster variables plus some administrative information (see Section 11.3.5). For many analyses, however, they use a random sample containing 30% of the insured population. The advisory board cannot use data external to the risk adjustment system such as the health surveys as is done in the Netherlands. As there is no other mechanism but risk adjustment at present (in particular, no high expenditure pool), performance of the risk adjustment system in terms of explanatory power at the individual and group level is the only element evaluated. Efficiency in the delivery of health care is not evaluated, and risk selection by sickness funds is not measured.

The BVA and the advisory board distinguish between performance measures on the individual level and on the group level. On the individual level, adjusted $R^2$, Cumming's prediction measure (CPM), and mean absolute prediction error (MAPE) are used. Also reported are the shares of the subsidies allocated according to morbidity, age, gender, and reduced earning capacity. On the group level, predictive ratios and MAPE on the level of sickness funds are used.

Table 11.2 presents the development of $R^2$, CPM, and MAPE from 2009 (first year of morbidity-based risk adjustment) until 2014 (most recent publication of data); the table does not include IRA or sick leave payments. As

**TABLE 11.2 Development of Goodness-of-fit Measures**

|                         | 2009 | 2010 | 2011 | 2012 | 2013 | 2014 |
|-------------------------|------|------|------|------|------|------|
| $R^2$ (%)               | 20.2 | 21.0 | 23.9 | 23.6 | 22.6 | 24.0 |
| CPM (%)                 | 22.5 | 22.6 | 22.6 | 22.8 | 23.3 | 23.7 |
| MAPE (€)                | 1817 | 1891 | 1922 | 1970 | 2036 | 2141 |
| MAPE standardized (%)   | 97.9 | 97.0 | 94.7 | 94.3 | 94.2 | 95.5 |

Bundesversicherungsamt (2015), MAPE standardized: own calculation.

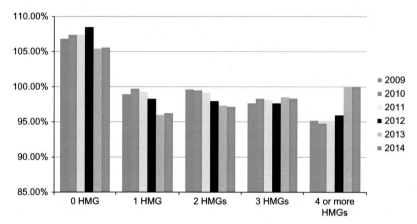

**FIGURE 11.4** Predictive ratios according to number of HMGs.
Bundesversicherungsamt (2015).

MAPE is influenced by the absolute level of health insurance expenditures, we also present a standardized figure for MAPE for which we divided its raw value by the basic allocation. The table demonstrates that all three figures on the individual level have modestly improved since the introduction of morbidity-based risk adjustment. This is especially a result of a rising number of HMGs which increased from 106 in 2009 to 199 in 2017. The "jump" in $R^2$ from 2010 to 2011 was basically achieved by adding a few high-cost HMGs, e.g., by splitting HMGs due to different forms of medication (see also Table 11.1). Only a few insured are affected by these changes, which is also reflected in the CPM that remained stable in these 2 years at 22.6%.

On the group level, predictive ratios are calculated, e.g., according to the risk factor of sickness funds (which is measured as the average subsidy per insured of a sickness fund in relation to the average subsidy per insured across all sickness funds) or according to the number of HMGs of insured. MAPE is also used on the level of sickness funds (MAPE$_{SF}$) as a criterion for certain analyses and special groups of insured, such as those who switched sickness funds. Fig. 11.4 presents the development of the predictive ratio for groups according to the number of HMGs per insured. Given that only 80 diseases are included in the risk adjustment, that insured with HMGs have a higher rate of comorbidity with the diseases not included in risk adjustment, and that there are also interactions between morbidities which are not addressed in the model, there is an overpayment for insureds without any HMG. The underpayment for insureds with at least one HMG corresponds to this overpayment.

The report evaluating the risk adjustment for 2009 also analyzed predictive ratios for sickness funds according to their number of insured (via a risk-neutral correction factor, the predictive ratio over all insureds was set to be equal to 100%). The 33 funds insuring between 30,000 and 100,000 insured had in sum the highest predictive ratio with 100.99%. The lowest predictive ratio of 99.87% was calculated for the 16 sickness funds that each insured more than 1 million people. But the range for over- and underpayment was highest for the smallest sickness funds that insured less than 30,000 lives each. In sum, the predictive ratio for these 73 sickness funds was 100.71%, but the most underpaid sickness fund had a predictive ratio of only 90.57%, and the most overpaid had a predictive ratio of 124.81% (Drösler et al., 2011). As we will discuss below, a crucial question is whether these outcomes are due to shortcomings of the risk adjustment system or variation in efficiency across sickness funds.

Besides the evaluation of the advisory board, few studies have been conducted on the performance of plan payment in Germany. Bauhoff (2012) showed that sickness funds are less likely to respond to applicants for insurance if they originate from high-cost regions. He interprets this as an indication of regional risk selection. A study by Brosse (2016) confirmed this finding. Other academic studies have been conducted in the context of reform proposals (see Section 11.5).

Another academic group has studied interactions of risk adjusters in the German risk adjustment formula by using regression trees (Buchner et al., 2017). The improvement of adjusted $R^2$ that could be achieved by their approach is only marginal (from 25.43% to 25.81%). The authors concluded that according to the sample level performance measures used, leaving out morbidity interactions leads to an insignificant loss in accuracy.

## 11.5  ONGOING ISSUES AND REFORMS

Risk adjustment has been controversial in Germany from the beginning. Sickness funds drawing more healthy insureds and high-income members vigorously opposed the idea from the beginning of the 1990s, and again a decade later, lobbied against the move to a morbidity-based risk adjustment. At present, there are also intense discussions about the future development of risk adjustment. Typically, those sickness funds who insure the sicker part of the population and therefore receive higher subsidies per capita argue for expanding morbidity-based risk adjustment (e.g., AOK-Bundesverband, 2016), whereas the other sickness funds argue for "less risk adjustment," what they call a "purification" (BKK-Bundesverband, 2011; BKK-Dachverband, 2016). There are a number of issues on the agenda and in what follows we present a short overview of the main topics.

One of the main drivers of the discussion is over- and undercompensation. As described above (see Section 11.3.2), sickness funds at present are, on average, undercompensated by subsidies from the central fund by 6% (which was implemented by government to ensure that all sickness funds need to charge an ACR). Sickness funds who are undercompensated to a higher degree request changes in risk adjustment. From our point of view, the crucial question is: What are the reasons for over- and undercompensation beyond the intended systematic 6% undercompensation mentioned above. If overcompensation is the result of efficient management (e.g., in tendering for generics, intelligent contracts of integrated care) these differences should not be levelled out. But if the over- and undercompensations are due to differences in morbidity, missing risk adjusters should be identified. It is then a political decision, whether sickness funds should be held responsible for these factors or whether they should be compensated for these factors (Schokkaert and van de Voorde, 2006).

## 11.5.1 Selection of Diseases

An ongoing issue is the selection of diseases for which morbidity-based risk adjustment is performed. On the one hand, there are sickness funds that request that the present limitation to 50−80 diseases should be abolished altogether, and that instead morbidity groups should be built for all diseases, because this increases model fit and reduces possibilities for risk selection (AOK-Bundesverband, 2016). On the other hand, there are sickness funds (especially those with many healthy enrollees) who object that although the law gives room for 50−80 diseases, it is always the upper limit which is chosen by the advisory board and the BVA (BKK-Dachverband, 2015); they argue that the system gets more complex with more diseases included. The impact of different numbers of diseases being included in risk adjustment was studied by the advisory board in 2011 (Drösler et al., 2011).

Also, there is an intense discussion about the algorithm used for selecting the 80 diseases: in the ranking and selection process the average annual costs of a disease in year $t-3$ are multiplied by the square root of the number of insured with this disease in year $t-4$ (see Section 11.3). Many sickness funds (see, e.g., Meyers-Middendorf and Baumann, 2016) and some studies (Dietzel et al., 2015; Häckl et al., 2016a) recommend that the square root be replaced by the logarithm. By that algorithm, less prevalent diseases with higher costs per individual would replace more common but less cost-intensive diseases. In this context, some players argue that measures of prevention are available for many of the diseases with high prevalence, and that paying subsidies for these diseases discourages sickness funds to engage in preventive activities.

The prevalence of diseases greatly varies across sickness funds. Consequently, alternative specifications of how the prevalence is weighted may result in different sickness funds winning and losing; this typically determines the side for which a sickness fund is arguing. In addition, the question of whether prevention should be included in considerations of the risk adjustment scheme is a matter of discussion. In any case, the simple exclusion of preventable diseases from risk adjustment would create clear incentives for risk selection.

## 11.5.2   Upcoding and Manipulation

A main concern with morbidity-based risk adjustment is to keep its vulnerability to manipulation as low as possible. The German risk adjustment scheme has several features to impede manipulation: the requirement of diagnoses from inpatient stays, the validation of secondary inpatient and outpatient diagnoses through the M2Q-criterion and the obligation to show certain levels of drug prescriptions for certain diseases (see Section 11.3). As described in Section 11.3.5, there are also extensive algorithms to check the data for unusual increases in costs and diagnoses to prevent manipulation.

Nevertheless, from the start of morbidity-based risk adjustment, "upcoding" was actively discussed (Meißner, 2009). This discussion reached a new height in 2016 after the chairman of one of the largest sickness funds declared publicly that sickness funds are urging doctors to document more severe diseases (Scherff, 2016). This led to an upheaval not only among sickness funds but also among doctors and insureds, culminating in patient representatives pressing charges against sickness funds (Rybarczyk, 2016). An explicit regulation for ambulatory physicians regarding coding diagnoses is under discussion (AOK-Bundesverband, 2016); for hospitals mandatory coding guidelines have existed since the introduction of the DRG payment system in 2003. There is also a proposal to limit the selection of diseases for risk adjustment to those diseases for which there is little discretion with regard to coding (Dietzel et al., 2015). The latter would, however, increase incentives for risk selection.

## 11.5.3   Region as (Additional) Risk Adjuster Variable

Since the introduction of risk adjustment, regional issues have been discussed intensively (Jacobs et al., 1998). At present, region is not included as a variable in the risk adjustment formula. However, expenditures vary considerably among regions after adjusting for the current risk factors of risk adjustment. Since region is not accounted for in the risk adjustment scheme, regions with a well-established infrastructure of healthcare institutions, especially some urban areas such as Berlin and Hamburg, have a predictive ratio below 1 (Drösler et al., 2011; Ulrich et al., 2016). As those sickness funds which are active nationwide are not allowed to differentiate their ACR according to region, some regions are "profitable", while others are "unprofitable" for them. Sickness funds that have a larger share of insured in the unprofitable areas (Meyers-Middendorf and Baumann, 2016), in addition to some federal states (Bayerische Staatsregierung, 2016), demand that the region becomes a variable in the risk adjustment system. Others argue that regional differences in expenditures should not be equalized as they reflect medical supply, which falls under the responsibility of the individual sickness fund (Jacobs, 2015). Another consideration has to do with the cost containment incentives that play a role in the negotiations between sickness funds and the associations of office-based physicians and hospitals on the state level, as described in Section 11.2. From the perspective of sickness funds, these incentives may be considerably reduced in the case that region is included in the risk adjustment formula in the form of a state variable. There is also a discussion of whether sickness funds with nationwide activity should be allowed or even forced to enact regional differentiation of ACR (Jacobs et al., 1998; Felder, 1999).

### 11.5.4 Insured with Reduced Earning Capacity

When risk adjustment was introduced in 1994, no direct morbidity measures were available. Only the status of reduced earning capacity as an indirect morbidity measure was at hand and thus implemented in the German risk adjustment system. Critics argue that reduced earning capacity is only a proxy for morbidity, which they claim has become redundant with the introduction of direct morbidity variables. Until now, it has been kept in the system. The rationale is that although direct morbidity measures are now implemented in the system, the insured with reduced earning capacity would be significantly underfunded if the variables were to be deleted. This is, for instance, because reduced earning capacity is a proxy for socioeconomic status, which is not included in the model. Since sickness funds have the information readily available, insured with reduced earning capacities could become an easy target for risk selection.

Use of this variable has also been criticized because only insured who have been employed before falling ill can get the status of reduced earning capacity. Retired persons, students and the unemployed might be as severely ill but are not eligible and thus the sickness fund will get no additional surcharge (Dietzel et al., 2016). Sickness funds with an above-average undercompensation but with a below-average number of insured with reduced earning capacity call for exclusion of this variable.

### 11.5.5 Insured Residing Abroad

The current risk adjustment for IRA suffers from insufficient data availability. The per capita expenditures per IRA in different countries are partly unknown and the current risk adjustment method creates substantial over- and undercompensations within the IRA group because of large differences in the cost levels for health care of different countries. Reasons for the insufficient data availability are, e.g., time lags of several years for invoices from abroad to reach the domestic sickness funds, and the fact that the accounts of sickness funds for healthcare expenditure abroad also include the invoices of domestic insured who use health care during their holidays abroad. Another reason is that the lump sum for the dependents is booked to the account of the member and is not distributed to each dependent covered by the lump sum.

The government commissioned a study that recommended differentiating the subsidies for IRA according to their country of residence and to ensure that the sum of all subsidies for IRA across all sickness funds equals the sum of all sickness funds' expenditures for these insured (Lux et al., 2016).

### 11.5.6  Sick Leave Payments

With the introduction of risk adjustment, the design of the subsidies for sick leave payments was discussed (Wasem, 1993b) and since then, several studies have been performed (Jacobs et al., 2002; Reschke et al., 2005; Drösler et al., 2011). Although sick leave payments are income-related, and therefore sickness funds with high-income insured have above-average obligations to pay sick leave payments per day of sick pay, this income dependency is not presently accounted for in risk adjustment.[10] At the same time, morbidity is not accounted for either, creating a disadvantage for sickness funds with high-morbidity members who are entitled to sick leave payments. More recent studies suggest that a model that predicts days of sick leave by using morbidity, and thus pays for each day of predicted sick leave subsidies according to the individual income of the insured, would outperform the status quo considerably (Wasem et al., 2016; Häckl et al., 2016b).

### 11.5.7  Socioeconomic Factors

Besides a variable for insured with reduced earning capacities, no other variables for socioeconomic factors are used in risk adjustment. There is an ongoing discussion, however, that socioeconomic status may influence healthcare expenditures and could be used in risk adjustment. One example is a study on insured who are exempted from copayments due to low income. The study showed that these insured are clearly undercompensated by risk adjustment, and that the model could be improved by integrating that information (Lux et al., 2015).

### 11.5.8  Drug Prescriptions in Risk Adjustment

As described in Section 11.3, drug prescriptions are used in risk adjustment in Germany to validate outpatient and secondary inpatient diagnoses for some diseases. In a number of cases, the morbidity group (for instance, for HIV) has been split into a group *with* continuous drug consumption and a group *without* continuous drug consumption. At present, all drugs that can reasonably be prescribed for a given morbidity can qualify for the drug consumption group, regardless of their costs. There is an ongoing debate about whether drug consumption groups should be split into groups for expensive drugs and groups for inexpensive drugs. This would lead to better performance of the model. There are concerns, however, that this would lead to incentives for inefficiency (Bundesversicherungsamt, 2012).

## 11.5.9 Outlier Risk Sharing

The distribution of healthcare expenditures is extremely skewed with very few insured causing extremely high expenditures. Although the refinements of the German morbidity-based risk adjustment took several extremely costly diseases with surcharges up to half a million euros per year (see Table 11.1) into account, the problem of underpayment for high-cost cases remains. The reason for this is twofold: On the one hand, morbidity-based risk adjustment in Germany is prospective, and therefore, extremely high costs caused by acute diseases and accidents are not picked up in risk adjustment. This leads to financial problems for smaller sickness funds and even for large sickness funds due to the respective financial volatility in claims expenditure. On the other hand, even for the very cost-intensive chronic diseases within the risk adjustment, a surcharge representing the average cost of those with the disease will underpay the high-cost outliers within the disease category. Insured who are systematically at the high-cost end of the variance produce predictable losses for the sickness funds and incentives for risk selection.

Introduction or reintroduction of measures to tackle the problem of outliers has been discussed since the elimination of the high-cost pool (see, e.g., Jacobs 2009; Dietzel et al., 2016). Several propositions have been made to deal with extreme outliers: Dietzel et al. (2016) as well as Drösler et al. (2011) pick up the idea of the old high-cost pool described in Section 11.3.3. Through the partial compensation of actual costs in their models, the studies reach an $R^2$ ranging between 28% and 55%, depending on the design of the pool. Schillo et al. (2016) propose different ways of dealing with high-cost cases, including a high-cost pool in which insured are included based on their undercompensation *after* risk adjustment and not on the actual costs; in addition, a model that integrates the calculation of surcharges for high-cost cases into the risk adjustment regression formula, reaching an $R^2$ between 28% and 78%, depending on the design and, in particular, on the reimbursement rate.

## ENDNOTES

1. As these social health insurance institutions are entities of public law, which are established by law and most of their insured are mandatorily insured with these institutions, and as they do not offer various "health plans" but primarily provide a benefit package regulated by law and directives of the Joint Federal Committee, the term "health insurers" is not adequate. Therefore, in this chapter we consistently call them "sickness funds."
2. In fact, only the net flow of these two financial streams was transferred via a clearing house which was established at the Federal Social Pension Insurance Scheme, and it was embedded in a broader stream of financial flows between social health insurance and social pension insurance.
3. From 2009 until 2010, sickness funds could choose between raising additional income-related contributions and raising additional flat-rate premiums for funding additional resources (or giving a respective rebate in case of a surplus). From 2011 until 2014, the only options were flat rate premiums or rebates. Starting from 2015, this was changed to the ACR described above (Wasem, 2015).

4. There are about 300,000 insured residing abroad (IRA). They consist of three main groups of insured: (1) retired persons with a German pension and residing abroad, (2) family members living abroad but covered by the family insurance of the member with a German health insurance coverage, (3) persons living abroad but with employment in Germany—they commute between Germany and a foreign country and are called "Grenzgänger" (cross-border commuters) (Lux et al., 2016).

5. Various publications on the website of the German Federal Social Insurance Authority (Bundesversicherungsamt, BVA) describe the model and the procedure in German language: www.bundesversicherungsamt.de/risikostrukturausgleich.html.

6. German Institute for Medical Documentation and Information.

7. For the 1.5-threshold condition average annual costs for the diseases are calculated. In this context the coefficients of a multiple linear regression (to control for multimorbidity) in a concurrent approach are used as average annual costs.

8. Pharmazentralnummer: unique identifier for pharmaceuticals.

9. Sickness funds therefore to a certain extent face the risk that their premiums are based on wrong assumptions about relative risk adjustment subsidies, in comparison to a situation in which the coefficients determined in year $t-1$ for year $t$ remain stable. However, they otherwise face the risk that relative expenditure for diseases develops differently than they assumed.

10. As mentioned in Section 11.3.3, in a transitional arrangement, 50% of subsidies for sick leave payments are according to actual spending, as a reaction to these problems.

# REFERENCES

AOK-Bundesverband, 2016. Vorschläge für eine systematische Weiterentwicklung des Risikostrukturausgleichs. AOK-Bundesverband, viewed 17 December 2016, http://aok-bv. de/presse/pressemitteilungen/2016/index_17346.html.

Andersen, H., Grabka, M.M., 2006. Kassenwechsel in der GKV 1997 - 2004. Profile - Trends - Perspektiven. In: Göpffarth, D., Greß, S., Jacobs, K., Wasem, J. (Eds.), Jahrbuch Risikostrukturausgleich 2006. Zehn Jahre Kassenwahlfreiheit. Asgard, St. Augustin.

Andersen, H., Grabka, M.M., Schwarze, J., 2002. Wechslerprofile-Risikoprofile. Relativer Beitragsbedarf der Kassenwechsler 1997−2001. Arbeit und Sozialpolitik 56 (7-8), 19−32.

Ash, A.S., Ellis, R.P., Pope, G.C., Ayanian, J.Z., Bates, D.W., Birstin, H., et al., 2000. Using diagnoses to describe populations and predict costs. Health Care Financing Rev. 21 (3), 7−28.

BKK-Bundesverband, 2011. BKK-Vorschläge für eine Reform des morbiditätsorientierten Risikostrukturausgleichs. BKK-Bundesverband, viewed 17 December 2016, http://www. bkkmitte.de/fileadmin/PDF/DownloadCenter/Positionspapier_BKK_BV_Morbi-RSA.pdf? PHPSESSID = 63e752cbeafcca7096d3341c750d1c0e.

BKK-Dachverband, 2015. Weiterentwicklung der Krankheitsauswahl im Risikostrukturausgleich (RSA). BKK-Dachverband, viewed 17 December 2016, http://www.bundesversicherungsamt. de/risikostrukturausgleich/festlegungen.html.

BKK-Dachverband, 2016. Stellschrauben im Morbi-RSA. Sondergruppen im Fokus. Jetzt entschlacken!. BKK-Dachverband, viewed 17 December 2016, http://www.bkk-dachverband.de/publikationen/risikostrukturausgleich/.

Bauhoff, S., 2012. Do health plans risk-select? An audit study on Germany's Social Health Insurance. J. Public Econ. 96, 750−759.

Bayerische Staatsregierung, 2016. Gesundheitsministerin Huml: Freistaat muss endlich entlastet werden − Gutachten untermauert Forderung Bayerns nach gerechterer Krankenkassen-Finanzierung. Bayerische Staatsregierung, viewed 24 December 2016, http://www.bayern.de/gesundheitsministerin-huml-freistaat-muss-endlich-entlastet-werden-gutachten-untermauert-forderung-bayerns-nach-gerechterer-krankenkassen-finanzierung/.

Brosse, F., 2016. Direct risk selection in the German social health insurance system: a field experiment. Abstract presented at EUHEA conference 2016, Hamburg.

Buchner, F., Wasem, J., 2003. Needs for further improvement: risk adjustment in the German health insurance system. Health Policy 77, 21−35.

Buchner, F., Göpffarth, D., Wasem, J., 2013. The new risk adjustment formula in Germany: implementation and first experiences. Health Policy 109, 253−262.

Buchner, F., Wasem, J., Schillo, S., 2017. Regression trees identify relevant interactions: can this improve the predictive performance of risk adjustment? Health Econ. 26 (1), 74−85.

Bundesversicherungsamt, 2012. Erläuterungen zur Festlegung von Morbiditätsgruppen, Zuordnungsalgorithmus, Regressionsmodell und Berechnungsverfahren für das RSA-Ausgleichsjahr 2012. Bundesversicherungsamt, viewed 23 December 2016, http://www.bundesversicherungsamt.de/risikostrukturausgleich/festlegungen.html#c144.

Bundesversicherungsamt, 2015. Ergebnisse des Jahresausgleichs 2014. Bundesversicherungsamt, viewed 18 December 2016, http://www.bundesversicherungsamt.de/fileadmin/redaktion/Risikostrukturausgleich/Info-Dateien%20und%20Auswertungen/Auswertung_JA2014.pdf.

Bundesversicherungsamt, 2016. Erläuterungen zur Festlegung von Morbiditätsgruppen, Zuordnungsalgorithmus, Regressionsmodell und Berechnungsverfahren für das RSA-Ausgleichsjahr 2017. Bundesversicherungsamt, viewed 17 December 2016, http://www.bundesversicherungsamt.de/risikostrukturausgleich/festlegungen.html#c5594.

Busse, R., Blümel, M., 2014. Germany: health system review. Health Syst. Trans. 16 (2), 1−296.

Cassel, D., 1984. Wettbewerb in der Krankenversicherung: Möglichkeiten und Grenzen. Bundesarbeitsblatt (12), 31−33.

Dietzel, J., Glaeske, G., Greiner, W., 2015. *Begleitforschung zum Morbi-RSA (Teil 1) - Kriterien, Wirkung und Alternativen.* IGES Institut, viewed 14 December 2016, http://www.iges.com/e6/e1621/e10211/e13470/e13612/e13614/e13616/attr_objs13620/IGES_RSA-Begleitforschung_Teil_1_WEB_ger.pdf.

Dietzel, J., Neumann, K., Glaeske, G., 2016. Begleitforschung zum Morbi-RSA - Erwerbsminderungsrenten als Morbiditätsindikatoren? IGES Institut, viewed 14 December 2016, http://www.iges.com/e6/e1621/e10211/e13470/e13890/e13891/e13893/attr_objs13894/160303_IGES_MorbiRSA_Erwerbsminderungsrenten_WEB_ger.pdf.

Drösler, S., Hasford, J., Kurth, B.M., Schaefer, M., Wille, E., Wasem, J., 2011. Evaluationsbericht zum Jahresausgleich 2009 im Risikostrukturausgleich. Endfassung. Bundesministerium für Gesundheit, viewed 17 December 2016, http://www.bmg.bund.de/fileadmin/dateien/Publikationen/Forschungsberichte/2011/Evaluationsbericht_morbi-rsa.pdf.

Enthoven, A., 1980. Health Plan: The Only Practical Solution to the Soaring Cost of Medical Care. Addison-Wesley, Reading, MA.

Felder, S., 1999. Regionalisierung, Risikostrukturausgleich und Wettbewerb in der gesetzlichen Krankenversicherung. Zeitschrift für die gesamte Versicherungswissenschaft 88, 59−76.

GKV-Spitzenverband, 2016. Krankenkassenliste. GKV-Spitzenverband, viewed 12 December 2016, https://www.gkv-spitzenverband.de/service/versicherten_service/krankenkassenliste/krankenkassen.jsp.

Gitter, W., 1991. Zur Verfassungsmäßigkeit unterschiedlicher Beitragssätze in der Gesetzlichen Krankenversicherung. In: Schwartz, F.W., Hoffmann, W., Badura, B., Brecht, J.G., Jöckel, K.H., Trojan, A. (Eds.), Public health. Springer, Heidelberg.

Gitter, W., Oberender, P., 1987. *Möglichkeiten und Grenzen des Wettbewerbs in der Gesetzlichen Krankenversicherung - Eine ökonomische und juristische Untersuchung zur Strukturreform in der GKV.* Nomos, Baden-Baden.

Griesewell, G., 1985. Kostendämpfungs- und Strukturpolitik in der Bundesrepublik Deutschland. In: von Ferber, C. (Ed.), Kosten und Effizienz im Gesundheitswesen: Gedenkschrift für Ulrich Geißler. Oldenbourg, München.

Häckl, D., Weinhold, I., Kossack, N., Schindler, C., 2016a. Gutachten zu Anreizen für Prävention im Morbi-RSA. Wissenschaftliches Institut für Gesundheitsökonomie und Gesundheitssystemforschung, Leipzig, viewed 17 December 2016, http://www.wig2.de/ fileadmin/content_uploads/PDF_Dateien/Gutachten_zu_Anreizen_fuer_Praevention_im_ Morbi-RSA.pdf.

Häckl, D., Neumann, K., Greiner, W., Wille, E., Dietzel, J., Kossack, N., Degenkolbe, B., 2016b. Verbesserung der Deckungsquoten im Krankengeld - eine Analyse auf Basis von Daten der gesetzlichen Krankenversicherung. Wissenschaftliches Institut für Gesundheitsökonomie und Gesundheitssystemforschung, Berlin, viewed 17 December 2016, http://www.iges.com/e6666/e13520/e14655/e14657/e14658/attr_objs14666/IGES_WIG_ Greiner_Wille_Verbesserung_der_Deckungsquoten_im_Krankengeld_ger.pdf.

Hofmann, J., Hühne, P., 1988. GKV-Solidarprinzip, Wettbewerb und Finanzierungsverfahren. Arbeit und Sozialpolitik 42, 238−246.

Höppner, K., Greß, S., Rothgang, H., Wasem, J., 2006. Instrumente der Risikoselektion − Theorie und Empirie. In: Göpffarth, D., Greß, S., Jacobs, K., Wasem, J. (Eds.), Jahrbuch Risikostrukturausgleich 2006 − 10 Jahre Kassenwahlfreiheit. Asgard, St. Augustin.

Huppertz, P.H., Jaschke, H., Kops, M., 1981. Beitragssatzdifferenzen und adäquate Finanzausgleichsverfahren in der gesetzlichen Krankenversicherung. Bundesministerium für Arbeit und Sozialordnung, Bonn.

Hustadt, A., Wasem, J., 1993. Pflegeversicherung: Risikostrukturausgleich nur bei Wettbewerb. Sozialer Fortschritt 42, 279−281.

Igl, G., 2007. Die Entstehung der sozialen Pflegeversicherung und ihre Konsequenzen. In: Ritter, G.A. (Ed.), Geschichte der Sozialpolitik in Deutschland seit 1945. Band 11: 1989-1994: Bundesrepublik Deutschland. Sozialpolitik im Zeichen der Vereinigung. Nomos, Baden-Baden.

Jacobs, K., 2009. 'Hohe Risiken besser absichern?'. G + G 12 (10), 14−15.

Jacobs, K., 2015. 'Bayern lässt nicht locker - Zur Einführung eines Regionalfaktors im Risikostrukturausgleich'. GGW 15 (2), 23−30.

Jacobs, K., Reschke, P., Wasem, J., 1998. Zur funktionalen Abgrenzung von Beitragssatzregionen in der gesetzlichen Krankenversicherung. Nomos, Baden-Baden.

Jacobs, K., Reschke, P., Cassel, D., Wasem, J., 2002. Zur Wirkung des Risikostrukturausgleichs in der gesetzlichen Krankenversicherung. Nomos, Baden-Baden.

Leber, W.D., Wasem, J., 1989. Risikostrukturausgleich in der gesetzlichen Krankenversicherung. Wirtschaftsdienst 69, 87−93.

Lisac, M., Reimers, L., Henke, K.D., Schlette, S., 2010. Access and choice−competition under the roof of solidarity in German health care: an analysis of health policy reforms since 2004. Health Economics, Policy and Law 5, 31−52.

Lux, G., Schillo, S., van der Linde, K., Walendzik, K., Wasem, J., 2015. Die Berücksichtigung von Zuzahlungsbefreiungen im RSA-Ausgestaltungsmöglichkeiten und Wirkungen einer erweiterten Berücksichtigung sozioökonomischer Faktoren. IBES, viewed 13 December 2016, https://www.wiwi.uni-due.de/forschung/publikationen/ibes-diskussionsbeitraege/.

Lux, G., Schillo, S., Wasem, J., 2016. Die Berücksichtigung von Auslandsversicherten im RSA. In: Repschläger, U., Schulte, C., Osterkamp, N. (Eds.), Gesundheitswesen Aktuell 2016. Barmer GEK, Köln.

Meißner, M., 2009. Morbi-RSA: Gerangel um "korrekte" Codierung. Deutsches Ärzteblatt 106 (5), A172.

Meyers-Middendorf, J., Baumann, M.G., 2016. Morbi-RSA reformieren — Kassenwettbewerb fair gestalten. Ersatzkassen-Magazin 100 (5/6), 21−26.

Reiners, H., 1993. Das Gesundheitsstrukturgesetz - 'Ein Hauch von Sozialgeschichte'? Werkstattbericht über eine gesundheitspolitische Weichenstellung. In: Abholz, H.H., Borgers, D., Klosterhuis, H., Kühn, H., Reichelt, A., Rosenbrock, R., Schafstedde, F., Schagen, U. (Eds.), Jahrbuch für kritische Medizin 20. Die Regulierung der Gesundheit. Argument-Verlag, Hamburg.

Reschke, P., Sehlen, S., Schiffhorst, G., Schräder, W.F., Lauterbach, K.W., Wasem, J., 2005. Klassifikationsmodelle für Versicherte im Risikostrukturausgleich. Bundesministerium für Gesundheit und Soziale Sicherung, Referat Information, Publikation, Redaktion, Bonn.

Rybarczyk, C., 2016. Gesetzliche Krankenkassen streiten um Betrugsvorwürfe. Hamburger Abendblatt, viewed 10 October 2016, http://www.abendblatt.de/ratgeber/gesundheit/article208388403/Gesetzliche-Krankenkassen-streiten-um-Betrugsvorwucrfe.html.

Scherff, D., 2016. Wir Krankenkassen schummeln ständig. Frankfurter Allgemeine Sonntagszeitung, 9. October, 35.

Schillo, S., Lux, G., Wasem, J., Buchner, F., 2016. 'High cost pool or high cost groups - How to handle high(est) cost cases in a risk adjustment mechanism?'. Health Policy 210, 141−147.

Schmitz, H., Ziebarth, N.R., 2016. Does framing prices affect the consumer price sensitivity of health plan choice? J. Human Resour. 51, . Available from: https://doi.org/10.3368/jhr.52.1.0814-6540R1viewed 30 December 2016.

Schokkaert, E., van de Voorde, K., 2006. Incentives for Risk Selection and Omitted Variables in the Risk Adjustment Formula. Annales d'Économie et de Statistique 83/84, 327−351.

Schut, F., Greß, S., Wasem, J., 2003. Consumer Price Sensitivity and Social Health Insurer Choice in Germany and the Netherlands. Int. J. Health Care Finance Econ. 3, 117−139.

Smigielski, E., 1982. Möglichkeiten und Grenzen des Wettbewerbs zwischen den Trägern der gesetzlichen Krankenversicherung. Sozialer Fortschritt 31, 234−243.

Tamm, M., Tauchmann, H., Wasem, J., Greß, S., 2007. Elasticities of market shares and social health insurance choice in Germany: a dynamic panel data approach. Health Econ. 16, 243−256.

Tennstedt, F., 1983. Die Errichtung von Krankenkassen in deutschen Städten nach dem Gesetz betreffend die Krankenversicherung der Arbeiter vom 15.6.1883. Zeitschrift für Sozialreform 29, 297−338.

Ulrich, V., Wille, E., Thüsing, G., 2016. Die Notwendigkeit einer regionalen Komponente im morbiditätsorientierten Risikostrukturausgleich unter wettbewerbspolitischen und regionalen Aspekten. Bayerisches Staatsministerium für Gesundheit und Pflege, München.

van de Ven, W.P., Ellis, R., 2000. Risk Adjustment in competitive health plan markets. In: Culyer, A.J., Newhouse, J.P. (Eds.), Handbook of Health Economics, Vol. 1A. Elsevier North Holland, Amsterdam.

van de Ven, W.P., Schut, F.T., 1994. Should catastrophic risks be included in a regulated competitive health insurance market. Soc. Sci. Med. 39, 1459−1472.

van de Ven, W.P., Beck, K., Buchner, F., Schokkaert, E., Schut, F.T., Shmueli, A., Wasem, J., 2013. Preconditions for efficency and affordability in competitive healthcare markets: Are they fulfilled in Belgium, Germany, Israel, the Netherlands and Switzerland? Health Policy 109, 226−245.

Verband der privaten Krankenversicherung, 2016. Rechenschaftsbericht der privaten Krankenversicherung 2015. Verband der privaten Krankenversicherung, viewed 28 December 2016, http://www.pkv.de/service/broschueren/verband/rechenschaftsbericht-2015/.

Wasem, J., 1989. Perspektiven einer Organisationsreform der gesetzlichen Krankenversicherung. Informationsdienst Nr. 212 der Gesellschaft für Versicherungswissenschaft und -gestaltung e.V. Köln.

Wasem, J., 1993a. Der kassenartenübergreifende Risikostrukturausgleich - Chancen für eine neue Wettbewerbsordnung in der GKV. Sozialer Fortschritt 42, 31−39.

Wasem, J., 1993b. Berücksichtigung des Krankengeldes beim Risikostrukturausgleich: Statement II. In: Paquet, R., König, W. (Eds.), Der Risikostrukturausgleich und die Konsequenzen für den Wettbewerb. Bundesverband der Betriebskrankenkassen, Essen.

Wasem, J., 2015. GKV-Finanzarchitektur als Eckpfeiler der Wettbewerbsordnung: Stand und Weiterentwicklung. Gesundheits- und Sozialpolitik 69 (3/4), 28−33.

Wasem, J., Schillo, S., Lux, G., Neusser, S., 2016. Gutachten zu Zuweisungen für Krankengeld nach § 269 Abs. 3 SGB V i.V.m. § 33 Abs. 3 RSAV − Endbericht. Universität Duisburg-Essen, viewed 23 December 2016, http://www.bundesversicherungsamt.de/fileadmin/redaktion/Risikostrukturausgleich/Weiterentwicklung/Gutachten_Krankengeld.pdf.

Weber, R., 2010. Risikoausgleichsverfahren in der privaten Krankenversicherung. In: Göpffarth, D., Greß, S., Jacobs, K., Wasem, J. (Eds.), Jahrbuch Risikostrukturausgleich 2010 - Von der Selektion zur Manipulation? medhochzwei Verlag, Heidelberg.

Zöllner, D., 1981. Ein Jahrhundert Sozialversicherung in Deutschland. Duncker&Humblot, Berlin.

# Chapter 12

# Health Plan Payment in Ireland

John Armstrong

*Erasmus School of Health Policy and Management, Erasmus University Rotterdam, Rotterdam, The Netherlands*

## 12.1 INTRODUCTION

### 12.1.1 Overview

Ireland has long had a voluntary health insurance market regulated to meet a stated public policy goal of achieving risk solidarity in order to promote affordability of private health insurance coverage for all (Department of Health, 1956, 1999a, 2016). Risk solidarity means cross-subsidies from low-risk to high-risk people. Many other elements of regulated competition have also been present in the market for many years, including community rating and a risk equalization system to support risk solidarity and deter risk selection.

Successive Irish governments have seen the voluntary insurance system as an important part of health policy and aim to use community rating, combined with risk equalization, as tools to make insurance affordable to the entire population regardless of their risk profile (Armstrong, 2010; Department of Health, 1999a). The role of health insurance within the Irish health system has been extensively discussed in earlier publications (Armstrong, 2002; Nolan, 2006; Colombo and Tapay, 2003). This chapter presents and updates the Irish experience on issues related to the premium regulation and risk equalization arrangements that have evolved over the last 60 years.

Nearly half the Irish population purchases private health insurance that duplicates their coverage within the public health system. Since the establishment of the Voluntary Health Insurance Board (Vhi) in 1957, the health insurance market has developed significantly. According to the industry regulator, the Health Insurance Authority (HIA), approximately 46% of the population, or slightly over 2.1 million persons, had health insurance as of the end of June 2017 (HIA, 2017a). It is estimated that health insurance funds approximately 13% of all health expenditure in Ireland (CSO, 2016). This small percentage understates the role of private health insurance, given that

Risk Adjustment, Risk Sharing and Premium Regulation in Health Insurance Markets.
DOI: https://doi.org/10.1016/B978-0-12-811325-7.00012-9

health insurance pays for approximately 26% of hospital care costs, giving it a significant role in the health sector (CSO, 2016).

Following Armstrong (2010), I outline risk-related subsidies in the form of risk equalization and, in the remainder of this section, I present some important historical background as to the development of the private health insurance market. I then outline how the health insurance market is organized (Section 12.2). I go on to discuss some of the design issues, including outlining the nature of risk equalization and the calculation of cross-subsidy payments (Section 12.3). In Section 12.4, I evaluate the effectiveness of the risk equalization system using some of the published data that are available from the industry. Finally, I discuss some possible future developments regarding premium regulation and risk equalization (Section 12.5), and I present some final conclusions.

## 12.1.2 Historical Background

In 1957, the Voluntary Health Insurance Board was established by the Irish parliament, the Oireachtas, under primary legislation to provide private health insurance to the Irish population. The significance of creating the Vhi under primary legislation meant that it became a statutory organization[1] with the sole task of providing health insurance to the Irish population on a voluntary basis. Three important aspects are notable.

First, the legislation required the Vhi to set premiums to be no higher than sufficient to meet the cost of providing benefits to its members (Voluntary Health Insurance Act, 1957). Second, the legislation gave absolute power to the Irish Minister for Health to grant or refuse a license for another insurer to enter the market. Third, the Vhi was exempt from the Insurance Acts. The significance of these aspects of the legislation meant that Vhi operated on a not-for-profit basis; that Vhi was a monopoly insurer until the mid-1990s;[2] and that capital and consumer protection requirements did not apply in the health insurance market.[3]

The Vhi and creation of a private health insurance market were important milestones in that they provided another tool for the government to meet its social objective of ensuring that the entire population gained access to health insurance at an affordable cost.[4] A key element in achieving affordability was community rating, ensuring that an individual's premium was independent of their own risk. Until the mid-1990s, when competition was introduced, community rating was not explicitly set out in legislation. Community rating applied in practice, however, because all premium changes for the monopoly state organization Vhi, had to be approved by the Minister of Health and successive Ministers of Health ensured community rating was applied.

Establishing the (monopoly) health insurance market needs to be seen in the historical context of the 1940s and 1950s in Ireland. Ireland gained independence from the United Kingdom in 1921. The healthcare system at that time was structured in a similar manner to that of the United Kingdom prior to the creation of the National Health Service (NHS) in 1948. While government and, likely, most of the population, would have preferred to replicate the NHS, it was not feasible given the economic position of Ireland in 1948. Encouraging development of a tightly regulated private health insurance sector was considered to be an expedient way to meet social objectives and enabled Ireland to finance health insurance collectively with limited public outlays.

At an early stage, the government gave income tax subsidies to individuals to encourage the take-up of private health insurance. The level of subsidies changed over time. Initially, an individual's total health insurance premium was credited against income tax obligations at the marginal tax rate for that individual. With Ireland's progressive tax schedule, the subsidy was more valuable to those with higher income. In the period 1995−97, for equity reasons, the tax subsidy on the premium was reduced to the standard rate of tax for all, regardless of income.[5] Since October 2013, tax relief is set at a standard rate (currently 20% of premiums) for all, but capped at a monetary threshold (currently €200 per adult and €100 per child), eliminating favorable tax treatment for higher-income groups.

Tax subsidies supported enrollment in private health insurance, particularly for individuals who otherwise would have had to pay for their own hospitalization costs. Although the main objective of establishing the private health insurance system was to provide coverage for those without an entitlement to public health services, health insurance was also perceived as improving access to private healthcare services in the state and voluntary hospitals and in the increasing number of private hospitals, most of which, until the mid-1980s, were not-for-profit charitable institutions.

Over the period 1957−94, enrollment in private health insurance grew significantly with Vhi as the sole insurer. By 1967, approximately 300,000 persons (about 10% of the population at the time) had private health insurance, and by 1977, this figure had increased to 600,000 persons (about 18% of the population). By the end of the 1980s, 1.2 million persons had health insurance (approximately 34% of the population) and by 1994, just before the market opened to competition, that figure had increased to approximately 1.3 million persons, about 40% of the population (Nolan, 1991; various Vhi Annual Reports; Department of Health, 1999a). The HIA attributes much of this growth to the perceptions that private health insurance improved access to better-quality health services (HIA and Millard Brown, 2015). In fact, the most substantial growth in the market came during periods when the alternate tax-funded public health system was struggling due to the macroeconomic situation in the country.

With the Third Directive on NonLife Insurance on July 1, 1994, the monopoly position of the Vhi became problematic (European Commission,

1992). This Directive was part of the "Single Market" process, intended to open up European Union markets to competition. Consequently, Ireland was required to open the private health insurance market to competition while retaining the principles of advancing the "general good" and solidarity in financing health care. New regulation was necessary to open the market and maintain solidarity at the same time.

The Health Insurance Act (1994) set regulations for insurers based on principles of regulated competition (Armstrong, 2010), as first articulated by Enthoven (1988). In the next section I outline some of the features of the newly created market in relation to these principles.

## 12.2 ORGANIZATION OF THE HEALTH INSURANCE SYSTEM

### 12.2.1 The Role of Health Insurance

Ireland now finances health care from a number of sources including government funding (about 70% of total funding), voluntary health insurance premiums (about 13% of total funding), and out-of-pocket expenditure (17% of total funding).[6]

Under the state health system, all members of the population are entitled to a defined level of coverage, depending upon their income relative to a threshold level, age, and the nature and severity of their illness. In general, those with income below a threshold are entitled to free primary, secondary, or tertiary care services.[7,8] The income thresholds are higher for those 70 years and over with the income assessment for a couple based on the age of the older partner. Individuals with certain illnesses (e.g., children with cancer) are entitled to free care automatically or on discretionary basis following an assessment of need. Those not entitled to free care pay a modest daily fee for hospital services within the state statutory and voluntary hospitals, subject to an annual out-of-pocket maximum, currently €750. As of December 31, 2016, approximately 2.175 million people (about 46% of the population) had access to free care under the medical card scheme (HSE, 2017; CSO, 2017).

Currently, private health insurance provides benefits for primary care and hospital-related services. Primary care benefits include contributions towards the cost of general practitioner and specialist services, and the cost of ancillary health services such as physiotherapy. Primary care benefits cover, on average, about 60% of the cost of the treatment for the patient based upon the application of various cost-sharing mechanisms such as coinsurance, benefit ceilings, or copayments.[9] For a hospital in an insurer's network, hospital-related benefits typically cover close to the full cost of the treatment including the doctor and hospital costs. Since 2010, some insurers have introduced cost-sharing mechanisms[10] for certain orthopedic and ophthalmic benefits in private hospitals, equating to about 20% of the cost of the treatment, in return for reduced premiums (HIA, 2015). In addition, many products have overall small-sized deductibles applying for each treatment.[11]

Consumers are free to choose their health plan from those offered by their insurer, and though health plans that have both primary and hospital benefits are available, consumers have tended to choose health plans with relatively lower levels of primary care benefits but more comprehensive hospital benefits. Over 90% of the cost of private health insurance claims still corresponds to hospital treatment. Approximately 46% (HIA, 2017a) of the population buys insurance, one of the highest take-ups for a voluntary insurance market in the OECD (OECD, 2016).

Three open insurers currently operate within the market. An open insurer is one that allows anyone within the population to enroll. Other closed, occupational-related insurers cover, amongst others, the Gardai (the Irish police service), the prison service, and the state electricity body. These insurers act as self-insured bodies for a group of enrollees defined by employment.

At December 31, 2016, the largest open insurer, Vhi, insured about 1.06 million members. The other two insurers are Laya Healthcare (the successor of Bupa Ireland), with approximately 550,000 members and Irish Life Health (recently established from the integration of Aviva Health and GloHealth) with approximately 420,000 insured lives (HIA, 2016a).[12] Approximately a further 80,000 are insured with the closed insurers (HIA, 2016b).

## 12.2.2  Health Insurance Legislation

The Health Insurance Act 1994 and subsequent amendments set out a number of important requirements related to equity in financing and access to insurance:

1. All health plans must be community-rated.[13]
2. Open enrollment applies, which mandates that an insurer must accept all applicants. Waiting periods can be applied to reduce potential for adverse selection subject to maximums outlined in regulation.
3. Insurers must cover a minimum set of benefits. The minimum benefit limits are defined with respect to secondary care hospital services (inpatient, day patient, and hospital outpatient benefits), medical procedures provided by a consultant physician within a hospital setting together with limited outpatient services. Regulations do not require insurers to provide benefits in particular hospital with particular consultants or in particular hospital settings (e.g., a single room).
4. Open insurers must participate in a risk equalization system (explained below) that provides cross-subsidies among different insurers with different risk profiles.

## 12.2.3 Benefits Provided

Since the introduction of the Health Insurance Act and accompanying regulations (Statutory Instruments, 2003, 1996), insurers have routinely provided benefits in excess of the minimum benefit requirements on all their health plans. In practice, the benefits provided by all insurers are broadly similar and are principally related to hospital care with only a small portion of the benefits providing for primary care.[14] Thus, in effect, a market standard health plan has evolved over time, which the majority of customers choose to purchase and which is used as the basis for risk equalization. Table 12.1 compares the minimum benefits, the standardized benefits, and the benefits provided by supplemental health plans providing coverage above the standardized level of benefits.

**TABLE 12.1** Benefits Provided in the Irish Health Insurance Market

| Benefit category | Minimum benefit package | Most popular benefit package | Supplementary benefits |
|---|---|---|---|
| Cost of treatments in public/ voluntary hospitals | Covered | Covered | |
| Cost of treatments in private hospitals (excluding category 1 hospitals) | For certain procedures, defined in legislation as "Special Procedures" 35% of a monetary amount defined in the minimum benefit regulations | Covered for cost of multiple room occupancy in the range of hospitals covered by insurer | Single room cover can be purchased |
| Cost of treatments in category 1 private hospitals | For other treatments, the lesser of: (a) €171.41 for each in-patient day; or (b) 60% of (i) the charge made by the private hospital; less (ii) €50.78 for each day during which the insured person was accommodated in a single room | Not usually covered | Can be purchased |

*(Continued)*

**TABLE 12.1** (Continued)

| Benefit category | Minimum benefit package | Most popular benefit package | Supplementary benefits |
| --- | --- | --- | --- |
| Cost of treatment by specialist physician in all types of hospitals | Covered as defined by a monetary amount in the minimum benefit regulations for defined procedures | Covered in full | |
| General practitioner costs | Not covered with limited exceptions for certain procedures | Fixed monetary payment varying by health plan | Additional benefit can be purchased on higher plans |
| Consultation with specialist | Not covered | Fixed monetary payment varying by health plan | Additional benefit can be purchased on higher plans |
| Outpatient physiotherapy | Not covered | Fixed monetary payment varying by health plan | Additional benefit can be purchased on higher plans |
| Outpatient radiology services | Not covered | Usually covered | |
| Hospital drugs | For public/voluntary hospitals included in hospital payment. For private hospitals not covered explicitly | For public/voluntary hospitals included in hospital payment. For private hospitals covered with limited exceptions for high-cost drugs | No additional supplemental insurance can be purchased |
| Drugs dispensed outside hospitals | Not covered | Not covered | Very limited additional top-ups can be purchased |

In broad terms, for hospital care, the standard benefits health plans routinely pay the full cost, or close to the full cost (as outlined in Table 12.1) of the treating hospital and physicians. Insurers have the option, subject to minimum benefit requirements, not to cover all hospitals. However, until recently, most hospitals[15] have been covered by all insurers. More recently, insurers have introduced restricted networks of hospitals on each health plan consistent with preferred provider contracting strategies.[16]

Health plans with a deductible have recently become more popular. In fact, no health plans have been introduced in the last 5 years without a deductible. The HIA does not publish any figures on the precise number of individuals with such health plans. However, they have commented on this fact (HIA, 2016b). Though subject to meeting minimum benefit requirements, there are no limits on the level of a deductible.[17]

### 12.2.4 Premium Levels

Average premiums per person grew by 32% over the calendar years 2010–15, from €890 to €1,173 (Society of Actuaries in Ireland, 2016). This growth is partly driven by a reduction in the share of younger age groups buying insurance. As shown in Table 12.2, the rate of insurance for the 18–29 age group falls from 15% to 11% and the 30–39 age group from 17–15%. Consistent with the classic market response to community rating, those of lower risk, who pay an average premium, tend to drop from the

**TABLE 12.2** Number of Insured Persons and Percentage in Each Age Band 2009–15 (In Thousands)

| Age band | 2009 | 2010 | 2011 | 2012 | 2013 | 2014 | 2015 |
|---|---|---|---|---|---|---|---|
| 0–17 | 518 | 505 | 495 | 479 | 462 | 454 | 475 |
| | 24% | 24% | 25% | 24% | 24% | 24% | 24% |
| 18–29 | 310 | 284 | 256 | 230 | 211 | 203 | 210 |
| | 15% | 14% | 13% | 12% | 11% | 11% | 11% |
| 30–39 | 365 | 365 | 331 | 312 | 295 | 281 | 297 |
| | 17% | 18% | 16% | 16% | 15% | 15% | 15% |
| 40–49 | 321 | 321 | 308 | 302 | 296 | 293 | 322 |
| | 15% | 15% | 15% | 15% | 15% | 16% | 16% |
| 50–59 | 272 | 272 | 269 | 266 | 263 | 261 | 276 |
| | 13% | 13% | 13% | 14% | 14% | 14% | 14% |
| 60 and over | 337 | 337 | 361 | 371 | 383 | 394 | 412 |
| | 16% | 16% | 18% | 19% | 20% | 21% | 21% |

Source: Amended from Society of Actuaries in Ireland, 2016. Inflationary pressures in the Irish Private Health Insurance market, available at www.actuaries.ie Data taken from HIA Market Statistics, www.hia.ie

pool. Under community rating, the young (better risks) subsidize the old (relatively worse risks), only, of course, if the younger groups participate.[18]

Before considering the possible implications of these average premium increases, it is important to understand that, during the 2010−15 period, there was a significant economic downturn in Ireland that was even more severe than the global economic downturn. This meant, as shown in Table 12.3, that average premiums for health insurance became a larger proportion of consumers' incomes.

### 12.2.5   Competition in the Health Insurance Market

Insurers compete on the basis of premiums, the health plan/benefit package they provide to customers, the network of contracted healthcare providers, and the quality of the administrative services they provide to their insured membership. Major differences are summarized in Box 12.1.

As of July 27, 2017, there were 313 different health plans available within the market (HIA, 2017b). The rationale provided by insurers for the large number of health plans is to provide a greater range of choice for consumers. Tables 12.4 and 12.5 provide some data relevant for characterizing competition in the market over the period 2009−17.

Market concentration measures are one useful indicator of the state of competition in the market, often used in conjunction with other evidence of competitive effects (FTC, 2010). One commonly used measure is the Herfindahl−Hirschman Index (HHI), which is equal to the sum of the squares of the individual firms' market shares. As can be seen in Table 12.4, the HHI for insurers in Ireland has fallen steadily over the period in question. Nonetheless, the current concentration level is still significantly above the 2,500 used as a benchmark for classifying a market as "highly concentrated."

Table 12.4 also presents HHI for various age groups, a proxy for the various submarkets within the Irish health insurance market, namely for individuals and for group (corporate) business where health insurance is provided through an individual's employer.[19] As displayed, the level of market concentration significantly increases for the older ages.

Table 12.5 presents some information of some other indicators of competition including information on the entry and exit of insurers, profit margins, and details on the number of health plans over the period 2010−17. In summary, while the market continues to be highly concentrated over the period, entry data imply that the market is attractive for large global insurers, such as AIG and Great West Lifeco, both of whom entered the market during this period. In fact, the industry has been profitable as a whole, and profit margins for individual established insurers have been positive (ex-post net risk equalization costs) even in the face of an economic downturn in Ireland.[20] Insurers change their premium rates very regularly.

**TABLE 12.3 Change in Health Insurance Premiums 2006–14**

| Year | A<br>Avg. gross premium (€)[a] | B<br>Avg. gross premium (% change) | Health insurance take-up rate[b] | C<br>Avg. disposable income (€)[c] | D<br>Avg. disposable income (% change) | A/C<br>Avg. premium as % of avg. disposable income[d] | A minus D |
|---|---|---|---|---|---|---|---|
| 2006 | 607 | | 46.2% | 20,038 | | 3.0% | |
| 2007 | 667 | +10.0% | 46.6% | 21,148 | +5.5% | 3.2% | +4.4% |
| 2008 | 724 | +8.4% | 47.6% | 22,565 | +6.7% | 3.2% | +1.7% |
| 2009 | 822 | +13.6% | 46.6% | 21,123 | −6.4% | 3.9% | +20.0% |
| 2010 | 890 | +8.3% | 45.4% | 19,487 | −7.7% | 4.6% | +16.0% |
| 2011 | 926 | +4.0% | 44.1% | 18,935 | −2.8% | 4.9% | +6.8% |
| 2012 | 1,048 | +13.2% | 42.7% | 18,964 | +0.2% | 5.5% | +13.0% |
| 2013 | 1,150 | +9.7% | 41.5% | 18,707 | −1.4% | 6.1% | +11.1% |
| 2014 | 1,200 | +4.3% | 40.7% | 19,309 | +3.2% | 6.2% | +1.1% |

[a]The "Average Gross Premium" is the average gross health insurance premium (i.e., before the impact of tax relief) for both adults and children from 2006–2009 on open-enrollment policies derived from HIA published data ("Market Statistics"): http://www.hia.ie/publication/market-statistics. 2010–2014 are based on direct average premiums quoted from HIA quarterly newsletters: http://www.hia.ie/news/newsletters.

[b]"Health Insurance Take-Up Rate" is derived from published data from the HIA of year-end insured lives with open enrollment undertakings: http://www.hia.ie/publication/market-statistics. 2006 and 2008 are estimates based on the respective 2006/2007 and 2008/2009 changes in insured lives with inpatient cover (also from the same HIA source).

[c]"Average Disposable Income" is a per capita measure extracted from a database maintained by the CSO: www.cso.ie/px/pxeirestat/statire/SelectVarVal/Define.asp? MainTable = CIA01&TabStrip = Select&PLanguage = 0&FF = 1. It includes all employment income, benefits in kind, rent received, bank interest, share dividends, social welfare benefits, state pensions and other government transfers. Taxes on income and loan interest are then deducted to arrive at total disposable income for the whole Irish population before converting that to a per capita outcome. It implicitly takes account of increases in unemployment, salary/bonus cuts, and increases in income taxation seen from 2009 onwards.

[d]Average premium expressed as percentage of average disposable income.
Source: Amended from Society of Actuaries in Ireland, 2016. Inflationary pressures in the Irish Private Health Insurance market, available at www.actuaries.ie

BOX 12.1 Differences among health plans in the Irish health insurance market

Consumers have a choice of insurer and can choose one of the many offered health plans. The main differences among health plans are in:

1. The level and range of hospital-related benefits.
2. The particular hospitals covered by the health plan and the level of accommodation covered in each hospital.
3. The level of cost sharing (i.e., deductibles and coinsurance), referred to as excesses in the Irish market) that apply to the health plan both overall and specifically relating to orthopedic and ophthalmic services.
4. The extent of primary care benefits.
5. The range of nonmedical benefits (e.g., employee assistance or occupational health services).

TABLE 12.4 Competition in the Irish Health Insurance Market as Measured by the Herfindahl–Hirschman Indices (HHI), 2008–15

| Year | 0–49 | 50–59 | 60–69 | 70–79 | 80 + | Overall | Population weighted - 2015 base[a] |
|------|------|-------|-------|-------|------|---------|-----------------------------|
| 2008 | 4,931 | 5,912 | 6,958 | 8,514 | 9,226 | 5,401 | 5,653 |
| 2009 | 4,594 | 5,165 | 6,254 | 8,011 | 8,856 | 4,964 | 5,206 |
| 2010 | 4,362 | 4,952 | 5,846 | 7,493 | 8,669 | 4,780 | 4,939 |
| 2011 | 4,112 | 4,361 | 5,038 | 6,602 | 8,150 | 4,377 | 4,529 |
| 2012 | 4,012 | 4,283 | 4,850 | 6,309 | 7,993 | 4,273 | 4,407 |
| 2013 | 3,694 | 4,221 | 4,585 | 5,950 | 7,654 | 4,025 | 4,127 |
| 2014 | 3,531 | 4,045 | 4,317 | 5,609 | 7,342 | 3,892 | 3,935 |
| 2015 | 3,459 | 3,890 | 4,041 | 5,262 | 7,026 | 3,762 | 3,803 |

1. All data are from the HIA Market Statistics found at www.hia.ie. All data are at year-end.
2. The HHI is the sum of squared market shares in the market. It is the most commonly used measure of market structure (see Gaynor and Town, 2011). An HHI of greater than 2,500 is usually taken as demonstrating that the market is highly concentrated for the purposes of competition reviews (Federal Trade Commission, 2010). For comparison data for the Netherlands and United States see Kaiser Family Foundation (2011).
[a]We present population-weighted averages for all insurers using the market age profile by age band for 2015.

## 12.3   HEALTH PLAN PAYMENT DESIGN

This section outlines some of the important design issues affecting the health insurance market in Ireland. I begin by considering the role of community rating. I then consider risk equalization, and finally discuss how these two tactics work to establish risk solidarity in the market.

**TABLE 12.5 Select Measures of Competition in the Irish Health Insurance Market, 2010–17**

| Measure | Description |
| --- | --- |
| Profit margin[a] as % of earned premium | Range 1.4%–5.0% for 12 months to end December 2015. Market average 2.1% |
| Number of insurers | Year 2010: 3 |
| | Year 2017: 3 |
| Number of insurers for 50th percentile[a] | Year 2010: 1 |
| | Year 2017: 1 |
| Concentration levels for 75th percentile[b] | Year 2010: 2 |
| | Year 2017: 2 |
| Entry/exit | Over the period 2010–17, one insurer has entered the market as a start-up (GloHealth) in 2012. In 2016 two insurers were jointly and separately bought by Irish Life (a subsidiary of Great West Lifeco). Furthermore, the second largest insurer (Laya Healthcare) was sold to AIG over the period |
| Number of health plans[c] | Year 2010: 187 health plans |
| | Year 2017 (July): 313 health plans |

[a]*This is defined as the number of insurers that cover 50% of the market ranking the largest to the smallest insurer by market size.*
[b]*This is defined as the number of insurers that cover 75% of the market ranking the largest to the smallest insurer by market size.*
[c]*Source HIA various Annual Reports.*

## 12.3.1 Role of Community Rating as a Form of Premium Regulation

As already indicated, successive Irish governments have believed that private health insurance provides an important substitute for funding health care. By encouraging more people to purchase private health insurance, less pressure is placed on the public system with respect to the financing and delivery of services. However, risk rating of premiums, which would arise in an unregulated market, would lead to high, possibly unaffordable premiums for high-risk groups. Community rating is used as a risk-solidarity mechanism to channel subsidies to high-risk consumers from low-risk consumers. Community rating applies on a per plan (health plan) basis; in other words, each plan must be community-rated, but different plans can have different (community-rated) premiums.

There are no explicit income-related premium subsidies within the system. Instead, as outlined above, the government funds a portion of the premium through capped tax credits, effecting an implicit transfer (due to Ireland's progressive tax structure) from higher- to lower-income groups.

As is well known, community rating means that healthier groups are charged premiums above their expected costs. In a voluntary system, healthier individuals can choose to purchase, delay, or opt not to purchase health insurance.[21] The potential problems have been widely discussed in the economic literature and have been well-documented elsewhere (Buchmueller and DiNardo, 2002; Hartedny, 1994; Turner and Shinnick, 2013; Van de Ven, 2006). Community rating raises a threat of a troubling dynamic. As younger consumers react to high premiums and leave the market, the risk pool worsens and the community rate goes up, pushing yet more of the good risks to leave. In the extreme, this can lead to a "death spiral" in which the market disappears altogether (Cutler and Reber, 1998).

A number of case studies document these phenomena in a number of health insurance markets (Luft et al., 1985; Cutler and Zeckhauser, 1997; Lo Sasso and Lurie, 2009). Particularly relevant to Ireland is Buchmueller (2008) who indicated in the Australian private health insurance market that, prior to the introduction of penalties for individuals delaying purchase of health insurance, there were indications of adverse selection. Specifically, the private health insurance pool was older than the general Australian population. Australia and Ireland share many features of their private health insurance markets. Turner and Shinnick (2013) argue that, in Ireland, on balance, community rating of premiums has increased demand for private health insurance and reduced the burden on the public health system.

Mandating enrollment is one way to address adverse selection caused by community rating, a strategy adopted, with partial success, in the United States as part of the Affordable Care Act. Consistent with this approach and in response to the risk of adverse selection, a number of measures were introduced from May 2015.

1. Insurers have been allowed to provide, on a discretionary basis, a discount to younger persons aged 18−24 years up to a maximum of 50% of the adult rate.
2. Insurers can give up to a 10% discount on the adult premium to individuals who are part of group schemes. Insurers can select which groups can receive this discount, giving them a tool by which to accomplish risk selection at the group level.
3. A form of lifetime community rating has been introduced, under which consumers are penalized by higher premiums if they choose not to enroll after a threshold age. This penalty encourages younger, lower-risk individuals to purchase health insurance earlier in their lives. At present, the penalty applies from age 35 at a rate of 2% for each year of postponement to a maximum of 70%. This mechanism is similar to that of Australia's market.

The goal of these changes was to encourage enrollment in private health insurance by these younger age groups given the voluntary nature of the market, and the potential for them to opt out of the market when charged community-rated premiums.

## 12.3.2 Risk Equalization

### 12.3.2.1 History of Risk Equalization

As outlined earlier, the Health Insurance Act of 1994 made arrangements for the introduction of a risk equalization scheme. The power to introduce such a scheme was provided to the Minister for Health and the Act also envisaged the establishment of an independent regulator to administer the scheme. In their guide to risk equalization the HIA (2016c)[22] show that the current risk equalization evolved over a number of waves of reform from 1996 onwards.

### Period 1996–2000

In 1996, the Minister for Health issued the regulations to set out the terms of risk equalization and the circumstances in which transfers between insurers would commence. At the time, the proposed scheme was based upon 16 age–gender risk classes and differences in utilization rates among insurers (Armstrong, 2010). So, e.g., if the utilization rate for the market was 40% within a given age–gender risk group, the normative costs for all insurers would be calculated on the basis of having a 40% utilization rate. Of course, this meant that, with a small number of insurers making up the market average, any efficiencies (or inefficiencies) in the claims and provider management practices of one insurer would feed back into the market average, potentially affecting incentives for efficiency. Differences in utilization arising from risk profiles (not accounted for by age and gender) would also affect market averages. In effect, this payment system incorporated a high level of risk sharing, in the sense that the more a plan spent, the more the plan was paid.

The scheme also placed a monetary threshold for the level of risk equalization transfers that were needed among insurers before the scheme would apply. The logic for this monetary threshold was that, in an environment where market entry and competition among insurers was just commencing against the historic monopoly position of Vhi, it was anticipated that risk transfers would be paid by the new entrants and discourage their participation. This could, however, lead to efficiency problems as entering insurers might attempt to profit from selecting healthier members.

Bupa Ireland entered the market in 1997 as the first competitor to Vhi. By 2004, Bupa Ireland had approximately 400,000 members (a market share of approximately 21%) and the average "equalized benefit" cost per person was approximately 63% of the market average for the 6-month period July to December 2004 (HIA, 2005).[23]

No transfers were made under the 1996 risk equalization scheme given significant controversy about the rationale and logic for risk equalization, and the Minister for Health revoked the scheme prior to implementation. There then followed a period of public "consultation on the future of health insurance risk equalization" in Ireland and the publication of a number of expert reports advising on the nature of any new risk equalization scheme (HIA, 2016).[24] All of the reports reaffirmed the necessity of having a risk equalization system to support community rating and deter risk selection.

## Period 2001–2008

One of the key tasks of the HIA, established in 2001, was to create and administer a new risk equalization scheme. A new scheme was proposed in July 2003. The scheme had its genesis in the original 1996 scheme but included a number of important modifications. These modifications included a mechanism under which the Minister of Health, with the advice of the HIA, would decide if and when risk equalization transfers would commence.

In addition, while age and gender continued to be used as risk adjusters, the utilization-based factor outlined above was modified so that only up to 50% of differences among risk profiles resulting from this factor were used in determining transfers.[25] Though this modification cut the degree of risk sharing in the payment system, a considerable degree of risk sharing remained.[26]

These modifications introduced a degree of subjectivity and administrative discretion into the risk equalization mechanism. First, the industry regulator now had the role of recommending to the Minister for Health whether risk equalization should commence based upon possible consideration of wider issues relating to the extent of competition within the market. Second, the Minister for Health could separately decide whether to follow the recommendation of the industry regulator. These elements of administrative discretion created another channel by which potential new entrants, who were opposed to risk equalization, might attempt to limit transfers.

It was not until the end of 2005 that the Minister and the HIA agreed to commence transfers under this scheme. However, again, no transfers ever took place under this scheme as Bupa Ireland commenced a number of legal challenges to the risk equalization scheme in both the Irish and European courts. The grounds for the legal challenges were based upon a range of legal and economic arguments. These included:

1. **Risk equalization is a form of state aid** as it involves financial transfers from some insurers to the largest private insurer in the market, namely the Vhi, which is a quasi-state body.

2. Risk equalization interferes with the property rights of the shareholders of contributing insurers;
3. The risk equalization mechanism used was inappropriate, disproportionate, and unfair to the contributing insurer; and;
4. The Minister for Health went outside their legal powers in introducing such a system.

Legal challenges took place in the Irish High Court (the second highest court) and the Irish Supreme Court together with the European Court of First Instance. Both Irish and European courts decided in favor of the use of risk equalization (Armstrong, 2010). However, the Irish Supreme Court decided that the Minister went outside their powers in introducing the 2003 risk equalization scheme and, therefore, further changes were needed to be undertaken to the proposed risk equalization scheme. The challenges effectively delayed, for many years, the commencement of any monetary risk equalization transfers among insurers (Armstrong, 2010).

### Period 2009 onwards

To move forward, the Irish Government rapidly introduced a new risk equalization scheme. The scheme was significantly altered to avoid the risks of legal challenge. Furthermore, the Irish Government sought the approval of the European Commission to limit any possibility of challenge in the European Courts. An initial version of the scheme was introduced in 2009 on an interim basis. The current system took shape in 2013,[27] and consists of two parts:

1. First, a scheme under which risk-related prospective payments are made to insurers (equating to approximately 80% of plan payments (HIA, 2016b p. 37); and
2. Second, a cost-sharing mechanism under which a fixed payment is made to each insurer for each inpatient night a patient spends in hospital or for each hospital day-case episode.

### 12.3.2.2  Payment Flows Under the 2013 Risk Equalization System

Fig. 12.1 provides an overview of the financing arrangements for health insurance since 2013. As outlined previously, subject to a limited number of exceptions, all insured persons pay a community-rated premium to their insurer. This premium is used to meet the cost of benefit payments by their insurer. Separately, each insurer pays a flat stamp duty for each insured person to the Irish tax authorities who pass it to the Risk Equalization Fund administered by the industry regulator, the HIA. This stamp duty funds the risk equalization payments calculated on a prospective basis among insurers. Disbursements are made from the Fund to each insurer based upon a number of risk adjusters.

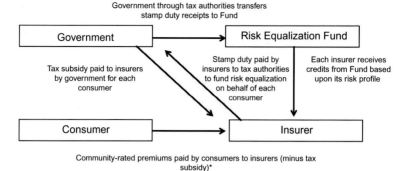

FIGURE 12.1    Financing scheme under the Irish Health Insurance Act.

Separately, all consumers receive a tax subsidy towards the cost of their health insurance. This subsidy is the lesser of €200 per adult or 20% of the gross cost of the premium per adult and is made directly from the tax authorities to insurers. While the tax subsidy thus varies by person, the premium for all persons after the tax subsidy remains the same (i.e., community rating is defined after the tax subsidy).

Total gross earned premium in the year 2015 within the market for the nonoccupational-based schemes amounted to €2,353 million (HIA, 2016b) and in the year 2016 to €2,402 million (HIA, 2017c). The HIA projected information for the risk equalization scheme for policies commencing in the 12-month period ending March 31, 2018 and, as part of this, estimated that the stamp duty receipts would be €719.4 million.[28] Separately, the author's own estimate suggests income tax relief during the year 2016 was between €330 and €335 million.[29]

### 12.3.2.3   Risk Adjusters

The current risk equalization system uses age, gender, and level of cover as risk adjusters to determine transfers under risk equalization. For the purposes of risk equalization, the level of cover refers to whether a health plan is classified as either a "nonadvanced" or "advanced" type of contract. The determination of whether a health plan is either "nonadvanced" or "advanced" depends upon whether the health plan in question provides a level of indemnity of more than 66% of cover for private hospital accommodation.

The legislation underpinning the Irish risk equalization scheme sets out eight age classes for both males and females and the two types of cover categories. Thus, there are 32 risk groups in the Irish risk equalization system. The age bands used are 50–54 years, 55–59 years, 60–64 years, 65–69 years, 70–74 years, 75–79 years, 80–84 years, and 80 years and over.

A number of important elements to this design need to be noted:

- The legislation explicitly excludes any risk transfers for individuals within the 0−49 age range. The principal logic for this exclusion is that to include them would make the monetary-based stamp duty much greater, and, given there are no indicators for illnesses, the variability in health costs among young people is relatively small. Furthermore, at present, no transfers are made for persons aged between 50 and 64 years as the HIA has determined that the relative risk profile of the group is identical among insurers and including transfers for this group would increase the required level of stamp duty.
- The use of a type of cover as a risk factor reflects two considerations. First, greater coverage tends to cause higher utilization among persons with a given risk profile, and it was decided not to have this systematic higher cost being reflected in premiums to enrollees through risk equalization. Second, higher-risk persons may select the plans with better coverage, and this selection may not be fully captured by the age and gender adjusters. Including coverage as an adjuster goes against the classic model of regulated competition, under which consumers pay higher premiums for cover beyond the standard level of benefit (Enthoven, 1988), although the metal level of plan in the US Marketplaces also bases transfers partly on the level of coverage.

### 12.3.2.4 Estimation Procedure for Risk Equalization Subsidies

**Risk Equalization Payments**

The payments (referred to as credits) provided under the scheme are updated annually upon approval by the Irish Parliament following a recommendation to the Minister for Health by the HIA. In determining its recommendation, the HIA reviews the relevant profile of consumers in the market and their claims experience based upon returns submitted by the open market insurers every 6 months. The HIA projects the average costs for each risk group together with the market profile of risks for the next 12-month risk equalization projection period. Assumptions are made regarding changes in the risk profile of the market and for utilization and medical cost inflation over time.

In simple terms, the risk subsidy for each risk group is calculated from the projected average cost of that risk group compared to the overall average cost across all risk groups. Adjustments are made to the calculation to ensure that, first, no subsidies are derived for risk groups for which no subsidy is to be paid (i.e., currently the 0−64 age groups) and, second that the requirements from the European Commission that the level of subsidy within a given risk group cannot exceed a certain threshold. This second requirement arises because, in order to receive approval from the European Commission for the current risk equalization scheme, the Commission required that the net cost (post risk equalization) in any risk class shall not be more than 125% of the average net cost across all groups.[30]

Regression techniques are not used to determine the level of subsidies. Instead, the calculation involves projecting average risk costs in each risk group, using market-wide historic average risk costs in each risk group and assumed levels of cost increases, and then calculating the subsidy in that group as being the difference between the expected cost for that risk group and the overall risk cost. This calculation is subject to the constraints outlined previously that no subsidy applies for all age groups below age 65 years.

There are also a significant number of judgments that the HIA must make to perform these calculations. For example:

1. Determining the expected rate of cost increase between the base period of data and the projection period.
2. Determining the take-up of health insurance in each risk group in the projection period.
3. Determining how the calculation should work for risk groups with few members and where an average cannot be reliably estimated. For example, there may be few individuals in a given age/gender risk group who have a particular type of cover.[31]

Box 12.2 provides a simplified example of how this part of the system operates.

## Hospital Utilization Payments

In addition to the risk equalization payments outlined above, the remaining approximately 20% of payments are made through a utilization based cost- or risk-sharing payment to each insurer based upon the experience of its insured population in hospitals. A fixed monetary payment is made per day in the case of inpatient treatment or per stay in the case of day-case ambulatory treatment. As of April 2018, these payments are €100 for each overnight stay in hospital and €50 for each day-case admission to hospital. While this is accepted to be a crude measure by policy-makers, its use has been justified given the lack of available data for a more sophisticated, health status-type measure. The levels of fixed payments have been set to contribute in small part towards the cost of such care but are still a low percentage of the full cost of the treatment. At present, the fixed contributions are less than 15% of the cost of the treatment, so the contribution is modest.[32]

A separate projection is made of the cost of providing the hospital utilization credit. The credit is paid retrospectively based upon actual utilization in past periods, though the projection is used in order to determine the stamp duty required to fund the credit. In making the projection, estimates are made of the expected numbers of inpatient nights and day-case episodes

---

**BOX 12.2 A simplified example of the calculation of risk equalization credits in Ireland**

*Assume:*

1. During the risk equalization projection period, there will be 10,000 insured lives, with 60% of them aged less than 65 years and 40% aged 65 years and over;
2. The average projected cost per person aged 0–64 years will be €500; for persons over 65 years the average cost per person will be €1,500, and;
3. Only for the purposes of this simplified example risk equalization is only based upon age and not by gender/type of cover or health utilization.
4. Risk equalization payments are set so as to ensure that the total cost of the credits and the revenues from stamp duties are matched (i.e., budget neutrality).

*Calculations of credits and stamp duty:*

1. The overall projected average cost of claims = (500 × 0.6 + 1500 × 0.4) = €900 per person.
2. The first-stage risk equalization payment to be given to the age group 65 years and over is therefore = €600 = €1500 − €900.
3. As under the Irish risk equalization system, no payments are given for persons under 65 years.
4. Total size of risk equalization subsidies for the differential for the average cost of claims overall = (4000) × (600) = €2,400,000.
5. The cost of the stamp duty must also be subsidized under risk equalization for those persons 65 years and older. This is notated by the letters *SD*.
6. The total cost of the credits is therefore the sum of these the two parts (identified in steps 4 and 5) = (4000 *SD* + €2,400,000).
7. The total revenue received from the stamp duty = 10,000 × *SD*.
8. Setting the total cost of the credits equal to the total revenues received from the stamp duty (to ensure the budget neutrality condition is met) the unit cost of the stamp duty is calculated as €400 per person.
9. This gives a total credit for persons 65 years and over of €1,000.

*Check on answers:*

1. Claims plus stamp duty minus risk equalization payment for persons less than 65 years = €500 + €400 + €0 = €900.
2. Claims plus stamp duty minus risk equalization payment of persons 65 years and over = €1500 − €1000 + €400 = €900 (the market average cost).

---

during the projected period. Using an assumed level of compensation per inpatient night or for each day-case episode[33] the total expected payments for this utilization variable are estimated. The basis for the calculation of the fixed monetary compensation has not been set out in legislation and is left to the Irish Parliament to choose, with the recommendation of the Minister for Health and the HIA.

### Required Stamp Duty Payments

A stamp duty is collected from each insurer for each person insured with them to fund the overall cost of both the age/gender/type of cover risk-sharing payments and the hospital utilization (cost-sharing) payments. The stamp duty varies depending upon whether the person is an adult or a child (i.e., less than 18 years with limited exceptions) and the type of cover they choose (i.e., "nonadvanced" or "advanced" cover).[34]

### 12.3.2.5  Implementation and Maintenance

The Irish Parliament must approve the level of subsidies (risk equalization payments) and stamp duties. The process for approval by Parliament normally ends in December of the preceding year in the case of payments to be implemented for health insurance contracts renewed or taken up from April onwards of each year.[35] Before a proposal is made to Parliament, the industry regulator, the HIA, carries out the required technical analysis and issues a report to the Minister for Health (normally in October) with a recommendation as to the required levels of subsidies and stamp duty for the following year. The Minister can accept this recommendation or not and bring forward legislative change as he/she believes is appropriate.

## 12.3.3  Risk Sharing

There are two forms of explicit risk sharing in the Irish health plan payment system.

### 12.3.3.1  Hospital Utilization Credit

This credit, discussed above, can be considered to be a form of risk-sharing mechanism given its retrospective nature.

### 12.3.3.2  Overcompensation

A second risk-sharing mechanism within the risk equalization scheme is oriented to insurers that are net beneficiaries from risk equalization to check whether there may have been overcompensation.[36] The HIA using ex-post analysis of the financial performance of insurers determines whether the return received by an insurer exceeds a "reasonable profit." For the purposes of the current scheme, this normalized return is considered to be greater than a profit margin of 4.4% (gross of any reinsurance and excluding investment income) over a 3-year period. If the HIA finds that there has been overcompensation, the overcompensated health insurance undertaking must repay the amount of the overcompensation to the Risk Equalization Fund (managed by the HIA). Such an arrangement is similar, in effect, to a one-sided risk corridor with no shared savings for the plan after exceeding the threshold of profits. The Affordable Care Act (ACO) in the US operates primarily one-sided risk corridors, but the threshold is defined in terms of risk-adjusted costs, not profits, and some shared savings remain for the ACO after the cost threshold is crossed.

## 12.4  EVALUATION OF RISK EQUALIZATION (HEALTH PLAN PAYMENT)

Each year, as part of their review of the market, the HIA evaluates both the quantitative performance of the market and also presents an analysis of current developments. This section briefly presents some recent findings on these topics.

### 12.4.1  Evaluation of the Payment System

Before making a recommendation, the HIA engages actively with each of the insurers and, with actuarial input, undertakes a review of market data, including evaluating the assumptions that were used in determining the previous year's recommendation. More substantive changes to the structure of the risk equalization system are considered through the engagement of the Department of Health and the HIA with insurers and other stakeholders.

Unfortunately, given commercial considerations, data to evaluate the payment system are difficult to access and no published data are available regarding the fit of payments to costs, such as that which would be measured by an $R$-squared from either the risk equalization part or the utilization-based, risk-sharing components.

One measure that is often used to determine the effectiveness of risk equalization is whether there is ex-post (risk equalization) over- or undercompensation in each defined risk group. Fig. 12.2 presents these numbers for the most recent reported years for female consumers who purchased the advanced type of cover for each age cell.[37] It demonstrates that, after risk equalization for females in this level of cover, there continues to be significant potential gains from selecting average risks on an age basis, even for an average person within a risk cell.[38] It also shows that there are some age cells for which risk equalization does not sufficiently compensate.

These over-/undercompensations are caused by a number of factors. The most important factor is that the calculation only provides subsidies for certain ages, while the stamp duty is equal across age groups. If the stamp duty was to vary by age band then it would be possible to avoid such a scenario, though having a stamp duty varying by age would significantly add to complicating the risk equalization system. As a consequence of the current approach, the health cost–risk curve is not flat across age groups.

One approach to avoid over-/undercompensation would be to provide subsidies across all risk groups. However, extending subsidies to all groups

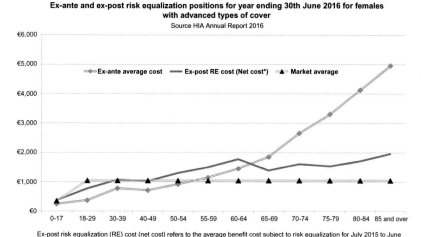

Ex-post risk equalization (RE) cost (net cost) refers to the average benefit cost subject to risk equalization for July 2015 to June 2016, plus the risk equalization stamp duty for that age/type of cover less the age/gender/type of cover and hospital utilization credits for renewals from 1 march 2016 onwards

**FIGURE 12.2**    Measuring the ex-post risk equalization position.

would require a substantial change in the stamp duty level of payments to fund the risk equalization mechanism.

The measure presented here is informative but is far from a comprehensive review of the effectiveness of the risk equalization scheme. In research on other countries, most checks for group-level performance are related to disease groups, not simply age and gender. Nonetheless, it does present an indication of the strong incentive for selection of healthy people within each age/gender cell in the absence of proper health status risk adjustment. Unfortunately there is no published evidence on the extent to which this occurs.

It is also clear from recent reports of the HIA that there is considerable variation in the risk profile and claims experience of the market from 1 year to the next (HIA, 2015, 2016b, 2017b) potentially leading to considerable uncertainty as to whether calculated risk equalization payments will be appropriate in future periods in a given age cell. For example, the 2016 report highlights that overall claims paid by insurers in the first half of 2016 grew 10.5% compared to the same period in 2015 (HIA, 2016b, p. 16).

While the growth in claim payments between periods does not necessarily mean that the variation between insurers' risk profiles is changing over time, it can still have a significant impact on the absolute level of risk equalization transfers between periods and it demonstrates the importance of assumptions used in the calculation of the payments. For example, the overall market growth in claims costs between periods is used as a central assumption to calculate the risk equalization payments into the future.

Such growth between periods may not affect all risk cells equally, introducing additional uncertainty into the calculation of prospective payments. It may also reflect the fact that the overall growth in claims costs may differ among insurers, which may be indicative of many other factors that need to be considered by the regulator in calculating the prospective payments, such as changes in the risk profile of individual insurers, changes in the benefits provided to consumers from one period to the next, and changes in reimbursement arrangements of individual insurers with particular providers over time.

More generally under the Irish risk equalization system, with only a small number of insurers and particularly with one having a significant market share, if an insurer spends one more euro in any given risk cell in a given market average the level of subsidies within that cell will increase. This is another important example of risk sharing within the Irish system.

## 12.4.2   Monitoring of Risk Selection

There are a number of ways in which risk selection could occur within the Irish health insurance market. Of course, disentangling risk selection from efficient behavior of insurers is difficult (Van de Ven et al., 2017). Nonetheless, examples of ways in which insurers might seek to attempt to engage in risk selection include the choice of benefits to cover, the use of deductibles, the use of health plan proliferation (i.e., introducing more plans with similar levels of benefit but at significantly different price points—see below) that may make it difficult for individuals to make informed choices as to the suitability of individual health plans, changing prices regularly on individual health plans, and selective contracting on health providers. It is clear from the annual report to the Minister compiled by the HIA that all of these tactics have been used in the Irish market (HIA, Reports to Minister, 2010–2017e). Specific details on some of them are outlined below.

### 12.4.2.1   Health Plan Proliferation and Health Plan Development

Both the number of health plans provided and the type of product development within the market provide evidence of potential risk selection in the market. An insurer developing a new health plan can target benefits and premiums that are attractive to a very specific favorable profile of risks for a defined period. For example, an insurer may have a health plan that is priced very competitively that is only available for customers during certain months of the year and is uncompetitive at other periods of the year. The HIA has reported that insurers continue to develop more and more health plans that provide cover attractive to younger and healthier customers but less attractive to older, less healthy customers (HIA, 2017b, 2016b). They also report that this, along with the greater reluctance amongst older people to change health plan/insurer and the fact that older customers are likely to have health plans with higher benefits, has resulted in older consumers paying, on average, significantly higher premiums than younger people, as shown in Table 12.6. This is symptomatic of risk selection behavior of insurers based upon competition to attract preferred risks rather than on the basis of efficiency.

These behaviors and outcomes not only raise significant challenges for risk solidarity within the market but they also reveal some issues relating to consumer choice and transparency. The greater the volume and complexity of health plans, the more difficult it is for consumers to make informed choices.[39]

### 12.4.2.2    Greater Use of Deductibles

The industry regulator reports that plans with higher deductibles (referred to as excesses in Ireland) of up to €500 for private hospitals are becoming more popular with consumers. They do not report any data as to what risk groups these are popular with, but it is known from other research that high deductible plans tend to be more popular with low-risk groups (Van de Ven and Van Praag, 1981; Van Winssen et al., 2017).

**TABLE 12.6** Average Premium per Person by Age Band, 2013−15 in Euros[a]

| Age band | 2013 | 2014 | 2015 |
|---|---|---|---|
| 0−17 | 1147 | 1242 | 1324 |
| 18−29 | 1310 | 1231 | 1139 |
| 30−39 | 1359 | 1272 | 1148 |
| 40−49 | 1431 | 1332 | 1202 |
| 50−54 | 1578 | 1457 | 1320 |
| 55−59 | 1734 | 1601 | 1458 |
| 60−64 | 1890 | 1735 | 1595 |
| 65−69 | 2041 | 1874 | 1744 |
| 70−74 | 2131 | 1984 | 1888 |
| 75−79 | 2206 | 2062 | 1993 |
| 80−84 | 2260 | 2133 | 2098 |
| 85 and over | 2289 | 2173 | 2170 |
| Overall | 1147 | 1242 | 1324 |

[a]The difference in average premiums by age band is not because of risk rating but results from the fact that older consumers are found in higher-priced health plans more often than younger consumers.
Source: Society of Actuaries in Ireland, 2016. Inflationary pressures in the Irish Private Health Insurance market, available at www.actuaries.ie.

## 12.5 ONGOING ISSUES AND REFORM

The conclusions from the experience of Ireland can be summarized as follows.

First, the experience of Ireland would suggest that it is possible to introduce risk equalization even in a voluntary health insurance environment in spite of considerable challenges to its adoption. Regulators, if they do not succeed at first, may need to modify the arrangements to fit the legal and regulatory requirements of the country.

Second, while introducing risk equalization is obviously an important first step, the risk equalization formula needs improvement to more fully respond to risk selection actions of insurers. This has not been done sufficiently in Ireland, as of yet, and there are a range of important changes required in the risk equalization system to improve its functioning.

Third, community rating should be reconsidered as a basis of premium setting. Community rating poses problems, particularly in a voluntary health insurance market, when insurers have tools for risk selection. While removing community rating completely may not be politically acceptable, removing community rating for benefits provided on health plans in excess of what is considered to be meaningful, from a solidarity perspective, seems logical. To do this, of course, a standardized benefit package would need to be developed. Moreover, a complete shift to risk rating with risk-related cross-subsidies could be considered.

Ireland has a long history of using premium rate regulation and health plan payments (risk equalization) in a voluntary health insurance market with competition while facilitating consumer choice (Armstrong, 2010) to meet over-arching solidarity goals, and the Irish experience may be relevant to other countries (Armstrong et al., 2010a,b). In particular, it is relevant for countries with a developed, voluntary health insurance market attempting to limit risk selection and increase affordability to meet over-arching health policy goals (e.g., the United States), while facilitating consumer choice, and who are likely to need to grapple with the same challenges that have occurred in Ireland. It is also relevant, more generally, for countries attempting to introduce more elements of "regulated" or "managed competition" within their health system.

It has taken many years for risk equalization to become embedded in the health insurance system in Ireland. There are still a number of important challenges to consider in terms of its future development, including the need for improving the risk adjustment methodology, improving the ability to monitor risk selection in the market, and considering the linkages between community rating and risk equalization. These issues are considered below.

### 12.5.1 Improving the Risk Adjustment Methodology

#### 12.5.1.1 Improving the Risk Adjusters

A more sophisticated system of risk equalization needs to be introduced that would allow for more accurate predictions of health expenditure, thereby reducing the incentive for risk selection. An immediate example would be to introduce a health status measure in line with international approaches. To implement a health status risk adjuster, significant extra morbidity-related data would need to be collected. This has proved challenging to establish. The balance for regulators in introducing new risk adjusters will be to ensure that insurers are encouraged to adopt behaviors that are innovative in terms of their engagement with medical providers and the benefit design, while protecting risk solidarity.

### 12.5.1.2 Use of Type of Cover Risk Adjuster

The type of cover as a risk adjuster needs reconsideration. If it were to be removed to discourage risk selection, consumers on nonadvanced health plans would end up paying a higher stamp duty to fund the risk equalization payments and, thus, at least from an actuarial perspective, it would lead to higher premiums for these nonadvanced health plans. While premiums for the advanced level of health plans should correspondingly decrease, in a voluntary health insurance market there is a risk that lower-risk consumers opt out of the market, thereby destabilizing the market.

### 12.5.1.3 Moving to a Statistical Approach to Calculating Subsidies

It is clear that moving to a more sophisticated, statistical basis for the calculation of risk equalization payments has an important part to play in developing more accurate risk equalization.

### 12.5.1.4 Removing the Subjectivity From the Risk Equalization Calculations

As presented above, there are still a considerable number of subjective elements in the Irish equalization system. By reducing the number of subjective elements within the system it could lead to greater transparency and reduce the possibility of challenge relating to the system.

## 12.5.2 Monitoring Risk Selection

Risk selection is inherently difficult to monitor. The use of regression analysis would allow regulators to identify factors that affect risk within a given risk equalization risk category. However, it would allow insurers to identify better factors that would facilitate risk selection also. It is the case that there would probably be variables that would not be considered to be appropriate for risk equalization purposes that may allow insurers to identify preferred risk groups (e.g., lifestyle groups). A debate similar to that occurring internationally is needed to determine the appropriate risk factors for the purposes of risk equalization (Van de Ven and Ellis, 2000). This gets to the heart of the blurred lines between risk selection and efficiency outlined by McGuire et al. (2014).

### 12.5.3 Reconsideration of Community Rating

There is a need for further discussion as to the benefits of retaining community rating in its current form. Although community rating is popular politically and is readily understood by consumers, it can encourage adverse selection by consumers and risk selection by insurers, as discussed by Armstrong (2010).

The introduction of penalties for delayed purchase of health insurance was an important starting point in its reform. However, as a next step the range of health plans that are subject to community rating needs to be reconsidered. It makes no sense for supplemental insurance health plans to have community rating, even if community rating is to be retained for the publicly regulated level of health plan. To introduce a publicly regulated level of health plan, a formal level of standard health plan would need to be introduced.

More generally, as discussed by Van de Ven (2006), it is necessary to consider whether the alternative of risk-rated premiums combined with risk-related subsidies may be more effective in meeting solidarity goals. In the case of Ireland, risk rating would encourage consumers to shop around more actively for their health insurance. It would also remove the incentive for health plan proliferation that undermines the basis for risk solidarity.

### DISCLAIMER

The author has previously worked for two of the insurers currently operating in the Irish health insurance market—namely the Voluntary Health Insurance Board (Vhi) and Aviva Health Insurance Ireland now part of Irish Life Health. He was been centrally involved in both the discussions and court cases surrounding the regulation of the health insurance market in Ireland for the period 1995–2016.

### ENDNOTES

1. A statutory organization in Ireland is a state organization subject to oversight by the Irish Parliament and with no shareholders.
2. Successive Ministers refused to grant such licenses until required to do so under European Union Directives in the mid-1990s, with the exception of limited permissions being given for some occupational-type schemes serving, principally, the Irish police and prison services and the national electricity company.
3. When competition was introduced health insurers with the exception of Vhi had to meet the requirements of the Insurance Acts. This was changed for Vhi in 2015.

4. The term "private health insurance market" might seem unconventional to use given it was provided by a state organization and no competition was initially allowed, but it reflects the fact that government saw health insurance as being principally available to individuals who privately funded their own premiums. Furthermore, from the date of Ireland joining the European Union in 1973 (then referred to as the European Economic Community) health insurance in Ireland was considered to be an insurance market under the Third Non-Life Insurance Directive. For these reasons I will continue to use the phrase "private health insurance market."

5. To give an indication of the effect of this change the current standard rate of tax is 20% while the highest marginal rate is 40%.

6. Source: Central Statistics Office (2016).

7. Those entitled to "free care" are said to have what is called a "medical card."

8. The thresholds are set based upon the income level of the family and also the family status, number of children, and age of the adults and they vary between hospital and primary care. Income is defined as gross income less income taxes and various other social security-related contributions. For example for hospital care, the income threshold for a single person aged less than 66 years is €184 per week and for a couple where the adults were under age 66 years the combined threshold is €266.50 per week. Further allowances are made for dependent children (Citizens Information, 2018).

9. Market practice is that the type of cost-sharing mechanism used depends upon the type of benefit. For example, diagnostic services typically are based on a coinsurance arrangement, while general practitioner benefits are most usually based upon either coinsurance or defined benefit up to a monetary benefit ceiling.

10. The cost-sharing mechanisms are typically referred to as "excesses" in Ireland and apply as fixed monetary amounts (i.e., deductibles) or on the basis of a percentage of the cost of the treatment (i.e., coinsurance).

11. To provide an indication of their significance these deductibles are typically between €75 and 150 per hospital episode and only apply to treatment received in private hospitals.

12. These are calculated from data available on the website of the HIA.

13. Limited exceptions are made to community rating for certain risk groups. For example, the premium for children should be no more than 50% of the adult premium. Furthermore, a discount of up to 10% is permissible for group of individuals joining together to purchase health insurance business. There are no restrictions as to how these groups of individuals join together.

14. Since 2001, insurers have been allowed to separately sell ancillary health plans that are not subject to the minimum benefit requirements on a standalone basis. These ostensibly cover primary care benefits and do not cover hospital benefits.

15. The exceptions apply to what have historically been perceived as the most sophisticated hospitals which have normally been measured as being the most expensive hospitals for the insurer.

16. This is an interesting development, but it is too early to assess its effectiveness as either a tool for risk selection or as a method of managing costs for insurers.

17. Because minimum benefits have not been updated since their introduction in 1996, the level of minimum benefit, with the exception of public hospital coverage, represents a small proportion of the actual current cost of the care and, therefore, for practical purposes there is a limited constraint on the extent to which deductible (cost-sharing) mechanisms can apply.

18. Figures published in May 2017 suggested that the average premium in 2016 was only marginally higher at €1,177 per person (HIA, 2017e).

19. While this is an imperfect measure, the way in which the market is organized makes the use of HHI by age band a reasonable indicator of the extent of competition across risk groups. The largest employers, which have the lowest risk profile, tend to have the youngest age profiles.

20. The aggregate level of profitability (ex-post risk equalization) has been published in various publications over the years including by the European Commission (2013) and in the HIA Reports to the Minister for Health (2012–2017).
21. Evidence presented to the Oireachtas Committee on Health would suggest this is the case (Armstrong and Aviva Health, 2014).
22. Comprehensive guides to the various versions of risk equalization in Ireland are provided in multiple HIA documents (HIA 2003, 2008, 2013b, 2016c, 2017b).
23. "Equalized benefit" was the term used to quantify the value of benefits that were subject to the risk equalization mechanism as some elements of the cost of claims for insurers were excluded from risk equalization.
24. Report of Advisory Group on Risk Equalization (1998), Department of Health (1999a,b).
25. Thus, for example, if in a given age and gender risk group the utilization rate was 40% for the market and the insurer's own utilization rate was 20% then normative costs for this insurer in the given risk group would be calculated using 30%, i.e. $0.5 \times (40\%) + 0.5 \times (20\%)$.
26. It cut the degree of risk sharing by less than half because, with a small number of plans in the market, the spending of an individual health plan affects the market average, even without any risk sharing based on rates of utilization.
27. See "Guide to 2016–2020 Risk Equalization Scheme" (HIA, 2016c) for some more details on the current scheme not covered here.
28. This is the amount available for risk equalization transfers. Actual transfers in a year will differ from this slightly due to differences in the timing of inflows and outflows.
29. This is based upon data available in HIA (2016b) and HIA (2015).
30. This requirement is unusual in that the European Commission has brought in such a requirement for the Irish risk equalization scheme but not for any other scheme within other Member States. The logic of this stems from the previous legal challenges to risk equalization in Ireland and the fact that on a prima facia basis risk equalization payments may be considered a state aid under European Union competition rules.
31. For example, in practice, according to the Report of the HIA to the Minister 2016, the projected male membership as of April 1, 2018, for a nonadvanced level of cover will be 105 persons. This is not sufficiently credible from an actuarial perspective. Given the relatively few members, it is difficult to determine what should be the assumed average benefit costs for these members.
32. The fixed contributions as of April 1, 2018, are 100 per inpatient night and 50 per day-case episode. The cost charged to insurers per inpatient night is €813 for the basic level of coverage for most hospitals and 407 for a day-case episode.
33. A day-case episode refers to a day admission to a hospital where the patient is admitted and discharged on the same day.
34. A number of simplifying assumptions are made to determine the relative size of the stamp duty that applies for children versus adults and for nonadvanced compared to advanced types of cover. For example, it is currently assumed that the child stamp duty is one-third the cost of the adult stamp duty and that the stamp duty for nonadvanced coverage is 50% of that for advanced coverage.
35. From the year 2017, an implementation date of April 1 is being used. Previously the implementation date was March 1.
36. No corresponding calculation is made to assess whether undercompensation applies.
37. For the purposes of this measure the ex-ante position is defined as the overall average cost of benefits per person across all age cells less the average cost of benefits per person in each age cell. The ex-post position is defined as the overall average cost of benefits across all age cells less the average cost of benefits per benefits plus the cost of the stamp duty for each person in that age cell less the combined risk equalization credit and the utilization credit in that age cell.

38. For example, it appears that based on all ages over 55 years that the level of risk equalization compensation for females is, on average, insufficient to neutralize the differences in risk profiles between these ages and the overall market average position.

39. Many studies have considered the impact of consumer choice in health insurance. McGuire (2012) lists many of these studies and has a fuller discussion on this important topic. Such studies include Dafny et al (2013) and Bundorf et al. (2012). Of particular relevance here is the statement quoted by McGuire (2012, p. 380) from Leibman and Zeckhauser (2008) that "Health Insurance is too complicated a product for most consumers to purchase intelligently."

## REFERENCES

Armstrong, J., 2002. Overview of Health Insurance in Ireland, Paper compiled as a submission to European Union study on Voluntary Health Insurance in Europe.

Armstrong, J., 2010. Risk equalization in voluntary health insurance markets: the case of Ireland. Health Policy 98 (1), 15−26.

Armstrong, J., Aviva Health, 2014. Submission to Oireachtas Committee on Health, available at www.oireachtas.ie.

Armstrong, J., McCleod, H., Paolucci, F., van de Ven, W.P.M.M., 2010a. Risk equalization in voluntary health insurance markets. Health Policy 98 (1), 39−49.

Armstrong, J., Paolucci, F., van de Ven, W.P.M.M., 2010b. Risk equalization in voluntary health insurance markets: editorial. Health Policy 98 (1), 1−2.

Buchmueller, T., 2008. Adverse selection in private health insurance in Australia. The Geneva Papers on Risk and Insurance. Issues and Practice 33 (4), 588−609.

Buchmueller, T., DiNardo, J., 2002. Did community rating induce an adverse selection death spiral? Evidence from New York, Pennsylvania, and Connecticut. Am. Econ. Rev. 92 (1), 280−294.

Bundorf, M.K., Levin, J., Mahoney, N., 2012. Pricing and welfare in health plan choice. Am. Econ. Rev. 102, 3214−3248.

Central Statistics Office, 2016. National Health Accounts for Ireland. Available at www.cso.ie, Government of Ireland, Dublin.

Central Statistics Office (CSO), 2017. Figures taken from CSO website, Dublin. Available at www.cso.ie, viewed on 1 February 2017.

Citizens Information, 2018. Figures taken from CSO website. Available at www.citizensinformation.ie, viewed on 2 January 2018.

Colombo, F., Tapay, N., 2003. Private Health Insurance in Ireland: A Case Study, OECD Health Working Paper No. 10, 2003.

Cutler, D., Reber, S., 1998. Paying for Health Insurance: the trade-off between competition and adverse selection. Quart. J. Econ. 113 (2), 434−466.

Cutler, D., Zeckhauser, R., 1997. Adverse Selection in Health Insurance, NBER Working Paper No. 6107, National Bureau of Economic Research, Cambridge MA.

Dafny, L., Ho, K., Varela, M., 2013. Let them have choice: gains from shifting away from employer-sponsored health insurance and toward an individual exchange. Am. Econ. J. Econ. Policy 5 (1), 32−58.

Department of Health and Children, Government of Ireland, 1956. Speech by Minister Tom O'Higgins during Oireachtas debate on Voluntary Health Insurance Bill 1956. Government of Ireland, Dublin. Available at debates at http://www.oireachtas-debates.gov.ie/.

Department of Health, Government of Ireland, 1999a. White Paper on Private Medical Insurance. Government of Ireland, Dublin.

Department of Health, Government of Ireland, 1999b. Technical Paper on Risk Equalization. Government of Ireland, Dublin.

Department of Health, Government of Ireland, 2016. Speech by Minister Simon Harris during Oireachtas debate on Health Insurance (Amendment) Bill, 2016. Government of Ireland, Dublin.

Enthoven, A.C., 1988. Theory and practice of managed competition in health care finance, North Holland.

European Commission, 1992. Third Non Life Insurance Directive, Directive 92/49/EEC of 18 June 1992. European Commission, Brussels.

European Commission, 2013. State aid SA.34515 (2013/NN) – Ireland Risk equalisation scheme for 2013. Available at www.ec.europa.eu.

Federal Trade Commission (Department of Justice), 2010.Horizontal Merger Guidelines, available at https://www.ftc.gov/sites/default/files/attachments/merger-review/100819hmg.pdf.

Gaynor, M., Town, R., 2011. Competition in Health care markets, National Bureau of Economic Research Working Paper 17208, Available at: http://www.nber.org/papers/w17208; 1050 Massachusetts Avenue, Cambridge, MA 02138.

Hartedny, J.A., 1994. You can't buy insurance when the house is on fire. Postgrad. Med. 95 (7).

Health Insurance Act 1994 (subsequently amended in 2001) Debates at http://www.oireachtas-debates.gov.ie/, Government of Ireland, Dublin.

Health Insurance Authority, 2003. Guide to risk equalisation. Available at www.hia.ie.

Health Insurance Authority, 2005. Report to the Minister on Risk Equalisation for the period January to June 2005. Available at www.hia.ie.

Health Insurance Authority, 2008. Update Guide to the Risk Equalisation Scheme. Available at www.hia.ie.

Health Insurance Authority, 2010. Report to the Minister for Health and Children on Risk Equalisation. Available at www.health.gov.ie.

Health Insurance Authority, 2011. Report of the Health Insurance Authority to the Minister for Health in accordance with Section 7E 1(b) of the Health Insurance Acts 1994–2009. Available at www.health.gov.ie.

Health Insurance Authority, 2012. Report to the Minister for Health on the Evaluation and Analysis of Returns for 1 July 2011 to 30 June 2012 including advice on Risk Equalisation Credits. Available at www.health.gov.ie.

Health Insurance Authority, 2013a. Report to the Minister for Health on the Evaluation and Analysis of Returns for 1 July 2012 to 30 June 2013 including advice on Risk Equalisation Credits. Available at www.health.gov.ie.

Health Insurance Authority, 2013b. Guide to Risk Equalisation Scheme 2013. Available at www.hia.ie.

Health Insurance Authority, 2014. Report to the Minister for Health on the Evaluation and Analysis of Returns for 1 July 2013 to 30 June 2014 including advice on Risk Equalisation Credits. Available at www.health.gov.ie.

Health Insurance Authority, 2015. Report to the Minister for Health on the Evaluation and Analysis of Returns for 1 July 2014 to 30 June 2015 including advice on Risk Equalisation Credits. Available at www.health.gov.ie.

Health Insurance Authority, 2016a.Market Statistics 2016. Accessed on 29 December 2017. Available at www.hia.ie.

Health Insurance Authority, 2016b.Report to the Minister for Health on the Evaluation and Analysis of Returns for 1 July 2015 to 30 June 2016 including advice on Risk Equalisation Credits. Available at www.health.gov.ie.

Health Insurance Authority, 2016c. Guide to 2016 – 2020 RE Scheme. Available at www.hia.ie.

Health Insurance Authority (HIA), 2017a. Newsletter June 2017 Available at www.hia.ie.

Health Insurance Authority, 2017b. Report to the Minister for Health on the Evaluation and Analysis of Returns for 1 July 2016 to 30 June 2017 including advice on Risk Equalisation Credits. Available at www.health.gov.ie.

Health Insurance Authority, 2017c. Annual Report for 2016, available at www.hia.ie.

Health Insurance Authority, 2017d. Guide to Risk Equalisation Scheme 2017. Available at www.hia.ie.

Health Insurance Authority, 2017e. Newsletter, May 2017, available at www.hia.ie.

Health Insurance Authority / Millard Brown Consulting, 2015. Consumer survey on the Private Health Insurance Market in Ireland.

Health Services Executive (HSE), 2017. Figures taken from HSE website, Dublin. Available at www.hse.ie viewed on 1 February 2017.

Kaiser Family Foundation, 2011. How Competitive are State Insurance Markets Available at: https://kaiserfamilyfoundation.files.wordpress.com/2013/01/8242.pdf.

Leibman, J., Zeckhauser, R., 2008. Simple Humans, Complex Insurance, Subtle Subsidies. NBER Working Paper 14330. National Bureau of Economic Research, Cambridge MA.

Lo Sasso, A.T., Lurie, I.Z., 2009. Community rating and the market for private non-group health insurance. J. Public Econ. 93 (1–2), 264–279.

Luft, H.S., Traener, J.B., Maerki, S.C., 1985. Adverse selection in a large, multi-option health benefits program: a case study of the California public employees' retirement system. In: Scheffler, Richard M., Rossiter, Louis F. (Eds.), Advances in Health Economics and Health Services Research, Vol. 6. JAI Press, Greenwich, CT, pp. 197–230.

McGuire, T.G., 2012. Demand for health insurance. Handbook Econ. 2, 317–396. Elsevier.

McGuire, T.G., Newhouse, J.P., Normand, S.L., Shi, J., Zuvekas, S., 2014. Assessing incentives for service-level selection in private health insurance exchanges. J. Health Econ. 35, 47–63.

Nolan, B., 1991. The utilisation and financing of health services. ESRI General Research Series.

Nolan, B., 2006. The interaction of public and private health insurance: Ireland as a case study. Geneva Papers Risk Insurance Issues Practice 31 (4), 633–649.

Organisation for Economic Co-operation and Development, 2016. Health at a Glance. OECD, Paris.

Report of Advisory Group on Risk Equalization, Department of Health, Ireland, 1998. Available at www.health.gov.ie, Government of Ireland, Dublin.

Society of Actuaries in Ireland, 2016. Inflationary pressures in the Irish Private Health Insurance market, available at www.actuaries.ie.

Statutory Instruments Numbers 80–84/1996, 1996. Government of Ireland, Dublin.

Statutory Instruments Numbers 261/2003, 2003. Government of Ireland, Dublin.

Turner, B., Shinnick, E., 2013. Community rating in the absence of risk equalisation: Lessons from the Irish private health insurance market. Health Econ. Policy Law 8 (2), 209–224.

Van de Ven, W.P.M.M., 2006. Response: The case for risk-based subsidies in public health insurance. Health Econ. Policy Law 1, 195–199.

Van de Ven, W.P.M.M., Ellis, R.P., 2000. Risk adjustment in competitive health plan markets. Handbook Health Econ. 1, 755–845.

Van de Ven, W.P.M.M., Van Praag, B.M., 1981. The demand for deductibles in private health insurance: A probit model with sample selection. J. Econ. 17 (2), 229–252.

Van de Ven, W.P.M.M., Van Vliet, R.C.J.A., Van Kleef, R.C., 2017. How can the regulator show evidence of (no) risk selection in health insurance markets? Conceptual framework and empirical evidence. The European Journal of Health Economics 18 (2), 167–180.

Van Winssen, K.P.M., Van Kleef, R.C., Van de Ven, W.P.M.M., 2017. A voluntary deductible in health insurance: the more years you opt for it, the lower your premium? European Journal of Health Economics 18 (2), 209–226.

Voluntary Health Insurance Act, 1957. Government of Ireland, Dublin.

Voluntary Health Insurance Board (Vhi) Annual Reports various, Dublin.

Chapter 13

# Regulated Competition and Health Plan Payment Under the National Health Insurance Law in Israel—The Unfinished Story

Shuli Brammli-Greenberg[1], Jacob Glazer[2,3] and Amir Shmueli[4]

[1]University of Haifa, Haifa, Israel, [2]Tel Aviv University, Tel Aviv, Israel, [3]University of Warwick, Coventry, United Kingdom, [4]The Hebrew University, Jerusalem, Israel

## 13.1 INTRODUCTION

Israel has a National Health Insurance (NHI) Law. Every citizen or permanent resident of Israel is required to choose one of the four competing, not-for-profit health plans (HPs), which function as managed care organizations. Since 1995, the HPs have been required by the NHI Law to provide a uniform benefits package and ensure reasonable accessibility and availability.

The system is financed primarily via progressive taxation, and the government distributes the NHI funds among the HPs according to a capitation formula that takes into account the number of members in each plan, as well as their characteristics in terms of age, gender, and general place of residence (periphery vs. center of the country). While public financing remains the primary source of the health system's resources, the share of private financing in national health spending has been increasing, reaching 40% in recent years.

### 13.1.1 Early History of the Israeli Health System

The structure of the Israeli health system was shaped before the establishment of the state of Israel (1948). The four Israeli not-for-profit HPs, established between 1912 and 1940 by political parties or trade unions as mutual-help organizations, insured their members and provided medical services. In 1948, the Ministry of Health took over planning, regulating, and

Risk Adjustment, Risk Sharing and Premium Regulation in Health Insurance Markets.
DOI: https://doi.org/10.1016/B978-0-12-811325-7.00013-0

supervising the HPs, and began providing selected health services and running hospitals (Gross and Anson, 2002). Although health insurance was voluntary, almost all citizens (95%) were insured by 1994, mainly by Clalit, which had a 66% share of the market. The HPs were only loosely regulated by the Ministries of Health and Finance, and could set their own benefit packages and members' dues (based on the households' income). The HPs could also reject applicants.

Between 1948 and 1995, the structure of the health system was repeatedly examined by government committees, but major stakeholders (i.e., the Ministry of Finance, the General Federation of Labor in Israel, smaller HPs) opposed reforms, fearing nationalization of the health system and loss of power (Yishai, 1982; Gross and Anson, 2002; Schwartz et al., 2006).

## 13.1.2 The National Health Insurance Law of 1995

Around 1990, the huge immigration waves from the former USSR and Ethiopia brought in relatively old, sick, and poor new immigrants, many of whom were rejected by two of the HPs (Maccabi and Meuhedet). The Clalit HP, on social-ideological grounds, accepted these unprofitable groups, and consequently reached the verge of bankruptcy, dragging the system into total collapse. An urgent reform was needed. The NHI Law came into effect in January 1995, adopting many elements of Enthoven's 1993 managed (or regulated) competition model (Chinitz, 1995; Gross et al., 2001; Gross and Anson, 2002; Gross, 2003). It stipulates that all Israeli residents are entitled to a specified package of benefits (largely adopting what was then Clalit's package) that includes primary, secondary, and tertiary care, emergency and preventive care, listed medications, diagnostic procedures and medical technologies, dental health for children, and mental health. It excludes long-term care (funded by the MoH) and dental care for adults (financed privately). The Ministries of Health and Finance update the benefits package annually. Participation is mandatory, which means that all residents must be insured in one of the competing HPs. HPs must, by law, accept all applicants.

In 2015, Clalit had the largest market share (52%), followed by Maccabi (25%), Meuhedet (14%), and Leumit (9.0%) (National Insurance Institute, 2015).

Within the public system, the HPs provide care themselves (as listed in the NHI benefits package) within communities and purchase inpatient and outpatient care from hospitals (about 80% of hospitals' revenues come from services covered by HPs).

Every year, the government determines the level of funding for the NHI, which is financed predominantly through public sources. Private sources include the HPs' supplemental insurance and copayments. NHI funds are collected primarily via earmarked health taxes and general tax revenues. While public financing remains the primary source of health system

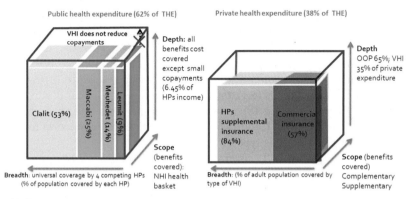

**FIGURE 13.1**  The Israeli health insurance market. THE, total health expenditure; OOP, out-of-pocket expenditures. *Source: Brammli-Greenberg et al. (2014).*

resources, the share of private financing has been increasing in recent years. The share of public financing declined to 61% of the national health expenditure (NHE) in 2012, well below the OECD average of 72%. Accordingly, the share of private financing increased to 39%, constituting one of the highest rates among OECD countries (see Fig. 13.1). According to data from the Ministries of Health and Finance, this increase corresponds to a sharp increase in spending on voluntary health insurance (VHI) premiums (MoF, 2012; MoH, 2012).

### 13.1.3  Voluntary Health Insurance

The voluntary health insurance (VHI) market in Israel offers two products: supplemental insurance (SI) provided by the HPs and commercial insurance (CI) provided by for-profit commercial insurance companies. The SI is an integral part of the public health system. The NHI Law (State of Israel 1994: Clause 10) allows the HPs to offer SI in addition to the mandatory NHI benefits package, supervised by the Ministry of Health. The MoH oversees benefits, premiums, and user charges, as well as the financial stability of the SI providers, approving their annual budgets and actuarial reports. The Ministry also regulates the interface with NHI benefits for two reasons: First, the Ministry must ensure that HPs do not give preference to SI members. For example, SI is not allowed to cover shorter waiting times or offer an extended choice of provider at HP facilities (as they can do at private clinics). Second, the Ministry ensures that the SI compensates the NHI budget for use of HP facilities and staff.

In practice, however, the HPs encourage their members to use their particular SI to obtain healthcare services in the private market, including services guaranteed in the NHI benefits package. This way, the HPs' expenditure decreases, while their income remains the same. In the last few decades, this trend has contributed to the constant increase of private financing as a share of the NHE (MoH, 2014).

The CI is offered by private insurers and regulated by the Insurance Commissioner at the Ministry of Finance. As for other insurance types, the Commissioner oversees policies to ensure the financial stability of insurers and protect consumer rights (e.g., through fair pricing and proper disclosure). Since the NHI legislation in 1995 and the subsequent growth of the commercial market, the Insurance Commissioner has strengthened regulation to protect consumer rights for this type of health insurance.

VHI policies (SI and CI) cover (1) services that are not included in the NHI basic healthcare package (e.g., dental care or alternative medicine); (2) services that are covered by the NHI, but only to a limited extent (e.g., in vitro fertilization [IVF] and physiotherapy); and (3) care purchased in the private sector (which may also be available in the public system) that provides enhanced choice of provider, faster access, or improved facilities. The VHI does not cover or reduce copayments in the public system (Brammli-Greenberg et al., 2016b).

### 13.1.4   Mental Health Care

Until June 2015, the MoH provided and funded mental health services directly through its own clinics and hospitals as well as by purchasing care from private facilities. Since then, HPs have become the providers and purchasers of mental health services and can purchase these services from the MoH-operated community clinics, which provide outpatient mental health and psychosocial services such as psychotherapy, group therapy, mental health rehabilitation (post hospitalization), social work, and pharmacological management and follow-up. For each patient, the HP pays the mental health clinic for two initial "diagnostic" visits. Then HPs pay prospectively for the treatment itself according to a treatment plan set by the clinic, depending on the diagnosis. There are different treatment weights based on (1) age (children and adults), (2) average length of treatment (short or long term), and (3) type of treatment (individual or group) (Rosen, Waitzberg and Merkur 2015).

The remainder of this chapter focuses on the NHI system. In the next sections, we describe the institutional setting of the NHI system (Section 13.2) and the central role of HP compensation by the government (Sections 13.3 and 13.4). In Section 13.5 we discuss ongoing issues and reforms as well as ways to improve the HPs' compensation mechanism.

### 13.2   ORGANIZATION OF THE NATIONAL HEALTH INSURANCE SYSTEM

The HPs' managed care model is structured to create strong incentives to contain utilization and cost. The financial environment in Israel is one of strict rationing of funding for the public health system. The cost containment objective on the one hand, and the inability to add significant resources to the public system on the other, raise concerns that members may be (1) deterred from obtaining adequate health care or (2) persuaded to purchase and use VHI.

The following sections describe the relevant aspects of the current system in terms of regulation, monitoring, consumer choice, and instruments for HPs to promote efficiency in the delivery of care.

## 13.2.1   Health Plan Market Regulation and Monitoring

Alongside the MoH, the MoF plays a major role in the Israeli healthcare system and must approve all MoH decisions that have budgetary implications. The two ministries share responsibility for monitoring the HPs' financial performance, setting the NHI annual budget, negotiating contracts of physicians' salaries, setting official price lists, and so on (Zwanziger and Brammli-Greenberg, 2011).

As mentioned above, the structure of the HP market regulation and monitoring was determined by the National Health Insurance (NHI) Law. The NHI Law ensures that all Israelis are covered by health insurance and spells out the list of benefits to which they are entitled.

The total amount of government financing allocated to the NHI system is regulated by government, with separate decisions regarding the amount to be paid for the existing benefits package (to reflect population growth, aging, and changes in input prices) and the amount to be made available for expansions of the benefits package. The risk-adjustment (capitation) system that governs how the bulk of NHI funds are distributed among HPs is set by the government. In part, this involves determining what parameters (i.e., risk adjusters) will be included in the capitation formula (e.g., determining whether health status, socioeconomic status, and/or quality measures should be added). In addition, the coefficients of the existing parameters need to be updated periodically. A related decision is the extent and nature of payments to the HPs outside the capitation formula, such as the payments for "severe illnesses" and various safety net payments (see Section 13.3). With regard to the HP—consumer interface, regulation involves determining the extent and nature of the copayments that HPs and others can charge their members (Rosen, Waitzberg and Merkur, 2015).

The government specifies the HPs' financial reporting requirements and ensures that the HPs' financial and operational activities are consistent with other various legal requirements (e.g., spending limits on advertisement).

Originally, the NHI Law called for a reduction in the government's provision of services, specifically in personal preventive care, long-term care (LTC), and mental health care. The idea was to transfer these responsibilities to the HPs. To date, however, the transfer has only been successful for mental health care and dental care for children, although efforts have been made in the LTC area as well. Lately, the MoH and the MoF are working together to formulate recommendations to streamline and improve the treatment of the LTC disabled elderly in Israel, up until now, no recommendations have been published.

Most analysts interpret the NHI Law as increasing government control of the main elements of the healthcare system. Prior to its enactment, the HPs had been largely unregulated, whereas under the Law the government has substantial powers regarding the benefits to be provided and the level of HP revenues. Nevertheless, the HPs remain separate legal entities with considerable latitude for strategic and managerial discretion.

The government uses regulation to promote access to care, quality of care, financial stability, and equity. These objectives are mainly realized through regulation directed at the HPs, but hospitals, private insurers, manufacturers, and health professionals also face extensive regulations. Israel also has a formal, highly sophisticated process for setting priorities for the adoption of new technologies by the NHI benefits package. The prioritization process draws upon technical information on costs and health benefits and on an intuitive sense of public preferences and aspirations.

SI, which is a part of the VHI market, is also regulated by the MoH. As mentioned above, all applicants must be accepted, and the content and pricing of supplemental insurance packages offered by individual HPs, as well as the interface with the NHI benefits package, are regulated as well. This regulation includes provisions such as whether the SI packages can include coverage for life-saving pharmaceuticals and choice of hospital-based physicians.

## 13.2.2 Health Plan Choice Options for Consumers

### 13.2.2.1 Consumers' Choice of HP

Every Israeli must be a member of one of the four HPs; however, they are free to choose among the HPs. Enrollment is open, meaning that HPs must accept all applicants. Members can switch from one HP to another at six pre-specified points of time during a calendar year (up to two moves in a period of 12 months). Since 2011, members have been able to switch at no cost using the internet or for a nominal fee at the post office. In reality, that all residents of Israel are entitled to the open enrollment is not clear, especially for residents in rural Israel where Clalit insures 70% of the population and operates the majority of services. For example, in the southern part of Israel, the only university public hospital is owned by Clalit.

In practice, each year only 1−2% of the population switches plans. In 2016, 164,398 members switched HP (2% of the population), of which 57% used the post office and 43% used the internet. Interestingly, switching is relatively more common among lower-income individuals (Keidar and Plotnic, 2016). A possible explanation for this is the intense competition among the HPs regarding children, for which the capitation rate is generous (see the discussion below). Large families (many of whom are Orthodox Jews and Arabs) are relatively poor.

### 13.2.2.2 Consumers' Choice of Healthcare Provider

Within communities, patients have a considerable choice of primary care physicians and specialists with whom their HP contracts. They also have a choice of hospitals that have an agreement with their HP. Services at hospital outpatient clinics are included in the NHI package and hence are usually covered by the HPs. Noncontracted care is not covered.

When it comes to inpatient care, all physicians and medical staff are salaried employees of the hospitals. When a patient is hospitalized or visits an outpatient clinic, the hospital chooses the patient's physician or surgeon. Furthermore, the hospital is not required to inform the patient in advance about the identity of the surgeon. If a patient wishes to choose a specific surgeon or physician, she must turn to the private system of medical services at one of Jerusalem's hospitals or at a private institution (mostly in the center of the country, in the Tel Aviv area) and has to pay out-of-pocket or through her VHI.

As mentioned above, the data indicate that private health expenditure has increased in the past decade. Some private spending is for services that are not included in the NHI package (e.g., dental treatment for adults) and copayments for services that are in the NHI package. However, a substantial amount of private spending is the result of patients' willingness to pay for "the right to choose" for services available under the NHI package that lack the option to choose the provider.

Over the past two decades, there has been extensive public and academic discussion about the option of choosing specialists (nonsurgeons) and/or surgeons through the private system. Recently there have been initiatives within and outside the MoH to promote choice of surgeon in public hospitals without additional payment.

### 13.2.3 Instruments for Health Plans to Manage the Utilization and Costs of Care

The HPs are third-party payers that manage the utilization and costs of healthcare services through mechanisms that affect the behavior of both providers and consumers, taking into account three key organizational objectives: cost containment, quality improvement, and equity promotion (Enthoven, 2014). Cost containment is one of the HPs' main organizational objectives. Their efforts to control costs include managed-care tools: reviewing and preauthorizing the utilization of hospital care, arranging discounts when purchasing from hospitals and pharmaceutical manufactures, enforcing strict rationing of some services (especially through gatekeeping and waiting times), applying high-powered incentive schemes to providers (e.g., a flat salary, or capitation), and creating a network of primary care providers, throughout the country, that serve as gate-keepers and substitutes for specialists, in some cases (Brammli-Greenberg and Waitzberg, 2013).

Israel has successfully built a high-quality primary care system through changing the structure of supply by promoting larger health clinics to gain economies of scale, and by reorganizing doctors, working in teams within communities, which allows them to deliver follow-up support, preventive care, and regular monitoring of health indicators of patients (OECD, 2016). Other efforts include implementing an information technology infrastructure for monitoring utilization and expenditures at the level of physicians (Rosen, 2011).

In 2002, the HPs—in cooperation with the National Program for Quality Measures in Community Care—established a system of quality measures to enhance community care, a move which has been praised by the OECD.

## 13.3   HEALTH PLAN PAYMENT DESIGN

The NHI Law of 1995 replaced member dues collected by HPs with a health tax collected by the National Insurance Institute. Under NHI, the total annual funding level of the health system is no longer determined by market forces, but rather—primarily—by the parliament.

The NHI Law is financed through a combination of an earmarked health tax and general government revenues, each contributing approximately half of the financing. Both are progressive, and equity is maintained in that high-income and low-risk individuals subsidize low-income and high-risk individuals. Moreover, due to the combination of earmarked and general government funding, when there are economic slowdowns and the health tax revenue decreases, the government can increase its share of funding so as not to decrease the NHI funding. On the other hand, there is always a constant, predictable part of NHI funding that does not depend on year-to-year government decisions and priority settings. Fig. 13.2 provides a summary of the financing scheme of the NHI with the arrows representing the major money flows. In the following sections we elaborate on the different aspects of the HPs' payment design.

### 13.3.1   Contributions and Premiums Regulation

#### 13.3.1.1   The NHI Premium

The NHI Law broke the link between members' income and health plan revenue. The HPs no longer charge premiums for the basic benefit package.

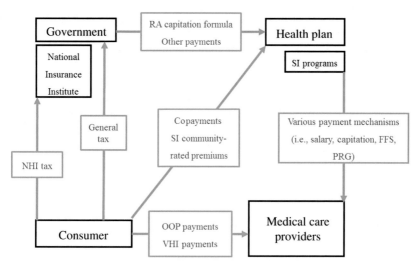

**FIGURE 13.2** Financing scheme of the NHI.

They collect only the SI premiums, which vary by age and gender but are otherwise community-rated.

All permanent residents above the age of 18 must pay a health tax. The health tax is 3.1% over income up to 60% of the average wage (to date about 1,160€), and 5% over income above this threshold. The self-employed pay the same rates as employees from their total income, and retired individuals pay either 21€ or 40€ depending on the amount of their pension. Married women who do not have paid work are exempt from paying the health tax. Students and the unemployed must pay 5% of their income or cash transfers (such as unemployment benefits, income support, National Insurance Institute allowances, or scholarships). Those who have no income pay a minimum rate of 103 NIS (about €20) (NII, 2017). Income five times or more than the average national wage is not taxed for NHI purposes. Failure to pay the required health tax results in government action to enforce payment, but in no way jeopardizes the individual's right to NHI benefits. Populations excluded from the NHI include undocumented migrants, temporary residents, foreign workers, and tourists. Soldiers and prisoners are insured under separate arrangements.

### 13.3.1.2 Additional Contributions

Primary and inpatient care are provided free of charge. Visits to Emergency Departments require a payment, which is determined by the medical necessity and urgency of the visit. Secondary care, such as visits to specialists and diagnostic exams, requires small copayments (~€5). Copayments for medication and other medical technologies are generally 10−15% of the price with a minimum of $\sim €5$. There are also small copayments for rehabilitation care and paramedical care such as physiotherapy and speech therapy. Discounts and spending caps are provided for the chronically ill, the elderly, and other disadvantaged families.

Copayments for medical care and medical technologies, paid out of pocket (OOP) by members, account for around 7% of the total NHI budget.

While the HPs can compete on the levels of copayments, in general the levels are similar. The HPs submit their copayment schedule for approval by the MoH and the Finance Committee of the Israeli Parliament.

Services outside the NHI system are financed via VHI, and direct OOP payments.

## 13.3.2 The Capitation Formula and Risk Adjustment

In 2015, the NHI budget was about €9.1 billion, or about €1,100 per capita. The National Insurance Institute combines the revenues from the NHI tax with direct government contributions and transfers the funds to the HPs using three main mechanisms: (1) financing of HPs primarily via prospective payments based on a capitation formula with simple and objective risk adjusters; (2) conditioning specific payments for patients with some prespecified "severe illnesses," and (3) supplementary HP funding via retrospective payments based on performance. This section discusses these compensation mechanisms in more detail.

### 13.3.2.1 The Capitation Formula

The NHI Law specifies that the capitation formula has two objectives: (1) to reduce the incentives for the HPs to favor certain types of members; and (2) to distribute resources among the HPs in a way that relates to the needs of the members, in order to protect HPs who insure disproportionate numbers of high-risk members from financial insolvency (Hadley et al., 2002).

In 1995, the capitation formula had only one risk adjuster: age. Therefore, the HP revenues were primarily a function of the size of its membership and the age distribution of its members. The age "weights" reflected estimates of the relative cost of providing health services to nine age groups.[1] The prospective capitation formula is the main funding source for the HPs. In 2015, it constituted 88% of the total NHI budget, the other 12% consisting of copayments and payments for individuals with severe illnesses.

In 2003, Clalit, the largest HP, initiated a lawsuit against the MoH and the MoF at the Supreme Court. The main claim of Clalit was the alleged unfair distribution of the funds among HPs and the resulting incentives for selection. A study published by Clalit, based on Clalit's actual cost data, showed that the compensation by the capitation formula for members with chronic illness was, on average, 60% lower than the plan's real expenditures.

For diabetic patients, the level of undercompensation reached 71%. Conversely, on average, Clalit was about 60% overcompensated for members without a chronic illness (Shmueli et al., 2003).

As a result, the MoH came up with a new formula in which the number of age groups was extended from 9 to 11 and the rate for the elderly was somewhat increased. The new 2003 formula did not add any new risk adjusters.

In 2010, two additional risk adjusters were introduced: gender and residence in the geographic periphery. Currently, as of summer 2018, a joint MoH and MoF capitation committee is discussing adding more risk adjusters to the formula. The issue of the weak set of risk adjusters will be discussed in more detail in Section 13.4.

### 13.3.2.2 The Procedure for Deriving Risk-Adjustment Coefficients

The calculation of the risk-adjustment weights has historically been based on quantities of care rather than expenditure data. The main reason (in 1995) was the limited availability and quality of individual (cost) data at the HPs. The argument for the continued use of the original methodology is twofold. First, the cost data are not "uniform" across the HPs due to accounting and calculation discrepancies. Second, the HPs might manipulate the data (Shmueli, 2015).

Medical expenditures within the budget of services are broken down into so-called "major services headings." In 1995, there were three of these major services headings: visits to physicians, visits to outpatient clinics, and general inpatient days. Data on age-specific, mean number of visits to doctors was obtained from the 1993 use of health services survey of the Central Bureau of Statistics (CBS) (about 30,000 individuals). Data on the number of visits to outpatient clinics was obtained from the government hospitals for the year 1993, and age-specific mean number of inpatient days was obtained from the CBS's 1987 hospitalizations data file. The three quantity scales were then combined with weights reflecting the share of each of the expenditure headings in the National Health Expenditure. The 1995 weights were: 45% for visits to doctors, 13% for outpatient visits, and 42% for inpatient days. In 2005, a fourth major service heading was added—visits to emergency departments—and the data on the other expenditure headings were updated using the 1999 CBS survey on the use of health services and the MoH's 2002 hospitalizations file. The weights (out of the total HPs' expenditures) were: 50% for visits to doctors, 8% for outpatient visits, 40% for inpatient days, and 2% for visits to the emergency department. In 2010, a third and, so far, last, update was performed, still keeping the 1995 methodology. A fifth major service heading was introduced—the number of prescription drugs consumed. Use of hospital services was obtained from the

**TABLE 13.1** Weights of Major Services Headings as Defined by the 2010 Capitation Committee

| Expenditure heading | Weight |
| --- | --- |
| Inpatient days | 0.38 |
| ER | 0.03 |
| Outpatient clinics visits | 0.09 |
| Visits to doctors | 0.40 |
| Prescription drugs | 0.10 |
| Total | 1.00 |

MoH's 2007 hospitalizations file. The number of prescription drugs by age was obtained from the HPs (Brammli-Greenberg et al., work in progress; Shmueli, 2015). The 2010 capitation weights of major services headings are presented in Table 13.1.

More formally, the calculation of the Israeli capitation weights for each group j is as follows:

$$W_j = \sum_q W_q \frac{\text{Average use of service q in group j}}{\text{Average use of service q in the population}} \qquad (13.1)$$

where groups are defined by age (0−1, 1−4, 5−14, 15−24, 25−34, 35−44, 45−54, 55−64, 65−74, 75−84, 85+), gender (women, men), and place of residence (residence in the periphery or not, where "periphery" is defined as the locations included in the four bottom clusters of the CBS's Geographic Periphery Index).[2] $W_q$ is the share of costs of service q in of total healthcare costs.[3] Table 13.2 presents the 2010 capitation weights for each group and compares these to the 2005 weights.

### 13.3.3 Prospective Payments for "Severe Illnesses"[4] and Other Supplementary Payment Mechanisms

Prospective payments for severe illnesses apply to 0.07% of the population and constitute €444 million of the NHI health benefits package funding. HPs are paid prospectively according to the number of patients and a predetermined cost set for each of the following diseases: thalassemia major (1.3% of the total payments), Gaucher's disease (6.8%), kidney dysfunction (68.4%), hemophilia (5.8%), and AIDS (17.7%). In 2015, Clalit, which insured a high proportion of patients with severe illnesses, got 66.5% of the total payments, Maccabi 18.2%, Meuhedet 7.5%, and Leumit 7.8%. The

**TABLE 13.2** 2005 and 2010 Capitation Formula Rates (1 = Overall Mean)

| | 2010 Capitation rates | | | | 2005 Capitation rates |
|---|---|---|---|---|---|
| | Center | | Periphery | | |
| Age | Female | Male | Female | Male | |
| Newborn | 1.41 | 1.87 | 1.45 | 1.92 | 1.55 |
| 1−4 | 0.75 | 0.94 | 0.80 | 0.99 | 0.96 |
| 5−14 | 0.38 | 0.41 | 0.42 | 0.45 | 0.47 |
| 15−24 | 0.43 | 0.36 | 0.47 | 0.40 | 0.40 |
| 25−34 | 0.73 | 0.41 | 0.77 | 0.46 | 0.57 |
| 35−44 | 0.78 | 0.57 | 0.82 | 0.62 | 0.68 |
| 45−54 | 1.14 | 0.99 | 1.18 | 1.03 | 1.07 |
| 55−64 | 1.70 | 1.79 | 1.74 | 1.84 | 1.69 |
| 65−74 | 2.63 | 3.14 | 2.67 | 3.18 | 2.86 |
| 75−84 | 3.40 | 4.13 | 3.45 | 4.18 | 3.56 |
| 85 + | 3.52 | 4.23 | 3.57 | 4.27 | 4.06 |

copayments from the members for consumption of services constitute 6.5% of the NHI health benefits package funding, the lowest rate in a decade (MoH, 2016).

Besides the NHI budget, HPs can receive some additional financial support from the government at the end of each year. The size of such payments is determined primarily by the extent to which the HPs meet various targets regarding fiscal responsibility, efficiency, and reduction of inequality. The main goals of this retrospective financial support from the government are to ensure the HPs' economic stability and to implement government policy goals. This mechanism is called "criteria for support," because the allocation of the money is contingent upon meeting certain criteria set by the MoH and MoF. Most of the support monies are funneled toward meeting expenditure goals and balancing the budget. However, in the past, some of these monies have been allocated to improving the quality of care of the elderly in the community, providing flu vaccinations without copayments for the elderly and children, and to HPs that reduced the cost of medicines for the elderly (over 75). In 2013−2014, the targets included providing preventive care and oral health care without copayments for children, preventing hospital readmissions, promoting healthy lifestyles, tackling geographic and social disparities in health, and providing care for chronic obstructive pulmonary disease (MoH, 2014).

In 2015, the amount of additional financial support from the government was about €0.4 billion (about 3% of the HPs' total income). The amount allocated according to criteria of meeting fiscal and financial goals constituted more than the 93% of the support. The other 7% was divided according to specific criteria such as providing discounts for the elderly in copayments for medications (3.5%), operating preventive care programs and programs to reduce inequalities (1.5%), providing flu vaccines for the elderly and children (1%), and other (1%).

In all, the support monies are divided among the HPs according to criteria that are established every budget year (usually every 3 years).

### 13.3.4 Implementation and Maintenance

The capitation formula is reviewed periodically by the "capitation committee," which consists of representatives of the MoH and MoF. Capitation weights are reviewed every 3 years, based on the previous year's average use of each capitation group. The committee invites representatives of the HPs as well as academic experts to raise their suggestions and criticism regarding the formula. Capitation weights and major services headings are reviewed every 3 years, based on previous years' average use of each capitation group. The recommendations of the committee must be approved by the government.

The 2016 capitation committee is presently finalizing its recommendations. The main changes will be as follows:

- At least two additional service headings will be added to the formula calculation; one of them will be children's dental care; the other one has not yet been announced;
- The calculation of the risk adjustment weights will be based more on national datasets (such as national registries) and less on surveys;
- Compensation mechanisms for HP expenditures for members who have suffered from work injuries will be set.

The MoH brought up the following possible changes for discussion in the committee:

- Adding indicators for socioeconomic status and health/disability status as new risk adjusters;
- Considering some supplementary mechanisms for specific health status (e.g., diabetes). The exact mechanisms have not yet been specified;
- Adding orphan diseases to the list of "severe illnesses."

As mentioned above, the amount of additional financial support to the HPs is determined primarily by the extent to which they meet various targets regarding fiscal responsibility, efficiency, and reduction of inequality. These targets are also set by the MoH every 3 years, in accordance with key policy objectives. Nonetheless, in 2016, a meaningful legislative modification to the NHI Law was set. Now the Ministers of Health and Finance have the authority to compensate the HPs for providing the NHI health benefits package not only prospectively, via capitation, but also retrospectively, via various risk-sharing and pay-for-performance mechanisms. Among other things, this legislative modification brought with it the initiative to pay a portion of the HPs' fixed costs out of capitation.

## 13.3.5 Health Plans' Payments for Their Community-Based Healthcare Providers

The HPs work as managed care organizations. Most of the physicians working with the HPs are paid via capitation and/or salary arrangements, thereby largely avoiding the cost-promoting effects of fee-for-service reimbursement. The HPs purchase inpatient care from hospitals through per diem fees and activity-based payments based on procedure-related groups (PRGs). The government publishes maximum-price lists for inpatient care and sets hospital revenue caps to contain the HPs' expenditures. Moreover, due to their dominance, the HPs are further able to obtain discounts from hospitals (Rosen, Waitzberg and Merkur, 2015).

Most physicians work as salaried employees of the HPs or as independent physicians paid by capitation contracts. A collective bargaining agreement between the Israeli Medical Association and the major employers governs the payment terms for employed physicians. Physicians working independently are not covered by the agreement and instead are engaged via individual contracts.

In all HPs the primary care physicians (PCPs) or specialists who work as employees of the HP, are paid a salary on a monthly basis. In Clalit, the largest HP, self-employed PCPs are paid according to a risk-adjusted capitation (according to their patients' age and chronic conditions). This is referred to in Israel as "passive capitation" as it does not depend on whether the member visited the physician but rather on whether the member is on the PCP's list. Specialists are paid on an active capitation basis (i.e., a set amount for each patient who has visited the doctor's clinic at least once during a quarter-year, irrespective of the number of visits) plus fee for service (FFS) payments for various procedures (according to a fixed-fee schedule) up to a quarterly ceiling.

In Maccabi, the second largest HP, the majority of physicians (over 80%) are independent contractors (self-employed). Both self-employed PCPs and specialists in the Maccabi network are paid on an active capitation basis plus FFS for various procedures, with the FFS component being a large share of compensation for the specialists. The other two HPs also use a mix of passive and active capitation to pay their PCPs and specialists (Vardy et al., 2008; Rosen, Waitzberg, and Merkur, 2015).

## 13.4 EVALUATION OF HEALTH PLAN PAYMENT

The capitation formula is reviewed periodically by the "capitation committee" as mentioned above. The fairness of the distribution of the funds among HPs and the financial stability of the HPs are constantly monitored by the MoH and MoF. Also monitored are the operational activities and fiscal responsibility of HPs as well as their efficiency and inequality-reducing efforts. This monitoring serves mainly to determine the amount of additional compensation (above the capitation payments) each plan will receive (as mentioned in Section 13.3.3).

Each year, the Government determines the level at which the NHI system will be funded. It is based on the previous year's budget, adjusted for demographic growth, technological developments, and a price index. However, it seems that these adjustments are insufficient to cover cost growth, and studies show that the "real value" of the NHI budget has eroded since the enactment of the NHI Law (Shmueli and Chinitz, 2001; Shmueli et al., 2008; Arieli et al., 2012). The capitation payments increased only from €4.1 billion in 2005 to €7.3 billion in 2015 (nominal), including the annual update of the NHI health benefits package for new technologies. The NHI budget per capita (adjusted for changes in the official health cost index) was essentially the same in 2013 as it was in 1995. If we deduct the additional funds received for additions to the benefits package (which of course also had concomitant additional costs) then the per capita budget in 2013 was 12% lower than it was in 1995 (MoH, 2014). The main reasons for this erosion are the inadequate adjustments for the health cost index, demographic growth, and population aging.

Therefore, not surprisingly, we notice fiscal instability of the HPs. Indeed, in 2015 alone the four HPs ran a total deficit of €545 million (MoH, 2016).[5] Many researchers and policy-makers argue that the main reason for this deficit is the lack of sufficient public funds (the budget of the package of benefits) provided by the government, to finance the package of services that the HPs are required to provide under the NHI Law.

### 13.4.1 An Evaluation of the Israeli Capitation Formula

In a capitation system such as the one used in Israel, where HPs cannot charge premium and must accept every applicant, the main form at which adverse selection may appear is "service distortion" (Glazer and McGuire 2000, 2002).

The HPs cannot engage in direct selection of members (i.e., reject individuals ex-ante). Consequently, they have strong incentives to perform (ex-ante) service selection and ex-post individual selection. Ex-ante service selection refers to a situation where the plans distort the quality of services they provide in order to attract the profitable enrollees and discourage the unprofitable ones. Ex-post individual selection refers to a situation where, at the time of treatment, the plan provides a high-quality service to some individuals (the profitable ones) and a low-quality service to others (the unprofitable ones) in order to affect the mixture of individuals that choose to stay with the plan. Both of these selection mechanisms can be conducted easily by HPs.

Service distortion is likely to take place if plans are either over- or undercompensated for some enrollees. Service distortion occurs when a provider chooses to overprovide services used by low-risk/low-cost individuals in order to attract them; or underprovide the services that attract unprofitable enrollees (Frank, Glazer, and McGuire, 2000, 2002; Cao and McGuire, 2003).

There are two main causes of under-/overcompensation: (1) under-/overcompensation of specific subgroups due to an insufficient set of risk adjusters; and (2) shortcomings of the methodology of calculating the weights of the major services heads included in the formula.

### 13.4.1.1 Under-/Overcompensation of Subgroups due to the Weak Set of Risk Adjusters

Two types of risk-adjusters are missing in the Israeli risk-adjustment scheme: chronic health conditions and socioeconomic characteristics.

While most risk-adjustment schemes in Europe and the US have been enriched with sophisticated health-based risk adjusters, such as DCGs (diagnostic cost groups) or PCGs (pharmacy cost groups), the Israeli scheme compensates for only five "severe diseases" (see Section 13.3.3) and ignores other "common" high-cost chronic conditions such as cancer, diabetes, asthma, and heart disease. Since chronic patients cost, on average, 2–3 times more than nonchronic patients, the health plans have no incentive to compete on chronic patients by developing services for chronic diseases and to excel in the provision of good-quality chronic care.

The consideration of socioeconomic risk adjusters is more complex. Since poor and less-educated enrollees suffer from worse health, when health-related risk adjusters are not included in the risk-adjustment scheme, the poor are unprofitable for the health plans. While the health plans do not know the socioeconomic status of the enrollees, they may rely on their place of residence. The socioeconomic status of the Israeli locations (towns and neighborhoods within cities) is known (it is published by the Central Bureau of Statistics). Since health services are provided on a local basis, the Israeli health plans compete in rich locations, resulting in high levels of supply of care, and do not compete on enrollees residing in poor localities, which are often located in the periphery.

Indeed, based on a sample of 20% of the members of Clalit, Achdut and Shmueli (2015) find that the socioeconomic characteristics are highly correlated with individuals' medical expenses (Table 13.3). While the size of

**TABLE 13.3** Average Marginal Effects (AME) Calculated Based on One Part GLM Model

|  | AME as % From the average estimated health expenditures |
| --- | --- |
| **Age (ages 5−14 base)** | |
| 0−1 | 147.3 |
| 1−4 | 50.3 |
| 15−24 | 12.6 |
| 25−34 | 33.7 |
| 35−44 | 39.8 |
| 45−54 | 59.1 |
| 55−64 | 87.4 |
| 65−74 | 136.1 |
| 75−84 | 163.8 |
| 85 + | 180.7 |
| Gender (female base) | − 4.4 |
| Heart disease | 84.1 |
| Diabetes | 91.4 |
| Transplants | 699.8 |
| Cancer | 130.7 |
| Charlesson Index | 32.8 |
| Socioeconomic index of the locality | 5.1 |
| Social insurance allowances | 45.4 |
| Periphery index | 1.6 |

Note: All results in the table are statistically significant.
From Achdut, L., Shmueli, A., 2015. Re-examination of then Israeli risk-adjustment: the introduction of socio-economic risk adjuster, Van Leer Policy Study number 19 (Hebrew).

the effects depends on the estimation method, the direction is clear—Clalit's costs are higher for individuals living in wealthy or more central locations. Since the rich enjoy better health, this effect might reflect the lower supply of (ambulatory) health services in poor and remote locations. In 2010, a higher risk-adjustment rate was introduced for enrollees residing in the periphery in order to promote competition among the health plans by increasing the supply of services (this measure was accompanied by financial incentives to physicians to serve in peripheral locations). The effect of these measures on the supply of care in the periphery is presently under investigation.

Another finding of this study shows that, beyond the influence of residential location, the need for social insurance allowances (i.e., disability or income maintenance allowance) is highly correlated with costs. Among the allowances, the dominant influence is that of the receipt of a disability allowance, which combines low economic status and higher health needs.

Achdut and Shmueli (2015) emphasize the need for additional risk adjusters in the Israeli risk-adjustment mechanism, especially an index of socioeconomic status of the residential location in addition to the periphery/center status, which is already included in the capitation formula. The authors also propose to consider adding a risk-adjustment variable indicating the enrollee's need for welfare allowances, and, in particular, the receipt of a disability allowance for those aged 25−65.

In summary, at least two sets of risk adjusters are missing from the Israeli risk-adjustment formula. The first, and most important, is health-related risk adjusters. The second is socioeconomic characteristics that are known to affect the expected medical care costs.

Ideally, the set of risk adjusters, to be used in the formula, and the risk-adjustment weights, should be explored using individual data from the HPs' administrative files combined with the NII's data on income sources and allowances. This will require some standardization of the "acceptable costs" of the different HPs. This course of action seems infeasible at present. What seems feasible is improvement of the current methodology.

### 13.4.1.2    Under-/Overcompensation of Subgroups due to Incorrect Weights

Brammli-Greenberg et al. (work in progress) refined calculation of selection incentives by comparing the weights of the actual use to the payment weights under the current Israeli capitation formula. The comparison shows which of the capitation groups (by gender and age) are profitable to the HPs and which are unprofitable. Fig. 13.3 reveals that the current formula overcompensates for girls aged 0−14, boys aged 0−4, and men aged 55 + . The situation is reversed for women aged 55 + .

The conclusion from this comparison is that, under the current compensation scheme, there are incentives for positive selection of children and older men. On the other hand, there are incentives for negative selection of older women. Since the HPs cannot reject applicants, they have an incentive to engage in service selection, such as developing fewer services for older women. Very similar results were found by Shmueli (2015) who calculated the profits/losses of each age group, showing that the HPs make significant

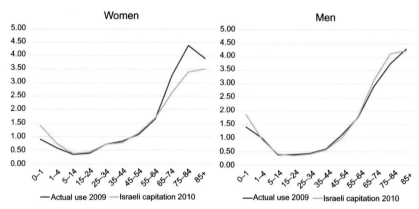

**FIGURE 13.3** Weights of the Israeli capitation versus weights of actual (public) use, by age and gender. *Source: Brammli-Greenberg et al. (work in progress).*

profits on children aged 0−14, but suffer significant losses on persons over 55.

### 13.4.1.3  Evidence of Incentives For Selection

Because of the complex nature of the provision of medical care, it is difficult to identify evidence of risk selection. There is, however, some limited evidence that confirms that the incentives discussed above do exist and that they lead to ex-ante individual selection and service distortion.

One of the most obvious tools for ex-ante individual selection is using marketing campaigns in order to alter open enrollment to encourage profitable individuals to join the HP without denying the unprofitable individuals. In recent years, all HPs have launched aggressive marketing campaigns aimed to attract children, young people, and the healthy (Shmueli, 2015). The results are reflected in the switching rates between HPs. In 2015, the switching rates between HPs were the highest in the Arab and Orthodox Jewish localities (switching rates of 8% and 5% in these localities, respectively, compared to a total average of 2%). These localities are characterized by large young families (Keidar and Plotnic, 2016).

Shmueli and Nissan-Engelcin (2013) found that the availability of physicians' services (measured as reception hours per age-adjusted inhabitant) in the locations with worse health state (measured by standardized mortality rates) and in poor locations is significantly lower than that in healthy locations. They interpreted this finding as evidence of implicit selection: since medical care is provided locally, there is less competition among the HPs— and hence lower supply—in sick and poor locations because sick and poor members are unprofitable, while the competition in healthy locations among the HPs is stronger, resulting in a higher supply of care.

Brammli-Greenberg et al. (work in progress) use data from the 2009 CBS Health Survey ($N = 28,968$) to study the HPs' incentives for service distortion under the NHI Law in Israel. Their preliminary findings indicate that among the groups exposed to negative selection are individuals with chronic illness or physical disability as well as those with cancer or depression. These characteristics were found to have the strongest independent effect on the probability and amount of health services used. Furthermore, applying an index proposed by Layton, Ellis, McGuire, and Van Kleef (2017), to measure incentives to select within groups, Brammli-Greenberg et al. (work in progress) demonstrate that even under an improved risk-adjustment scheme, HPs would have incentives to discourage members with a high probability of being hospitalized, regardless of the risk-adjustment group to which they belong. The incentives-for-selection index also indicates that HPs have more incentives to select low-risk individuals among the chronically ill than among the healthy. Moreover, calculation of Pearson's correlation between actual use of major services and the HPs' profit from supplying these services found a negative correlation between use and profit in *all* major services and for *all* groups. It seems that HPs have very strong incentives to control operating expenses (primarily administrative employee compensation) and to constrain their payments to providers.[6]

## 13.5   ONGOING ISSUES AND REFORMS

### 13.5.1   The Israeli Procedure to Set the Risk-Adjustment Weights

As was mentioned above, the Israeli risk-adjustment mechanism is quite simple compared to the mechanisms employed in other countries. Another weakness of the mechanism relates to the way the weights are derived, which is not based on the HPs' expenditure data but on the use of services. Furthermore, the formula has been updated only four times over the past 20 years.

### 13.5.2   The Problem of Weight Calculation Based on Actual Use of Services

A more general problem with the calculation of the risk-adjustment weights comes from the fact that these weights are often calculated on the basis of actual use. Such a procedure is likely to reinforce existing inefficiencies in the healthcare system (Layton et al., 2016). The actual use is influenced by the existing supply, the supply is affected by the average payment that is set according to the capitation formula, and the payment is determined on the basis of the actual use. This procedure creates a "snapshot" of the current situation. However, the current situation does not necessarily reflect the real *need* for health services by the population and the variance in needs among population groups. For example, if elderly women face barriers to a certain service's accessibility, and the actual use is lower than the need, the capitation formula will facilitate this underuse, since it is based on the current usage.

### 13.5.3 The Shortcomings of the Major Services Weights Calculation Methodology

To date there are three major services (visits to doctors, inpatient services, and medications) whose weights are calculated as the proportional of the service cost of use out of the total expenditure. The straightforward actions recommended to improve the capitation formula are to add major service categories and to base the calculation of the major service weights more on national datasets rather than surveys. These two recommendations are now on the agenda of the capitation deliberations.

However, there is a fundamental weakness in the methodology of calculating the weights that has not yet been dealt with by the capitation committee. When the risk-adjustment weights—the (normalized) mean costs of the risk adjustment groups—are derived from a national sample of insurers, as is done in most systems, the quantities of services are weighted by the unit-costs of the services in the different HPs. The Israeli methodology is based on quantities-scales of the major services (derived nationally from surveys and MoH data), as is clear from Eq. (13.1). These quantities-scales are weighted by the share of the service in total HPs' expenditures. This methodology would be correct (i.e., one which is based on actual HPs' individual cost data) if there were one HP or when the unit-costs are similar across HPs.

Shmueli (2015) identified several reasons that the unit costs of at least three major services are expected to differ across HPs:

- *Visits to physicians*: As mentioned above (Section 13.3.5), there is a variation in the way doctors are paid by the HPs. The HPs differ not only by the payment methods (e.g., salary vs. capitation) but also by the level of reimbursement for a given payment method. Furthermore, the doctors visited represent a mix of specialties differing in their level of payment. If the mix is not identical across the HPs, the "average" payment will not be similar. Finally, the productivity of doctors varies across HPs and payment methods. As a result, it is not likely that the unit cost of a visit to a doctor will be similar across HPs.
- *Hospitalization*: The MoH's reimbursement prices for inpatient days serve as benchmarks in the system. Typically, in return for guaranteeing a minimum revenue stream, the HPs are given additional price discounts.

The HPs differ in their market power when negotiating with hospitals, as there are only four HPs, and hence, each has a different market segment (with concentration levels even higher at the regional level than at the national level). Furthermore, two of the HPs, Clalit and Maccabi, cover almost 80% of Israel's residents. Both HPs own general hospitals: Clalit owns eight general not-for-profit hospitals, whereas Maccabi owns five for-profit hospitals. Since there is no law in Israel that forbids HPs from channeling patients to particular hospitals, both Maccabi and Clalit have additional negotiation power for price discounts (Rosen, Waitzberg, and Merkur, 2015). This situation creates differences in the hospitalization cost structure among the four HPs. For example, the overall weight of hospitalization (including inpatient days, ER, and outpatient visits) is 50%. However, this rate differs widely across the four HPs: 45.5% for Clalit, 41% for Leumit, 34% for Maccabi, and 35% for Meuhedet.

- *Prescription drugs*: The unit costs of prescription drugs are typically determined in large global agreements between each of the HPs and the pharmaceutical firms. Therefore, the unit costs of prescription drugs are not equal among HPs. In 2009, Clalit's expenditure for medication, covered under the NHI health benefits package, per adjusted capita, was €131, in Maccabi it was €158, Meuhedet €122, and in Leumit €174 (MoH, 2010).

Unit costs of the four plans are very different. One of the main purposes of paying health plans prospectively by capitation is to incentivize them to be cost-efficient; and, indeed, in the long run one would expect this to be the case. However, such a process may take many years, as it requires the plans to make major changes that are not easy to implement, especially when some of these changes involve other players. In the meantime, however, using a risk adjustment rate that ignores historical differences among plans creates strong incentives for service selection. If, e.g., in one plan, the ratio between the cost of a 79-year-old man and the cost of a 7-year-old girl is much higher than the same ratio in another plan, the first plan has stronger incentives to distort services against the elderly and in favor of the young. Furthermore, differences in the production function and care management among the health plans that are associated with differences in unit-costs of services might lead to an over- or underprovision of specific services by the different health plans, when facing an arbitrary unit-cost implied by the capitation weights.

While the current methodology enabled the calculation of the risk-adjustment weights in 1995, in the context of limited and uncomputerized data of the HPs, today, with the development of data management and information technologies, there should be no reason not to use national samples of enrollees to calculate the risk-adjustment weights.

### 13.5.4 Expanding the Set of the Risk Adjusters and Improving the Methodology of Setting Their Weights

Since the implementation of the NHI Law and constitution of the capitation formula, there has been an ongoing public debate about which risk adjusters should be added to the formula. Socioeconomic status, health status, and disability status have all been suggested as necessary additions to the scheme. However, thus far, none of these adjusters has been added to the formula, due to a mix of concerns about data availability and reliability, potential adverse incentives, and the effect of changing in the balance of the current pooling of funds.[7]

Recently, the MoH brought to the 2016 committee for discussion the possibility of adding socioeconomic status and health/disability status as new risk adjusters. Political courage and policy management skills are vital if these risk adjusters are to be incorporated into the capitation formula.

Moreover, in order to improve the methodology by which risk adjusters are set and calculated, serious discussions should take place regarding (1) the technical feasibility (given data and other limitations), (2) the method for adding new risk adjusters, and (3) the acceptability of various analytic compromises that could speed up the preparation of a concrete capitation formula that includes socioeconomic status and health measures.

Evidence is still lacking to evaluate whether the funds allocated to improve healthcare provision in the periphery (through the new risk adjuster added in 2010 to the capitation formula) have achieved their purpose. Many analysts believe that these funds are insufficient and might have been used for other, more profitable, purposes.

Even the most advanced mechanisms of prospective risk adjustment explain only a small share of the variation in expected expenditure. The system paying Medicare Advantage plans in the US explains about 12%. It is unlikely that prospective payment-based systems eliminate plans' incentives for selection (Van de Ven et al., 2015). Adding to this the ability of HPs to perform service selection raises the need for complementary mechanisms.

### 13.5.5 The Use of Compensation Mechanisms to Maximize Outcomes

The question of the "right amount" of funds to be allocated to the HPs to enable them to provide the package of services, as defined by the NHI Law, is at the center of a heated debate among many researchers, policy-makers, healthcare leaders, and more. The MoF has been able to persuade the government to agree to relatively small increases in the NHI budget because the system is apparently showing good performance in comparison to other countries, according to measures such as life expectancy, infant mortality, and more. The health system has, moreover, shown itself to be relatively efficient and has continued to improve health outcomes (OECD, 2015). However, the significant deficit of the four HPs, which reached €545 million in 2015 alone, as well as the over €1 billion deficit of all general hospitals in Israel, together with worrying data on long waiting times (especially in hospitals) and disparities of availability and quality of services among Israeli groups, raise two important questions. First, by how much should the government increase the public health system budget in order to compensate for the continual erosion of resources? Second, how should the compensation mechanisms be modified in order to maximize outcomes under the current budget? The first question is outside the scope of this chapter and therefore, we will focus only the second one.

### 13.5.6    Risk-Sharing as a Supplement to Imperfect Risk Adjustment

Up to this point, most of the discussion in this chapter—as well as most of the research and debate in Israel—regarding the issue of HPs' compensation, has focused on mechanisms to improve the capitation formula and the risk-adjustment scheme. In the remainder of this section, we broaden the discussion and consider other payment mechanisms that could be implemented, alongside the capitation mechanism, in order to reduce plans' incentives for selection.

As mentioned above, the MoF sets the annual government funding level for the NHI. Until 2016, the government had to distribute the NHI funds among the HPs according to a capitation formula. There was no flexibility in choosing the compensation mechanism (i.e., risk sharing or capitation). Only the additional financial support could be distributed using a risk-sharing mechanism. A recent, meaningful amendment to the NHI Law enables the Ministers of Health and Finance to compensate the HPs for providing the NHI health benefits package not only by a capitation formula but also by a risk-sharing mechanism (RSM). The 2016 capitation committee mentioned above (Section 13.3.4) could use this amendment when finalizing its recommendations.

RSMs are designed to complement the capitation formula. The economic literature lists several types of mechanisms with risk-sharing characteristics:

- Retrospective payment of expenditures for certain individuals according to predetermined criteria (e.g., by serious illness, or old age);
- Predetermination of the type (and sometimes the price) of treatment for which all or part of the expenditure is paid—for all or some individuals;
- Retrospective payment for the most expensive individuals;
- Setting a proportion of an HP's individuals for whom the HPs may receive the real expenditures;

- Determination of the level of normative expenditures, beyond which the funder will pay retrospectively.

RSMs are aimed at reducing the incentives for selection, but at the cost of increasing the incentives for inefficiency and overprovision (moral hazard). Generally, a combination of prospective and retrospective mechanisms best serves economic efficiency (see Chapter 5: Evaluating the Performance of Health Plan Payment Systems).

Based on the literature and in-depth interviews with Israeli researchers and policymakers, Brammli-Greenberg et al. (2016a) identified several types of RSMs as well as other mechanisms, which are feasible in Israel and could reduce incentives for implicit and service selection. Some mechanisms operate at the individual level and are designed to benefit the target individuals.

### 13.5.7   Mental Health Patients

As mentioned above, since June 2015, the HPs have been carrying the responsibility for providing mental health services. Two billion NIS (€0.4 billion) was added to the budget and the funds are allocated to the plans using two compensation mechanisms: one for mental health hospitalization and the other for mental health ambulatory care. For the mental health ambulatory care, the budget allocation was implemented simply by changing weights of the current capitation formula groups.

This policy raises two potential problems. First, HPs can claim that the budget is insufficient since it was calculated on the basis of previous use, which is much lower than use will be after the reform is fully implemented, as mental health services will be more accessible. Second, allocating the entire budget for ambulatory care via capitation does not guarantee that the money will go to mental health services. On the contrary, since mental health patients are usually very expensive (in terms of both physical and mental health services they use), and given that there has been no change in the capitation formula to include mental health ambulatory care (nor as a risk adjuster or as a major service) mental health patients could be targeted for implicit selection and service distortion. A recent study confirmed the need to develop a specific risk adjustment formula for mental health and the high costs of care involved (Cohen and Shmueli, in press; Cohen and Shmueli, in progress).

A supplemental mechanism that is feasible in Israel, and that could reduce incentives for selection of mental health patients, would be to carve out the budget for mental health and to compensate the HPs on the basis of a separate capitation formula with different risk coefficients and different weights than the health capitation formula. It should be mentioned here that such a mechanism is part of a proposal now being discussed in Israel, which would make the HPs responsible for providing long-term care in addition to their current package of services.

## 13.5.8    Patients With Exceptional Expenditure

The "severe illnesses" mechanism, discussed above, constituted 7% of the HPs' revenue in 2015 and covers about 0.07% of the population (see Section 13.3.3). As noted, HPs are paid prospectively according to the number of patients and a predetermined cost set for each of the following diseases: thalassemia major, Gaucher's disease, kidney dysfunction, hemophilia, and AIDS. The current capitation formula completely ignores other, more common chronic conditions such as cancer, diabetes, asthma, heart diseases, and less common conditions such as transplants. People with one or more of these conditions are, of course, particularly vulnerable to implicit and service selection.

In addition to the prospective mechanism, several different supplemental RSMs could be easily implemented and used, under the Israeli system, in order to reduce incentives for selection. Here we discuss three of them, but one could consider several others (or various modifications of the ones mentioned below). It should be mentioned that these mechanisms are not perfect substitutes for one another and all three of them could be implemented simultaneously.

- *Outlier risk sharing.* Retrospective compensation for patients for whom the HPs have had exceptionally high expenditures (the threshold of expenditures above which such a payment would be made, as well as the level of risk sharing, would be determined in advance). This mechanism is also known as reinsurance. Layton et al. (2017) show how reinsurance can complement risk adjustment to counteract plans' incentives for ex-post individual selection.
- *Risk sharing for services potentially subject to underprovision.* Retrospective compensation for patients whose use of some prespecified services was above a certain threshold. Such services are predictable, predictive, and their use is negatively correlated with the plan's compensation under the capitation formula (Ellis and McGuire, 2007; Frank, Glazer, and McGuire, 2000). Such a mechanism can be especially effective to counter plans' incentives to underprovide services that attract unprofitable enrollees.
- *Risk sharing for high risks.* Retrospective or prospective compensation for preselected high-risk patients. The prospective payment would be made so as to cover (at least some of) the predicted costs of these patients. Even though plans must accept every applicant, they may still apply some mechanisms in order to deter certain individuals or groups of

individuals from joining the plans. By paying separately for these individuals, the incentives for such selection will be reduced.

### 13.5.9   Pay-for-Performance Mechanisms

Various supplementary mechanisms could be easily implemented in the public system in Israel to supplement the capitation mechanism and to enhance the quality of care. Here we mention two of them.

- *Retrospective payments based on improvement of health status over time.* Under this mechanism, plans would be reimbursed for reducing the number of members with specific illnesses (e.g., diabetes or high blood pressure).
- *Retrospective payments for "targeted" services.* The MoH would choose a (small) set of services that it would like to advance (e.g., preventive medicine) and pay the plans some additional amount for providing these services. These payments could be based on the number of patients receiving these services or the number of times the service is performed. The payment could also be a lump sum payment to cover a certain, verifiable investment.

To summarize, the current payment mechanism employed under the Israeli NHI Law is almost purely prospective. Both economic theory and empirical evidence suggest that moving towards a more "balanced" system, where some of the funds would be allocated to the plans on a retrospective basis, could be welfare-improving. Using both prospective and retrospective compensation mechanisms would improve the efficiency of the healthcare system, by redistributing healthcare spending away from services that the healthy are likely to use toward services likely to be used by less healthy enrollees.

### ENDNOTES

1. The nine age groups (until 2005) were: 0−4, 5−14, 15−25, 25−34, 35−44, 45−54, 55−64, 65−74, and 75 + .
2. The Israeli Central Bureau of Statistics calculates the Periphery Index of the local authorities (the index ranges from 1 to 10). The Periphery Index is calculated as a combination of two components (with equal weights): Potential Accessibility Index of local authority and proximity of local authority to the boundary of the Tel Aviv District. The proximity between the geographical units is measured by the shortest distance in the available road network, with some roads unavailable due to construction or for security reasons.
3. It is easy to see that if the costs of all services were the same for services across plans, the use weights would be equivalent to spending weights and $W_j$ would be the ratio between the average cost of individuals in group j and the average cost in the entire population.
4. As will be discussed below, the payments for "severe illnesses" under the NHI Law are prospective and, as such, can be viewed as just another element of the capitation formula. However, since, historically, in Israel, it has been referred to as a separate mechanism and

since the payments under this mechanism are calculated differently than the other capitation payments, we treat them as a separate mechanism in this chapter.

5. Excluding the governmental support and one-time profits or losses.
6. Even though all four HPs are not-for-profit and even though it is likely that if a plan performed relatively poorly, the government would prevent it from going bankrupt, it is also true that no HP manager would like to have his name associated with a bankrupt HP. Furthermore, it is usually the case in Israel that if and when the government comes to the rescue of a particular organization it comes with much more involvement of the MoF in operating that organization.
7. Obviously, this last argument goes against the whole idea of using risk-adjustment mechanisms. Nevertheless, it is an argument often raised by the Ministry to oppose advanced changes in the risk-adjustment formula.

## REFERENCES

Achdut, L., Shmueli, A., 2015. Re-examination of then Israeli risk-adjustment: the introduction of socio-economic risk adjuster. Van Leer Policy Study, number 19 (Hebrew).

Arieli, A., Horev, T., Keidar, N., 2012. National Health Insurance Law — statistical data from 1995-2011. Ministry of Health, Jerusalem (Hebrew). Available from: http://www.health.gov.il/PublicationsFiles/stat_LB1995_2011.pdf.

Brammli-Greenberg, S & Waitzberg, R 2013, Using waiting times as a tool for rationing care in a managed care setting: is it a good idea, and if so, for whom? 5th International Conference on Health Policy in Jerusalem. http://www.israelhpr.org.il/1059/, accessed 15.7.2014.

Brammli-Greenberg, S., Glazer, J & Waitzberg, R., *work in progress. Payment mechanisms to mitigate incentive for (Adverse)* Service Selection among Health Plans in Israel.

Brammli-Greenberg, S., Waitzberg, R., Medina-Artom, T., Adijes-Toren, A., 2014. Low-budget policy tool to empower Israeli insureds to demand their rights in the healthcare system. Health policy 118 (3), 279−284.

Brammli-Greenberg, S., Waitzberg, R., & Glazer, J. 2016a. *Evaluation of the mechanisms for distributing funds among the health plans and a proposal for complementary mechanisms*, Research report submitted to the Israel National Institute for Health Policy research (in Hebrew) http://www.israelhpr.org.il/.

Brammli-Greenberg, S., Waitzberg, R., Gross, S., 2016b. Integrating public and private insurance in the Israeli health system: an attempt to reconcile conflicting values. In: Thomson, S., Mossialos, E. (Eds.), Private health insurance and medical savings accounts: history, politics, performance. Cambridge University Press, Cambridge.

Cao, Z., McGuire, T.G., 2003. Service-level selection by HMOs in Medicare. Journal of health economics 22 (6), 915−931.

Chinitz, D., 1995. Israel's health policy breakthrough: the politics of reform and the reform of politics. Journal of Health Politics, Policy and Law 20 (4), 909−932.

Cohen, Y., Shmueli, A., (in press). Identifying Predictors of Mental Health Services Consumption in Israel, Harefuah (in Hebrew).

Cohen, Y., Shmueli, A., (work in progress). Towards a Capitation Formula in Mental Health in Israel.

Ellis, R.P., McGuire, T.G., 2007. Predictability and predictiveness in health care spending. Journal of health economics 26 (1), 25−48.

Enthoven, A.C., 2014. Theory and practice of managed competition in health care finance. Elsevier.

Frank, R.G., Glazer, J., McGuire, T.G., 2000. Measuring adverse selection in managed health care. Journal of Health Economics 19 (6), 829−854.

Glazer, J., McGuire, T.G., 2000. Optimal risk adjustment in markets with adverse selection: an application to managed care. The American Economic Review 90 (4), 1055−1071.

Glazer, J., McGuire, T.G., 2002. Setting health plan premiums to ensure efficient quality in health care: minimum variance optimal risk adjustment. Journal of Public Economics 84 (2), 153−173.

Gross, R., 2003. Implementing health care reform in Israel: Organizational response to perceived incentives. Journal of health politics, policy and law 28 (4), 659−692.

Gross, R., Anson, O., 2002. Health care reform in Israel. In: Twaddle, A.C. (Ed.), Health Care Reform around the World. Greenwood publishing group, pp. 198−218. , 2002. Health care reform around the world.

Gross, R., Rosen, B., Shirom, A., 2001. Reforming the Israeli health system: findings of a 3-year evaluation. Health Policy 56 (1), 1−20.

Hadley, J., Rosen, B., Shmueli, A., 2002. Towards the inclusion of a health status parameter in the israeli capitation formula. RR-372-02. Myers-JDC Brookdale Institute, Jerusalem Israel.

Keidar, N., Plotnic, R., 2016. *HPs transfers in 2016, on who HPs compete, The Administration for strategic and economic planning*. MoH (in Hebrew). Available at: https://www.health. gov.il/PublicationsFiles/economy_18022013.pdf.

Layton, T., Ellis, R., McGuire, T., Van Kleef, R., 2017. Measuring Efficiency of Health Plan Payment Systems in Managed Competition Health Insurance Markets. Journal of Health Economics forthcoming.

Layton, T.J., McGuire, T.G., van Kleef, R.C., 2016. Deriving Risk Adjustment Payment Weights to Maximize Efficiency of Health Insurance Markets (No. w22642). National Bureau of Economic Research.

Ministry of Finance 2012, *Annual report of the commissioner of the capital market, insurance and savings*, prepared by The Ministry of Finance, Jerusalem. (in Hebrew). Available at: http://www.anet.co.il/anetfiles/files/6199.pdf.

Ministry of Health 2010, *The 2009 public summary report on HP activities*, prepared by The Ministry of Health, Jerusalem. (in Hebrew). Available at: http://www.health.gov.il/ PublicationsFiles/dochhashavut2009.pdf.

Ministry of Health 2012, *Issues on policy and regulation of private health insurance*, prepared by The Ministry of Health, Jerusalem. (in Hebrew). Available at: http://www.health.gov.il/ PublicationsFiles/281112_11122012.pdf.

Ministry of Health 2014, *Committee for strengthening the public healthcare final report*, prepared by The Ministry of Health, Jerusalem. (in Hebrew). Available at: (http://www.health. gov.il/PublicationsFiles/publichealth2014.pdf.

Ministry of Health 2016, *The 2015 public summary report on HP activities*, prepared by The Ministry of Health, Jerusalem. (in Hebrew). Available at: http://www.health.gov.il/ PublicationsFiles/dochhashavut2015.pdf.

National Insurance Institute, 2015. Annual report. National Insurance Institute, Jerusalem (Hebrew) https://www.btl.gov.il/Publications/survey/Documents/seker_280.pdf.

National Insurance Institute (NII), 2017. National and Health Insurance premiums. https://www. btl.gov.il/Insurance/Rates/Pages/default.aspx.

OECD, 2015. Health at a Glance 2015. https://doi.org/10.1787/health_glance-2015-en.

OECD, 2016. Health policy in Israel. OECD Health Policy Overview. Available from: https:// www.oecd.org/israel/Health-Policy-in-Israel-April-2016.pdf.

Rosen, B., 2011. How health plans in Israel manage the care provided by their physicians. The Smokler Center for Health Policy research at Myers-JDC-Brookdale Institute. Available at: http://brookdaleheb.jdc.org.il/_Uploads/PublicationsFiles/136-11-Manage-Physician-5-REP-ENG.pdf, accessed 15.7.2014.

Rosen, B., Waitzberg, R., Merkur, S., 2015. Israel: Health System Review. Health systems in transition 17 (6), 1−212.

Schwartz, S., Doron, H., Davidovitch, N., 2006. Between vision and deficit − the historical political struggle for national health insurance legislation. In: Bin Nun, G., Ofer, G. (Eds.), Ten years of National Health Insurance 1995−2005. Israel National Institute for Health Policy and Health Services Research, Tel Hashomer, pp. 69−106. (in Hebrew).

Shmueli, A., 2015. On the calculation of the Israeli risk adjustment rates. The European Journal of Health Economics 16 (3), 271−277.

Shmueli, A., Chinitz, D., 2001. Risk-adjusted capitation: the Israeli experience. The European Journal of Public Health 11 (2), 182−184.

Shmueli, A., Nissan-Engelcin, E., 2013. Local availability of physicians' services as a tool for implicit risk selection. Social Science & Medicine 84, 53−60.

Shmueli, A., Chernichovsky, D., Zmora, I., 2003. Risk adjustment and risk sharing: the Israeli experience. Health Policy 65 (1), 37−48.

Shmueli, A., Achdut, L., Sabag-Endeweld, M., 2008. Financing the package of services during the first decade of the National Health Insurance Law in Israel: trends and issues. Health Policy 87 (3), 273−284.

van de Ven, W.P., van Kleef, R.C., van Vliet, R.C., 2015. Risk selection threatens quality of care for certain patients: lessons from Europe's health insurance exchanges. Health Affairs 34 (10), 1713−1720.

Vardy, D.A., Kayam, R., Kitai, E., 2008. Community health: How to incentivize physcians. Harefuah 147 (12), 999−1003.

Yishai, Y., 1982. Politics and medicine: The case of Israeli national health insurance. Social Science & Medicine 16 (3), 285−291.

Zwanziger, J., Brammli-Greenberg, S., 2011. Strong Government influence over the Israeli health care system has led to low rates of spending growth. Health Affairs 30 (9), 1779−1785.

# Chapter 14

# Health Plan Payment in the Netherlands

Richard C. van Kleef, Frank Eijkenaar, René C.J.A. van Vliet and
Wynand P.M.M. van de Ven
*Erasmus School of Health Policy and Management, Erasmus University Rotterdam, Rotterdam,*
*The Netherlands*

## 14.1 INTRODUCTION

The Dutch health insurance system has a long tradition of both public and private initiatives. Until the 1940s, there was no regulation with respect to healthcare financing, but from 1940 to 1970 the government implemented several laws to establish universal access to medical care. In this period two major health insurance schemes were introduced. The first was the so-called "Sickness Fund Scheme" (1941), a mandatory insurance program for low- and middle-income people which covered mostly curative short-term care, such as physician services, hospital care, and prescription drugs. At the end of the 20th century about 65% of the population was enrolled in the sickness fund insurance. The vast majority of high-income people (who were not eligible for the sickness fund insurance) purchased private health insurance with similar coverage.[1] The second program was the so-called "Exceptional Medical Expenses Act" (1968), which still exists today (though under a different name, i.e., the "Long Term Care Act"). This program is mandatory for all people working or living in the Netherlands and provides coverage for long-term care such as nursing home care for the elderly and disabled people. On top of the extensive coverage provided by these two programs, the majority of the Dutch population also purchases supplementary insurance coverage, e.g., for dental care, physiotherapy, alternative medicine, and acute care in foreign countries. Box 14.1 describes some key features of the three "layers" in the Dutch health insurance system in place from 1968 to 2006.

From 1970 to 1990 the government implemented stringent supply-side regulation to better control medical spending. Key reforms in this period included the replacement of free prices and open-ended reimbursement by

**Risk Adjustment, Risk Sharing and Premium Regulation in Health Insurance Markets.**
DOI: https://doi.org/10.1016/B978-0-12-811325-7.00014-2

---

**BOX 14.1 Three layers of the Dutch health insurance system in place from 1968 to 2006**

| | | |
|---|---|---|
| *Layer 1* | *Exceptional Medical Expenses Act:*<br>• Public insurance for long-term care (e.g., nursing home care for the elderly and disabled)<br>• Mandatory for the entire population<br>• Regulated by the government<br>• Executed by regional noncompeting administration offices that bear no financial risk | |
| *Layer 2* | *Sickness Fund Insurance:*<br>• Public insurance for curative care (e.g., physician services, hospital care, and prescription drugs)<br>• Mandatory for people with income below a certain threshold<br>• Regulated by the government<br>• Executed by sickness funds that started bearing financial risk in the mid-1990s | *Private Health Insurance:*<br>• Private insurance for curative care (e.g., physician services, hospital care, prescription drugs)<br>• Enrollment on a voluntary basis by those not eligible for Sickness Fund Insurance<br>• Minor regulation by the government<br>• Executed by private insurance companies that bear full financial risk |
| *Layer 3* | *Supplementary Health Insurance:*<br>• Private insurance for supplemental benefits (e.g., dental care and physiotherapy)<br>• Enrollment on a voluntary basis<br>• No specific regulation by the government (other than the usual insurance regulation)<br>• Executed by competing private insurance companies that bear full financial risk | |

---

regulated prices and volumes. Cost containment was considered crucial since the Sickness Fund Scheme and the Exceptional Medical Expenses Act had led to significant increases in medical spending. However, in the early 1980s, dissatisfaction about the stringent supply-side regulation started to grow: the regulatory mechanisms had become too complex, the financing structure of the healthcare system had become fragmented and incentives for innovation and efficiency in the delivery of care were absent, both for insurers, consumers, and healthcare providers. These shortcomings led to a stream of new reform proposals. Among these proposals was the advice of the Dekker committee in 1987 which recommended market-oriented reforms in combination with a national health insurance program. In retrospect, the advice of the Dekker committee turned out to be a landmark proposal that

---

**BOX 14.2  Three layers of the Dutch health insurance scheme since 2006**

| Layer 1 | *Exceptional Medical Expenses Act (since 2015: Long-term Care Act):*<br>• See Box 14.1 |
|---------|------|
| Layer 2 | *Health Insurance Act:*<br>• Private insurance covering, e.g., physician services, hospital care, and prescription drugs<br>• Mandatory for the entire population<br>• Regulated by the government<br>• Executed by competing insurance companies that bear financial risk |
| Layer 3 | *Supplementary Health Insurance:*<br>• See Box 14.1 |

---

led to several reforms underpinning the "Health Insurance Act" that was implemented in 2006.

The Health Insurance Act introduced a national plan for mandatory private health insurance based on principles of regulated competition (Van de Ven and Schut, 2008). The Health Insurance Act replaced the second layer in Box 14.1 (i.e., the sickness fund insurance and the former private health insurance), leading to the new situation shown in Box 14.2 which remains, with some modifications, in place today.

Recently, several services originally covered by the first layer were transferred to the second layer. Among others, these include short-term mental health care (2008), geriatric rehabilitation care (2013), home care (2015), and long-term mental health care (2015). Possibly, other types of long-term care will follow in the (near) future, implying that more types of care will be exposed to principles of regulated competition. For 2017, the projected spending in the three layers sums to about 65 billion euros (9.2% of GDP), consisting of 18 billion euros (2.6% of GDP) for the first layer, 43 billion euros (6.1% of GDP) for the second layer, and 4 billion euros (0.5% of GDP) for the third layer (Tweede Kamer, 2017; Vektis, 2016).

The remainder of this chapter focuses on the Health Insurance Act. In the next sections we describe the institutional setting (Section 14.2) and the central role of health plan payment in this system (Sections 14.3 and 14.4). In Section 14.5 we discuss some ongoing issues and reforms.

## 14.2  ORGANIZATION OF THE HEALTH INSURANCE SYSTEM

The Health Insurance Act is based on principles of regulated competition, meaning that insurers and providers of care *compete* on price and quality, while the government establishes *regulation* to protect public objectives such as individual affordability and accessibility of health plans (Enthoven and Van de Ven, 2007; Van de Ven et al., 2013). The following sections describe some relevant aspects of the current system in terms of regulation, consumer choice, and instruments for insurers to promote efficiency in the delivery of care.

## 14.2.1   Health Plan Market Regulation

The Health Insurance Act contains various features to enforce individual affordability and accessibility of health plans (Box 14.3). First, every person who lives or works in the Netherlands is obliged to enroll in a health plan offered by a private insurer. The contract between the consumer and the insurer is on an individual basis (i.e., family contracts are not allowed). Second, the benefit package is standardized in terms of types of medical care (e.g., physician services, hospital care, and prescription drugs), implying that the nature, content, and extent of services are specified by law (while insurers have substantial freedom with respect to network design as will be described in Section 14.2.3). Moreover, insurers are obliged to ensure that services are available to the consumer within a reasonable travel/waiting time. Third, insurers must accept all applicants and charge a community-rated premium. In addition to premium regulation, there are premium subsidies, the so-called "health allowances," for low- and middle-income families. In order to mitigate the potential for risk selection (induced by community-rated premiums) insurers are compensated for some of the variation in medical spending by a risk equalization system (and risk-sharing mechanisms), which will be described in Section 14.3.

In addition, there are numerous rules and directives regarding the protection of market efficiency. One example is the European antitrust regulation (supervised by the Authority for Consumers and Markets) aimed at protecting the market against anticompetitive behavior via cartels, mergers, or dominant market shares. Other examples include various types of quality

---

**BOX 14.3 Regulation to achieve individual affordability and accessibility of health plans in the Health Insurance Act**

- Individual mandate to enroll in a health plan (offered by a private insurer)
- Standardized benefit package in terms of types of medical care (regulated by the government)
- Open enrollment
- Community-rating per health plan
- Income-related healthcare allowances for low- and middle-income families
- Risk equalization (and risk sharing)

regulation that apply to healthcare organizations and physicians (supervised by the Health Care Inspectorate), solvency regulation for health insurers (supervised by the Authority for Financial Markets), and specific market regulation (e.g., with respect to transparency of prices and products) for both insurers and providers (supervised by the Health Care Authority). Although these types of regulation are crucial for the functioning of the healthcare system, the primary focus of this chapter is on the rules and systems regarding the protection of individual affordability and accessibility of health plans, and health plan payment in particular.

## 14.2.2  Health Plan Choice Options for Consumers

Under the Health Insurance Act, consumers have an annual choice of health plan. Contracts start on January 1 and have a maximum duration of one year, leading to a concentration of health plan switching at the end of the calendar year. Box 14.4 summarizes the main dimensions in which health plans (can) differ. The consumers' choice of insurer mainly implies a choice of customer service, e.g., in terms of communication, (medical) advice, and the way claims are handled. Note, however, that customer service can also vary among health plans provided by the same insurer. The deductible option means consumers can increase their deductible from the mandatory minimum of 385 euros per person per annum (2017) by an amount of 100, 200, 300, 400 or 500 euros; the higher the deductible, the lower the premium. Another choice option for consumers is to enroll via a so-called "group arrangement." Although all enrollees have an individual-based contract, insurers are allowed to offer specific pluses to groups of people (e.g., in terms of a premium discount with a maximum of 10% and/or discounts on other products). Group arrangements can be organized for employees of a particular firm, members of a sports club, or people gathered by a private initiative, among others. In practice, over 50,000 group arrangements exist (Dutch Health Care Authority, 2015). Although consumers cannot join more than one of these arrangements, they can generally choose among multiple groups (e.g., their employer and their sports club). Finally, health plans are allowed to differ in terms of network of contracted providers and out-of-network coverage. This flexibility is the main instrument for insurers to promote efficiency in the delivery of care. We will elaborate on this aspect in the next section.

---

**BOX 14.4  Health plan choice options for consumers**

- Insurer
- Level of voluntary deductible
- Yes/no group arrangement
- Network of contracted providers and out-of-network coverage

### 14.2.3 Instruments for Insurers to Promote Efficiency in the Delivery of Care

Under the Health Insurance Act, insurers have several instruments to promote efficiency in the delivery of care (Box 14.5). First, they are allowed to selectively contract and restrict their provider network. In the early years of the Health Insurance Act, almost all health plans provided access to (all healthcare services of) all providers. In recent years, however, the number of health plans with a restricted provider network increased (Dutch Health Care Authority, 2015). Instead of contracting with healthcare providers, insurers can also choose to set up their own healthcare facilities. So far, this so-called vertical integration has been limited, but is growing slightly. Some insurers have set up their own pharmacies or some primary care facilities (Dutch Health Care Authority, 2014). In order to channel patients toward contracted providers, insurers can charge copayments (on top of the deductible) for out-of-network spending. In practice, these copayments go up to 50% of the average market price for a particular treatment (Dutch Health Care Authority, 2015). In addition, insurers can channel patients toward preferred providers (within their network) by eliminating the out-of-pocket expenses due to the deductible in case consumers visit these providers; so far, this option is not widely used. In addition to network design, insurers also have some freedom to exploit utilization management and to decide on the design of provider payment systems, e.g., fee-for-service, bundled payments, and pay-for-performance. Although insurers negotiate with providers on prices and volumes, innovative payment systems—such as pay-for-performance—are hardly applied yet. An important reason is the current lack of information on the quality of medical services to use as a basis for payment (Van de Ven et al., 2013).

---

**BOX 14.5 Instruments for insurers to improve efficiency in delivery of care**

- Insurers have substantial freedom to restrict their provider network
- Insurers are free to set up their own healthcare facilities
- For out-of-network spending insurers can charge copayments (on top of the deductible)
- For preferred providers insurers can waive out-of-pocket payments under the deductible
- Insurers can exploit utilization management
- Insurers are increasingly free to decide on the design of provider payment systems

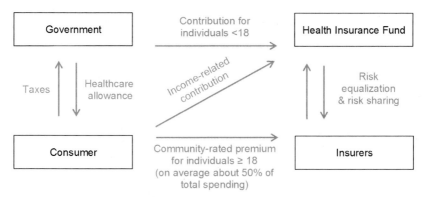

**FIGURE 14.1**　Financing scheme of the Health Insurance Act.

## 14.3　HEALTH PLAN PAYMENT DESIGN

Fig. 14.1 provides a summary of the financing scheme of the Health Insurance Act with the *arrows* representing the major flows of money. All people 18 years or older pay a community-rated premium to their insurer. The total premium revenues cover about 50% of average medical spending. Since this premium is considered to be too high for low- and middle-income families, they receive an income-related premium subsidy (the so-called "healthcare allowance"), which is financed with general tax revenues. The other 50% of total spending is covered by an income-related contribution (partly paid by consumers and partly by their employer) and a direct contribution from the government to compensate for the zero premiums of people under the age of 18 (financed with general tax revenues). These contributions are collected in the "Health Insurance Fund," and distributed to insurers via the risk equalization system and some risk-sharing mechanisms. In the risk equalization system insurers receive a contribution for enrollees with expected spending above the average premium and pay a contribution for enrollees with expected spending below the average premium. In the next sections these elements of the financing scheme will be explained in more detail.

### 14.3.1　Regulation of Premiums and Contributions

In order to achieve individual affordability of health plans, the Dutch regulator aims at establishing cross-subsidies from the healthy to the sick (referred to as risk solidarity) and from high-income to low-income people (referred to as income solidarity). Risk solidarity is enforced by the requirement of community-rating per health plan (in combination with risk equalization and risk sharing as will be explained in later sections). Income solidarity is organized by the income-related contribution, which is a fixed percentage of income and has a maximum of about 2900 euros per person per year (in 2017), and by the healthcare allowance, which increases with a lower income and has a maximum of about 1050 euros per year for individuals and about 2050 euros per year for households (in 2017). Depending on political decision making, the precise percentages and maximum values for the income-related contribution and healthcare allowance can (slightly) differ from year to year.

## 14.3.2 Risk Equalization

The Dutch risk equalization system was first implemented in the sickness fund insurance in 1993 together with some modest financial risk for sickness funds which has increased over time (see Fig. 14.2). In 2017, the system includes four different risk equalization models, one for each of the following types of care: somatic health care (projected spending for 2017: 39.9 billion euros), short-term mental health care (i.e., outpatient mental treatments and first year of inpatient mental treatments, 3.7 billion euros), long-term mental health care (i.e., second and third years of inpatient mental treatments, 0.2 billion euros), and out-of-pocket payments due to the mandatory deductible (3.2 billion euros). Each of these four models leads to a prediction of medical spending per individual, which forms the basis of the risk equalization payment. Below, we will discuss the risk adjustor variables applied in the different models, the estimation techniques used for deriving the risk adjustor coefficients, and the procedures applied to go from predicted spending to the actual payments for insurers. Readers might wonder why mental health care is not simply included in the model for somatic care. The reason is that once mental health care was transferred to the Health Insurance Act, specific risk-sharing mechanisms were applied to this type of care. For example, a risk corridor was applied to the gap between realized and predicted spending on mental care. Since this risk corridor was not applicable to

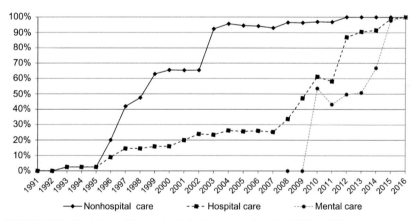

**FIGURE 14.2** Evolution of financial risk for insurers in the period 1993–2016.

somatic care, predicted spending had to be calculated separately for mental care requiring a separate risk equalization model. This led to some path dependency: although the specific risk-sharing mechanisms for mental care no longer exist, the models for mental care and somatic care have not yet been merged, probably due to the fact that these models now differ in terms of performance, risk adjusters, and estimation technique.

### 14.3.2.1  Risk Adjustor Variables for Somatic Care

The risk equalization model for somatic care dates back to the model implemented in the sickness fund insurance in 1993. Over the course of time a large number of risk adjusters have been added to the model based on the following characteristics: age interacted with gender (1993), zip-code clusters for somatic care (1995), source of income interacted with age (1995), pharmacy-based cost groups (2002), diagnosis-based cost groups (2004), socioeconomic status interacted with age (2008), multiple-year high-cost groups (2012), durable medical equipment cost groups (2014), yes/no morbidity in interaction with age (2015), physiotherapy-diagnoses cost groups (2016), groups based on prior spending on specific services (2016), and household size interacted with age (2017). Box 14.6 summarizes the risk adjustors used in the model of 2017.

---

**BOX 14.6  Risk adjustors used in the risk equalization model for somatic care (2017)**

*Age interacted with gender:* 20 classes for men and 20 classes for women. The age classes are: 0 years, 1–4 years, 5–9 years, 10–14 years, 15–17 years, 18–24 years, 5-year cohorts up to the age of 90, and finally a class for people of 90 years or older.

*Pharmacy-based cost groups (PCGs):* 33 classes based on the individual's prior use of pharmaceuticals. Enrollees are categorized in one or more of 33 PCGs if they received a predefined amount of specific pharmaceuticals in the previous year (in most cases: more than 180 defined daily doses). Enrollees that are not classified in one or more of the 33 PCGs are categorized in a separate PCG. For the main principles and technical details on the construction of the Dutch PCGs, see Lamers (1999).

*Diagnoses-based cost groups (DCGs):* 15 clusters of specific hospital inpatient and outpatient diagnoses from the previous year (with diagnoses clustered on the basis of residual spending resulting from a risk equalization model without DCGs). Enrollees with multiple diagnoses are classified in only one DCG (that with the highest residual spending). Enrollees without any of these diagnoses are categorized in a separate DCG. For more information and technical details on the construction of the Dutch DCGs, see Lamers (1998), Prinsze and Van Vliet (2007), and Van Kleef et al. (2014).

*(Continued)*

**BOX 14.6 (Continued)**

*Multiple-year high-cost groups (MHCGs)*: Seven classes based on high health-care spending on somatic care in year $t-1$, $t-2$, and $t-3$. The assumption is that those with multiple-year high costs suffer from a chronic disease. The following seven classes are distinguished. Based on information from three prior years: $3 \times$ costs in the top 0.5%, $3 \times$ costs in the top 1.5%, $3 \times$ costs in the top 4%, $3 \times$ costs in the top 7%, $3 \times$ costs in the top 10%, $3 \times$ costs in the top 15%. Based on information from 2 prior years: $2 \times$ costs in the top 15%. Enrollees are classified in one class only, which is the one in which they first appear (in the aforementioned order of classes). Enrollees who are not classified in one of these seven classes are categorized in a separate class. For more information, see Van Kleef and Van Vliet (2012).

*Durable medical equipment cost groups (DMECGs)*: 10 classes based on the use of durable medical equipment in the previous year related to specific chronic conditions. Enrollees with use of more than one device are classified in only one DMECG (that with the highest residual spending). Those without any DMECG are categorized in a separate class. For more information, see Van Kleef and Van Vliet (2011).

*Physiotherapy-diagnoses cost groups (PDCGs)*: Four classes of specific diagnoses obtained from physiotherapy visits in the previous year (with diagnoses clustered on the basis of residual spending resulting from a risk equalization model without PDCGs). Enrollees with multiple diagnoses are classified in only one PDCG (that with the highest residual spending). Enrollees without any of these diagnoses are categorized in a separate PDCG (Eijkenaar and Van Vliet, 2017).

*Home care spending in the previous year*: Seven classes based on the level of home care spending in the previous year. The following classes are distinguished: top 0.25%, top 0.5%, top 1.0%, top 1.5%, top 2.0%, top 2.5%, and bottom 97.5%. Enrollees are classified in one class only, which is the one in which they first appear (in the aforementioned order).

*Geriatric rehabilitation care spending in the previous year*: Two classes based on the level of spending on geriatric rehabilitation care in the previous year. The following classes are distinguished: top 0.275% and bottom 99.725% (a threshold that more or less reflects yes/no spending).

*Yes/no morbidity in interaction with age*: Four classes based on yes/no classification in one or more PCGs, DCGs, MHCGs, DMECGs, and/or PDCGs in interaction with two age groups (below/above 65).

*Zip-code clusters for somatic care*: 10 clusters based on the four digits of the zip code, which represents a village or town or parts of either. The clustering is based on the relation between somatic healthcare spending and information at the regional level (e.g., proportion of non-Western immigrants, degree of urbanization, and distance to healthcare providers).

*Socioeconomic status (SES) in interaction with age*: 12 classes based on total household income (operationalized as total income per street address) in interaction with age. Those in the bottom 20% of the income distribution are categorized in SES class 1, those in the left-middle 20%–40% in SES class 2, those in the middle 40%–70% in SES class 3, and those in the top 30% in SES class 4.

*(Continued)*

**BOX 14.6 (Continued)**

*Source of income/education in interaction with age*: 23 classes derived from source of income or education in interaction with age. The following groups are distinguished: completely disabled, partly disabled, social security beneficiaries, students, fully self-employed, high educational degree, and other (including employed). Enrollees are classified in one class only, which is the one in which they first appear (in the aforementioned order). This classification only applies to people in the age of 18−65.

*Household size in interaction with age*: 13 classes based on the number of residents per street address in interaction with age. The following classes are distinguished: street address with one registered person, street address with 2−15 registered persons, and street address with >15 registered persons (the assumption being that they are living in a nursing home, an institution for physically or mentally handicapped or similar facility). The latter category is divided into two subclasses, one for people living on a >15 person street address in both year *t* and *t* − 1 and one for people living on a >15 person street address in year *t* only (i.e., those who first enter an institution or facility).

---

*Note: most of the articles referred to in this box describe previous versions of a risk adjustor variable.*

## 14.3.2.2    Risk Adjustor Variables for Mental Care

The risk equalization model for short-term mental health care dates back to the transfer of this type of care from the Exceptional Medical Expenses Act (see Box 14.2) to the Health Insurance Act in 2008. In terms of risk adjustor variables the model started with age interacted with gender, zip-code clusters for mental care, source of income interacted with age, pharmacy-based cost groups for mental diseases, socioeconomic status interacted with age, and household size interacted with age. In later years the model was extended with (multiple-year) high-cost groups for mental care (2010), diagnoses-based cost groups for mental diseases (2014), and need-severity level (2017). Until 2016, this model only applied to short-term mental health care, but this changed with the transfer of long-term mental care from the Exceptional Medical Expenses Act (see Box 14.2) to the Health Insurance Act in 2015. In its first year under the Health Insurance Act (2015) long-term mental care was subject to full risk sharing (implying no financial risk for insurers), but since 2016—with the introduction of a separate risk equalization model for this type of care—insurers started to bear financial risk. The risk equalization model for long-term mental care mimics the model for short-term mental care with one additional risk adjustor: spending on inpatient mental care in the previous year (2016). Box 14.7 briefly describes the design of these risk adjustor variables for 2017. Both models for mental care solely apply to people of 18 years or

## BOX 14.7 Risk adjustors used in the risk equalization model for mental care (2017)

*Age interacted with gender*: 30 classes, only for 18 years and older, see Box 14.6.

*Zip code clusters for mental care*: 10 clusters based on the four digits of the zip code, which represents a village or town or parts of either. The clustering is based on the relation between mental healthcare spending and information at the regional level (e.g., proportion of non-Western immigrants, degree of urbanization, and distance to healthcare providers).

*Source of income/education*: 23 classes derived from source of income or education in interaction with age, only for 18 years and older. For further information, see Box 14.6.

*Pharmacy-based cost groups (PCGs)*: Seven classes based on the individual's prior use of pharmaceuticals specifically used for treatment of mental diseases. For further information, see Box 14.6.

*Diagnoses-based cost groups (DCGs)*: Five clusters of specific hospital inpatient and outpatient mental diagnoses from the previous year. For further information, see Box 14.6.

*Socioeconomic status (SES)*: 10 classes based on household income in interaction with age, only for 18 years and older. For further information, see Box 14.6.

*Multiple-year high cost groups (MHCGs)*: Seven classes based on healthcare spending on mental care in year $t-1$, $t-2$, $t-3$, $t-4$, and $t-5$. The assumption is that those with (multiple-year high) spending on mental care probably suffer from a (chronic) mental disease. The following seven classes are distinguished. Based on cost information from five prior years: 5 × costs in the top 0.25%, 5 × costs in the top 0.5%, 2 × costs in the top 0.1%, 2 × costs in the top 0.25%, 2 × costs in the top 0.5%, and 2 × costs in the top 1%. And based on costs information from three prior years: 1 × costs >0. Enrollees are categorized in one class only, which is the one in which they first appear in the aforementioned order. Enrollees who are not classified in one of these seven groups are categorized in a separate class.

*Household size in interaction with age*: 12 classes based on the number of persons per street address in interaction with age, only for 18 years and older. For further information, see Box 14.6.

*Need-severity level*: Five classes based on the amount/type of mental healthcare individuals needed in the previous year. The following five classes are distinguished: low severity, moderate severity, high severity, very high severity, and acute care. Enrollees are categorized in one class only. Enrollees who are not classified in one of these five groups are categorized in a separate class.

*Use of inpatient mental care in the previous year*: Four classes based on the use of inpatient short-term mental health care and the use of long-term mental health care in the previous year. Individuals who are not classified in one of the four classes are categorized in a separate class.

older. For people under the age of 18, mental care is financed by a public program.

### 14.3.2.3  Risk Adjustor Variables for Out-of-Pocket Expenses Under the Mandatory Deductible

The risk equalization model for out-of-pocket expenses under the mandatory deductible dates back to the no-claim rebate in 2006 and 2007 (which was replaced by a mandatory deductible in 2008). This model is applied to correct the risk equalization payments for (differences in) out-of-pocket spending (between high-risk and low-risk individuals) under the deductible. This is necessary because the risk equalization models for somatic care and mental care lead to a prediction of *total* spending (including the out-of-pocket payments due to the mandatory deductible). As will be explained below, the risk equalization payment that an insurer receives is based on the prediction of total spending minus the prediction of out-of-pocket payments.

The deductible applies to all healthcare services covered by the Health Insurance Act (both somatic and mental care) except for primary (GP) care, maternity care, obstetrics, and home care. Because the consumer pays the out-of-pocket payments due to the deductible directly to the insurer (and not to the provider of care) all these expenses are known in the insurers' administration. Box 14.8 briefly describes the design of the risk adjustor variables used in this model in 2017. The model only applies to people of 18 years and above (since those under the age of 18 are exempted from the mandatory deductible) and to those without a PCG, DCG, MHCG, DMECG, and PDCG. For individuals with a PCG, DCG, MHCG, DMECG, and/or PDCG—who generally exceed the deductible—the predicted out-of-pocket payments equal the average out-of-pocket spending in this group, which nearly equals the deductible amount.

---

**BOX 14.8  Risk adjustors used in the risk equalization model for out-of-pocket spending due to the mandatory deductible (2017)**

*Age interacted with gender:* 30 classes, only for 18 years and older, see Box 14.6.

 *Zip code clusters for somatic care:* 10 clusters of zip code areas. For further information, see Box 14.6.

 *Source of income/education:* 23 classes derived from source of income or education in interaction with age, only for 18 years and older. For further information, see Box 14.6.

---

*Note: for individuals with a PCG, DCG, MHCG, DMECG, and/or PDCG the predicted out-of-pocket payments equal the average out-of-pocket spending in this group, which nearly equals the deductible amount.*

### 14.3.2.4    Procedure for Deriving Risk Adjustor Coefficients

In all of the four risk equalization models risk adjustors take the form of dummy variables. The risk adjustor coefficients for year $t$ follow from an individual-level regression of medical spending in year $t - 3$ on the dummy variables from year $t - 3$ (or before, depending on the definition of risk adjustor variables). Data on medical spending and risk characteristics cover the entire Dutch population with a health plan in year $t - 3$. Before estimation, some modifications are applied to make the lagged data representative for year $t$. First, the number of enrollees per risk class (i.e., the classes distinguished by the risk adjustor variables, see Boxes 14.6–14.8) in year $t - 3$ is brought in line with the projected prevalence for year $t$. This is done by a reweighting procedure. Second, the spending data from year $t - 3$ is corrected for particular system changes between $t - 3$ and $t$, such as changes in the benefit package and/or modifications in provider payment systems, as well as for (projected) cost inflation. After these corrections the sum of spending in the dataset equals total spending for year $t$ as projected by the regulator.

For both the somatic model and the model for out-of-pocket payments under the mandatory deductible, risk adjustor coefficients are derived by an ordinary least-squares regression. For the mental care models, the coefficients are derived by a restricted least-squares regression (in order to avoid negative predictions of medical spending that can occur in a multivariate regression model due to a large zero mass). For all models the regression is based on annualized spending weighted by the fraction of the year an individual was enrolled in $t - 3$ (which can be smaller than 1.0 due to birth, death, migration, and within-year switching of health plans which occasionally occurs, e.g., when children turn 18 or when people change jobs and leave the group arrangement of their old employer). For example, a person with a half-year enrollment and 2000 euros spending is given a weight of 0.5 and annualized spending of 4000 euros (2000/0.5). Every year, all models are reestimated as new data—from year $t - 3$—become available. Moreover, an extensive program led by the Ministry of Health is carried out in order to improve the models. Each year this leads to changes in terms of risk adjustor variables (Box 14.9).

### 14.3.2.5    How to Go from Predicted Spending to Risk-Adjusted Payment?

Box 14.10 summarizes the way risk equalization payments are calculated. For people of 18 years or above the risk equalization payment equals the sum of predicted spending for somatic care and mental health care (short term and long term) minus the predicted out-of-pocket spending due to the deductible and minus a fixed amount $p$. The level of $p$ is determined by the government and reflects a political choice on the amount of spending

---

**BOX 14.9 Key features of the procedure for deriving risk adjustor coefficients for year $t$**

- Spending data: from year $t-3$, made representative for year $t$ and covering the entire population
- Risk adjustor variables: from $t-3$ or before (depending on the definition of the risk adjustor); correction for differences between prevalence in year $t-3$ and projected prevalence for year $t$
- Estimation procedure: individual-level regression of annualized medical spending on dummy variables, separately for somatic care, short-term mental health care, long-term mental health care, and copayments under the mandatory deductible
- Estimation method: ordinary least-squares and restricted least-squares
- Weighting: in the regression individuals are weighted with the duration of enrollment
- Frequency of reestimation of risk adjustor coefficients: every year

---

**BOX 14.10 Calculation of risk equalization payment (REP) for individual $i$**

$$REP_{i(18-)} = \hat{y}_{i,somatic}$$

$$REP_{i(18+)} = \hat{y}_{i,somatic} + \hat{y}_{i,mental\_short} + \hat{y}_{i,mental\_long} - \hat{y}_{i,oop} - p$$

$$\text{Total projected spending} = \sum_i \left( \hat{y}_{i,somatic} + \hat{y}_{i,mental\_short} + \hat{y}_{i,mental\_long} - \hat{y}_{i,oop} \right)$$

---

insurers must finance via their premiums. On average $p$ equals about 50% of the average per person spending (see Fig. 14.1). Since $p$ is fixed, the risk equalization payment is independent of the efficiency of health plans, implying that relatively efficient plans can charge lower premiums than inefficient plans. As mentioned earlier, people under the age of 18 are exempted from paying a premium to the insurer and do not face a deductible. Moreover, mental health care for this group is financed by another program. Therefore, the risk equalization payment for people under the age of 18 simply equals the sum of predicted spending for somatic care. For enrollees with incomplete enrollment in year $t$ the payment is in proportion to the duration of enrollment.

In September of year $t-1$ insurers receive notification of their tentative risk equalization payment based on their expected portfolio for year $t$ (in terms of the prevalence of risk adjustor variables). Publication of the tentative payments in September of year $t-1$ allows insurers to calculate and publish their premium in November of year $t-1$, a deadline set by the regulator. Due to enrollees switching plans (mostly on January 1 of year $t$) the final portfolio of health plans may differ from their expected portfolio. Once the final portfolio is known, the definitive risk equalization payments are calculated by combining the final portfolio characteristics with the prospectively estimated risk adjustor coefficients.

## 14.3.3    Risk Sharing

The regulated health insurance market in the Netherlands has a long tradition of risk sharing. Over the past decades different forms of risk sharing have been applied, e.g., risk corridors (at the insurer level), proportional risk sharing, and outlier risk sharing. The main motives for risk sharing in the Netherlands have been (1) to mitigate systematic under- and overcompensations caused by the risk equalization model and (2) to mitigate financial risk regarding specific types of spending largely outside of insurers' influence (e.g., elements of hospital spending that were subject to price regulation). The first motive explains the connection between the extent of risk sharing and the evolution of the risk equalization model over time. As illustrated in Fig. 14.2, the introduction of risk equalization (in 1993) came with a substantial degree of risk sharing: for each euro under/overcompensation on average 97 cents were shared with the Health Insurance Fund (i.e., insurers were liable for only 3 cents). However, as the risk equalization model improved, the financial risk for insurers increased. Since 2016, risk sharing has been almost absent, implying that insurers bear full financial risk for nearly all medical spending covered by the Health Insurance Act. One exemption is the spending on specific newly included treatments for which the historical data necessary to estimate risk equalization payments are not (yet) available.

Closely related, but different from the types of risk sharing mentioned above, is a mechanism called "flankerend beleid" in Dutch, which roughly translates to "flanking policy" in English. This mechanism consists of three elements aimed at protecting insurers against specific risks they are not held responsible for (see Box 14.11).

## 14.3.4    Implementation and Maintenance

In the Netherlands, health plan payment design is primarily the responsibility of the government. For the implementation and maintenance of the health plan payment system, the government contracts with research institutes and consultancy firms. Research includes development of risk adjustor variables, collection and preparation of required data, and annual updating of the risk adjustor coefficients. The calculation of insurers' risk equalization payment (Box 14.10) and the administrative and legal aspects of payment transfers between insurers and the Health Insurance Fund are delegated to the National Health Care Institute; the same holds for the "flanking policy"

**BOX 14.11 "Flanking policy" in 2017**

Three elements of "Flanking policy" aimed to protect insurers against specific risks they are not held responsible for are:

1. Protection against increases in the projected spending for year $t$ due to changes to the benefit package *after* insurers have published their premiums. In case a service is added to (or removed from) the benefits package, the coefficients for risk adjustor variables are multiplied by a factor equal to (new projected spending) divided by (old projected spending).

2. Protection against increases in insurance claims because of "exceptional circumstances," like a catastrophe (e.g., an explosion in a city center). In case the government has decided that an increase in medical spending for one or more insurers is due to exceptional circumstances, the insurer(s) can be provided with a compensation for the spending resulting from the catastrophe. The increase in medical spending needs to be at least 4% of an insurer's total spending. Since the introduction of "flanking policy" in 2012 this measure has not been applied.

3. Protection against a mismatch between total projected spending (see bottom line of Box 14.10) and total actual spending at the population level. In the case of a mismatch (e.g., projected spending for year $t$ < actual spending in year $t$), the financial consequences will generally be worse for insurers with relatively many high-risk people than for plans with relatively few of these people. Once actual spending for year $t$ is known (usually in year $t+3$), individual-level equalization payments are corrected in the following way: (1) determine total predicted spending for year $t$ by combining the prospective risk adjustment coefficients with the *actual* 0/1 values of risk adjustor variables, (2) calculate the difference between total predicted spending for year $t$ and total actual spending in year $t$, (3) distribute this difference across enrollees relative to the individual-level predicted spending, resulting in an additional payment per enrollee which is positive (negative) in case actual total spending in year $t$ exceeds (falls below) projected spending for year $t$. These payments are financed by the plans themselves via a flat contribution per enrollee of 18 years or above.

(Box 14.11). Box 14.12 roughly summarizes the main steps in the process of estimating and calculating risk equalization payments.

## 14.4   EVALUATION OF HEALTH PLAN PAYMENT

From an economic perspective, the most important aspects of health plan payment evaluation in the Netherlands include "incentives" and "market response".[2] This section reports on the measures used to quantify these aspects and highlights some empirical findings.

> **BOX 14.12 Main steps in the process of estimating and calculating risk equalization payments**
>
> 1. Collecting individual-level data on spending and characteristics of the population of year $t-3$
> 2. Correcting $t-3$ data for mutations in the benefit package between year $t-3$ and year $t$
> 3. Correcting prevalence of risk classes in $t-3$ data for differences with projected prevalence in year $t$
> 4. Political decision on the design of risk equalization models in year $t$
> 5. Political decision on the projected spending for year $t$
> 6. Aligning total spending in the dataset (after steps 1–3) with the projected spending for year $t$
> 7. Estimating payment weights on the modified dataset of step 6
> 8. Calculating tentative risk equalization payments for year $t$ (usually in September of year $t-1$) based on the expected portfolio of insurers (in terms of risk adjusters) using weights from step 7
> 9. Correcting risk equalization payments for year $t$ as the actual risk portfolio becomes known
> 10. Calculating definitive risk equalization payments for year $t$ when the actual risk portfolio of insurers is fully known (usually in September of year $t+3$)

## 14.4.1 Evaluation of Incentives

Three types of incentives are considered to be particularly relevant for the functioning of the health insurance market. These include incentives for risk selection, incentives for upcoding, and (dis)incentives for promoting efficiency in the delivery of care. For each of these categories we will describe how "incentives" are measured and present some empirical findings.

### 14.4.1.1 Selection Incentives

In the Netherlands selection incentives are assessed by measures of payment fit. Two families of measures can be distinguished: (1) measures for assessing individual-level payment fit and (2) measures for assessing group-level payment fit. Members of the first family include, among other measures, the $R$-squared of the regression model and Cumming's prediction measure (CPM). Fig. 14.3 shows the development in these measures regarding the risk equalization model for somatic care over the period 2010–17. It might be surprising to see that the $R$-squared substantially dropped in some of these years. The explanation can be found in changes in the underlying patterns of healthcare spending contained in the data used for estimating the risk equalization model. In 2011, the $R$-squared decreased by more than 0.05 due to a

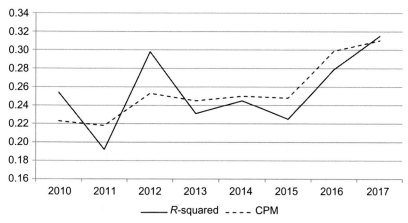

**FIGURE 14.3**    *R*-squared and CPM of the risk equalization model for somatic care.

substantial reduction in prices for kidney dialysis. Since people with kidney failure are classified in a separate DCG, the variation associated with prices of dialysis was well explained by the risk equalization model. The loss of this explained variation—due to the price reduction—decreased the *R*-squared. The reductions in *R*-squared in 2013 and 2015 are due to expansions of the benefits package that increased the (unexplained) variance in spending. The improvements in *R*-squared are mainly the result of the introduction of new risk adjustor variables, i.e., MHCGs (in 2012), DMECGs (in 2014), PDCGs (in 2016), home care spending in the prior year (in 2016), spending on geriatric rehabilitation care in the prior year (in 2016), and the introduction of new PCGs for people with rare diseases (in 2017). These results illustrate how the development in *R*-squared over time is determined by both improvements in the risk equalization model and developments in the underlying data. The CPM is less sensitive to changes in the variance of spending and shows a more gradual improvement over the period 2010–2017.

Although the measures in Fig. 14.3 are informative, they do not directly indicate incentives to attract or deter particular risk types. A more direct measure for assessing such incentives is group-level fit (Van Veen et al., 2014). Over the past 10 years researchers have combined residual spending from the risk equalization model with individual-level health survey information. This procedure allows calculating under- and overcompensations for selected groups in the population. For example, Van Kleef et al. (2013) have quantified the reduction in under/overcompensations for the period 1993–2012. Fig. 14.4 shows a subset of their results. The connected dots clearly show that over the course of time the Dutch risk equalization model for somatic care improved substantially. The endpoints of the lines, however, indicate that the risk equalization model of 2012 did not eliminate selection incentives completely.

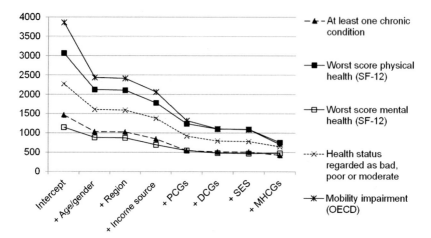

**FIGURE 14.4**   Mean per-person undercompensation for five subgroups under eight risk equalization models for somatic care (in Euros of 2009).
*Note*: The lines show the reduction in undercompensation for five subgroups when going gradually from a risk equalization model with an intercept only (far left) to a model that also includes risk adjustor variables based on age/gender, region, source of income, PCGs, DCGs, socioeconomic status, and MHCGs (far right). Subgroups are based on survey information from 2008 ($N = 8735$). Risk adjustor variables are defined according to the risk equalization model of 2012. Risk equalization models are estimated on spending for somatic care in 2009. *From Van Kleef, R.C., Van Vliet, R.C.J.A., Van de Ven, W.P.M.M., 2013. Risk equalization in the Netherlands: an empirical evaluation. Expert Rev. Pharmacoeconom. Outcomes Res. 13, 829–839.*

Van Kleef et al. (2017) have calculated mean per person under/overcompensations by the risk equalization model of 2016. Based on individual-level claims data from 2013 ($N = 16.6$ million) they estimated all four risk equalization models in place for 2016 (i.e., the models for somatic care, short-term mental care, long-term mental care, and out-of-pocket spending under the mandatory deductible). Based on individual-level survey data from a sample of 381,283 individuals, they identified a variety of selected groups. Table 14.1 presents the outcomes for some of these groups. The second column shows the population frequency, the third column shows the mean spending per person per year, and the fourth column shows the mean overcompensation per person per year. The latter is calculated as the mean predicted spending for a group minus the mean actual spending for that group (where spending equals the sum of the costs for somatic care and mental care, minus the out-of-pocket spending due to the mandatory deductible). Based on these figures one can easily calculate the extent to which the risk equalization models compensate for spending variation among groups. For the groups based on general health, for instance, the difference in mean spending of 4282 euros (5636 minus 1354) between those with the best score and those with the worst score is reduced by 86% to 592 euros (194 minus

**TABLE 14.1** Overall Mean Overcompensation by the Risk Equalization Models of 2016 for Five Sets of Mutually Exclusive Groups[a]

| Subgroup based on survey data from the prior year ($N = 381,283$) | Population frequency (%) | Mean spending in Euros per person per year | Mean overcompensation in Euros per person per year[b,c] |
|---|---|---|---|
| Best score on general health | 77 | 1354 | 194** |
| Worst score on general health | 23 | 5636 | −398** |
| No self-reported condition | 40 | 997 | 183** |
| One self-reported condition | 28 | 2097 | 98** |
| Two self-reported conditions | 15 | 2966 | −22 |
| Three self-reported conditions | 8 | 4230 | −211** |
| Four or more self-reported conditions | 9 | 6316 | −314** |
| Low risk of incurring anxiety disorder or depression | 60 | 1712 | 170** |
| Moderate risk of incurring anxiety disorder or depression | 34 | 2981 | −81** |
| High risk of incurring anxiety disorder or depression | 6 | 5164 | −544** |
| Norm-active (3 or more days of sufficient exercise per week) | 61 | 2018 | 120** |
| Semi-active (1−2 days of sufficient exercise per week) | 31 | 2111 | 22 |
| Inactive (0 days of sufficient exercise per week) | 8 | 5352 | −313** |

(Continued)

**TABLE 14.1** (Continued)

| Subgroup based on survey data from the prior year (N = 381,283) | Population frequency (%) | Mean spending in Euros per person per year | Mean overcompensation in Euros per person per year[b,c] |
|---|---|---|---|
| Nonsmoker | 81 | 2348 | 106** |
| Moderate smoker | 15 | 2248 | −150** |
| Heavy smoker | 4 | 2938 | −244** |

\*\*$P < .01$.
[a]*Subgroups and population frequency are conditional on the population of 19 years and older.*
[b]*Within a mutually exclusive set of groups the sum product of population frequency and mean overcompensation is positive (contrary to any mutually exclusive grouping based on the entire population for which this sum product always equals zero) since the survey sample is slightly healthier than the total population.*
[c]*Overcompensation is calculated as the mean predicted spending for 2013 (using the risk equalization models of 2016) minus the mean actual spending in 2013.*
*Source*: From Van Kleef, R.C., Eijkenaar, F., Van Vliet, R.C.J.A., 2017. Risicoverevening 2016: Uitkomsten op subgroepen uit de Gezondheidsmonitor 2012 (English translation: Risk Equalization 2016: Outcomes for Subgroups Based on a Health Survey From 2012)

−398). For the other categories this figure is 91% (zero vs four or more self-reported conditions), 79% (low vs high risk of incurring anxiety disorder or depression), 87% (0 vs 3 or more days of sufficient exercise per week), and 41% (no smoking vs heavy smoking). On the one hand these results imply that the Dutch risk equalization system of 2016 substantially reduces incentives for risk selection; on the other hand they show that some selection incentives to attract or deter particular risk types remain.

### 14.4.1.2 Incentives for Upcoding

Many risk adjustor variables in the Dutch risk equalization system are based on prior utilization of medical care. A well-known disadvantage of such risk adjustors is that they might provide insurers with incentives for upcoding (see also Chapter 3: Risk Adjustment for Health Plan Payment). Incentives for upcoding are quantified by comparing the incremental payment of risk classes in the risk equalization model with the price of the treatment that leads to assignment to these classes. This measure captures the incentives to undertake the costs necessary to achieve a higher-risk equalization payment. This can be illustrated with Table 14.2, which provides the relevant information for 14 risk classes based on the use of durable medical equipment (DME). These risk classes were analyzed in a study that explored the potential of DME to serve as a basis for risk adjustment (Van Kleef and Van Vliet, 2011). A DME group consists of individuals who have used that

**TABLE 14.2** Incremental Payment for DME Groups in Year $t$ (in an Extended Version of the Dutch Equalization Model of 2008) and the Costs of the Particular DME in Year $t-1$

| DME groups | Population frequency | Incremental payment in year $t$ | "Cost" of DME in $t-1$ |
|---|---|---|---|
| No DME | 98.95 | 0 | – |
| Users of antibedsore equipment | 0.06 | 1661 | 372 |
| Users of CPAP equipment | 0.08 | 1816 | 1116 |
| Users of bandage shoes | 0.03 | 2775 | 115 |
| Users of elastic arm socks | 0.04 | 2682 | 229 |
| Users of catheters and supplies | 0.28 | 3761 | 1009 |
| Users of insulin infusion pump | 0.03 | 4220 | 2255 |
| Users of ergonomic chairs and bikes | 0.03 | 4194 | 1658 |
| Users of foot/leg prosthesis | 0.06 | 4805 | 2606 |
| Users of stoma equipment | 0.25 | 5038 | 2050 |
| Users of oxygen equipment | 0.11 | 5869 | 1450 |
| Users of voice prosthesis | 0.01 | 7071 | 2798 |
| Users of infusion pump (not insulin) | 0.04 | 7659 | 1536 |
| Users of orthotic equipment | 0.01 | 10,408 | 1523 |
| Users of tube-feeding equipment | 0.04 | 13,628 | 1542 |

Source: From Van Kleef, R.C., Van Vliet, R.C.J.A., 2011. Prior use of durable medical equipment as a risk adjuster for health-based capitation. Inquiry, 47, 343–358.

particular DME in the prior year. For each group, the second column shows the population frequency and the third column shows the incremental payment (i.e., the risk adjustor coefficient) if these DME groups would have been added to the risk equalization model of 2008. The fourth column shows the average price of the DME. A comparison of the third and fourth columns reveals that for each DME group the incremental payment in year $t$ is much higher than the average price of the particular DME required for assignment to that group. These results imply that a DME-based risk adjustor comes with substantial incentives for upcoding.

### 14.4.1.3 Incentives for Promoting Efficiency in the Delivery of Care

Another type of incentive includes those for promoting efficiency in the delivery of care. Although these incentives are related to incentives for upcoding there is a subtle difference: upcoding refers to the action of actively endorsing use of more (expensive) medical care, while incentives for efficiency in the delivery of care refer to actions of exploiting possibilities for cost containment. The latter can be (partly) measured by the extent to which insurers are risk bearing with respect to medical spending. Over the course of time insurers' financial risk substantially increased as risk sharing was gradually abolished (Fig. 14.2). The *lines* in Fig. 14.2 can be interpreted as the average proportion of savings (losses) an insurer is responsible for. This roughly indicates an insurer's incentives for cost containment. Since 2016, these incentives are maximal. When it comes to incentives for efficiency, however, it is not only the relationship between cost in year $t$ and health plan payment in year $t$ that matters, but also the relationship between cost in prior years and health plan payment in year $t$. For example, the positive association between use of DME in the prior year and the risk equalization payment in the next year (Table 14.2) weakens a plan's incentives to promote prudent use of DME.

## 14.4.2 Evaluation of Market Response

The Health Care Authority monitors the health plan market and the behavior of actors operating in that market.[3] One particular aspect being monitored is risk selection. The Health Care Authority has operationalized risk selection as "Actions (other than risk rating per product) by consumers and insurers with the intention and/or the effect that the desired cross-subsidies from low-risk to high-risk people are not fully achieved," a definition that originates from Newhouse (1996) and has been customized by Van de Ven et al. (2016). This definition roughly implies that risk selection involves actions with the *intention* and/or the *effect* that profitable and unprofitable enrollees sort into different health plans. Risk selection can be about explicit actions by insurers to selectively attract profitable (i.e., overcompensated) enrollees, but also includes simple correlations between plan features and specific preferences of under- or overcompensated enrollees. Such correlations can occur, for instance, when a health plan provides access to a first-best physician (in order to improve the quality of his network) that is particularly popular by specific groups of (undercompensated) high-risk enrollees. Given this broad definition of risk selection, any dimension in which plans can differ is a potential source of risk selection (for an overview of these dimensions, see Boxes 14.4 and 14.5). In addition, risk selection can take place via the selling process of health plans (e.g., advertisement and marketing strategies) and the connection with other insurance products (e.g., supplementary health insurance, which 85% of the population buys, typically from the same insurer as the basic health insurance).

As a first step in monitoring risk selection, the Health Care Authority has examined the extent to which profitable and unprofitable consumers do enroll with different insurers. A challenge for assessing this sorting effect is that under/overcompensation at the insurer level can be confounded by variation in efficiency among insurers. To overcome this challenge, the Health Care Authority uses a method developed by Van de Ven et al. (2016) that focuses on the average under/overcompensation of people who *switched* insurer. For people who switched to insurer S, this method calculates the average under/overcompensation in the year *before* the switch. Since these people come from different insurers, this under/overcompensation will be hardly affected by variation in efficiency across insurers. Analogously, for people who switched from insurer S to other insurers, the Health Care Authority calculates the average under/overcompensation in the year *after* the switch. Since these people spread out over different insurers, this under/overcompensation will be hardly affected by variation in efficiency across insurers. Table 14.3 shows the outcomes of this analysis for the year 2009,

**TABLE 14.3** Average Overcompensation (Euros) in 2008 of "New Enrollees on January 1, 2009" and Average Overcompensation in 2009 of "Disenrollees on January 1, 2009," for Each of the 25 Insurers, After Applying the Risk Equalization Model 2012 (Excluding the Costs of Mental Care)

| Health insurer (in 2009) | New enrollees on 1 January 2009: Average overcompensation in the year *before* the switch (2008) | Disenrollees on 1 January 2009: Average overcompensation in the year *after* the switch (2009) |
| --- | --- | --- |
| 1 | 123* | − 27 |
| 2 | 35 | − 54 |
| 3 | − 45 | − 142 |
| 4 | 39* | 17 |

*(Continued)*

**TABLE 14.3** (Continued)

| Health insurer (in 2009) | New enrollees on 1 January 2009: Average overcompensation in the year *before* the switch (2008) | Disenrollees on 1 January 2009: Average overcompensation in the year *after* the switch (2009) |
|---|---|---|
| 5 | 77* | − 5 |
| 6 | 68* | 66* |
| 7 | 45* | 129* |
| 8 | 60* | 78* |
| 9 | 132 | − 47 |
| 10 | 70* | − 12 |
| 11 | − 10 | − 35 |
| 12 | 81* | 41* |
| 13 | 108* | 5 |
| 14 | 75* | 55* |
| 15 | 112* | 13 |
| 16 | 13 | 40 |
| 17 | 81* | 38 |
| 18 | 123* | 89* |
| 19 | 197* | 26 |
| 20 | 115* | 58* |
| 21 | 163* | − 50 |
| 22 | 126* | 57 |
| 23 | 116* | − 3 |
| 24 | 76 | 30 |
| 25 | 201* | − 192* |

*$P < .05$.
Source: From Van de Ven, WPMM, Van Kleef, RC & Van Vliet, RCJA 2016, 'How can the regulator show evidence of (no) risk selection in health insurance markets? Conceptual framework and empirical evidence', Eur. J. Health Econ., DOI 10.1007/s10198-016-0764-7.

for each of the 25 insurers that were on the market that year. For most insurers, Table 14.3 shows significant risk selection among their switchers on January 1, 2009. In the year after disenrollment, the average overcompensation ranged from −192 to +129 euros per insured. Most remarkable is insurer 25, who had both the highest average overcompensation on new enrollees and the highest average undercompensation on those who disenrolled. This insurer also had the lowest "average residual expenses" per insured for nonswitchers. In a next step the Health Care Authority has evaluated the sorting pattern in Table 14.3 in the light of consumer and insurer behavior and health plan characteristics. The Authority found that in some cases the average (un)profitability of switchers into particular health plans can be explained by marketing strategies of the insurers selling these plans and/or specific characteristics of these plans (Dutch Health Care Authority, 2016).

Note that Table 14.3 provides an underestimation of risk selection. First, positive and negative selection effects may cancel out. For example, an insurer may have attracted groups of undercompensated enrollees (e.g., due to offering the best care for the chronically ill) as well as groups of overcompensated enrollees (e.g., due to selective advertising). Second, there may be selection within insurers' portfolios since most insurers offer multiple health plans. Since risk selection can take place at the health plan level, measurement of residual spending ideally takes place at that particular level (and not at the insurer level). At the health plan level, market segmentation may be more severe than at the insurer level. Finally, actions by insurers with the intention that profitable and unprofitable enrollees sort into different health plans may not be successful and therefore not be reflected in the insurers' average residual expenses. Nevertheless these unsuccessful actions can have undesirable outcomes (such as a reduction in the quality of care when insurers do not contract first-best physicians in order to deter high-risk consumers).

## 14.5 ONGOING ISSUES AND REFORMS

Regulated competition in the Netherlands was not implemented overnight. Instead, the transition from a public noncompetitive system to a private market-based system is an ongoing process. In this transition, health plan payment design plays a crucial role. On the one hand, extensive policy research has led to major improvements in this area. On the other hand, however, it has been shown that further improvements are necessary in order to avoid market failure. Below we highlight some of the main issues that remain to be tackled.

### 14.5.1 Under/Overcompensation Discourages Insurers from Investing in the Quality of Their Plans

The empirical results in this chapter have shown that, in 2016, insurers are still undercompensated for groups of high-risk people and overcompensated for groups of low-risk people. At the same time, risk sharing has been abolished almost completely. Due to the premium regulation these under- and overcompensations provide insurers with incentives for risk selection. In the early years of the Health Insurance Act the policy debate about risk selection

---

**BOX 14.13 Disincentives to meet preferences of a particular group**

Health insurer Eno offered a health plan that was particularly attractive to women who expect to deliver a baby in the contract year. Since the Dutch risk equalization model lacks risk adjustors that explicitly indicate pregnancy and compensate for the associated costs, this insurer was confronted with substantial losses (i.e., thousands of euros per pregnant woman per year). This discouraged the insurer from continuing with the health plan (ultimately resulting in withdraw of the plan in 2016) and also discouraged other insurers from starting offering such products. This is the direction in which insurers are being pushed for under-compensated groups of consumers.

*Source: Dutch Health Care Authority, 2016.*

---

mainly focused on selection actions by insurers with the goal of attracting overcompensated enrollees (e.g., via selective advertisement and group arrangements). In recent years, however, the focus is shifting toward actions by insurers with the goal of deterring undercompensated enrollees, e.g., by quality skimping (Van de Ven et al., 2015). Triggers for this shift were complaints by insurers that the imperfections of the risk equalization model discourage them from actively investing in the quality of their provider network (e.g., Achmea, 2011). In a recent evaluation of the Health Insurance Act, representatives from health insurance companies (who participated in focus groups) actually admitted that insurers are reluctant in making such investments (KPMG, 2014). Box 14.13 provides an illustration in this context.

In response to the policy debate on quality skimping the government announced that "the chronically ill must become financially attractive for insurers" (Tweede Kamer, 2015), putting political pressure on further improvement of the health plan payment system.

## 14.5.2 Endogenous Risk Adjustor Variables Discourage Insurers From Improving Efficiency

The Dutch risk equalization system includes many risk adjustor variables based on prior cost or utilization (see Boxes 14.6 and 14.7). Although these variables are good predictors of future spending (Van Veen et al., 2014)—and substantially reduce selection incentives—they have an important downside: they create a (positive) correlation between spending in the current year and the risk equalization payment in later years. This reduces the incentives for insurers to promote efficiency in the delivery of care and introduces incentives for upcoding. These incentives can be illustrated by the DME-based risk adjustor shown in Table 14.2: for each DME group the incremental risk equalization payment is much higher than the average price of the particular DME required for assignment to that group. This not only mitigates incentives for insurers to promote efficient use of DME, but also provides them with the perverse incentive to promote inefficient use of DME (i.e., upcoding). Though the DME-based risk adjustor currently in place differs from the classification presented in Table 14.2, the direction of incentives is similar. The same holds for the other risk adjustors based on prior cost or utilization. Whether these incentives will actually lead to undesired behavior depends on the possibilities for insurers to influence healthcare provision. So far, insurers' response to these incentives has hardly been monitored, which is an important shortcoming of the current evaluation process. Given the growing international evidence on upcoding we strongly recommend the Dutch government to develop and apply measures for this purpose.

When particular risk adjustors are expected or found to result in unacceptable levels of upcoding, the regulator might be confronted with a dilemma. On the one hand, inclusion of these risk adjustors in the risk equalization model will eliminate incentives for risk selection with respect to the groups identified by these risk adjustors; on the other hand, this will reduce incentives for efficiency and introduce incentives for upcoding. Researchers have proposed an interesting procedure to escape from this dilemma: instead of directly including these variables as risk adjustors in the model, they can be used as a basis for "constraints" on the estimated coefficients. The idea is very simple and can be illustrated for the variable "use of home care in the previous year." Instead of including this variable as a risk adjustor in the risk equalization model, the coefficients for the existing risk adjustors can be estimated under the constraint that the undercompensation for this group equals zero (or any specific amount). A "constrained regression" can reduce under- and overcompensation of groups that are *not* explicitly recognized in the model; at the same time, however, it introduces under- and overcompensations for groups that *are* explicitly recognized in the model (e.g., DCGs). Under certain circumstances, however, the benefits can be worth the costs (Van Kleef et al., 2016).

## 14.5.3 Accurate Risk Equalization May Not be Possible for All Types of Care

Since 2008, several types of care have been transferred from the Exceptional Medical Expenses Act (since 2015: Long Term Care Act) to the Health Insurance Act. These include short-term mental health care (2008), geriatric rehabilitation care (2013), home care (2015), and long-term mental health care (2015). Due to the lack of incentives for efficiency in the public scheme for long-term care, other types of long-term care (e.g., nursing home care for the elderly) may follow the same path. It is questionable, however, whether appropriate risk equalization can be developed for these types of care. Compared to the traditional types of care under the Health Insurance Act (e.g., physician services, hospital care, and prescription drugs), the types of care under the former Exceptional Medical Expenses Act (e.g., home care, geriatric rehabilitation care, mental care, and elderly care) have particular characteristics that complicate risk equalization design (Bakx, 2015). First, the group of users is relatively small, implying a substantial zero mass. Multivariate regression models may lead to negative spending predictions which may be considered undesirable. Second, these people incur high spending that is quite predictable for insurers. For example, when a patient is in a long-term care facility in year $t$, it is very likely that the patient will be in the same facility in year $t + 1$. This implies that insurers can easily identify high-cost patients by checking the claims history of their enrollees. In order to avoid selection incentives, claims history can be included as a risk adjustor variable in the risk equalization model. As explained above, however, such an endogenous risk adjustor reduces incentives for efficiency in the delivery of care. It is highly questionable, however, whether sufficient non-endogenous risk adjustor variables are available for these types of care.

### 14.5.4  Measurement of Risk Selection is Complex

In the policy debate on health plan payment some people argued that the system works fine because no (or only limited) risk selection is observed in practice. When it comes to the measurement of risk selection, however, it is practically impossible to prove its absence. Only if risk equalization is perfect then risk selection is absent (by definition). However, it is impossible to show that the risk equalization is perfect. Perfect risk equalization exists if and only if there exists no group of over- or undercompensated insured. Because in principle the number of subgroups is unlimited, it is practically impossible to show that there exists no single group of over- or undercompensated insured. If risk equalization is found to be imperfect, the number of actions that can be qualified as risk selection is unlimited. It is impossible to show the absence of all these actions. Showing that all health plans have a similar risk portfolio of insured is also no proof of the absence of risk selection, because all plans could be equally successful in risk selection. It could also mean that within portfolios there is both positive selection (e.g., an underrepresentation of chronically ill insured) and negative selection (e.g., an overrepresentation of low-educated low-income people), and that these selection effects cancel out. Finally, not rejecting the null-hypothesis "that a selected group of insured is not over- or undercompensated" with a certain level of statistical significance is not a proof that "the selected group of insured is not over- or undercompensated." Possibly, this group is over- or undercompensated, but the size of the group is too small to come to statistically reliable conclusions, e.g., in the case of rare diseases. These complexities limit the possibilities for detecting risk selection. Consequently, one should be very careful with judging the performance of the health plan payment system by the extent to which risk selection is actually "detected" in practice.

## 14.5.5    For Some Types of Spending Variation the Regulator Might Not Want Cross-Subsidies

In the bylaws of the Health Insurance Act, the Dutch regulator states that risk equalization should exclusively compensate for spending variation due to differences in age, gender, and health status of individuals. In this light, two interesting observations are that (1) risk adjustor coefficients are estimated by a regression of *observed* spending on risk adjustor variables and (2) insurers are not allowed to differentiate health plan premiums according to any risk factor. With respect to the first observation the regulator should be aware that variation in observed spending is not only due to differences in age, gender, and health status, but also due to factors for which compensation is not desired, referred to in the literature as "N-factors," e.g., inefficiency of health plans, life-style of consumers, and moral hazard. When the N-factors are correlated with the risk adjustor variables included in the model, a simple regression of observed spending on these risk adjustor variables may lead to coefficients that (partly) reflect spending variation for which compensation is not desired (Schokkaert and Van de Voorde, 2004; Van Kleef et al., 2010). In order to avoid such "unintended" compensation, the regulator can either correct observed spending for the effect of N-factors (e.g., see Stam et al., 2010) or replace the current one-step estimation method by the two-step method used in Belgium (see Chapter 7: Risk Adjustment in Belgium: Why and How to Introduce Socioeconomic Variables in Health Plan Payment). The latter means that—in the first step—risk adjustor coefficients are estimated with a regression model that includes both S-type and N-type variables. For the calculation of the risk equalization payments (i.e., the second step) the coefficients for the N-type factors are neutralized. If the regulator explicitly avoids compensation for particular sources of spending variation, insurers should be given the possibility to reflect this variation in their health plan premiums. For example, if the regulator decides that the difference in residual spending between smokers versus nonsmokers (see Table 14.1) is not to be compensated for by the risk equalization model (e.g., because this residual spending is partly due to healthy/unhealthy lifestyle), then insurers should be allowed to charge smokers a higher premium than nonsmokers. Without this possibility, plans will be confronted with selection incentives on the basis of smoking behavior.

## ACKNOWLEDGMENTS

The authors gratefully acknowledge the valuable comments on earlier versions of this chapter by Frank Bakker, Rudy Douven, and Tom McGuire. The responsibility for the content of this chapter rests fully with the authors.

## ENDNOTES

1. Next to the sickness fund insurance and the private health insurance there was a separate public insurance for civil servants. In terms of coverage and organization this scheme was quite similar to the sickness fund insurance.
2. Other aspects of evaluation include measurability of risk adjustor variables and spending, validity of risk adjustor variables, stability of coefficients, simplicity, and transparency. Although these criteria are highly relevant from a practical perspective (e.g., for getting and maintaining public and political support for the payment system), they are less relevant for the economic functioning of the health plan market.
3. The general role of the Health Care Authority is to "protect the interests of citizens with regard to accessibility, affordability, and quality of health care in the Netherlands."

## REFERENCES

Achmea, 2011. Brief van Achmea aan de leden van de Vaste Commissie voor Volksgezondheid, Welzijn en Sport (English translation: Letter from ACHMEA to the Members of the Permanent Commission of Health, Welfare and Sports), September 7, 2011.

Bakx, P.L.H., 2015. Financial Incentives in Long Term Care, Dissertation, Erasmus University Rotterdam.

Dutch Health Care Authority, 2014. Marktscan Zorgverzekeringsmarkt 2014 (English translation: Marketscan Health Insurance Market 2014).

Dutch Health Care Authority, 2015. Marktscan Zorgverzekeringsmarkt 2015 (English translation: Marketscan Health Insurance Market 2015).

Dutch Health Care Authority, 2016. Risicoselectie en risicosolidariteit zorgverzekeringsmarkt (English translation: Risk Selection and Risk Solidarity on the Health Insurance Market).

Eijkenaar, F., Van Vliet, R.C.J.A., 2017. Improving risk equalization using information on physiotherapy diagnoses. Eur. J. Health Econ. Available from: https://doi.org/10.1007/s10198-017-0874-x.

Enthoven, A.C., Van de Ven, W.P.M.M., 2007. Going Dutch — Managed-competition health insurance in the Netherlands. New Engl. J. Med. 357, 2421—2423.

KPMG, 2014. Evaluatie Zorgverzekeringswet (English translation: Evaluation of the Health Insurance Act).

Lamers, L.M., 1998. Risk-adjusted capitation payments: developing a diagnostic cost groups classification for the Dutch situation. Health Policy 45, 15—32.

Lamers, L.M., 1999. Pharmacy costs groups: a risk-adjuster for capitation payments based on the use of prescribed drugs. Med. Care 37, 824—830.

Newhouse, J.P., 1996. Reimbursing health plans and health providers: efficiency in production versus selection. J. Econ. Literature 34, 1236—1263.

Prinsze, F.J., Van Vliet, R.C.J.A., 2007. Health-based risk adjustment: improving the pharmacy-based cost group model by adding diagnostic cost groups. Inquiry 44, 469—480.

Schokkaert, E., Van de Voorde, C., 2004. Risk selection and the specification of the conventional risk adjustment formula. J. Health Econ. 23, 1237—1259.

Stam, P.J., Van Vliet, R.C.J.A., Van de Ven, W.P.M.M., 2010. Diagnostic, pharmacy-based, and self-reported health measures in risk equalization models. Med. Care 48, 448—457.

Tweede Kamer, 2015. Brief Kwaliteit loont (English translation: Letter from the Minister of Health to the Parliament), 2014-2015, 31 765, nr. 116.

Tweede Kamer, 2017. Vaststelling van de begrotingsstaten van het Ministerie van Volksgezondheid, Welzijn en Sport voor het jaar 2017 (English translation: Budget 2017 for the Ministry of Health, Welfare and Sports). 2016-2017, 34 550 XVI.

Van de Ven, W.P.M.M., Schut, F.T., 2008. Universal mandatory health insurance in the Netherlands: a model for the United States? Health Affairs 27, 771−781.

Van de Ven, W.P.M.M., Beck, K., Buchner, F., Schokkaert, E., Schut, F.T., Shmueli, A., et al., 2013. Preconditions for efficiency and affordability in competitive healthcare markets: are they fulfilled in Belgium, Germany, Israel, the Netherlands and Switzerland? Health Policy 109, 226−245.

Van de Ven, W.P.M.M., Van Kleef, R.C., Van Vliet, R.C.J.A., 2015. Risk selection threatens quality of care for certain patients; lessons from Europe's health insurance exchanges. Health Affairs 34, 1713−1720.

Van de Ven, W.P.M.M., Van Kleef, R.C., Van Vliet, R.C.J.A., 2016. How can the regulator show evidence of (no) risk selection in health insurance markets? Conceptual framework and empirical evidence. Eur. J. Health Econ. Available from: https://doi.org/10.1007/s10198-016-0764-7.

Van Kleef, R.C., Van Vliet, R.C.J.A., 2011. Prior use of durable medical equipment as a risk adjuster for health-based capitation. Inquiry 47, 343−358.

Van Kleef, R.C., Van Vliet, R.C.J.A., 2012. Improving risk equalization using multiple-year high cost as a health indicator. Med. Care 50, 140−144.

Van Kleef, R.C., Beck, K., Buchner, F., 2010. Risk-type concentration and efficiency incentives: a challenge for the risk adjustment formula. The Geneva Papers 35, 503−520.

Van Kleef, R.C., Van Vliet, R.C.J.A., Van de Ven, W.P.M.M., 2013. Risk equalization in the Netherlands: an empirical evaluation. Expert Rev. Pharmacoeconom. Outcomes Res. 13, 829−839.

Van Kleef, R.C., Van Vliet, R.C.J.A., Van Rooijen, E.M., 2014. Diagnoses-based cost groups in the Dutch risk-equalization model: The effects of including outpatient diagnoses. Health Policy 115, 52−59.

Van Kleef, R.C., McGuire, T.G., Van Vliet, R.C.J.A., Van de Ven, W.P.M.M., 2016. Improving risk equalization with constrained regression. Eur. J. Health Econ. Available from: https://doi.org/10.1007/s10198-016-0859-1.

Van Kleef, R.C., Eijkenaar, F., Van Vliet, R.C.J.A., 2017. Risicoverevening 2016: Uitkomsten op subgroepen uit de Gezondheidsmonitor 2012 (English translation: Risk Equalization 2016: Outcomes for Subgroups Based on a Health Survey From 2012).

Van Veen, S.C.H.M., Van Kleef, R.C., Van de Ven, W.P.M.M., Van Vliet, R.C.J.A., 2014. Improving the prediction model used in risk equalization: cost and diagnostic information from multiple prior years. Eur. J. Health Econ. 16, 201−218.

Vektis, 2016. Zorgthermometer: Verzekerden in beeld 2016 (English translation: Health Insurance Market Monitor).

## FURTHER READING

Van Veen, S.C.H.M., Van Kleef, R.C., Van de Ven, W.P.M.M., Van Vliet, R.C.J.A., 2015. Is there one measure-of-fit that fits all? A taxonomy and critical assessment of measures that are used for assessing the predictive performance of risk-equalization models. Med. Care Res. Rev. 72, 220−243.

# Chapter 15

# Health Plan Payment in the Russian Federation

Igor Sheiman
*National Research University High School of Economics, Moscow, Russia*

## 15.1 INTRODUCTION

Prior to the 1990s, the Russian National Health System was financed by a combination of national and regional government contributions. It featured universal coverage, but due to substantial underfunding (public health funding was less than 2.5% of GDP) health care was often of poor quality. Higher-income individuals could buy some health care outside of the public system, but this represented a small fraction of healthcare resources. There was no health insurance, and individuals had little choice about where to receive care.

Although the previous Russian healthcare system dramatically improved the health status of the Russian people, the system had noticeable problems with inefficiency of service provision and weak incentives for providers (Telyukov, 1991). Budgets of providers were based on their capacity, i.e., the number of doctors and hospital beds, and were not related to their performance (Davis, 1988; Thompson, 2007). Therefore, hospitals had strong incentives to increase bed numbers and fill the beds as much as possible. The rate of admission was around 25 per 100 residents at the end of the 1980s, about 2−3 times higher than in European countries (Twigg 1998; Davis, 2010). Primary care physicians who worked as salaried workers for multispecialty clinics lacked the incentives to treat patients themselves; they frequently referred patients to specialists and hospitals. The referral rate was 30%−35%, much higher than in the United Kingdom and France (Sheiman, 1995). Waiting time was also a serious problem. Patients often had to pay under-the-table to doctors in order to move rapidly to the front of a queue or acquire services of better quality (Telyukov, 1991). Thus, the combination of poor quality and inefficiency promoted the search for a new health finance and provision model.

Risk Adjustment, Risk Sharing and Premium Regulation in Health Insurance Markets.
DOI: https://doi.org/10.1016/B978-0-12-811325-7.00015-4
**431**

After the collapse of the USSR in the 1990s, Russia reformed healthcare financing to introduce a role for insurers, including a Mandatory Health Insurance (MHI) system with some features of "regulated competition." This introduction briefly reviews the main sources of financing currently operating in Russia, putting the MHI system, the main focus of the chapter, in context.

The general aim of the reform was to enhance the efficiency of the medical service delivery by creating a prudent purchaser of health care while maintaining universal coverage and practically a universal package of medical benefits. According to the Constitution of the Russian Federation (1993), all citizens of the country are entitled to free care provided in publicly owned medical facilities and funded from health insurance and public budgetary sources.

The purchasing of health care and provision of health care were separated by setting up what will be referred to as "health insurers." They were expected to use their authority as purchasers to select providers, including private ones, and to influence their performance, replace input-based allocation of resources with contracting and performance-based payment. The insureds are allowed to choose among insurers. Competition among insurers for enrollees was deemed to be the major policy instrument for reforming the healthcare sector (Xu et al., 2010).

The Health Insurance Law (1994) introduced both MHI and voluntary health insurance (VHI). The MHI coverage, according to this law, includes physician services, day care, home care, hospital and emergency care, rehabilitation services, and most dental care. Most prescription drugs are not covered. Collection of funds in MHI is based on contributions by employers (employees do not contribute) and regional governments. All citizens are allowed to select a health insurer with no additional premium contribution.

VHI is optional, offers similar benefits to MHI but gives enrollees access to more advanced medical facilities with a higher quality of care. Similar to MHI, prescription drugs are generally not covered, but must be paid for mostly out-of-pocket. The rates of VHI premiums are not regulated, nor are the prices of medical facilities contracted by insurance companies. Most VHI health plans are offered to big groups of employees on a community-rated basis. Individual purchases account for less than 5% of the VHI market. VHI plays a limited role in financing health care in Russia, covering only 6% of the population in 2016 (Shishkin et al., 2016).

The 2010 Law on Mandatory Health Insurance (MHI Law) modified insurance regulation, but left unchanged the split between MHI and VHI. MHI is highly regulated, whereas VHI insurers are regulated only in terms of financial solvency (i.e., the standard insurance regulation).

Governments pay directly for care for mental care, infectious diseases, AIDs, some other conditions, the most complicated and costly tertiary care, and public health. These services are provided by a set of public facilities and funded by the federal government and governments of 85 regions of the country (each with the population ranging from 1 to 11 million people), with little involvement of local governments. In total, governments pay directly for about 40% of publicly funded care, with the balance controlled by MHI Funds. "Budgetary" and MHI parts of total public health system currently function with their own regulation. Integrating these funding streams is on the agenda of health reforms (Shishkin et al., 2016).

Finally, more than one-third of health expenditure (37%) is outside of publicly regulated and funded schemes (Flek, 2015). Private out-of-pocket payment relates to so-called "chargeable" services provided by publicly owned medical facilities. Most of these are the same services that are covered under MHI, but the government allows these charges due to a serious underfunding from public sources. The rhetoric behind this decision is to expand patient choice, but the actual reason is to strengthen the financial basis of public medical facilities, since the rates of payment for services under MHI often don't cover their actual cost. The most popular facilities collect 25%−30% of their revenue from out-of-pocket payments (an estimate by the author).

The border between free care and "chargeable" services is not clear, which causes continual debate about the entitlements of the MHI enrollees. Furthermore, direct informal payments to health workers to motivate better quality and access are common though officially prohibited. The ultimate reason for these payments is also underfunding of health care from public sources. Including all "official" sources, the country spends only 5.9% GDP on health, while the government contribution is about 3.7% (Flek, 2015).

Private providers are a fast-growing subsector paid by private out-of-pocket payments. Most of these providers are not involved in MHI, and therefore charge their patients either directly or through VHI. But the most substantial area of out-of-pocket payment is prescription drugs. Box 15.1 summarizes the major funding sources of health care in Russia.

The remainder of this chapter focuses on the second layer—MHI. The following sections describe the institutional setting of this system (Section 15.2) and the role of health plan payment (Sections 15.3 and 15.4). In Section 15.5 we discuss some ongoing issues and reforms.

## 15.2   ORGANIZATION OF THE HEALTH INSURANCE SYSTEM

The term "regulated competition" is not used in the official documents, but the MHI health funding system in Russia bears some resemblance to models implemented in a number of countries. 67 health insurers are involved in the MHI scheme now (much less than the around 200 in the 1990s). In each region there are 3−10 insurers competing for enrollees. The MHI Law specifies individual rather than collective choice of insurers, and is effective in this regard. Consumers can change insurer at any time. Also, the benefit package is standardized in terms of the type and quantity of medical care

---

**BOX 15.1 Layers of the healthcare financing system in Russia**

| | |
|---|---|
| *Layer 1* | *Direct governmental funding socially important care* |
| *Layer 2* | *Mandatory health insurance (MHI Law of 2010):*<br>• Mandatory contributions by employers and regional governments for the entire population without contributions (premiums) by the insured<br>• Insurance covering most outpatient and inpatient care<br>• Regulated by the government<br>• Executed by private insurance companies who are supposed to bear some financial risk |
| *Layer 3* | *Voluntary health insurance (Health Insurance Law of 1991):*<br>• Enrollment on a voluntary basis<br>• Medical benefits cover practically the same types of care as in MHI, but provided in better medical facilities<br>• Little regulation by the government<br>• Executed by private insurance companies who bear financial risk<br>• VHI and MHI have separate financial reserves and reporting systems. They don't interact with each other in terms of common packages of medical benefits |
| *Layer 4* | *Out-of-pocket payment:*<br>• Payment for "chargeable" services provided by publicly owned clinics and hospitals<br>• Informal payment to medical workers of publicly owned medical facilities<br>• Payment for services provided by private medical facilities that are not involved in MHI<br>• Payment for outpatient drugs |

---

covered, rules for referrals (patients not following them must pay out-of-pocket), and conditions of care delivery, including maximum waiting time.

The coverage of services is comprehensive, although in practice informal rationing is present due to a serious underfunding. The coverage of outpatient drugs is limited to around 5% of beneficiaries. The share of public expenditure in total drug expenditure is 11% in Russia, while the average for Europe is 48% (WHO Database, 2015).

Since coverage is comprehensive, regional variation in the scope of the medical benefits is limited. Richer regions can enhance the coverage of outpatient drugs by increasing the number of beneficiaries with drug coverage and expanding the list of reimbursable drugs. Generally, funding of the benefits package is more generous in the richer regions. This allows insurers from these regions to set higher rates of payment for medical services. Health insurers in richer regions are more likely to deliver on benefits consumers are entitled to by law and rely less on explicit and implicit rationing.

Health insurers negotiate volumes of care with providers and therefore become responsible for the accessibility of care. They are supposed to bear some financial risk for overutilization of care and overspending, although as will be shown in later sections, the actual financial risk for insurers has been limited so far. Some simple risk equalization is used as well, as will be explained below. Finally, the MHI Law allows contracts with any licensed public and private provider. The choice is based on the providers' performance.

Deviations from the "classic" regulated competition model are, however, substantial. First, consumers do not pay a premium to their insurer; therefore, there can be no price competition in the MHI. Also, there is no formal copayment at the time of services use.

Second, product competition is essentially nonexistent. Since insurers in MHI cannot collect additional premiums, they cannot offer additional benefits.[1] The concept of "health plans" is even absent in the MHI Law. MHI compete only in the relatively narrow area of implementing the universal package of medical benefits—the "Program of state guarantees of free care" (referred to hereinafter as the Program).

Third, quality competition exists in theory because health insurers are responsible for what is stated in the legislation as "health care quality control." They are responsible for a set of activities—control of providers' medical records, control of underprovision of care (by comparing it with clinical standards and recommendations), control of appropriateness of hospital care, overviews of the prevailing clinical patterns in the selected clinical areas (so-called "thematic review"). In practice, as will be explained below, MHI insurers cannot affect quality of care substantially.

Regulated completion approaches rely on consumers to make informed evaluations of the characteristics and practices of alternative insurers. In practice, the lack of information impedes effective choice, and therefore people are more concerned with customer services provided by insurers rather than quality of providers. Consumers tend to select the insurer which can issue the MHI policy quicker, better process patients' complaints, have a good call center, consult on the organization of care, protect enrollee's rights in court if necessary, etc. Health insurers are very active in attracting enrollees through marketing campaigns demonstrating actual and alleged quality of customer services. All these activities are of course helpful but they are not directed to the insurer function of expanding medical benefits, enhancing quality and efficiency.

The following subsections review the major features of the current system in terms of regulation, consumer choice, and instruments for health insurers to encourage efficiency in the delivery of care.

## 15.2.1 Health Plan Market Regulation

The MHI Law directly affects the accessibility and affordability of medical benefits through: (1) strict requirements for solvency of insurance companies (supervised by the Ministry of Finance); (2) regulation requiring the provision of specific information on both insurers' and providers' performance (supervised by the Federal Fund of MHI); (3) quality of care standards (supervised by the Ministry of Health); and (4) subsidizing of health insurers in case of additional cost related to overprovision of medical care (supervised by the Federal Fund of MHI). There is no antitrust regulation aimed at protecting the market against anticompetitive behavior via cartels, mergers, or dominant market shares. Box 15.2 summarizes some of these regulations.

## 15.2.2 Health Plan Choice Options for Consumers

Under MHI, consumers have a choice of insurer, but the price and coverage is the same in all options. As mentioned earlier, a consumer chooses the insurer mostly on the basis of the quality of customer services. The biggest and most well-known insurers are perceived as being better able to establish relationships with providers, organize the settlement of patient complaints, help with referrals to providers whose services are in short supply, and provide more consumer information.

Although the focus of this chapter is on MHI, the term "health plan" is more relevant for the VHI, where insurers sell the plans which differ in price and in the package of medical benefits (health plans for outpatient care only, for outpatient and inpatient care, with or without dental care, as well as the network of contracted healthcare providers).

## 15.2.3 Instruments for Health Plans to Promote Efficiency in the Delivery of Care

Under MHI, health insurers have several instruments to promote efficiency in the delivery of care. First, insurers negotiate volumes of care with providers with the focus on more efficient structure of service delivery. Operating

---

**BOX 15.2 Regulation to achieve individual affordability and accessibility of a package of medical benefits under MHI in Russia**

- Individual mandate to enroll in a health plan (offered by a private insurer) and open enrollment
- Standardized benefit package
- Risk equalization
- Strict requirements for solvency of insurance companies
- Insurers are required to disclose extensive information on both insurers and providers' performance
- Establishing quality of care standards
- Risk-sharing arrangements

under the umbrella of the special regional commissions that include also representatives of regional health authority and the MHI Fund, health insurers have a voice in decisions on questions of healthcare delivery in the regions, such as shifting care from inpatient to outpatient settings and day care centers, moving volumes of care and money among providers. They collect information on providers' performance and come up with proposals on the best allocation of resources, the selection of providers, and the allocation of volumes among providers. In the course of these activities, health insurers are expected to follow utilization targets (e.g., bed-days, physician visits per capita) established by the Program. Recent policy efforts have been to decrease inpatient care volumes, increase day treatment, rehabilitation services, and others. Health insurers may not exceed the target aggregates for their insured set by the regional commission.

The final decisions on the size and allocation of volumes of care among providers are made by the regional commissions. Their decisions are the basis for contracting between insurers and specific providers. Contracts are standard for all insurers and providers, the only variable elements are the volume of care and expected level of funding (volumes multiplied by rates of payment).

Second, insurers are incentivized to identify areas of inefficiency in the provision of care. According to the MHI Law, they can keep 10% of savings (insurers' revenue minus actual healthcare payment). Some regions introduce additional incentives. For example, in Moscow City, insurers control the appropriateness of inpatient care by identifying the cases of hospital admissions that can be served in outpatient settings. They are allowed to keep 80% of the payments avoided for care demonstrated to be inappropriate. These cases are usually identified through comparison with clinical guidelines. Insurers may deny payment to providers. Also, the readiness of a patient for admission is checked. If insurers identify an elective admission without prior necessary diagnostic tests, they can keep 70% of the potential payments and the multispecialty clinic that referred a patient pays a penalty (Moscow MHI Fund, 2015). Thus, there are some elements of managed care in MHI.

Third, health insurers are responsible for healthcare quality control and so-called "medical-economic expertise," that is checking the claims of providers, identification of underprovision of care ("incomplete cases of care"), denials of care provision, cases of charging patients for the services included in the Program, as well as defects in medical recording (the latter is most common). They are also allowed to penalize medical facilities for the identified violation of established rules and keep a certain portion of the imposed penalties (it varies from 30% to 50%). Thus insurers are incentivized to conduct some cost and quality control activities.

There were approximately 11 million instances in which insurers applied medical-economic expertise in 2014. Some violation of the rules was identified in 25% of these. Even at this frequency of control activities, the share of penalties kept by insurers is less than 1% of their revenue. Also, around 3 million of "thematic reviews" were conducted in 2014 (FOMS, 2015).

Finally, health insurers are involved in a large-scale state program of periodic check-ups and screenings (referred to as "dispanserization"). The program is designed to reveal major diseases at an early stage. Around 45 million children and adults (31% of the population) are covered by this program (Stadchenko, 2016). Apart from the reimbursement of preventive services, health insurers are responsible for control of their comprehensiveness (matching the authorized list of services) and revealing false claims.

Contrary to many European models, Russian law does not allow insurers to set up their own healthcare facilities, e.g., general practitioner offices, day care centers, or pharmacies. Also, insurers may not establish networks of providers with limited patient choice, specific rates of copayment, or out-of-network payment rates. The list of providers in MHI is the same for all insurers in the region. The insured can see any provider irrespective of the enrollment with the specific insurer. Thus, selective healthcare contracting is not presently part of MHI.

Provider payment methods are determined by the federal and regional health authorities and MHI Funds, not insurers. There is a tendency for all regions to use the payment methods recommended by the Federal MHI Fund—simple capitation for outpatient care and the Russian version of the Diagnosis-Related Group (DRG) method for inpatient care. Capitation payments are made to multispecialty clinics that serve a specified catchment area. Individuals can choose a clinic once a year and enroll irrespective of where he or she lives within the region. The total number of enrollees is the basis for clinic budgeting. Additionally, they are paid by fee-for-service for the services provided to the enrollees of other settings (if the latter can't provide the necessary services). Thus, the payment system allows for some flexibility in terms of choice and cross-border patients flows. The peculiarity of this scheme is that capitation does not provide strong incentives for provision of preventive services and better management of chronic diseases, because the clinics contract for a certain number of patient visits (according to the negotiated volumes of care) and therefore face contradictory incentives: to enhance quality of care and provide preventive services (capitation) or to supply the contracted number of visits.

Around 10 of the 85 regions in the country chose a fundholding scheme in which clinics control a portion of inpatient care expenditure and the regional authority plays the role of health insurers in monitoring patients' flows and clinic's performance indicators—in addition to reimbursement of services. Clinics can keep savings from lower inpatient care utilization only when they meet a certain number of performance targets. This mitigates the risk of overly aggressive denial of referrals to hospitals (Sheiman, 2016). Health insurers are also interested in this scheme, since they can keep 10% of savings.

**BOX 15.3 Instruments for MHI insurers to improve efficiency in delivery of care**

- Insurers negotiate volumes of care with the focus on more efficient structures of service delivery, but they don't act as the main purchasers of care
- Insurers control appropriateness of hospital admissions and are allowed to keep 10% of savings
- Insurers penalize medical facilities for the identified underprovision of care and are allowed to keep a portion of the penalties paid by providers
- Insurers conduct the reviews of clinical patterns in the selected clinical areas, with the obligatory feedback by providers
- Insurers have limited freedom in restricting their provider network and are not allowed to set up their own medical facilities
- Insurers have limited choice of provider payment methods

A DRG-type method for paying hospitals started in 2013, and is now used in 63 regions. The others use rates for each diagnosis. The number of groups is 426 and is growing. A system of subsidies compensates hospitals for losses under the DRG payment method (Shishkin et al., 2016). The size of subsidies is determined by health authorities and regional MHI Funds. Again, health insurers act as operators of the payment method, rather than purchasers of care who can choose appropriate incentives for providers (Box 15.3).

## 15.3  HEALTH PLAN PAYMENT DESIGN

Fig. 15.1 summarizes the current MHI financing scheme with the *arrows* representing the major money flows. Collection of funds is based on contributions of employers and regional governments. The former pays for their employees, the latter for the nonworking population, including children, pensioners, disabled, and the unemployed. The contribution of employers is income-related with a ceiling of the annual income against which a contribution is assessed. At the start of the reform, employers paid 3.6% of payroll; currently the rate is 5.1%. As mentioned earlier, there are no premiums paid directly by individuals.

Contributions of employers and regional governments are pooled in the Federal Fund of MHI, and distributed to 85 Regional MHI Funds according to the number of people in the region (with no risk-adjustment) and their financial capacity (poorer regions receive higher subsidies). The MHI Funds act as the governmental agencies responsible for organization and funding MHI in the region. They contract health

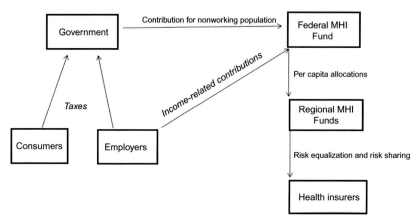

**FIGURE 15.1** Financing scheme of the Mandatory Health Insurance Law in Russia.

insurers and fund them according to the number of the enrollees with some risk equalization explained below. Health insurers contract with health providers and reimburse their services, control quality of care, and protect the insureds' rights. Planning and purchasing health care are the functions of the above-mentioned regional commissions with the involvement of health insurers. Their input in purchasing decisions is discussed in Section 15.4.

## 15.3.1 Regulation of Premiums and Contributions

As noted earlier, premiums are prohibited in MHI. (Community-rated premiums are used in the VHI system.) The MHI funds rely on income-related contributions of employers. The MHI Law sets regional rates of contribution for the nonworking population according to their fiscal capacity. Relatively rich regions pay much more for the nonworking population per person than relatively poor regions. The latter receive higher allocations per capita from the Federal MHI Fund. To provide the incentive for regional governments to contribute directly to the Regional MHI Funds (in addition to the federal pool), the MHI Law introduced the category of the "supplementary contribution for the nonworking population"; this is a contribution that exceeds the regional rate of contribution. Thus, the revenue of each Regional MHI Fund consists of federal allocations and contributions collected in the region.

This relatively new scheme has contributed to the leveling out of health funding by region but has not fully eliminated regional disparities. In 2010, the per capita health spending of the richest regions was 4.2 times higher than the poorest ones, in 2014 this variation reduced to 1.9 times (Shishkin et al., 2016).

## 15.3.2    Risk Equalization

The Russian risk equalization system is simple, based only on the age and sex of the enrollee. It is applied to all types of care without differentiation for the specific services. Six or more age—gender combinations are recognized in risk equalization (see Box 15.4). The estimates of health spending are made for each group. The curve of age and sex utilization of health care was estimated in the 1990s (based on the data in four regions) and then updated in early 2000 with more groups than required by the regulation (Fig. 15.2). The figure shows a very high average utilization of care for infants and a steep drop in the following 3—5 years. For adults there is an upward tendency from working age to old age as expected. The ratio of use

---

**BOX 15.4  Risk adjustors used in the risk equalization model for MHI**

*Age and sex are the basis* for six groups: 0—4 years, males and females; 5—17 years, males and females; 18—54 years, men; 18—54 years, women; more than 55 years, men; more than 55 years, women.

*Each region sets its own capitation rates across age/sex groups.*

*Risk-equalization weights are influenced by health policy priorities, particularly the focus on child care.*

---

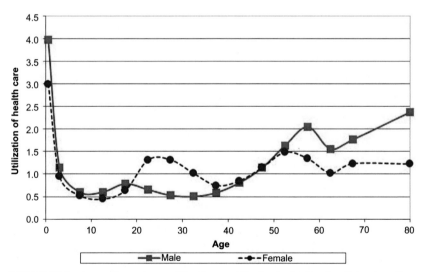

**FIGURE 15.2**    Age and sex curves of healthcare utilization in the Russian Federation. *From Frid, E., Isakova, L., Okushko, N., 2003. Development of methodological recommendations on capitation rates of the regional MHI programs funding. Report to the Federal Fund of MHI, (in Russian) (Frid et al., 2003).*

by the old to the young in Russia seems generally less than in other countries. For example, in the US Marketplaces, the ratio of premiums charged to 64-year-olds compared to 18-year-olds must be constrained to be no more than 3−1 (the unconstrained ratio is approximately 6−1) (see Layton, Ellis, McGuire, and Van Kleef, 2017). In Russia, the ratio of use for the 60s to the 20s is lower for both sexes, particularly for men. Some special circumstances in Russia may account for these results. At the age of 17−18 many young men have large-scale medical check-ups before military service. Also, prior to age 60 (retirement age for men) some may tend to hide their diseases to protect their employment. Utilization after 60 is growing steadily for men.

The estimates in Fig. 15.2 are used for setting differentiated capitation weights across age/sex groups. The regions are allowed to set their own weights (The Russian Federation Ministry of Health, 2011). In most regions they are based on six or more age/sex groups. Table 15.1 provides an example of the actual weights of capitation rate for one of the biggest health insurance companies in Russia. They differ across six regions where this company operates.

The weights represent ratios of spending relative to the entire population average. Risk equalization payment is the result of a simple multiplication of the ratio with the average capitation in a region for each age/sex group.

Table 15.1 demonstrates the age/sex variability of capitation rates across regions. For the group of working age (18−59 years) the range is 12%−15%, and for the youngest group it is 25%−30% (see the range of values in the respective columns). The higher range for the youngest group (even higher than for the over 60 group) can be attributed to the special policy of MHI Funds to support child and maternity care. The poorer regions (with lower average capitation rate) tend to have higher payment rates for the youngest group. The relatively higher underfunding makes these regions focus on child care as the first priority.

This simple scheme of risk equalization applies to all 85 regions of Russia. No other risk adjusters have been developed yet.

## 15.3.3 Risk Sharing

According to the MHI Law, in case of "underspending" (when an insurer's healthcare spending falls below the insurer's revenues), health insurers must return most of savings to the Regional MHI Fund. The presumption is that MHI financial resources belong to the federal government, except for administration costs (its rate is specified by the regulation) and the allowed 10% of savings. In the more common case of overspending, health insurers can apply to the Fund for subsidies. The estimate of overspending is based on the healthcare utilization targets per capita set by the Regional Program of state guarantees, as well as the volumes of care planned and negotiated for the

**TABLE 15.1 Age/Sex Coefficients for the Average Capitation Rate Adjustment in Six Regions of the Russian Federation**

| Regions | 0—4 years | | 5—17 years | | 18—59 years | | 60 and older | | Average capitation, Roubles per month |
|---|---|---|---|---|---|---|---|---|---|
| | Male | Female | Male | Female | Male | Female | Male | Female | |
| 1 | 1.94 | 1.80 | 0.95 | 0.92 | 0.57 | 0.90 | 1.60 | 1.39 | 660 |
| 2 | 2.21 | 2.02 | 0.87 | 0.90 | 0.56 | 0.82 | 1.60 | 1.37 | 619 |
| 3 | 1.69 | 1.54 | 0.80 | 0.76 | 0.58 | 0.88 | 1.66 | 1.46 | 560 |
| 4 | 1.72 | 1.59 | 1.06 | 0.97 | 0.60 | 0.98 | 1.44 | 1.22 | 645 |
| 5 | 1.50 | 1.34 | 0.75 | 0.75 | 0.74 | 1.11 | 1.48 | 1.36 | 972 |
| 6 | 1.54 | 1.34 | 0.78 | 0.78 | 0.61 | 1.00 | 1.67 | 1.47 | 720 |

*Source:* Database of one of the biggest health insurance companies in Russia.

specific providers (number of bed-days, day care cases, emergency calls, physician visits, etc.).

The MHI Law establishes vague grounds for insurers' application for subsidies—an unexpected increase in morbidity, changes in the size of tariffs (prices) used for provider reimbursement. Insurers are supposed to substantiate the need for and the size of the expected subsidy. Each application is considered on a case-by-case basis by the Regional MHI Fund. The work of health insurers is heavily scrutinized to check how they interact with providers of care: are there inappropriate referrals and hospital admissions, are utilization targets met in practice? The Fund has the right to reject the subsidy application. In this case a health insurer is required to cover overspending from its own reserves. Subsidies are paid from the so-called "normalized insurance reserve," funds set aside in the course of financial planning (5% of regional revenue). This is operated by the Regional MHI Fund. The allocation of these subsidies is discussed in Section 15.4.

### 15.3.4   Implementation and Maintenance

The design of financial flows and payment schemes in MHI is the responsibility of the Federal Ministry of Health and the Federal MHI Fund. They issue regulations for the entire country. The regional health authorities and MHI Funds add regulations which are required by the federal legislation. The implementation and maintenance of the schemes is the responsibility of health authorities and MHI Funds of federal and regional levels.

### 15.4   EVALUATION OF THE PAYMENT SYSTEM

This section explains some quantitative measures used for the assessment of payment schemes in MHI, including the stability of regional weighted capitation rates, the actual practice of insurers' subsidization, and their role as health purchasers. The criteria for choosing these measures are the following: (1) to assess the predictability of insurers' revenue from public sources (based on capitation); (2) to determine the degree of insurers' dependence on subsidies, as well as the fairness of subsidy allocation across insurers (whether they relate to insurers' performance); and (3) to evaluate insurers' leverage to manage cost of care and their financial risks. The weak purchasing role complicates the development of a system employing more risk bearing.

The evaluation is based on two surveys of health insurers conducted by the National Research University High School of Economics in cooperation with the Federal MHI Fund in 2012 and 2014. The questions were addressed to the heads of 78 insurance companies involved in MHI at that time (the number is now lower) in 50 regions of Russia. Almost all Russian insurers were covered by the surveys (Shishkin et al., 2015).

### 15.4.1 Stability of Regional Weighted Capitation Rates

Regional MHI Funds set weighted capitation rates for insurers funding for the period of one year. But they are allowed by the Law to adjust the rate during the year when health expenditure is not balanced with the expected Funds' revenue. The survey of 2014 indicates that in 2013 the rates were adjusted for 54% insurers at least once a year. For some of them it was done every quarter. Only 8% of insurers reported a stable rate. Thus capitation rates for insurers are not stable.

### 15.4.2 Subsidization of Insurers

As mentioned earlier, the MHI Law allows for substantial discretion in the use of MHI Funds in the allocation of subsidies. The surveys demonstrate how this scheme actually works. The share of health insurers that applied for a subsidy increased from 24.4% in 2012 to 65.3% in 2014. The average number of applications during the year increased from 1.8 to 3.7 per insurer. Some insurers submitted 10−12 applications. It is unclear how these applications are reviewed and how decisions are made, indicating a lack of transparency in insurers' subsidization.

65% of insurers reported a rise in the share of subsidies in their revenue, 29.7%—a stable share, and only 5.4%—a decrease. There is thus overall an upward trend in the level of subsidization, which implies a decrease in the share of financial risks borne by insurers. A more precise figure of the effective financial risk is unavailable due to the absence of statistical reporting on this issue.

The diversity in the share of funds coming from subsidies among insurers also indicates unclear grounds for decisions and a lack of transparency. This point is recognized by insurers themselves. 53% of respondents consider the prevailing pattern as unfair, 47% as fair. In sum, the subsidization system is: (1) mostly retrospective, (2) has an upward trend, (3) not predictable by insurers, (4) not transparent, and (5) of questionable fairness.

### 15.4.3 The Role of Health Insurers in Purchasing Care

As indicated earlier, health insurers share the function of care purchasing with health authorities and MHI Funds. The survey assessed the degree and forms of their involvement in this process.

The share of health insurers involved in planning and negotiating volumes of care with providers is 62%. Another 20% are involved in collective negotiations as members of insurers associations in the regions. The rest are not active contractors.

Another question was "What is your assessment of the results of your participation in determining planned volumes of care for the individual health providers?" 66% of respondents indicated that their involvement had actually affected the plans of volumes of care. The rest were skeptical about their input. The share of the latter went up over 2012–14.

Also, the role of insurers in quality assurance was explored. The surveys indicated a growing share of health insurers that provided reports with their analysis of quality problems in health organizations to health authorities. However, the level of feedback was low. Less than 30% of reports were actually taken into account in the planning process.

## 15.5 ONGOING ISSUES AND REFORMS

Competition among health insurers in Russian MHI is in place and growing. Consumers choose insurers. According to the above-mentioned surveys, the switching rate increased from 3.8% in 2010 to 4.6% in 2012 and 7.1% in 2014. Regional markets are becoming more competitive in the view of insurers: in 2012, 66% leaders of health insurers reported high competition, in 2014 it was 88% (Shishkin et al., 2015).[2]

However, competition is directed to areas which are not very important for the health system and the insured—mostly customer services. Insureds may choose the company which provides more information and courtesy but at present they are unable to purchase health plans with higher benefits or lower price. The potential of health insurers to offer new products in MHI is minimal. The financing system is not set up to absorb and direct the purchasing power of the rising middle class, one consequence of which is a high incidence of formal and informal direct payments to providers from consumers.

### 15.5.1 Ongoing Problems in Mandatory Health Insurance Design

The impact of competition on efficiency of service delivery is limited by the design of MHI and the following ongoing problems.

1. The MHI system is built as a command-and-control system. Contrary to the Netherlands, Germany, and other countries with a regulated competition model, in Russia the MHI authorities seek to directly control health insurers' performance and treat them as outsourcing agents. The purchasing function of insurers is limited. While participating in negotiating volumes of care with health providers, insurers have little leverage to influence resource allocation and manage healthcare cost. The major decisions are made by administrative bodies. The scope for risk bearing is limited by the administrative system.
2. Related to this is the problem of the legal treatment of health insurers' revenue. The Law states that most of the financial resources of the MHI system are owned by the federal government. The only exception is the

administrative costs, including 10% savings and the penalties revenue collected by insurers. As a result, the bulk of possible savings of insurers cannot be reinvested by insurers into improvements in efficiency. The alternative is to give insurers at least some stake in savings; a necessary condition for the introduction of a system based on the regulated competition model.

3. Financial parameters of MHI (capitation rates, services prices, the level of subsidization) are not stable and predictable by insurers. The subsidies are retrospective, not transparent enough and unrelated to insurers' performance. The predictability of insurers' revenue is low. There is an inadequate basis at present for building viable risk-bearing schemes.

   The major reason for instability is embedded in the design of the MHI system, which makes regional MHI Funds strong administrative bodies with wide discretion about the allocation of funding across insurers and providers. Depending on the actual MHI revenue and the approved volumes of care, capitation rates and subsidies are adjusted retrospectively in the so-called "manual" regime. Not surprisingly, in the current economic crisis the legislative provision of keeping 10% of savings has been almost canceled. According to a survey, in many cases, authorities adjusted capitation rates downward to eliminate the possibility of savings (Shishkin et al., 2015).

4. The MHI Law introduced a strict pattern of health provider reimbursement—paying only for the volumes of care that have been authorized by the regional commissions. Overprovision of services is either not reimbursed at all or reimbursed after a new round of voluminous negotiation with administrative bodies playing the decisive role. Providers bear a financial risk for overprovision of services. By contrast, risk bearing by health insurers has gone down compared to previously when actual volumes of care were reimbursed. This model of risk bearing has reduced insurers' incentives to negotiate a more rational structure of service delivery.

## 15.5.2 Developing Trends

Risk equalization improvement is not a high priority for the current MHI system.[3] In spite of the individual choice of insurers, risk selection among insurers is not perceived as a problem. This is partly because of large insurance pools (sometimes millions of insureds), partly due to the low level of risk bearing by insurers, and partly because of the limited tools for insurers to differentiate health plans. Currently, health insurers do not question the simple risk equalization system. However, they do argue that a move to a new model with more substantial risk bearing will make risk selection stronger. In that case, improved payment models will be needed.

Unmet expectations of health reform in Russia have led to serious public dissatisfaction with the healthcare system. Health insurers have become the focus of criticisms over the last few years. Some advocate for eliminating insurers in the MHI system leaving only MHI Funds (Kravchenko et al., 2013). Moreover, some critics suggest eliminating the entire MHI system and to reestablish the national health system (Gontmaher, 2015). In the current political context, the closure of the competitive model of MHI seems quite likely.

The interest in the regulated competition model has been revitalized by the message of the President to the Federal Chamber. It states that "in health care it is necessary to finish the shift to the insurance principles and improve the current system" (President of the Russian Federation, 2014). This signal has been picked up by the Ministry of Health which has set about the task of developing a supplementary health insurance system to the MHI.

Two research centers were commissioned by the government to develop this model with the special focus on making health insurers "real" risk-bearing entities and developing a new health plan payment design. Below are the major points of the document developed by the National Research University—High School of Economics, presently under discussion in Russia (HSE, 2015).

A set of proposals is based on the assumption that building a sound regulated competition model requires substantial groundwork to make the current financial arrangements in MHI more predictable and transparent. This system must be ready to attract additional money in the form of premiums paid by consumers together with the government (in the form of subsidies). Therefore, the following major changes are proposed for the initial stage of reform:

- Shift to the more stable annual financial parameters—prices of services, weighted capitation rates, the level of subsidies. A "manual" management of subsidies should be replaced by a more stable and transparent system—mostly in the form of a fixed percentage of overspending to be funded by MHI Funds.
- Increase in the share of MHI Fund reserves in their total revenue to ensure predictability of financial parameters.
- A shift from the collective (through regional commissions) to volume negotiations between insurers and providers, in other words, a shift from the administrative to the market principles of determining volumes of care.
- Collecting more information and negotiating quality indicators of providers' performance.
- A rise in the share of savings (due to lower spending) kept by health insurers from the current 10% to 20%−30% to encourage effective care purchasing by health insurers.

- Preparative work for building other foundations of regulated competition, including completion of product standardization (e.g., improving classifications of DRGs), accumulation of cost data for improving the risk equalization system, setting up anticartel legislative arrangements, reconsideration of health insurers functions—a shift from the current quality control to quality assurance and higher role of insurers as prudent purchasers of care.

The proposed reforms would radically change financial flows, making insurers real risk-bearing entities. It is suggested to split the current income-related MHI contribution into two parts: (1) contribution to MHI Funds, and (2) premium paid by the insured to the selected insurer with the legislative provision that it can vary depending on health plans (but community rated within an insurer). These reforms would make insurers responsible for a specified share of overspending and underspending.

It is further recommended that the current division of MHI and VHI schemes should give way to the division of basic and supplementary health plans which are offered and operated by the same insurer. The latter would then compete on price, product, and quality of customer and health services.

The major controversial point of this program is the participation of the insureds in health plan payment. Many critics oppose direct payment from consumers, making reference to a deeply rooted tradition of free care in Russia. Another area of concern is that an increase in financial risk for health insurers will require stable funding which may not be possible in the current economic situation. It may be best to start this model during an economic recovery.

The design of health insurance plan payment depends on the future model of financial flows, as well as the political willingness and the financial capacity of the government to subsidize premiums. But in any scenario an improvement of the current risk equalization model will be needed.

Although geographic inequity does not directly correspond to risk solidarity in the way that term is usually used in the context of the regulated competition model, it is an important characteristic which needs to be contended with in any future model for Russia. The elimination of the imbalance of a package of medical benefits (and health plans) with financial resources available has been referred to as a precondition for an effective regulated competition model (Van de Ven et al., 2013; Van de Ven, 2014). For a big country like Russia, overcoming this imbalance is possible only through a broad geographic equalization policy which goes beyond risk equalization of health plans. Similarly, stable financial parameters of the entire payment system are another important precondition for a more transparent risk-sharing scheme, and, in a broader sense, for the regulated competition model.

## ACKNOWLEDGMENT

This chapter is an output of a research project implemented as part of the Basic Research Program at the National Research University Higher School of Economics (HSE) in 2015−16.

## ENDNOTES

1. Operators of VHI can offer additional benefits (shorter waiting time, better amenities, more choice of provider, etc.
2. A direct question was asked in the survey: "How do you assess the level of competition?" with options "high," "medium," "low," and "can't say."
3. Comments in this section are based on the personal experience of the author.

## REFERENCES

Davis, C., 1988. The organization and performance of the contemporary Soviet health system. In: Lapidus, G., Swanson, G. (Eds.), State and Welfare, USA/USSR: Contemporary Policy and Practice. Institute of International Studies, University of California Berkeley, Berkeley.

Davis, C., 2010. Understanding the legacy: health financing systems in the USSR and central and Eastern Europe prior to Transition. Reforms and Challenges Implementing Health Financing Reforms − Lessons From and for Countries in Transition. Open University Press, Buckingham.

Flek, V., 2015. Russian Health Finance Based on Health Accounting System. Moscow (in Russian).

FOMS, 2015. Federal Fund of mandatory health insurance. Report on the Mandatory Health Insurance System in the Russian Federation in 2014. Objazatelnoemeditsinskoestrahovanie № 4 2015, pp. 12, 37 (in Russian).

Frid, E., Isakova, L., Okushko, N., 2003. Development of methodological recommendations on capitation rates of the regional MHI programs funding. Report to the Federal Fund of MHI, (in Russian).

Gontmaher, E., 2015. Health System Diagnosis. Vedomosti №3883, (in Russian).

HSE, 2015. National Research University High School of Economics. Report on the Development of Competitive (Risk) Model of Health Insurers Involvement in Mandatory Health Insurance, (in Russian).

Kravchenko, N., Ragozin, V., Rozanov, V., 2013. Why Does not the Dutch Model Meet Russian Situation. Objazatelnoemeditsinskoestrahovanie № 2 2013 (in Russian).

Layton, T., Ellis, R., McGuire, T., Van Kleef, R., 2017. Measuring efficiency of health plan payment systems in managed competition health insurance markets. J. Health Econ. 56, 237−255.

MHI Fund, 2015. Tariff Agreement for 2015. Moscow (in Russian).

President of the Russian Federation, December 4, 2014. The Message of the Russian Federation President to the Federal Chamber (in Russian).

Sheiman, I., 1995. New methods of financing and managing health care in the Russian Federation. Health Policy 32, 167−180.

Sheiman, I., 2016. Payment methods for integration: typology, evidence and pre-conditions of implementation. J. Pharm. Care Health Syst. 3 (2). Available from: https://doi.org/10.4172/2376-0419.1000154.

Shishkin, S., Sazchina, S., Selezneva, E., 2015. Insurance Medical Organizations in Mandatory Health Insurance system: What Has Changed After the Reform? National Research University High School of Economics, Preprint WP8/2015/04. Public Administration WP8, Moscow (in Russian).

Shishkin, S., Sheiman, I., Abdin, S., Boyrski, S., Sazchina, S., 2016. Russian Healthcare in the New Economic Situation: Challenges and Prospective. Publishing House of National Research University High School of Economics, Moscow, 84 pp. (in Russian).

Stadchenko, N., April 20, 2016. Interview of the Federal MHI Fund Director to the Medical Gazette, (in Russian).

Telyukov, A., 1991. A concept of health-financing reform in the Soviet Union. Int. J. Health Services 21, 493−504.

The Russian Federation Ministry of Health, 2011. Order # 158 N, 28.02.2011. Moscow, (in Russian).

Thompson, W., 2007. Healthcare reform in Russia: problems and prospects. *OECD Economics Department Working Papers*, No. 538. OECD Publishing, Paris.

Twigg, J., 1998. Balancing the state and the market: Russia's adoption of obligatory medical insurance. Europe-Asia Studies 50, 583−602.

Van de Ven, W., 2014. Health insurance in Russia: is there a Dutch solution? In: Seminar "Reforming Healthcare: Global Challenges/Dutch Solutions" organized by the Dutch embassy in Moscow on 31 March 2014.

Van de Ven, W., Beck, K., Buchner, F., Schokkaert, E., Schut, E., Shmueli, A., et al., 2013. Preconditions for efficiency and affordability in competitive health markets: are they fulfilled in Belgium, Germany, Israel, the Netherlands and Switzerland? Health Policy 109, 226−245.

WHO Database, 2015. European Health for All Database. <http://data.euro.who.int/hfadb/shell_ru.html>.

Xu, W., Sheiman, I., Van de Ven, W., Zhang, W., 2010. Prospects for regulated competition in the health care system: what can China learn from Russia's experience? Health Policy Plan. 26, 199−209.

# FURTHER READING

Sheiman, I., Shevski, V., 2014. Evaluation of health care delivery integration: the case of the Russian Federation. Health Policy 115 (2−3), 128−137.

Chapter 16

# Health Plan Payment in Switzerland

Christian P.R. Schmid[1,2], Konstantin Beck[1,3] and Lukas Kauer[1,4]
[1]CSS Institute for Empirical Health Economics, Lucerne, Switzerland, [2]University of Bern, Bern, Switzerland, [3]University of Lucerne, Lucerne, Switzerland, [4]University of Zurich, Zurich, Switzerland

## 16.1 INTRODUCTION

The foundations for the Swiss health insurance system were laid in 1890 when the parliament established the constitutional basis for regulating accident and health insurance. Although the voters approved the constitutional change soon afterwards with 75.4% affirmative votes in a public referendum, it took more than 20 years until the first Sickness and Accident Insurance Law (KUVG) was passed by the parliament in 1911 and approved by the voters in 1912 with 54.4% affirmative votes. Under the KUVG, all health insurers offering a defined minimal coverage and meeting some entry standards received annual federal subsidies that differed between the four age classes 0−15, 16−59, 60−69, and 70 + . In addition, the subsidies were different in the age class 16−59 for men and women and insurers received additional subsidies for women who gave birth. In 1993, subsidies ranged from CHF 11.45 to 744.25 for young men and for elderly consumers (70 + ), respectively (Beck et al., 1995). Although the cantons (i.e., states) were empowered to introduce compulsory insurance for (parts of) the cantonal population, health insurance remained predominantly voluntary (Bundesrat, 1992). Note that Switzerland consists of 26 cantons with an average (median) population of 322,768 (232,683) in 2016. The smallest canton in terms of population has 15,948 inhabitants (Appenzell I.Rh.) while the largest canton has 1,482,650 inhabitants (Zurich). Around the turn of the 20th century, the federal laws on nutrition, epidemics, free movement of medical staff, and protection of workers in factories covered additional areas of health and healthcare provision. After the Second World War, health protection and access to medical care were further improved through a series of new laws including the federal law on Old-age Pension Insurance (AHVG) and the

Risk Adjustment, Risk Sharing and Premium Regulation in Health Insurance Markets.
DOI: https://doi.org/10.1016/B978-0-12-811325-7.00016-6

federal law on Disability Insurance (IVG). The first revision of the KUVG in 1966 enhanced the minimum coverage (maternity) and reorganized the federal subsidies, while the second revision in 1981 created a separate accident insurance (Leu et al., 2008). An accident is defined as the sudden, unintentional, harmful influence of an exceptional external force on the human body, resulting in the impairment of physical, mental, or psychological health, or death (General Section of Social Insurance Law (ATSG) Art. 4). The accident insurance covers all accident-related expenditures including spending for medical treatments, that is, health insurance and accident insurance are separated in Switzerland. However, several structural problems could not be tackled by these revisions. In particular, health insurers could charge premiums depending on gender and age at enrollment, irrespective of previous health insurance status, and limit coverage for preexisting conditions for 5 years. Thus, bad risks could not move freely between health insurers. Moreover, differences in the risk structures led to premium differences among health plans, which in turn created adverse selection (Colombo, 2001). Finally, risk solidarity and affordability of health plans were difficult to achieve. By risk solidarity we mean cross-subsidies from low-risk to high-risk individuals. Nevertheless, the share of voluntarily insured grew from 48% in 1945 to almost 100% in 1990.

In response to these shortcomings, the Federal Council proposed in 1991 a new Federal Health Insurance Law (*Bundesgesetz über die Krankenversicherung, KVG; Loi fédérale sur l'assurance-maladie, LAMal*) with three main goals (Bundesrat, 1992): First, to strengthen the risk solidarity regarding gender, age, and health status while maintaining affordability of health plans for low-income individuals. In order to achieve risk solidarity, health insurance became compulsory and the law introduced community-rated premiums and periodic open enrollment. In addition, the law established a certain degree of risk equalization (RE) to reduce risk-related differences in premiums within 10 years. To maintain affordability, means-tested health insurance subsidies were introduced. Second, to contain health-care expenditures (HCEs) through various demand-side and supply-side measures including mandatory as well as voluntary copayments, managed care, and enforced competition among health insurers as well as among healthcare providers. However, insurers are not allowed to make profits on compulsory health plans, i.e., surpluses can only be used to accumulate insurance reserves. On the other hand, health insurers are allowed to offer profitable supplemental health plans. Supplemental health plans cover, for instance, dental care, alternative medicine, or more comfort and choice in hospital care. Compared to compulsory health plans, the market for supplementary insurance is less regulated and allows inter alia for risk-rated premiums, constrained enrollment, and coverage limitations regarding preexisting conditions. Third, to maintain quality of health care through competition among healthcare providers as well as among health insurers and to expand coverage. The KVG was passed by the Federal Parliament in March 1994, approved by the voters in December of the same year with 51.8%

affirmative votes, and came into effect at the beginning of 1996. Thereafter, different proposals for revision were discussed but in most instances not put into practice. Notable exceptions are two reforms implemented in 2012, namely the improvement of the RE formula and the introduction of case rates based on diagnosis-related groups (DRGs) for inpatient care cofunded by the cantons (at least 55%) and the health insurers.

According to the Federal Statistical Office (FSO, 2016) and shown in Table 16.1, total HCE in 2014 amounted to 71.3 billion Swiss Francs (11.1% of GDP). (In 2016, 1 Swiss Franc bought on average 1.02 US$ and 0.92 €, respectively.) Compulsory health insurance covered 26.0 billion Swiss Francs (or 36.5%) of total HCE while total copayments under the KVG additionally accounted for 4.0 billion Swiss Francs (5.6%). The contributions of

**TABLE 16.1** Funding Sources of HCE in Switzerland in 2014 (in 1000 Swiss Francs)

| | | |
|---|---|---|
| **Total healthcare expenditures** | **71,334.8** | **100.0%** |
| **Compulsory health insurance (KVG)** | **30,031.0** | **42.1%** |
| Covered expenditures | 26,041.8 | 36.5% |
| Copayments | 3,989.2 | 5.6% |
| **Public contributions** | **14,228.8** | **19.9%** |
| Federal state | 156.9 | 0.2% |
| Cantons | 12,058.5 | 16.9% |
| Municipalities | 2,013.4 | 2.8% |
| **Supplementary (private) insurance** | **5,207.5** | **7.3%** |
| Covered expenditures | 5,158.7 | 7.2% |
| Copayments | 48.9 | 0.1% |
| **Social insurance** | **7,651.6** | **10.7%** |
| Accident insurance | 2,237.6 | 3.1% |
| Invalidity insurance | 2,621.0 | 3.7% |
| Old-age pension insurance | 2,375.1 | 3.3% |
| Other | 417.8 | 0.6% |
| **Out-of-pocket and private expenditures** | **14,215.9** | **19.9%** |

This table shows the relative importance of the different funding sources of total HCE in Switzerland in 2014 (based on FSO, T 14.05.02.01). Total HCE includes all physician services and services after referrals, prescription drugs, dental care, hospital and long-term care, home care, support for disabled individuals, prevention, emergency services, and administration costs. The bulk share of public contributions is cofunding of inpatient care and is, thus, subject to regulated competition.

the federal state, the cantons, and the municipalities summed up to 14.2 billion Swiss Francs, accounting for 19.9% of total HCE. Note, however, that the bulk share of public spending is triggered by the KVG and includes inter alia cofunding for inpatient care and expenditures for public health and prevention. In other words, roughly 60% of total HCE is regulated under the KVG (see also INFRAS, 2010). Moreover, compulsory health insurance covers basically all individuals with a Swiss domicile (in 2015: 8.3 million individuals). Finally, supplementary (private) insurance including copayments amounts to 5.2 billion Swiss Francs (7.3%) and the remaining 21.9 billion Swiss Francs (30.7%) are either funded by other social insurances such as Accident Insurance, Invalidity Insurance, and Old-age Pension Insurance or not covered by any insurance and thus paid out-of-pocket. Regarding the latter, it is important to note that dental care and stays as well as nonmedical assistance in nursing homes are in principle not covered by any social insurance. Consequently, health services paid out-of-pocket accounted for more than 14 billion Swiss Francs.

The remainder of this chapter focuses on regulated competition and, therefore, on the KVG and the corresponding by-law for the Compulsory Health Insurance (*Verordnung über die Krankenversicherung, KVV*; *Ordonnance sur l'assurance-maladie, OAMal*). In the following sections we will describe the health insurance system (Section 16.2) and health plan payment (Sections 16.3 and 16.4) in more detail. Finally, we will discuss some ongoing issues and reforms in Section 16.5.

## 16.2 ORGANIZATION OF THE HEALTH INSURANCE SYSTEM

The health insurance system under the KVG is organized according to principles of regulated competition to maintain risk solidarity, affordability of health plans, and efficiency, implying that health plans and providers compete on price and quality while regulation ensures individual affordability of health plans and risk solidarity between low- and high-risk individuals. In what follows, we focus on health plan market regulations, consumer choice options, and instruments for insurers to promote efficiency. However, the Swiss healthcare system has a decentralized structure reflecting the strong federal structure of the country. In other words, tasks and responsibilities are dispersed over all three state levels, i.e., the federation, the cantons, and the municipalities (Leu et al., 2008). Therefore, we also describe the division of tasks and the coordination mechanisms between the three state levels where necessary.

### 16.2.1 Health Plan Market Regulation

All Swiss residents, including refugees, asylum seekers, and individuals with habitual residence as well as posted workers of companies based in

Switzerland are obliged to purchase compulsory health insurance (KVG Art. 3) offered by private insurers. Cantons are responsible for enforcing this obligation (KVG Art. 6). All contracts between the consumer and the insurer are on an individual basis, i.e., health plans do not cover dependents, are independent of employment, and group contracts are not allowed (Leu et al., 2008). Insurers are obliged to accept consumers who wish to enroll regardless of health status, age, gender, and so on (open enrollment). In principle, insurers have to charge premiums that are community-rated per health plan and canton with some flexibility regarding age and cantonal region. Premiums may differ between "young adults" (19−25) and "adults" (26+) and among up to three premium regions per canton (defined by the regulator). In addition, health plan premiums for "children" (0−18) have to be lower than the adults' premiums (KVG Art. 61). In other words, an insurer must offer the same premium to all individuals who purchase the same health plan, are in the same age group, and live in the same canton or cantonal premium region. In addition, RE should ensure that community-rating does not incentivize insurers to practice risk selection (see Section 16.3). There are, however, no risk-sharing mechanisms between insurers.

Regarding the services covered by compulsory health insurance, the benefit package is standardized and comprehensive. In case of sickness, outpatient and inpatient services performed by physicians and chiropractors are covered as well as physician-directed and chiropractor-directed services performed by other healthcare providers including pharmacists (e.g., prescription drugs), physiotherapists, psychotherapists, midwifes, laboratories, birth houses, and hospitals (KVG Art. 25). In addition, compulsory health insurance covers some preventive services, maternity services, and services due to birth defects that are not covered by disability insurance, and it partly covers costs related to spa therapies, emergency transportation, ambulance services, and (long-term) care. In contrast, dental services are in principle not covered by compulsory health insurance unless the dental problems are related to a severe illness (preventive dental care for children is provided for free and financed by the municipality). Finally, the specified services are also covered in case of accident (KVG Art. 28). However, all consumers with more than 8 hours of paid work per week have to be covered by an employer-sponsored accident insurance. Therefore, they can opt out of accident coverage by compulsory health insurance (KVG Art. 8).

All insurers have to offer the *standard* health plan (*ordentliche Versicherung*) in regions they operate in. That is, health insurers can operate in the entire country, in a subset of cantons, or merely in a few municipalities. The standard health plan has a standard deductible (CHF 300) and is the default option for consumers. Enrollees in standard health plans can freely choose among general practitioners and specialists providing outpatient care. Regarding inpatient care, consumers can choose among all hospitals listed on a cantonal list of hospitals defined by the cantonal authority (the so-called "hospital list"). In contrast to outpatient care, health plan reimbursement of inpatient care is limited to the costs that would typically arise in the canton of residence (KVG Art. 41) (see Section 16.2.3).

To maintain affordability means-tested premium subsidies are awarded (KVG Art. 65). Basically, these subsidies are decreasing in (family) income to fade out completely above a certain threshold (see Gerritzen et al., 2014, for details). As cantons have decisive power on the design of the subsidies, the subsidies vary across cantons in terms of the relevant income and asset thresholds, the subsidy amount, and how the family structure is taken into account. Depending on income and family structure, the subsidy may fully cover the health plan premium (Kaufmann et al., 2017). Since 2014, cantons have transferred the subsidies directly to the insurer to reduce the individuals' out-of-pocket premiums. The subsidies are financed jointly by the canton of residence and the federal government through tax revenues. The federation provides a total amount of 7.5% of the HCE covered by compulsory health insurance to the cantons; its contributions are mainly allocated according to the number of cantonal residents (KVG Art. 66) (Box 16.1).

In addition to the aforementioned health plan market regulations, the KVG includes inter alia federal regulations on the provider licensing, regulations regarding the quality of health care and providers, and several legal issues. In addition, further laws and regulations exist concerning the solvency of health insurers and specific markets such as pharmaceuticals and supplementary health insurance plans. Although some regulations against restraints of competition exist in the KVG (e.g., Art. 46), it is worth noting that antitrust regulation is generally not applicable to the compulsory healthcare market (Leu et al., 2008), which is especially important for the regulations

---

**BOX 16.1 Regulation to achieve risk solidarity and individual affordability of health plans**

- Obligation to purchase an individual health plan (offered by a private insurer)
- Comprehensive standardized benefit package
- Insurers have to offer a *standard* health plan with the *standard* deductible (CHF 300) and free physician choice
- Open enrollment
- Community-rated health plan premium
  - may differ between "young adults" (19–25) and "adults" (26 + )
  - may differ among up to three premium regions per canton
  - premiums for "children" (0–18) have to be lower than the adults' premium
- Means-tested premium subsidies
- Risk equalization

described in Section 16.2.3. While all these regulations have an effect on the market structure and might be important for the functioning of the healthcare system as a whole, we solely focus on the regulation regarding risk solidarity, individual affordability, and health plan payment.

## 16.2.2    Health Plan Choice Options for Consumers

In principle, health plans differ in three dimensions, namely the health insurer offering the plan, the deductible of the plan, and access restrictions with respect to healthcare providers commonly referred to as managed care options.

Regarding the insurer, consumers can freely choose among all approved health insurers (KVG Art. 4). The contract period basically corresponds to the calendar year and starts on January 1. Health insurers have to announce the change in the plan premium no later than October 31 of the prior year and consumers can give notice to quit the current plan of the insurer until November 30 (KVG Art. 7). There are two notable exceptions. First, consumers enrolled in a standard health plan can additionally switch insurer biannually within a notice period of 3 months. Second, if the insurer has to extraordinarily increase the premium during the year due to a sudden and significant drop in solvency, enrollees can give notice to quit until 1 month before the new premium takes effect. To prevent consumers from shirking the obligation to obtain insurance, the termination does in either case not take effect until the new insurer notifies the former insurer about the contract closing with the consumer. Although the coverage in compulsory health insurance is the same across all health insurers, insurers differ in terms of customer services such as availability, communication, time to process claims, chronic disease management programs, and the payment flow between health insurers, healthcare providers, and consumers (see Section 16.2.3). Note, however, that the available choices regarding insurers have shrunk over the past 20 years as the number of health insurers has diminished from 145 in 1996 to 52 in 2017.

Instead of the standard deductible of CHF 300, adults can opt for a deductible of CHF 500, 1000, 1500, 2000, or 2500 where all consumers aged 19 or older are considered as adults. Note that the year of birth is relevant and not the exact date of birth, i.e., individuals turn adult at the beginning of the year during which they turn 19 (KVG Art. 61). For children, the standard deductible is zero and voluntary deductibles range from CHF 100 to 600 (KVV Art. 93). Health plan premiums are decreasing in the deductible level though the maximum reduction is regulated (see Section 16.3.1). In addition, all consumers have a coinsurance rate of 10% for healthcare costs exceeding the deductible until a stop-loss amount is hit. The stop-loss amount is CHF 700 for adults and CHF 350 for children. If more than two children from one family are insured by the same insurer, their cumulative stop-loss amount is

CHF 700 (KVV Art. 103). Cost sharing is not applied to HCE related to maternity and de facto cost-sharing exemptions exist for social-assistance beneficiaries and recipients of supplementary old-age and disability benefits (Leu et al., 2008). Note that the deductible levels as well as the stop-loss amounts have been adapted on a nonregular basis. The latest adaptation was the increase in stop-loss amounts from CHF 600 (300) to CHF 700 (350) for adults (children) in 2004 and the increase of the standard adults' deductible levels by CHF 70 as well as an expansion of the choice set of voluntary deductible levels in 2005 (Schmid, 2017).

The third choice dimension relates to managed care health plans. From the consumer's perspective, these plans primarily apply gatekeeping tactics with respect to physician services in exchange for a premium rebate (KVG Art. 41 and Art. 62). However, insurers differ in the availability of managed care health plans and managed care options vary considerably across health insurers as managed care is only lightly regulated (see Section 16.2.3). Today, the majority of consumers (64.7% in 2015) enroll in managed care plans and more than half of consumers in managed care plans also have a voluntary deductible. In contrast, among the consumers not in a managed care health plan, only 39.3% have a voluntary deductible. Overall, the vast majority of consumers (78.6% in 2015) enroll in health plans that apply demand-side and/or supply-side controls for containing costs (Box 16.2).

## 16.2.3 Instruments for Health Plans to Promote Efficiency

For several reasons, the health insurers' possibilities to promote efficiency are limited. First, insurers are obliged to contract with all licensed healthcare providers in the *standard* plan. On the one hand, consumers are guaranteed free physician choice in standard health plans and all health insurers have to offer this plan. Therefore, health insurers do not have the possibility to suspend physicians. Moreover, standard health plans have to reimburse all physicians according to a standard fee-for-service (FFS) schedule (see next paragraph). It is important to note that this default reimbursement schedule combined with the contract obligation is very attractive for providers, i.e., they have only small incentives to selectively contract with insurers. On the other hand, cantonal authorities are responsible for planning inpatient services in hospitals. All cantons compile a list of hospitals and health plans

---

**BOX 16.2 The three dimensions of health plan choice options for consumers**

- Insurer
- Level of voluntary deductible
- Restriction of access to healthcare providers (managed care options)

have to cover inpatient services provided by the hospitals listed (KVG Art. 41). Besides regulating hospital care, the majority of hospitals in Switzerland are canton-owned enterprises which potentially results in conflict of interest and weakens cost containment incentives. This is reflected in the fact that canton-owned hospitals are always included on the hospital list while this is not the case for privately owned hospitals.

Second, the dominant types of provider remuneration are FFS and case rates based on DRGs for outpatient and inpatient services, respectively. The general structure of these tariffs is determined by collective negotiations between insurer and provider organizations, mainly because the general structure of each tariff has to be identical throughout Switzerland (KVG Art. 43 and 49). The base rate is then negotiated either on the cantonal or the provider level and registered in a tariff contract. For instance, the base rate for the DRG tariff can be determined on the provider level while the base rate for outpatient physician services is generally negotiated on a cantonal basis. Because tariff structure and base rate are predominantly collectively negotiated, providers do virtually not compete on prices. Regarding outpatient care, health insurers and providers are allowed to individually negotiate and agree on other tariff structures as far as the negotiated tariff is *not* based on FFS (KVG Art. 43). However, such negotiations rarely happen, most likely because outpatient providers prefer the default FFS tariff.

Third, FFS and DRG tariff contracts have to be approved either by cantonal authorities or by the federal council depending on whether the contract applies to a canton or to the entire country (KVG Art. 46). In addition, the federal council can adapt the general structure of the tariff if the negotiations fail or the tariffs seem to be no longer appropriate (KVG Art. 43). On the cantonal level, similar rules apply to tariff contracts. The latter is rather crucial as hospitals owned by the cantons negotiate with the insurers on the base rates for inpatient and outpatient care. At best, health insurers can appeal to the Federal Administrative Court if they do not agree with a tariff contract decreed by the canton, and there have been some cases where the insurers have won their case.

Given the obligation to contract and the tariff regulations, health insurers are in a rather weak position when bargaining with healthcare providers. Nevertheless, health insurers have at least three instruments to promote efficiency in the delivery of care: Supply-side measures, complementary demand-side measures, and improving claim processing.

### 16.2.3.1 Supply-Side Measures

Gatekeeping applied by managed care plans is lightly regulated and, therefore, the variety of such health plans is large but can yet be summarized into three different types: health maintenance organization (HMO) health plans, telemedicine health plans, and preferred provider organization (PPO) health plans. In contrast to the above-discussed obligation to contract with all licensed healthcare providers, insurers have the possibility to contract selectively given a gatekeeper plan. By doing so, health insurers implement supply-side controls. In HMO health plans, they usually contract with a group of outpatient providers or a managed care organization. Unlike in the United States, health insurers and healthcare providers are nowadays generally not vertically integrated. The contracts often include a bonus for efficiency gains or a risk-adjusted capitation payment per plan enrollee (see Section 16.3 for details). The latter implies budget responsibility for the entire clinical pathway, i.e., also for services provided after referrals. While these health plans partly rely on gatekeeping, efficiency gains are additionally achieved by incentivizing providers to deliver care more efficiently and to reduce (unnecessary) referrals.

The second type are telemedicine health plans. Consumers purchasing these health plans are obliged to phone a telemedicine service before visiting any physician (Grandchamp and Gardiol, 2011). The medical call center employs medical staff who approve physician visits. On the other hand, employed physicians can give advice over the phone, prescribe drugs, and send the prescription to a pharmacy, and write certificates of incapacity for the consumer's employer. The medical call center receives a small capitation payment per plan enrollee, but physicians visited after approval are still paid by FFS. Consequently, efficiency gains are mainly achieved by avoiding unnecessary physician visits.

The third type are so-called family doctor health plans (PPO plans with provider lists). In contrast to the first and second types of health plans, family doctor health plans typically have no contract with the listed general practitioners, avoiding costs and time associated with insurer–provider negotiations. The insurer can define on its own a list of selectable preferred providers to its consumers and restrict the access in the first instance to a general practitioner (gatekeeper) on that list. Consumers are required to consult the family doctor first before they can seek specialized care (e.g., specialists, hospitals). The physicians (on the list) are paid by FFS. In other words, efficiency is increased by gatekeeping only: guiding consumers to the physicians who were identified by insurers to work more efficiently, deterring consumers from visiting several providers until they receive the desired treatment, and preventing them from directly consulting a specialist for trifles.

### 16.2.3.2    Complementary Demand-Side Measures

Health insurers can incentivize consumers to choose managed care plans and to stick to the gatekeeper. On the one hand, consumers opting for managed care plans with restricted provider access enjoy premium rebates. On the other hand, insurers can either partly or fully waive the deductible and the coinsurance rate (KVV Art. 99). Waiving the copayments would make managed care plans especially attractive for consumers with chronic conditions. Nevertheless, health plans rarely include this waiver, either because individuals with chronic conditions are undercompensated by the current RE scheme or due to (demand-side) moral hazard, i.e., overutilization of services by patients (see Boes and Gerfin, 2016). On the other hand, health plans are allowed to refuse reimbursement of out-of-network spending. Health plans cover out-of-network spending in case of an emergency or when the gatekeeper approved it ("gatekeeper rule"). In addition, prior approval is commonly not required for services provided by gynecologists, pediatricians, and ophthalmologists. Besides refusing reimbursement, any consumer continuously disregarding the gatekeeper rule is also automatically enrolled in the corresponding health plan (i.e., with the same deductible) without the managed care option. As the premiums of health plans without managed care option are considerably higher, the threat of exclusion in addition to the threat of nonreimbursement incentivizes consumers to stick to the gatekeeper. Finally, managed care plans can charge higher coinsurance rates for some services, e.g., if the consumer purchases a drug for which there is a cheaper alternative.

### 16.2.3.3 Improving Claim Processing

Claim processing can improve the efficiency of the health insurance market as well as the efficiency of the administration of care considerably. On the one hand, the electronic processing of (standardized) health insurance claims reduces administrative costs. Today, the claims are either handed in on paper and scanned afterwards or sent electronically to the insurer. Regarding the latter, consumers have the possibility to submit their claims using their smartphone, while healthcare providers can use electronic billing for reimbursement by the health insurance. The latter is, however, only possible if healthcare providers agree in the tariff contract to send their bills directly to the insurers (see Schmid, 2017, for further details). While hospital and pharmacy claims are generally processed electronically and directly sent to the insurers, most physicians prefer to bill their patients, implying that a large fraction of invoices for outpatient care is still handed in on paper. From the insurers' perspective, direct reimbursement of healthcare providers is appealing because it reduces administrative costs and claims can be electronically processed. However, patients might reduce their efforts in reviewing bills of their healthcare providers, which in turn reduces error and fraud detection. In any case, the processing of claims using information technology reduces the employment of labor and thus administrative costs. Moreover, efficient claim processing has grown in importance over the past two decades as the growth rate of claims is 1.6 times the growth rate of HCE. Between 1996 and 2015, the share of electronically processed claims has increased from 0% to 74% (according to the claims department of one of the largest Swiss health insurers. Comparison of growth rates is based on FOPH (2016), T2.03, 2.25, and 11.04). On the other hand, electronic processing implies that claim details can be fully gathered. This in turn means that the behavior of health-care providers can be observed. For instance, health insurers are able to identify efficient physicians and offer health plans where these physicians act as gatekeepers. In addition, information can be provided to managed care organizations in order to improve their delivery of care and referral behavior. Moreover, monitoring of healthcare providers helps to detect inadvertent payments as well as fraudulent billing. While the direct effect of monitoring might be rather small, it has also a preventive effect and thus reduces over-provision of services (Box 16.3).

## 16.3   HEALTH PLAN PAYMENT DESIGN

Fig. 16.1 depicts the payment flows within the KVG. The size of the arrows represents the importance of the component in terms of the amount involved. The left-hand side of Fig. 16.1 shows the contributions involved in the KVG:

- The consumer finances almost two-thirds of the expenditures (27.1 billion CHF of 43.4 in 2015) through premiums paid to the insurer. The premium is community-rated by region and age category and amounts to a yearly average of CHF 3289 in 2015 paid by every enrollee. A substantial part of the population receives a subsidy cofinanced by the cantons and the federation (see Section 16.2.1), which reduces their premium burden. In 2015, 26.9% of the population was awarded a subsidy with an average amount of CHF 1853.
- Almost 10% of total expenditures are also financed by the consumers through copayment. Copayment includes the deductible, coinsurance, and a daily fee for every day spent in a hospital. It is completely waived for maternity care (KVG Art. 64), while the daily fee is waived for children and young adults (19−25 years old) still studying (KVV Art. 104).
- Cantons provide the only payment which is not passed through the insurer but directly disbursed to the provider. As a form of risk sharing, reimbursement of inpatient hospital care is divided by cantons and insurers, with cantons obliged to pay at least 55% (KVG Art. 49a; see also Section 16.3.3). Like the premium subsidy, these payments by the cantons are financed through general tax revenues.
- RE is administered directly between the insurers. For every consumer with below (above) average medical spending in its subgroup the insurer pays (receives) a certain amount into (from) a fund (see Section 16.3.2). By construction, these transfers sum up to zero.

The right-hand side of Fig. 16.1 shows the payments involved in the KVG:

- Since 2012, inpatient care has been reimbursed by a flat-rate payment based on DRGs, while most outpatient care is still paid FFS.

**BOX 16.3  Health plans and insurers' instruments to improve efficiency**

*Compulsory health plans (with open enrollment, not for profit)*
- A *Standard plan* (default option)
  - **a)**  access: free choice among all healthcare providers in the (cantonal) market
  - **b)**  copayment structure
    - standard deductible of CHF 300 (children: CHF 0)
    - coinsurance rate of 10%, stop-loss amount of CHF 700 (children: CHF 350)
  - **c)**  premium: community-rated
- B *Voluntary deductibles* (consumer choice option)
  - **a)**  access: as in A
  - **b)**  copayment structure
    - deductible options for adults: CHF 500, 1000, 1500, 2000, and 2500
    - deductible options for children: CHF 100, 200, 300, 400, 500, and 600
    - coinsurance as in A
  - **c)**  premium: as in A minus (regulated) rebate
- C *Managed care plans* (consumer choice option)
  - **a.i)**  access: several types of gatekeeping
    - HMO health plan
    - Telemedicine health plan
    - PPO health plan (based on lists of preferred providers)
  - **a.ii)**  all with selective contracting with the (network of) providers
    - providers are financed by risk-adjusted capitation, FFS with bonus payments to award efficient providers, or simple FFS
    - as this is a free market, new types of contracts and networks appear regularly
  - **b)**  co-payment structure
    - all deductible options from A and B selectable
    - coinsurance as in A, but the coinsurance rate can be doubled for certain services
    - health plan can waive the copayments fully or partly
    - no coverage of out-of-network care
  - **c)**  premium: premiums of the standard plan minus rebate (regulated, depends on the chosen deductible and the managed care plan type)

*Insurer's instruments to contain costs not directly related to (specific) health plans*
- *Claim processing improvements:* Insurers process increasing shares of claims electronically and can monitor physicians by advanced data analysis.
- *Disease management programs:* Insurers are free to offer any form of disease management to their enrollees independent of the type of health plan in which they are enrolled.

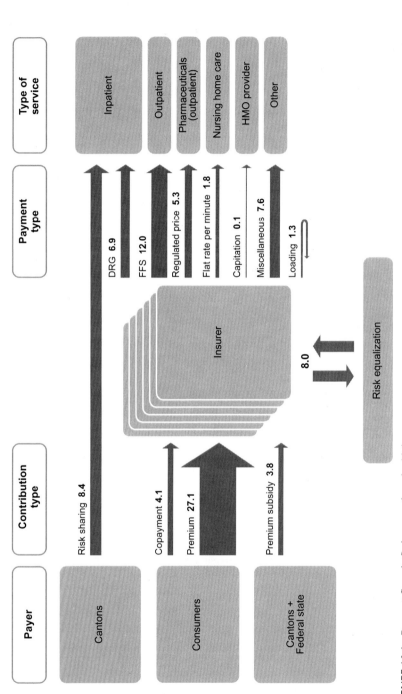

**FIGURE 16.1** Payment flows in Swiss compulsory health insurance.

This figure shows payment flows between consumers, insurers, providers, and government in Swiss compulsory health insurance. Numbers from 2015, in billions of Swiss Francs. Authors' own illustration based on Federal Office of Public Health, 2016. Statistic of the Compulsory Health Insurance 2015 (Statistik der obligatorischen Krankenversicherung 2015), FOPH, Bern T2.17, T10.02, T11.06.

- The arrow representing payments for pharmaceuticals includes drugs dispensed by pharmacists and physicians only (unlike in many other countries, physicians are partially allowed to sell drugs to their patients, see Kaiser and Schmid, 2016). Drugs dispensed in hospitals are included in the flat-rate payment, so that their total share is underestimated.
- Expenditures for nursing home care include care services related to the illness or disability only. All other costs emerging in a nursing home (assistance, room, food) are paid out-of-pocket and by the state.
- Risk-adjusted capitations are used in managed care plans both for calculations of bonus payments and capitation budgets. In that sense, the arrow for capitation in Fig. 16.1 is biased, underestimating the importance of (risk-adjusted) capitation in health plan payment.
- The most important components of the residual category are expenditures for laboratory tests, physiotherapy, home care (*Spitex*), and materials and objects (e.g., crutches).
- Finally, about 1.3 billion CHF (4% of the plan revenues) are used for loading.

In the following subsections, we discuss the components of plan revenues in detail.

## 16.3.1  Premium Regulation

All health plan premiums need to be approved by the regulator, i.e., the Federal Office of Public Health (FOPH). The insurers have to submit their premiums for the upcoming year by the end of July. The regulator checks whether the premiums ensure the solvency of the insurer, do not result in excessive reserves (though the term 'excessive' remains undefined), and cover costs according to the combined ratio (sum of claim ratio and loading ratio). Note, however, that the combined ratio may be a problematic and too static measure as the variance of costs can be very high in some cantons. If an insurer has only a few enrollees (i.e. less than 300) in one canton or if an insurer enters a new market (e.g., canton), the premium must not fall short of the average premium of that region (KVV Art. 91). After approval, the FOPH publicly announces the new premiums by the end of September. As noted in Section 16.2, the premiums are community-rated by canton and age group. Within a canton up to three regions may be formed to grade the premium while the regulator defines which municipality belongs to which region. The premium rebate between the second (third) and the first (second) region must not exceed 15% (10%). Premiums for children (0−18 years old) need to be reduced by law (KVG Art. 61) but cannot be set to zero (maximum rebate offered in 2017 relative to adults 26 years and older: 82%, median: 76%; rebates can be higher for the second child). Premium rebates for young adults (19−25 years old) are voluntary. Since the introduction of

KVG, these rebates have plummeted (see Section 16.5 for details), and some insurers have stopped providing a rebate altogether (maximum rebate offered in 2017 relative to adults 26 years and older: 22%, median: 6%).

Further premium rebates are allowed if the consumer has employer-sponsored accident insurance (and is thus allowed to suspend health insurance-based accident coverage), increases the deductible, or chooses to restrict the free access to providers in managed care plans. The basis for these rebates is always the premium for the *standard* health plan. The accumulated rebate for these three choices (accident coverage, deductible level, managed care plan) is limited to 50% (KVV Art. 90c). If the accident coverage is provided by the employer, the premium has to be reduced but not by more than 7% (KVV Art. 91a). The maximum rebate for a higher deductible amounts to 70% of the incremental deductible amount (KVV Art. 95). For instance, the increase from the standard (CHF 300) to the maximum (CHF 2500) deductible equates to CHF 2200, implying that the annual rebate for choosing the highest deductible cannot exceed CHF 1540 (70% of CHF 2200). For managed care plans, the rebate must stem from actual cost savings and not be due to a more favorable risk portfolio in these plans. This has to be verified by a statistical procedure defined by the regulator. If the plan has been offered for less than 5 years, the rebate must not exceed 20% (KVV Art. 101) (Box 16.4).

## 16.3.2 Risk Equalization

To mitigate risk selection incentives, a consequence of community-rated premiums, RE was introduced. Fig. 16.2 provides an overview of the evolution of RE since the introduction of KVG. The lower panel of Fig. 16.2 juxtaposes the evolution of the risk-adjusted capitation payment in managed care plans. (The chronology stems from a large health insurer. Other insurers most likely had different timing but similar risk adjustors.) In capitation calculations many risk adjustors were tested in the market, while some of them

---

**BOX 16.4 Premium regulation**
- Every premium must be approved by the regulator to ensure solvency, coverage of costs, and to prevent build up of excessive reserves.
- Premiums are community-rated by health plan, canton, and age group.
- Premium rebates are allowed but strictly regulated for
  - regional differences within cantons (max. 15%−25%),
  - exclusion of accident coverage (max. 7%),
  - higher deductible levels (max. 70% of incremental deductible amount),
  - and choice for managed care plans (max. the efficiency gain proven by a standardized risk-adjusted analysis defined by the regulator).

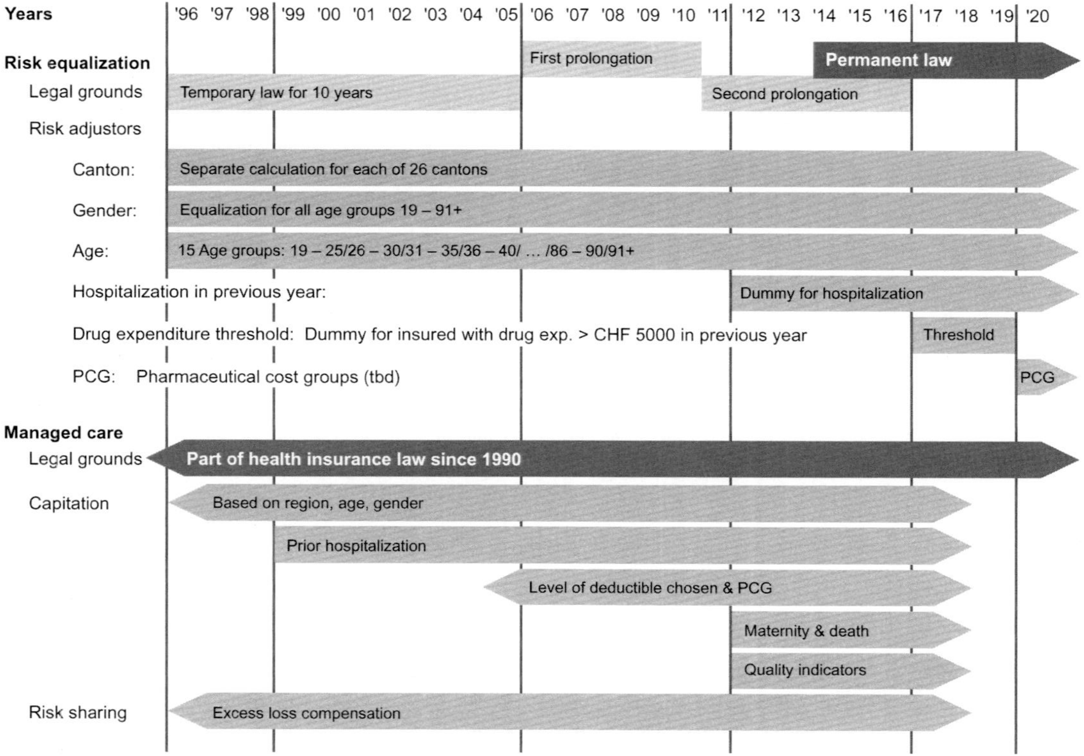

**FIGURE 16.2** Development of plan payment.
This figure shows chronological development of plan payment. Authors' own illustration.

were later used in RE. Since its start, RE has been calculated separately but with the same formula in each of the 26 cantons so that there are no transfers between cantons. The other two initial risk adjustors are age and gender. Children have always been excluded from RE (as have asylum seekers since 2007). For adults, 15 age groups are formed. Unlike in most other countries with RE, but in common with the Marketplaces in the United States, the RE fund is not filled with external contributions. RE payments thus sum to zero. The calculation and transfer are administered by a common institution (*Gemeinsame Einrichtung KVG* or *Institution commune LAMal*) based on the so-called cell-based approach, which is equivalent to a regression with a dummy for every group (see Beck, 2013, p. 407). The dependent variable is total spending net of copayment and of the cantonal contribution for inpatient stays. Every insurer reports their gross HCE, copayments, and number of months insured for each risk group per canton to this institution. The institution then calculates average net HCE per group and for the canton. The RE payment to a group equals the deviation between the average net HCE for that group in canton $c$ and the total average net HCE in canton $c$. For example, 26−30-year-old men have below-average costs and insurers pay a contribution for each insured in that age class while 86−90-year-old women have above-average costs and insurers receive a contribution. In the gross calculation, every insurer pays (receives) for every consumer who is in a group with below (above)-average costs. This would result in 7.7 billion CHF reported in Fig. 16.1. However, since every insurer has consumers with above- and below-average costs, their contributions are internally offset, resulting in a net transfer of 1.6 billion CHF between insurers in 2015. Starting from 0.5 billion CHF in 1996, the transfer volume constantly increased until 2009 but has more or less stabilized since then. Of 58 health insurers in 2015, 35 were net-payers, while 23 were net-recipients. The number of net-recipients has been rather stable in the past decade, while the number of net-payers has gradually decreased, balancing the relative proportion (Gemeinsame Einrichtung KVG, 2017).

As demographic RE reduces risk selection incentives only weakly (see Section 16.4), several reforms have aimed at improving RE in Switzerland. First, hospitalization in the previous year was identified as a readily available predictor of HCE in the following year (Beck, 2000). It was quickly implemented in the calculation of capitation payment in managed care. Yet, it took several years until this additional risk adjustor was included in RE. Parliament passed the reform only in 2007 but it took another 5 years to be implemented in 2012. More precisely, this risk adjustor is an indicator for whether or not consumers spent at least three consecutive nights in a hospital or nursing home, excluding maternity-related stays. Therefore the number of cells in the RE formula doubled to 60. Besides its availability, an important feature of this risk adjustor is the low ability for gaming by the insurer. Since hospital stays are paid by a flat-rate payment, the hospital has no financial interest in keeping a patient one day longer. Moreover, the RE payment for previously hospitalized consumers does not cover the additional cost the insurer faces for a three-night hospital stay. Also in 2012, RE was switched from a concurrent to a prospective calculation, i.e., expenditures from year $t-1$ are used to predict HCE in year $t$ for RE in year $t$, while the hospitalization indicator stems from year $t-2$. The next reform passed in 2014, which included two important modifications. First, after being temporarily extended twice RE was permanently established. Second, the authority to decide which risk adjustors to include in RE was transferred from the parliament to the federal council. Since then, the reforms to include more risk adjustors have been tackled more quickly. It is well known that there are a number of high-cost morbidities which rarely require hospitalization so that prior hospitalization alone is an insufficient morbidity risk adjustor. In 2017, an easily implementable pharmaceutical threshold was included. Insurers receive contributions for consumers who were dispensed with pharmaceuticals for a total amount of more than CHF 5000 in the previous year. This adjustor is hierarchical in the sense that all consumers with drug expenditures below the threshold are divided into the 60 previously known groups. Those above the threshold are only divided into two groups with or without prior hospitalization independent of age and gender, resulting in a total of 62 groups. The threshold was selected because it increases fit considerably (Pirktl, 2015) and is readily available for the insurer. Yet, as it is prone to gaming, its inclusion is only temporary and it is to be replaced by pharmaceutical cost groups (PCGs) starting in 2020. If consumers receive over a certain period certain drugs that are mostly prescribed for a specific condition, they are assigned to groups which will then be used as a morbidity indicator. The Swiss regulator follows Lamers and Vliet (2003) who argue PCGs are less gameable if a (high) number of prescribed daily doses is used to assign persons to PCGs, double counting due to comorbidities are not allowed for, and PCGs with low future costs are removed. Like the indicator for prior hospitalization, the PCG indicator has been used for many years in risk-adjusted capitation calculation in managed care plans.

The RE is administered at low cost. In 2015, the annual report of the common institution reported administrative costs of less than one million CHF for a transfer volume of 1.6 billion CHF (Box 16.5).

## 16.3.3   Risk Sharing

In addition to RE, the insurers' financial risk is limited by two forms of risk sharing. First, cantons pay at least 55% of inpatient hospital costs directly to the provider, leaving the remaining maximum of 45% to the insurer. Second, as a sanction in case of insufficient solvency the regulator can urge the insurer to buy reinsurance. It is commonly underwritten by other health insurers, which need at least 300,000 customers to qualify. Before 2017,

---

**BOX 16.5  Characteristics of risk equalization in 2017**

- Zero-sum system where contributions from insurers with a below-average risk profile are fully transferred to insurers with an above-average risk profile
- Same procedure for the entire country but calculated separately in each of the 26 cantons, resulting in no transfers between the cantons
- Risk adjustors as of 2017:
  - Gender
  - 15 age groups
  - Indicator for at least three consecutive nights in a hospital or nursing home in the previous year (prior hospitalization)
  - Hierarchical indicator for drug expenditures of at least CHF 5000 in the previous year
- Risk equalization contribution$_{ic} = \bar{x}_{ic} - \bar{x}_c$

$$i \in \{1, 2, \ldots, 62\}$$

$$c \in \{1, 2, \ldots, 26\}$$

$\bar{x}$ = average net health care expenditures per month covered where

$$i = \text{risk group}$$

$$c = \text{canton}$$

- Prospective calculation

---

reinsurance was mandatory for insurers with less than 50,000 customers. However, the current solvency criteria now imply a de facto reinsurance obligation for small insurers.

Risk sharing is also applied to healthcare providers since excess loss compensation is common within risk-adjusted capitation payments in managed care plans. As an example, the scheme of a large insurer is provided: If the provider exceeds annual costs of CHF 20,000 for a patient, the (re-)insurer bears 90% of every additional Franc up to CHF 120,000. Amounts above this threshold are fully covered by the (re-)insurer. The provider is thus charged with a 10% coinsurance rate up to a stop-loss amount of CHF 10,000. Overall, the provider faces budget responsibility in the order of CHF 30,000 per patient and year.

## 16.4   EVALUATION OF HEALTH PLAN PAYMENT

This section briefly summarizes the measures and criteria used for evaluating the health plan payment system. In what follows, we focus on incentives for risk selection, risk selection actions, and the evaluation of managed care and demand-side controls.

## 16.4.1    Incentives for Risk Selection

The FOPH is responsible for monitoring the efficacy of the KVG and for evaluating its impact on the situation and behavior of healthcare providers, consumers, and health insurers (KVV Art. 32). In general, to conduct these evaluations it mandates private research institutes which are selected in a public tendering process. However, risk selection incentives are neither systematically monitored nor frequently evaluated by public authorities. In fact, Spycher and Olar (1999) are the only ones who restrict their evaluation to the RE scheme then in force. Subsequent, publicly mandated studies focus primarily on improving RE by introducing high-risk pooling (Spycher, 2003, 2004b) or by adding morbidity indicators such as PCGs (Trottmann et al., 2010, 2015) and information on DRGs from inpatient treatments (McKinsey, 2015). In addition, Spycher (2004a) discusses several potential changes and improvements.

However, these studies focus on changes to the RE formula and most studies do not provide any empirical results on risk selection incentives, mainly due to limited data availability. Notable exceptions are McKinsey (2015), Trottmann et al. (2015), and Pirktl (2015) who had access to health insurance (claims) data covering roughly 37%, 63%, and 87%, respectively, of the insured population. Regarding risk selection incentives, the reported payment fit in terms of the $R$-squared given the RE scheme in place from 2012 to 2016 ranges from 12.2% to 17%. In addition, it is shown that including more risk adjustors in the RE formula would increase the $R$-squared to roughly 25% and, thus, decrease risk selection incentives. It is important to note that although the application of the $R$-squared is controversial in the context of RE evaluations (see Layton et al., 2015, for a recent critique), it is the principal measure for risk selection incentives in Switzerland preferred by the regulator. Consequently, only a few studies report other measures such as the mean absolute prediction error (Trottmann et al., 2015) or the root mean squared error (Trottmann et al., 2010, 2015).

Besides the publicly funded but privately conducted research, some additional academic research on RE in Switzerland exists. The main focus of this research is also only on improving the RE formula using health insurance claims data. Initially, Beck and Zweifel (1998) point out that RE merely based on demographic factors yields an $R$-squared of 3.9%. As an additional risk adjustor, the authors propose an indicator for death that increases the $R$-squared to 11.1%. Similarly, Holly et al. (2004) find that *concurrent* RE based on age, gender, and canton of residence yields an $R$-squared of 5.9%. In addition, the authors estimate that including prior hospitalization, DRGs, and an alternative classification system for inpatient diagnoses (SQLape) could increase the $R$-squared of *prospective* RE to 9.9%, 14.3%, and 17.4%, respectively. Beck and Trottmann (2007) and Beck et al. (2010) compare three RE formulas and analyze the long-term effectiveness of RE. Regarding the predictive power, they estimate that RE based on age and gender achieves an $R$-squared of 11%. Including prior hospitalization and additionally including PCGs increases the $R$-squared to 21% and 30%, respectively. In addition, the authors are the first to analyze how RE affects risk selection incentives in the long run. They consider several risk types with different profit potential and analyze long-run profits associated with risk selection under the different RE schemes. Their results suggest that RE based on gender, age, prior hospitalization, and PCGs is effective enough in the longer term to redirect insurers' efforts away from risk selection in favor of innovation aiming at containing costs.

Finally, Schmid and Beck (2016) analyze potential improvements of a reinsurance in the context of the Swiss RE formula. Without reinsurance, they estimate that *prospective* RE based on age and gender yields an $R$-squared of 8.2%. Including prior hospitalization, PCGs, or an indicator for high drug costs, the $R$-squared increases to 14.7%, 21.2%, and 25%, respectively. Overall, the academic research corroborates the aforementioned findings, i.e., risk selection incentives as measured by potential long-term profits from risk selection and in terms of the $R$-squared were prevalent between 1996 and 2011 (see Table 16.2). Future developments may, however, reduce these incentives considerably (see Section 16.3.2 for details) (Box 16.6).

## 16.4.2    Risk Selection Actions

Like risk selection incentives, risk selection actions are neither systematically monitored nor frequently evaluated by public authorities. In addition, the insurers' instruments to improve efficiency (e.g., introducing managed care plans) can also be used for the purpose of risk selection, which makes it difficult to distinguish between efficiency attempts and risk selection actions. Consequently, little is known about the risk selection actions of health insurers. Beck et al. (2013a) provide some examples of risk selection activities undertaken by Swiss health insurers between 1996 and 2002. The reported activities include ignoring of or slow processing of applications, misinformation regarding insurance choice and health plans, and the closure of insurance agencies in certain regions. Similar examples are also mentioned in Spycher and Olar (1999, p. 76) for the period between 1992 and 1996. In addition, Trottmann and Telser (2013) mention that insurers perhaps do not apply direct provider reimbursement to practice risk selection as direct provider reimbursement is convenient for patients with chronic conditions. Still, these examples provide merely anecdotal evidence on risk selection actions and are rather single cases (see also Ombudsman, 2009, p. 22). Till now, only Baumgartner and Busato (2012) have provided some evidence

**TABLE 16.2** Risk Selection Incentives Measured by *R*-Squared in Switzerland (Since 1996)

| Risk Equalization | | | | Evaluation | | |
|---|---|---|---|---|---|---|
| Based On | In Force | R-squared | Year | Data | Number of Individuals | Study |
| Age, gender | 1996–2011 | 3.9% | 1993 | Single insurer, canton Zurich only | 4539 (0.5%) | Beck and Zweifel (1998) |
| | | 11.0% | 2000 | Single insurer, French- and Italian-speaking cantons | 182,529 (14%) | Beck et al. (2010) |
| | | 5.9% | 2002 | Two insurers, cantons Vaud and Zurich only | NA | Holly et al. (2004) |
| | | 9.0% | 2012 | Several insurers | 4,732,538 (73%) | Pirktl (2015) |
| | | 8.3% | 2012 | Single insurer | 235,420 (3.7%) | Schmid and Beck (2016) |
| Age, gender, prior hospitalization | 2012–2016 | 21.0% | 2000 | Single insurer, French- and Italian-speaking cantons | 182,529 (14%) | Beck et al. (2010) |
| | | 14.3% | 2002 | Two insurers, cantons Vaud and Zurich only | NA | Holly et al. (2004) |
| | | 17.0% | 2012 | Several insurers | 4,732,538 (73%) | Pirktl (2015) |
| | | 14.7% | 2012 | Single insurer | 235,420 (3.7%) | Schmid and Beck (2016) |
| | | 15.1% | 2013 | Several insurers | 4,089,493 (63%) | Trottmann et al. (2015) |
| | | 12.2% | 2014 | Several insurers | 2,400,000 (37%) | McKinsey (2015) |

*(Continued)*

**TABLE 16.2 (Continued)**

| Risk Equalization | | | | Evaluation | | |
| --- | --- | --- | --- | --- | --- | --- |
| Based On | In Force | R-squared | Year | Data | Number of Individuals | Study |
| Age, gender, prior hospitalization, indicator for high drug expenditures | 2017–2019 | 28.0% | 2012 | Several insurers | 4,732,538 (73%) | Pirktl (2015) |
| | | 25.0% | 2012 | Single insurer | 235,420 (3.7%) | Schmid and Beck (2016) |
| Age, gender, prior hospitalization, pharmaceutical cost groups | 2020– | 30.0% | 2000 | Single insurer, French- and Italian-speaking cantons | 182,529 (14%) | Beck et al. (2010) |
| | | 21.2% | 2012 | Single insurer | 235,420 (3.7%) | Schmid and Beck (2016) |
| | | 25.3% | 2013 | Several insurers | 4,089,493 (63%) | Trottmann et al. (2015) |
| | | 23.8% | 2014 | Several insurers | 2,400,000 (37%) | McKinsey (2015) |

This table shows estimated R-squared for past, current, and future risk equalization formulas. Estimates are based on claims data from one or more health insurers that, however, do not cover the entire market. Market shares of the analyzed market (e.g., canton) are reported in parentheses next to the number of observations (i.e., individuals). Numbers of individuals are not available for the study by Holly et al. (2004) as they report only the total number of observations over 4 years. The analysis of Beck et al. (2010) is based on the cantons Fribourg, Ticino, Vaud, Geneva, Neuchâtel, and Jura. See text for further details on the listed studies.

---

**BOX 16.6 Risk selection incentives**

- Risk selection incentives are neither systematically monitored nor frequently evaluated.
- Publicly funded research and academic research suggest that risk selection incentives were prevalent between 1996 and 2011.
- Since 2011, risk selection incentives as measured by $R$-squared and in terms of potential profits from risk selection in the longer run have decreased but are still fairly large.

---

on risk selection actions in the application process based on a sound empirical analysis. In a so-called correspondence test they requested quotes from all health insurers operating in the canton of Bern. The overall response *rate* is similar for all types of consumers. Yet, with respect to response *time* consumers who are considered as "bad risks" wait on average longer (5.68 days instead of 4.75 days) and are less frequently offered a managed care health plan. Consequently, the difference between the expected premium and the offered premium is smaller for "bad risks" than for "good risks" (CHF 11.05 and 18.75 per month, respectively). These findings are statistically significant but negligible in economic terms, implying that direct risk selection in the enrollment process is of limited relevance.

An empirical approach to measure risk selection in the entire market is presented in von Wyl and Beck (2016). These authors exploit the fact that health insurers are allowed to establish subsidiary firms that are, however, marketed under the same brand name. Together, the health insurer and its subsidiary firms form a so-called "conglomerate" consisting of so-called "insurance carriers." This structure enables the health insurer to separate good risks from bad risks by internally redirecting applications to the different insurance carriers. Indeed, Baumgartner and Busato (2012) report that 21.5% of the applications sent to a conglomerate are internally redirected. In addition, subsidiary firms entering the market can charge lower health plan premiums. Due to adverse selection, young and healthy consumers are attracted, reinforcing the lower premium. As a result, the goal of risk solidarity is undermined. Overall, establishing conglomerates was a very successful strategy for insurers to practice risk selection and to increase the market share (see Fig. 16.3). However, this strategy also increases the variation in the market premium. Thus, the basic idea of von Wyl and Beck (2016) is to estimate the additional variation in health plan premiums due to conglomerates; the resulting index of risk selection is presented in Fig. 16.3 for the period 1997–2015.

Fig. 16.3 suggests that risk selection leads to considerable differences in health plan premiums with a peak in 2009. Von Wyl and Beck (2016) argue

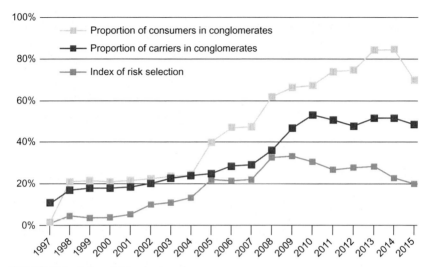

**FIGURE 16.3** Index of risk selection.
This figure shows the evolution of conglomerates over time. A conglomerate is a group of insurance carriers with the same ownership. Index of risk selection calculates the variance in premiums within conglomerates compared to the entire market. Source: *Kauer and Beck (2016) as an update of von Wyl and Beck (2016).*

that health insurers adapted their behavior in 2010 due to an anticipated change in the RE formula in 2012. In other words, the evolution of the selection index suggests that profits from risk selection declined because of better RE. However, this analysis exhibits at least three important limitations. First, it implicitly assumes that all premium variations within the conglomerates are based on selection even though differences in efficiency of health plans may occur as well. Second, it focuses on a very particular form of risk selection and does not capture all risk selection actions. In other words, an index of zero does not necessarily imply that insurers do not risk select. Third, the index is not informative about the potential welfare losses of this particular selection strategy.

In summary, some limited evidence on risk selection actions of Swiss health insurers exists. However, these activities are not systematically monitored by public authorities and the welfare implications remain unknown (Box 16.7).

### 16.4.3 Evaluation of Managed Care and Demand-Side Controls

Besides the evaluation of the efficacy of RE, other research studies the efficiency in the delivery of care. This strand of literature focuses on the efficiency gains achieved by managed care health plans. Lehmann and Zweifel (2004) provide the first thorough analysis for Switzerland. They estimate

---

**BOX 16.7  Risk selection actions**

- Risk selection actions are not systematically monitored.
- Some anecdotal and little empirical evidence on risk selection actions exists.
- Extent of risk selection and welfare implications remain unknown.

---

that HMOs reimbursed by risk-adjusted capitation payments generate on average lower HCE in the order of 62%. However, the efficiency gain is about two-thirds of the total cost advantage. Similar patterns are found for PPO health plans with and without bonus payments where the efficiency gains are 10% and 21%, respectively. In other words, managed care plans benefit from some risk selection effects. Indeed, separating risk selection effects and efficiency gains is the major challenge in this literature. Basically, one has to take into account that consumers enrolled in managed care health plans are on average healthier than enrollees in traditional FFS plans. Controlling for differences in the individuals' health status have become easier over recent years as data availability has improved. In more recent studies, Trottmann et al. (2012) and Reich et al. (2012) still estimate that managed care health plans with risk-adjusted capitation payment achieve efficiency gains in the order of 12%−19% and 21%, respectively. Reich et al. (2012) also corroborate the earlier finding that the efficiency gains of PPO health plans with bonus payments are considerably smaller compared to health plans with risk-adjusted capitation payments. In addition, telemedicine health plans generate savings due to an efficiency of about 4% (Grandchamp and Gardiol, 2011; Reich et al., 2012). Table 16.3 provides an overview over the aforementioned studies. Finally, it is worth noting that the efficiency gains in Switzerland seem to persist over time. By comparing consumers in standard FFS and managed care plans over 10 years, Kauer (2017) shows that cost savings are substantial and sustainable, while the mortality rate is lower in managed care plans. As the probability of visiting a provider at least once per year is similar or even higher for consumers in managed care plans, the author argues that efficiency gains are achieved within the HMO due to fewer follow-up consultations and fewer days in hospital care. In summary, the empirical literature for Switzerland provides clear evidence that health plans increase the efficiency in the delivery of care by applying supply-side measures and gatekeeping.

A related strand of literature analyzes the reduction in demand-side moral hazard resulting from (voluntary) deductibles. As with managed care plans, the researcher has to take into account the self-selection of healthier consumers into health plans with voluntary deductibles. Early moral hazard estimates for Switzerland are thus either based on structural approaches and strong assumptions (e.g., Gardiol et al., 2005), or the deductible choice is

**TABLE 16.3** Efficiency Gains of Managed Care in Switzerland

| Study | Period | Health plan | Savings relative to FFS | |
|---|---|---|---|---|
| | | | Raw | Efficiency |
| Lehmann and Zweifel (2004) | 1997–2000 | HMO with capitation | 62% | 40% |
| | | PPO with bonus | 34% | 10% |
| | | PPO | 39% | 21% |
| Grandchamp and Gardiol (2011) | 2003–2006 | Telemedicine | 57–62% | 4% |
| Trottmann et al. (2012) | 2003–2006 | HMO/PPO with capitation | 42% | 12–19% |
| Reich et al. (2012) | 2006–2009 | HMO/PPO with capitation | 30% | 21% |
| | | PPO with bonus | 21% | 16% |
| | | Telemedicine | 22% | 4% |
| Beck et al. (2013b) | 2006–2007 | HMO/PPO with capitation | 59% | 9% |
| Kauer (2017) | 2003–2014 | HMO with capitation | NA | 14–36% |

This table shows estimated efficiency gains of managed care health plans in Switzerland. The raw difference corresponds to the average cost difference between consumers in FFS and managed care health plans; savings due to efficiency gains are corrected for morbidity disadvantages in the FFS population. See text for further details.

instrumented somehow (e.g., Gerfin and Schellhorn, 2006) or assumed to depend on observables (e.g., Werblow and Felder, 2003; van Kleef et al., 2008). In addition, Trottmann et al. (2012) analyze the interaction of managed care and moral hazard using a control function approach. These studies consistently provide evidence for moral hazard in the Swiss health insurance market although endogeneity might still be an issue. However, Gerfin and colleagues corroborate the general findings on moral hazard based on quasiexogenous changes in the consumers' price for medical care. On the one hand, Gerfin et al. (2015) exploit the resetting of the deductible at the start of each calendar year. They find that high deductible plans (CHF 1000 and above) reduce demand for health care by roughly 27%. On the other hand, Boes and Gerfin (2016) analyze the introduction of deductibles and coinsurance in a managed care plan that was previously offered with no copayments. Based on panel data, they find a demand elasticity of about $-0.14$. Thus, there is clear evidence that deductibles increase the efficiency in the Swiss health insurance market.

However, it is worth noting that voluntary deductibles and managed care health plans are basically ignored in the Swiss RE formula and that research in that regard is scarce. A notable exception is van Kleef et al. (2008), who point out that the potential rebate for the highest deductible in Switzerland is higher than the actual (and regulated) rebate, implying that consumers choosing that deductible are on average more profitable to the insurer than those without a voluntary deductible. The choice of a (high) voluntary deductible provides an unambiguous signal to the insurer that a potential enrollee is a good risk. This is likely to hold for managed care plans as well due to a similar self-selection of good risks. Therefore, the interaction of voluntary deductibles, managed care health plans, and RE is important but yet not empirically assessed in Switzerland (Box 16.8).

## 16.5   ONGOING ISSUES AND REFORMS

With respect to continuing debates on reforms of the compulsory health insurance, we identify three crucial obstacles for regulated competition in Switzerland: Cantonal subsidies for and cantonal provision of inpatient care, the insurers' obligation to contract with every physician in the standard health plan, and risk selection. Within the last 25 years, five reforms addressing risk selection and RE have been adopted. Surprisingly, no reform regarding the two other obstacles has been successful, even though these issues hinder effective competition. On the one hand, the cantonal hospital subsidies distort the price between inpatient care and outpatient care. In addition, cantons face conflicting incentives because they own hospitals and regulate the provision of inpatient care. On the other hand, the contract obligation protects inefficient physicians and facilitates supply-side moral hazard. Thus, disentangling the role of cantons regarding inpatient care and

---

**BOX 16.8 Evaluation of managed care and demand-side controls**

- Managed care health plans increase the efficiency in the delivery of care.
- The highest efficiency gains are achieved in managed care plans with risk-adjusted capitation payments; the lowest gains are generated with telemedicine health plans.
- Voluntary deductibles reduce demand-side moral hazard considerably.
- Empirical evidence on the interaction of voluntary deductibles, managed care health plans, and risk equalization is scarce.

introducing selective contracting in the standard health plan combined with effective RE would most likely increase welfare.

In contrast, the welfare effects of the use of additional variables for RE are less clear. First, reducing risk selection incentives is not free of (social) costs because RE also decreases cost containment incentives (Geruso and McGuire, 2016; Schmid and Beck, 2016). This point is particularly important for Switzerland as health insurers should be the main driver for cost containment according to the KVG. It is neither necessary nor welfare-maximizing to completely eliminate risk selection incentives. Second, the Swiss regulator commonly uses $R$-squared to evaluate RE, which is not informative about any welfare effects. This in turn implies that the target value for $R$-squared is unknown. Moreover, an increase in $R$-squared is not necessarily associated with less undercompensation for vulnerable groups (see Chapter 5: Evaluating the Performance of Health Plan Payment Systems), e.g., consumers with chronic conditions. If society has a preference for better compensating these groups, $R$-squared becomes additionally inappropriate for evaluating RE. Thus, improving the measurement of risk selection incentives is an important issue.

Based on the issues mentioned here, we describe more in-depth three possible starting points for future developments in the design of the health plan payment system. First, how the RE formula can be adapted and how risk selection incentives could be measured. Second, why changes in the formula are necessary to make RE and premium regulations consistent. Third, which prominent role RE is expected to have in solving the problem of distorted prices between inpatient and outpatient hospital care.

## 16.5.1   Changes in the Risk Equalization Formula and Measuring Selection Incentives

Regarding changes in the RE formula, McKinsey (2015) considers inpatient diagnoses as risk adjustors and Schmid and Beck (2016) analyze the effect of insurer risk sharing in the form of mandatory reinsurance. While the inclusion of inpatient diagnoses has a negligible effect on $R$-squared, risk sharing seems to considerably reduce selection incentives. However, there are already planned changes to the RE formula, in particular the inclusion of PCGs in 2020. With regard to the Swiss political system, it is therefore unlikely that additional risk adjustors, complementary risk sharing, and other potential changes will be considered meanwhile. Note that, instead of further improving RE, one could consider introducing risk-rated premiums. This would make RE obsolete as the risk selection incentive for the insurer disappears. However, the financial burden of risk-rated premiums, e.g., for the elderly and consumers with chronic conditions, would additionally call for risk-adjusted subsidies.

More importantly, the regulator lacks a concept for properly measuring risk selection incentives. The currently used $R$-squared is a statistical not an economic measure, and has some important limitations. For example, it does not take into account the (insurers') costs associated with risk selection. Beck et al. (2010) provide a potential framework for such an analysis, which also allows to separately evaluate risk selection incentives for groups with high predictable expenditures. Besides analyzing the effect of additional risk adjustors and risk sharing, the analysis of selection action prevention is also possible. For instance, the regulator has actually banned reserve transfers between insurers within conglomerates since 2016 (see Section 16.4.2). While $R$-squared is not affected by this ban, it made the conglomerate strategy substantially less profitable. Therefore, a risk selection measure should take into account the profits from and costs of risk selection.

Based on the method proposed by Beck et al. (2010), the regulator could design RE such that the expected (long-run) profits of risk selection are zero. This is an objective and measurable target value. However, it is not necessarily the case that zero profits are welfare-maximizing. For instance, society could allow for some risk selection profits in order to maintain cost containment incentives on a certain level. Therefore, the acceptable level of risk selection incentives is a normative and thus political decision.

## 16.5.2    Inconsistency of Risk Equalization and Premium Regulation

RE and premium regulations are not consistent in Switzerland because premium regulations allow for rebates that are not taken into account in the RE formula. As a result, rebates are either impossible or limited to a certain extent implying that, e.g., the choice of a high deductible plan becomes less attractive. In what follows, we consider three specific cases: The premium rebate for young adults, regional premium variation within the canton, and the premium rebates for managed care health plans as well as health plans with a voluntary deductible.

### 16.5.2.1    The Premium Rebate for Young Adults

By regulating the children's premium to be lower than the adults' premium, the legislator takes into account that community-rated health plan premiums without age differentiation would put a financial burden on families. Because children are not included in RE, their premium equals roughly the covered expenditures (see Beck et al., 2014). In Switzerland, it is beyond debate that children do not cross-subsidize adults' health plan contributions. There is, however, an ongoing discussion in the Swiss parliament about a separate RE scheme for children (Bundesrat, 2016). Similar to the children's premium, the regulation aims at reducing premiums for young adults, aged

19—25 (see Section 16.2.1). However, young adults are included in RE, implying that any cost differences between their age group (19—25) and all adults (19+) are equalized. In other words, the feasible premium rebate is zero and the observed average rebate in the market has indeed decreased from 32.4% in 1997 to 5% today (see Section 16.3.1). Positive rebates are only possible due to risk selection among the young adults or by cross-subsidizing the young adults' premium. The result is a paradoxical situation in which the young adults' premium when rebated does not fully cover the sum of their HCE and their RE contribution (Beck et al., 2014), although this group shows minimal HCE.

In order to again render possible premium rebates for young adults, the Swiss parliament has approved a revision of the KVG concerning the RE contributions in March 2017. The basic idea is to limit the RE contribution of young adults to 50% of the difference between their average costs and the average costs of all adults (19+). This reform will remove the current inconsistency between RE and premium regulations after its expected implementation in 2018.

### 16.5.2.2 Regional Premium Rebates Within the Cantons

Health plan premiums vary among cantons, reflecting differences in demand-side and supply-side factors. To avoid cross-subsidies across cantonal borders, RE contributions are calculated on a cantonal basis (see Section 16.3.2). Because HCE also vary considerably within cantons, health plan premiums may differ among up to three premium regions per canton (see Section 16.2.1). However, due to the regulation of maximum premium rebates premiums may not completely reflect these intracantonal cost differences. On the one hand, these differences can be relatively small resulting in a nonbinding regulation where premium rebates mirror cost differences and incentives to select with respect to region dissolves. On the other hand, the differences can be relatively large, implying that the regulation is binding. In this case, premiums do not fully reflect the cost differences and individuals in regions with below-average HCE cross-subsidize the premium of individuals in regions with above-average HCE. Put differently, the premium in regions with below-average (above-average) HCE exceeds (falls below) the actual costs. Because RE contributions are invariant with respect to regions within the canton, health insurers are incentivized to practice risk selection, i.e., to prefer consumers living in rural regions over consumers living in urban regions.

In principle, there are two solutions to this issue. First, one could weaken the regulation and no longer determine the maximum rebates. Thus, premiums would fully reflect differences in HCE between regions. Second, one could take residual regional cost differences not reflected in premium differences into account in the RE formula, implying that limited premium differences between regions are possible and insurers' incentives to risk select are neutralized. However, there are currently no reforms planned to alleviate this issue. Quite the contrary, the responsible member of the federal council and head of the FOPH intends to reduce the intracantonal premium differences by decreasing the overall number of premium regions and by reducing the legally accepted premium rebates (Federal Department of Home Affairs, 2016). If successful, risk selection incentives based on intracantonal cost differences are thus very likely to be reinforced.

### 16.5.2.3   Demand-Side and Supply-Side Cost Sharing

Managed care health plans and voluntary deductibles reduce supply-side and demand-side moral hazard. In other words, these measures increase the efficiency in the healthcare market and reduce HCE (see Section 16.4.3). However, consumers enrolled in these plans are on average also healthier, younger, and more often male than female (e.g., Trottmann et al., 2012; Gerfin et al., 2015). Therefore, the demographic factors in the risk adjustment formula capture both the moral hazard effect and the expenditure difference between gender and age (van Kleef et al., 2010; Schokkaert and van de Voorde, 2004). This means that the efficiency gains are partially redistributed and potential premium rebates (for choosing these health plans) are reduced. However, note that simply including health plan choices as risk adjustors does not solve the problem. Quite the contrary, and similarly to the rebate for young adults, the possible rebate would be zero and efficiency gains fully redistributed. Instead, Schokkaert and van de Voorde (2004) propose to include health plan choice in the RE calculation and to neutralize the effect of the choice afterwards when calculating the RE contributions. Although the theoretical solution exists, there has never been an attempt to implement it. In addition, empirical evidence on the efficiency gain reduction does not exist for Switzerland so the importance of this issue is unknown.

## 16.5.3   Cantonal Hospital Financing

Health insurers and cantons jointly reimburse inpatient care in hospitals (see Section 16.3) implying that the relative price between inpatient care and outpatient care is distorted. From the insurers' point of view, inpatient care is subsidized and the insurer has in many cases no incentive to promote the corresponding but overall less expensive outpatient treatment. Thus, there is an ongoing debate on how to solve this issue. One possibility is to jointly finance all hospital care by the cantons and the insurers, another possibility is that insurers solely finance all care (so-called "Monismus"). The latter is likely to be more efficient and the purpose of a parliamentary initiative (09.528, 2009). Without the cantonal contributions financed through general taxes, however, the premiums would increase considerably and the income solidarity would decrease. Thus, these contributions have to be allocated somehow to the healthcare system. Note that flat payments to the insurers per enrollee would incentivize the insurers to practice risk selection. Consequently, it would be reasonable to allocate the cantonal contributions through the RE fund. While risk selection incentives are unlikely to be affected, this change in the payment system could increase overall efficiency. Admittedly, this solution might not be politically feasible as cantons want to keep decisive power over the allocation of their tax money.

## 16.6   CONCLUDING REMARKS

To ensure risk solidarity in the Swiss compulsory health insurance, health plan premiums have to be community-rated, which in turn incentivizes insurers to practice risk selection. RE mitigating such incentives is thus essential for regulated competition. The Swiss regulator started with a very crude and insufficient demographic RE formula in the early 1990s. Over the years this formula has been developed gradually becoming more sophisticated and morbidity-oriented. This progress, although very slow and hesitant, has usually been in line with the recommendations of the literature. In addition, increased enforcement of the existing law by the FOPH reduced the profitability of and incentives for selection. Concurrently, albeit much faster, health insurers developed capitation formulas for reimbursing contracted provider networks. A variety of morbidity indicators was tested in this context. Some of these indicators have been included as risk adjustors in RE afterwards, and even more of these risk adjustors will be added in 2020. However, there is an immanent trade-off between containing cost and mitigating risk selection incentives. Therefore, the regulator should become capable of answering the question, which level of RE is optimal conditional on the preferences of the Swiss population. In addition, some health plan regulations clearly generate inefficiencies in the healthcare market. Given the latest progress in RE, solving other issues such as adapting cantonal hospital financing and removing inconsistencies between premium regulations and RE might become more relevant in order to maintain the efficiency of the healthcare market and to ensure affordability of health plan premiums.

## ACKNOWLEDGMENTS

We would like to acknowledge the very helpful comments by Thomas G. McGuire and Richard van Kleef. We also thank Boris Kaiser, Robert E. Leu, Markus Moser, Stefan Spycher, Maria Trottmann, and Werner Widmer for their perceptive and valuable comments. We are grateful to Claudia Müller-Hensch for her assistance in preparing the artwork.

# REFERENCES

Baumgartner, C., Busato, A., 2012. Risikoselektion in der Grundversicherung – Eine empirische Untersuchung. Schweizerische Ärztezeitung 93, 510–513.

Beck, K., 2000. Growing importance of capitation in Switzerland. Health Care Manage. Sci. 3, 111–119.

Beck, K., Trottmann, M., 2007. Der Risikostrukturausgleich und die langfristigen Profite der Risikoselektion: Wie erfolgreich sind verschiedene Formeln? In: Göpffarth, D., Gress, S., Jacobs, K., Wasem, J. (Eds.), Jahrbuch Risikostrukturausgleich. Asgard Verlag, St. Augustin.

Beck, K., Zweifel, P., 1998. Cream-skimming in deregulated social health insurance: evidence from Switzerland. In: Zweifel, P. (Ed.), Health, the Medical Profession, and Regulation. Kluwer, Dordrecht.

Beck, K., Debever Hilfiker, A., Kocher, G., Schmocker, E., Bardenhofer, D., 1995. Die Solidarität im Wandel. Meinungen, Fakten und Analysen zur Krankenversicherung, Schriftenreihe der SGGP, No. 48. SGGP, Bern.

Beck, K., Trottmann, M., Zweifel, P., 2010. Risk adjustment in health insurance and its long-term effectiveness. J. Health Econ. 29, 489–498.

Beck, K. (Ed.), 2013. Risiko Krankenversicherung. Haupt, Bern.

Beck, K., Käser, U., von Wyl, V., 2013a. Stabilität, Mobilität, Gerechtigkeit und Risikoselektion im Krankenversicherungsmarkt: Ist ein Risikoausgleich notwendig? In: Beck, K. (Ed.), Risiko Krankenversicherung. Haupt, Bern.

Beck, K., Käser, U., Buholzer, M., Kunze, U., Engler, N., Trottmann, M., 2013b. Problematik einer fairen Risikoteilung zwischen Versicherern und Leistungserbringern in Managed-Care-Modellen. In: Beck, K. (Ed.), Risiko Krankenversicherung. Haupt, Bern.

Beck, K., von Wyl, V., Biener, C., Martin, E., 2014. Brennpunkt Solidarität. Diskussionsbeiträge zur Weiterentwicklung der Sozialen Krankenversicherung, Schriftenreihe der SGGP, No. 125. SGGP, Bern.

Boes, S., Gerfin, M., 2016. Does full insurance increase the demand for health care? Health Econ. 25, 1483–1496.

Bundesrat, 1992. Botschaft über die Revision der Krankenversicherung vom 6. November 1991, vol. 144. Bundesblatt, Bern, pp. 93–292, no. 1.

Bundesrat, 2016. Parlamentarische Initiativen Prämienbefreiung für Kinder/KVG Änderung der Prämienkategorien für Kinder, Jugendliche und junge Erwachsene, Bericht der Kommission für soziale Sicherheit und Gesundheit des Nationalrates vom 7. Juli 2016, Stellungnahme des Bundesrates, 12. Oktober 2016, Bern.

Colombo, F., 2001. Towards more choice in social protection? Individual choice of insurer in basic mandatory health insurance in Switzerland. OECD Labour Market and Social Policy Occasional Papers, No. 53. OECD Publishing.

Federal Department of Home Affairs, 2016. Änderung der Verordnung des EDI vom 25. November 2015 über die Prämienregionen: Eröffnung des Vernehmlassungsverfahrens. EDI, Bern.

Federal Office of Public Health, 2016. Statistic of the Compulsory Health Insurance 2015 (Statistik der obligatorischen Krankenversicherung 2015). FOPH, Bern.

Federal Statistical Office, 2016. Costs and Financing of Health Care (Kosten und Finanzierung des Gesundheitswesens). FSO, Neuchâtel.

Gardiol, L., Geoffard, P., Grandchamp, C. 2005, Separating selection and incentive effects: an econometric study of Swiss health insurance claims data, PSE Working Papers, 2005/38.

Gemeinsame Einrichtung KVG, 2017. Bericht über die Durchführung des Risikoausgleichs im Jahr 2016, Solothurn.

Gerfin, M., Schellhorn, M., 2006. Nonparametric bounds on the effect of deductibles in health care insurance on doctor visits — Swiss evidence. Health Econ. 15, 1011−1020.

Gerfin, M., Kaiser, B., Schmid, C., 2015. Health care demand in the presence of discrete price changes. Health Econ. 24, 1164−1177.

Gerritzen, B., Martinez, I., Ramsden, A., 2014. Cantonal Differences in Health Care Premium Subsidies in Switzerland. University of St. Gallen, School of Economics and Political Science SEPS, Discussion Paper NO. 2014-20.

Geruso, M., McGuire, T.G., 2016. Tradeoffs in the design of health plan payment systems: fit, power and balance. J. Health Econ. 47, 1−19.

Grandchamp, C., Gardiol, L., 2011. Does a mandatory telemedicine call prior to visiting a physician reduce cost or simply attract good risks? Health Econ. 20, 1257−1267.

Holly, A., Gardiol, L., Eggli, Y., Yalcin, T., Ribeiro, T., 2004. Health-Based Risk Adjustment in Switzerland: An Exploration Using Medical Information from Prior Hospitalisation. Final Report for the Swiss National Fund, National Research Program 45, University of Lausanne.

INFRAS, 2010. Finanzströme der OKP. Studie im Auftrag von santésuisse, Zürich.

Kaiser, B., Schmid, C., 2016. Does physician dispensing increase drug expenditures? Empirical evidence from Switzerland. Health Econ. 25, 71−90.

Kauer, L., 2017. Long-term effects of managed care. Health Econ. 26, 1210−1223.

Kauer, L., Beck, K., 2016. Analyzing risk selection in the Swiss market: the conglomerate strategy revisited. In: Unpublished Presentation at RAN Meeting, Berlin.

Kaufmann, C., Schmid, C.P.R., Boes, S., 2017. Health insurance subsidies and seductible choice: evidence from regional variation in subsidy schemes. J Health Econ. 55, 262−273.

Lamers, L.M., Vliet, R.C.J.A., 2003. Health-based risk adjustment: improving the pharmacy-based cost group model to reduce gaming possibilities. Eur. J. Health Econ. 4, 107−114.

Layton, T.J., Ellis, R.P., McGuire, T.G., 2015. Assessing Incentives for Adverse Selection in Health Plan Payment Systems. NBER Working Paper No. 21531.

Lehmann, H.-J., Zweifel, P., 2004. Innovation and risk selection in deregulated social health insurance. J. Health Econ. 23, 997−1012.

Leu, R.E., Rutten, F., Brouwer, W., Rütschi, C., Matter, P., 2008. The Swiss and the Dutch Health Care Systems Compared. A Tale of Two Systems. Baden-Baden, Nomos, Germany.

McKinsey & Company, 2015. Verfeinerung des Risikoausgleichs auf Basis von Daten zur stationären Abrechnung (Abschlussbericht). Studie im Auftrag des Bundesamtes für Gesundheit, Bern.

Ombudsman der sozialen Krankenversicherung, 2009. Tätigkeitsbericht 2008, Lucerne.

Parliamentary Initiative 09.528, 2009. Finanzierung der Gesundheitsleistungen aus einer Hand. Einführung des Monismus, filed by Mrs. Ruth Humbel, member of the National Council, 11. December 2009, Bern.

Pirktl, L., 2015. Verfeinerung des Risikoausgleichs durch Berücksichtigung der Arzneimittelkosten, Soziale Sicherheit CHSS, 1/2015, pp. 42−46.

Reich, O., Rapold, R., Flatscher-Thöni, M., 2012. An empirical investigation of the efficiency effects of integrated care models in Switzerland. Int. J. Integrated Care 12, 1−12.

Schmid, C.P.R., 2017. Unobserved healthcare expenditures: how important is censoring in register data? Health Econ. 26, 1807−1812.

Schmid, C.P.R., Beck, K., 2016. Re-insurance in the Swiss health insurance market: fit, power, and balance. Health Policy 120, 848−855.

Schokkaert, E., van de Voorde, C., 2004. Risk selection and the specification of the conventional risk adjustment formula. J. Health Econ. 23, 1237−1259.

Spycher, S., 2003. Risikoausgleich und Poollösungen ("Grossrisikopool") in der obligatorischen Krankenversicherung, Beiträge zur sozialen Sicherheit, 19/03.

Spycher, S., 2004a. Der Risikoausgleich im Rahmen der Teilrevision des Krankenversicherungsgesetzes. Definitiver Schlussbericht der vom Bundesamt für Sozialversicherung eingesetzten Arbeitsgruppe "Risikoausgleich", im Auftrag des Bundesamtes für Sozialversicherung (BSV), Bern.

Spycher, S., 2004b. Risikoausgleich im KVG − wie weiter? Soziale Sicherheit CHSS, 2/2004.

Spycher, S., Olar, S., 1999. Wirkungsanalyse des Risikoausgleichs in der Krankenversicherung. Beiträge zur sozialen Sicherheit, Forschungsbericht im Auftrag des Bundesamtes für Sozialversicherung (BSV), Bern.

Trottmann, M., Telser, H., 2013. Evaluation zu den Auswirkungen des verfeinerten Risikoausgleichs auf den Krankenversicherungswettbewerb. Studie im Auftrag des Bundesamtes für Gesundheit (BAG), Zwischenbericht zur ersten Etappe, Bern.

Trottmann, M., Weidacher, A., Leonhardt, R., 2010. Morbiditätsbezogene Ausgleichsfaktoren im Schweizer Risikoausgleich. Gutachten im Auftrag des Bundesamts für Gesundheit (BAG), Bern.

Trottmann, M., Zweifel, P., Beck, K., 2012. Supply-side and demand-side cost sharing in deregulated social health insurance: which is more effective? J. Health Econ. 31, 231−242.

Trottmann, M., Telser, H., Stämpfli, D., Hersberger, K.E., Matter, K., Schwenkglenks, M., 2015. Übertragung der niederländischen PCG auf Schweizer Verhältnisse. Schlussbericht, Studie im Auftrag des Bundesamtes für Gesundheit (BAG), Bern.

Van Kleef, R.C., Beck, K., Van de Ven, W.P.M.M., Van Vliet, R.C.J.A., 2008. Risk equalization and voluntary deductibles: a complex interaction. J. Health Econ. 27, 427−443.

Van Kleef, R.C., Beck, K., Buchner, F., 2010. Risk-type concentration and efficiency incentives: a challenge for the risk adjustment formula. The Geneva Papers 35, 503−520.

Werblow, A., Felder, S., 2003. Der Einfluss von freiwilligen Selbstbehalten in der Gesetzlichen Krankenversicherung. Evidenz aus der Schweiz. Schmollers Jahrbuch 123, 235−264.

von Wyl, V., Beck, K., 2016. Do insurers respond to risk adjustment? A long-term, nationwide analysis from Switzerland. Eur. J. Health Econ. 17, 171−183.

# Chapter 17

# Health Plan Payment in US Marketplaces: Regulated Competition With a Weak Mandate

Timothy J. Layton[1], Ellen Montz[2] and Mark Shepard[3]

[1]*Department of Health Care Policy, Harvard Medical School and the NBER, Boston, MA, United States,* [2]*Department of Health Care Policy, Harvard Medical School, Boston, MA, United States,* [3]*Kennedy School of Government, Harvard University and the NBER, Cambridge, MA, United States*

## 17.1 INTRODUCTION

The Patient Protection and Affordable Care Act (ACA) of 2010 called for the creation of state-based health insurance markets known as Health Insurance Exchanges or Health Insurance Marketplaces (Marketplaces). These markets are intended to provide a new, affordable source for health insurance for Americans who do not receive insurance through their employers or through public programs providing coverage for the elderly (Medicare) and for low-income families (Medicaid). The law included a number of reforms to the nonemployer-based private health insurance market (the "individual" market) in the United States that shifted this market toward a model of regulated competition. These reforms included (partial) community rating of premiums, mandated coverage of a basket of "essential health benefits," and guaranteed issue and renewal provisions prohibiting insurers from rejecting applicants based on their health status. These reforms represented a dramatic shift in the individual market in most states, where previously many insurance products were limited in the scope of what they covered, insurers were allowed to charge higher premiums for sicker enrollees, and some individuals with chronic conditions were unable to find insurers willing to sell them coverage.

The US health insurance market can be broken down into three sectors: employer-sponsored insurance, public insurance (i.e., Medicare and

*Risk Adjustment, Risk Sharing and Premium Regulation in Health Insurance Markets.*
DOI: https://doi.org/10.1016/B978-0-12-811325-7.00017-8

Medicaid), and individual private insurance. The first two sectors, employer and public, are perceived to function relatively well, at least in terms of coverage (although high costs are a perennial concern). These sectors feature relatively high rates of take-up among eligible people and benefits that are perceived as adequate. The individual market is the third and smallest sector, covering only around 11 million Americans prior to the implementation of the ACA. It also acts as a sort of "market of last resort" for individuals without access to employer or public coverage. Unlike employer and public coverage, the individual market has historically featured low take-up (contributing to the high rate of uninsurance in the United States) as well as insurer underwriting and limited benefits driven by adverse selection. In an attempt to increase take-up and address adverse selection problems in this market, the ACA created the Marketplaces and made income-based premium subsidies available to individuals purchasing Marketplace plans. Additionally, a new tax penalty (or "mandate") was introduced for individuals neglecting to purchase coverage.

As of 2016, about 18 million Americans are enrolled in a Marketplace plan, 85% of whom receive premium subsidies. This represents over 60% of the individual market (US Department of Health and Human Services, 2016b). Recent research has shown that the premium subsidies have had a meaningful impact on the rate of uninsurance in the United States, accounting for 40% of the decrease in the uninsurance rate due to the ACA (Frean et al., 2017).[1] Overall growth in the individual market has been significant postimplementation of the ACA. This can be seen in Fig. 17.1, which plots enrollment in the individual market between 2011 and 2015, with the ACA reforms going into effect in 2014 (Box 17.1).

Data from the first 3 years (2014—16) suggested that (despite initial technical difficulties) the Marketplaces were functioning reasonably well. Insurer premiums came in below the levels expected by the Congressional Budget Office (Adler and Ginsburg, 2016), and premium growth was relatively slow. Many Marketplaces were initially highly concentrated—the average federally facilitated market in 2014 had 3.9 insurers, and almost 30% had just one or two insurers (Dafny, Gruber, and Ody, 2015). In 2014, Marketplaces were more concentrated than the wider individual market (U.S. Government Accountability Office, 2016). However, there was net insurer entry in 2015—16, with large national companies like United Healthcare expanding their presence.

More recent developments make for a less favorable picture. Two large national insurers (United and Aetna) exited many Marketplaces in 2017, and many smaller "co-op" insurers (which were established and subsidized as part of the ACA) have exited amid insolvency. Additionally, premiums rose markedly among the remaining insurers, with an average premium increase of 24% between 2016 and 2017. These developments became an important political issue in the 2016 US presidential election, with Donald Trump elected on promises to repeal the ACA (and, by implication, end the Marketplaces).

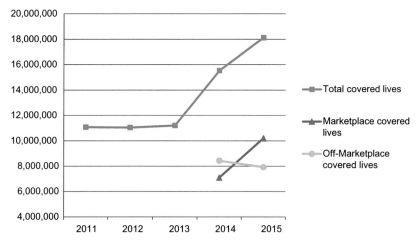

**FIGURE 17.1**   Growth of the individual market (2011–15).
The number of total covered lives in the individual market is calculated by summing the "life years" reported across all insurers in the individual market in the medical loss ratio data from the Department of Health and Human Services (CMS, 2015). Life years are calculated by summing the number of individuals enrolled on a given day in each month divided by 12. The number of Marketplace covered lives is taken from the "effectuated enrollment" numbers as reported by the Office of the Assistant Secretary for Planning and Evaluation at the Department of Health and Human Services. Effectuated enrollment numbers represent the number of confirmed customers paying premiums at a given point during the year, in this case, March. The number of off-Marketplace covered lives is calculated by taking the difference between total and on-Marketplace enrollment. The authors note there is measurement error in this calculation because of the manner in which covered lives are calculated in the MLR data compared to effectuated enrollment data. There does not exist a consistent measure of total and on- and off-Marketplace enrollment overtime. As such, this figure should be taken as representative.

There is much speculation about the reasons for these disruptions in the Marketplaces. Many insurers have cited a sicker-than-expected risk pool, an inadequate risk adjustment system, the only partially funded risk corridor program, and the end of federal reinsurance payments as important reasons for exiting and raising premiums. A key factor potentially behind many of these issues—and a difference from the standard ideas of managed competition—is that many (likely healthier) eligible individuals have remained uninsured due to a relatively weak coverage mandate (Newhouse, 2017). These developments suggest that the future success of the Marketplaces is unknown and likely depends on continual adaptation of the health plan payment system to the new issues raised in the ACA.

We proceed as follows. In Section 17.2, we describe the organization of the individual market in the United States under the ACA. In Section 17.3, we describe the payment system used to pay health plans in the individual market. In Section 17.4, we review the (limited) literature evaluating the

> **BOX 17.1 Marketplace versus individual market**
>
> While the introduction of the Marketplaces reformed the individual market, the Marketplaces did not replace the individual market. Instead, the Marketplaces entered as a platform where insurers could choose to compete and consumers could choose to purchase coverage within the larger individual market. Private individual health insurance can still be purchased outside of a Marketplace.
>
> This generates two types of plans in the individual market: on-Marketplace plans and off-Marketplace plans. Many ACA reforms apply to both on-Marketplace and off-Marketplace plans, such that both sets of plans are subject to the same regulations on premium rating rules, cost-sharing categories, and minimum benefit standards. Importantly, both on- and off-Marketplace plans are part of a single risk pool, meaning (1) risk adjustment transfers occur at the level of the entire individual market, not separately for the on- and off-Marketplace subsets of the market, and (2) insurers cannot assign different prices to the on-Marketplace and off-Marketplace versions of the same plan due to anticipated differences in health status of on-Marketplace and off-Marketplace enrollees.
>
> While the same rules apply to on- and off-Marketplace, insurers are not typically required to participate in the Marketplaces. In most states insurers can choose to offer off-Marketplace plans but not to offer on-Marketplace plans. The reverse is not true: Any plan offered on-Marketplace must also be offered off-Marketplace. The biggest difference between on- and off-Marketplace plans is that when an individual purchases off-Marketplace coverage they are ineligible to receive a subsidy.

Marketplace payment system. Finally, in Section 17.5 we discuss several issues with the Marketplace payment system and their potential implications for the future stability of the individual health insurance market.

## 17.2 ORGANIZATION OF THE HEALTH INSURANCE SYSTEM

The ACA created Marketplaces within the individual market as part of a package of reforms, and also as a vehicle to increase access to and affordability of health insurance coverage. Each state has its own Marketplace, operated either by a state entity or the federal government in accordance with the state's choice. As of 2016, the federal government ran 34 of the 51 Marketplaces. All Marketplaces must be operated according to federal regulations, but states can set standards that go beyond federal rules.

Health insurers offering coverage in the individual market (both on- and off-Marketplace) must offer plans that cover a minimum set of benefits, called "essential health benefits." They must offer plans that fall within four levels of increasing generosity: bronze, silver, gold, and platinum. Plans include a number of cost-sharing parameters, including deductibles, coinsurance rates, copays for various drugs and services, and out-of-pocket maximum payments. Due to the complexity of the cost sharing, generosity is summarized by the plan's "actuarial value," the percentage of spending on covered services the plan is expected to pay, on average, for a fixed sample of individuals.[2] Actuarial values must be 90% for platinum plans, 80% for gold, 70% for silver, and 60% for bronze.[3] Plans must also meet other minimum requirements set by federal and state regulators, including network adequacy rules, maximum out-of-pocket cost caps, and marketing standards. While some of these additional regulations are related to plan actuarial value, they are separate requirements.

Each state defines rating areas within the state, and eligible individuals within each rating area can choose from among all plans offered to them. The Marketplace functions as a common platform where all on-Marketplace competing plans are offered to consumers in one place. Health insurance issuers meeting minimum federal and state standards are generally allowed to offer as many health plan options in as many rating areas within the state as they wish—although a few states, most notably California (see Box 17.2) and Massachusetts, take a more active role in managing the number and type of plans available to consumers. As such, health insurers typically have wide discretion in plan pricing and flexibility in designing cost-sharing rules (conditional on actuarial value), provider network size, coverage for out-of-network spending, care management rules, and other difficult-to-observe measures of quality and generosity. This flexibility differentiates the Marketplaces from regulated insurance markets in other countries and provides potentially important avenues through which insurers can engage in behaviors related to risk selection.

Plans for the upcoming year are available to consumers on the first day of open enrollment, which now runs from November 1 to January 31. Outside of open enrollment, health insurers are not required to accept new enrollees unless they fall under special enrollment rules—cases such as losing eligibility for employment-based insurance or Medicaid or the birth of a baby (Box 17.2).

## 17.3   HEALTH PLAN PAYMENT DESIGN

Health plan payment in the Marketplaces consists of a number of components. First, insurers set and collect premiums for each of their plans. Second, insurers receive premium and cost-sharing subsidies from the government for their subsidy-eligible enrollees. Third, insurers receive or pay risk adjustment, reinsurance, and risk corridor transfers. Fig. 17.2 describes payment flows across the different actors in the market. We will discuss each of these components of the plan payment system in this section.

### BOX 17.2 Covered California

Covered California, California's Health Insurance Marketplace, is widely viewed as one of the most successful of the ACA Marketplaces. Covered California chose to adopt an "active purchaser" model where the state chooses to play a more active role than other states following the "clearinghouse" model. California has implemented the active purchaser role by limiting insurer entry (only allowing one-third of the insurers who originally expressed interest to actually enter the market), standardizing cost-sharing benefit designs, and negotiating prices and benefits with insurers (including provider network size and composition and insurers' use of non-FFS "alternative" payment arrangements with providers). California has also limited new entry after the initial year of 2014. Entry has been restricted to insurers newly entering California after 2012, insurers that offer MediCal plans, and insurers entering low-competition areas (Qualified Health Plan Recertification, 2015). The goal of this entry limitation was to stabilize the Marketplace. The regulator also prevented insurers from charging prices that they deemed "too low" as well as "too high." While state regulators rarely ask insurers to *raise* their premiums, Covered California wanted to ensure that insurers were not engaging in "invest-then-harvest" dynamic pricing strategies, where insurers offer low prices and take losses in order to capture market share the first year but then ramp up prices over time, exploiting consumer inertia. Finally, Covered California used their access to administrative hospital discharge data to aid insurers in pricing by providing estimates of each plan's risk adjustment transfer payments based on information about the relative rates of various chronic conditions for each insurer's members.

In addition to using active purchasing, Covered California also chose to implement an "active marketer" strategy where the Marketplace invested substantial resources in outreach to groups of enrollees (such as non-English speakers) that insurers were not targeting with their own outreach campaigns. In addition, insurers were required to invest substantial marketing dollars of their own. The rationale for this form of centralized marketing is that individual insurers may underinvest in outreach due to a free-riding problem, since consumers induced by marketing efforts to purchase insurance through Covered California may choose to buy a competitor's plan. Covered California's active marketer strategy may help solve this free-riding problem.

While the effects of California's active purchaser and active marketer strategies are still unclear, what is clear is that Covered California has achieved several measures of success in its individual market. First, Covered California has high levels of enrollment, with around 1.5 million enrollees in 2016. This comprises 47% of eligible individuals, placing California ninth among states with respect to this measure of Marketplace success (Marketplace Enrollment, 2016). Second, adverse selection between on- and off-Marketplace plans seems to be fairly limited. Finally, and most importantly, adverse selection between the insured and uninsured populations in California also seems to be fairly limited.

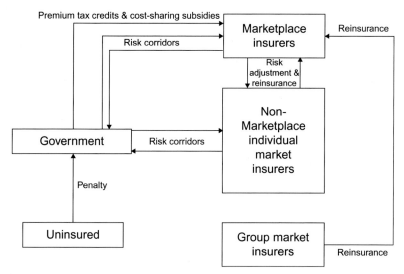

**FIGURE 17.2**    Payment flows under the Marketplace plan payment system.
This figure illustrates payment flows across actors in the US health insurance market under the
Marketplace payment system. Six components of the Marketplace payment system are illustrated: the penalty for remaining uninsured, premium tax credits, cost-sharing subsidies, risk corridor payments, risk adjustment transfers, and reinsurance transfers/payments. Penalties are paid
by the uninsured to the government. The government pays premium tax credits to Marketplace
plans. Risk corridor payments are made by profitable Marketplace and non-Marketplace insurers
to the government and by the government to unprofitable Marketplace and non-Marketplace
insurers. Risk adjustment payments are made by Marketplace and non-Marketplace insurers with
relatively more low-risk enrollees to Marketplace and non-Marketplace insurers with relatively
more high-risk enrollees. All insurers (individual and group market) make reinsurance contributions.
Marketplace insurers and non-Marketplace insurers with high-cost enrollees receive reinsurance
payments.

## 17.3.1    Premiums

Plan premium setting in the Marketplaces is subject to a variety of regulations that makes the process differ from a textbook insurance market.
Typically, economists think of firm pricing decisions as taking place at the
level of the product (i.e., a specific plan in a given market), with product-
specific demand and cost factors determining firm pricing incentives. In
insurance markets, economists also consider the possibility that insurers price
discriminate across enrollees based on observable risk factors like age and
preexisting conditions. The ACA Marketplaces limit both of these aspects of
the insurer premium-setting decision.

   First, the Marketplaces regulate how insurers set the premium for a given
plan in a given market. Insurers are supposed to adhere to a "single risk pool
rating" requirement, which means that insurers must consider all enrollees in
all health plans (both on- and off-Marketplace) in a given state as one single

risk pool when developing premiums. The ACA limits the reasons that an insurer can vary premiums across its individual market plans in a state and subjects these decisions to regulatory oversight.

In practice, this works as follows. Each insurer first develops an "index rate" for a given state. This index rate can be thought of as an "insurer price" that will influence the price of every plan the insurer offers. The index rate then acts as the starting point for building the "plan price" that is assigned to a particular plan offered by the insurer in a particular rating area.[4] Regulation allows the insurer price and plan price to vary only based on specific factors (which differ between the two). The insurer price is allowed to incorporate average claims for essential health benefits for the insurer's anticipated risk pool (which can be influenced by risk selection) as well as market-wide adjustments for items such as risk adjustment, fees, and reinsurance. The plan price then builds off the insurer price via a set of allowed plan-specific adjustments. Plan-specific adjustments to the insurer price are allowed based on geographic factors, benefit generosity (captured in the metal level and the provision of any additional benefits), network size, and plan management factors (e.g., HMO versus PPO).

Importantly, plan prices—i.e., for different plans offered by the same insurer—are not supposed to incorporate differential selection on health status across plans.[5] Nonetheless, since insurers may adjust plan-specific premiums for a number of other plan factors (listed above), insurers do have flexibility to incorporate selection- and demand-related factors into *plan* prices via tweaks to their expectations of the allowed adjustment factors. For example, an insurer anticipating that its HMO plans will attract healthier individuals than its PPO plans might tweak its HMO/PPO adjustment factor to incorporate differential selection in addition to structural cost differences between these two plan types.

After the premium for a particular plan (in a particular rating area) is determined in the manner just described, the Marketplaces also restrict how this plan's premium can vary across individuals. Plan prices may vary across individuals only by age and smoking status. Age-based premium variation is fixed by regulation. Insurers first submit a base price for each plan. Then, the base price is multiplied by a fixed set of age weights (varying from 1.0 for a 21-year-old to 3.0 for a 64-year-old) to produce age-specific premiums. Smoking status is incorporated by multiplying a "smoking" weight by the individual's age-specific premium. The smoking weight is chosen by the insurer, but it must be between 1.0 and 1.5.

All insurers seeking to offer coverage in the individual market in a given year must submit their plan offerings and premium proposals by June 1 of the prior year. Plan and pricing submissions are reviewed by state and/or federal regulators.[6] The interactions between regulators and issuers often leads to changes—generally minor but sometimes larger for premiums. This pricing process applies to the entire individual market, not just on-Marketplace plans.

## 17.3.2 Subsidies

There are two forms of subsidies in the Marketplaces: (1) premium tax credits, which lower the premiums that low-income enrollees must pay, and (2) cost-sharing subsidies, which make silver plans more generous for a subset of low-income enrollees. We describe these two forms of subsidies in turn.

While the same plans available on-Marketplace are available off-Marketplace, individuals below 400% of the Federal Poverty Line (FPL) have access to premium tax credits only if they buy an on-Marketplace plan. Additionally, those households eligible for cost-sharing subsidies have access to those subsidies only when purchasing an on-Marketplace silver plan. Premium tax credits are applied directly to reduce health insurance premiums owed by eligible enrollees. They are calculated based both on an individual's household income for the year and on the second-lowest price silver plan available on the Marketplace. Specifically, the tax credit is set so that the *postsubsidy* enrollee premium for the second-cheapest silver plan equals a target amount intended to be affordable based on an enrollee's income. This target amount rises on a sliding scale from 2% of income for a household with income of 100% of FPL up to 9.7% of income for a person with income of 400% of FPL.

This calculation—the premium of the second-cheapest silver plan minus the income-specific target amount—determines the dollar amount of the tax credit. This tax credit can then be used toward the purchase of any plan on the Marketplace. However, the tax credit cannot be used to reduce the enrollee premium of a plan below $0—a constraint that has been binding for some bronze plans for lower-income households.

Individuals may claim their tax credit in two ways. First, an individual can receive an advance premium tax credit (APTC) based on projected household income for the year at the time of enrollment. In this case, individuals pay premiums, net of the tax credit directly to insurers each month, and the federal government pays the tax credit directly to the health insurance issuers. APTCs are an estimate and the individual must reconcile the amount they received based on actual income when they file their income taxes.[7] Second, an individual may choose to pay the full amount of their premium directly to insurers during the year and then use the tax credits against their tax obligations, receiving any remaining balance in the form of a tax refund from the federal government.

The second type of Marketplace subsidies are cost-sharing reductions. Cost-sharing reductions lower the amount eligible individuals have to pay for out-of-pocket costs like deductibles, copayments, and coinsurance. To qualify, households must have income below 250% FPL and enroll in a silver plan on the Marketplace. Cost-sharing reductions increase the actuarial value of the silver plan (70% at baseline) to 94% for individuals below 150% FPL, to 87% for individuals between 151% and 200% FPL, and to

73% for individuals between 201 and 250% FPL. When insurers submit their plans and rates for the year, they also include 73%, 87%, and 94% versions of all of their silver plans. Eligible individuals are automatically enrolled in the increased actuarial value silver plan of their chosen silver plan on the Marketplace and, unlike tax credits, do not need to reconcile any subsidy received when filing their taxes. Health insurers receive money from the federal government based on a per capita enrollee estimate of cost-sharing subsidies during the course of the year. Then, during the following year, health insurers reconcile with the federal government the per capita dollars they received during the year with the actual dollar amount of cost-sharing reductions received by the enrollees throughout the year.

### 17.3.3   Risk Adjustment

To mitigate problems caused by risk selection across plans in the individual market, the ACA established a permanent risk adjustment program. This program transfers funds from (both on- and off-Marketplace) plans with healthier enrollees to plans with sicker enrollees, after accounting for age and other factors on which premiums already vary at an individual level. Risk adjustment aims to make plan premiums charged to enrollees reflect differences in scope of benefits and network coverage rather than differences in enrollee health status. It also aims to mitigate incentives for plans to avoid high-cost individuals.

The individual market risk adjustment program is made up of two components: a *risk adjustment model* (which determines individual risk scores) and a *risk transfer formula* (which determines monetary transfers across plans). We will discuss these two components of the program separately.

#### 17.3.3.1   Risk Adjustment Model

The risk adjustment model assigns risk scores to enrollees based on their demographics and observed diagnoses during the concurrent plan year (i.e., calendar year). The risk score reflects the individual's predicted costliness to the insurer relative to an average enrollee. Risk scores are calculated using a model developed by the Department of Health and Human Services (HHS), the HHS Hierarchical Condition Categories (HHS-HCC) model. The HHS-HCC model predicts an enrollee's medical spending in the current year by mapping diagnoses coded on insurance claims into one of 100 HHS-selected HCCs, which were selected from the full 264 HCCs in the diagnostic classification system (Kautter et al., 2014). To determine which HCCs to include in the HHS-HCC model, HHS used four main criteria: (1) that the HCC had to represent clinically significant, well-defined, and costly medical conditions; (2) that the HCCs are not especially vulnerable to discretionary diagnostic coding; (3) that the HCCs do not primarily represent poor-quality or avoidable complications of medical care; and (4) that the HCCs should identify chronic, predictable, or other conditions that are subject to insurer risk selection, risk segmentation, or provider network selection, rather than random acute events that represent insurance risk. The HCC indicators enter into a linear regression model predicting individual-level total cost.

The starting point for the HHS-HCC model is the model used in Medicare Advantage, the CMS-HCC model (see Chapter 19: Medicare Advantage: Regulated Competition in the Shadow of a Public Option). The CMS-HCC model was modified to reflect three major differences between Medicare Advantage and the individual market. The HHS-HCC model: (1) uses concurrent year diagnoses and demographics to predict spending (rather than the past year's variables used by the CMS-HCC model); (2) reflects HCCs more relevant to the under-65 population (such as those related to childbirth); and (3) predicts total spending including drug costs (which in Medicare are covered by Part D). The full HHS-HCC risk adjustment model incorporates 15 different variations—one model for each age group (adult, child, and infant) by cost-sharing level (platinum, gold, silver, bronze, and catastrophic). The separate models are meant to capture major differences across the age groups and differences across the cost-sharing levels in the portion of medical spending covered by the insurer. The adult and child models include the same variables (with the exception of a few interactions) but differ in the payment weights because the adult model is estimated on a sample of adults and the child model is estimated on a sample of children. The infant model uses a different set of risk variables: a set of 20 mutually exclusive categories based on a subset of HCCs that are relevant to infant health status. Additional details on the HHS-HCC risk adjustment model are provided in Box 17.3.

### 17.3.3.2 Risk Transfer Formula

Next, HHS inputs enrollee risk scores into a "risk transfer formula" that determines transfer payments across insurers. Transfer payments are intended to offset cost differences due to risk selection while preserving cost differences due to plan features (e.g., moral hazard, actuarial value, provider network) and allowable rating factors like age. Transfer payments depend on a plan's average risk score relative to the market average risk score and are constructed to be budget neutral in a given year. Payment transfers occur among (both on- and off-Marketplace) platinum, gold, silver, and bronze plans as a single risk adjustment pool, with a separate risk pool for catastrophic plans.

The risk transfer formula is complex and not always intuitive from an economic standpoint. Here, we try to provide some insight into the regulator's thought process in constructing the formula based on the discussion in Pope et al. (2014). Later, we will discuss some of the potential problems that the formula may introduce.

## BOX 17.3 Details of the Marketplace (HHS-HCC) risk adjustment model

The HHS-HCC risk adjustment model is designed to determine individual risk scores, which measure how costly an individual is relative to the average market enrollee, for individuals enrolled in Marketplace plans. To determine such risk scores, HHS constructed a linear model using age, sex, and diagnosis information to predict individual-level total costs. The HHS-HCC model consists of separate models for adults (age > 20), children (age 1−20), and infants (age < 1).

The HHS-HCC model uses the Hierarchical Condition Category (HCC) classification system. This system consists of 254 Condition Categories (CCs) that map the universe of ICD-10 diagnoses to unique clinical conditions. The system takes all of the diagnoses submitted for a given individual and maps them to CCs. A binary variable for each CC is created, and if the individual has at least one eligible diagnosis appearing on a health insurance claim that maps to the CC, the individual is given a value of 1 for that CC. The system then takes the Condition Categories and produces Hierarchical Condition Categories. For sets of related Condition Categories, hierarchies are prespecified so that more-severe conditions are higher in the hierarchy than less-severe conditions. The HCCs are generated by setting to zero for an individual any CCs for which there is a CC "higher up" in the CC's hierarchy that is set equal to 1. This ensures that for each individual, only the most severe CC in a hierarchy is turned "on" and all less-severe CCs are turned "off." The mapping from ICD-10 diagnoses to HCCs is described in Fig. 17.3.

Of the 254 HCCs, the same 127 were chosen for inclusion in the child and adult HHS-HCC models. Variables were chosen based on how discretionary diagnoses were and how well they predict spending as well as other considerations laid out in Kautter et al. (2014). Of these 127 HCCs, 53 were combined into 17 HCC groups for the adult model in order to improve the precision of the coefficient estimates. For the child model 50 HCCs were combined into 17 groups. A "Severe Illness Indicator" was also formed, equal to 1 if one of eight high-severity HCCs is equal to 1. This indicator was not included in the model but was instead used to form two interaction groups, indicating interactions between severe conditions. These interaction groups were included in the adult model but not the child model. The final adult model includes 18 age-by-sex groups, 74 individual HCCs, 17 groups of HCCs, and two interaction groups for a total of 111 variables. The final child model includes eight age-by-sex groups, 77 individual HCCs, and 17 groups of HCCs for a total of 102 variables.

The infant HHC-HCC model also starts with the HCC classification system. A total of 108 relevant HCCs are grouped into five severity groups. A hierarchy is then imposed on the severity group such that each infant is only in the most severe severity group for which he has an HCC. HCCs describing prematurity are then mapped to five maturity levels: extremely immature, immature, premature multiples, term, and age 1. A hierarchy is then imposed on the maturity level so that each infant is assigned only to the most severe maturity level for which he has an HCC. Neither the maturity level nor the severity level variables are included directly in the infant model. Instead, they are interacted with one

*(Continued)*

**BOX 17.3  (Continued)**

another to form a set of 25 mutually exclusive severity-by-maturity cells. The model then consists of these 25 cells.

In the absence of actual claims data from a yet-to-be formed Marketplace, HHS used data from Truven MarketScan Commerical Claims and Encounter Data, a dataset of individuals in employer-sponsored plans, to calibrate the model. For each of the three populations, five models were estimated, one for each plan tier (platinum, gold, silver, bronze, catastrophic). For each model, total spending was first calculated for each individual and then a standard cost-sharing schedule (deductible, coinsurance, out-of-pocket maximum) was applied to determine the total plan spending for the tier. Models were then estimated separately for adults, children, and infants using ordinary least squares, constraining coefficients to be greater than or equal to zero, and constraining coefficients on more-severe categories within a hierarchy to be larger than less-severe categories within the same hierarchy.

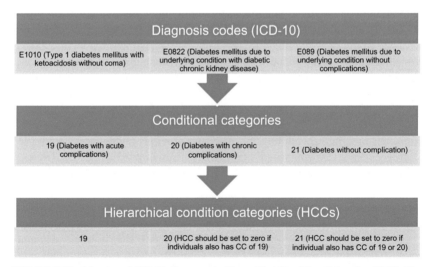

**FIGURE 17.3**   Mapping of ICD-10 diagnoses to Hierarchical Condition Categories (HCC): The case of diabetes.

This figure illustrates the mapping from ICD-10 diagnosis codes to Hierarchical Condition Categories (HCCs) for the case of diabetes. The HCC system starts by mapping every diagnosis code to a Condition Category (CC). HCCs are then generated by setting to zero any CC for which the individual has a more severe CC in the same hierarchy. *Source: Risk Adjustment: HHS-Developed Risk Adjustment Model Algorithm Software. https://www.cms.gov/CCIIO/ Resources/Regulations-and-Guidance/index.html#Premium Stabilization Programs.*

First, the regulator constructs an estimate of what a plan's premium *would be* without risk adjustment. To do this, the regulator starts with the statewide (enrollment-weighted) average premium and accounts for the following factors driving differences between the underlying costs for a given plan and the statewide average: health risk, coverage (i.e., actuarial value), demand-response (i.e., moral hazard), and geography. Other factors contributing to differences in premiums across plans, such as plan type (HMO vs PPO), are not accounted for in the risk transfer formula. The regulator constructs her estimate via the following formula:

$$\hat{P}_j = \left( \frac{Risk_j \cdot IDF_j \cdot Geo_j}{(Risk \cdot IDF \cdot Geo)_s} \right) \cdot \overline{P}_s$$

$\overline{P}_s$ represents the statewide (enrollment-weighted) average premium. $Risk_j$ is the average risk score among plan $j$'s enrollees, $IDF_j$ is a plan-specific "induced demand factor" calibrated by the regulator and meant to capture differences in costs across plans with different actuarial values caused by demand-response (moral hazard) to the coverage level, and $Geo_j$ is a geographic factor meant to capture differences in costs across plans due to differences in the geographic distribution of a plan's enrollees. The denominator is a statewide (enrollment-weighted) average of the product of these factors. Note that a plan's actuarial value does not explicitly enter the formula. The regulator argues that this is because it implicitly enters via $Risk_j$ due to the fact that there are different risk adjustment models for plans with different actuarial value levels, as explained in Box 17.3 (Pope et al., 2014).

Next, the regulator constructs an estimate of what a plan's premium would be without risk selection, conditional on the "allowable rating factors." To do this, the regulator again starts with the statewide average premium, but this time accounting for all of the previous factors contributing to differences in underlying costs across plans *except for health risk* ($Risk_j$). The regulator constructs this estimate via the following formula:

$$\tilde{P}_j = \left( \frac{AV_j \cdot Age_j \cdot IDF_j \cdot Geo_j}{(AV \cdot Age \cdot IDF \cdot Geo)_s} \right) \cdot \overline{P}_s$$

For this estimate, the regulator again includes the induced demand factor, $IDF_j$, and the geographic factor, $Geo_j$. But now two additional factors are also included: the actuarial value of the plan, $AV_j$, and an age factor equal to the average age weight (the age-based premium factors discussed above) for the plan's enrollees. While these two factors were not explicitly included in the regulator's estimate of the plan's premium without risk adjustment ($\hat{P}_j$), the regulator argues that they were implicitly included via the risk score calculation, which incorporates both the plan's actuarial value (different models for each actuarial value level) and age distribution (age groups are included in the risk adjustment model).

The risk adjustment transfer is defined as the difference between the estimate of the premium with risk selection, $\hat{P}_j$, and the estimate of the premium without risk selection, $\tilde{P}_j$:

$$T_j = \hat{P}_j - \tilde{P}_j = \left\{ \frac{Risk_j \cdot IDF_j \cdot Geo_j}{(Risk \cdot IDF \cdot Geo)_s} - \frac{AV_j \cdot Age_j \cdot IDF_j \cdot Geo_j}{(AV \cdot Age \cdot IDF \cdot Geo)_s} \right\} \cdot \bar{P}_s$$

The use of the statewide (enrollment-weighted) average premium combined with the normalization of the numerators of both terms in brackets by their statewide averages ensures that transfers are budget neutral within a given year and market. This is true even in the presence of insurer "upcoding" of enrollee risk scores—in contrast to the Medicare Advantage market where upcoding increases government spending (Geruso and Layton, 2015). The transfer is meant to eliminate premium differences stemming from risk selection. Thus, if the difference between the estimate of the premium with risk selection and the estimate of the premium without risk selection is positive, a plan receives a transfer payment, and if the difference is negative, a plan owes transfer funds.

Risk adjustment and payment transfer calculations occur annually after the coverage year ends, following a period to allow all claims to be submitted by providers. Only the summary measures necessary to calculate the transfer payments are provided to HHS. Individual claims and risk score data are kept by the insurer and are not required to be reported, except in the case of an audit. After health insurance issuers run the HHS software to get a risk score for each of their enrollees, issuers report the average risk score for their enrollees, the average enrollment-weighted premium for their enrollees, and other demographic and enrollment details necessary for HHS to implement the risk adjustment transfer formula. After HHS completes the risk adjustment transfer calculation, HHS reports balances to issuers and transfers across insurers are routed through HHS. Apart from a small administrative fee to HHS, the transfers are budget neutral.

### 17.3.4 Risk Sharing

The Marketplace payment system featured two risk-sharing features. Both were temporary, in place from 2014 to 2016, with the goal of stabilizing the market in the short term to encourage insurer entry. The first was a reinsurance policy, reimbursing insurers for a portion of individual-level spending exceeding a threshold. The second was a risk corridor program, compensating insurers for a portion of any losses exceeding a prespecified threshold and extracting a portion of profits.

### 17.3.4.1 Temporary Reinsurance Program

The ACA established a temporary reinsurance program for plans in the individual market (both on- and off-Marketplace). The program was in place from 2014 to 2016 and was intended to stabilize premiums during the initial years of reform by helping cover the costs of very high-cost enrollees. While it is not totally clear why reinsurance was temporary, a possible reason was the hope that, over time, insurers would learn the extent to which these high-cost cases affected their costs and incorporate that information into plan premiums.

The program, run by HHS, collected per-capita fees from all commercial insurance (both in the individual *and* group market, including self-insured plans) in amounts totaling $10 billion in 2014, $6 billion in 2015, and $4 billion in 2016, and transferred these funds to individual market plans when their enrollees incurred high costs. Individual market plans received reimbursement for an enrollee's annual costs above an attachment point— $45,000 for 2014−15 and $90,000 for 2016—up to a reinsurance cap of $250,000. Because the reinsurance program could not pay out more than the amount collected, the percentage of costs reimbursed for a given year depended on the total funding available. In 2014, 100% of the costs were reimbursed, but this fell to 51% in 2015.

The reinsurance program differed from risk adjustment in two notable ways. First, it was based on enrollees' *actual* costs—rather than predicted costs as used in the risk adjustment model. Second, unlike risk adjustment, the reinsurance program involved a net transfer of funds *into* the individual market from the group market (which helped fund the fees). This meant that the end of reinsurance in 2017 involved a net funding reduction. Insurers' large premium increase in 2017 partly reflects the one-time loss of reinsurance as a funding source.

### 17.3.4.2 Temporary Risk Corridors

The ACA also set up a temporary risk corridor program for 2014−16. Underlying this program is the idea that, with uncertainty about the costliness of enrollees in a new market, issuers might stay out of the market or price higher than otherwise. Because the Marketplaces represented an entirely new market, and the risk mix of the individuals who would enroll in the market was previously unknown, there was a great deal of uncertainty around the consequences of entry for a particular insurer. Many of the insurers also had little experience with risk adjustment in general, having previously participated mostly in the individual market or in the employer market (neither of which used risk adjustment). Additionally, the risk adjustment system used in the Marketplaces was different from the systems used in other US markets such as Medicaid and the Medicare Advantage program, in that the Marketplace system was "balanced budget," and depended on transfers across insurers rather than from the government to insurers. Because of these issues, it was difficult for insurers to predict (1) what the costs of their enrollees would be and (2) what their risk adjustment payments would look like (including whether they would be positive or negative). This uncertainty provided a rationale for implementing this temporary risk corridor program.

The program—which applies only to Marketplace-certified plans (Qualified Health Plans)—worked like a profit-and-loss-sharing program between insurers and the government. Plans first calculated a "benchmark" rate, equal to 80% of their premium revenue, and the amount spent on health care plus quality improvement.[8] The state shared in "profits" when spending was less than 97% of the benchmark and shared in "losses" when spending exceeded 103% of the benchmark. The profit-sharing rate was 50% for the first 5% of costs (i.e., between 92%−97% or 103%−108% of the benchmark). For instance, a plan with spending between 92% and 97% of its benchmark owed HHS 50% of the difference between 97% of the benchmark and their actual spending. The profit-sharing rate was 80% for all profits/losses beyond this amount.

As originally enacted, risk corridor payments were not required to be budget neutral. As a result, the program gave insurers a strong incentive to lower premiums. Each $1 of lower premiums could be passed onto enrollees, increasing demand, but a portion of the lower per-enrollee profit (or increased losses) would be offset by additional risk corridor payments. Perhaps as a result, many insurers "underpriced" their plans, setting premiums such that spending exceeded their benchmark.

However, following a backlash against what some Republicans labeled as a "bailout" of money-losing insurers, Congress changed the original program by specifying that payments could not exceed charges for a given year. Such a change meant that the risk corridor program could pay out very little of its liabilities. HHS was only able to pay out 12.6% of claims for 2014 and has announced that any revenues collected for 2015 will go toward (but far from cover) existing 2014 issuer claims. This change was made after plan prices were set for 2015, implying that any issuer that incorporated the original risk corridor payments into their 2014 or 2015 pricing decision experienced an unexpected negative shock to revenues. This shock may have contributed to the forced (co-ops) or voluntary (Aetna and United) exit of many insurers from the Marketplaces in 2016 and 2017.

## 17.4    EVALUATION OF HEALTH PLAN PAYMENT

Generally, evaluations of health plan payment systems come in two forms. The first is ex-ante evaluations that use data from other markets and simulate plan payments and costs under a given payment system. The second is ex-post evaluations that use data from the actual market of interest to determine how well the payment system works in practice. Because the Marketplaces are so new and access to data is so limited, most studies evaluating the Marketplace plan payment system fall into the ex-ante category, with a few notable exceptions that we discuss below.

## 17.4.1    Ex-ante Evaluations

All of the ex-ante studies of the Marketplace plan payment system use data from large employers or the Medical Expenditure Panel Survey (MEPS). The first evaluation was produced by the Marketplace payment system designers (Kautter et al., 2014). They found that for the different risk score models (by age group and metal level, as described above) the R-squared statistic (in a regression predicting costs) varied between 0.3 and 0.36. They also looked at predictive ratios (the ratio of simulated revenues to realized costs) for subgroups of the population, focusing largely on groups defined by quantile of the distribution of predicted spending. They find that predictive ratios for most quantiles are close to 1, indicating little incentive to attract or deter these groups of individuals. This result is not surprising because individuals were grouped by quantile of *predicted* spending rather than *actual* spending, meaning that any spending not picked up by the risk adjustment model would also not be picked up by the grouping of individuals.

McGuire et al. (2014) also evaluate the performance of the Marketplace plan payment system. In their evaluation, McGuire et al. again use predictive ratios but for subgroups of individuals with four chronic conditions: cancer, heart disease, diabetes, and mental health conditions. In addition, they use measures based on Ellis and McGuire's (2007) "predictability and predictiveness" index of the incentives for a profit-maximizing plan to ration a particular service to attract healthy enrollees and avoid sick ones. They find that, even after accounting for risk adjustment, strong incentives remain to avoid individuals with chronic conditions, with the strongest disincentives attached to cancer and mental health conditions.

Montz et al. (2016) delve further into the payment system's performance with respect to individuals with mental health conditions. They find evidence of service-level selection incentives within the HHS-HCC risk adjustment system as individuals with mental health conditions are undercompensated by the model, especially those with anxiety, mood, and adjustment disorders. Examining differences between the HHS-HCC risk adjustment system and those used in Medicare Advantage and Medicare Part D, the study suggests that the treatment of prescription drugs in the HHS-HCC system may contribute to this undercompensation. The reliance on a model not optimized for predicting drug spending may result in the HHS-HCC model failing to adequately account for conditions that do not typically result in high medical spending but that do result in high prescription drug spending.

Handel et al. (2015) and Layton (2017) evaluate the Marketplace payment system with respect to its ability to limit welfare losses due to adverse selection. Both focus on selection between bronze and platinum plans and both find that with no risk adjustment, the platinum plan death spirals, leaving all enrollees in the limited coverage bronze plan. Handel, Hendel, and Whinston find that a risk adjustment system that bases transfers on realized costs corrects part of this market failure. Layton presents similar findings for a simulation of the actual Marketplace payment system, implying that the payment system seems to perform well with respect to its ability to weaken adverse selection. Both of these studies simulate plan prices and consumer choices using data from large employers.

Layton et al. (2017) introduce new measures of payment system performance that are "valid, complete, and practical," where valid refers to their being based in a formal model of welfare economics, complete refers to their incorporation of all components of the payment system, and practical refers to their ability to be readily implemented by researchers and policymakers. The main measure they develop is "payment system fit" which is the R-squared from a regression of individual-level spending on the revenue (from premiums, risk adjustment, reinsurance, etc.) a plan would receive from enrolling the individual. They also show the additional importance of "premium fit" or how well premiums match an individual's expected cost. They make the important conceptual point that, because no single premium can typically achieve first-best sorting of individuals across plans, any payment system evaluation must take account of premium fit *and* payment system fit separately. Finally, they present a measure of incentives for service-level selection under a given payment system recently developed by Layton et al. (2017). They use all of these measures to evaluate the Marketplace plan payment system relative to an alternative system. They simulate the payment systems using data from the Marketscan database of employer-provided health insurance claims. Unlike the other studies that use Marketscan data, they restrict the dataset to individuals who look similar to individuals eligible for coverage through the Marketplaces, as identified in the MEPS.[9] They find that the Marketplace's concurrent risk adjustment system performs well with respect to payment system fit and the service-level selection measure. They also find that the reinsurance system in place in 2014 produces dramatic improvements in these measures. Premium fit is weak because premiums vary only by age, but it is better than in other markets where premium discrimination is not allowed at all.

Geruso and McGuire (2016) introduce a new evaluation criteria, the "power" of the payment system, and apply it to the 2017 Marketplace payment system as well as several alternatives. Power is defined as the portion of the marginal dollar a plan spends on an enrollee that is borne by the plan. The concept stems from the observation that under a given payment system, when a plan spends an extra dollar on an individual, the revenue the plan receives for that individual may be affected. Consider a payment system incorporating reinsurance. Under such a payment system, a plan only bears $(100-X)\%$ of the marginal dollar it spends on an individual whose spending exceeds the reinsurance cutoff, where X is the reinsurance policy's reimbursement rate. Intuitively, power captures the strength of a plan's incentive to control their enrollees' costs. It is clear that reinsurance weakens power by reimbursing plans for a portion of the marginal dollar spent on high-cost individuals. Geruso and McGuire argue that risk adjustment has similar properties: risk scores are based on diagnoses coded in insurance claims, and these diagnoses cannot appear unless an enrollee visits a doctor. Thus, the first doctor visit for an individual with a chronic condition generates a large increase in revenue, weakening the incentive to limit the cost of physician visits. Geruso and McGuire operationalize power by randomly eliminating outpatient days and inpatient admissions and observing how costs and simulated revenues respond. They show via simulation that the power of the Marketplace's concurrent risk adjustment system is relatively low, around 0.25 with reinsurance and around 0.6 without it (where 1.0 indicates full power). On the other hand, they find that payment system fit is relatively high, around 0.6 with reinsurance and around 0.4 without. Finally, they bring these two measures together with another novel measure, "balance," to show that the 2017 Marketplace payment system is dominated by a payment system consisting of prospective (rather than concurrent) risk adjustment and a reinsurance policy compensating plans for 80% of an individual's annual spending above $60,000.

A final ex-ante evaluation is by Layton et al. (2016). They focus on the final component of the Marketplace plan payment system, risk corridors, and compare the Marketplace risk corridor and reinsurance programs with respect to insurer risk protection and the power measure developed by Geruso and McGuire (2016). They find that both Marketplace policies offer substantial risk protection, and that they perform similarly when compared on both power and risk protection simultaneously.

## 17.4.2 Ex-post Evaluations

Due to the relatively young age of the Marketplaces, as well as limited data availability, there are few ex-post evaluations of the Marketplace payment system. One exception is evidence from Massachusetts, which established a health insurance marketplace (the Connector) in 2006 that was a model for the ACA Marketplaces. The Connector shared many of the features of the ACA Marketplaces including strict limits on premium discrimination, generous subsidies, a coverage mandate, and risk adjustment payments.

Shepard (2016) studies the subsidized portion of the Connector for low-income people, called Commonwealth Care. He studies the role of adverse selection in affecting insurers' incentives to offer a more generous hospital network that covers certain "star" academic hospitals. He finds that plans covering star hospitals attracted a much higher-cost set of members—in particular those with existing relationships with the star hospitals and their affiliated physicians. The Connector's risk adjustment system compensated these plans for about two-thirds of these patients' higher costs. But even after risk adjustment, these patients were substantially more expensive (about 28% higher) than other individuals. Shepard shows that much of their higher costs reflect differential "moral hazard," in the sense that these enrollees' costs increase more when their plan covers the star hospitals and they shift their care to those hospitals and away from cheaper providers.

Geruso et al. (2016) combine ex-ante and ex-post techniques to study the performance of the Marketplace payment system with respect to insurer incentives to inefficiently ration access to prescription drugs that attract unprofitable enrollees. They first use Marketscan data and simulated revenues under the Marketplace payment system to assess for each drug class the over-/underpayment for individuals taking drugs in the class as well as the "predictability and predictiveness" measure of insurer incentives to distort coverage developed by Ellis and McGuire (2007). They find that the Marketplace payment system performs reasonably well. Figure 2 from their paper is reproduced here as Fig. 17.4. It plots for each drug class the average

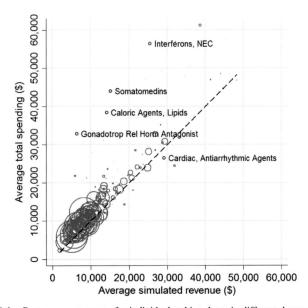

**FIGURE 17.4** Costs versus revenues for individuals taking drugs in different therapeutic classes. This figure is reproduced from Geruso et al. (2016a). Each point represents a drug class, with the size of the point indicating the importance of the drug class in terms of individuals. The x-axis shows average simulated revenue for individuals taking a drug in the class. The y-axis shows average total (drug and nondrug) spending for individuals taking a drug in the class.

cost versus the average revenue associated with people taking drugs in the class. It is clear that most classes lie close to the 45-degree line, implying an alignment of costs and revenues. A few classes, however, are far from the 45-degree line. Geruso, Layton, and Prinz then go to ex-post data on the drug formularies of Marketplace plans. They show that the generosity of the Marketplace formularies for a given drug class is highly correlated with their measures of the insurer's incentive to ration access to the drugs in the class in order to avoid unprofitable enrollees. This result holds even when adding data on employer formularies (where there is no selection incentive) and including drug class fixed effects to control for drug characteristics that are fixed across the employer and Marketplace markets. They also find that the result is largely driven by the most salient drugs in a class, the drug spending component of an individual's profitability, and the drug classes in the far right tail of the distribution of selection incentives. They conclude that while the Marketplace payment system performs well for the vast majority of drug classes, it performs poorly with respect to a few (such as classes that include fertility drugs and drugs used to treat multiple sclerosis) and that insurers respond to the incentives generated by that poor performance.

## 17.5 ONGOING ISSUES AND REFORMS

### 17.5.1 High-Cost Cases

One of the major issues cited by insurers exiting the Marketplaces between 2016 and 2017 was the end of the federal reinsurance program, described in Section 17.3. Under this program, a per capita assessment was collected from most insurers (including from plans in the separate group insurance market), and the proceeds of the assessment were paid out to reimburse individual market insurers for spending on extremely high-cost cases. This program was intended to limit insurer risk during the Marketplaces' early years in order to encourage entry and boost competition. It was intended to be a complement (rather than a substitute) for private reinsurance that insurers themselves can purchase, in that it covered a range of high-cost cases that typically fall below the cutoffs in private reinsurance contracts.

It also differed from private reinsurance in two important respects likely to favor higher-cost plans (and those that attract sicker enrollees). First, the program involved a net transfer of funds into the individual market, since fees were collected from both group and individual market plans but payouts were made only to individual market plans. Second, the fees funding the program were a flat per-capita amount for all plans, regardless of their cost structure or likelihood to attract sicker enrollees. A private reinsurer, by contrast, would likely charge a higher fee to plans that were *predictably* higher-cost or adversely selected (e.g., plans with broad networks) and therefore more likely to draw on reinsurance. Together, these factors suggest that the

ACA reinsurance program involved a net subsidy to the individual market and specifically to its highest-cost plans.[10]

The recent exit of insurers citing the end of the reinsurance program as a factor in their decision suggests that the program may have been successful at inducing entry into the Marketplaces. Some insurers may have been induced to enter but later decided they could not remain viable in these markets without the reinsurance subsidy. This has spurred some discussion about a way to embed a permanent, budget-neutral version of the original reinsurance program in the Marketplaces, while complying with statutory language requiring the original reinsurance program to end in 2016.

There are several potential motivations for an extension of this program. First, the program has the potential to reduce the risk faced by insurers in the Marketplaces. Many insurers purchase private reinsurance, suggesting risk aversion (Layton and McGuire, 2017). A public reinsurance program can provide insurers with risk protection without the profit margin collected by private reinsurers. Second, reinsurance acts as a subsidy to plans that attract costly individuals, potentially combatting adverse selection problems and weakening insurer incentives to distort plan benefits to attract healthy enrollees (Layton et al., 2017). Of course, these motivations must be weighed against the standard concern that reinsurance weakens plan incentives to control costs.

HHS recently proposed to modify the risk adjustment formula to include effective reinsurance for high-cost cases, though budget-neutral transfers across plans within the individual market rather than a transfer from group market plans to individual market plans (US Department of Health and Human Services, 2016a). The proposal calls for extremely high-cost cases to be pooled across insurers via the risk adjustment transfer formula discussed in Section 17.3. This option is explored along with an additional option of incorporating reinsurance into the risk adjustment formula developed in Layton and McGuire (2017), who show analytically that both the HHS proposal and their alternate plan (which incorporates spending above a threshold as a risk adjustment factor) are equivalent to a conventional budget neutral reinsurance policy. They also show that with a minor modification (accounting for reinsurance when estimating risk adjustment weights), these methods actually improve upon conventional reinsurance in terms of payment system fit. They argue that incorporating reinsurance into the risk adjustment system is better than a conventional public reinsurance system because all reinsurance-related administrative costs are eliminated. Finally, they show via simulation that all policies have significant effects on the probability that a small insurer faces a catastrophic loss, but essentially no effect on the level of risk faced by a large insurer. Notably, however, their proposal would not include the inflow of funds into the individual market that occurred under the ACA's reinsurance program.

HHS is currently implementing the risk adjustment formula modification just discussed for 2017. The current HHS rule calls for a policy that protects insurers from cases exceeding $1 million in a year. Choosing the "correct" level of protection is a difficult task because the benefits of insurer risk protection must be weighed against the possibility of weakening insurer incentives to control costs (e.g., via care management or aggressive price negotiations with providers). A policy providing partial coverage can mitigate this problem but will not fully eliminate it. Despite these difficulties, it is likely that a great deal of risk protection can be achieved with limited effects on insurer incentives: Layton and McGuire (2017) show that with a cutoff of $500,000, only 0.02% of their sample is affected, but risk of a large loss is greatly reduced for small insurers. Additionally, recent evidence shows that in Medicaid managed care insurers' ability to affect the spending of the high-cost cases affected by these reinsurance policies is fairly limited (Geruso et al., 2016b), suggesting that the weakening of insurer cost-control incentives for these extremely high-cost cases may be a second-order concern. It is important to note, however, that while this policy will protect insurers against risk, it will not provide a net subsidy to individual market plans as the previous reinsurance policy did.

## 17.5.2 Selection Against the Marketplaces Within the Individual Market

While the ACA established the Marketplaces, it did not require that all individual market policies be sold through them. It is not widely known that 38% of individuals with individual market coverage are enrolled in an off-Marketplace plan (US Department of Health and Human Services, 2016b). When individuals purchase off-Marketplace coverage, however, they are not eligible for the subsidies available when purchasing a plan on the Marketplace.

While all new off-Marketplace plans are required to comply with ACA rating and benefit rules, there are plans offered off-Marketplace in the individual market that are not subject to some of the new rules. These so-called "grandfathered" and "grandmothered" plans—the first a construct of the ACA law and the second the result of an administrative ruling—were intended to create a smooth transition to the fully reformed ACA individual market. However, these plans likely contribute to adverse selection against the ACA-compliant market, since healthier individuals are more likely to find the pre-ACA health-rated premiums to be attractive. These plans are decreasing in number and will likely be all but gone by 2018.

A grandfathered health plan is a plan that was in place on the date of enactment of the ACA (March 23, 2010) which has continuously covered at least one person and has not changed coverage terms. These plans are essentially exempt from all of the ACA market changes. Grandmothered plans were created as a transitional policy (to end December 31, 2017) by the administration to allow plans newly created between March 23, 2010 and January 1, 2014 to continue to operate under the post-2010 and pre-2014 rules for their existing enrollees if allowed by their regulating states. Grandmothered plans must comply with more ACA regulations than grandfathered plans (e.g., prohibition on annual and lifetime limits on coverage) but do not have to comply with rating and benefit rules put in place in 2014.

Even without the grandfathered and grandmothered plans, this off-Marketplace/on-Marketplace distinction presents a potential for adverse selection. While the entire individual market (both on- and off-Marketplace) makes up a single risk pool (for risk adjustment) and is subject to the same pricing and guaranteed issue regulations, the off-Marketplace individual market may still have more attractive enrollees. If lower-income individuals eligible for subsidies are higher cost *conditional on risk adjustment*, plans may wish to avoid them by only offering their products off-Marketplace, where subsidies are not available, an action allowed by most states. Many of the large insurers exiting the on-Marketplace market in 2017 remained in the off-Marketplace individual market, suggesting differential risk selection patterns in these two segments of the market (Families USA, 2012).[11] However, at this point there is no empirical evidence regarding the differential risk profiles on- and off-Marketplace. More research is needed to understand whether and to what extent this is a problem, and to what extent the price-linked subsidies available in the Marketplaces counteract the consequences of adverse selection.

### 17.5.3  Adverse Selection Into the Individual Market

While in the previous section we discuss selection against the Marketplaces within the individual market, we now turn to the topic of adverse selection into the entire individual market, both on- and off-Marketplace. The ACA includes both carrots (subsidies) and sticks (coverage mandates/penalties) to encourage Americans to obtain insurance. Both subsidies and mandates/penalties can address the consequences of adverse selection (Einav and Finkelstein, 2011). In the Marketplaces, the system of carrots and sticks has not led to complete take-up of insurance. Subsidies are only available to low- and middle-income enrollees, and the size of the subsidy declines with income, reaching zero for people whose incomes exceed 400% of the FPL. In contrast, in Medicare *all* consumers effectively receive a voucher equal to (or approximately equal to in the case that they choose a Medicare Advantage plan) their expected cost in Fee-for-Service Medicare. These limited subsidies mean that healthy middle- to high-income people may be unwilling to buy coverage at Marketplace prices, which reflect higher demand for insurance among the sick.

The stick in the ACA is an income-based tax penalty on all individuals who do not obtain insurance. While this stick encourages coverage, it appears to not be large enough to lead to universal take-up of insurance. In 2016, 10.7 million individuals eligible for coverage through the Marketplaces remained uninsured. A total of 8.1 million households paid a penalty for not purchasing insurance in 2015, with the average annual penalty equal to $210.

This mix of carrots and sticks makes the Marketplaces an experiment with regulated competition that allows for empirically relevant levels of "opting out" of the market. Allowing consumers to "opt-out" of coverage may interact in important ways with the payment system. Specifically, a budget-neutral risk adjustment system like the one embedded in the Marketplace payment system can only alleviate problems of adverse selection across plans *within* the market. Such a policy does nothing to weaken the forces of adverse selection *into* the market (i.e., healthier people choosing to remain uninsured).

Newhouse (2017) considers the design choice between the "zero-sum" Marketplace risk adjustment system versus the Medicare Advantage system. He makes the conceptual point that the zero-sum system protects the government from payment increases due to "upcoding" of conditions by insurers. But the cost is that the zero-sum system does not protect insurers from adverse selection into the market. He argues that selection into the market can still lead to death spirals, despite the presence of risk adjustment.

In fact, risk adjustment may have unintended consequences in this voluntary environment. Consider the case of an insurer that offers low-cost basic coverage and an insurer that offers high-cost enhanced coverage. With no risk adjustment, the price of the basic plan will be low due to its low costs *and* its healthy enrollees. If risk adjustment is implemented, the basic plan will be required to pay transfers to the enhanced plan to compensate the enhanced plan for its sicker enrollees. This will increase the price of the basic plan and decrease the price of the enhanced plan, leading some individuals to shift from basic to enhanced coverage. But it may also lead some individuals in the basic plan to drop out of the market due to the plan's higher price, possibly worsening welfare. The net efficiency consequences of risk adjustment in this environment are thus theoretically ambiguous.[12]

Panhans (2016) provides recent evidence on the extent of this problem. He exploits price variation due to rating area boundaries to find that a 1% increase in premiums in a given market leads to a 0.8% increase in the average cost in the market. He also estimates willingness-to-pay for insurance, allowing him to use the Einav et al. (2010) framework to assess the welfare losses due to adverse selection in these markets. His analysis suggests that the current premium subsidies are "too low," and that higher subsidies would improve welfare. He also finds that age-targeted subsidies that are higher for younger consumers are a more efficient way to improve welfare than the income-based subsidies currently in place (a point also made by Tebaldi [2016]).

### 17.5.4 Transfer Formula

The mechanism by which risk adjustment is implemented in the Marketplaces is the so-called risk adjustment "transfer formula" presented in Section 17.3. Interestingly, the transfer formula used in the Marketplaces differs from that of most other public health insurance programs. One key feature of the transfer formula may have important implications for adverse selection and the incentive for an insurer to offer generous plans.

Other public insurance markets (e.g., Medicare Advantage (MA) and the pre-ACA Massachusetts Connector) use an "own-price" transfer formula. After calculating an enrollee's risk score—which captures the person's expected costliness relative to an average individual—the risk score multiplies the *plan's price* to determine what the insurer receives. So a plan with price $P_j$ that covers an enrollee with risk score $r_i$ receives a payment of $r_i P_j$. This payment can be written as the sum of the plan's price plus a transfer amount:

$$Payment_{ij} = P_j + (r_i - 1) \cdot P_j \qquad \text{(MAFormula)}$$

The key feature of the MA's own price formula is that the transfer amount scales with both the enrollee's risk score and the plan's price.

The ACA Marketplaces use a different transfer formula, which we call an "average price" transfer. Conceptually, the transfer is based on the enrollee risk score times the *average plan price* in the market, $\overline{P}$.[13] Formally:

$$Payment_{ij} = P_j + (r_i - 1) \cdot \overline{P} \qquad \text{(ACAFormula)}$$

Because Marketplace risk scores are normalized to have mean 1.0 (as discussed above), the ACA formula ensures that transfers are budget neutral when averaged over all enrollees and plans. Guaranteeing budget neutrality seems to be the practical reason this formula was adopted (Pope et al., 2014).

However, the different format has real implications for payments to different types of plans and therefore insurer incentives. Specifically, high-price plans (i.e., $P_j > \overline{P}$) that attract sicker enrollees ($r_i > 1$) do worse under the ACA's average price formula than under the MA own-price formula. If high-price plans have a higher cost structure (e.g., because they have a broader provider network), then the transfer for sicker enrollees may not make up for these enrollees' extra costs.[14] Insurers would then have an incentive to discontinue high-cost, high-price plans that are adversely selected on *observable* risk—even if there is no unobserved risk selection. This dynamic would augment any incentive to reduce generosity because of unobserved risk selection (as we discussed earlier).[15]

This brief analysis of differences between these two risk adjustment systems serves to cast light on a component of risk adjustment systems that has not received much attention from researchers but that can have important implications for the plan payment and thus market outcomes. All countries implicitly use some form of a transfer formula. This analysis shows that it may be beneficial for policymakers and researchers to study these formulas more explicitly. More research is needed in this area to understand the empirical significance of the differences between transfer formulas. Additional work is also needed in order to understand the efficiency consequences of transfer formula design. For example, in the case of the MA versus the Marketplace formula it is not clear whether the ACA's formula is more or less desirable than MA's for achieving efficient market outcomes. It is possible that the MA formula overpays high-price plans for sick enrollees, leading to levels of generosity that are "too high" from a social efficiency perspective and too little competition on prices.

## 17.5.5 Price-Linked Subsidies

A key feature of the Marketplaces' subsidies is that they are linked to insurers' prices, specifically the price of the second-cheapest silver-tier plan in a given market. Subsidies are set so that this plan's postsubsidy price equals an "affordable" amount based on a consumer's income (which varies between 2% and 10% of monthly income). If a consumer buys a higher- or lower-price plan, they pay or save the incremental price, as long as this does not push their payment below zero.

Jaffe and Shepard (2017) and Tebaldi (2016) analyze what this "price-linked" subsidy design means for competition, relative to a system in which policymakers set a "fixed" subsidy amount based on their best estimate of what prices will be. They show that price-linking weakens price competition, since insurers that expect to be "subsidy pivotal" have a greater incentive to markup their plans' prices.

However, the price-linked design also has desirable properties in the presence of uncertainty about medical costs or the selection of consumers into the Marketplaces. In particular, if all prices rise in tandem (e.g., because of a cost increase from an expensive new drug), government subsidies automatically increase to bear the costs. Essentially, the government bears the risk of unexpected price/cost shocks, which Jaffe and Shepard (2017) argue is desirable in some circumstances. In particular, they argue that price linking may stabilize participation and the level of coverage. For instance, if prices increase sharply—as was occurring in the Marketplaces in 2017—the automatic adjustment to subsidies means that *postsubsidy* prices (for the benchmark plan) will not increase for the ~85% of enrollees who are below 400% of poverty and receive federal subsidies. Therefore, it is unlikely that there will be a substantial reduction in coverage for this group. Price-linked subsidies therefore may be able to arrest an adverse selection death spiral before it starts. Of course, the inverse is true as well: if costs decline unexpectedly, there will not be gains in coverage, as federal subsidies will instead fall.

## ENDNOTES

1. The ACA has had much larger impacts on the uninsurance rate, but most of those impacts seem to have come via expansion of the Medicaid program and the "woodwork" effect of increasing take-up of Medicaid among already eligible individuals who were not enrolled.
2. In practice, the regulator selected a large sample of individuals with employer-provided health insurance and used that sample to construct an actuarial value calculator used by the regulator to determine plan actuarial value (and, thus, metal tier) and by the insurer to design the cost-sharing features of their plans.
3. For reference, 90% actuarial value (platinum) is similar to a generous employer-sponsored insurance plan, while 60% actuarial value (bronze) is equivalent to a high-deductible plan.
4. Throughout this section a plan refers to a product-by-rating area pair, so we consider the same plan offered in two rating areas as two plans.
5. Recall that the "insurer price" is allowed to vary because of risk selection. A single insurer, however, is not supposed to vary premiums across its plans because of anticipated risk selection. The motivation for this asymmetric restriction on including risk selection factors in premiums is not totally clear.
6. Regulators review not only the premiums themselves but the assumptions that map from the insurer premium to the plan premiums. It is this review that allows the regulator to (loosely) enforce the regulations outlined above regarding what factors can and cannot be considered in the development of plan premiums.
7. At the time of tax filing, households with incomes greater than 400% FPL must pay back the full difference between the tax credit they actually received and the tax credit they should have received. Households with incomes less than 400% FPL repay only part of this difference.
8. Costs are defined in the same manner in which the medical loss ratio is defined for the same market.
9. See Rose et al. (2015) for a discussion of the methods that produced this dataset.
10. As a result, the end of reinsurance has been cited as a contributing factor for the large (and politically damaging) premium increases in 2017.
11. An HIPAA provision may also have contributed to the decision by these insurers to remain in the off-Marketplace individual market. The provision states that if an insurer exits the individual market, it is banned from re-entering the market for 5 years.
12. We note that the mechanism discussed in this paragraph applies only to the Marketplaces' unsubsidized enrollees. For subsidized enrollees, the ACA's "price-linked" subsidy design (see discussion below) means if there is adverse selection into the market, subsidies automatically increase to keep the postsubsidy price of the basic plan equal to a target "affordable" amount.
13. The full ACA transfer formula is conceptually similar but more complicated (see Section 17.3.3).
14. Note that the logic we have discussed requires that the cost increase of a high-cost plan for sicker enrollees must be greater than for healthier enrollees. This would be true, for instance, if a high-cost plan raised all enrollees' costs proportionally (e.g., by 20%), but would not be true if it raised all enrollees' costs by a fixed amount (e.g., $50).

15. Interestingly, low-price ($P_j < \overline{P}$) plans that attract healthy ($r_i < 1$) enrollees also do worse under the ACA's formula. This suggests that rather than a "race to the bottom"—as typically occurs under adverse selection—there could be a "race to the middle." In practice, if enrollees are highly price-sensitive, the average price will be close to the cheapest plans' prices, making this issue more significant for high-price plans. Additionally, if the "own-price" transfer formula were modified to be budget neutral by adding a per capita risk adjustment fee equal to the average risk adjustment transfer, low-cost plans would likely be worse off under the "average price" formula relative to the "budget neutral own-price" formula.

## REFERENCES

"2016 Qualified Health Plan Recertification and New Entrant Regulation." In Proceedings of California Health Benefit Exchange Board Meeting. Sacramento, CA. January 15, 2015. Accessed January 10, 2017. http://board.coveredca.com/meetings/2015/1-15/QHP%20Recert%20and%20New%20Entrant%20Regulation%20text%20and%20docs.pdf.

Adler, L., Ginsburg, P., 2016, July 16. Obamacare Premiums Are Lower Than You Think. Retrieved from: http://healthaffairs.org/blog/2016/07/21/obamacare-premiums-are-lower-than-you-think/.

Center for Medicare and Medicaid Services: The Center for Consumer Information & Insurance Oversight, 2015. Medical Loss Ratio Data and System Resources. 10 Jan. 2017. Retrieved from: https://www.cms.gov/CCIIO/Resources/Data-Resources/mlr.html.

Dafny, L., Gruber, J., Ody, C., 2015. More Insurers, Lower Premiums: Evidence from Initial Pricing in the Health Insurance Marketplaces. Am. J. Health. Econ. 1 (1), 53–81.

Einav, L., Finkelstein, A., 2011. Selection in insurance markets: theory and empirics in pictures. J. Econ. Perspect. 25 (1), 15–138. Winter.

Einav, L., Finkelstein, A., Cullen, M., 2010. Estimating welfare in insurance markets using variation in prices. Quart. J. Econ. 123 (3), 877–921.

Ellis, R., McGuire, T., 2007. Predictability and predictiveness in health care spending. J. Health Econ. 26 (1), 25–48.

Families USA, 2012. When a Health Insurer Leaves the Individual Market: What States Can Do Before Certain Affordable Care Act Changes Take Effect in 2014. May 1. Accessed 10 January 2017. Retrieved from: http://familiesusa.org/sites/default/files/ product_documents/When-Insurers-Leave-Individual-Market.pdf.

Frean, M., Gruber, J., Sommers, B., 2017. Premium subsidies, the mandate, and Medicaid expansion: coverage effects of the Affordable Care Act. J. Health Econ. 53, 72–86.

Geurso, M., Layton, T.J., 2015. Upcoding or Selection? Evidence from Medicare on Squishy Risk Adjustment. NBER Working Paper 21222.

Geruso, M., Layton, T.J., Prinz, D., 2018. Screening in contract design: evidence from the aca health insurance exchanges. Forthcoming at Am. Econ. J. Econ. Policy.

Geruso, M., Layton, T., Wallace, J., 2016b. Are All Managed Care Plans Created Equal? Evidence from Random Plan Assignment in New York Medicaid Managed Care. In preparation.

Geruso, M., McGuire, T.G., 2016. Tradeoffs in the design of health plan payment systems: fit, power, and balance. J. Health Econ. 47, 1–19.

Handel, B., Hendel, I., Whinston, M., 2015. Equilibria in health exchanges: advrse selection vs. reclassification risk supplement. Econometrica 83 (4), 1261–1313.

Jaffe, S., Shepard, M., 2017. Price-Linked Subsidies and Health Insurance Markups. NBER Working Paper 23104.

Kaiser Family Foundation, Marketplace Enrollment as a Share of the Potential Marketplace Population. March 31, 2016. http://kff.org/health-reform/state-indicator/marketplace-enroll-ment-as-a-share-of-the-potential-marketplace-population-2015/?currentTimeframe = 0#.

Kautter, J., Pope, G.C., Ingber, M., Freeman, S., Patterson, L., Cohen, M., et al., 2014. The HHS-HCC risk adjustment model for individual and small group markets under the afford-able care act. Med. Med. Res. Rev. 4 (3), E1−E11.

Layton, T.J., 2017. Imperfect risk adjustment, risk preferences, and sorting in competitive health insurance markets. J. Health Econ. 56, 259−280.

Layton, T.J., McGuire, T.G., 2017. Marketplace plan payment options for dealing with high-cost enrollees. Am. J. Health Econ. 3 (2), 165−191.

Layton, T.J., McGuire, T.G., Sinaiko, A.D., 2016. Risk corridors and reinsurance in health insur-ance exchanges: insurance for insurers. Am. J. Health Econ. 2 (1), 66−95.

Layton, T.J., Ellis, R.P., McGuire, T.G., van Kleef, R., 2017. Measuring efficiency of health plan payment systems in managed competition health insurance markets. J. Health Econ. 56, 237−255.

McGuire, T., Newhouse, J., Normand, S.-L.T., Shi, J., Zuvekas, S., 2014. Assessing incentives for service-level selection in private health insurance marketplaces. J. Health Econ. 35 (1), 47−63.

Montz, E.J., Layton, T.J., Busch, A.B., Ellis, R.B., Rose, S., McGuire, T.G., 2016. Risk-adjust-ment simulation: plans may have incentives to distort mental health and substance use cov-erage. Health Aff. 25 (6), 1022−1028.

Newhouse, J.P., 2017. Risk adjustment with an outside option. J. Health Econ. 26, 256−258.

Panhans, 2016. Adverse selection in ACA markets: evidence from Colorado. Working paper.

Pope, et al., 2014. Risk transfer formula for individual and small group markets under the Affordable Care Act. Med. Med. Res. Rev. 4 (3), E1−E23.

Shepard, M., 2016. Hospital Network Competition and Adverse Selection: Evidence from the Massachusetts Health Insurance Exchange. NBER Working Paper 22600.

Tebaldi, P., 2016. Estimating Equilibrium in Health Insurance Exchanges: Price Competition and Subsidy Design under the ACA. Working paper.

U.S. Department of Health and Human Services, September 6, 2016a. Patient Protection and Affordable Care Act; HHS Notice of Benefit and Payment Parameters for 2018" 81 Fed. Reg. 61455.

U.S. Department of Health and Human Services, 2016b. ASPE Data Point: About 2.5 Million People Who Currently Buy Coverage Off-Marketplace May Be Eligible for ACA Subsidies. https://aspe. hhs.gov/sites/default/files/pdf/208306/OffMarketplaceSubsidyeligible.pdf. Updated October 4, 2016. Accessed January 10, 2017.

U.S. Government Accountability Office, A Report to Congressional Committees on Private Health Insurance. GAO-16-724. http://www.gao.gov/assets/680/679500.pdf. Published September 6, 2016. Accessed January 10, 2017.

# FURTHER READING

Layton, T.J., Ellis, R.P., McGuire, T.G., 2015. Assessing Incentives for Adverse Selection in Health Plan Payment Systems. NBER Working Paper 21531.

U.S. Department of Health and Human Services, 2014. ASPE Issue Brief: How Many Individuals Might Have Marketplace Coverage After the 2015 Open Enrollment Period? https://aspe.hhs.gov/sites/default/files/pdf/208306/OffMarketplaceSubsidyeligible.pdf. Updated October 4, 2016. Accessed January 10, 2017.

U.S. Department of Health and Human Services, 2015. March 31, 2015 Effectuated Enrollment Snapshot. https://www.cms.gov/Newsroom/ MediaReleaseDatabase/ Fact-sheets/2015-Fact-sheets-items/2015-06-02.html. Updated March 31, 2015. Accessed January 10, 2017.

Chapter 18

# Health Plan Payment in Medicaid Managed Care: A Hybrid Model of Regulated Competition

**Timothy J. Layton[1], Alice Ndikumana[2] and Mark Shepard[3]**
[1]*Department of Health Care Policy, Harvard Medical School and the NBER, Boston, MA, United States,* [2]*Harvard University, Cambridge, MA, United States,* [3]*Kennedy School of Government, Harvard University and the NBER, Cambridge, MA, United States*

## 18.1 INTRODUCTION

Medicaid, the public program for providing low-income and disabled Americans with health insurance coverage, is the largest payer for healthcare services in the United States. As of August 2016, over 73 million Americans (almost one quarter of the US population) were enrolled in the Medicaid program (CMS, 2016a). In 2015, total Medicaid spending exceeded $550 billion (almost one-fifth of total US healthcare spending) (Kaiser Family Foundation, 2016).

Unlike Medicare, a federal program that is nationwide and uniform across states, Medicaid is a joint state-federal program. The federal government provides substantial funding for the program and in return regulates which populations must be covered by a state's Medicaid program and what benefits must be provided. States, in turn, have significant flexibility to cover additional populations and provide additional benefits. Importantly for this chapter, states can also choose whether to provide Medicaid benefits through a publicly managed fee-for-service (FFS) program or to contract out the provision of Medicaid benefits to private managed care organizations (MCOs), also known as Medicaid Managed Care (MMC) plans. Over time, states have increasingly moved toward managed care, with around 60% of Medicaid recipients enrolled in a private managed care plan by 2014 (CMS, 2016b). As part of these MMC programs, states often let individuals choose among multiple competing MMC plans and/or between a private MMC plan and a

Risk Adjustment, Risk Sharing and Premium Regulation in Health Insurance Markets.
DOI: https://doi.org/10.1016/B978-0-12-811325-7.00018-X
**523**

public FFS Medicaid plan—an arrangement similar to competition between private Medicare Advantage plans and Traditional Medicare.

As in the other individual health insurance markets covered in this volume, MMC exhibits some features of regulated competition, though, as we explain below, MMC uses a unique and interesting flavor of regulated competition that leverages procurement rules to introduce the forces of competition at the initial procurement stage rather than at the level of consumer plan choice. In a sense, state Medicaid agencies can use their regulatory position to construct a low-cost, high-quality "network of health plans"—analogous to how health plans themselves attempt to construct low-cost, high-quality networks of healthcare providers.

State experimentation with regulated competition in Medicaid began in the early 1970s, with California leading the way (Sparer, 2012). Growth was slow until the "managed care revolution" of the 1990s when managed care enrollment increased dramatically both in Medicaid and in other sectors of the US health insurance market. However, managed care in Medicaid continued to grow dramatically even during the subsequent "managed care backlash" in the late 1990s and 2000s.[1] Most of the initial enrollment in MMC was concentrated among pregnant women, mothers, and children, but more recently MMC enrollment has been growing among aged, disabled, and chronically ill Medicaid recipients (MACPAC, 2011).

In addition to the expansion of managed care enrollment, there has been an increase in the use of regulated competition principles by MMC programs. Initially, when states adopted managed care, payments to health plans were negotiated individually with each plan on an annual basis; risk adjustment was primitive and limited to demographics and eligibility category; and "competition" consisted of one plan competing with the public FFS plan. Today, plan payments are often either based on competitive bids or set administratively, more sophisticated risk adjustment is widely used, and competition among MMC plans is more robust in many areas. Increasingly, MMC programs look like traditional health insurance markets organized around the principles of regulated competition—including markets like Medicare Advantage and national health insurance systems in the Netherlands, Germany, and Switzerland.

While MMC is adopting more features of regulated competition, its design is also rooted in its history as a public program for the poor. In many ways, state Medicaid programs treat MMC plans as *contractors* administering welfare benefits rather than as *competitors* in a regulated health insurance market. This theme shows up in several ways in MMC programs. First, there are generally no premiums in Medicaid. The program is largely free to recipients. While a few states have adopted nominal premiums for select (and small) populations, these premiums are charged for entry into Medicaid, not based on a recipient's plan choice. In other words, even when they exist, Medicaid premiums do not vary across plans. This implies that insurers cannot "pass through" any savings to Medicaid enrollees in the form of lower premiums. As we discuss below, this policy effectively rules out the standard form of price competition used in typical markets and which was a key principle of Enthoven and Kronick's (1989) regulated competition model. Instead, this channels consumer-driven competition into the quality dimension of the product. This forces state Medicaid agencies to employ other tools to restrain spending growth, such as administrative rate-setting, exclusion of high-price plans from the market, and auto-assignment targeted to lower-price plans.

Second, most benefits (including cost sharing and covered services) are fixed across plans, following a state-specified schedule. Per federal rules, this schedule has minimal cost-sharing, removing demand-side incentives from the insurer's toolkit for encouraging efficient use of health care. This design is based on the idea that almost any cost sharing is considered "unaffordable" for indigent Medicaid recipients and therefore an undue barrier to accessing care. Insurers do, however, have flexibility to design medical provider networks (subject to minimum network adequacy rules), prescription drug formularies, and utilization review/care management practices.

Finally, health plan choice differs substantially from the traditional model of regulated competition. Many Medicaid recipients fail to actively choose an MMC plan, leaving the state to administratively assign them to one—assignment which is often random or quasirandom. States often use this assignment policy as part of the contracting process with MMC plans. A common policy is to use assignment to equalize market share, effectively ensuring all plans with a contract receive an adequate number of enrollees. More recently, as we describe in more detail below, states have also begun to experiment with assignment rules that are tied to elements of a plan's bid such as the plan's capitation rate or plan quality ratings.

It is also important to understand that unlike Medicare, Medicaid differs substantially across states, making it not one program but 52 programs (50 states plus DC and Puerto Rico). States differ both in whether they use managed care at all and in which features of regulated competition they adopt. For example, some states like Connecticut do not contract with private managed care plans, relying exclusively on the public FFS plan.[2] On the other hand, states like New York have robust managed care programs that use regulated competition principles like plan choice, open enrollment periods, and risk adjustment. Then there are states like Missouri, which uses administratively set government payments to plans but restricts entry to three plans per region via a competitive procurement process aimed at extracting the highest level of quality out of the competing health plans. Using the state's power over entry into the market as a tool to improve outcomes is an example of how procurement policy can shape competitive dynamics in Medicaid markets. This tool perhaps represents a new instrument to be considered in the "regulated competition" toolkit. This can also be thought of as a form of "selective contracting," analogous to the way health plans use the threat of exclusion from their provider networks to induce competition among providers.

Because of these significant differences across states, instead of going into great detail describing a particular state's payment system, below we attempt to describe broadly how plan payment works across different types of states. The remainder of the chapter is organized as follows. Section 18.2 discusses the organization of the MMC system. Section 18.3 discusses health plan payment design, and Section 18.4 discusses the (very limited) research evaluating MMC plan payment. Section 18.5 concludes by discussing ongoing issues and reforms.

## 18.2 ORGANIZATION OF THE HEALTH INSURANCE SYSTEM

The organization of the MMC health insurance system is complex. State MMC programs vary in plan design requirements, procurement methods, and plan options for beneficiaries. Each state, subject to federal regulations, defines a set of covered health services, allowable cost-sharing amounts, and provider network adequacy requirements for participating managed care plans. Some states contract with any insurer that complies with its requirements. Other states are selective, contracting only with insurers that win a competitive procurement process on the basis of price and/or other features of plan bids, such as the use of alternative payment models, care management practices, and other state priorities. Prices (also known as "capitation rates") paid by the state Medicaid program to insurers may be determined through the competitive plan selection process or may be set administratively or through negotiation with private insurers.

Once a menu of plans has been determined, Medicaid recipients either choose a plan or are assigned to a plan, following the regulations of their state. If recipients choose their plan, their choice may be influenced by marketing, outreach programs, and brokers or "navigators" provided by Medicaid. In this section we will discuss plan design, procurement, and choice in greater detail to provide an overview of how the MMC health insurance market operates.

### 18.2.1 Plan Design Regulations

State Medicaid programs determine which benefits must be covered by managed care plans. This decision consists of three components. First, states decide which services will be covered in their Medicaid programs beyond the services required by the federal government (if any). Second, states decide who will provide the services: a private MMC plan, a specialty MCO, or the state's FFS Medicaid program. Third, the state chooses certain parameters regulating how managed care plans provide the services.

## 18.2.1.1    Covered Services

The federal government defines a set of mandatory benefits that states are required to provide for Medicaid enrollees, outlined in Table 18.1. For example, Early and Periodic Screening, Diagnostic, and Treatment (EPSDT) services are required for enrollees under 21 years of age to facilitate early identification and diagnosis of physical and mental disorders, as well as early initiation of the appropriate treatment. States are also required to provide pregnancy-related services, including prenatal care, delivery, postpartum care, and family planning. Federal rules prohibit cost sharing for both EPSDT and pregnancy-related services.

States may elect to also provide optional benefits for Medicaid enrollees, listed in Table 18.2. While prescription drug coverage is technically optional, all states provide the benefit, though 22 states require nominal copayments for covered drugs (KFF, 2017a). Other notable optional benefits include adult dental, physical therapy and rehabilitation, and optometry. Federal regulations require that benefits are equivalent across beneficiaries and across the state in duration, amount, and scope (MACPAC, 2017).

## 18.2.1.2    Managed Care Carve-Outs

When states adopt managed care, they may not do so for all covered Medicaid services[3] or traditional FFS Medicaid. The most commonly carved

**TABLE 18.1** Mandatory Covered Benefits

| Mandatory Benefits | |
|---|---|
| Inpatient hospital services | Laboratory and X-ray services |
| Outpatient hospital services | Nursing facility services (for ages 21 and over) |
| Physician services | Nurse midwife services |
| Early and Periodic Screening, Diagnostic, and Treatment services (for individuals under age 21) | Certified pediatric or family nurse practitioner services |
| Family planning services and supplies | Rural health clinic services |
| Federally qualified health centers | Tobacco cessation counseling and pharmacotherapy for pregnant women |
| Freestanding birth centers | Nonemergency transportation to medical care |
| Home health services | |

Source: Centers for Medicare &Medicaid Services (CMS) https://www.medicaid.gov/medicaid/benefits/list-of-benefits/index.html.

**TABLE 18.2** Optional Covered Benefits

**Optional Benefits**

| | |
|---|---|
| Prescribed drugs | Dentures |
| Intermediate care facility services for individuals with intellectual disabilities | Personal care services |
| Clinic services | Private duty nursing services |
| Occupational therapy services | Program of All-inclusive Care for the Elderly (PACE) services |
| Optometry services | Chiropractic services |
| Physical therapy services | Critical access hospital services |
| Targeted case management services | Respiratory care for ventilator dependent individuals |
| Prosthetic devices | Primary care case management services |
| Hospice services | Services furnished in a religious nonmedical health care institution |
| Inpatient psychiatric services for individuals under age 21 | Tuberculosis-related services |
| Dental services | Home- and community-based services |
| Eyeglasses | Health homes for enrollees with chronic conditions |
| Speech, hearing, and language disorder services | Other licensed practitioners' services |
| Inpatient hospital and nursing facility services for individuals age 65 or older in institutions for mental diseases | Emergency hospital services in a hospital not meeting certain Medicare or Medicaid requirements |
| Other diagnostic, screening, preventive, and rehabilitative services | |

Source: Centers for Medicare & Medicaid Services (CMS) https://www.medicaid.gov/medicaid/benefits/list-of-benefits/index.html

out benefits are prescription drugs, behavioral health, and dental services. Table 18.3 outlines which states carved out each of these services in 2014. States may carve out benefits that they conclude would be more effectively administered and financed outside of a comprehensive managed care plan. Carve-outs may also have the beneficial property of protecting services that may be vulnerable to risk selection. Frank et al. (1996) and Frank et al. (2000) note that MMC plans have strong incentives to inefficiently ration services that are predictably used by high-cost, unprofitable individuals. By removing these services from the MMC plan contracts and financing them

**TABLE 18.3** Benefit Carve-Out

| State | Comprehensive MCO | Dental | Behavioral health | Prescription drugs |
|---|---|---|---|---|
| Alabama | | – | – | – |
| Alaska | | – | – | – |
| Arizona | ♦ | ✓ | ✗ | ✓ |
| Arkansas | | – | – | – |
| California | ♦ | ✗ | ✗ | ✓ |
| Colorado | ♦ | ✗ | ✗ | ✓ |
| Connecticut | | – | – | – |
| Delaware | ♦ | ✓ | ✓ | ✓ |
| District of Columbia | ♦ | ✓ | ✓ | ✓ |
| Florida | ♦ | ✓ | ✗ | ✓ |
| Georgia | ♦ | ✓ | ✓ | ✓ |
| Hawaii | ♦ | ✓ | ✓ | ✓ |
| Idaho | ♦ | ✓ | ✓ | ✓ |
| Illinois | ♦ | ✗ | ✓ | ✗ |
| Indiana | ♦ | ✗ | ✓ | ✗ |
| Iowa | ♦ | ✗ | ✗ | ✓ |
| Kansas | ♦ | ✓ | ✓ | ✓ |
| Kentucky | ♦ | ✓ | ✗ | ✓ |
| Louisiana | ♦ | ✗ | ✗ | ✗ |
| Maine | | – | – | – |
| Maryland | ♦ | ✓ | ✗ | ✓ |
| Massachusetts | ♦ | ✓ | ✓ | ✓ |
| Michigan | ♦ | ✗ | ✗ | ✓ |
| Minnesota | ♦ | ✓ | ✓ | ✓ |
| Mississippi | ♦ | ✓ | ✗ | ✓ |
| Missouri | ♦ | ✓ | ✓ | ✗ |
| Montana | | – | – | – |
| Nebraska | ♦ | ✗ | ✗ | ✗ |
| Nevada | ♦ | ✓ | ✓ | ✓ |

*(Continued)*

**TABLE 18.3** (Continued)

| State | Comprehensive MCO | Dental | Behavioral health | Prescription drugs |
|---|---|---|---|---|
| New Hampshire | ♦ | ✗ | ✓ | ✓ |
| New Jersey | ♦ | ✓ | ✓ | ✓ |
| New Mexico | ♦ | ✓ | ✓ | ✓ |
| New York | ♦ | ✓ | ✓ | ✓ |
| North Carolina | | − | − | − |
| North Dakota | ♦ | ✓ | ✓ | ✓ |
| Ohio | ♦ | ✓ | ✓ | ✓ |
| Oklahoma | | − | − | − |
| Oregon | ♦ | ✓ | ✓ | ✓ |
| Pennsylvania | ♦ | ✓ | ✗ | ✓ |
| Puerto Rico | ♦ | ✓ | ✗ | ✓ |
| Rhode Island | ♦ | ✗ | ✓ | ✓ |
| South Carolina | ♦ | ✗ | ✓ | ✓ |
| South Dakota | | − | − | − |
| Tennessee | ♦ | ✗ | ✓ | ✗ |
| Texas | ♦ | ✗ | ✓ | ✗ |
| Utah | ♦ | ✗ | ✗ | ✓ |
| Vermont | ♦ | ✓ | ✓ | ✓ |
| Virginia | ♦ | ✗ | ✓ | ✓ |
| Washington | ♦ | ✗ | ✗ | ✓ |
| West Virginia | ♦ | ✓ | ✗ | ✓ |
| Wisconsin | ♦ | ✓ | ✓ | Varies |
| Wyoming | | − | − | − |
| **Total Comp. MCO:** | **42** | − | − | − |
| **Total carved-in:** | − | 26 | 26 | 34 |
| **Total carved-out:** | − | 16 | 16 | 7 |

✓carved in; ✗ carved out; ♦ state contracts with comprehensive MCO; − N/A
Source: Compiled from the Centers for Medicare and Medicaid Services (CMS) Managed Care State Profiles https://www.medicaid.gov/medicaid/managed-care/state-profiles/index.html.

separately, states can ensure access to these services is maintained under MMC.

Behavioral health care is the most prominent example of a service often carved out of managed care contracts. Specialized behavioral health providers are often separate from the rest of the healthcare system—such as psychiatric hospitals or outpatient behavioral health clinics. Some professionals are nonphysician healthcare providers who specialize in behavioral health, such as clinical social workers and psychologists.[4] While carving out behavioral health has been the norm in MMC, a growing number of states have reversed course, "carving in" behavioral health into MMC plan contracts. Among the 42 states that offered MMC plans in 2014, 16 states carved out behavioral health (CMS, 2016b) whereas in 2010, 21 of 36 states offering MMC plans carved out behavioral health (Gifford et al., 2011).

States may also carve out benefits in response to federal policies. For example, prior to the Affordable Care Act (ACA), prescription drugs provided through MMC plans were not eligible for the Medicaid drug rebate program, which required pharmaceutical companies to provide substantial discounts to Medicaid programs. As of 2010, the rebate program was expanded to include drugs financed through MMC, prompting some states (such as New York) to carve prescription drug coverage into managed care plan contracts (MACPAC, 2011; KFF, 2011).

### 18.2.1.3 Regulation of MMC Plan Benefits

Premiums and cost sharing are restricted to nominal levels in MMC plans, and prohibited for certain services and populations. Medicaid serves low-income individuals and families, for whom cost sharing typical in commercial insurance plans is perceived as unaffordable. Because of this, states impose maximum allowable amounts for premiums and cost sharing that vary by service, income level, and beneficiary type, in accordance with federal regulations. Cost sharing is prohibited for emergency services, family planning services, pregnancy-related services, or preventive services for children (Brooks et al., 2016). Furthermore, the sum of premium and cost-sharing liabilities cannot exceed 5% of a family's income (Medicaid and Children's Health, 2013).

Some cost sharing, however, is allowed in a few cases. For example, some states allow the use of variable copayments for prescription drugs to steer beneficiaries to more cost-effective drugs included on a preferred drug list. Federal regulations limit the maximum allowable copay for prescription drugs to $4 for preferred drugs and $8 for nonpreferred drugs, though state limits may be more restrictive. MMC plans may also elect to include lower cost sharing than the maximum allowed by the state. As a result, cost sharing may vary between MMC plan offerings and the FFS option, or between participating MMC plan offerings.

While cost sharing is strictly regulated, MMC plans have more flexibility in other areas of plan benefit design. The most important area is provider network design. Medicaid plan provider networks are perceived as some of the narrowest in the American health insurance market (though hard evidence to support this perception is limited), indicating that MMC insurers use this tool to limit healthcare costs among their enrollees (Draper et al., 2004; Mershon, 2016). In practice, the de facto networks for these plans may be even smaller than the set of providers listed in the network. A 2013 study by the US Department of Health and Human Services found that about half of listed providers in managed care networks did not offer appointments to enrollees (OIG, 2014).

Managed care plans are permitted to limit provider networks in accordance with network adequacy standards. Federal regulations require that all states define access standards for MMC plans to ensure that enrollees have adequate and timely access to all covered services. States must also develop a plan to monitor access, including an external review of access standards. Network adequacy standards must require MMC plans to consider anticipated enrollment, utilization, and geographic location when constructing their provider network. If a covered service cannot be delivered by an in-network provider, a managed care plan must cover the service at an out-of-network provider with no additional cost to the beneficiary (OIG, 2014).

MMC plans are generally health maintenance organizations (HMOs), which do not cover out-of-network services when an in-network provider is available. However, federal regulations require that MMC plans must cover out-of-network care for emergency and family planning services, both of which are also exempt from patient cost sharing. MMC plans are required to communicate which benefits may be obtained out-of-network and how to obtain those benefits. For example, insurers may require prior authorization for nonemergency services obtained at an out-of-network provider when an in-network provider was not available. Out-of-network providers are prohibited from billing the patient for the difference between the amount reimbursed by the MMC plan and the provider's customary charge. Additionally, payments to providers for out-of-network care are not governed by predetermined contracts. As a result, costly case-by-case negotiations between insurers and providers may arise to determine reimbursement. The 2005 Deficit Reduction Act attempted to address this issue by requiring providers to accept payments made for out-of-network emergency services at the equivalent Medicaid FFS rate (Center for Medicaid and State Operations, 2006). Some states have established policies to govern reimbursement for nonemergency out-of-network payments as well. For example, in Florida, a Medicaid plan must reimburse an out-of-network provider the lesser of the Medicaid FFS rate or the provider's customary charges (Lewin Group).

Federal network adequacy regulations discussed so far leave states considerable flexibility to develop state-specific network adequacy standards, leading to significant variations across states. Common criteria for network adequacy used by states include distance or time of travel to provider, availability of appointments within a given timeframe, and a defined ratio of providers to enrollees. Standards may or may not be specified differently for different types of providers, such as a PCP or obstetrician. Additionally, for a given network adequacy criterion, the exact requirement may vary significantly across states. For example, in 2013, among states that had a provision for the maximum enrollee-to-PCP ratio, the maximum allowed ratio varied from 100 enrollees per PCP to 2,500 enrollees per PCP (OIG, 2014).

### 18.2.2  Procurement and Competition

States use varying procurement methods to select insurers for MMC programs. Some states contract with all insurers that meet specified requirements. Most states, however, use competitive procurement to select insurers on the basis of cost and/or other features of plan bids such as quality and proposals for fulfilling particular state priorities such as the adoption of alternative models of provider payment. States generally contract with MCOs for 1–3 years and may include an option for 1-year renewals.[5]

Table 18.4 indicates which states use competitive versus noncompetitive selection methods. In a competitive procurement model, states issue a request for proposals (RFP) that informs insurers about the Medicaid program requirements and solicits a cost bid and/or a technical proposal from insurers. The cost bid may include factors such as the insurer's historical financial performance, administrative costs, projected costs for delivering Medicaid benefits, or a proposed capitation rate. States may communicate a range of acceptable (i.e., "actuarially sound") capitation rate bids in the RFP. In some cases, the cost bid is used to determine the capitation rate. Alternatively, some states use competitive procurement to select plans, but capitation rates are set administratively or through negotiation.[6] Next, the technical proposal outlines the insurer's plan for delivering covered services in accordance with the state's regulations, incorporating information on provider networks and alternative provider payment models (e.g., use of medical homes or Accountable Care Organizations). Bids are reviewed by state Medicaid programs, and insurers are selected using state-specific rubrics that weigh the cost bid and technical proposal.[7]

The insurers that participate in MMC programs vary significantly in size, scope, and structure. Prior to 1997, there was a "75/25" rule that required MMC insurers have at least 25% of their membership in the private, commercial health insurance market. The Balanced Budget Act of 1997 eliminated the "75/25" rule, making it possible for Medicaid-only insurers to participate (MACPAC, 2011). This flexibility has led to the rise of insurers like Centene and Molina that focus almost exclusively on the MMC market. Nonetheless, more traditional, predominantly commercial insurers continue

**TABLE 18.4** Procurement and Enrollment Options

| State | Comprehensive MCO | Procurement method | Enrollment option in managed care | | |
| --- | --- | --- | --- | --- | --- |
| | | | Adult | Child | Disabled |
| Alabama | | – | – | – | – |
| Alaska | | – | – | – | – |
| Arizona | ◆ | Competitive Selection | Varies | Varies | Varies |
| Arkansas | | – | – | – | – |
| California | ◆ | ** | Mandatory | Mandatory | Varies |
| Colorado | ◆ | ** | Voluntary | Voluntary | Voluntary |
| Connecticut | | – | – | – | – |
| Delaware | ◆ | Competitive Selection | Mandatory | Mandatory | Mandatory |
| District of Columbia | ◆ | Competitive Selection | Mandatory | Mandatory | Not Eligible |
| Florida | ◆ | ** | Mandatory | Mandatory | Mandatory |
| Georgia | ◆ | Competitive Selection | Mandatory | Mandatory | Not Eligible |
| Hawaii | ◆ | Competitive Selection | Mandatory | Mandatory | Mandatory |
| Idaho | ◆ | Competitive Selection | Mandatory | Mandatory | Not Eligible |
| Illinois | ◆ | Competitive Selection | Voluntary | Voluntary | Mandatory |
| Indiana | ◆ | Competitive Selection | Mandatory | Mandatory | Not Eligible |
| Iowa | ◆ | ** | Mandatory | Mandatory | Not Eligible |
| Kansas | ◆ | Competitive Selection | Mandatory | Mandatory | Mandatory |

| State | | | | | |
|---|---|---|---|---|---|
| Kentucky | ● | Competitive Selection | Mandatory | Mandatory | Mandatory |
| Louisiana | ● | Competitive Selection | Mandatory | Mandatory | Varies |
| Maine | | — | — | — | — |
| Maryland | ● | Noncompetitive | Mandatory | Mandatory | Mandatory |
| Massachusetts | ● | Competitive Selection | Mandatory | Mandatory | Varies |
| Michigan | ● | Competitive Selection | Varies | Mandatory | Mandatory |
| Minnesota | ● | Competitive Selection | Mandatory | Mandatory | Varies |
| Mississippi | ● | Competitive Selection | Mandatory | Mandatory | Mandatory |
| Missouri | ● | Competitive Selection | Mandatory | Mandatory | Mandatory |
| Montana | | — | — | — | — |
| Nebraska | ● | Noncompetitive | Mandatory | Mandatory | Mandatory |
| Nevada | ● | Competitive Selection | Mandatory | Mandatory | Mandatory |
| New Hampshire | ● | Competitive Selection | Mandatory | Mandatory | Mandatory |
| New Jersey | ● | Competitive Selection | Mandatory | Mandatory | Mandatory |
| New Mexico | ● | Competitive Selection | Mandatory | Mandatory | Mandatory |
| New York | ● | Competitive Selection | Mandatory | Mandatory | Mandatory |
| North Carolina | | — | — | — | — |
| North Dakota | ● | ** | Not Eligible | Not Eligible | Not Eligible |
| Ohio | ● | Competitive Selection | Mandatory | Mandatory | Mandatory |
| Oklahoma | | — | — | — | — |

(Continued)

**TABLE 18.4** (Continued)

| State | Comprehensive MCO | Procurement method | Enrollment option in managed care | | |
| --- | --- | --- | --- | --- | --- |
| | | | Adult | Child | Disabled |
| Oregon | ◆ | ** | Mandatory | Voluntary | Voluntary |
| Pennsylvania | ◆ | Competitive Selection | Mandatory | Mandatory | Mandatory |
| Puerto Rico | ◆ | Competitive Selection | Mandatory | Voluntary | Mandatory |
| Rhode Island | ◆ | Competitive Selection | Mandatory | Mandatory | Mandatory |
| South Carolina | ◆ | Competitive Selection | Mandatory | Mandatory | Mandatory |
| South Dakota | | – | – | – | – |
| Tennessee | ◆ | Competitive Selection | Mandatory | Mandatory | Mandatory |
| Texas | ◆ | Competitive Selection | Mandatory | Mandatory | Mandatory |
| Utah | ◆ | Competitive Selection | Mandatory | Mandatory | Mandatory |
| Vermont | ◆ | Other | Mandatory | Mandatory | Mandatory |
| Virginia | ◆ | Competitive Selection | Mandatory | Mandatory | Mandatory |
| Washington | ◆ | Competitive Selection | Varies | Varies | Mandatory |
| West Virginia | ◆ | Noncompetitive | Mandatory | Mandatory | Not Eligible |
| Wisconsin | ◆ | Other | Mandatory | Mandatory | Mandatory |
| Wyoming | | – | – | – | – |

**Procurement method unknown; ◆ state contracts with comprehensive MCO; – N/A
Noncompetitive procurement method—States that use noncompetitive procurement contract with any MCO that agrees to meet their requirements.
Other procurement method—States use different procurement methods for different populations or regions or an alternative procurement method.
Compiled from the Centers for Medicare and Medicaid Services (CMS).
Source: Managed care state profiles: https://www.medicaid.gov/medicaid/managed-care/state-profiles/index.html

to participate in MMC (KFF, 2017b). For example, in 2016, Aetna and United Healthcare had MMC contracts with 12 and 22 states, respectively (KFF, 2017b). Insurers also vary by geographic scope, with some operating in a single state or region (or even metropolitan area) and others operating across states.

Another notable feature of MMC insurance markets is the prevalence of small, local provider-owned insurers. Some safety-net hospitals and community health centers, which serve a high share of low-income, Medicaid-eligible patients, also operate MMC plans. These plans may operate within relatively small geographic areas—e.g., Metroplus in New York City or Chinese Community Health Plan (CCHP) in San Francisco. While providers have entered the insurance market with Medicaid plans, some Medicaid insurers have likewise entered the provider market by building their own health centers in areas with a high density of Medicaid eligibility. Examples of these are Trusted Health Plan in the District of Columbia and L.A. Care in Los Angeles.

### 18.2.3   Plan Choice

Plan choice in Medicaid varies significantly across states on a variety of dimensions. First, the *enrollment options* available to Medicaid beneficiaries vary by state and beneficiary type. Table 18.4 shows how these enrollment options vary across states. Medicaid beneficiaries are either (1) required to enroll in a managed care plan ("mandatory"), (2) given a choice between MMC and the publicly managed FFS Medicaid program ("voluntary"), or (3) excluded from MMC ("not eligible"). Federal rules require states that use MMC to provide Medicaid recipients with some form of choice, either between FFS and MMC or among different MMC plans. In the 1990s, MMC served mainly low-income children and families, often via mandatory enrollment but sometimes as a voluntary choice. Aged and disabled Medicaid beneficiaries, who tend to have more complex health needs, were generally served by FFS Medicaid. More recently, states have started to enroll aged and disabled beneficiaries into managed care plans (MACPAC, 2011). Table 18.4 indicates that of the 42 states with MMC programs in 2014, 28 of them required all disabled Medicaid recipients to enroll in an MMC plan.

Second, the *enrollment process* varies by state and recipient type. In some states, all new enrollees are preassigned to a managed care plan and then given a period of time during which they are allowed to switch. In others, there is an initial enrollment choice period (just after eligibility verification) for new enrollees to select a plan. During this choice period, recipients are covered by the FFS program. After the choice period, enrollees who do not make an active plan choice are "autoassigned" to a plan using algorithms that vary by state. This enrollment process varies across states and within a state by recipient type. For example, pregnant women in Louisiana are preassigned, whereas other beneficiaries have a 30-day enrollment choice period.

In many states, autoassignment—using an algorithm to automatically enroll Medicaid recipients who do not actively choose a plan in a (typically randomly) selected plan—is very common. A recent survey of state Medicaid programs found that the median state has an autoassignment rate of 45%, with the autoassignment rates for 10 states exceeding 60% (Smith et al., 2016). Autoassignment algorithms sometimes consider existing provider–patient relationships and may also consider geographic location and enrollment of family members. In some states, preferential autoassignment rewards plans with superior cost or quality performance. In many states, however, preferential autoassignment focuses on balancing market shares across MMC plans—i.e., assigning more enrollees to the plans that fewer people have actively chosen.[8] Autoassigning more enrollees to smaller plans helps prop up these insurers, making them more likely to succeed and giving them more leverage in contract negotiations with providers). If enrollment in managed care is not mandatory, enrollees who do not make a plan selection may instead be enrolled in FFS Medicaid.[9] Once the initial plan assignment has been made, enrollees are often given a period of time to freely switch plans, after which they are often "locked-in" to a managed care plan for 6−12 months. However, the allowed time when enrollees can switch plans also varies across states. Even during the "open enrollment" period during which recipients can switch plans, assignments are relatively "sticky," with low levels of switching. However, switching is more likely among sicker recipients who tend to move from lower-quality to higher-quality plans, indicating that while autoassignment may weaken adverse selection problems, it does not remove them entirely (Geruso et al., 2016; Marton et al., 2016).

Plan choice can be influenced by marketing, outreach programs, and support from insurance brokers. Most states allow insurers to conduct marketing and outreach campaigns aimed at enrolling Medicaid-eligible populations. Provider-owned insurers generally use their own emergency rooms or community health centers to identify and enroll eligible but uninsured patients. Most states also use third-party enrollment brokers who help beneficiaries compare plan options and make a selection (CMS, 2016b).

In summary, the plan choice process in Medicaid differs significantly from the process in other settings such as employer-sponsored insurance, Medicare Advantage, and the ACA Marketplaces. The large share of passive enrollees means that state-defined autoassignment rules play an outsized role in shaping insurer competitive incentives. This represents both a distinction from standard insurance markets—where demand is based on enrollee preferences and choices—and a powerful tool for states to use to shape the competitive environment.

## 18.3 HEALTH PLAN PAYMENT DESIGN

Health plan payment policies in Medicaid are complex and vary significantly across states. MMC insurers are generally paid a monthly, risk-adjusted per enrollee payment (also known as a capitation rate) and may also receive supplemental payments for certain services or populations. In the rate development process, a "base payment" is developed based on the expected cost of the average Medicaid enrollee. The base payment is either set administratively or set as part of the procurement process (through competitive bidding or negotiation). The base payments are typically risk-adjusted by multiplying the payment by individual (or group) risk scores to account for the health risks of a given insurer's Medicaid enrollees. Risk adjustment factors include demographic factors, health status, and eligibility type. Some states also use risk-sharing methods such as risk corridors, reinsurance, or stop-loss programs. Though states have flexibility to define state-specific health plan payment policies, federal regulations have led to some similarities across states. We discuss the development of the base payment rate first, and then outline risk adjustment in more detail.

### 18.3.1 Rate Development

Beginning in 2002, federal regulations required that capitation payments to MMC insurers be certified as "actuarially sound" based on cost and utilization data from Medicaid enrollees or a comparable population (MACPAC, 2011). As part of the rate development process, states work with actuaries to develop a range of capitation rates based on national or state healthcare cost trends, provider reimbursement levels, FFS data, and encounter data collected from participating insurers.[10]

There are three basic methods for setting insurer capitation rates. Table 18.5 shows which states use each method. Some states use a single rate-setting method, whereas other states use a combination of multiple methods. In the first, *administrative rate setting*, states select a capitation rate within the actuarially sound range and communicate it to insurers during procurement. This method gives the state more control over its costs and avoids the administrative hassles of a bidding process. Rather than using its bargaining position to minimize costs while providing a given level of quality, the state has a set level of Medicaid spending and uses its position to maximize quality given that spending level.

A second method is for the state to conduct a *competitive bidding* process in which the actuarially sound range effectively serves as a price floor and ceiling.[11] Interestingly, some states do not reveal the actuarially sound range during bidding but impose it on rates after bids are collected. The bidding method introduces price competition into Medicaid procurement and lets the state save money if insurers submit low bids. However, just a handful of

**TABLE 18.5** Rate Setting and Payment

| State | Comprehensive MCO | Administrative | Negotiated | Competitive bid | Pay for performance |
|---|---|---|---|---|---|
| Alabama | | – | – | – | – |
| Alaska | | – | – | – | – |
| Arizona | ◆ | | | ✓ | |
| Arkansas | | – | – | – | – |
| California | ◆ | ✓ | | | |
| Colorado | ◆ | ✓ | ✓ | | |
| Connecticut | | – | – | – | |
| Delaware | ◆ | ✓ | ✓ | | ✓ |
| District of Columbia | ◆ | ✓ | ✓ | | |
| Florida | ◆ | ✓ | | | ✓ |
| Georgia | ◆ | ✓ | | | ✓ |
| Hawaii | ◆ | | ✓ | ✓ | ✓ |
| Idaho | *◆ | | | | |
| Illinois | ◆ | ✓ | | | |
| Indiana | ◆ | | | ✓ | ✓ |
| Iowa | *◆ | | | | |
| Kansas | ◆ | | | ✓ | |
| Kentucky | ◆ | ✓ | | | |

| State | | | | | |
|---|---|---|---|---|---|
| Louisiana | ◆ | ✓ | — | | — |
| Maine | ◆ | — | | — | ✓ |
| Maryland | ◆ | ✓ | | | ✓ |
| Massachusetts | ◆ | ✓ | | | |
| Michigan | ◆ | ✓ | | | ✓ |
| Minnesota | ◆ | ✓ | | | |
| Mississippi | ◆ | ✓ | | | |
| Missouri | ◆ | ✓ | | | ✓ |
| Montana | ◆ | — | — | — | — |
| Nebraska | ◆ | ✓ | | | |
| Nevada | ◆ | ✓ | | | |
| New Hampshire | ◆ | ✓ | | | ✓ |
| New Jersey | ◆ | ✓ | | | ✓ |
| New Mexico | ◆ | ✓ | | ✓ | ✓ |
| New York | ◆ | ✓ | | | ✓ |
| North Carolina | ◆ | — | — | — | — |
| North Dakota | ◆* | | | | — |
| Ohio | ◆ | ✓ | | | ✓ |
| Oklahoma | ◆ | — | — | — | — |
| Oregon | ◆ | ✓ | ✓ | | ✓ |

*(Continued)*

**TABLE 18.5** (Continued)

| State | Comprehensive MCO | Administrative | Negotiated | Competitive bid | Pay for performance |
|---|---|---|---|---|---|
| Pennsylvania | ♦ | ✓ | ✓ | | ✓ |
| Puerto Rico | ♦ | ✓ | | | |
| Rhode Island | ♦ | ✓ | | | ✓ |
| South Carolina | ♦ | ✓ | | | ✓ |
| South Dakota | | – | – | – | – |
| Tennessee | ♦ | | | ✓ | ✓ |
| Texas | ♦ | ✓ | | | ✓ |
| Utah | ♦ | ✓ | | | |
| Vermont | ♦ | ✓ | | | |
| Virginia | ♦ | ✓ | | | |
| Washington | ♦ | ✓ | | | |
| West Virginia | ♦ | ✓ | | | |
| Wisconsin | ♦ | ✓ | | | |
| Wyoming | | – | – | – | – |
| **Total** | **42** | **32** | **6** | **6** | **18** |

*Rate setting method unknown.
✓ state uses rate setting method; ♦state contracts with comprehensive MCO; – N/A
Note: Some states use a combination of rate-setting methods.
Source: Compiled from the Centers for Medicare and Medicaid Services (CMS) Managed Care State Profiles https://www.medicaid.gov/medicaid/managed-care/state-profiles/index.html

states use competitive bidding to set rates—perhaps due to a perception that plans that bid very low also offer lower-than-acceptable levels of quality.

The final method for rate setting is to conduct a *negotiation* with MMC plans. In these cases, states generally begin negotiations at the low end of the actuarially sound range. Insurers then present their case for higher capitation rates, citing evidence of plan performance or quality. Negotiation was historically the norm for rate setting in MMC. However, today it is used in only a few states. The initial rate agreed upon during a competitive bid or negotiation is generally adjusted annually during the duration of the contract period to account for benefit changes and medical cost inflation.

## 18.3.2   Risk Adjustment

Starting from the base capitation payment (just discussed), states use various factors to adjust payment rates to account for differing health statuses of enrollees in each plan. Demographic factors—such as age, sex, geography, and Medicaid eligibility category—are generally included in rate adjustment. Medicaid eligibility category may not be used as a rate adjustment factor in states that only enroll children and families into managed care, excluding aged, disabled or otherwise medically needy populations. Over time, more states have incorporated medical diagnoses into risk adjustment. Risk scores are generated for each enrollee based on the included variables, and the average risk score of a plan's enrollees determines its risk-adjusted capitation rate. The precise method by which this occurs varies across states, as we describe below.

Diagnosis information may be gleaned from medical claims, encounter data, or pharmacy claims. The type of risk adjustment model chosen by a given state depends on the type and quality of claims data available to the state. For example, Florida moved from using Medicaid Rx (a model based on pharmacy claims) to the Chronic Disability Payment System (CDPS, a model based on medical diagnoses codes) after the reporting of encounter data improved. Moreover, a single state may use different risk-adjustment models for different populations. A study of 20 managed care programs in 2010 found that 17 states used a risk-adjustment model incorporating health status, though the exact models used varied by state (Courtot et al., 2012). CDPS, a risk-adjustment model originally developed for Medicaid plan payment, was the most frequently used model. Eleven study states used CDPS, and three states used Adjusted Clinical Groups (ACGs). Other models used include Ingenix Symmetry, Medicaid Rx, Clinical Pharmaceutical Groups (CRxG), and Diagnostic Cost Groups (DxCG).

States also differ in whether they implement risk adjustment based on concurrent diagnoses or diagnoses from the prior year (prospective) and in whether they use individual or "aggregate" risk adjustment (Winkelman and Damler, 2008). Under all risk-adjustment methods, an average risk score for the plan is generated, and plan payments are equal to the base payment multiplied by the average risk score. The methods differ in how the average risk score is generated. Under individual risk adjustment—the standard method used in programs like Medicare Advantage and the ACA Marketplaces— plan payments are adjusted based on the risk scores of the individuals actually enrolled in the plan for each month. In this case, the plan's average risk score is the mean risk score of all of its enrollees in a given month. This method makes prospective risk adjustment difficult due to relatively short enrollment spells of most Medicaid recipients. Because of this difficulty, many states use "aggregate" risk adjustment, where a plan's per member per month payment in year $t$ is adjusted based on the average risk score of its population during year $t-1$. In this case, the plan's average risk score is the mean risk score of all of its enrollees during the prior year. In other words, plan payments are not adjusted based on the risk scores of their *current* enrollees but based on the risk scores of their *prior* enrollees. This solves the problem of short enrollment spells, but may make risk adjustment less accurate if the risk composition of a population changes across years. According to a 2008 survey, at that time most states used prospective aggregate risk adjustment (Winkelman and Damler, 2008).

Health plans may also receive payment adjustments in the form of incentive payments or efficiency adjustments. Some states incorporate incentive payments into capitation rates to reward insurers for meeting performance benchmarks. This payment model is often referred to as "pay-for-performance." Often, these payments are implemented as "quality withholds" where the state withholds a portion of a plan's payment until they can determine whether the plan met the quality benchmarks for the year. Similarly, states may adjust capitation payments for efficiency factors to incentivize plans to meet efficiency targets or reward plans for achieving cost savings. For example, rates may be adjusted to account for targeted or achieved reduction in unnecessary inpatient admissions.

## 18.3.3 Risk Sharing

In addition to risk-adjusted capitation payments to MMC plans, some states also use risk-sharing methods such as risk corridors, stop-loss protection, and reinsurance for extremely high-cost cases. Other policies related to risk sharing include service and population carve-outs and supplemental payments to health plans for certain services. The objectives of these policies vary, with risk corridors and stop-loss protection intended to protect insurers against financial risk and carve-outs and supplemental payments intended at least in part to weaken selection incentives. These methods are adopted differently across states and multiple risk-sharing methods may be used collectively.

Risk corridors work like a profit-sharing scheme with the state. Plans whose claims costs exceed capitation payments by a given percentage are reimbursed for a portion of their losses. Conversely, a plan whose claims fall short of capitation payments by a given percentage must reimburse the state for a portion of their profits. With stop-loss protection, plans are not accountable for claims above a defined threshold. For example, New York limits plan risk for inpatient care to $100,000 per enrollee per year, with the state covering remaining costs. Similarly, Arizona will cover 75% of an enrollee's annual inpatient claims above $25,000 or $35,000 (depending on the beneficiary) and 100% of inpatient claims exceeding $650,000. Some states do not offer stop-loss protection or reinsurance but require that plans purchase private reinsurance coverage (Courtot et al., 2012).

In addition to these risk-sharing policies, carve outs of certain services and populations also act as risk-sharing mechanisms. For example, New York automatically defaults low-birthweight babies into the FFS program, protecting managed care plans from very high neonatal intensive care unit costs. Many states also default disabled individuals and other individuals with complex chronic conditions into FFS, weakening selection incentives faced by managed care plans.

Some states also use supplemental "kick" payments to insurers for certain services or types of individuals. Supplemental payments are typically made to compensate managed care plans for services for which the state does not want them to bear the risk. The most common supplemental payment is for maternity services, to cover the cost of prenatal care and delivery, with additional payments for low-birthweight babies. These payments act as a form of risk sharing to compensate insurers for the added cost of delivery. Pregnancy and childbirth are often difficult to include explicitly in the prospective risk-adjustment models typically implemented in Medicaid given that (1) there typically are not diagnoses from year $t-1$ indicating that a delivery will take place in year $t$ and (2) many pregnant women who have Medicaid coverage became eligible for Medicaid only when they become pregnant. Supplemental payments may also be made for HIV care, organ transplants, and other high-cost populations or services.

A final form of risk sharing that takes place in MMC is as part of the MMC plan's base payment. In some cases, MMC plans are not actually at risk for the spending of their enrollees. This typically occurs with provider-owned plans. The plan/provider organization is charged with managing the care of its enrollees and then reimbursed for any services that it provides to its enrollees on a FFS basis. For example, the University of Utah has an MMC plan that participates in Utah's Medicaid program, and until 2013 this plan was reimbursed FFS for all services it provided its enrollees. This form of plan payment is similar to another form of payment (known as "cost-plus" payment) that used to be common in Medicaid. Under cost-plus payment, MMC plans would present the state each year with records of their enrollees' spending. The state would then set each plan's payment equal to the plan's prior spending plus a mark-up to cover administrative costs and provide profits. While there was typically some negotiation between the state and the MMC plans, this form of payment was closer to FFS reimbursement, leaving MMC plans with some short-term risk but limiting the medium- and long-term risk they faced. New York used "cost-plus" payment in its MMC program until 2008 when it transitioned to administratively set regional rates with risk adjustment.

## 18.4 EVALUATION OF HEALTH PLAN PAYMENT

Medicaid does not have a single health plan payment system; instead, each state has its own payment system that may vary across different Medicaid populations. This makes an overall evaluation of health plan payment close to impossible. Thus, in this section we focus our attention on two types of evaluations. First, we present results on the statistical performance of each of the five risk adjustment models most commonly used in state Medicaid programs. For each model, we present R-squared and/or predictive ratio statistics from the initial research papers outlining the development of the models. While risk adjustment is far from the only component of Medicaid plan payment systems, it is an important component and is the only component that we know of that has been evaluated. Second, we review the small set of papers that have studied indirect consequences of plan payment systems, such as effects on health outcomes, benefit distortions, and risk selection of profitable enrollees by managed care plans. These papers provide insights into the inadequacies of the overall payment system, rather than focusing solely on risk adjustment.

### 18.4.1 Statistical Performance of Common Risk Adjustment Models

The five most commonly used risk adjustment models that have been incorporated into MMC payment systems are the Chronic Illness and Disability Payment System (CDPS), the Medicaid Rx model, the Adjusted Cost Groups (ACG) system, the Clinical Risk Groups (CRG) system, and the Diagnostic Cost Group (DxCG)/Hierarchical Condition Category (HCC) system. For each of these risk adjustment systems, the researchers who developed the system produced a report describing the development of the system and reporting some key statistics that are often used to evaluate payment system performance. While we recognize that there has been additional research on each of these systems, because of the large number of systems, we restrict our review to these initial reports except in a few exceptional cases. Additionally, we are limited to discussing the measures of performance that have been used, with the only available measures being R-squared statistics and predictive ratios. While these metrics do not directly measure the performance of the payment system with respect to common objectives such as inducing efficient sorting across plans and providing plans with incentives to provide efficient levels of benefits, (1) they are available and (2) they are not too different from metrics that do measure performance on these objectives (Layton et al., 2017).

The CDPS system was developed specifically for risk adjustment in Medicaid. It categorizes chronic conditions by the part of the body they affect. Each category is then divided into levels of severity. Kronick et al. (2000) report statistical measures of model performance using FFS Medicaid data from seven states. They estimate separate weights for disabled and low-income Medicaid recipients. The model is estimated prospectively, using diagnoses from the prior year to predict current-year spending. The model performs particularly well for the disabled population, achieving an R-squared of 0.18 for this group. Performance is weaker for nondisabled adults and children enrolled in Medicaid, with R-squared statistics of 0.08 and 0.04 for these groups. When considering predictive ratios, the model also performs poorly for individuals with multiple chronic conditions, resulting in payments that fall below costs for these individuals. The developers of the CDPS also compare their model to the HCC and ACG systems, finding that with respect to the R-squared statistic the CDPS model outperforms both of its competitors in the Medicaid population they study. This result holds for all three eligibility categories: the disabled, nondisabled adults, and nondisabled children.

The Medicaid Rx Model uses pharmacy claims rather than diagnosis codes from claims to group individuals by chronic condition. This model is also prospective, using drug utilization from the prior year to predict current spending. Gilmer et al. (2001) show that this model performs better for disabled Medicaid recipients than it does for nondisabled adults and children using FFS Medicaid data from California, Colorado, Georgia, and Tennessee (Gilmer et al. 2001). The model produces R-squared statistics of 0.15, 0.11, and 0.06 for the disabled, nondisabled adults, and nondisabled children, respectively. However, the developers of the model compare the model to the CDPS model and find that the CDPS model performs better.

The ACG model is similar to the CDPS in that it uses diagnoses to group individuals by condition. Unlike the other models, this model was developed on a commercial managed care population (Starfield et al., 1991). The developers found that in that population, the model produced an R-squared statistic of 0.19, implying reasonably good performance. However, other work indicates much weaker performance in a Medicaid population (Kronick et al., 2000).

The CRG model is also a diagnosis-based model. It differs from the ACG and CDPS models in that the categories to which it assigns individuals are mutually exclusive, i.e., each individual belongs to a single category. The developers of this model find that in a Medicare population the model produces an R-squared of 0.11 when used prospectively and around 0.43 when used concurrently (Hughes et al., 2004). The model performs reasonably well across all subgroups analyzed by the developers, with predictive ratios ranging from around 0.9 to around 1.1, implying that for these groups costs never exceed or fall below revenues by more than 10%. This is not surprising given that the authors only analyzed subgroups of individuals incorporated into the model (age, number of chronic diseases, etc.).

The DxCG/HCC system is another diagnosis-based risk adjustment model. The developers of this model find that it performs well in a Medicaid population, with an R-squared statistic between 0.21 and 0.23 (Ash et al., 2000). The developers analyze predictive ratios for a variety of medical condition-based subgroups. They find that the DxCG model dramatically outperforms basic age/sex risk adjustment and that it performs well overall: All predictive ratios exceed 0.8 with the exception of the arthritis and sexually transmitted diseases groups, and many groups including most cancers, heart failure, diabetes, and alcohol/drug dependence have predictive ratios close to 1.0.

## 18.4.2 Indirect Consequences of Inadequate Risk Adjustment

While statistical measures of payment system performance can be useful—in that these measures are similar to measures derived from a formal model of a regulator's objective in addressing adverse selection incentives (Layton et al., 2017)—studies of the actual consequences of payment systems for enrollment and health outcomes provide a more complete picture of whether a payment system achieves the desired goals. Here, we focus on studies that consider potential indirect outcomes of payment systems.

Frank et al. (2000) study insurer incentives to distort plan benefits to attract health enrollees in a Medicaid population. They construct a theoretical model that provides a measure of an insurer's incentive to distort coverage for a particular service, calling the insurer's behavior in response to that incentive "service-level selection." They then use the measure to evaluate service-level selection incentives in Michigan's Medicaid program using data from FFS Medicaid recipients. They show that insurer service-level selection incentives are particularly strong for mental health services and that this result holds under a payment system with no risk adjustment and systems using ACGs and HCCs. They also show that both the HCC and ACG risk adjustment systems tend to weaken distortionary incentives.

An early paper showing evidence of MMC plan behavior consistent with a potential failure of an MMC plan payment system was Currie and Fahr (2005), who study the effect of the switch to managed care on the composition of the Medicaid caseload. They find that Medicaid enrollment increases for poor white and Hispanic children but decreases for black children. They also find that enrollment decreases among toddlers but not for school-aged children. Given that toddlers and black children are generally sicker than other Medicaid populations (Currie and Fahr, 2005), these results are consistent with "cream-skimming" behaviors, potentially implying that the payment systems in place during the study period (1989−94) were inadequate.

Kuziemko et al. (2013) study transitions to managed care in Texas' Medicaid program. Again, they focus on evidence of cream-skimming behavior among MMC plans, though they focus on the mechanism by which plans engage in cream-skimming rather than the ultimate enrollment consequences. Specifically, they show that when Texas counties transitioned from FFS Medicaid to MMC, black infant mortality rates increased while Hispanic infant mortality rates decreased. They argue that this is consistent with plans reducing quality of care for high-cost Medicaid recipients and improving quality of care for low-cost Medicaid recipients because the average black birth costs almost twice as much as the average Hispanic birth. Again, this suggests that the MMC plan payment system was imperfect in Texas during the authors' study period (1993−2001).

Clearly, more research is needed in this area. Medicaid is a population with extreme variation in healthcare spending, with kids and pregnant women sometimes combined in the same risk pool as the disabled and low-income aged individuals. This unpriced risk heterogeneity represents a challenge for policymakers seeking to minimize adverse selection problems. Thus, work focusing on more recent years and investigating standard questions about the extent of selection in these MMC markets and the adequacy of current payment systems for compensating plans for that selection is critical to improving the economic performance of these markets.

## 18.5  ONGOING ISSUES AND REFORMS

There is a great deal we do not know about the economics of MMC. MMC market design, in particular, is an issue that is ripe for study and reform, and an issue clearly linked to decisions about the form of health plan payment. As a large and growing budget item, Medicaid reform is an issue high on states' priority lists. MMC regulation is also a federal priority, with the Center for Medicare and Medicaid Services (CMS) in 2016 issuing the first large regulatory revamp in over a decade. Finally, as we have emphasized in this chapter, the principles of regulated competition have been applied to Medicaid only incompletely and in varying ways across states. This makes Medicaid a potential "laboratory for regulated competition"—a setting where researchers can test ideas underlying regulated competition and inform state Medicaid reform efforts. This sort of research can improve our understanding of the consequences of various policies underlying the regulated competition model.

In this section, we highlight several areas where the principles of regulated competition could be more fully applied in MMC. We discuss both potential reforms suggested by these principles and the actual reform activity in these areas.

### 18.5.1 Enrollee Premiums

The lack of enrollee premiums in Medicaid is a major departure from the basic idea of regulated competition, for instance as laid out by Enthoven and Kronick (1989). Price signals are central to the standard economic theory of market functioning. They steer consumers towards lower-cost options and also let them indicate their level of valuation for higher-quality goods by paying extra. These demand signals, in turn, encourage producers to cut costs and improve quality. This standard form of competition is not possible in Medicaid where enrollees can typically choose any plan for free.

The implications of Medicaid's "price-free" competition model are not well understood. Its consequences are particularly interesting because of well-known market failures associated with price competition in insurance markets with adverse selection (Akerlof, 1970; Rothschild and Stiglitz, 1976). One way of mitigating these inefficiencies is to cross-subsidize *price differences* between plans of varying generosity, lowering the relative price of the (more generous) adversely selected plan. Cross-subsidizing price differences can lead to two beneficial effects. First, it can improve the *sorting* of beneficiaries across plans by narrowing price differences towards cost differences for the marginal enrollee (or "marginal costs"; see Culter and Reber, 1998; Einav et al., 2010). Second, it can increase the *quality of plans in equilibrium*, making it possible for generous plans to survive (Miyazaki, 1977; Handel et al., 2015).

Medicaid's zero-premium design works like a 100% subsidy on price differences. For improving sorting among plans, this is only optimal if marginal cost differences are truly zero. Recent evidence from Layton et al. (2016) studying New York Medicaid suggests that cost differences may in fact be quite large (as large as 30% among MMC plans in New York City). Thus, Medicaid's 100% cross-subsidies likely go too far for the purpose of optimal sorting (i.e., "too many" individuals enrolling in high-cost plans and "too few" enrolling in low-cost plans).

For increasing equilibrium quality, the effects of Medicaid's subsidy policy are ambiguous. On the one hand, firms are likely to compete more on quality when enrollees are not price-sensitive (Dorfman and Steiner, 1954). Further, the absence of premiums may eliminate a powerful tool for low-cost, low-quality plans to selectively attract profitable consumers—the mechanism at the heart of the Rothschild and Stiglitz (1976) model.[12] Alternatively, the sick and healthy might value different *aspects* of quality— e.g., the sick might value good specialist networks, whereas the healthy value good PCP networks. The latter is the mechanism in the literature on "service-level selection" (Frank et al., 2000; Ellis and McGuire, 2007)). On the other hand, the zero-premium setup means that Medicaid must either set insurer prices administratively or (if bidding is used) impose caps on price bids. Otherwise, a plan could charge an arbitrarily high price and make unlimited profits. Binding price caps can reduce equilibrium quality because a plan cannot raise its price to pay for the associated costs of improving quality. Thus, the net effect on quality is ambiguous. Additional research is needed to understand the tradeoffs involved with Medicaid's price-free competitive model.

We are not aware of any states that apply different enrollee premiums to MMC plans based on their price bids. Several states have recently adopted reforms requiring higher-income enrollees (above the poverty line) to pay modest premiums to enroll in Medicaid.[13] Some of these reforms allow lower-income enrollees to get slightly more generous benefits if they pay a modest premium (though they are not disenrolled if they fail to pay). However, these reforms do not apply *different* premiums to managed care insurers based on their price bids, costs of care, or observed/unobserved quality.

One concern with premiums in Medicaid is that even modest amounts may deter enrollment (Dague, 2014), leaving low-income individuals uninsured. This concern, however, can be addressed within the regulated competition framework if premiums can be *negative*—that is if the state can rebate money to consumers. The state could make a benchmark plan (e.g., the most expensive plan) free and share savings with consumers if they choose a cheaper option. There are questions about whether such a system would be administratively feasible, but if so, it could allow for premium differences without deterring coverage.

## 18.5.2    Competitive Procurement

Absent enrollee premiums, the main way Medicaid programs can encourage insurers to compete on prices is via states' power to limit and shape choices. We highlight two "competitive procurement" tools: regulators' power to determine *plan availability* and to set *autoassignment* rules.

One way states can encourage competition is by selecting insurers in the procurement process based on criteria like price and quality. If these criteria are clear in advance and there is a credible threat of rejection, the procurement process may encourage insurers to lower prices and/or improve quality. Notice the counterintuitive logic: by limiting choice (or at least threatening to do so), the program promotes competition on desired outcomes. While many states use a "competitive" process to select MMC plans, the extent to which there is a real threat of rejection is unclear. Some states (like Missouri) explicitly limit the number of insurers that can participate in Medicaid (either statewide or regionally). The desired number of MMC plan contracts may be communicated to insurers during the RFP process, as in the case of Iowa's 2015 RFP release.[14] But it is not clear how binding these limits are or how states select the winning insurers. In Minnesota's 2012 RFP, a scoring rubric based on quality, efficiency, and cost was used to select the top three plans in each region (Spencer et al., 2012).

Another way of using plan availability to encourage competition is for states to accept all insurers but limit plan availability for certain enrollees (e.g., new enrollees) to plans with the lowest prices. This method has been used in two hybrid Medicaid/exchange programs: Massachusetts' pre-ACA CommCare program and Arkansas' "private option" Medicaid expansion. It has the advantage that the Medicaid program can limit choice without having to kick current enrollees out of an existing plan if it fails in the competitive procurement process.

An additional competitive procurement tool is states' power to *autoassign* passive beneficiaries. In theory, plans with lower prices (or better quality) could be favored with larger shares of autoassignees. Interestingly, while 10 states consider quality in autoassignment, as far as we know only Kentucky appears to use insurer prices as a factor (Marton et al., 2016). Indeed, 23 states use autoassignment to "balance enrollments" across plans, giving larger shares to plans with fewer people (Smith et al., 2016). This method has the odd (and likely perverse) effect of favoring plans that actively choosing enrollees have signaled to be less desirable. Given the high rates of auto-assignment in many states (45% in the median state), a state's decision of how to allocate these enrollees is likely to have a significant effect on MMC plan behavior. Overall, competitive autoassignment seems like a simple and underexplored avenue for reform.

### 18.5.3  Scope of Benefits and Carve-Outs

Standard theory suggests that managed care plans will have more efficient cost control incentives if they cover a broad set of benefits. An insurer that covers all benefits will internalize "offset effects," whereby benefit changes in one area affect spending in another. For instance, reducing access to prescription drugs has been shown to increase hospitalizations for the elderly (Chandra et al., 2010). An insurer that covered only prescription drugs (as in Medicare Part D) would not internalize these offset effects (Starc and Town, 2016; Lavetti and Simon, 2016).

In the presence of adverse selection, however, it may be efficient to "carve-out" certain services that are used by individuals with predictably high costs (Frank et al., 2000; Ellis and McGuire, 2007). If these services are not carved out and risk adjustment is inadequate, then insurers face incentives to inefficiently ration these services. Because of this selection issue, it can be better for the state to pay for a service via FFS or to contract it out separately to a specialized plan (e.g., a behavioral healthcare organization), despite the potential inefficiency induced by noninternalized offset effects.

In Medicaid, benefits like behavioral health, prescription drugs, and dental care are in fact often "carved out" of managed care contracts. However, the recent trend has been to begin carving some of these services back into managed care contracts. The shift in strategy may be driven by more favorable federal policies for drug reimbursement or improved integration of dental and behavioral health provider networks by insurers. The shift may also be driven by improvements in state MMC plan payment systems that use sophisticated risk adjustment systems that combat the selection-related inefficiencies that the carve-outs may have partially been intended to prevent. Alternatively, even without a carve-out insurers may still subcontract with more specialized insurers to provide behavioral health services.[15]

More research is needed to understand the efficiency consequences of these carve-outs. Given that many states are currently shifting away from carve-outs, there should be many natural experiments with which researchers can study their consequences in the coming years.

### 18.5.4    Plan Regulation and Payment

A key feature of regulated competition is that the market designer regulates benefits and risk adjusts payments to offset incentives to stint on quality due to adverse selection. MMC regulators have widely adopted both approaches: benefits are heavily regulated (indeed, typically completely specified) and risk adjustment is standard. But there are several ways in which these areas are ripe for reform.

First, while states are increasingly adopting risk adjustment methods that use enrollee diagnoses (Smith et al., 2016), these methods are still imperfect. For instance, many states use "aggregate" risk adjustment, which is based on the risk scores of a plan's enrollees in the *prior* year (see discussion in Section 18.3). This is likely to offset selection incentives less well than the standard risk adjustment methods based on a plan's actual enrollees (though it may also reduce incentives to upcode). Further, an important lesson from the literature is that when risk measures are imperfect, optimal risk adjustment "overpays" based on observed risk to compensate for adverse selection on unobserved risk (Glazer and McGuire, 2000). We are not aware of any states that have tested this approach.

Second, some aspects of quality—like how well the insurer coordinates care or how smooth its claims-paying process is—are difficult to measure and regulate in plan contracts. Instead, Medicaid programs are increasingly using quality reporting and pay-for-performance incentives to encourage insurers to improve on these softer aspects of quality.[16]

Third, Medicaid programs are increasingly specifying in contracts that plans pay their providers using value-based purchasing or non-FFS "alternative" payment models. This new focus of Medicaid programs has the goal of reforming the delivery system. In 2016, 12 states had contracts requiring or encouraging alternative payments, with eight states planning to adopt such contract provisions in 2017 (Smith et al., 2016). In addition to these plan payment requirements, several states are adopting reforms to require plans to provide services that address the "social determinants" of health, including screening beneficiaries and referring them to nonmedical community support services.

Finally, Medicaid programs are increasingly adopting regulations on medical loss ratios (MLRs), to constrain plan profits and administrative costs. New federal regulations in 2016 mandated an 85% minimum MLR for Medicaid plans, though many states already had similar or higher requirements. MLR regulation has little basis in standard regulated competition principles—though it may make sense given the limits on price competition in the Medicaid program. However, it is unclear how it can work in a program where provider-owned plans are so common. These plans can directly adjust their costs via the transfer price embedded in their plan's payment rates to the owning provider (Boxes 18.1–18.4).

---

**BOX 18.1 MO HealthNet—Missouri's Medicaid program**

In most regions of Missouri, nondisabled adults and children, as well as disabled Medicaid recipients, are required to enroll in a private comprehensive MMC plan. Prior to 2012, Missouri allowed "any willing plan" to participate in its MMC program, and paid plans using administratively set rates. Rates were adjusted using demographic factors. There were three rating regions, and plans could choose which regions to enter. In each of the eastern and western regions, there was at least one hospital-owned plan in the program.

Starting in 2013, Missouri switched to a competitive bidding system. Under the new system, the state awards only three managed care contracts, and the plans must operate in all three rating regions. Plan bids do not include prices, however. Instead, bids are purely technical proposals that outline provider networks and how the plans will achieve a set of priorities outlined by the state, including the adoption of medical homes and alternative payment models. This results in a procurement process that is highly subjective. The process is an example of a state that uses the threat of exclusion to attempt to extract higher levels of quality out of health plans for a given administratively set payment.

Despite the subjectivity involved in the process, the threat of exclusion turned out to be highly credible: one large plan owned by Molina that had participated in MO HealthNet for a number of years was excluded in 2013, despite Molina's attempts to force the state to accept its contract via litigation. The three plans chosen to participate in the market were HealthCare USA (owned by Aetna), Home State Health Plan (owned by Centene), and Missouri Care (owned by Wellcare). Because the chosen plans were required to operate in all three regions of the state, local hospital-owned plans were effectively eliminated from the program.

*(Continued)*

**BOX 18.1 (Continued)**

Plan payments under the newly reformed program include a few interesting features. First, the state began to risk adjust payments using the Medicaid Rx risk adjustment model. The state decided to use the pharmacy-only model initially due to concerns about the completeness of diagnosis data for some health plans (Dockendorf et al., 2014). Starting in 2015, the state began to pay under the CDPS + Rx model which incorporates both diagnoses and pharmacy information for risk adjustment. Second, plan payments include quality withholds, where the state doesn't pay plans the full payment until after the year is over and the state determines whether the plan met certain quality thresholds.

**BOX 18.2 MassHealth—Massachusetts' Medicaid program**

Massachusetts operates a state-run Primary Care Clinician (PCC) plan alongside a set of private comprehensive MMC plans. Many Medicaid recipients have a choice between the PCC and MMC plans, though the childless adults covered under Massachusetts' Medicaid expansion do not have the PCC option. Unlike most states, recipients who neglect to choose a plan are autoassigned to both PCC and MMC plans rather than exclusively to MMC plans. In March 2015 about half of Massachusetts Medicaid recipients were enrolled in a private MMC plan.

Massachusetts contracts with six health plans: Boston Medical Center (BMC) HealthNet Plan, Fallon Community Health Plan, Health New England, Neighborhood Health Plan, Network Health, and Celticare (owned by Centene, and only available in the CarePlus program open to Massachusetts' Medicaid expansion population). Plans are not required to participate in all regions of the state. Two of the five plans, BMC HealthNet and Neighborhood Health Plan, are hospital-owned. The state does not restrict the number of health plans, but does require all plans to go through a procurement process. The state also contracts with a specialty managed care plan, MA Behavioral Health Partnership, to provide behavioral health services to individuals in the PCC plan.

Massachusetts pays plans based on regional administratively set rates. Payments to health plans are risk adjusted using the DxCG risk adjustment system. The state is currently developing a variant of their current risk adjustment model that incorporates "social determinants of health" information.

### BOX 18.3 Kentucky's Medicaid program

In 2011, Kentucky ended its PCCM program and expanded mandatory enroll-ment in private risk-based managed care plans statewide. The state chose to contract with three managed care plans: Aetna Better Health of Kentucky (owned by Aetna), Wellcare of Kentucky (owned by Wellcare), and Kentucky Spirit (owned by Centene). More recently, the state also initiated a contract with Anthem to serve its Medicaid expansion population. All plans are comprehensive MMC plans and there are no service "carve-outs."

In April 2011, the state issued an RFP seeking bids from managed care insurers to cover Medicaid recipients residing outside the Louisville area. They received bids from nine insurers and chose three. After the state selected the three plans, regional rates were negotiated with each managed care plan. Overall, Wellcare negotiated the highest rates and Spirit negotiated the lowest rates. It is not clear whether a promise of favorable autoassignment to plans with lower rates was part of the negotiation process, but ultimately the state did assign more enrollees to the lowest-cost plan in each region than to the other plans (Palmer et al., 2012).

In November 2011, the state autoassigned all Medicaid recipients to one of the three plans and then opened a 90-day open enrollment period during which recipients were able to switch to a different plan (Marton et al. 2016). The autoassignment algorithm took into account prior physician relationships, family relationships, "load balancing," and cost (Palmer et al., 2012).

Following autoassignment, there was substantial switching out of the Kentucky Spirit plan, which had the lowest negotiated rate and was viewed as low-quality, especially in one region where it was unable to contract with a dominant provider group (Marton et al., 2016). Marton et al. find that sicker recipients were more likely to switch out of Spirit and into Wellcare, potentially leading to an adverse selection problem for Wellcare. However, the advanta-geously selected plan, Spirit, exited the market in 2013, citing large financial losses under the low rate it had negotiated with the state.

### BOX 18.4 Chronic Illness and Disability Payment System (CDPS)

The Chronic Illness and Disability Payment System was developed to enable states to calculate risk-adjusted payments to health plans for their Medicaid ben-eficiaries. CDPS groups ICD-9-CM diagnostic codes into 20 major diagnostic cat-egories, which are further subdivided into subcategories by expected expenditure (i.e., high-cost, medium-cost, low-cost). To develop CDPS, regres-sion analysis of Medicaid claims was used to identify which diagnosis in year one predicted expenditure in subsequent years. Then, clinical consultants helped to identify poorly defined diagnoses that were omitted from the set of diagnostic predictors to help mitigate the likelihood of inaccurate reporting. The model also

*(Continued)*

**BOX 18.4 (Continued)**

features separate weights based on demographic and eligibility information, such as disability status.

CDPS uses individual diagnosis and demographic data to calculate individual risk scores which are used to adjust the payments made to health plans. CDPS + Rx is a revised version of CDPS that combines diagnostic predictors from CDPS with pharmacy claims-based predictors using the Medicaid Rx risk adjustment model. Pennsylvania has used the CDPS + Rx risk adjustment model (Courtot et al., 2012). CDPS and CDPS + Rx can be used concurrently, based on current claims, or prospectively based on previous claims. (Kronick et al., 2000)

## ENDNOTES

1. By 2014, 60% of Medicaid recipients were enrolled in a private MMC plan (CMS, 2016b). Often estimates of Medicaid managed care penetration of 70% or higher are cited by policymakers and researchers. The "greater than 70%" estimates include additional forms of "managed care," specifically the use of "primary care case management" (PCCM) programs. These programs are essentially government-run fee-for-service plans with bonuses to primary care providers (PCPs) for each Medicaid PCCM enrollee in their panel. The use of this type of "managed care" arrangement does not fit the mold of regulated competition, and, thus, for the purpose of this chapter we do not count it as managed care.
2. This is becoming less common, however, with only 10 states not enrolling at least some Medicaid recipients in a private MMC plan in 2014 (CMS, 2016b). Throughout this chapter we do not consider state Programs of All-Inclusive Care for the Elderly (PACE) as comprehensive Medicaid Managed Care plans. This differs from the CMS definition.
3. Often, some covered benefits are "carved out" of managed care plan contracts and instead provided and financed via a separate insurance scheme, such as a limited benefit plan or traditional FFS Medicaid. States may contract with insurers to provide a subset of benefits or services to enrollees, such as behavioral health, transportation, dental, or prescription drugs. These contracts, referred to as "limited benefit plans" or "prepaid health plans," are generally paid through capitation. Enrollment into limited benefit plans may include managed care enrollees, fee for services enrollees, or both.
4. This separate nature of the behavioral health system is one reason why states may carve out these services from MMC plans. Behavioral health carve-outs are used in the private health insurance market as well. Large employers may contract separately with a managed behavioral health organization. Alternatively, an employer-sponsored health plan may subcontract with a managed behavioral health organization.
5. For instance, Florida and Missouri have used 1-year contracts with two 1-year renewals for a total contract length of 3 years. Virginia has used 1-year contracts.
6. More details on rate-setting methods are provided in Section 18.3.
7. In some states, such as Missouri, the MMC plan bids do not include a cost bid, thereby focusing the bid entirely on the technical proposal.
8. This policy therefore rewards plans that—based on revealed preference in enrollees' active plan choices—appear to be less desirable. While this policy seems odd, it is consistent with the theme of MMC plans as contractors or partners in administering a welfare program (rather than competitors in a market). Autoassigning more enrollees to smaller plans helps prop up these insurers, making them more likely to succeed and giving them more leverage in contract negotiations with providers.

9. Massachusetts autoassigns Medicaid recipients first to FFS versus MMC and then those individuals who are assigned to MMC are autoassigned to a specific MMC plan.
10. Encounter data include records of services provided to enrollees in a given plan. As the quality of encounter data has improved over the years, some states have begun relying exclusively on encounter data (rather than fee-for-service data) for determining the actuarially sound rate range.
11. Rate ceilings are a natural check on high prices, especially since beneficiaries do not pay higher premiums for plans that are more expensive to the state. Rate floors seem less natural given the state's desire to save money. Our understanding is that they are intended to prevent an MMC plan from mistakenly charging an unsustainably low price and then being forced to drop out mid-way through a contract period.
12. Adverse selection can still occur in zero-premium Medicaid markets, but the mechanism would have to be different. Sicker people might be more aware that certain plans are better quality (or more likely to actively choose a plan).
13. For instance, five states (Arkansas, Indiana, Iowa, Michigan, and Montana) have received federal waivers allowing them to charge premiums to enrollees newly eligible under the ACA (Smith et al., 2016). The "Healthy Indiana Plan" is a typical example. It requires enrollees between 101% and 138% of poverty to pay premiums of 2% of income (about $25/month) to stay enrolled.
14. Iowa stated plans to reward two to four MMC plan contracts in the 2015 Iowa Medicaid Managed Care RFP release (Herman, 2015).
15. Section 18.2 includes more detail on the incentives to carve-out certain Medicaid services.
16. In 2015, nearly all states with risk-based managed care had quality reporting programs, and 28 of the 39 states had pay-for-performance initiatives. Many states were adopting or expanding these initiatives in 2016 and 2017.

# REFERENCES

Akerlof, G., 1970. The market for "lemons": quality uncertainty and the market mechanism. Quart. J. Econ. 84 (3), 488–500.

Ash, A., Ellis, R., Pope, G., et al., 2000. Using diagnoses to describe populations and predict costs. Health Care Finance Review 21 (3), 7–28. Spring.

Brooks, T., Miskell, S., Artiga, S., et al., 2016. Medicaid and Chip Elligibity, Enrollment, Renewal, and Cost-Sharing as of January 2016: Findings from a 50-State Survey. Kaiser Family Foundation, January21. Accessed January 10, 2017. http://kff.org/report-section/medicaid-and-chip-eligibility-enrollment-renewal-and-cost-sharing-policies-as-of-january-2016-premiums-and-cost-sharing/.

Center for Medicaid and State Operations, 2006. Letter to State Medicaid Directors. Center Medicaid and Medicare Services, Retrieved from https://www.medicaid.gov/Federal-Policy-Guidance/downloads/SMD06010.pdf.

Chandra, A., Gruber, J., McKnight, R., 2010. Patient cost sharing in low income populations. Am. Econ. Rev. 100 (2), 303–308.

Courtot, B., Coughlin, T.A., Lawton, E.A., 2012. Medicaid and CHIP managed care payment methods and spending in 20 states. Office of the Assistant Secretary for Planning and Evaluation, US Department of Health and Human Services. Urban Institute, Washington, DC.

Currie, J., Fahr, J., 2005. Medicaid managed care: effect on children's Medicaid coverage and utilization. J. Public Econ. 89 (1), 85–108.

Culter, D., Reber, S., 1998. Paying for health insurance: the trade-off between competition and adverse selection. Quart. J. Econ. 113 (2), 433−466.

Dague, L., 2014. The effect of Medicaid premiums on enrollment: a regression discontinuity approach. J. Health Econ. 37, 1−12.

Dockendorf, M., Larson, E., WasDyke, A., 2014. MO Healthnet Managed Care Rate Development July 1, 2015- June 30, 2016. Mercer. November 10, 2014. Accessed January 10, 2017. https://dss.mo.gov/business-processes/managed-care/bidder-vendor-documents/mercer-presentationmohealthnet-managed-care-rate-development.pdf.

Dorfman, R., Steiner, P., 1954. Optimal advertising and optimal quality. Am. Econ. Rev. 44 (5), 826−836.

Draper, D.A., Hurley, R.E., Short, A.C., 2004. Medicaid managed care: the last bastion of the HMO? Health Affairs 23 (2), 155−167.

Einav, L., Finkelstein, A., Cullen, M., 2010. Estimating welfare in insurance markets using variation in prices. Quart. J. Econ. 123 (3), 877−921.

Ellis, R.P., McGuire, T.G., 2007. Predictability and predictiveness in health care spending. J. Health Econ. 26 (1), 25−48.

Enthoven, A., Kronick, R., 1989. A consumer choice health plan for the 1990s. N. Engl. J. Med. 320, 29.

Frank, R., Huskamp, H., McGuire, T., Newhouse, J., 1996. Some economics of a mental health carve out. Arch. Gen. Psychiatry 56.

Frank, R., Glazer, J., McGuire, T., 2000. Measuring adverse selection in managed health care. J. Health Econ. 19, 829−854.

Geruso, M., Layton, T., Wallace, J., 2016. Are All Managed Care Plans Created Equal? Evidence from Random Plan Assignment in New York Medicaid Managed Care. In preparation.

Gifford, K., et al., 2011. Profile of Medicaid Managed Care Programs in 2010: Findings from a 50-State Survey, A.

Gilmer, T., Kronick, R., Fishman, P., Gianats, T., 2001. The medicaid Rx model: pharmacy-based risk adjustment for public programs. Med. Care 39 (11), 1188−1202.

Glazer, J., McGuire, T.G., 2000. Optimal risk adjustment in markets with adverse selection: an application to managed care. Am. Econ. Rev. 90 (4), 1055−1071.

Handel, B., Hendel, I., Whinston, M., 2015. Equilibria in health exchanges: advrse selection vs. reclassification risk supplement. Econometrica 83 (4), 1261−1313.

Herman, B., 2015. Iowa opens Medicaid program to managed-care bidding. Modern Health Care. Retrieved from http://www.modernhealthcare.com/article/20150224/NEWS/150229971.

Hughes, J., Averill, R., Eisenhandler, J., et al., 2004. Clinical Risk Group's (CRG): a classification system for risk-adjusted capitation based payment and health care management. Med. Care 42 (1), 81−90.

Kaiser Family Foundation (KFF), 2011. A Profile of Medicaid Managed Care Programs in 2010: Findings from a 50 state survey. September 13 Retrieved from http://kff.org/medicaid/report/a-profile-of-medicaid-managed-care-programs-in-2010-findings-from-a-50-state-survey/

Kaiser Family Foundation (KFF), 2016. Total Medicaid Spending. The Henry J Kaiser Family Foundation September. Available from: http://kff.org/medicaid/state-indicator/total-medicaid-spending/?currentTimeframe = 0.

Kaiser Family Foundation (KFF), 2017a. Medicaid Benefits: Prescription Drugs. State Health Facts: Medicaid Benefits Data Collection, Retrieved from http://kff.org/medicaid/state-indicator/prescription-drugs/?currentTimeframe = 0.

Kaiser Family Foundation (KFF), 2017b. Medicaid MCO Parent Firm Activity, by State and Insurance Market. State Health Facts: Medicaid Managed Care Market Tracker, Retrieved from http://kff.org/other/state-indicator/medicaid-mco-parent-firm-activity-by-state-and-insurance-market/?currentTimeframe = 0.

Kronick, R., Gilmer, T., Dreyfus, T., Lee, L., 2000. Improving health-based payment for medicaid beneficiaries. Healthcare Finan. Rev. 21 (3), 29−64. Spring.

Kuziemko, I., Meckel, K., Rossin-Slater, M., 2013. Do Insurer's Risk Select Against Each Other? Evidence from Medicaid and Implications for Health Reform. NBER Working Paper 19198.

Lavetti, K., Simon, K., 2016. Strategic formulary design in medicare Part D plans. Am. Econ. J., Forthcoming.

Layton, T., Geruso, M., Wallace, J., 2016. Are All Managed Care Programs Created Equal? Evidence From Random Plan Assignment in New York Medicaid Managed Care. In preparation.

Layton, T.J., Ellis, R.P., McGuire, T.G., Van Kleef, R., 2017. Measuring efficiency of health plan payment systems in managed competition health insurance markets. J. Health Econ. 56, 237−255.

Lewin Group, July 2009. ACAP, and MHPA. Medicaid Non-Emergency Out-of-Network Payment Study.

Marton, J., Yelowitz, A., Talbert, J.C., 2017. Medicaid program choice, inertia and adverse selection. J. Health Econ. 56, 292−316.

Medicaid and Children's Health, 2013. Medicaid and Children's Health Insurance Programs: Essential Health Benefits in Alternative Benefit Plans, Eligibility Notices, Fair Hearing and Appeal Processes, and Premiums and Cost Sharing; Exchanges: Eligibility and Enrollment. 78 Federal Register 42159. September 15.

Medicaid and CHIP Payment and Access Commission (MACPAC), 2011. Report to the Congress: The Evolution of Managed Care in Medicaid.

Medicaid and CHIP Payment and Access Commission (MACPAC), 2017. Mandatory and Optional Benefits. Retrieved from https://www.macpac.gov/subtopic/mandatory-and-optional-benefits/.

Mershon, E., 2016, May 23. Medicaid Plans Succeed in Obamacare Exchange as Others Struggle. Washington Health Policy: Week in Review. Retrieved from http://www.commonwealthfund.org/publications/newsletters/washington-health-policy-in-review/2016/may/may-23-2016/medicaid-plans-succeed-in-obamacare-exchange-as-others-struggle.

Miyazaki, H., 1977. The rat race and internal labor markets. Bell J. Econ. 8 (2), 394−418.

Office of the Inspector General (OIG), US Department of Health and Human Services, 2014. State Standards for Access to Care in Medicaid Managed Care.

Palmer, A., Howell, E., Costich, J., Kenney, G.M., 2012. Evaluation of Statewide Risk-Based Managed Care in Kentucky. University of Kentucky, Lexington.

Rothschild, M., Stiglitz, J., 1976. Equilibrium in competitive insurance markets: an essay on the economics of imperfect information. Quart. J. Econ. 90 (4), 629−649.

Smith, V., Gifford, K., Ellis., E., 2016. Medicaid Reforms to Expand Coverage, Control Costs, and Improve Care: Results from a 50-State Medicaid Budget Survey for State Fiscal Years 2015-2016. Kaiser Family Foundation, Accessed January 10, 2017. http://files.kff.org/attachment/report-medicaid-reforms-to-expand-coverage-control-costs-and-improve-care-results-from-a-50-state-medicaid-budget-survey-for-state-fiscal-years-2015-and-2016.

Sparer, M., 2012. Medicaid Managed Care: Costs, Access, and Quality of Care. Robert Woods Johnson Foundation, September. Accessed January 10, 2017. http://www.rwjf.org/content/dam/farm/reports/reports/2012/rwjf401106.

Spencer, D., Dybdal, K., Johnson, K., 2012. Stakeholder Analysis of Medicaid Competitive Bidding in Minnesota: Final Report. State Health Access Data Assistance Center (SHADAC), Retrieved from http://archive.leg.state.mn.us/docs/2014/mandated/140686.pdf.

Starc, A., Town, R.J., 2016. Externalities and Benefit Integration in Health Insurance, NBER Working Paper 21783.

Starfield, B., Weiner, J., Mumford, L., Steinwachs, D., 1991. Ambulatory care groups: a categorization of diagnoses for research and management. Health Services Res. 26 (1), 53−74.

US Department of Health and Human Services Centers for Medicare and Medicaid Servies. (CMS), 2016a. Medicaid & CHIP: August 2016 Monthly Applications, Eligibility Determinations and Enrollment Report. Novemer 3. Accessed January 10, 2017. https://www.medicaid.gov/medicaid/program-information/downloads/august-2016-enrollment-report.pdf.

US Department of Health and Human Services Centers for Medicare and Medicaid Servies. (CMS), 2016b. Medicaid and Managed Care Enrollment and Program Characteristics 2014. Spring. Available from: https://www.medicaid.gov/medicaid-chip-program-information/by-topics/data-and-systems/medicaid-managed-care/downloads/2014-medicaid-managed-care-enrollment-report.pdf.

Winkelman, R., Damler, R., 2008. Risk adjustment in state Medicaid programs. Health Watch 57, 1−34.

Chapter 19

# Medicare Advantage: Regulated Competition in the Shadow of a Public Option

Thomas G. McGuire and Joseph P. Newhouse

*Department of Health Care Policy, Harvard Medical School and the NBER, Boston, MA, United States*

## 19.1 INTRODUCTION

The Medicare Advantage (MA) health insurance sector in the US is one of the oldest (dating from 1985 under a different name) and largest markets operated as regulated competition. In 2016, Medicare paid $202.5 billion to MA plans on behalf of 19 million beneficiaries. In terms of spending, MA is one of the three largest regulated competition markets in the world, along with the German Social Health Insurance system and US Medicaid managed care.[1] Some of the technology of risk adjustment of plan payments in use worldwide, notably its clinical grouping, was developed under contract for Medicare. MA has also been subject to a great deal of published research on cost, quality and selection.

### 19.1.1 Medicare Advantage (Medicare Part C)

Since 1985, Medicare beneficiaries have had the option to choose health insurance through a private plan in Medicare Part C, a program now known as MA. MA plans must offer the same coverage as the other option for beneficiaries, Traditional Medicare (TM), consisting of hospital inpatient care (Part A) and office-based care and other services (Part B), and may in addition offer greater coverage and/or offer additional benefits. Prescription drug coverage, which is voluntary but subsidized for both TM and MA beneficiaries, is covered through Part D of Medicare. If they choose to purchase drug coverage, however, virtually all MA beneficiaries must buy it through their MA plan, so-called MA-PD plans.[2] In contrast, beneficiaries choosing TM can choose among several stand-alone drug plans, so-called PDP plans. The subsidy for Part D plans is the same in TM and MA.[3]

Risk Adjustment, Risk Sharing and Premium Regulation in Health Insurance Markets.
DOI: https://doi.org/10.1016/B978-0-12-811325-7.00019-1
**563**

A key difference between TM and MA is that MA enrollees pay much more than TM enrollees to use a provider that is not part of the MA plan's network. For many persons, however, MA will be considerably cheaper over-all because the cost sharing in an MA plan for using an in-network provider is less than TM. Alternatively, many TM beneficiaries have Medigap plans to cover the higher cost sharing, but unless the plan is provided by a former employer or the beneficiary is eligible for Medicaid, beneficiaries will have to purchase it, thus raising the relative cost of TM.[4] Lower out-of-pocket costs in MA make the program particularly attractive to those lower-income beneficiaries with incomes just above the full Medicaid eligibility limit (McWilliams et al., 2011; MedPAC Data Book, 2016, Chart 9−11).[5]

A second key difference is that TM has historically passively reimbursed for services a physician orders, whereas MA plans apply utilization management methods and are more active in denying coverage for services they do not consider justified. From an economic perspective one can regard the MA plans' utilization management as an effort to reduce moral hazard, albeit one subject to error since the beneficiary's willingness-to-pay for a service the MA plan did not deliver may have been above the cost to the MA plan.

Fig. 19.1 shows the steady growth in enrollment in MA for the past 10 years, with its share of beneficiaries roughly doubling over this time period. Currently, MA's share is at an historic high of about 33% (Kaiser Family Foundation, 2017). For the most part, MA plans resemble the private plans offered to the working population through employer-based health insurance, though the provider networks in MA plans may be less broad than plans offered to large employers (Jacobson et al., 2016). The most common type of MA plan is an HMO (like Kaiser Permanente); such plans accounted for 66% of MA enrollment in 2015 (see Box 19.1). Local and regional PPO plans accounted for 24% and 8%, respectively. Private fee-for-service plans, which grew rapidly in the mid-2000s, were for some time not true managed care plans, and have declined sharply in popularity after they were required to have provider networks.

## 19.1.2 In the Shadow of a Public Option

The MA plan market differs from most regulated competition health insurance markets because it operates in the shadow of a public option for Medicare beneficiaries: traditional Medicare. TM is a federally operated social health insurance system modeled on the Blue Cross and Blue Shield plans predominant in the 1960s, at the birth of Medicare. TM pays an open network of providers by service, does not manage care, and attempts to reduce moral hazard with significant deductibles and coinsurance for beneficiaries. Because of the continuing prominence of TM in terms of number of beneficiaries and program costs, most policy interest and research on MA is concerned with MA *in relation to* TM: Are MA plans *less expensive*

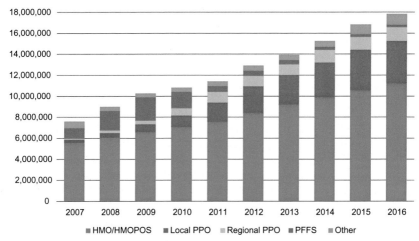

HMO/HMOPOS ■ Local PPO ■ Regional PPO ■ PFFS ■ Other

**FIGURE 19.1** Medicare Advantage enrollment by plan type, 2007 to 2016. *Data are from January of each year (source: https://www.cms.gov/Research-Statistics-Data-and-Systems/ Statistics-Trends-and-Reports/MCRAdvPartDEnrolData/Monthly-MA-Enrollment-by-State-County-Contract.html).*

---

### BOX 19.1 Major types of plans in Medicare Advantage

*HMOs and local Preferred Provider Organizations (PPOs):* These plans have provider networks and use tools such as selective contracting and utilization management to coordinate and manage care and control service use.

*Regional PPOs:* These plans are required to offer a uniform benefit package and premium across designated regions made up of one or more states. Regional PPOs have more flexible network requirement than local PPOs.

*Private Fee-for-Service (PFFS):* Before 2011, PFFS plans typically did not have provider networks and paid providers Medicare rates. Currently, PFFS plans must have provider networks.

Source: *MedPAC (March, 2016, pp. 331–332.)*

---

than TM? Do beneficiaries in MA cost Medicare *less* than beneficiaries in TM? How well does risk adjustment pick up the expected *cost differences* between MA plans and TM? How does the quality of care and beneficiary satisfaction in MA plans *compare to* TM? How should plan payment and beneficiary premiums be set so as to encourage the right beneficiaries to *choose* MA?

A TM-like public option is an anomaly in many health insurance markets. A few states still offer a TM-like option in their Medicaid plans in the United States, though, as described in Chapter 17, Health Plan Payment in

US Marketplaces: Regulated Competition With a Weak Mandate, states are moving away from such open systems and, unlike TM, many physicians do not accept Medicaid patients. Such plans have virtually disappeared from the offerings by private employers. Open network plans could in principle be offered by private insurers in the Marketplaces, as discussed in Chapter 18, Health Plan Payment in Medicaid Managed Care: A Hybrid Model of Regulated Competition, but in fact, no such plans have even been offered, let alone purchased, presumably because the required premiums would render them noncompetitive.[6] In short, when exposed to market tests in employer-based health insurance or on the Marketplaces, open network plans simply cannot compete. Chile and Colombia share some features of the MA-TM set up, with private insurance plans as an option to public health insurance (see Chapter 8: Health Plan Payment in Chile and Chapter 10: Health Plan Payment in Colombia). In most countries, however, a TM-like public option is not offered in the other countries covered in this volume that have implemented regulated competition.

Despite the singularity of the institutional structure of the market for health insurance in Medicare, research and experience in MA have wide applicability. We seek in this chapter to write both for readers interested in MA policy per se and for those with a general interest in regulated competition. We cover some research on MA in relation to TM in terms of cost, quality, and selection but at a high level.[7]

## 19.2 THE CURRENT MEDICARE ADVANTAGE SYSTEM

Regulation of MA plan premiums, coverage, and payment methods is defined in relation to TM. Beneficiaries must pay the premium associated with Part B in TM first, and then any supplemental premium that the MA plan charges (positive or negative). As mentioned above, the types of services covered and the actuarial value of the benefits, including any supplemental premium, must at least equal those offered in TM. Risk adjustment of plan payments is based on relative costs of observably similar patients in TM as well.

### 19.2.1 Premiums, Coverage, and Benefits

MA is an alternative to TM's Part A (hospital and other institutional care) and Part B (mostly physician services). Part A has no premium; Part B, which is optional, does have a premium, but it is sufficiently subsidized that over 90% of Medicare beneficiaries elect it (low-income beneficiaries have it purchased on their behalf by Medicaid).

The premium a Medicare beneficiary pays when choosing an MA plan has two parts, a mandatory and fixed part paid to Medicare, and a variable part set by and paid to the plan. The mandatory part is the standard Part B premium, which in 2016 was $121.80 per month (although through something of a quirk most beneficiaries continued to pay the 2015 premium of $104.90).[8] The vast majority of beneficiaries receive Social Security retirement payments, and for them the Part B premium is simply deducted from their monthly Social Security check.

Subject to the constraint that the actuarial value of the plan's benefits, including any premium the plan charges, must equal or exceed that of TM, the plan can choose its premium and cost sharing. In principle, the premium the plan charges may be positive or negative because of the subsidy the plan receives from Medicare for each enrollee. An MA plan declares its premium in the course of making its "bid" each year in each of its service areas for an average Medicare beneficiary. The mechanics of the bidding in relationship to the Medicare subsidy are described below.

An MA plan can also make itself more attractive in the marketplace by reducing the Medicare Part A and Part B cost sharing and/or offering coverage for additional services. Table 19.1 lists some of the information contained in Medicare's Plan Finder website[9] for Boston zip code 02116 for the top four plans that also offer drug coverage (among 19 such plans) ranked by Medicare's estimate of lowest total cost to the enrollee (premium plus cost sharing).[10] Only one of the plans (Fallon) charged a premium (above the mandatory Part B premium to Medicare). All plans eliminated Medicare's deductibles, provided an out-of-pocket maximum, and offered some coverage for optional dental, hearing, and vision services.[11] Interpreting and comparing information about coinsurance and drug copayments required consulting the detailed benefit information about each plan available by clicking through options on the website.

An MA plan can also buy down the beneficiary premium to a negative value. To do this, the MA plan pays part of the mandatory Part B premium to Medicare on behalf of the beneficiary, reducing the amount deducted from the Social Security check. Positive and negative premiums, however, may have unequal salience for beneficiaries. When a positive premium is required, the beneficiary must pay this directly, typically by writing a check or charging a credit card. When a negative premium is offered, the automatic deduction for the Part B premium from the Social Security check is reduced, and the beneficiary may notice and react less to this form of premium. A zero premium may then serve as a powerful reference price, in which case beneficiaries will be highly responsive to small increases in price above zero while much less responsive to prices below it, effects that have been found empirically both in the United States (Buchmueller and Feldstein, 1997) and in Germany (Schmitz and Ziebarth, 2017).[12]

In fact, fully 50% of MA plans in 2016 charged a premium exactly equal to zero. Fig. 19.2 shows a bunching of 2016 monthly premiums at the value of $104.90, indicating the plans charge a zero premium and beneficiaries simply pay the required Part B premium directly to Medicare. We return to

**TABLE 19.1** Example of Selected Benefits Offered in Medicare Advantage Plans

| Name | Premium | | Deductible | | Coinsurance/Copay | | OOP Max in Network | Other Benefits | Star Rating (of 5) |
| --- | --- | --- | --- | --- | --- | --- | --- | --- | --- |
| | Health | Drug | Health | Drug | Health | Drug | | | |
| Tufts Health Plan (HMO) | $0 | $0 | $0 | $300 | 26% | $6–100 | $3,400 | Dental, Vision, Hearing | 5 |
| Fallon Health (HMO) | $30.20 | $25.80 | $0 | $0 | 33% | $1–86 | $6,700 | Dental, Vision Hearing | 4.5 |
| United Health Care (HMO) | $0 | $0 | $0 | $190 | 28% | $3–95 | $6,700 | Vision, Hearing | 4 |
| Harvard Pilgrim Health Care (HMO) | $0 | $48 | $0 | $320 | 25% | $0–$100 | $3,400 | Vision, Hearing | Not enough data |

Source: https://www.medicare.gov/find-a-plan/results/planresults/plan-list.aspx, accessed September 29, 2016. Zip code 02116 (Suffolk Co., Boston, MA); First four listed plans among 19 MA plans offering drug coverage; sorted by lowest estimated annual health and drug costs. Dental, vision, and hearing indicate some but incomplete coverage for these services. It is necessary to consult the plan's benefit information for details.

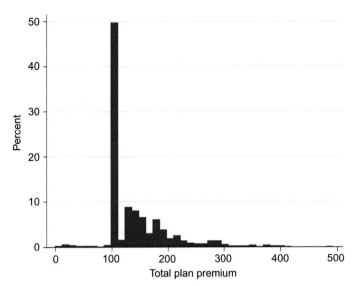

**FIGURE 19.2**   Enrollment weighted distribution of total plan premiums in 2016. *Source: CMS 2016 Landscape, Enrollment, and Benefits Files. Includes MA-PD Local CCP plans (HMOs and PPOs) only and excludes SNPs and employer-sponsored group plans. Also excludes demonstrations, HCPPs, PACE plans, and plans for special populations.*

the potential problems created by this premium system at the close of this chapter.

The package of more generous MA benefits seemingly free at a zero premium is perhaps responsible for an overrepresentation of lower-income beneficiaries in MA plans; they may be more willing than the more affluent to give up the free choice of provider afforded by TM to save money. By contrast, the difference in benefits historically was less relevant for those also eligible for Medicaid ("full dual eligibles") and those with retiree health insurance from their prior employer; if they enrolled in TM, both of these groups had low cost sharing, either from Medicaid in the case of full dual eligibles or from a subsidized supplementary policy from their prior employer in the case of retirees. As a result, most of these two groups, which comprise roughly half of Medicare beneficiaries, historically enrolled disproportionately in TM.

## 19.2.2   Consumer Choices and Lock-In Provisions

Medicare presents beneficiaries, virtually all of whom are elderly or disabled or both, with a set of health insurance choices far more complex than the choices faced by younger, active workers in the United States. If they have a choice of insurance plan at all—and only about half do—active employees typically choose among the two or three plans preselected by their employer, presumably for value. When moving to Medicare, however, a beneficiary's choices proliferate. The beneficiary must first decide whether to enroll in TM or MA, defaulting into TM if no active choice is made. If the beneficiary chooses MA, he or she must choose a plan type (Health Maintenance Organization or HMO, Preferred Provider Organization or PPO, Private Fee-for-Service or PFFS) and within the plan type a specific insurer and plan. If the beneficiary instead chooses TM, he or she must decide whether to enroll in Part B (as noted above, Part B enrollment is mandatory for MA) and whether to purchase a supplementary (Medigap) policy, and if so which one. In either case the beneficiary must decide whether to enroll in Part D, and, if he or she is enrolled in TM (or the PFFS version of MA), which Prescription Drug Plan to choose.

A well-known finding from behavioral economics is that greater choice does not always lead consumers to better decisions (Iyengar, 2004). In conventional economic theory, more choices always benefit a consumer because more choices make for a better match between what is bought and the consumer's preferences. It follows from conventional theory that adding MA plan options should move more beneficiaries out of TM because of the potential for an improved match with consumer preferences. This prediction, however, is inconsistent with the data. Greater plan choice in a county does lead to higher enrollment in MA, but only up to about a menu of about 15 plans. If between 15 and 30 MA plans are offered, the proportion of beneficiaries choosing MA is little affected, but if more than around 30 plans are offered, the proportion choosing MA actually declines (McWilliams et al., 2011).[13] Beneficiaries with higher cognitive scores, however, were more responsive in their plan choice to this greater generosity, supporting the interpretation that the complexity of choice inhibited good decisions for some beneficiaries (McWilliams et al., 2011)).

As an example of excessive choice, beneficiaries in Miami-Dade County in 2008 faced a choice among 123 MA plans, 32 of which were PFFS plans. Sinaiko et al. (2013) document the stickiness in choices among beneficiaries in the richly served Medicare health insurance market in Miami-Dade and interpret the stickiness as resulting from "choice overload."

Originally, Medicare beneficiaries could move between MA and TM, or among MA plans, on a monthly basis. Although originally seen as a beneficiary protection, the ability to change plans monthly facilitated selection and was notably different from employment-based insurance where employees with a choice of plans could typically only change plans annually. Easy movement raised the danger that a beneficiary might switch temporarily into TM to avoid network or other managed care restrictions in times of illness, and then return to MA to save on premiums when less care was needed.[14] In order to reduce such opportunities for selection, the 2003 Medicare Modernization Act changed the policy that beneficiaries could move between MA and TM monthly. The new, more restrictive rules on changing between MA and TM did not take effect until 2006, at which time Medicare beneficiaries who chose MA were locked into their choice for the last 6 months of the year (i.e., they could still change monthly in the first 6 months). In 2007 beneficiaries were locked in for the last 9 months of the year, and in 2011 the lock-in period was further tightened to the last 10.5 months of the year.

### 19.2.3   Instruments Plans Can Use to Manage Cost and Affect Selection

Plans have several sets of instruments to manage costs and quality and to affect the mix of beneficiaries who choose them. Plans generally increase coverage in relation to TM by reducing beneficiary out-of-pocket payments and covering additional services, such as eyeglasses not covered in TM. As do other managed care plans in the United States, they choose how many and which physicians and hospitals are in their networks, although they are subject to Medicare regulations that their networks must be "adequate." They choose the formulary placement of various drugs, along with the copayment for those drugs, though like choices around networks, their choices are somewhat constrained by regulation. Provider reimbursement rates are negotiated, and plans can use the level of reimbursement to induce greater supply of care in some services than others. Plans, however, do not have to pay more than TM reimbursement for out-of-network providers, and patient cost sharing for in- and out-of-network providers is determined by the plan, subject to the constraint that the plan's actuarial value equals or exceeds that of TM. As a result, plans can structure cost sharing to induce most members to use in-network providers, which in turn gives providers an incentive to be in-network at approximately TM reimbursement rates.

### 19.3   HEALTH PLAN PAYMENT

The structure of the MA plan payment is based on TM in two major ways. First, the level of payments: average costs in TM in the county of residence of a beneficiary are the basis of the benchmark in the plan payment formula. Second, the adjustments: the risk adjustment scheme used to adjust plan payments is based on patterns of care in TM rather than in MA.

### 19.3.1   Defining Payments: Benchmarks and Bids

Prior to 1998, plans were reimbursed at a take-it-or-leave-it amount that was a percentage of risk-adjusted average costs in TM, at that time 95% of the county's average.[15] To encourage MA plan entry into low-spending TM markets, in 1998 Congress set floors on MA payments in those markets, which raised benchmark levels above TM. To maintain budget neutrality, the growth of payments in high-spending markets was limited, and in those markets growth in reimbursement fell below the growth of TM spending. In response plans cut benefits or in some cases exited the market.

In 2006 the take-it-or-leave-it system was changed to a bidding system in which MA plans submit bids for care of an average Medicare beneficiary. Each plan's bid is compared with a benchmark; if the bid exceeds the benchmark, Medicare pays the plan the benchmark and the plan has to pass the excess of the bid less the benchmark to beneficiaries in the form of a higher premium. If the bid is below the benchmark, the plan is paid its bid plus a rebate equal to a share of the difference between the benchmark and the bid. The rebate, however, must be passed through to beneficiaries in the form of a lower premium, lower cost sharing, or additional services, or some combination. In practice, virtually all bids are below the benchmark, and plans not receiving a rebate are not competitive. Prior to 2012, plans received 75% of the difference between the benchmark and their bid as a rebate.

At the outset of the bidding system in 2006 the benchmark was set equal to 100% of the prior take-it-or-leave-it price. Between 2006 and 2012 Medicare updated benchmarks by a combination of local and national growth rates, and periodically "rebased" the rates to local TM costs (if this rebasing increased the local benchmark payment).

Since 2012, as specified in the Affordable Care Act (ACA, 2010), the rebate percentage has been reduced and now ranges from 50% to 70% depending on plan quality scores. Medicare summarizes the quality of each plan using a 1−5 star rating (5 is best; half stars are possible).[16] Scoring is based on a combination of measures from administrative data, such as rates of colorectal cancer screening, and patient ratings, for example, ability to access care when needed. Administrative data are from the Healthcare Effectiveness Data and Information Set (HEDIS), and the patient ratings from the Consumer Assessment of Healthcare Providers and Systems—MA (CAHPS-MA) and Health Outcomes Survey (HOS). Rates of complaints and appeals are also incorporated. About a third of the weight is on the plan's Part D offering.

Average plan ratings have crept up over the years since 2012 when the star system was introduced. In 2016, 70% of beneficiaries were enrolled in plans with a 4-star rating or above (the rating at which plans qualify for a quality bonus payment to the benchmark).[17] The increase in star ratings reflected plans' efforts to maximize their rebate, which enhances their competitive position in the local market.

Medicare rules partially connect the premium a plan charges to beneficiaries to the bid. As described above, if the bid exceeds the benchmark, the plan must charge the difference to beneficiaries in a premium as well as charge for any extra benefits over the basic Medicare benefits. This, however, is uncommon. Much more common is that the bid is below the benchmark, in which case the plan must pass 50%−70% of the difference, which is termed the rebate, through to beneficiaries in the form of lower premium or increased benefits; Medicare retains the other 30%–50%. Thus, Medicare's sharing rules are asymmetric around the bid = benchmark point. This is illustrated in Box 19.2.

There are important differences in the financial consequences to an MA plan of raising its bid in the ranges below and above the benchmark implied by the rules in Box 19.2. Holding any extra benefits fixed, when the bid is above the benchmark, an increase in the bid increases the revenue to the plan and the premium charged to the beneficiary dollar-for-dollar. In the range below the benchmark, this is not necessarily true. If we assume for simplicity that the entire adjustment from a change in its bid is in the premium (and not in cost sharing or additional services) and that plan markets are competitive, in the range below the benchmark, $\Delta$premium $= s(\Delta b - R)$. Thus, when the bid increases by \$1, the premium goes up by only \$s (since the plan shares the benchmark–bid gap with Medicare in this range). This asymmetry implies that to achieve a premium reduction to beneficiaries of \$1 in the range of the bid above the benchmark, the plan needs to give up \$1 in revenue per person. To achieve a premium reduction of \$1 in the range of the bid below the benchmark, however, the plan must give up \$1/s > \$1 in revenue per person (still assuming for simplicity that cost sharing and additional services are constant). This asymmetry makes it less attractive for a plan to cut the premium below zero (i.e., charge a negative premium), contributing to the observed bunching of premiums at point of asymmetry observed in Fig. 19.2. It is straightforward for a plan with a zero premium to choose to keep the zero premium even if its rebate changes since it can adjust on the margins of cost sharing or additional services.

---

**BOX 19.2 Bids and benchmarks in Medicare Advantage plan payments**

Let the benchmark be $R$, the plan's bid be $b$, and the share the plan keeps of the benchmark minus bid if the bid falls below the benchmark be $s$, determined by the quality score. Then the premium a beneficiary pays or rebate a beneficiary receives is:

$$\text{Premium} = b - R \text{ if } b \geq R$$

$$\text{Rebate} = s(b - R) \text{ if } b < R$$

Medicare's payment (before risk adjustment) to the plan is:

$$\text{Medicare pays} = \begin{cases} R \text{ if } b \geq R \\ b + s(R - b) \text{ if } b < R \end{cases}$$

The rebate is to be used to reduce the plan's premium, its cost sharing, or to cover services that TM does not cover, or some combination. In addition, the actuarial value of the plan before the rebate must equal or exceed that of TM.

The ACA modified benchmark rules. After a transition that began in 2012 and was completed in 2017, MA benchmark levels are 95−115% of risk-adjusted TM costs according to the TM cost quartile of the county.[18] Counties in the highest-cost quartile have benchmarks equal to 95% of TM cost, whereas those in the lowest have benchmarks set at 115%.[19] MedPAC (March, 2016, 329) estimates that for 2015 the federal average payment including all rebates was 102% of TM average costs. Plan bids, the apples-to-apples comparison of the cost of supplying the TM benefit package in MA, averaged 94% of TM costs; Medicare intends the difference between the 102% federal payment and the 94% bid should go to beneficiaries as additional benefits relative to the TM benefit package. In MA HMO's, federal payments were 101% of TM costs and bids averaged 90% of TM costs, with the 11 percentage point difference available for additional benefits.

## 19.3.2    Risk Adjustment Model

There is one last major component to determining Medicare payment, the role of risk adjustment. Medicare adjusts each plan's reimbursement to be above or below its bid, depending on its mix of enrollees.[20] Prior to 1999 the beneficiary characteristics that Medicare used to adjust consisted of age, gender, Medicaid status, institutional status, and employment status, but those demographic variables explained only about 1% of the variation in the annual spending of individual beneficiaries. Pushed by a Congressional mandate to account for health status in the risk adjustment formula, Medicare moved beyond this primitive risk adjustment scheme to use diagnostic information from claims or encounter data. Thus, Medicare would pay a plan more for enrolling a beneficiary with a more costly diagnosis such as breast cancer than for a beneficiary with a less costly diagnosis such as pneumonia. The relative payment for more costly diagnoses was based on the relative cost of treatment for various diagnoses in TM as recorded on TM claims.

The use of diagnoses to adjust for health status, however, posed a problem because in 2000 coding of diagnoses on TM outpatient claims was incomplete, probably because provider reimbursement for outpatient services did not depend on diagnosis. By contrast, coding of diagnoses in the inpatient setting was accurate because since 1983 such coding had formed the basis of Diagnosis-Related Groups (DRGs), the basis for Medicare hospital reimbursement. Given the coding problem with outpatient claims, CMS in 2000 only added diagnoses coded on inpatient claims as a risk adjuster and ignored diagnoses recorded on outpatient claims. But it gave the method incorporating inpatient diagnoses only 10% weight in calculating reimbursement; the remaining 90% of reimbursement continued to be based on the old method of only demographic adjusters.[21]

In addition to initiating the use of diagnoses to adjust reimbursement, CMS began to enforce a requirement that plans report diagnoses recorded on outpatient claims or encounter forms. In turn, plans took steps to ensure more complete coding of outpatient diagnoses when physicians submitted their claims to the plan.[22] By 2004 outpatient coding was deemed sufficiently reliable that CMS began a transition to the current CMS-HCC method of risk adjustment, which adjusts reimbursement to plans using diagnoses recorded on both inpatient and outpatient claims in addition to demographic variables (Pope et al., 2011). Each CMS-HCC category has a weight, estimated from data on the cost of treating the diagnosis in TM. If a beneficiary has multiple diagnoses, the weights for each are generally added together to form a risk score, and reimbursement is approximately proportional to the risk score.[23] In 2004 the new CMS-HCC method received 30% weight (with the remaining 70% on the prior 90%-demographic−10%-inpatient-diagnosis method described above), in 2005 50%, in 2006 75%, and from 2007 on the new method has been fully in place. Compared with the method used prior to 2000, incorporating the diagnostic information through the CMS-HCCs raised the percentage of explained variance in annual individual spending from 1% to about 11% (Pope et al., 2011, p. 6)

The last publicly available evaluation of the CMS-HCC model by Research Triangle Institute (RTI), the contractor that developed the model, is Pope et al. (2011), which contains an evaluation of the 2005 recalibration of Version 12 (V12) of the model and a comparison with the then-new Version 21 (V21) that was never implemented. A later Version 22 (V22) was implemented, but its evaluation has not been released by CMS as of 2016. In Section 19.4.1 we report the statistics on the evaluation of V21. The major difference between V22 and V21 is that V22 dropped some HCCs from the model, including two for dementia and two for chronic kidney disease; performance in terms of R-squared will thus be worse for V22 than V21, and may be worse in terms of predicted ratios as well.[24]

### 19.3.2.1   Choice of Adjusters

Box 19.3 summarizes the (0,1) variables used as adjusters in the current CMS-HCC model for community-dwelling aged and disabled beneficiaries, by far the largest group of beneficiaries. The clinical grouping begins with the more than 14,000 ICD-9-CM diagnostic codes on claims. These 14,000 codes are grouped into 189 Condition Categories (CCs), at which point a hierarchy among these CCs is imposed (meaning less severe manifestations of a conditions are zeroed out and the more severe manifestation is retained) to arrive at 170 Hierarchical Condition Categories (HCCs). A committee convened by CMS then decides which of these to include as payment HCCs. Version 21 contains 87 payment HCCs.

CMS balances a number of considerations in selecting HCC indicators to include for payment. For example, judgments must be made about achieving higher predictive value at the expense of introducing discretionary codes. CMS also tinkers with estimated coefficients, disallowing negative estimates for any HCC. Pope et al. (2011, pp. 8–9) contains a list of 10 "principles" used in the development of the CMS-HCC model, listed here in Box 19.4.

---

**BOX 19.3 Risk adjusters: the MA CMS-HCC for the aged and disabled**

**Continuing Enrollees**

*Age and gender:* 24 age–gender cells covering the full age range; 0–34, 35–44, 45–54, 5-year bands beginning at 55 to 94, 95 and above.

*Hierarchical Condition Categories:* 70 HCCs for V12; 87 HCCs for V21. Includes selected interactions, such as diabetes and chronic heart failure.

*Other variables:* Medicaid status and an indicator for original eligibility due to disability.

**New Enrollees**

Without a prior year's diagnoses, HCCs cannot be calculated. The new enrollee model uses gender, age in 1-year increments, 65–69, but otherwise same age categories as the continuing enrollees model, Medicaid status, and an indicator for original eligibility because of disability as for continuing enrollees.

Source: *Pope et al. (2011).*

---

**BOX 19.4 Principles for risk adjustment model development in the MA CMS-HCC model**

1—Diagnostic categories should be clinically meaningful.

2—Diagnostic categories should predict medical expenditures.

3—Diagnostic categories that will affect payments should have adequate sample sizes to permit accurate and stable estimates of expenditures.

4—In creating an individual's clinical profile, hierarchies should be used to characterize the person's illness level within each disease process, while the effects of unrelated disease processes accumulate.

5—The diagnostic classification should encourage specific coding.

6—The diagnostic classification should not reward coding proliferation.

7—Providers should not be penalized for recording additional diagnoses (monotonicity).

8—The classification system should be internally consistent (transitive).

9—The diagnostic classification should assign all ICD-9-CM codes (exhaustive classification).

10—Discretionary diagnostic categories should be excluded from payment models.

Source: *Pope et al. (2011, pp. 8–9).*

### 19.3.2.2 Estimating Weights

Weights on all variables are estimated by an ordinary least squares (OLS) linear regression (Pope et al., 2011), with right-hand side variables from Box 19.3 from a prior year. The left-hand side (dependent) variable is Medicare paid amounts from the current year, excluding any beneficiary cost-sharing obligation.[25] Estimates are conducted on data from TM. For example, V12, which went into effect in 2009, was based on a 5% sample of TM data from 2004 and 2005 (Pope et al., 2011, p. 6).

In terms of payment, the MA plans report HCC indicators to Medicare which then plugs these into the risk adjustment formula to determine plan payments.

### 19.3.2.3 Implementation and Maintenance

The underlying classification system on which the CMS-HCC risk adjustment formula is based is continually evaluated and revised by a private contractor, the Research Triangle Institute (RTI). At irregular intervals, CMS either recalibrates the existing model's weights with more recent data, or, less frequently, changes model versions. Currently, MA plans are being paid with CMS-HCC Version 22.

Performance of the MA and TM plan payment systems more broadly is regularly scrutinized on an annual basis by the Medicare Payment Advisory Commission (MedPAC) in its annual March and June reports (MedPAC, March, 2016; MedPAC, June 2016) to Congress. MedPAC's recommendations, together with recommendations from the Secretary of Health and Human Services, form the basis for annual updates to the benchmarks decided by Congress. These analyses may also lead to modification of risk scores, quality scores, rebate rules, beneficiary premium requirements, lock-in requirements, and other features of the plan payment system.[26] The research community also addresses aspects of MA plan payment. Some of these policy evaluations by the public sector and the private research community are noted in Section 19.4.

### 19.3.3 Payment Flows

Fig. 19.3 describes the payment flows to Medicare overall and within that to MA plans. Federal Medicare payments are financed by a combination of general federal tax revenue, contributions to a Medicare Hospital Insurance (HI) Trust Fund through ear-marked payroll taxes, and premiums paid by beneficiaries (MedPAC, March, 2016). Currently, the HI Trust Fund pays for about 44% of Medicare expenses but the Fund is running a deficit and is projected by Medicare Trustees to reach a zero balance by 2028 (2016 Boards of Trustees 2016 Annual Report, pp. 4−5). A second trust fund, The Supplementary Medical Insurance (SMI) Trust Fund, is funded from general revenues, which come primarily from personal and corporate income taxes,

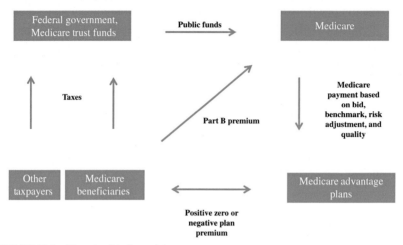

**FIGURE 19.3**   Financing Medicare Advantage.

and covers the balance of expenditures. Premiums for Part B are set to roughly 25% of expected costs, and these flow into the SMI Trust Fund, with the balance of Part B expenses being met from general revenues at the federal level. The SMI Trust Fund is considerably smaller than the HI Trust Fund and essentially functions as a working cash balance; if it is in need of funds, it simply draws on federal tax revenues.

Currently, general revenues pay for 42% of Medicare spending, and this is projected to grow to 48% by 2030 (MedPAC, March, 2016, p. 18). Unlike a universal system where everyone participates in the same financing system, Medicare draws the bulk of its funds from younger taxpayers who are not currently beneficiaries. Although the current beneficiaries paid into the HI Trust Fund when they worked, these payments do not cover the costs of current beneficiaries, implying that purchasing power is transferred across age cohorts. The general revenue component of Medicare costs is covered by current taxpayers (some of whom of course are Medicare beneficiaries, including the two coauthors of this chapter).[27]

## 19.4   EVALUATION OF HEALTH PLAN PAYMENT AND PERFORMANCE OF THE MA MARKET

The various parties evaluating the MA plan payment methodology have used several perspectives. Developers of the risk adjustment model evaluate the risk adjustment formula based on fit criteria at the individual and group level (Pope et al., 2014). MedPAC evaluates the policy performance of the overall payment method in terms of Medicare's goals. The research literature covers the full range of issues, tending to focus on comparing MA to the public option of TM.

### 19.4.1    RTI Evaluations of the Risk Adjustment Model

Using Medicare claims data, Pope et al. (2011) report that the CMS-HCC V21 model produced an R-squared statistic, which describes fit at the individual level, of 0.1246 for the largest group of beneficiaries, the aged-disabled community sample of continuing enrollees (those for whom a prior year of claims data are available for estimation). V21 improves the fit over V12 which was 0.1091.[28]

Most of RTI's evaluation of V21 assesses fit at the group rather than the individual level using predictive ratios (PRs), with a numerator equal to the average of predicted values from the risk adjustment model for a given group and a denominator equal to the actual average cost of the group. PRs for groups defined by variables used in the model will be 1.0 for in-sample predictions by properties of OLS. Consequently, it is more informative to investigate PRs for groups defined by variables not in the model, particularly by variables that could be included in the model. The Swiss risk adjustment model, for example, includes indicators for prior hospitalization as a risk adjustor variable. In the CMS HCC V21 model, beneficiaries with no hospitalization in the prior year have a PR of 1.037 (See Table 3.33, p. 76 from the RTI report). The PR is below 1.0 for beneficiaries with hospitalization in the prior year, falling to 0.831 for beneficiaries with three or more hospitalizations in the prior year. These are likely to be very expensive beneficiaries so the "underpayment" of 16.9% probably corresponds to a substantial absolute dollar loss for this high-need group.[29]

### 19.4.2    MedPAC Reports: Policy Analysis

MedPAC evaluates the policy performance of the entire MA payment system (as well as the TM system), but relative to the academic literature on MA it tends to focus on budgetary expenditure rather than social efficiency. MedPAC evaluates in relation to two primary goals Medicare had in implementing Part C (McGuire, Newhouse, and Sinaiko, 2011, p. 289):

1. "Giving beneficiaries a choice of health insurance plans beyond the fee-for-service Medicare program, and
2. Transferring to the Medicare program the efficiencies and cost savings achieved by managed care in the private sector."

MedPAC also has had a long-standing view that reimbursement should be financially neutral between TM and MA. It reports annually on access, cost, and quality in the MA program.

According to the March 2016 MedPAC *Report* (March, 2016, p. 335), with respect to the first objective, "access to MA plans remains high." In 2016, continuing a pattern from earlier years, virtually all Medicare beneficiaries had access to at least one HMO/local PPO type MA plan. Eighty percent of beneficiaries had access to at least one plan offering drug coverage at a "zero premium." The average beneficiary-weighted number of MA plan choices was 18.

Evaluating the cost of the MA program involves a comparison of what Medicare pays for a beneficiary in MA (which can be known) to what Medicare would have paid for that beneficiary had the beneficiary stayed in TM (which must be estimated or inferred). At the beginning of the Part C program, favorable selection into MA (not accounted for by risk adjustment) led Medicare to pay more for beneficiaries in MA than it would have had they stayed in TM, in spite of some cost saving in MA plans, and in spite of payment rules that initially paid MA plans at 95% of the TM average. Because of the floors (minimum MA reimbursement above TM) in low-spending TM counties that were described above, more intensive coding, and favorable selection, overpayments continued, with MedPAC (2009) estimating that the average beneficiary in 2008 would have cost 12% less in TM than what Medicare paid the MA plans. As noted above, the ACA (2010) reduced benchmarks and made coding adjustments which reduced government payment, but added payments for quality scores, which as of 2016 left MA payments on average at 102% of average TM costs, though as explained above the actual cost of delivering the same benefits in MA was 94% of average TM cost; the excess went to beneficiaries as additional benefits above TM. Risk adjustment and lock-in provisions have reduced but likely not eliminated selection (discussed below), leaving Medicare still in a position of likely paying more for beneficiaries in MA than if the same beneficiaries had stayed in TM. Paying more, of course, is not a sufficient condition to establish social inefficiency.

## 19.4.3   Research Literature on MA and TM

### 19.4.3.1   Use and Costs in MA and TM

The quantity of health care provided, e.g., admissions, surgeries, and length of stay in hospitals, tends to be lower in MA than TM for otherwise similar beneficiaries. Landon et al. (2012) used national survey data to match beneficiaries in MA and TM by location and personal factors affecting use to compare procedure rates in MA and TM. Rates of ambulatory surgery and emergency department use were 20%−30% lower in MA, with differences concentrated in "discretionary" procedures like hip replacements. In other work, Landon et al. (2015) compared resource use for episodes of care for diabetes and cardiovascular disease and found a 20% lower rate of service use in MA for both disease groups. Cost comparisons at the end of life also favored MA (Stevenson et al., 2013). In 2009 emergency department use, for example, was less than half as great in the last 6 months of life for decedents enrolled in MA relative to decedents enrolled in TM after matching on age, sex, race, and location. Hospital admissions were 13% less.

Duggan et al. (2015) followed Medicare beneficiaries in New York State who were involuntarily disenrolled from their MA plan following plan exit and joined TM, finding that inpatient hospital utilization went up 60%, with rates of increase higher for elective procedures. With hospital costs about 40% of the total (and assuming no offsetting increase in outpatient costs), these estimates correspond to about a 20% lower cost for MA plans. Curto et al. (2014) backed out MA costs implied by MA bidding patterns (and profit maximization with some market power) to conclude that MA plans provide TM benefits at 12% lower cost than TM.

Setting aside deadweight loss from financing, quantity differences, not price differences, are relevant for comparisons of social costs. From Medicare's standpoint, however, cost differences include both a price and quantity component. MA plans can pay out-of-network providers at the TM rate, and negotiate prices with in-network providers. In-network physician payments tend to be at or a little above the Medicare fee schedule.[30,31] Indeed, MA plans could likely not compete with TM unless their unit prices were roughly similar. The Affordable Care Act required that MA plans pay out 85% or more of their premium dollar as medical benefits, and firms that are not price competitive on 85% of their input costs are not likely to remain in business very long. Moreover, MA plans have a credible threat; if they collectively fail to get unit prices near those of TM and exit the market, their beneficiaries would default to TM, in which case the provider would simply get the TM price.

### 19.4.3.2   Quality of Care

Medical management methods that MA plans employ could in principle improve or degrade the quality of care they give relative to TM. It is difficult to compare quality of care in TM and MA because the data necessary to do so are sparse (Landon et al., 2012; Ayanian et al., 2013b, *Health Affairs*) A small number of comparisons can be made from the beneficiary reported data on the Consumer Assessment of Health Plans (CAHPS) surveys, but beneficiaries' ability to assess the technical quality of their care is clearly limited. HEDIS process measures are available to assess technical quality among MA plans, which must report such measures to CMS, but there is no comparable reporting for TM. Most HEDIS process measures cannot be calculated from the claims data available for TM because the measures require data from the medical chart, for example, the proportion of controlled hypertensives or the proportion of beneficiaries with Hba1c values over 7.

Some comparable HEDIS measures however, can be calculated from TM claims, and some measures of patient satisfaction can be compared using CAHPS. For those measures that can be compared, MA plans generally score better than TM (Newhouse and McGuire, 2014). In addition, there is a small amount of evidence MA plans ameliorate healthcare disparities by race and ethnicity compared to TM. In particular, a comparison of differences by racial and ethnic group in mammography rates shows that MA plans not only reduce disparities but that the traditional differential between whites and minority groups in TM reverses in MA (Ayanian et al., 2013a, *JCNI*).[32]

### 19.4.3.3   *Favorable Selection into MA Conditional on Risk Score*

Prior to the mid-2000s, risk adjustment of MA plan payments was primitive, and switching rules allowed beneficiaries to enroll/disenroll on a monthly basis as described above. Early research on MA showed considerable favorable selection into MA plans even after the risk adjustment of plan payments (Newhouse and McGuire, 2014). Improvements in the risk adjustment formula and tightening of switching rules have greatly reduced the degree of favorable selection into MA (Newhouse et al., 2015).

There are two reasons why beneficiaries might be healthier/less costly in TM conditional on risk score. The first is differences in coding practices; the same person could be coded as sicker in MA than in TM, resulting in the person being placed in a higher weighted CMS-HCC category. Physicians in TM are not paid according to diagnosis (they are paid by procedure), whereas MA plans have an incentive to encourage more intensive coding among their providers to increase the measured risk score. For example, some MA plans encourage providers to conduct "health risk assessments" to find and code otherwise overlooked diagnoses. Geruso and Layton (2015) find that MA plans code 6−16% higher for the same person as TM, and that elevated coding is greater in the vertically integrated MA plans where a plan is in a better position to transmit incentives to providers. Other studies substantiate this finding (GAO, 2013; Kronick and Welch, 2014). In response, the ACA mandated annual coding adjustments each year that by 2016 had cumulated in a 26% cut in the MA benchmark. Nonetheless, MedPAC (March 2016) recommends further downward adjustments in Medicare payments, fundamental revision of the coding formula (using two instead of one year of diagnostic data), and disregarding diagnoses from health risk assessments not supported by active treatment—all because of aggressive coding in MA.[33]

The second reason is selection. Measured risk scores capture only a portion of the variation in expected costs, and individuals with higher expected costs conditional on risk scores may prefer TM with its unlimited provider choice and freedom from managed care techniques. Additionally, MA plans may structure their product to deter higher-cost beneficiaries conditional on risk score. A long line of early research established favorable risk selection into MA. Prior to Medicare policy changes in the mid-2000s, the consensus in the health economics and policy literature was that MA plans benefited from favorable selection net of any risk adjustment transfers.[34] The Congressional Budget Office (1997) concluded that selection more than undid Medicare's practice at the time of paying on 95% of the risk-adjusted TM average, leading to a net average overpayment of 8% for every MA enrollee relative to their costs in TM. Stronger evidence of selection was the finding by Medicare Payment Advisory Commission analysts that mortality rates among MA enrollees in 1998 were 15% lower than among TM enrollees after adjusting for age, sex, and Medicaid status (MedPAC, 2000).

Recent research continues to find favorable selection into MA conditional on risk scores, but a lower magnitude than prior to improvements in risk adjustment and introduction of longer lock-in periods for enrollment.[35] McWilliams, Hsu, and Newhouse (2012) compare selection in the early 2000s to years later in the decade and find declining selection as measured by self-assessed health status and utilization. Although these comparisons are not net of risk adjustment, they are particularly helpful because they compare the entire stock of MA enrollees versus the entire stock of TM enrollees, whereas most of the other studies compare the small number of switchers with nonswitchers and show that much of the favorable selection within the age–sex categories that constituted risk adjustment prior to the advent of the CMS-HCCs had disappeared. (The proportion of switchers in the 2004–2008 period was 1%–4% of enrollees in each year [Newhouse et al., 2012].) Furthermore, Newhouse et al. (2012) find mortality differences between MA and TM declined from 15% to 7% between 1998 and 2008 and was an insignificantly 1% different for those enrolled in MA or TM for five or more years. Since the MA share was growing substantially in the five years prior to 2008 but has been relatively stable in the past few years and disenrollment is only a few percent each year, the picture from a more recent year would probably show a considerably higher proportion of MA enrollees having been in MA for five or more years.

Switchers into MA are 2.3% less expensive than stayers in TM (conditional on risk score) in Curto et al. (2014). Newhouse et al. (2015), in an analysis of MA switchers, find recent declines in selection with some remaining selection.[36] Another finding supports a view of some remaining selection in each year between 2004 and 2008: over half of nondecedents who disenroll from an MA plan re-enrolled in MA within a year of disenrolling (Newhouse et al., 2012). Why did they disenroll and then re-enroll shortly thereafter? A likely possibility is that they wanted to have a procedure done by an out-of-network provider and after the procedure was complete, they re-enrolled. Consistent with this view, those disenrolling have higher risk scores. However, as just noted, the proportion of disenrollees in any one year is small, only about 2%–3%, so their influence on the amount of selection overall is small.

In their structural model of the MA sector, Curto et al. (2014) use mortality to check for selection differences net of risk adjustment.[37] They find lower mortality in MA, conditional on risk score, though again, the mortality gap with TM is lower in the more recent periods.[38] By comparing costs conditional on risk score, Curto et al.'s estimate that MA plan enrollees are about 7% less costly than TM conditional on risk score captures both differences due to coding practices and differences due to selection.

### 19.4.3.4   Service-Level Selection in MA compared to TM

Service-level selection refers to a second inefficiency associated with adverse selection: plans distorting their benefits or service offerings in order to attract financial winners and deter losers. Although nominal benefits are regulated in MA, plans can work around the regulations by creating networks and drug formularies that favor/disfavor certain conditions or that impose more or less strict care management techniques across different categories of care. Breyer et al. (2012, p. 729) refer to these activities as "indirect selection." Incentives for service-level selection have been studied theoretically, and there is also empirical literature on the existence of extensive service-level selection. The empirical estimates of the extent of service-level selection, of course, are conditional on the risk adjustment method that is in place.

Ellis and McGuire (2007) show that when plans are designed to maximize profits, plans have an incentive to ration services more tightly that are predictive of plan losses, predictable by beneficiaries, and exhibit high demand elasticity. They measure plan incentives for various sets of services in Medicare, and note the general confirmation with empirical findings from an earlier paper by Cao and McGuire (2003). Ellis et al. (2013) rank services in Medicare according to incentives to undersupply them. Consistent with service-level selection, they show that HMO-type plans tend to spend less on predictable and predictive services than unmanaged plans just as the selection index predicts. Brown et al. (2014) and Newhouse et al. (2015) study how selection into MA changed after the introduction of the CMS-HCC method of risk adjustment. Both studies find that after the new method was introduced, MA plans attracted sicker Medicare beneficiaries, a result consistent with a decline in service selection with improved risk adjustment and tighter lock-in policies. This result is also consistent with the mortality and utilization changes described above. Newhouse et al. (2013) study relative margins in one MA plan across HCCs to determine if beneficiaries in HCCs with high profit margins were overrepresented relative to their presence in TM; surprisingly they were not.[39]

## 19.5   ONGOING ISSUES AND DIRECTIONS FOR REFORM

Topics for reform of the health plan payment system to MA relate both to supply—how plans are paid—and to demand—how plans are priced to beneficiaries. We identify and make some brief comments on each side of the market, noting some ongoing research. The supply side has tended to receive more attention in US policy circles. Premium policy deserves attention as well.

## 19.5.1    Choosing Data to Use for MA Risk Adjustment Modeling

Currently, the data used to estimate the relative weights of risk adjuster variables in the CMS-HCC risk adjustment models used to pay MA plans comes from the beneficiaries in TM; in other words, from the beneficiaries who *chose not to join MA*. Are the patterns of use of these beneficiaries the right patterns to set for MA plans?

One can think of this issue as being composed of two components. First is the question of which beneficiaries should be used to estimate a risk adjustment model. Should these be beneficiaries in MA or beneficiaries in TM? Second is the issue of the patterns of use. Should the patterns be drawn from TM or from MA (for whatever population is deemed appropriate)?

In terms of the population, since MA plans are responsible for providing health care to the beneficiaries that choose to join them, it seems clear that, ideally, the population joining MA is the relevant one. Suppose, for example, that 50% of the male Medicare beneficiaries joined MA plans but none of the females did, and that males had different patterns of need than females. Would we want to estimate a risk adjustment model on the TM sample, more than half of which was female to set payment weights for the males in TM?

Probably not, and this example points to a possible direction for addressing the issue: use the males in TM to estimate relative weights for the MA joiners. Ongoing research by Rose and colleagues, following up on similar research on data selection in US Marketplaces (Rose et al., 2015) pursues this idea, applying matching and weighting methodologies to identify a sample in TM with the same distribution of characteristics as the beneficiaries who join MA, and developing methods for evaluating the potential contribution of the sample selection. Regression techniques, as for example in Pope et al. (2011) adjust for some differences in characteristics across the samples. The potential value of matching methods is to escape the functional form assumptions in conventional regression methods.

With regard to "what patterns?," the use of the TM data may be a plus, not a minus, for two reasons. First, suppose MA could provide equal quality of care for much less cost for one group of beneficiaries, say those with diabetes, and not others. If one used patterns of relative cost in MA to pay plans, beneficiaries with diabetes would be no more attractive to plans than others. If one used TM patterns, however, the diabetics would be relatively attractive and plans would be given incentives to attract them out of the relatively inefficient TM. Second, in a related point, suppose one thought MA plans were using service-level selection to compete for the good risks and deter the bad risks, and thus, the patterns of care in MA were distorted by this unproductive competition. The patterns in TM, however, would be untainted by service-level selection and might therefore be a better choice for estimation. Note also that if the TM patterns were superior, once Rose et al. select the people in TM who are like the people in MA, they could use the TM data to estimate the preferred risk adjustment model.

### 19.5.2 Flat-of-the-Curve Research: More/Better Variables and the Risk Adjustment Formula

There is obviously a tradeoff between including more variables in a risk adjustment model to improve fit at both the individual and group levels and some of the unintended incentives created by adding variables: providing too many/unnecessary services to up the codes, or simply adding codes without changing services, not to mention resources expended to learn how to maximize under the new rules. In terms of the gains from adding variables, we may be at or near the flat of the curve within the indicators available in the CMS-HCC system. Going from V12 to V21 added about 0.01 to the R-squared, and the V21 system was regarded as too gameable for dementia and some other conditions so, after dropping eight variables, the system in use, V22, would have incremented the R-squared by an even smaller amount. Meanwhile, health plans and healthcare providers are investing billions of dollars into training and data systems to partly do a better job at extracting codes from records, as well as investing care resources to identify cases.[40]

There are feasible and attractive alternatives to adding more diagnostic indicators (or their interactions). Fit can be improved substantially (assuming that is at least one of the objectives) without generating adverse incentives by integrating a reinsurance-like feature in the payment system. Reinsurance refers to when, in exchange for a premium, a plan is reimbursed a share of costs after a threshold, for example, 80% of costs after $500,000 of cost for a person during a year. The very high-cost cases are responsible for the bulk of plan losses, and paying more for them via reinsurance can markedly improve payment system fit. A current example is the new targeted pharmacologic treatments for cancer that may cost $100,000 or more per treated patient per year. Diagnostic groups containing patients when a substantial fraction of them need the drug and another substantial fraction does not would leave underpayment for very high-cost cases since the current system has no adjuster for taking the drug and so the weight for such patients averages the costs of the two groups. Adding a drug indicator in the risk adjustment would improve fit but at the price of creating incentives for plans to use the expensive drugs too frequently. Reinsurance can address such a problem, and has the added virtue of being flexible in terms of accommodating expensive treatments as they appear without a revision to the coding formula. (See also Chapter 4 where risk sharing is discussed in more detail.)

The reinsurance function can be integrated into the risk adjustment formula. In data from Germany (Schillo et al., 2016), the Netherlands (Van Barneveld et al., 1998, 2001), and Switzerland (Schmid and Beck, forthcoming), all with regulated individual health insurance markets sharing features with MA, reinsurance is very effective at improving fit. Schillo et al. (2016) consider inclusion of (0,1) indicators of high-cost groups in the German risk adjustment formula. A single dummy variable for a "funding gap above €30,000" in the regressions reported in Schillo et al. (2016) increases the R-squared of the risk adjustment model from 27.6% to 51.0%.[41] A similar empirical approach was studied earlier in the Netherlands—including an indicator for exceeding a cost threshold in multiple past years as a risk adjuster (Van Kleef and Van Vliet, 2012), and subsequently included in the Dutch risk adjustment methodology. High thresholds would have very little effect on plans' incentives to control costs. Layton and McGuire (2017) find that in the US Marketplaces, a threshold of $500,000 per year would touch only 0.02% of enrollees. The percentage would likely be higher in Medicare with its higher-cost population, but would still amount to a very small share of the population.

### 19.5.3    Setting the Level of the Subsidy to MA

A decision about the level of government payment in Medicare can be framed as a decision about the level of the benchmark. In addition to government payments, the benchmark affects all the economic outcomes of the MA program: the supply of MA plans, the supplemental benefits these plans offer, any supplemental premium (positive or negative) charged to beneficiaries, and beneficiary enrollment. As a result, setting the level of the benchmark is among the most important decisions Medicare makes about the MA program. There are a number of economic forces that play into this decision, and these forces likely differ in different local MA markets.

The subsidy to MA plans has been controversial since the beginning of Medicare Part C more than 30 years ago. Originally, on the basis of anticipated efficiencies of managed care, the intended subsidy was negative; Medicare paid private plans 95% of local Medicare average costs.[42] The benchmark is now on average set at 107% of TM costs (MedPAC, March, 2016), whereas many policy analysts recommending reducing it to 100% of TM costs so as to achieve "payment neutrality," or "a level playing field."[43]While "payment neutrality" and "level playing field" sound intuitively appealing, the economics of health insurance markets imply that a level playing field is unlikely to be Medicare's optimal rule for setting the level of the benchmark.

The versatile model of health plan choice developed by Einav and Finkelstein (2011) can be applied to the MA-TM setting. The well-known EF result is that the regulator should set *unequal subsidies* to favor the plan attracting the higher-risk groups to counter the effect on premiums of risk selection into the more generous plan. The EF model was originally applied to a two-choice setting in employer-based health insurance where there is no risk adjustment. Applying this model to the MA-TM setting, the EF result holds only if there is some favorable selection into MA conditional on risk score (i.e., after risk adjustment) (Glazer and McGuire, 2017). If so, Medicare should set the subsidy (the benchmark level) to MA *below* that of TM.

In markets where MA plans have market power (see Section 19.5.5 for some evidence), however, Medicare can counter the monopolist's tendency to raise prices and restrict output (limit enrollment) by raising the benchmark.[44] It may be counterintuitive (and unappealing) to policymakers to raise payments in the face of an exercise of market power, but if market efficiency is the objective, the classic solution of subsidizing monopoly may apply in certain MA markets.

The presence of "spillovers" from MA to TM, if clearly demonstrated, should also feed into the decision about a benchmark. If expanding the MA presence in a market has a favorable impact on costs and quality for TM and/or for other payers, such as commercial insurers and Medicaid, membership in MA should be subsidized by a higher benchmark. Baicker et al. (2013) find that lower-cost practice patterns in MA plans do decrease costs in TM in the same locales.[45] More research on the possible policy externality associated with MA is needed to confirm and quantify any spillovers.

### 19.5.4 Framing the Beneficiary Premium to Increase Demand Response and Competition

As noted above, Medicare presents positive and negative premiums for MA plans to beneficiaries in different ways, creating an asymmetric demand response around a zero supplemental premium.[46] Actively writing a check for a positive premium is more salient than passively having less automatically deducted from a Social Security check. In another context, Finkelstein (2009) finds that automatic deductions of toll charges on the highway allowed states—acting just like monopoly sellers—to raise toll rates because of the reduced salience of the automatic deductions. Furthermore, research shows that zero is a special price (Shampanier, Mazar, and Ariely, 2007). In binary choice situations, the higher-priced option is more disadvantaged at $1 versus $0 than at $11 versus $10.

The kink in demand caused by the unequal salience of a positive and a negative price (and reinforced by asymmetry in the treatment of bids and benchmarks discussed above) has adverse consequences (Newhouse and McGuire, 2014). Reduced salience translates to demand inelasticity, and the less elastic is demand, the more a firm with market power can mark up costs in setting a market price. Second, the kink means that MA plans get little enrollment reward by reducing price below "zero" and so tend to stop there with respect to price reductions. The implication for the market is the bunching at zero shown in Figure 19.2. Any rebate plans return to beneficiaries is directed away into an inefficient enhancement of benefits rather than simple price reductions to beneficiaries.[47]

The kink in demand appears to be inhibiting the pass through of benchmark changes to beneficiaries.[48] Papers studying market circumstances where pass throughs vary are particularly informative about the role of market power and the presence of a kink contributing to the story contributing to the bunching and absence of a near full pass through. In Cabral et al. (2014), while the average pass through is around 50%, it is much higher, 74%, in the most competitive MA markets, and much lower, only 13%, in the least competitive markets. Stockley et al. (2014) found that the responsiveness of premiums and benefits to a change in the benchmark is greater when the plan is in the range of setting a positive premium than when in the negative range, consistent with the kinked demand curve idea. Pelech's (2015) study of regulatory shocks to the market structure in MA on premiums and benefits is also consistent with a kinked demand curve.[49] As plans gain market power, they ought to increase premium, decrease benefits, or both. In fact, there was little evidence for a premium increase overall, whereas benefits did decrease, consistent with plans being "stuck" at the kink of a zero premium. Furthermore, Pelech (2015) found benefits responded much more to a change in market structure for plans at zero premium than for plans charging a positive premium, as also would be predicted if premiums were stuck at zero.[50]

An administrative change not altering anything "real" could address this salience-related problem. Beneficiaries could pay for MA plans the same way they pay for Part B in TM by deducting any MA premium from Social Security checks. This would face beneficiaries with a choice of $104.90 per month for TM versus, for example, $109.90 for an MA plan that charged a $5 monthly additional premium (at 2016 rates). At a minimum, this would increase convenience to beneficiaries. In economic terms, such a change should increase demand elasticity (decreasing market power for MA plans) and decrease prices, leading to more MA enrollment, and a more efficient set of premium-coverage offerings by plans. Moreover, the tendency of beneficiaries to overweight premiums and underweight later cost sharing and higher benefits would work towards further increasing MA enrollment.

### 19.5.5   Competition in the MA Plan Market

The supply side of many MA markets is highly concentrated. At the national level in 2015, the top four insurers enrolled 54% of beneficiaries (United Health, 20%; Humana, 19%; Aetna, 7%; Kaiser, 7%) (MedPAC, March 2016). Potential mergers would push this concentration even higher. One insurer can offer multiple contracts in the same local market, for example, an HMO form and a PPO form, in order to compete in different market segments. Differentiation of products within MA, e.g., staff model HMO versus a PPO, tends to weaken competition for a given number of insurers. Thus, while many markets have a large number of plan options, concentration at the insurer level is what matters for market power.

On average, local MA markets are highly concentrated. Curto et al. (2014) report that for 2006−11, in the majority of counties, the three largest insurers had at least a 90% share of the MA market. In 2015, there was an average of just 3.2 insurers offering plans per county (MedPAC, 2016, 329). The average Herfindahl−Hirschman Index (HHI) in counties during 2010−2012 was 4,464 in Pelech (2015). (An HHI above 2,500 indicates "high concentration.")

Interpreting measures of MA market concentration, however, needs account for the presence of the public option. Even if only a few MA plans participate in a local market, to the degree that TM and MA plans are substitutes, the presence of TM would limit the market power of MA plans since TM is the dominant plan in almost all local markets. The market power of MA plans also should be assessed against the market power of local providers. Local providers with substantial market power may capture some rents that might otherwise go to plans with market power.

## 19.5.6    Ongoing Changes in TM and Effects on MA

Reforms in TM will also affect MA, in terms of both the supply of healthcare providers to MA plans, and in terms of the demand by beneficiaries. The most prominent current reform in TM, initiated by the Affordable Care Act of 2010, is the advent of Accountable Care Organizations (ACOs), a third arm of Medicare to go along with TM and MA. ACOs are formed at the discretion of provider groups "that are willing to become accountable for the quality, cost, and overall care of the fee-for-service Medicare beneficiaries assigned to it." (Section 1899(b)(2)(A) of the ACA.) ACOs agree to bear some risk in payment, although that risk may be asymmetric (only sharing in gains relative to a target) for the first few years. Beneficiaries do not actively choose ACO membership, but instead are assigned to the physician from whom they receive the plurality of their primary care services. If this physician is part of an ACO, then that ACO can share in any cost savings that may arise from treating the beneficiary, where savings are measured against estimated total TM costs for that beneficiary. From the beneficiary's point of view, the ACO program looks like TM except beneficiaries receive a letter advising them that they can opt out of having CMS share their claims data with the ACO.

The ACO program is something of a halfway house between TM and MA. Like MA, ACOs can profit from treating beneficiaries at lower cost than TM. Unlike MA, however, beneficiaries do not enroll in an ACO, and they can use any provider participating in TM with the same financial liability that they would have had in TM. In other words, because there are no networks there are no higher out-of-pocket payments from using a physician who is out-of-network. Any rationing of care or use of conservative specialists is left to the primary care physician and any medical management used by the ACO.

Many Medicare ACOs are also establishing ACO-like organizations in commercial insurance without the specific requirements for Medicare participation. Compared with Medicare ACOs, commercial ACOs look much more like classic HMOs, since unlike Medicare ACOs they can impose high charges for receiving services outside the ACO delivery organization. They differ from a commercial HMO with arms-length, fee-for-service contracts with provider groups in that typically the ACO and an insurer are joint residual claimants and thus share financial risk. ACOs have been reasonably well-accepted by many larger provider organizations, and so far have had a measurable but small effect on patterns of care in TM (McWilliams et al., 2016). If ACOs grow, and have more of an impact on costs and care, they will likely have an effect on choices providers and beneficiaries make between TM and MA.

## ACKNOWLEDGMENTS

The authors are grateful to Randy Ellis and Greg Pope for commenting on an earlier version of this chapter.

## ENDNOTES

1. For an overview of the place of the regulated competition sectors within the health insurance landscape in the United States, see Chapter 1: Regulated Competition in Health Insurance Markets: Paradigms and Ongoing Issues.
2. The 0.2% of enrollees in private fee-for-service MA plans are allowed to purchase their drug coverage outside their plan.
3. Although the premium and cost sharing in the underlying MA plan are constrained by the actuarial value of TM, as explained below, in Part D the government only constrains the actuarial value of the cost sharing. The government provides a subsidy of 74.5% of the national average bid to all Part D plans; beneficiaries are responsible for the other 25.5% plus or minus the difference between the bid of their chosen plan and the national average bid. Thus, the government relies on competition among plans to constrain premium bids. This strategy is particularly effective because beneficiaries overweight premiums relative to cost sharing in making plan choices (Abaluck and Gruber, 2011).
4. Medigap plans are private plans that pay some or all of deductibles, copayments for Medicare beneficiaries. They are regulated but not publicly subsidized.
5. These are called partial dual eligibility beneficiaries.
6. Unlike MA, Marketplace plans cannot impose TM's provider prices.
7. For more discussion of some of this research, readers can consult Newhouse and McGuire (2014) for a review of the research comparing cost and quality of MA plans and TM, recognizing the heterogeneity in the performance of MA plans. The review also considers the issue of selection and performance of risk adjustment in picking up selection between the MA and TM sectors. We will refer to other papers in specific contexts later in this chapter.

8. Although beneficiary premiums are generally to be set to cover 25% of the Part B cost, there was no cost-of-living increase in Social Security payments for 2016 and the law also limits Part B premium growth for existing beneficiaries to increases in Social Security payments. As a result, the Part B premium that the great majority of beneficiaries paid in 2016 towards either TM or MA was less than 25% of average TM costs. Beneficiaries that have the highest income, around 6% of all beneficiaries, pay a higher premium. See http://kff.org/medicare/issue-brief/whats-in-store-for-medicares-part-b-premiums-and-deductible-in-2016-and-why/. Part B is mandatory for MA enrollees since MA plans must cover Part B services.

9. https://www.medicare.gov/find-a-plan/questions/home.aspx. Accessed September 2016.

10. Beneficiaries can enter information about themselves, including drugs they use, and the Plan Finder will respond with some customization of the expected spending information. No information about the hypothetical beneficiary was included in this search.

11. Unlike TM, MA plans must have an out-of-pocket annual maximum that in 2016 could be at most $6700.

12. The power of the zero reference price is discussed in the general literature on consumer behavior in Shampanier et al. (2007).

13. Large numbers of Medicare beneficiaries failed to join the private fee-for-service (PFFS) form of plans at a time when these plans dominated TM for many beneficiaries. Until 2011, when policy toward PFFS plans changed to require such plans to have networks, PFFS plans were cheaper than TM for many beneficiaries, no more expensive for the many of the rest, and gave the same access to providers as TM for all enrollees. This occurred because PFFS plans were reimbursed by Medicare at higher than TM rates in many counties and thus could offer lower premiums and higher benefits than a TM beneficiary with no supplementary policy could obtain, while in the remaining counties it was reimbursed at the same rate as TM. In standard theory all beneficiaries in the counties with reimbursement rates above TM and without supplementary insurance should have enrolled in PFFS. In fact, using county averages in 2007, 95% of all beneficiaries would have faced lower expected out-of-pocket costs in a PFFS plan than if they had joined TM and paid for a Medigap policy out-of-pocket (McWilliams et al., 2011).

14. Beneficiaries switching back to TM and wanting to buy an individual Medigap policy, however, would find that policy could be medically underwritten.

15. TM costs were risk-adjusted using age, sex, institutional status, Medicaid eligibility, and employment status; at that time diagnosis was not used.

16. Ratings are actually made at the "contract" level. A contract with an insurer can include more than one plan. Information in this paragraph is from MedPAC (June, 2016), Chapter 12.

17. However, in 2012 when the star system went into effect, CMS announced a demonstration that lowered the threshold for a quality payment to 3 stars or above.

18. The ranking of counties for this purpose is not population weighted. In 2011 benchmarks were frozen at 2010 levels.

19. In addition to the rebates described, 5-star plans, of which there are few, receive a 5% add-on to the benchmark and plans in some counties also receive a 5% add-on.

20. More details can be found at http://medpac.gov/docs/default-source/payment-basics/med-pac_payment_basics_16_ma_final.pdf?sfvrsn=0. Unlike Medicare Part D, there is no risk sharing between Medicare and plans in Medicare Advantage.

21. This low weight was intended to minimize a plan's incentive to hospitalize a person unnecessarily solely to record a diagnosis.

22. Plans generally paid physicians fee-for-service and prior to the use of diagnosis for risk adjustment had no reason to question any incompleteness of outpatient diagnoses on the encounter forms physicians submitted to the plan for reimbursement.

23. There are a few allowances for interactions, meaning in a few cases reimbursement for a beneficiary with multiple diagnoses can reflect more than the sum of the weights for each diagnosis.

24. V22 dropped these eight HCCs from the payment model:

| | |
|---|---|
| 51 | Dementia With Complications |
| 52 | Dementia Without Complication |
| 138 | Chronic Kidney Disease, Moderate (Stage 3) |
| 139 | Chronic Kidney Disease, Mild or Unspecified (Stages 1−2 or Unspecified) |
| 140 | Unspecified Renal Failure |
| 141 | Nephritis |
| 159 | Pressure Ulcer of Skin with Partial Thickness Skin Loss |
| 160 | Pressure Pre-Ulcer Skin Changes or Unspecified Stage |

    In addition, some codes were moved between HCC 75 and 81 within the neurological condition categories.

25. TM hospice payments are excluded since MA plans are not responsible for those costs (TM pays them). Costs are annualized and each observation is weighted by the number of months of enrollment in a year. Months are excluded when Medicare is not the primary payer or the beneficiary is not resident in the US. We are grateful to Greg Pope from RTI for reviewing an earlier draft of this section.

26. CMS has some authority to modify quality scores on its own as well as to carry out demonstrations that can effectively, but modification of rebate rules, beneficiary premiums, and lock-ins would require new legislation.

27. Employer-sponsored health insurance is the primary insurer for working Medicare beneficiaries if the employer has 20 or more employees.

28. As noted above, however, V21 was never used for payment. V22, used for payment, drops eight HCC variables as described above, so would be characterized by a lower R-squared.

29. (As a rough idea, the average spending in the top 1% of spenders in 2006 was about $80,000 (from the tables in Section 3 of the RTI report); 16.9% of $80,000 is $13,520.

30. See Clemens and Gottlieb (2013) and Wallace and Song (2016) for comparison of TM prices to private managed care plans generally.

31. MedPAC, June 2013 report, Table 1-1; CBOhttps://www.cbo.gov/sites/default/files/113th-congress-2013-2014/reports/PremiumSupport_OneColumn.pdf p. 19.

32. See also Balsa et al. (2007) and Ayanian et al. (2013a) for evidence on disparities reduction in MA.

33. In 2013, MA plans were paid an additional $2.3 billion for higher-risk scores associated with diagnoses recorded from a health risk assessment only, in other words when there was no claim for a treatment for the condition (MedPAC, 2016, 348).

34. Cutler and Zeckhauser (2000) summarize a large literature documenting selection in health insurance markets generally.

35. In principle, "improved" risk adjustment, as measured by overall statistical fit, might be associated with greater or lesser opportunities to select (Brown et al., 2014).

36. The paper also contains a discussion of the literature documenting the decline in selection since Medicare improved risk adjustment and extended the lock-in period. The data in Brown et al. (2014)appear to differ from Newhouse et al. (2015), but Brown et al.'s data come from a markedly smaller sample and run only to 2006 as the new system was being phased in. Newhouse et al. find about a 2% favorable selection into MA for those switching, but that 2% was the same figure (conditional on risk score) before the CMS-HCC system was introduced.

37. Cabral et al. (2014) found evidence in their structural model estimates for an upward-sloping average cost curve in MA, indicating some adverse selection net of risk adjustment.

38. There are two potential limitations with this analysis. It is possible that MA plans have a small causal effect on mortality, though Curto et al. discount this possibility, following the interpretation of other authors comparing mortality across the two sectors. Furthermore, risk adjustment is intended to and is calibrated to adjust for cost differences, not mortality differences.

39. Two large insurers, however, are now offering plans designed for diabetics in the exchanges for the under 65. See http://khn.org/news/new-health-plans-offer-discounts-for-diabetes-care/. Diabetics had among the highest margins in the Newhouse et al. (2013) study of MA enrollees, emphasizing that incentives for selection are conditional on the risk adjustment scheme. Put another way, it is hard to imagine that diabetics would be profitable if there were only age–gender adjustment.

40. Policymakers could continue to adjust for more aggressive coding from plans by monitoring and making downward adjustments in the benchmark. A better general approach, however, might be to create fewer inefficient coding incentives in the first place, in part because it can be difficult to distinguish true changes from coding changes. See Carter, Newhouse, and Relles (1990) for an illustration of the analogous issue when DRGs began.

41. Schillo et al. (2016) first compute the conventional risk-adjusted payment, and compare this to cost to determine the "funding gap."

42. As explained above, however, the subsidy did not turn out to be negative; because of favorable selection, MA enrollees' cost in TM would have been less than 95%.

43. In its 2014 Report to Congress MedPAC (2014, p. 10) advised, "Policymakers may want a common benchmark to level the playing field and encourage beneficiaries to choose the model that will most efficiently give them the care and services that fit their individual preferences." MedPAC has held this position for many years.

44. This assumes that the MA plan can exercise market power. Medical loss ratio regulation in theory limits insurer profits, but the research literature discussed above implicitly treats this regulation as nonbinding or ineffective.

45. See Johnson et al. (2016) for more recent evidence that MA plan penetration in an area reduces spending patterns in TM.

46. This paragraph is based on a more thorough description in Stockley et al. (2014), which includes screen shots of the web pages referred to here. See also Newhouse and McGuire (2014) where the kinked demand curve due to asymmetry in Medicare price policy is shown.

47. Benefit enhancement may be efficient, however, if the MA plan can provide the benefit at lower cost than the individual can obtain it in other ways, for example purchasing it on the individual insurance market, assuming the benefit is sufficiently valued.

48. A pass through of around 50% has been found in a number of studies using different empirical methods for identifying the effect of the benchmark (Song et al., 2013; Cabral et al., 2014; Curto et al., 2014). An even lower pass-through rate was found by Duggan et al. (2014) who exploit the approximately 10% higher benchmark payments to plans in counties with populations about 250,000, finding no evidence of any effect on premiums, and a possibly small effect on coverage. Consistent with the interpretation that plans kept the higher payments as profits, they present suggestive evidence of higher advertising in the better-paid counties.

49. Pelech studied regulations that were part of the Medicare Improvements for Patients and Providers Act of 2008, which required MA plans referred to as Private Fee-for-Service plans create explicit networks by 2011 rather than just using Medicare prices and all providers. This led to large numbers of these Private Fee-for-Service plans exiting the market, which had differential effects on market structure in different MA markets.

50. Research in other health insurance markets shows how packaging the price can affect salience to consumers. Schmitz and Ziebarth (2017) study a natural experiment associated with a policy change in Germany in 2009 with very close parallels to the positive and negative price framing in MA. Prior to 2009 Germans joining one of the (mandatory) sickness funds paid via payroll deduction according to a "contribution rate" chosen by the fund expressed as a percentage of income. Post 2009, Germans faced a price expressed in euros that was paid (or in a few cases refunded) directly. The authors found that after prices were reframed in this fashion consumer response to premium differences increased fourfold and the premium distribution compressed.

# REFERENCES

<http://kff.org/medicare/issue-brief/whats-in-store-for-medicares-part-b-premiums-and-deductible-in-2016-and-why/>.

<https://www.medicare.gov/find-a-plan/questions/home.aspx>.

<http://medpac.gov/docs/default-source/payment-basics/medpac_payment_basics_16_ma_final. pdf?sfvrsn = 0>. (Page 16).

Abaluck, J., Gruber, J., 2011. Choice inconsistencies among the elderly: evidence from plan choice in the medicare Part D program. Am. Econ. Rev. 101 (4), 1180—1210.

Ayanian, J.Z., Landon, B.E., Zaslavsky, A.M., Newhouse, J.P., 2013a. Racial and ethnic differences in use of mammography between Medicare Advantage and traditional Medicare. J. Natl. Cancer Inst. 105 (24), 1891—1896. PMCID: PMC3866158.

Ayanian, J.Z., Landon, B.E., Zaslavsky, A.M., Saunders, R.C., Pawlson, L.G., Newhouse, J.P., 2013b. Medicare beneficiaries more likely to receive appropriate ambulatory services in HMOs than in traditional Medicare. Health Aff. (Millwood). 32 (7), 1228—1235. PMCID: PMC3925369.

Baicker, K., Chernew, M.E., Robbins, J., 2013. The spillover effects of Medicare Advantage. J. Health Econ. 32 (6), 1289—1300.

Balsa, A., Cao, Z., McGuire, T.G., 2007. Does managed care reduce health care disparities between minorities and whites? J. Health Econ. 26, 101—121.

Buchmueller, T.C., Feldstein, P.J., 1997. The effect of price on switching among health plans. J. Health Econ. 16 (2), 231—247.

Boards of Trustees Federal Hospital Insurance and Federal Supplementary Medical Insurance Trust Funds, 2016. Annual Report of the Boards of the Federal Hospital Insurance and Federal Supplementary Medical Insurance Trust Funds, available at https://www.cms.gov/ Research-Statistics-Data-and-Systems/Statistics-Trends-and-Reports/ReportsTrustFunds/ downloads/tr2016.pdf.

Breyer, F., Bundorf, K., Pauly, M.V., 2012. Health care spending risk, health insurance, and payment to health plans. In: Pauly, M., McGuire, T., Barros, P. (Eds.), The Handbook of Health Economics, Vol. 2. Elsevier.

Brown, J., Duggan, M., Kuziemko, I., Woolston, W., 2014. How does risk selection respond to risk adjustment? Evidence from the Medicare Advantage program. Am. Econ. Rev. 104 (10), 3335—3364.

Cabral, M., Geruso, M., Mahoney, N., 2014. Does privatized health insurance benefit patients or producers? Evidence from Medicare Advantage, NBER Working Paper.

Cao, Z., McGuire, T., 2003. Service-level selection by HMOs in medicare. J. Health Econ. 22 (6), 915—931.

Carter, G., Newhouse, J.P., Relles, D.A., 1990. How much change in the case mix index is DRG creep? J. Health Econ. 9, 411—427.

Clemens, J., Gottlieb, J.D., 2013. In the Shadow of a Giant: Medicare's Influence on Private Physician Payments. National Bureau of Economic Research, Working Paper 19503.

CBO.    https://www.cbo.gov/sites/default/files/113th-congress-2013-2014/reports/PremiumSupport_ OneColumn.pdf. p. 19.

Congressional Budget Office, 1997. Predicting How Changes in Medicare Payment Rates Would Affect Risk-Sector Enrollment.

Curto, V., Einav, L., Levin, J., Bhattacharya, J., 2014. Working Paper 20818 Can Health Insurance Competition Work? Evidence from Medicare Advantage. National Bureau of Economic Research.

Cutler, D.M., Zeckhauser, R., 2000. In: Culyer, A.J., Newhouse, J.P. (Eds.), The Anatomy of Health Insurance. Handbook of Health Economics. Elsevier, Amsterdam: North Holland.

Duggan, M., Starc, A., Vabson, B., 2014. Who Benefits when the Government Pays More? Pass-Through in the Medicare Advantage Program. National Bureau of Economic Research, Working Paper 19989, March.

Duggan, M., Gruber, J., Vabson, B., 2015. The Efficiency Consequences of Health Care Privatization: Evidence from Medicare Advantage Exits. National Bureau of Economic Research, Working Paper 21650, October.

Einav, L., Finkelstein, A., 2011. Selection in insurance markets: theory and empirics in pictures. J. Econ. Perspect. 25 (1), 115−138.

Ellis, R.P., McGuire, T.G., 2007. Predictability and predictiveness in health care spending. J. Health Econ. 26 (1), 25−48.

Ellis, R.P., Jiang, S., Kuo, T.-C., 2013. Does service-level spending show evidence of selection across health plan types? Appl. Econ. 45 (13), 1701−1712.

Finkelstein, A., 2009. E-Ztax: tax salience and tax rates. Quart. J. Econ. 124 (3), 969−1010.

General Accounting Office (GAO), 2013. Medicare Advantage: Substantial Excess Payments Underscore Need for CMS to Improve Accuracy of Risk Score Adjustments, Report to Congress, GAO-13-206.

Geruso, M., Layton, T., 2015. Upcoding: Evidence from Medicare on Squishy Risk Adjustment, NBER Working Paper #21222.

Glazer, J., McGuire, T.G., 2017. Paying medicare advantage plans: to level or tilt the playing field. J. Health Econ. 56, 281−291.

Iyengar, S., 2004. How much choice is too much?: determinants of individual contributions in 401(k) retirement plans. In: Mitchell, O.S., Utkus, S.P. (Eds.), Pension Design and Structure: New Lessons from Behavioral Finance. Oxford University Press, New York, pp. 83−97.

Jacobson, G., Trilling, A., Neuman, T., Damico, A., Gold, M., 2016. Medicare Advantage Hospital Networks: How Much do They Vary? Kaiser Family Foundation.

Johnson, G., Figuero, J., Zhou, X., Orav, J., Jha, A., 2016. Recent growth in Medicare Advantage enrollment associated with decreased fee-for-service spending in certain US counties. Health Affairs 35 (9), 1707−1715.

Kaiser Family Foundation, 2017. Medicare Advantage 2018 Data Spotlight: First Look. https://www.kff.org/report-section/medicare-advantage-2018-data-spotlight-first-look.

Kronick, R., Welch, P.W., 2014. Measuring coding intensity in the medicare advantage program. Med. Med. Res. Rev. 4 (2), E1−E19.

Landon, B.E., Zaslavsky, A.M., Saunders, R., Pawlson, L.G., Newhouse, J.P., Ayanian, J.Z., 2012. Analysis of medicare advantage HMOs compared with traditional Medicare shows lower use of many services during 2003-09. Health Affairs 31 (12), 2609−2617.

Landon, B.E., Zaslavsky, A.M., Saunders, R., Pawlson, L.G., Newhouse, J.P., Ayanian, J.Z., 2015. A comparison of relative resource use and quality in Medicare Advantage health plans versus traditional Medicare. Am. J. Manag. Care 21 (8), 559−566.

Layton, T., McGuire, T., 2017. Marketplace plan payment options for dealing with high-cost enrollees. Am. J. Health Econ. 3 (2), 1−27.

McGuire, T.G., Newhouse, J.P., Sinaiko, A., 2011. An economic history of medicare Part C. Milbank Quart. 89 (2), 289−332.

McWilliams, J.M., Afendulis, C., Landon, B.E., McGuire, T.G., 2011. Complex medicare advantage choices may overwhelm seniors − especially those with impaired decision making. Health Affairs 30 (9), 1786−1994.

McWilliams, J.M., Hsu, J., Newhouse, L., 2012. New risk adjustment system was associated with reduced favorable selection in medicare advantage. Health Affairs 31 (12), 2630−2640.

McWilliams, J.M., Hatfield, L.A., Chernew, M.E., Landon, B.E., Schwartz, A.S., 2016. Early performance of accountable care organizations in medicare. N. Engl. J. Med. April 13, 2016.

MedPAC, 2009. Report to the Congress: Improving Incentives in the Medicare Program, Washington, DC.

MedPAC Data Book, June 2016. http://www.medpac.gov/docs/default-source/data-book/june-2016-data-book-health-care-spending-and-the-medicare-program.pdf?sfvrsn = 0.

MedPAC, 2016. Report to the Congress: Medicare Payment Policy, Washington, DC, March.

MedPAC, 2000. Report to the Congress: Improving Risk Adjustment in Medicare, Washington, DC.

MedPAC, June 2013. Report to Congress, Table 1-1.

Newhouse, J.P., Price, M., Huang, J., McWilliams, J.M., Hsu, J., 2012. Steps to reduce favorable risk selection in medicare advantage largely succeeded, boding well for health insurance exchanges. Health Aff. 31 (12), 2618−2628.

Newhouse, J.P., McWilliams, J.M., Price, M., Huang, J., Fireman, B., Hsu, J., 2013. Do medicare advantage plans select enrollees in higher margin clinical categories? J. Health Econ. 32 (6), 1278−1288.

Newhouse, J.P., McGuire, T.G., 2014. How successful is medicare advantage? Milbank Quart. 92 (2), 351-194.

Newhouse, J.P., Price, M., McWilliams, J.M., Hsu, J., McGuire, T.G., 2015. How much favorable selection is left in medicare advantage? Am. J. Health Econ. 1 (1), 1−26.

Pelech, D., 2015. Paying More for Less? Insurer Competition and Health Plan Generosity in the Medicare Advantage Program, unpublished Ph.d. dissertation essay, Harvard University, April.

Pope, G. C., Kautter, J., Ingber, J.J., Freeman, S., Sekar, R., Newhart, C., 2011. Evaluation of the CMS-HCC Risk Adjustment Model, In Final Report, RTI Project Number 0209853.006, RTI International, March.

Pope, G.C., Bachofer, H., Pearlman, A., Kautter, J., Hunter, E., Miller, D., et al., 2014. Risk transfer formula for individual and small group markets under the affordable care act. Med. Med. Res. Rev. 4 (3), E1−E23.

Rose, S., McGuire, T.G., Shi, J., Nomrand, S.L., 2015. Matching and imputation methods for risk adjustment in the health insurance marketplaces. Statist. Biosci. Available from: https://doi.org/10.1007/s12561-015-9135-7 (special issue on big data) Advance online publication.

Schmid, C., Beck, K., forthcoming. Re-insurance in the Swiss Health Insurance Market: Fit, Power and Balance, Health Policy.

Schmitz, H., Ziebarth, N.R., 2017. Does Price Framing Affect the Consumer Price Sensitivity of Health Plan Choice? J. Human Resources 55(6): 799−819.

Schillo, S., Lux, G., Wassem, J., Buchner, F., 2016. High cost pool or high cost groups − how to handle highest cost cases in a risk adjustment mechanism? Health Policy 120, 141−147.

Shampanier, K., Mazar, N., Ariely, D., 2007. Zero as a special price: the true value of free products. Marketing Sci. 26 (6), 742−757.

Sinaiko, A.D., Afendulis, C.C., Frank, R.G., 2013. Enrollment in Medicare Advantage plans in Miami-Dade County: evidence of status quo bias? Inquiry 50 (3), 202−215.

Stevenson, D.G., Ayanian, J.Z., Zaslavsky, A.M., Newhouse, J.P., Landon, B.E., 2013. Service use at the end of life in medicare advantage versus traditional medicare. Med. Care 51 (10), 931−937.

Stockley, K., McGuire, T. G., Afendulis, C., Chernew, M.E., 2014. Premium Transparency in the Medicare Advantage Market: Implications for Premiums, Benefits and Efficiency, National Bureau of Economics Research Working Paper No. 20208, November 2014.

Song, Z., Landrum, M.B., Chernew, M.E., 2013. Competitive bidding in medicare advantage: effect of benchmark changes on plan bids. J. Health Econ. 32 (6), 1301−1312.

Van Barneveld, E., Lamers, L., Van Vliet, R., Van de Ven, W., 1998. Mandatory pooling as a supplement to risk adjusted capitation payments in a competitive health insurance market. Soc. Sci. Med. 47, 223−232.

Van Barneveld, E.M., Lamers, L.M., van Vliet, R.C.J.A., van de Ven, W.P.M.M., 2001. Risk sharing as a supplement to imperfect capitation: a tradeoff between selection and efficiency. J. Health Econ. 20 (2), 147−168.

Van Kleef, R.C., Van Vliet, R.C.J.A., 2012. Improving risk equalization using multiple-year high cost as a health indictor. Med. Care 50, 140−144.

Wallace J, Song Z. "Traditional Medicare versus private insurance: How spending, volume, and price change at age sixty-five." Health Affairs. 2016 May 1;35(5):864−872.

# Index

*Note*: Page numbers followed by "*f*," "*t*," and "*b*" refer to figures, tables, and boxes, respectively.